*Providing Specialized Distribution
for Independent Producers
Throughout the World*

*Theatrical
Non-Theatrical
Television
Video*

INTERNATIONAL FILM EXCHANGE, LTD.

An IFEX International Company

**201 WEST 52ND STREET
NEW YORK, NY 10019
TELEPHONE: (212) 582-4318
TELEX: 420748 RAPP UI
FAX: (212) 956-2257**

**9200 SUNSET BOULEVARD
LOS ANGELES, CA 90069
TELEPHONE: (213) 278-6490
TELEX: 4972966 CSP
FAX: (213) 278-7939**

The Second Annual Sarasota French Film Festival

November 15-19, 1990
Sarasota, Florida

PRESENTED BY: THE ASOLO CENTER FOR THE PERFORMING ARTS. SPONSORED BY: THE STATE OF FLORIDA IN ASSOCIATION WITH UNIFRANCE FILM INTERNATIONAL AND THE FRENCH CULTURAL SERVICES. DESIGN: KIDD&DRISCOLL DESIGN GROUP, TALLAHASSEE, FLORIDA

Following last year's successful debut, the Sarasota French Film Festival returns this fall offering the finest new French films. From November 15 - 19, you can gather with international stars, directors, producers, prominent film critics and film lovers in a dazzling seaside setting.

Share the excitement of:

• premiere screenings of the latest French films programmed by Artistic Director Molly Haskell

• an evening of tribute to a French cinema artist

• panels featuring nationally-renowned critics, industry leaders, directors, producers and actors

• celebrations with the stars

For more information on the Festival and available travel, lodging, and ticket packages, call 1-800-874-FILM.

EMPORiUM 91

First Euromarket
Exhibition of Production Services
for the TV, Motion Picture, and
Entertainment Industry.

■

November 21st - 24th, 1991
Acropolis Exposition
Nice - France.

■

Over 30 East and West
European countries will be
represented.

■

For further information, contact :
Remi Salette on (33) 93 56 28 18.
Or write to the Emporium 91 office,
Studios de la Victorine,
16 Ave. Edouard Grinda
06200 Nice - France.
Fax (33) 93 71 91 73.

■

ENTERTAINMENT DATA, INC.

"Access a world of information."

- WEEKLY RELEASE SCHEDULE
- OVERNIGHT GROSSES
- ON-LINE DATA BASE
- EDI INTERNATIONAL

ENTERTAINMENT DATA, INC. ▪ 331 N. MAPLE DRIVE ▪ BEVERLY HILLS, CA 90210 ▪ 213 · 271 · 2105
LOS ANGELES ▪ SAN FRANCISCO ▪ DALLAS ▪ CHICAGO ▪ WASHINGTON, D.C. ▪ NEW YORK

EDITED BY PETER COWIE

FILM GUIDE
1991

LONDON
ANDRE DEUTSCH

HOLLYWOOD
SAMUEL FRENCH INC.

CONTENTS

9 Editorial
13 Awards
16 Focus on European Institutions
19 Dossier: New Zealand Cinema Now
51 Anatomy of a Movie: Until the End of the World

WORLD SURVEY
60 Argentina
65 Australia
76 Austria
80 Belgium
83 Bolivia
85 Brazil
87 Bulgaria
91 Burma
92 Cambodia
92 Canada
117 Chile
119 China
122 Colombia
128 Cuba
131 Czechoslovakia
137 Denmark
145 Egypt
149 Finland
156 France
167 Germany
179 Greece
185 Hongkong
191 Hungary
199 Iceland
203 India
209 Indonesia
211 Iran
219 Ireland
224 Israel

CREDITS

Editor: Peter Cowie
Consulting Editor: Derek Elley
Editorial Assistant: Stephen Pemberton
New York Liaison: Fred Lombardi
Cover Design: Stefan Dreja

Editorial and Business Offices:
Variety
34–35 Newman Street
London W1P 3PD
Tel: (071) 637.3663
Fax: (071) 580.5555
Telex: 24377

ISBN 0 233 98613 8
U.S. Library of Congress Catalog Card No: 64–1706.
Copyright © 1990 by Cahners Publishing Ltd.
Photoset, printed and bound in Great Britain by Dotesios Printers Ltd.

229	Italy	325	Sweden
239	Ivory Coast	332	Switzerland
241	Japan	339	Taiwan
245	Korea (South)	343	Thailand
247	Laos	344	Turkey
248	Luxembourg	351	United Kingdom
251	Malaysia	365	U.S.A.
256	Mali	395	U.S.S.R.
257	Mexico	400	Venezuela
263	Mongolia	405	Vietnam
263	Nepal	406	Yugoslavia
265	Netherlands	410	Zaire
281	New Zealand	413	Guide to International Locations
287	Norway	423	Tribute to the Toronto Festival of Festivals
294	Pakistan		
297	Philippines	433	Guide to Leading Festivals
299	Poland	473	Film Schools
303	Portugal	478	Film Archives
305	Puerto Rico	490	Book Reviews
307	Senegal	493	Film Bookshops, Posters & Records
309	South Africa		
315	Spain	499	Magazines
323	Sri Lanka	504	Index to Advertisers

INTERNATIONAL LIAISON

Africa: Roy Armes
Argentina: Alberto Tabbia
Australia: David Stratton
Austria: Jack Kindred
Belgium: Patrick Duynslaegher
Bolivia: Pedro Susz K
Brazil: Luis Arbex
Bulgaria: Ivan Stoyanovich
Canada: Gerald Pratley
Chile: Hans Ehrmann
Cuba: Tim Barnard
Czechoslovakia: Deborah Young
Denmark: Ebbe Iversen
Egypt: Fawzi Soliman
Far East: Derek Elley, Fred Marshall

Finland: Matti Apunen
France: Michel Ciment
Germany: Jack Kindred
Greece: B. Samantha Stenzel
Hungary: Derek Elley
Iceland: Arnaldur Indridason
India: Uma da Cunha
Ireland: Michael Dwyer
Israel: Dan Fainaru
Italy: Lorenzo Codelli
Japan: Frank Segers
Luxembourg: Jean-Pierre Thilges
Malaysia: Baharudin A. Latif
Mexico: Tomás Pérez Turrent
Nepal: Kalendra Shahi
Netherlands: Pieter van Lierop

New Zealand: Mike Nicolaidi
Norway: J.R. Keith Keller
Pakistan: Aijaz Gul
Poland: Wanda Wertenstein
Puerto Rico: José Artemio Torres
Spain: Peter Besas
Sri Lanka: Amarnath Jayatilaka
Sweden: Peter Cowie
Switzerland: Christoph Egger
Turkey: B. Samantha Stenzel
U.K.: Mark Le Fanu
U.S.A.: William Wolf
U.S.S.R.: Verina Glaessner
Venezuela (and *Colombia*): Paul Lenti
Yugoslavia: Maja Vlahović

MANFRED DURNIOK PRODUKTION FÜR FILM UND FERNSEHEN
International Motion Picture
and Television Productions,
Co-Productions and Film Distribution.
Hausotterstraße 36, D-1000 Berlin 51 (West)
Germany, Phone (030) 491 80 45
Telex 1-81 717 Dufi D
Fax (030) 491 40 66

EDITORIAL

At a time when the global box-office returns for popular films are scaling unprecedented heights, it's worth assessing the state of the independents. And that makes for bleak reading.

In the United States, indie operations like Vestron, MCEG, Weintraub, Nelson, and Odyssey/Cinecom have all been suffering economically. The usual factors of mismanagement, poor judgement, and the innate hazards of investing in the movie business may all have come into play. But independence as such is on the wane, whether it be in production, distribution, or exhibition.

The worldwide trend is towards bigger units and bigger chains. Only a decade ago, for instance, Holland boasted a dozen thriving independent distributors/exhibitors. Now most have been devoured or absorbed by the American majors and their offshore offices. In Finland, almost 100% of distribution and exhibition is controlled by Finnkino.

Ironically, the Eastern European cinemas are bolting from one form of monopoly to another. The artistic repression that prevailed in communist countries for so long may well be replaced by an economic censorship. Instead of making independent films with universal themes, the talented directors of Poland, Czechoslovakia, Hungary, and the U.S.S.R. could be forced back into producing trashy pictures for local consumption only. The hard currency famine still afflicting these countries deprives their new, non-state companies of the ability to promote and sell films in the West.

In this Age of the Consumer, the role of the independent grows increasingly precious. The cinema *needs* risk-takers and mavericks, individuals who create a successful formula and not those who are content merely to clone the current megahits. Their integrity comes under heavier fire as Hollywood studios pay out millions of dollars for script outlines, and spend more millions on the release of new pictures around the world.

Independence spells freedom. From Warren Beatty to Jeremy Thomas, from King Hu to the Kaurismäki brothers, filmmakers willing to fight for their vision and take their chance at the box-office should be cherished and admired.

Peter Cowie

Missing Something?

A few back issues of the **International Film Guide** are still available. Tell us which ones you require, and send a cheque or International Money Order (payable to **Cahners Publishingh Ltd**) for £10.00 or $16.00 per copy – and that includes regular mail to anywhere in the world.
Issues in stock: **1968, 1971, 1972, 1974, 1975, 1976, 1977, 1978, 1979, 1980, 1981, 1982, 1983, 1984, 1986, 1987, 1988, 1989, 1990**
VARIETY, 34–35 Newman Street, London W1P 3PD. Tel: (071) 637 3663

NEW AND FORTHCOMING FILMS

Gérard Depardieu took the Best Actor prize at Cannes for his magnificent *Cyrano de Bergerac*

Akira Kurosawa's *Dreams* opened the Cannes Festival in 1990

Marcello Mastroianni in Giuseppe Tornatore's *Stanno tutti bene*
photo: Mario Tursi

Still from Michael Verhoeven's Berlin prizewinner, *The Nasty Girl*

Still from *Longtime Companion*, released by the Samuel Goldwyn Co.
photo: Gabor Szitanyi

Nina Petronzio makes her debut in Productions La Fête's *Vincent and Me*

Joe Mantegna and Faye Dunaway in *Wait Until Spring, Bandini*

Metropolitan has proved a sleeper hit with critics and audiences

photo: Carlo Ontal

Laura Dern and Nicolas Cage in the award-winning *Wild at Heart*

photo: Stephen Vaughan

Still from *Memphis Belle*, David Puttnam's production for release through Warner Bros.

Idrissa Ouedraogo won his second Cannes award with *The Law (Tilai)*

Delicate colour nuances in Katt Shea Ruben's *Streets*

UNITED INTERNATIONAL PICTURES

DISTRIBUTORS FOR

METRO-GOLDWYN-MAYER

PARAMOUNT

UNITED ARTISTS

UNIVERSAL

UNITED INTERNATIONAL PICTURES

UIP House, 45 Beadon Road, Hammersmith, London W6 0EG. Telephone 081 741 9041. Telefax No. 081 748 8990. Telex 8956521

U.S. ACADEMY AWARDS 1990 (for year 1989)

Best Film: *Driving Miss Daisy*.
Best Direction: Oliver Stone for *Born on the Fourth of July*.
Best Actor: Daniel Day-Lewis for *My Left Foot*.
Best Actress: Jessica Tandy for *Driving Miss Daisy*.
Best Supporting Actor: Denzel Washington for *Glory*.
Best Supporting Actress: Brenda Fricker for *My Left Foot*.
Best Original Screenplay: Tom Schulman for *Dead Poets Society*.
Best Adapted Screenplay: Alfred Uhry for *Driving Miss Daisy*.
Best Cinematography: Freddie Francis for *Glory*.
Best Art Direction: Anton Furst, Peter Young for *Batman*.
Best Costume Design: Phyllis Dalton for *Henry V*.
Best Editing: David Brenner. Joe Hutshing for *Born on the Fourth of July*.
Best Original Score: Alan Menken for *The Little Mermaid*.
Best Original Song: "Under the Sea" from *The Little Mermaid*. Music by Alan Menken. Lyric by Howard Ashman.
Best Sound: Donald O. Mitchell, Kevin O'Connell, Greg P. Russell, Keith A. Wester for *Black Rain*.
Best Foreign-Language Film: *Cinema Paradiso* (Italy).
Best Documentary Feature: *Common Threads: Stories from the Quilt*.
Best Documentary Short: *The Johnstown Flood*.
Best Live-Action Short: *Work Experience*.
Best Animated Short: *Balance*.
Best Special Effects: John Bruno, Dennis Muren, Hoyt Yeatman, Dennis Skotak for *The Abyss*.
Best Make-Up: Manilo Rocchetti, Lynn Barber, Kevin Haney for *Driving Miss Daisy*.
Best Sound-Effects Editing: Ben Burtt, Richard Hymns for *Indiana Jones and the Last Crusade*.

Gordon E. Sawyer Award: Pierre Angénieux.
Jean Hersholt Humanitarian Award: Howard W. Koch.
Honorary Oscar: Akira Kurosawa.

EUROPEAN FILM AWARDS: 1989

Best Film: *Landscape in the Mist* (Greece).
Best Young Film: *300 Miles to Heaven* (Poland).
Best Director: Géza Bereményi for *The Midas Touch* (Hungary).
Best Actor: Philippe Noiret for *Life and Nothing But* (France) and *Cinema Paradiso* (Italy).
Best Actress: Ruth Sheen for *High Hopes* (U.K.).
Best Supporting Performance: Edna Dore for *High Hopes* (U.K.).
Best Screenplay: Maria Khmelik for *Little Vera* (U.S.S.R.).
Best Cinematography: Ulf Brantås, Jörgen Persson for *The Women on the Roof*.
Best Score: Andrew Dickson for *High Hopes* (U.K.).
Best Documentary: *Recsk 1950–1953* (Hungary).
Special Jury Awards: *Life and Nothing But* (France), *Cinema Paradiso* (Italy), *A Tale of Wind* (Netherlands).
Special Mentions: *Pictures of the Old World* (Czechoslovakia), *The Road to God Knows Where* (Ireland).
European Cinema Society Lifetime Achievement Award: Federico Fellini.
European Cinema Society Special Award: Anatole Dauman.

BRITISH ACADEMY OF FILM AND TELEVISION ARTS AWARDS: 1990

Best Film: *Dead Poets Society*.
Best Original Screenplay: Nora Ephron for *When Harry Met Sally*.
Best Adapted Screenplay: Christopher

My Left Foot has won awards on both sides of the Atlantic

Hampton for *Dangerous Liaisons*.
Best Director: Kenneth Branagh for *Henry V*.
Best Actress: Pauline Collins for *Shirley Valentine*.
Best Actor: Daniel Day-Lewis for *My Left Foot*.
Best Supporting Actress: Michelle Pfeiffer for *Dangerous Liaisons*.
Best Supporting Actor: Ray McAnally for *My Left Foot*.
Best Score for a Film: Maurice Jarre for *Dead Poets Society*.
Best Foreign-Language Film: *Life and Nothing But* (France).
Best Short Film: *The Candy Show*.
Best Short Animated Film: *A Grand Day Out*.
Fellowship Award: Paul Fox CBE.
Michael Balcon Award: Lewis Gilbert.
Special Award: Dame Peggy Ashcroft.
Flaherty Award: Kevin Sim for *Four Hours in My Lai*.

INDEPENDENT SPIRIT AWARDS OF INDEPENDENT FEATURE PROJECT/WEST

Best Picture: *sex, lies and videotape*.
Best Director: Steve Soderbergh for *sex, lies and videotape*.
Best Actor: Matt Dillon for *Drugstore Cowboy*.
Best Actress: Andie McDowell for *sex, lies and videotape*.
Best Supporting Actor: Max Perlich for *Drugstore Cowboy*.
Best Supporting Actress: Laura San Giacomo for *sex, lies and videotape*.
Best Screenplay: Gus Van Sant Jr. and Dan Yost for *Drugstore Cowboy*.

Best Cinematography: Robert Yeoman for *Drugstore Cowboy*.
Best First Feature: Michael Lehmann for *Heathers*.
Special Distinction Award: Spike Lee for *Do the Right Thing*.
Friends of Independents (Findie) Awards: (*joint winners*) Miramax Films and the John D. and Catherine T. MacArthur Foundation.

FRENCH CESAR ACADEMY AWARDS 1990

Best Film: Bertrand Blier's *Trop belle pour toi*.
Best Foreign Film: Stephen Frears's *Dangerous Liaisons*.
Best Director: Bertrand Blier, for *Trop belle pour toi*.
Best Actor: Philippe Noiret, for Bertrand Tavernier's *La Vie et rien d'autre*.
Best Actress: Carole Bouquet, for *Trop belle pour toi*.
Best Supporting Actor: Robert Hirsch, for Denis Amar's *Hiver 54, l'Abbé Pierre*.
Best Supporting Actress: Suzanne Flon, for Georges Wilson's *La Vouivre*.
Best Promising Young Actor: Yvan Attai, for Eric Rochant's *Un Monde sans pitié*.
Best Promising Young Actress: Vanessa Paradis, for Jean-Claude Brisseau's *Noce blanche*.
Best First Film: Eric Rochant's *Un Monde sans pitié*.
Best Screenplay (original or adaptation): Bertrand Blier, for *Trop belle pour toi*.
Best Cinematography: Yves Angelo, for Alain Corneau's *Nocturne indien*.
Best Editing: Claudine Merlin, for *Trop belle pour toi*.
Best Art Direction: Pierre Guffroy, for Milos Forman's *Valmont*.
Best Sound: Pierre Lenoir, Dominique Hennequin, for Patrice Leconte's *M. Hire*.
Best Costumes: Theodor Pistek, for *Valmont*.
Best Music: Oswald d'Andrea, for *La Vie et rien d'autre*.
Best Animation Short: Marie-Christine Perrodin's *Le Porte-plume*.
Best Documentary Short: Bernard Aubouy's *Chanson pour un marin*.
Best Fiction Short: Patrick Bouchitey's *Lune froide*.

The smallest of the great festivals.

The greatest of the small festivals.

Every evening open-air screenings.

August 8-18 1991

44. festival internazionale del film Locarno / Switzerland

P.O. Box, Via della Posta 6   6600 Locarno   Phone: 093 31 02 32   Telefax: 093 31 74 65   Telex: 846 565

FOCUS ON EUROPEAN INSTITUTIONS

European Film Distribution Office

"If people don't sit up and take notice within the next year or so, European film will cease to exist," says European Film Distribution Office President Dieter Kosslick in a dire prediction.

To see that it does not come to pass, Kosslick and his EFDO crew are pushing their two-year-old system of grants for pre-distribution aid for low-budget films that otherwise might have no chance of being picked up for distribution within their own country, let alone in other European countries.

That is, in fact, the fate of the vast majority of European films.

"Two years ago we determined that 80% of all European films never found a distributor," Kosslick recalls. "Now I'd say the situation is even worse, and the figure is probably 90%. The market is getting tighter, and European film is in trouble."

But during that time, EFDO has provided EC-supplemented distribution grants for a total of 37 films, including such dark horses as Gabriel Axel's *Babette's Feast*, Terence Davies's *Distant Voices, Still Lives*, Peter Greenaway's *Drowning by Numbers* and Etienne Chatiliez's *La Vie est un long fleuve tranquille*.

"We have two years of experience under our belts," Kosslick says. "To cut a long story short, the initial period was successful, the system works." In its first two years, the system provided a total of $3.5 million in EC grant money through the Common Market's MEDIA programme to low-budget films. That money went to films with budgets under about $2 million.

Films chosen for participation in the EFDO system must have commitments by distributors in at least three participating countries to provide half such distribution pre-costs as making prints, developing promotional materials and subtitling prints. Eligible are films and distribution companies from 14 countries – the 12 EC countries plus Switzerland and Austria. Plans are in the offing to expand EFDO into Eastern Europe and Scandinavia, and to go worldwide with promotional efforts for European film, says Kosslick.

The grants are made available in the form of loans repayable if a film turns into a money-maker at the box-office. Kosslick says a number of EFDO-supported films have become successful. "I believe we've made an impact on the market and have stabilised. But we need more money to do the job thoroughly across the continent."

Additional funding from the EC would enable EFDO to expand its efforts and to raise its grant system to take in films with budgets of up to about $4.5 million.

Kosslick is optimistic that EC leaders will approve a large MEDIA '92 funding package which would make many of EFDO's dreams come true in time for implementation of the single market in the EC after 1992. "After 1992, we will have to expand our efforts and work with the American independents," Kosslick says. "After all, what we're doing is not aimed against the Americans. We just want a bigger market for everyone. But Europeans have to look beyond their own boundaries to do that. If they don't, then I'm not optimistic about the future of European film after 1992, because the American majors are taking steps now to secure their interests after that time. We at EFDO want to secure a place for European films with strong national identities seen by large audiences in many other European countries."

Ernest Gill

European Script Fund

The European Script Fund was founded as a pilot project of the Media 92 programme (of the Directorate General, Information Communication and Culture, Commission of the European Communities). The aim of the Fund is to encourage co-operation between talents and organisations in different countries, as well as between private financiers and public funding bodies.

The Fund provides seed money to European producers and writers in an attempt to redress the imbalance between indigenous production and the great amount of imported fictional material in European cinemas and TV.

Applicants should normally be European nationals. There is no quota for member states (and some non-EC countries have paid to join the Fund). Team applications receive at least 70% of the available funding, while 30% is allocated to individual writers.

All genres of fictional material for film or TV are eligible for funding, except animation which is funded by another Media 92 project. Priority is given to original ideas (rather than adaptations). Projects must have a reasonable chance of being produced and must be of interest to European audiences. Applicants from the smallest EC countries will be given special consideration. Some 2 million ECU (approx. $2.4 million) have been distributed to more than 120 projects since the Fund was launched in April 1989.

The Script Editor is Don Ranvaud, himself a film-maker and former writer on film. The Chairman of the Fund is Sir Richard Attenborough, and its governing Council of Management includes members from all the EC member states. The Secretary General is Renée Goddard.

Application forms may be obtained from the European Script Fund, 39c Highbury Place, London N5 1QP, U.K.

Distribution Aid for European Films

▶ efdo is an initiative of the MEDIA 92 Programme of the Commission of the European Communities
▶ Committee:
Dieter Kosslick (D), President,
Maria João Seixas (P), Vice-President,
Christiane Dano (B),
José L. Galvarriato (E),
David Kavanagh (IRL),
Tivi Magnusson (DK),
Claude-Eric Poiroux (F)
▶ Secretary:
Ute Schneider
▶ Friedensallee 14–16
▶ D - 2000 Hamburg 50
▶ Tel.: (0)40–390 90 25
▶ Telex: 216 53 55
▶ Fax: (0)40–390 62 49

Nissie Herewini in Barry Barclay's *Te Rua*

I.F.G. DOSSIER

NEW ZEALAND CINEMA NOW

In little more than a dozen years, the New Zealand cinema has made a powerful impact throughout the world, with names like Vincent Ward, Roger Donaldson, and Sam Neill achieving fame far beyond the Antipodes. MIKE NICOLAIDI traces the fascinating story behind this triumph over the handicap of a small population, slim financial resources, and a lack of tradition in movie-making.

> ... from a little land with no history.
> Making its own history, slowly and clumsily.
> Piecing together this and that, finding the pattern, solving the problem.
> Like a child with a box of bricks ...
> *Katherine Mansfield, in a letter, 1910*

The year 1990 was to be a watershed year for New Zealand in its commemoration of several important events that had shaped its heritage: 1,000 years of known habitation by its indigenous Maori people, 200 years of settlement by Europeans.

But most importantly, the year would be the 150th anniversary of the signing of the Treaty of Waitangi, the agreement between British representatives of Queen Victoria and the Maori people. This founding document for New Zealand as a nation has an importance not dissimilar to that of the U.S. Constitution. It embodies the desire for mutual respect and equality between all New Zealand's peoples – comparatively small in total at 3,300,000 as the last decade of the century commences, yet diverse in lifestyle, determinedly individualistic, strongly creative ... and free.

The fact that the celebrations were relatively low key and avoided great occasions for the masses, recognised the nature of New Zealand identity.

This identity is fundamentally idiosyncratic and tenacious. It is innovative, and inherently suspicious of pomp and ceremony and anything that has a whiff of nationalistic jingoism.

The collective raw emotions that can be aroused by prowess in sport are an exception. But the politicians best not seek to exploit such feelings for their own ends. While there have been times when populist leaders have been sought and supported, they have been unceremoniously dumped when national interest has appeared to override or not be in accord with the self-interest of individual electors.

These islands far in the south Pacific – next stop the South Pole – are still peopled by adventurers; indigenous and johnny-come-latelys. The contemporary urban ethics and concerns of Western Europe, North America and neighbouring Australia, have great difficulty taking root here.

Still from *Sleeping Dogs*

Small Population

Given the small population and the continuing dominance of a physical environment that can feed and offer natural space and clear air and light to most of the people, including those living in the most populous Auckland region, this may still be the situation when the country moves into the 21st century.

These are important matters to understand when considering the course taken by New Zealand cinema since its virtual inception in 1977. Its successes and shortcomings graphically mirror the nature of the society in which it exists.

The way it is seeking to survive in an increasingly global community reflects the same desire for economic and creative viability sought by other industries led by self-interested New Zealand "internationalists."

N.Z. cinema has had a relatively short history. How it matures over the decade ahead, increasing its impact at home and abroad and continually improving standards of accomplishment, will measure the country's own success in surviving and adapting to turbulent and complex economic times.

Where From

Itinerant showmen screened and produced the first moving pictures in New Zealand in the late 1890's. But few dramatic films were made before 1920. The basic diet comprised short topical films of important events like the Royal Visit by the Duke and Duchess of Cornwall and York in 1901.

Hinemoa, a 2,500-foot film based on a Maori legend, was made by George Tarr in 1914, and distributed throughout the country by Hayward's Pictures.

Rudall Hayward proved to be the key figure of N.Z. film making during the 1920's and 1930's. He produced six features and many single and two reel comedies. One of his best was the drama–romance, *Rewi's Last Stand*, made in 1925 and based on a famous incident in the Maori wars of the 1860's. A sound version was released by Hayward in 1940.

Between 1940 and 1970 only three N.Z. feature films were produced. All came from the Wellington studios of Pacific Films and were largely the inspiration – and work – of one man, John O'Shea, who continues to be an important figure and significant influence in the industry post-1977.

Three themes ignited O'Shea's passion at that time: race relations in *Broken Barrier* (1952), the man-alone syndrome in *Runaway* (1964), the impact of an essentially alien pop culture in *Don't Let It Get You* (1966). They remain important wells to be drawn from today.

O'Shea also became a force in moves to persuade the government of the importance to the country of a thriving film industry. Throughout the first half of the 1970's, a core group of individuals, dedicated to the task, worked through the Queen Elizabeth II Arts Council and other bodies to help achieve this goal.

In October 1977, the then Arts Minister Alan Highet established an Interim Film Commission with former Arts Council chairman, Bill Sheat, as its head. Sheat was to become founding chairman of the N.Z. Film Commission the following year, a position he held until 1985.

The dedicated few behind the scenes played important roles. But, ultimately the argument with politicians and bureaucrats about the benefits to the country of assisting film production, was won – as it had to be – by the film-makers themselves.

Lisa Peers in Tony Williams's *Solo*

Television, which began regular broadcasts in 1960, and the marauding counter-culture movement, which included N.Z. in its sweep through the world in the late 1960's, heightened the interest and ambitions of a new generation. They would practise what they preached – to drive the point home.

Among them were: Geoff Steven, a leading light of Alternative Cinema, the Auckland film-makers' co-operative; Geoff Murphy and Bruno Lawrence, who had won fame (if not fortune) throughout the country with their free-wheeling multi-media Blerta travelling roadshows; Tony Williams, who had photographed O'Shea's *Runaway* and moved into

DOSSIER: NEW ZEALAND CINEMA NOW

ALL-TIME NEW ZEALAND BOX-OFFICE WINNERS

		$NZ
1.	*Footrot Flats* 1986–87. Dir: Ball	2,200,000
2.	*Goodbye Pork Pie* 1981. Dir: Murphy	1,600,000
3.	*Came a Hot Friday* 1985. Dir: Mune	1,000,000
4.	*Utu* 1983. Dir: Murphy.	700,000
5.	*The Navigator* 1988. Dir: Ward	505,000
6.	*Smash Palace* 1982. Dir: Donaldson	500,000
7.	*Beyond Reasonable Doubt* 1980. Dir: Laing	450,000
8.	*Sleeping Dogs* 1977. Dir: Donaldson	450,000
9.	*The Quiet Earth* 1986. Dir: Murphy	450,000
10.	*Off the Edge* 1977. Dir: Firth	400,000
11.	*Never Say Die* 1988. Dir: Murphy	378,000
12.	*Other Halves* 1986. Dir: Laing	350,000

directing; and Roger Donaldson, an expatriate Australian who, with Auckland actor Ian Mune, set up a production company in 1974 to make short film dramas.

Steven, virtually single-handedly and on a shoe-string budget, produced an experimental film that could fairly claim to be the start of the final push. Released in 1975, *Test Pictures* was feature length, but understandably short on substance and craft. It would take Murphy, Williams, and particularly, Donaldson – along with a feature documentary maker, Michael Firth – to get there. That happened in 1976–77.

The films were: *Wild Man*, directed by Murphy; *Solo*, Williams; and *Sleeping Dogs*, Donaldson. Firth's documentary was *Off the Edge*. These films were popular when released throughout the country, and, as a group, they effectively mark the birth of modern N.Z. cinema.

The First Films

Wild Man is of interest for the talents it brought together as well as the hit-and-miss knockabout story of con-men and travelling boxers in colonial New Zealand. It was the first film to be directed by Geoff Murphy and, accepting its extended home movie look, established Murphy's exuberant, teasingly subversive style. On board were Bruno Lawrence (as lead actor/co-producer), Martyn Sanderson (co-writer, actor), Alun Bollinger (cameraman) and John Barnett (executive producer).

Barnett was to become a major figure in the industry in the first half of the 1980's. *Footrot Flats*, the animated feature he produced˙ in 1985–86, remains the industry's top money-spinner.

Sanderson went on to act in many N.Z. films and was writer/director of *Flying Fox in a Freedom Tree* in 1989, for which he won Best Screenplay Award at that year's Tokyo International Film Festival.

Tony Williams' **Solo** is a simple love story involving a man-alone forestry worker and a young hitch-hiking Australian woman. With finance from Seven Network, Australia, it was the first co-production involving the local industry and recognised the regular and easy movement of film artists between the two countries.

This trans-Tasman interchange was to deepen, if not gain official respectability and

Still from Tony Williams's *Solo*

positive acknowledgement, in the decade ahead.

Williams made one further feature – in Australia – and now lives in Sydney. His reputation today is as one of the world's best directors of television commercials.

Michael Firth's feature documentary, **Off the Edge**, a skiing/hang-gliding, tongue-in-cheek travelogue involving an American and a Canadian on holiday in N.Z., was marketed locally by independent distributor, Barrie Everard. It remains among the all-time top N.Z. box-office winners and won an Academy Award nomination in the documentary section in 1977.

From the early 1920's, film-makers began building a world-wide reputation for their ability to capture imaginatively the N.Z. scenic wilderness and thereby attract tourists. The leading exponents, post-1940 were employed by the state-owned and operated National Film Unit. This was a tradition Firth took advantage of and developed.

But Roger Donaldson's **Sleeping Dogs** was the decisive factor. It embodied all the elements to kick-start a feature film industry. It possessed a strong story, about political upheaval in a contemporary New Zealand, and universal themes that came from a distinctly N.Z. experience. It was not inhibited by self-consciously evading a Hollywood look or style.

The fine performance of Sam Neill, in the lead role of Smith, stood out. Neill's first feature was the little seen 16mm *Landfall* directed by Paul Maunder in 1975. Like Donaldson, he would move offshore in the 1980's and build a formidable career internationally.

Michael Seresin, D.O.P., would become cinematographer on most of Alan Parker's films of the 1980's.

Sleeping Dogs has rough edges. The momentum of the story slows badly at times and inexperience before the camera is obvious in several of the performances. But at the time, it looked a "big" picture, even though its budget was a paltry $NZ 300,000. More importantly, its taste for the irresponsible (like *Wild Man*), its macho emphasis and male-bonding of the two leading characters (a "buddy" movie before its time), appealed directly to many in heartland New Zealand.

The Bad Old Tax Days

Following establishment of the government-funded N.Z. Film Commission late in 1978, the making of feature films proceeded at some pace and in surprising quantity. In five years, 29 were produced – almost double the number to appear in the preceding 80 years.

The commission's mandate was, and still is, "to encourage, and also to participate and assist in the making, promotion, distribution and exhibition of films." It invested in more than half of those made during its first half decade of existence.

In 1984, 17 features were made. This was, by far, a record number for any single year – before or since. The commission invested in seven of them.

The circumstances that fired this flush of production were to cause anguish and debate within the industry for the greater part of the 1980's.

Argument revolved around such questions as: to what extent *quantity* of production is necessary to ensure *quality*, continuity of work and improving standards, and a way of keeping the best talent in the country; the respective roles of the government-funded commission and private investors in financing films; and the degree to which offshore productions should be encouraged to locate in N.Z.

The reason so many films were made in New Zealand in the early 1980's was because, initially, no tax restrictions were placed on film transactions. Financiers soon found ways to create tax shelters and some deals were made that allowed investors to put money into productions for tax reasons – purely and simply. In these cases, investors' interest in any particular film project – let alone its quality and likelihood of a return – was minimal, at best.

Neither was there anything in the Film Commission's brief to prevent it negotiating similar deals to finance those productions in which it intended to invest.

The government plugged the hole in 1982. The flow of unrestricted private investment into films was staunched. The one proviso was that projects approved before the government's 1982 budget could continue under the old tax regime. But they had to be completed by the end of September 1984 to qualify. Hence the avalanche of features which saw 12 New Zealand films being touted in the market at Cannes in 1985. After roller-coaster beginnings, which had seen an unnatural level of feature production in the early 1980's, N.Z. cinema was about to encounter raw reality.

Private investment, given the new tax situation and the N.Z. tax department's subsequent investigation into 90 special film partnerships operating between 1980–84, evaporated. The stock market crash of October 1987 was to further distance any likely financial players.

David Gascoigne, a founding member of the N.Z. Film Commission, succeeded Sheat as chairman in 1985. He believes the government's tax crack-down almost

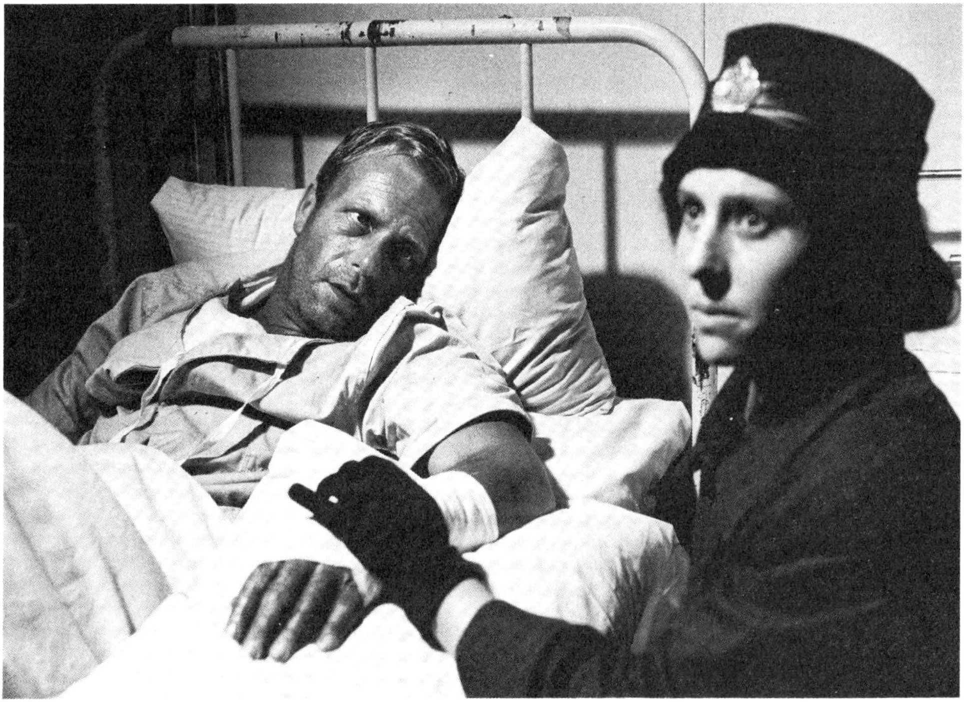

Jack Thompson and Carol Burns in *Bad Blood*

resulted in the extinction of New Zealand feature film-making.

Best Films 1978–84

Many of the best films emerged from those high-flying, tax-break years. Almost without exception, they were the fruit of combined Film Commission and private investor financing.

Films financed only by private investment varied greatly in quality – from low budget American-style "quickies" to brave attempts to beat Hollywood at its own game.

Two examples of the latter were the Lloyd Phillips/Rob Whitehouse action–adventure productions, **Battletruck** and **Savage Islands**, made in 1981 and 1982. Both had imported directors and stars and offshore investment. Both failed to make waves.

The best of the private investment only films were: **Bad Blood**, written and produced by expatriate New Zealander Andrew Brown, and directed by Englishman Mike Newell; and **Other Halves**, a rare entry into urban New Zealand, directed by John Laing and starring N.Z.-born actress, Lisa Harrow. *Bad Blood* was made in 1981 for British

Mark Pilisi in John Laing's *Other Halves*

Still from *Mr. Wrong*

television by Southern Pictures, and shown theatrically in other territories. It stars Australian actor Jack Thompson as farmer-turned-gunman, Stan Graham, who provokes one of the country's biggest manhunts. There is some fine acting and Newell proves adept at capturing the bleak edges of N.Z. rural/ small town paranoia circa 1940.

Other Halves is a story about love that attempts to break barriers of colour, age and class in contemporary Auckland. If a shade too genteel in its handling of the affair, the film offers more than competent performances from Harrow and young Polynesian actor, Mark Pilisi.

But the most entertaining and significant films of the period were three made by Murphy – *Goodbye Pork Pie*, *Utu*, *The Quiet Earth* – Donaldson's *Smash Palace*, Vincent Ward's *Vigil*, and Ian Mune's comedy, *Came a Hot Friday*.

Up there also were Gaylene Preston's first feature, the quirky femme thriller, **Mr Wrong**, David Blyth's deco-punk horror, **Death Warmed Up**, John Reid's suburban comedy **Middle Age Spread**, and Steven's ironic treatment of small town morality, **Skin Deep**.

Murphy's trio reveal a fast-developing talent on the loose. **Goodbye Pork Pie** is an anarchic road movie that thousands of young New Zealanders took to heart. **Utu** established his skills in the field of action and epic drama. **The Quiet Earth** revealed the kind of sensitivity and imagination he can bring to that enduring of N.Z. obsessions – Man Alone. With these three films, Murphy gave notice he was a director of international calibre.

Donaldson's **Smash Palace** remains one of the best examples of narrative skill in N.Z. cinema with strong central performances from Lawrence, Australian actress Anna Jemison, Keith Aberdein and young Greer Robson. Donaldson's next project would be *The Bounty*, for producer Dino De Laurentiis, to be followed by a slate of films that would place him in the top echelon of Hollywood directors.

Vigil, Vincent Ward's first feature, is an austere account of archetypal passion played through the eyes of an 11-year-old girl living on a farm in a remote valley. It was the first ever N.Z. film to be an official selection in competition at the Cannes Film Festival (1984) and revealed a unique talent. Four years later his second feature, **The Navigator** would be similarly honoured.

Ian Mune's **Came a Hot Friday** is the best N.Z. film comedy yet made with standout performances from actors Peter Bland and Phillip Gordon and Maori entertainer Billy T. James. James's Tainuia Kid is one of the great creations of local cinema – a Zorro-with-a difference who spins laughter from mayhem.

The film was a strong performer on the domestic market, but failed to have legs in the U.S. – despite enthusiasm from

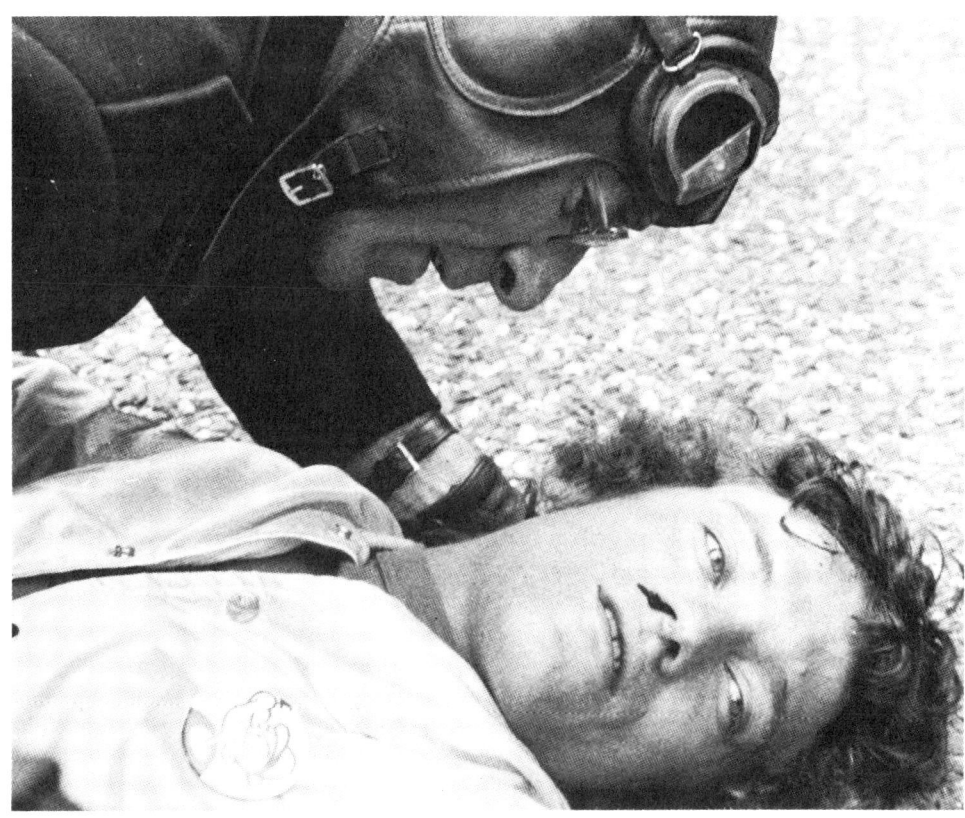

Scene from the adventure–comedy, *Goodbye Pork Pie*

distributors Orion Classics. It was further proof of the difficulty in making the New Zealand accent and sense of humour understandable to a greater audience.

This particular problem is of concern to feature film-makers, who have yet to come up with a major commercial hit in overseas markets. The matter of offshore sales are crucial to an industry where the domestic market is so small that even with a successful film locally it is virtually impossible to cover costs – let alone score a profit.

Brave Bid by Mirage
In March 1987 – seven months before The Big Crash wiped $NZ 8-billion off the value of shares on the N.Z. Stock Exchange in just one week – two of the country's leading producers, Larry Parr and Don Reynolds, linked companies to form Mirage Entertainment Corp. Between them they had been responsible for 12 features since 1983.

Parr, who produced *Came a Hot Friday*, had established an international sales arm in Auckland and New York as part of a bid to obtain better access to the world market. His priorities leaned towards projects possessing strong local content which might slot readily into acceptable Hollywood genres.

Reynolds's interests appeared not dissimilar. He also was involved on low

Still from *Came a Hot Friday*

budget features with first-up directors (Richard Riddiford's **Arriving Tuesday**) and such "difficult" projects as Leon Narbey's film about gold-mining Chinese in a foreign land, **Illustrious Energy**.

Still from *Utu*

Virtually all the projects in which they were involved received investments from the Film Commission.

Three other producers – John Barnett, and the Lloyd Phillips/Rob Whitehouse partnership – also announced a merger between their respective Wellington- based and Auckland-based companies. Their most recent films had been privately funded and Barnett was about to launch **Footrot Flats** in Australia after its huge gross of $NZ 2.5-million on home turf.

Jim Booth, film commission executive director at the time, said he believed the new mergers would ensure a range of more secure investment structures for the industry and provide the opportunity for a greater range of films to be made.

Two months before the crash, Mirage became the first N.Z. film company in 50 years to float publicly. Within a year it was in receivership, showing a bottomline loss of $NZ 12.1-million in its first year.

KEY DIRECTORS
Geoff Murphy

Born 1938. Talents as film-maker – and musician – forged in the pop circus foundry of the Blerta family roadshows of the late 1960's and early 1970's. Also there was actor Bruno Lawrence, who would star in several Murphy features and become country's leading film actor of the 1980's. The most gifted, original and commercially successful director to come out of the reborn N.Z. industry post-1978. Films blend high spirited rebellion, dark antipodean humour, and special effects – to great effect. Films include: *Wild Man*, 1977; *Goodbye Pork Pie*, 1980; *Utu*, 1982; *The Quiet Earth*, 1984; *Never Say Die*, 1988; *Young Guns 2*, 1990 (U.S.).

Geoff Murphy

Jane Campion

Born Wellington 1955. Parents both involved in theatre. Poised to become first antipodean director of the 1990's who is at ease working both in New Zealand and Australia. Studied anthropology and art history at Victoria University of Wellington before heading overseas. Involvement with film intensified at art school in London and led to the making of Super-8 films at Sydney College of Arts, Australia. Prize-winning short films were made at the Australian Film and Television School, Sydney, during the early 1980's. Her rare ability to invest the apparently mundane lives of ordinary and often disadvantaged people with strength and tenacity has been acclaimed. Films include: *Peel* (short), 1981; *A Girl's Own Story* (short), 1983–4; *Two Friends* (telemovie), 1986; *Sweetie*, 1989 – (all made in Australia); and *An Angel At My Table*, 1990.

Jane Campion

Still from *Illustrious Energy*

A major factor in this situation was Parr's production of **A Soldier's Tale**, which he also was directing, in France. It starred Gabriel Byrne, Marianne Basler and Judge Reinhold. The project, which originally was intended to be a French– New Zealand co-production under a 1987 treaty between

Gabriel Byrne in *A Soldier's Tale*

the appropriate government agencies, had continual cash flow problems.

At the same time a completed Mirage film, **Queen City Rocker**, released in the U.S. under the title *Tearaway*, failed to do any significant business. *A Soldier's Tale* was reviewed by *Variety* in the Cannes Film Festival market in May 1988, but has not yet been released anywhere theatrically.

The Barnett–Phillips–Whitehouse merger was a private one. In the early days of optimism Barnett spoke of making four low budget features during 1987–88 with finance from an unnamed private investor. Not one of those films had happened by July 1990.

At first Phillips, and then Whitehouse, shifted locale to Los Angeles. Barnett has moved strongly into local video and film distribution in Auckland. Don Reynolds is now general manager of Television New Zealand subsidiary and production house, South Pacific Pictures. Larry Parr is developing a new feature.

The collapse of Mirage and the failure of the Barnett–Phillips–Whitehouse merger to achieve production illuminated – and isolated – the N.Z. Film Commission as the major force and investor in the feature industry.

The Commission Strikes Back

In 1988, the year of Mirage's demise, the N.Z. Film Commission quietly celebrated its first ten years. Film production had plummeted, although five new films had been marketed in Cannes that year. They included Vincent Ward's second feature, **The Navigator**, which like his first was an official selection in competition.

Only one new film was to be included in the N.Z. Cannes catalogue of 1989, a low budget feature with an ominously prophetic title, *Zilch*.

From the moment of its establishment the commission was never short of critics. It had had some involvement in virtually every feature made in the country, with most

KEY PRODUCERS

John O'Shea

The greatest "enabler" of the N.Z. film industry as well as one of its most important creative talents. Through his Pacific Films studios in Wellington many film-makers continue to learn and develop their craft. His courage and idealism in making three features during the 1950's and 1960's provided the spark for an industry renaissance in the late 1970's. Appointed founder member of the N.Z. Film Commission, in 1978. Background pre-film was research historian (M.A.Hons.), and stint as Assistant Film Censor. In 1945

John O'Shea
photo: Alasdair Foster

helped establish New Zealand Film Society movement. Since early 1950's associated with the making of more than 200 films of all kinds. In recent years has worked closely, as producer, with director Barry Barclay. Still in the business. Films include: *Broken Barrier* 1952; *Runaway*, 1964; *Don't Let It Get You*, 1966; *Sons for the Return Home*, 1979; *Pictures*, 1981; *Among the Cinders*, 1983; *Leave All Fair*, 1984; *Ngati*, 1986; *Te Rua* (in production), 1990.

John Maynard

Australian born. Moved to N.Z. when appointed foundation director of Govett-Brewster Art Gallery, New Plymouth, 1967. Travelled, studied and worked in Australia, India, Europe and the U.K. before returning to N.Z. as Exhibitions Officer, Auckland City Art Gallery in 1975. Was a partner in Auckland-based Phase Three Films. Evaluates films on a project-by-project basis and is well-known for taking risks with new talent. A long producer–director association with Vincent Ward began with Ward's first feature. Was forced to return to Sydney, when the N.Z. financial structure for Ward's second feature collapsed and project was restructured as a co-production between N.Z. and Australia. Produced Jane Campion's first feature and co-produced her recent N.Z.-founded TV miniseries, also distributed theatrically. A director of the Len Lye Foundation. Films include: *Skin Deep*, 1979; *Strata*, 1983; *Vigil*, 1984; *The Navigator*, 1987; *Sweetie*, 1989 (Aus.); *An Angel at My Table*, 1990 (co-produced with Bridget Ikin).

---

film-makers (proven and aspiring) believing they had a natural right to its funds.

These funds, largely provided through direct government grant and the state lottery board, were forecast to be about $NZ 10-million for the 1988–89 financial year. The government grant was just under $NZ 4-million – a 250% lift since 1984.

A number of questions deeply concerned the commission at this time. They included:

FOUR DIRECTORS

Vincent Ward

Born 1956. Father a third-generation New Zealand farmer. Mother of German ancestry. Took film-making courses at Ilam

Vincent Ward

School of Fine Arts, Canterbury University, where he graduated Diploma in Fine Arts (Honours), 1979. Immediately established reputation as a film-maker of great originality with two short dramas. The two features completed to date were Official Selections in Competition at Cannes – in 1984 and 1988. Both works give primacy to the image in achieving a narrative style and have a distinctive archetypal quality. Films include: *A State of Siege*, 1978; *In Spring One Plants Alone*, 1980; *Vigil*, 1984; *The Navigator*, 1987.

Gaylene Preston

Born Greymouth 1947. Studied painting at Ilam School of Fine Arts, Canterbury

Gaylene Preston

University 1966–68. Film career began when involved in art and drama therapy at U.K. psychiatric institution. On return to N.Z. worked for Pacific Films, Wellington, before going freelance to make a series of outstanding documentaries. Her first feature films have been small, intimate dramas of idiosyncratic bent and surprising power. Films include: *All the Way Up There* (Docu), 1978; *Learning Fast* (Docu), 1981; *Making Utu* (Docu), 1982; *Mr Wrong*, 1984; *Ruby and Rata*, 1990.

Barry Barclay

Born 1944. Trained for the priesthood before working with Pacific Films, Wellington, as a director of trade films and commercials. His 1974 television series about Maori life and traditions, *Tangata Whenua*, broke new ground in its development of film-making techniques based on a deep respect for community values. Spent several years out of N.Z. from the late 1970's before returning to make a fine feature-length documentary and his first dramatic feature. Films include: *The*

Town That Lost a Miracle (Docu), 1972; *Tangata Whenua* (TV Series), 1974; *Ashes* (Docu), 1975; *Autumn Fires* (Docu), 1977; *The Neglected Miracle* (Docu), 1984; *Ngati*, 1986; *Te Rua* (*The Pit*) (in production), 1990.

Peter Jackson

Born 1961. Started making films featuring home-made monsters and space ships at age 8 when parents bought him a super 8mm camera. Left school at 17 and failed to get a job in the local film industry. Embarked on his first feature in 1983, shooting at weekends and funding it himself. Four years later, the N.Z. Film Commission viewed the footage and gave him finance to finish. It achieved cult movie status when released. Films: *Bad Taste*, 1987; *Meet the Feebles*, 1989.

Peter Jackson

Barry Barclay

- the level of production and the future prognosis given the flight of private investment and the collapse of such an important private player as Mirage.
- the apparent lack of impact upon N.Z. audiences of locally-made features. With the exception of the privately- funded *Footrot Flats*, no films in recent times had matched the local popularity of Murphy's *Goodbye Pork Pie* (1981) and Mune's *Came a Hot Friday* (1985). At the same time, while several films had received critical acclaim overseas there had been no real commercial hit on the all-important international markets.
- the quality of film scripts.

The commission's initial response was to adopt a harder line on investment in films and concentrate more on project development. Commission chairman Gascoigne confirmed "a more demanding" approach. "We have determined that the need now is to ensure films are made that appeal to audiences. If we cannot maintain and build audiences for New Zealand films then we're on a short-term route to long-term disaster."

He warned that continued government support for the industry depended on politicians knowing the New Zealand public valued what the industry was doing.

The commission's stance did not please everyone.

Barnett, a major player in the industry from its inception and at the time chairman of the Independent Producers' and Directors's Guild, described the major problem as being "no private finance and no diversity of product."

The commission had become preoccupied with "trying to pick winners." He feared a lack of new local features, coupled with the commission's policies, could see it making art films only.

Former commission chairman Bill Sheat said more energy should be spent achieving

Still from *Came a Hot Friday*

Still from Vincent Ward's *The Navigator*

DOSSIER: NEW ZEALAND CINEMA NOW

a non-concessional tax structure, accepted by film-makers and government financial advisers, that would restore private investment. He believed there was too much reliance placed on the commission. "This is bad, philosophically, politically, and artistically, because it places the commission in the position of 'playing God.'"

The commission was unmoved.

In March 1989, it announced it would allocate funds for six features and one miniseries (Jane Campion's *An Angel at My Table*) over the next year. It would fully underwrite four of the projects. The project budgets totalled $NZ 20-million.

This apparent change in policy reflected an absolute dearth of feature production and the new impetus provided by Judith McCann, commission executive director.

McCann, who had been deputy executive director of Canada's Telefilm, joined the commission in January following Jim Booth's move into independent production.

As a result of the policy, four new features were in the market at Cannes in 1990, with seven producers – operating under the umbrella of the commission – seeking offshore involvement for projects in advanced stages of development.

A new bullishness was apparent and McCann was able to announce commission financing priorities for the June 1990–91 year. These would preclude any 100% underwriting of any feature with unconfirmed overseas market interest – other than low budget or first features.

The commission also set about answering its critics on the issue of private investment regeneration. It said it had floated a scheme offering $NZ 30- million in film investment bonds to a limited number of major N.Z. institutional investors. The scheme is designed to return the original investment

ALL-ROUNDER
Ian Mune

Born Auckland 1941. As actor, director, scriptwriter, one of N.Z.'s most experienced film-makers. More than a dozen screen credits as director, and about two dozen as scriptwriter, including four features. Has won seven N.Z. awards for film and TV acting. Began career as stage actor, moving into theatre direction and TV work. Formed Aardvark/Mune Productions, with director Roger Donaldson, 1974, an association that led to the first full-scale feature to be made in N.Z. for 11 years. Co-wrote script and acted one of the two main roles (the other was played by Sam Neill). Sampled Hollywood and returned to N.Z. to direct first feature for producer Larry Parr, showing great skill in realising delicate moments of contact between actors. Films (as director, and/or writer) include: *The Woman at the Store*, (short drama), 1974; *Sleeping Dogs*, 1977; *Goodbye Pork Pie*, 1980; *The Silent One*, 1984; *Came a Hot Friday*, 1984; *Bridge to Nowhere*, 1985; *The Grasscutter* (telemovie), 1988; *The End of the Golden Weather* (in pre-production), scheduled 1991.

Ian Mune

John Bach in *Goodbye Pork Pie*

in five years – plus profits along the way.

As at July 1990, the scheme had failed to excite interest. Gascoigne gave the reason as being the high rates of interest then applying to ordinary fixed interest deposits in N.Z. banks.

With regard to generating greater interest for the local product among audiences, the commission intensified its promotion of recently completed and upcoming films.

Three of the Cannes features and the Campion miniseries, which will be released theatrically world-wide, were included in major film festivals in Wellington and Auckland during July and August. Following this showcasing, and with strong funding support from the commission, they would be promoted and exhibited throughout the country.

Effectively, the commission had come out of the closet and become N.Z. Cinema Inc. It was openly playing the role of studio head, rather than anonymous "encourager" of an industry long on dreams.

Films – 1985–80

Three important developments stand out when examining the catalogue of films made in N.Z. during the second half of the 1980's:

• Private investment only films virtually disappeared. The exception was *Footrot*

Lee Mete-Kingi and Yvonne Lawley in *Ruby and Rata*

photo: Geoff Short

Flats (1985–86). Two offshore productions located for varying periods, Lucasfilm's *Willow* and Disney's *The Rescue*. They could scarcely be deemed local or indigenous. But they did provide employment. All the action – and for a couple of those years there was very little – was with the Film Commission.

• The emergence of Maori film-makers and actors. In the forefront were directors Barry Barclay and Merata Mita and actor Wi Kuki Kaa. Both Barclay and Mita come from documentary film and made their first features in 1986–87. The growing number of Maori behind and before the cameras – developments positively encouraged by Barclay and Mita – is providing the industry with a new vein of talent and commitment.

• The return home in 1989 of Jane Campion to make a miniseries, that would also become a theatrical release. Campion's widely-acclaimed short films and first feature, *Sweetie*, made from her base in Australia, are notable for their implicit rendering of characteristics of European New Zealand. But her return for **An Angel at My Table** may be of greater importance in signalling new ways to embrace expatriate film talent and encourage its expression more obviously within the context of N.Z. cinema.

Three of the most significant films of this period – *An Angel at My Table*, Barclay's **Ngati**, and Gaylene Preston's **Ruby and Rata** – vary greatly, when compared one with the other, in quality and technical accomplishment. What they all share is an austerity of style and a rigorous attention to simple, apparently ordinary events and characters, that make the people and what happens to them extraordinary and entertaining.

It is surprising how both Campion and

FOUR ACTORS
Bruno Lawrence

Born U.K. 1949. Came to N.Z. as small boy. Was multi-talented drummer with the Blerta travelling roadshows of the late 1960's/early 1970's. Starred in the Blerta-inspired shoe-string mini-feature *Wild Man* and proceeded to become the country's most individual – and durable – film acting talent to date. Won best actor award at the 1982 Manila Film Festival for his performance as mechanic/racing driver, Al Shaw, in Roger Donaldson's *Smash Palace*. Parts have also come his way in Australia. Films include: *Goodbye Pork Pie*, 1980; *Smash Palace*, 1981; *Utu*, 1982; *Heart of the Stag*, 1983; *The Quiet Earth*, 1984; *Bridge to Nowhere*, 1985; *Rikky and Pete* (Aus.), 1988; *The Delinquents* (Aus.), 1989.

Bruno Lawrence

Wi Kuki Kaa

Born 1938. N.Z.'s leading Maori film actor. Returned home in 1983 after 15 years as an actor in Australia. Committed to the local industry and to working to secure the place of Maori film-makers and performers. Made a big impression in his first major film role as Wiremu in Geoff Murphy's *Utu*. Films include: *Utu*, 1982; *The Bounty* (U.S.), 1984; *Kingpin*, 1984; *Ngati*, 1986; *Te Rua* (in production), 1990.

Wi Kuki Kaa

John Bach

Born in 1946. Welsh ancestry. Began acting at school and has been dedicated to the craft ever since. A dramatic actor with presence and range he worked virtually non-stop in television and film in the 1970's and 1980's. He now works both in N.Z. and Australia. Films include: *Goodbye Pork Pie*, 1980; *Beyond Reasonable Doubt*, 1980; *Utu*, 1982; *The Lost Tribe*, 1983; *Pallet on the Floor*, 1984; *Other Halves*, 1984; *Blood Oath* (Aus.), 1989.

Phillip Gordon

Born 1959. Eight feature films since his debut in 1978. A N.Z. television best actor award winner. His films include: *Savage Islands*, 1983; *Came a Hot Friday*, 1984; *Bridge to Nowhere*, 1985; *Never Say Die*, 1988; *The Returning* (in post production) 1990.

John Bach

Philip Gordon
photo: Trishia Downie-Matte Box Films

Barclay, in different ways, have the capacity to generate emotional force through a technique of puritanical restraint in realising their stories. And this does not preclude compassion.

Ward's arresting and singular *The Navigator*, as severe in looks as his earlier *Vigil*, possesses similar characteristics in telling its mediaeval/contemporary tale of faith and redemption.

In a niche of his own is Peter Jackson, whose delight in Boy's Own Fodder Horror began with **Bad Taste** (1987) and continued with **Meet the Feebles** (1989). The films are uneven, outrageous and strictly late night material. He is new and has a natural talent, which suggests more and better lie ahead.

The Way Ahead

During the Cannes Film Festival and Market of 1990, the N.Z. Film Commission was not only concerned with selling product and aiding producers in their search for offshore partners for future projects. It began adjusting to the globalisation of film production that is proceeding apace in most Western countries.

One important move was to join agencies and production houses linking four countries – U.K., Canada, Australia and N.Z. – in a plan to make four medium-budget features a year over the next three years. One film will be financed by each country, with distribution guaranteed in the other three. Rights will be shared across the package.

TWO ACTRESSES
Donna Akersten

Born Auckland 1948. One of the Antipodes' most experienced dramatic and comedic actresses who has worked consistently on stage and screen in N.Z., and Australia, since the late 1960's. Good roles for women have been few in the born-again feature film industry post 1975. Akersten landed a couple of them. Films include: *Sleeping Dogs*, 1977; *Middle Age Spread*, 1979; *Bad Blood*, 1982; *Te Rua* (in production) 1990.

Alison Routledge
photo: Trishia Downie-Matte Box Films

Donna Akersten

Alison Routledge

Born U.K. 1960. Graduate of N.Z. Drama School. Made luminous impact in *The Quiet Earth*. Acted in many stage productions before commencing television and film career. Films include: *Other Halves*, 1984; *The Quiet Earth*, 1984; *Bridge to Nowhere*, 1985; *The Returning* (in post production), 1990.

The commission sees the plan as being important in regenerating private investment in New Zealand. David Gascoigne believes it might ignite interest in the commission's multi-million dollar film bond scheme.

With so many of the country's top directors currently located in the U.S. (Roger Donaldson, Geoff Murphy, Sam Pillsbury, David Blyth, Vincent Ward) the co-production pact conceivably also could be a way of attracting talent back from time to time. Equally, offshore projects in which they and/or other expatriate film talent might be involved in could come under the scheme.

This kind of view as to how N.Z. cinema, given its small domestic base, might better retain proven talent and expand production, will mean some adjustment in thinking. The country has a history of forever-pioneering and failing to secure its artistic enterprises so they can mature. It is still a national characteristic to bask in the glory of expatriate achievers, including filmmakers, yet not to welcome them home.

Cel from *Footrot Flats*

INTERNATIONAL AWARDS FOR NEW ZEALAND FILMS
A Selection in Alphabetical Listing

Bad Taste. Dir: Jackson 1988 17th Paris International Festival of Fantasy & Science Fiction Films: special jury prize, best Gore film

Flying Fox In A Freedom Tree. Dir: Sanderson 1989 Tokyo International Film Festival: best screenplay, Martyn Sanderson

Footrot Flats. Dir: Ball Los Angeles International Animation Celebration: first prize

Kingpin. Dir: Walker Moscow Festival: special prize

The Navigator. Dir: Ward 1988 Cannes Film Festival: official selection in competition 1988 Sitges Film Festival, Spain: best film

Ngati. Dir: Barclay 1987 Cannes Film Festival: Critics' Week 1987 Taormina Film Festival: Gold Charybdis, best film

The Scarecrow. Dir: Pillsbury 1982 Cannes Film Festival: selected for Directors' Fortnight

Smash Palace. Dir: Donaldson 1982 Manila Film Festival: best actor, Bruno Lawrence

Utu. Dir: Murphy 1983 Cannes Film Festival: official selection out of competition

Vigil. Dir: Ward 1984 Cannes Film Festival: off. selection in competition

THREE CINEMATOGRAPHERS

Leon Narbey

Born 1947. One of N.Z.'s best lighting cameramen. An earlier career as sculptor is widely credited as bringing a sophisticated feeling for light, colour, movement and form to his film work. Graduated with Diploma of Fine Arts (Honours) from University of Auckland 1969. Later established a film-maker's co-operative in Christchurch. As D.O.P. on a wide range of feature films has enjoyed close working relationships with several directors, including Gaylene Preston. Directed his first feature, *Illustrious Energy*, in 1987. Films include: *Skin Deep*, 1979; *Strata*, 1983; *Trespasses*, 1983; *Other Halves*, 1984; *Illustrious Energy*, 1987; *Ruby and Rata*, 1990.

Alun Bollinger

James Bartle

Alun Bollinger

Born Wellington 1948. Left school to work as cinecamera trainee in television. Freelancing by 1968. His association with the Blerta travelling roadshows of the early 1970's, resulted in his shooting *Wild Man*, 1977. He went on to be D.O.P. on many of the best N.Z. features of the next decade. Films include: *Middle Age Spread*, 1979; *Sons for the Return Home*, 1979; *Beyond Reasonable Doubt*, 1980; *Goodbye Pork Pie*, 1980; *Vigil*, 1984; *Came a Hot Friday*, 1984; *For Love Alone* (Aus.), 1987; *A Soldier's Tale*, 1988.

James Bartle

Born Melbourne, Aus., 1941. Entered television as cameraman 1963. Worked for Australian and British television before moving to N.Z. in 1974. Became a freelance lighting cameraman three years later shooting commercials, features and TV drama. Made a notable contribution as D.O.P. on Geoff Murphy's *The Quiet Earth*. Films include: *The Scarecrow*, 1982; *Heart of the Stag*, 1983; *Death Warmed Up*, 1984; *The Quiet Earth*, 1984; *I Was a Teenage Vampire* (U.S.), 1986; *Shrimp on the Barbie*, 1989.

Still from *Mauri*

What should help the country get out of this groove is the accelerating exchange of talent, in all fields, with Australia, and the global view of local programming now being taken by the state-owned enterprise network, Television New Zealand. It believes the emphasis must be on programmes that appeal to international viewers as well as consumers at home.

The network is also working hard to bring offshore "notables" back to work – on both sides of the camera.

Jane Campion's return for *An Angel at My Table*, hopefully, has established a most desirable pattern. (Hence her inclusion as a Key Director in this Dossier.) If something similar had happened to writer Katherine Mansfield back in the 1920's, the course of

44 | INTERNATIONAL FILM GUIDE

Still from *Shaker Run*

Still from *Mauri*

Still from *Starlight Hotel*

Still from The Quiet Earth, directed by Geoff Murphy

BEST-SELLING NEW ZEALAND FILMS ABROAD (a selection)

Footrot Flats 1986–87. Dir: Ball
Battletruck 1982. Dir: Cokliss
Smash Palace 1982. Dir: Donaldson
The Quiet Earth 1986. Dir: Murphy
The Navigator 1988. Dir: Ward
Never Say Die 1988. Dir: Murphy
Utu 1983. Dir: Murphy
Dangerous Orphans 1985. Dir: Laing
Shaker Run 1984. Dir: Morrison
Goodbye Pork Pie 1981. Dir: Murphy

Still from *Zilch!*

Still from *Death Warmed Up*

Still from *The Lost Tribe*

Still from *Constance*

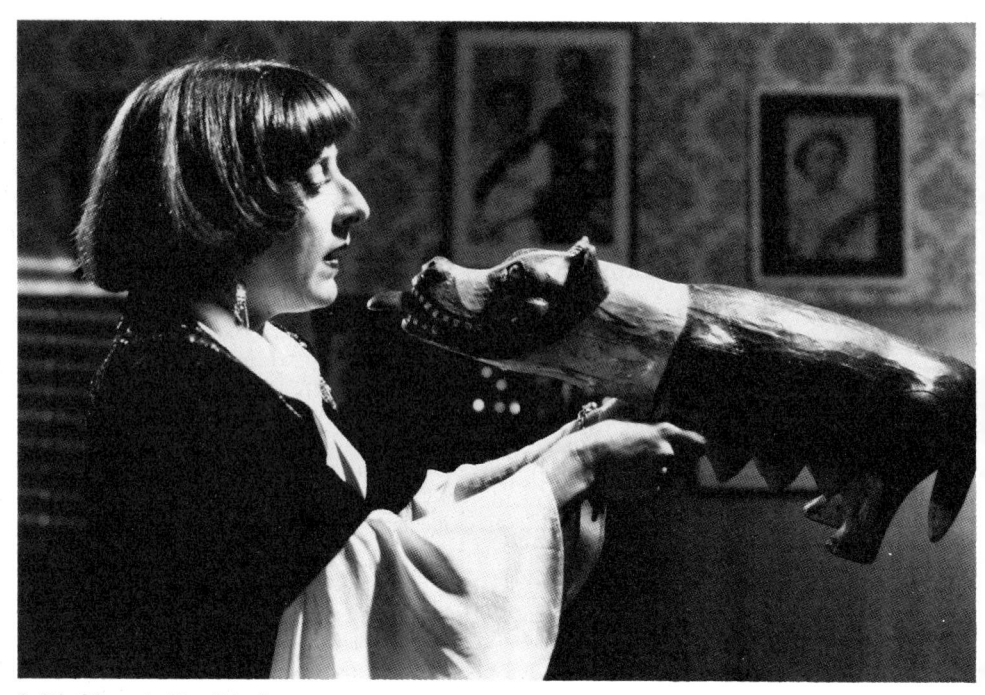

Judith Gibson in *User Friendly*

Still from *Ngati*

N.Z. literature, if not changed, certainly would have been deepened and embellished.

The record of N.Z. cinema stands. It is a creditable one. More than 60 films made and screened in a short life of just 12 years.

MIKE NICOLAIDI has been New Zealand correspondent for Variety since 1978. He was London correspondent for the New Zealand Press Association 1965–68 and is a former director of the Queen Elizabeth II Arts Council of New Zealand. He gratefully acknowledges the assistance of Lindsay Shelton, and the N.Z. Film Archive, in preparing this article. Nicholas Reid's book, A Decade of New Zealand Film, *was a valuable reference source.*

Still from Larry Parr's ill-fated *A Soldier's Tale*

Lee Meti-Kingi and Vanessa Rare in *Ruby and Rata*

photo: Geoff Short

DOSSIER: NEW ZEALAND CINEMA NOW

Useful Addresses

N.Z. Film Commission
PO Box 11546
Wellington
Tel: (04) 859.754
Fax: (04) 849.719

N.Z. National Film Unit
Fairway Drive
PO Box 46002
Lower Hutt
Tel: (04) 672.059
Fax: (04) 673.450

South Pacific All Media Distribution Ltd
PO Box 30948
Lower Hutt
Tel: (04) 678.285
Fax: (04) 670.484

TVNZ International
PO Box 3819
Auckland
Tel: (09) 391.414
Fax: (09) 794.907

Amalgamated Theatres Ltd
103–107 Hobson Street
Auckland
Tel: (09) 32.739
Fax: (09) 370.011

Endeavour Filmpac IFM Ltd
PO Box 37491
Auckland
Tel: (09) 781.900
Fax: (09) 781.905

Everard Films Ltd
PO Box 3664
Auckland
Tel: (09) 760.864
Fax: (09) 780.109

Proequity Entertainments Ltd
PO Box 46181
Auckland
Tel: (09) 788.336
Fax: (09) 766.061

Independent Producers & Directors
PO Box 3969
Wellington
Tel: (04) 854.344

N.Z. Federation of Film Societies
PO Box 9544
Wellington
Tel: (04) 850.162

Endeavour Entertainment Corp
PO Box 2689
Wellington
Tel: (04) 859.421
Fax: (04) 845.554

Finlayson Brewer Productions
PO Box 47141
Auckland
Tel: (09) 766.908
Fax: (09) 766.908

Gibson Group
PO Box 6185
Wellington
Tel: (04) 847.789
Fax: (04) 844.727

Training Media Services
PO Box 17096
Auckland
Tel: (09) 591.332
Fax: (09) 595.113

UIP (NZ) Ltd
PO Box 2606
Auckland
Tel: (09) 796.269
Fax: (09) 796.271

Hibiscus Films
PO Box 1852
Auckland
Tel: (09) 398.388
Fax: (09) 398.639

Matte Box Films
2 Balmoral Road
Epsom
Auckland
Tel: (09) 602.836
Fax: (09) 602.836

Midnight Film Prods.
PO Box 6357
Wellington
Tel: (04) 852.914
Fax: (04) 828.219

Pacific Films
PO Box 2040
Wellington
Tel: (04) 872.191
Fax: (04) 873.231

Pinflicks Productions
PO Box 9438
Wellington
Tel: (04) 844.496
Fax: (04) 851.807

The Partners Film Co
PO Box 1569
Wellington
Tel: (04) 856.509
Fax: (04) 859.790

Zee Films
PO Box 39020
Auckland
Tel: (09) 780.529

Anatomy of a Movie:
UNTIL THE END OF THE WORLD

In the second of our series on international productions, we focus on Wim Wenders' elaborate enterprise, set in the year 1999 and budgeted at $18 million, with location shooting here, there, and everywhere. DAVID STRATTON paid an exclusive visit to the closed set in Australia's Northern Territory . . .

Until the End of the World is described in advance publicity as "the ultimate road movie." It is certainly that, and it is unique in that shooting is taking place in no less than seven countries. The genesis for this remarkable production was over twelve years ago, when Wim Wenders made his first trip to Australia.

At the time, I was Director of the Sydney Film Festival, and had screened all Wenders' films from *The Fear of the Goalkeeper* (1971) on; despite several invitations, Wenders had never been able to come to the festival himself. Then, just a few days before Christmas in 1977, I received a call from Darwin, 3,000 miles away on Australia's sub-tropical north coast. Wenders, who had been attending a screening of some of his films in Djakarta,

Cameraman Robby Müller and Wim Wenders (centre) on location in Australia
photo: David Stratton

had hopped on a ship and arrived in the Top End. He started hitch-hiking down through the centre of the continent, in the intense summer heat, taking photographs of the remarkable scenery along the way. By the time he arrived in Sydney, he couldn't wait to develop the photos and to head back for the Centre. Already the seeds for a feature film set in the near-future were sown, a film Wenders planned to make in 1979 (after shooting *Hammett* for Francis Coppola).

July 4, 1990, Emily Gap, near Alice Springs

Day 67 of shooting. A large crew composed of Germans, French and Australians is clustered around this natural break in the McDonnell Ranges. This is the location for an Aboriginal Cultural Centre of the near-future (ten years hence). Living here are the parents (Max von Sydow, Jeanne Moreau) of Sam (William Hurt), who has crossed three continents already to be reunited with them in this remote spot.

The film commenced production on April 2 on a highway near San Remo in Italy. Since then, Wenders and his crew, and a cast that also includes Solveig Dommartin, Sam Neill, Rüdiger Vogler and Ernie Dingo, have filmed in Venice, the Southwest of France (Lozère region), Paris, Lisbon, Berlin, San Francisco and Tokyo.

Max von Sydow and Jeanne Moreau on location for *Until the End of the World*

photo: David Stratton

Dommartin plays Claire, a young woman who becomes involved with Sam and joins him on his inter-continental quest. They are followed by her former lover (Sam Neill) and two detectives (Rüdiger Vogler, Ernie Dingo).

Also involved in the Australian sequences are a large number of Aboriginal actors, including David Gulpilil (remembered from Roeg's *Walkabout* and Weir's *The Last Wave*), Justine Saunders (*The Fringe Dwellers*) and Bart Willoughby (*Wrong Side of the Road*).

Despite the extraordinary complexity of the production, and the fact that there is still a very long way to go, including scenes to be shot by a reduced crew in the less accessible Bungle Bungle range in the Kimberleys, everyone on set seems extremely cheerful. A helicopter is being used for a scene in which three CIA agents arrive and arrest the Max von Sydow character: Wenders cast Sydney playwright Michael Gow and French line producer Mark Monnet as two of the identically-clad spooks: the third is played by a local helicopter pilot, who is finding film-making a very different experience from flying scenic flights for tourists.

There are also scenes involving some 100 aborigines, men, women and children, who are forced to leave their homes because of radiation. They march past von Sydow, who is seated on the trunk of a dead tree. On the second take (for which two cameras are used), Wenders has some of the aboriginal children shake von Sydow by the hand as they go past. Everyone laughs at the enthusiasm with which the youngsters enter into the spirit of the scene.

When William Hurt comes on set, everyone unconnected with the production moves away to the base camp nearby. I notice that the character Rüdiger Vogler plays has the same name, Philip Winter, as the character he played in *Alice in the Cities* (1974), and the actor agrees that this could, indeed, be the same man who escorted young Alice across Germany in the earlier film. He is pleased with the irony that the character is reincarnated in a film where the chief location is close to a city called Alice.

Shooting lasts from dawn until sunset, and then the crew and many of the actors gather at the Alice Springs Casino where the nightclub has been converted into a screening room for the daily rushes. The film is being processed in Sydney, and the rushes we see are four days old. It's immediately clear that Wenders' regular DOP, Robby Müller, is doing another extraordinary job of work. An exhilarating crane shot is used for a majestic scene in which Sam (Hurt) is finally reunited with his blind mother (Moreau), and introduces her (in French) to Claire (Dommartin).

There's also a beautiful sequence in which the travellers, who have been stranded in the desert, are picked up by a one-armed man driving a truck full of aborigines; one old man sings a plaintive song, which Sam explains to Claire is his way of keeping the country, which is threatened by radiation, alive.

If all goes well, it's just possible that *Until the End of the World* might be ready for the 1991 Cannes festival. But whenever it's eventually completed and shown it seems evident that this unique road movie will make a considerable impact. Meanwhile, Wim Wenders' twelve-year dream is nearing reality.

Until the End of the World
Script: Wim Wenders, Peter Carey. Director: Wim Wenders. Photography: Robby Müller. Editor: Peter Przygodda. Produced by Jonathan Taplin. A Trans Pacific–Argos Films–Village Roadshow

Wenders lines up a shot with Max von Sydow, on location in Australia

photo: David Stratton

Rüdiger Vogler on location for *Until the End of the World*

photo: David Stratton

P/L-Road Movies production. (A French–Australian–German co-production.) *Players*: William Hurt, Solveig Dommartin, Sam Neill, Max von Sydow, Jeanne Moreau, Rüdiger Vogler, Ernie Dingo, David Gulpilil, Justine Saunders, Chishu Ryu.

SCREENWRITER: PETER CAREY

Peter Carey is a prizewinning Australian novelist (*Bliss, Oscar and Lucinda*) whose previous film assignment was to co-script the film version of *Bliss* (1985) with director Ray Lawrence. He is currently working with director Bill Bennett on a screenplay called *War Crimes*.

DIRECTOR: WIM WENDERS

Born in 1945, in Düsseldorf, Wenders started making short films, mostly about music, in the late 1960's. His German features all had a strong American influence ("America has colonised our sub-conscious" he once said): *Summer in the City* (1970), *The Fear of the Goalkeeper When the Penalty Is Kicked* (1971), *The Scarlet Letter* (1972), *Alice in the Cities* (1974), *Wrong Movement* (1975), *Kings of the Road* [or *In the Course of Time*] (1976), *The American Friend* (1977), *Lightning over Water* (1980), *Hammett* (1982), *The State of Things* (1982), *Paris Texas* (1984), *Tokyo-Ga* (1985), *Wings of Desire* (1987), *Until the End of the World* (1991).

STAR: WILLIAM HURT

Hurt was born in Washington D.C. in 1950 and was reared in the South Pacific where his father was a director of Trust Territories for the U.S. State Dept. He majored in theology at Tufts University before switching to drama.

After spending his senior year in London he returned to the U.S. and enrolled in Juilliard where he stayed for three years before joining the Oregon Shakespearean Festival. In New York Hurt joined the Circle Repertory Company and appeared in *The Fifth of July* and *The Runner Stumbles* among other plays. He also received a Tony nomination for best supporting actor for his performance in David Rabe's *Hurlyburly*.

Hurt's first film role was in *Altered States* in 1980 followed by *Eyewitness*, *Body Heat*, *The Big Chill* and *Gorky Park*. He won his Oscar for the 1985 *Kiss of the Spider Woman* and was subsequently nominated for *Children of a Lesser God* and *Broadcast News*. His more recent films include *A Time of Destiny*, *The Accidental Tourist*, *I Love You to Death* and the Woody Allen film *Alice*.

Fred Lombardi

William Hurt

DIRECTOR OF PHOTOGRAPHY: ROBBY MÜLLER

In addition to working on the Wim Wenders films listed above, Dutch-born Müller has shot films for Jim Jarmusch (*Down by Law*, 1986, and *Mystery Train*, 1989) and Andrzej Wajda (*Korczak*, 1990).

PRODUCER: JONATHAN TAPLIN

According to Jonathan Taplin, his involvement in one of the most complex financially-backed films and one of the most logistically difficult productions was triggered by a chance occurrence. In 1989 Wim Wenders was a late replacement for Francis Ford Coppola as president of the Cannes Film Festival jury and Taplin, an old friend of Wenders, sent him a teasing note asking if he could get in free to all events. Wenders in turn asked Taplin to look at a new script he wanted to direct. Taplin loved the script and committed his Trans Pacific Film, subsidiary of Trans Pacific Group, a Japanese–American partnership. In the process it helped relieve the difficulties with the French (Argos Films), Australian (Village Roadshow), and German (Road Movies) companies involved in the production. Trans Pacific then brought Majestic Films of London into the deal and a highly complex financial structure was set in place.

Trans Pacific was able to provide the bulk of the budget which now runs about $20 million. Distribution rights were established so that each of the original three companies had rights to their respective territories, Trans Pacific to

Jonathan Taplin

the U.S. and Japan and Majestic to all remaining areas.

Trans Pacific then sold American rights to Warner on a pure gross deal. Japanese rights were sold to Dentsu which also gives it an excellent marketing arm. The Japanese have good reason to feel confident about marketing the film since Wenders' last movie, *Wings of Desire*, enjoyed a phenomenal 67 week run in Tokyo.

Wenders' name was also a major factor in casting the film. According to Taplin, Willem Dafoe dropped out of the film because he was advised that he was working with too many arty directors. On the other hand William Hurt who replaced Dafoe was eager to work with Wenders. (According to Taplin, there are three directors in the world most sought after by actors: Wenders, Scorsese, and Bertolucci.) Taplin says it was also Hurt who suggested bringing Max von Sydow into the project.

Born in 1946, Taplin started his career in the music business (he was road manager for Bob Dylan and The Band), and moved over to film production with Martin Scorsese's *Mean Streets* (1973). His subsequent films have included Roger Spottiswoode's *Under Fire*, with Gene Hackman and Nick Nolte, and – currently in pre-production – Franc Roddam's *K2*.

Fred Lombardi

EXECUTIVE PRODUCER: ANATOLE DAUMAN

Described as a Renaissance Man among producers, Anatole Dauman is one of the most honoured figures of French and European film professionals. In four decades of activity, Dauman boasts a catalogue of films – some three dozen features, and over 100 shorts – of consistently high artistic calibre.

Of Polish-Russian extraction, Dauman (born in 1925) hoisted his Argos Films banner in Paris in 1949 and was one of the prime movers in the Golden Age of French shorts, which became the training ground for the New Wave film-makers. Alain Resnais' chillingly beautiful *Night and Fog* was one of many distinguished shorts produced under Argos. Chris Marker, Jean Aurel, Alexandre Astruc, Jacques Baratier, Georges Franju, Agnès Varda, Jan Lenica, Jean Rouch, Joris Ivens, Walerian Borowczyk, Henri Gruel, Mario Ruspoli, Jacques and Pierre Prévert, Pierre Kast all did some of their most imaginative films under Dauman's aegis.

Dauman's roster of features reflects his literate and literary tastes and his acumen in creating exciting artistic tandems, such as Alain Resnais' landmark collaborations with writers Marguerite Duras (*Hiroshima, mon amour*), Alain Robbe-Grillet (*Last Year at Marienbad*) and Jean Cayrol (*Muriel*). Dauman's faith in New Wave enfant terrible Jean-Luc Godard produced *Two or Three Things I Know about Her* and *Masculin-féminin* and his backing of Robert Bresson enhanced the art of film with *Mouchette* and *Au hasard, Balthazar*.

His cosmopolitan flair led to such unusual and controversial ventures as Nagisa Oshima's erotic dyptych, *In the Realm of the Senses* and *In the Realm of Passions*, Volker Schlöndorff's daring literary adaptations of *Le Coup de grace* and *The Drum*.

Until the End of the World is Dauman's third collaboration with the peripatetic Wim Wenders, begun with *Paris, Texas* and *Wings of Desire*, both Cannes honoured critical and commercial successes. He has a 50% stake in the new Wenders film.

Lenny Borger

FIPRESCI
Fédération Internationale de la Presse Cinématographique

In 1925 some film journalists from Paris and Brussels founded a "Professional Association of the Film Press." Soon after, the Belgian journalists took the initiative in making contact with others in foreign countries. The idea of an International Federation of Film Press took shape in Paris, during the Congress of Cinema in the autumn of 1926. The following communique was issued: "A strong representation of film critics from the daily press and the specialised press have attended the Congress of Cinema in Paris. After having heard a report by M.J.L. Croze, the Commission which was formed has demanded the constitution of an International Federation of the Film Press. This organisation should become a centre of international information as well as providing a group for the defence of professional interests."

Some Belgian critics took the initiative on their return home and made contact with other national associations for the film press within Europe. Negotiations took a considerable time until in 1929 it looked as though the whole thing would die before getting started. Then in June 1930 during the International Congress on Cinema held in the Palais des Académies in Brussels, some French, Italian and Belgian critics decided to take matters in their own hands and founded the Federation, based on the principle of individual membership.

The second General Assembly of the Federation was held in Rome in 1931, and efforts were made to contact countries who had not adhered into membership. The Italians also proposed that the name FIPRESCI be adopted. By June of that year a report drawn up by the Belgians had been published, which was sent to all European Journalist organisations. Governments became involved and in November an International Commission was created to reorganise FIPRESCI.

By June 1932 the third General Assembly, held in London, was in a position to approve the new international statutes proposed by the Commission, which subsequently dissolved itself.

In Paris during January the fourth General Assembly, Belgium assumed the posts of Secretary General and Treasurer and a logo and membership card were created.

During the late 1930's the Bureau of FIPRESCI had to tread a very wary line among the conflicting political storms taking place in Europe. On the whole FIPRESCI managed to maintain a position of neutrality, and during the first years of the Second World War the Bureau managed to assist members of FIPRESCI in Austria and Poland.

At the outbreak of the war FIPRESCI consisted of seven national sections, Germany, Austria, Belgium, France, Italy, Luxembourg and Czechoslovakia, with nine other countries represented by individual members, the Vatican City, Spain, United States, Holland, Portugal, Romania, Sweden and Switzerland. When the war finished it was again France and Belgium which started the process of getting FIPRESCI running again. At the Cannes Film Festival in 1946 FIPRESCI elected new officials, including Dilys Powell as President. In 1947 the organisation was fortunate enough to find Denis Marion, a man of great diplomacy and charm who helped to direct FIPRESCI towards its current situation.

The Organisation Today

FIPRESCI is run by its member sections, and holds a General Assembly each year, which has traditionally taken place during MIFED in Milan. There, the President, four Vice Presidents and a General Secretary are voted into office by delegates of sections present. Once appointed the General Secretary normally remains in office, unless voted out by the General Assembly. The President and four Vice Presidents are voted in for two years, normally renewable for a further two years when they retire from office. The office of the President has rotated between "Western" and "Socialist" sections, and two of the Vice Presidents represent "Western", and the other two "Socialist" sections.

Newsletters are sent to every section giving details of forthcoming FIPRESCI Juries and Seminars, as well as the General Assembly. In addition more substantial Bulletins are issued from time to time as well as reports on Seminars. FIPRESCI currently has virtually worldwide representation (Poland and Italy have two Associations), in addition there are 28 individual members. FIPRESCI Juries were constituted at 19 film festivals in 1989; these Juries are established on a rotational basis between the various countries.

The basic *raison d'être* of FIPRESCI is the defence of the rights and interests of professional film critics and the improvement of conditions in which they carry out their work. Over the years FIPRESCI prizes have been often as important as official jury prizes. The criterion for FIPRESCI Prizes is "To promote film-art and to encourage new and young cinema."

FIPRESCI accepts membership from any professional organisation of film critics in a country or region if a nation-wide organisation does not exist. It will also accept individual membership in countries where a section does not exist, but prefers membership on a sectional and national basis.

1990/91 Officers

Président d'Honneur – Lino Micciché.
President – Marcel Martin.
Vice Presidents – Peter Cargin
　　　　　　　　　Ninos Feneck Mikelides
　　　　　　　　　Andrei Plachov
　　　　　　　　　Eva Zaoralova

National Members:
AUSTRALIA – David Stratton, The Film Critic's Circle of Australia, P.O. Box 16, Spit Junction, N.S.W.
BRAZIL – Carlos Avellar, Rua Maria Eugenia 226 apt. 102 CEP 22261, Rio de Janeiro.
BELGIUM – Marc Turfkruyer, 71 van Maerlanstraat, B–2008 Antwerpen.

BULGARIA – Union des Cinéastes, Mme Iskra Dimitrowa, 6, September Str. 7, BG–1000 Sofia.
CANADA – Association Québécoise des Critiques de Cinéma, M. Bernard Boulad, C.P. 1143 succ. Place d'Armes, Montréal, H2Y 336.
CUBA – I.C.A.I.C. Centro de Informacion. Alex Fleites, Calle 23 No 1155 Vedado Ciudad, La Habana.
CZECHOSLOVAKIA – Eva Zaoralova, V. clavsk N m 57, 110 00 Prague.
DENMARK – Sammenslutningen af Danske Filmkritikers, Mrs. Nina Davidse, Sylows all. 8, DK–2000 Copenhagen.
EGYPT – Egyptian Film Critics Association, Hashea Nahhass, National Centre for Film Culture, 36, Sherif Str, Cairo.
FRANCE – Sydicat Français de la Critique de Cinéma, Claude Beylie, 11, rue de l'Abbé Gregoire, F–75009 Paris.
GERMANY – Verband der Journalisten der DDR, Film Critics Section, Horst Knietzsch, Friedrichstrasse 101, DDR–1080 Berlin 30
– Arbeitsgemeinschaft der Filmjournalisten, c/o Deutsches Filmmuseum, Schaumainkai 41, D–6 Frankfurt 70.
GREECE – Ninos Mikelides, 4, Lefkossias St, Athens 11252.
HUNGARY – Hungarian Film Critics Organisation, Agnes Koltai, Nepktzarsagag Utja 101, H– Budapest VI.
ISRAEL – Journalists' Association, Gideon Orsher, 4, Kalan St, Tel-Aviv 64734.
ITALY – Sindicato Nazionale Critici Cinematografici Italiani, Via Yser 8, 00198 Rome.
– Sindicato Nazionale Giornalisti Cinematografici Italiana, Via Basento 52, d I–00198 Rome.
JAPAN – Japan Film Pen Club, Tadao Sato, Ginza Hata Building, 4–5–4, Ginza, Chuo-Ku Tokyo.
NETHERLANDS – Kring van Nederlandse Filmjournalisten, KNF, Fred Bredschneyder, Snelliuslaan 78, 1222 TG Hilversum.

POLAND – Film Association, Film Literature Section, Wanda Wertenstein, Ul. Trbacka 3., PL–00 0744 Warsaw.
– Film Association, Film Literature Section, Dr Jerzy Plazewski, 10 m 6., PL–00378 Warsaw.
– Journalists Association, Film Critics Section, Jerzy Pelz, Ul Foksal 3/5, PL–00 366 Warsaw.
ROMANIA – Asociatia Criticilor, Uninuea Cineastilor, Florica Ichin, 28–30, Mendeleev Str, Bucharest 1.
SENEGAL – Association Sénégalaise des Critiques Cinématographiques AAECCI, Aly Kheury Ndaw, B.P. 5164 Fann, Dakar.
SPAIN (CATALONIA) – Associacio Catalana de Critics i Escriptors Cinematografics, José Luis Guarner, c/o Centre Internacional de Prensa, Rambla Catalunya 1 0/1er, E–08007 Barcelona.
SWEDEN – Svenska Filmkritikerforbundet, Hans Schiller, Karlbergsgatan 32 A., Stockholm.
SWITZERLAND – Association Suisse de la Presse Cinématographique, Walter Vian, Riehofstrasse 42, CH–8408 Winterthur.
TUNISIA – Association Tunisienne pour la Promotion de la Critique Cinématographique, Nelia Gharbi, C.C.P. 233–62 B.P.
VENEZUELA – Associacion Venezolana de Criticos Cinematograficos, Edificio AVP 2–piso Local 7, Avenida Andres Bello, Caracas.
UNITED KINGDOM – British Branch FIPRESCI, Peter Cargin, 82 Gladstone Road, Wimbledon, London SW19 1QT.
URUGUAY – Uruguay Section of FIPRESCI, Jorge Abbondanza, Juan Paullier 1168, Montevideo.
U.S.S.R. – Andrei Plachov, c/o Sojus Kinematografistow, Wassiliewskaja Ul, 13 UdSSR Moscow 125183.
YUGOSLAVIA – YU FIPRESCI, Nenad Dukić, c/o Institut za Film, Cika Ljubina 15/11, 11000 Belgrade.

General Secretary – Klaus Eder, Schliessheimer Str 83, D–8000 Munich 40, Germany.

WORLD SURVEY

ARGENTINA

by Alberto Tabbia

By mid-1990, Argentine cinema was on the verge of disappearing. New economic policies, aimed at reducing public expenditure and privatising those national industries deeply in the red, included the film industry among those no longer to be subsidised – only to grant it an exception, after a few weeks of public outcry from its professionals... However, without public money to maintain the previous policy of credits to ambitious Argentine films, an already difficult situation has become critical.

Earlier, inflation allowed the rare box-office hit a mere recoupment of its costs. Now, such commercial prospects seem only available to quick, mostly shoddy confections dumped on the screens no later than a few weeks after going into production.

Most damaging, Argentine audiences have shown a declining interest in Argentine films. Eliseo Subiela's ambitious *Last Images from the Shipwreck* (IFG 1990), with its high-flown symbolic treatment of current everyday malaise, failed to repeat the success of the director's previous *Man Looking Southeast* (1985). A broad farce, *One Hundred Times I Shouldn't*, has proved to be the only success of the 1990 season to date in terms of attendance though, again, this may be financially insignificant... It should be noted that the admission price is now between $2 and $2.50, high figures in a country where eight-tenths of the population earn under $200 a month.

Rates of exchange and low salaries have made shooting in Argentina very attractive for American and European producers, although local unions, mostly the actors', have reacted with ill temper to the "factory" status thus developed in the country. *Highlander II* featuring again Christopher Lambert and Sean Connery, was supposed to cost in Argentina one quarter of its budget if made in European studios and with European labour. Huge sets were built, local scenery and architecture were used as backdrops, hundreds of artisans and minor technicians momentarily escaped unemployment in its crew.

Co-productions seemed a short time ago (see IFG 1990) to provide an outlet for local talent, though it has not been easy to find

Assumpta Serna in *I, the Worst of All*

projects escaping the hybrid nature of most films shot here just for economic reasons. After the Paris-based Edgardo Cozarinsky's *Warriors and Captives* (IFG 1990), shot in Patagonia on a profoundly national theme, now the mostly London-based Miguel Pereyra, director of *The Debt*, is shooting **The Last Harvest** in his favourite far-North locations. Spanish television, an increasingly frequent partner for Argentine producers, has launched a series of TV movies based on Borges short stories. Héctor Olivera is directing one of them, Carlos Saura is to shoot another.

Argentina being, in spite of its by now endemic crises, such an unpredictable country, it should not come as a surprise that a Festival of Films Made by Women should have survived into its third year with great success, this time in Buenos Aires. In spite of very uneven material, this mostly private endeavour is the kind of crusade that has proved rewarding in this country.

Profile: María Luisa Bemberg

After three years of uninterrupted struggle, María Luisa Bemberg has finally succeeded in making *Yo, la peor de todas* (*I, the Worst of All*), a project that often seemed impossible only to become her most cherished obsession. For a woman who directed her first feature film when already into her fifties, this is only typical of her courage and resilience.

Like other scions of a traditional upper class, it was only after her children were grown-up and she separated from her husband that Bemberg found an outlet for her long-repressed creative energy – first in feminist militancy, then as a scriptwriter, finally as a director.

Together with her associate, producer Lita Stantic, she founded Gea Cinematográfica and made a rather timid debut with *Moments* (*Momentos*, 1980), of which she was already scriptwriter and director. Her second feature, *Nobody's Wife* (*Señora de nadie*, 1982) was more daring in its observation of Argentine mores and behaviour – it was very unexpected, under the puritanical censorship of the period's régime, to see this story of a happy divorce ending with the wife in bed with her best friend, a battered homosexual home from an evening of rough cruising...

Bemberg's first commercial success, *Camila* (1984), described in intensely romantic tones the story of a doomed love affair from the 1820s – that of an upper-class girl and a priest. Their escape, rebirth through change of identity and life close to nature, sexual passion, hunting and final execution by rival political factions equally interested in setting an example, impressed young moviegoers, and made the film a favourite of teenagers throughout Argentina. Less easy but richer, *Miss Mary* (1986) starred Julie Christie as an English governess imported by a rich landowning family to the Argentine countryside in the 1930's. A settling of accounts with Bemberg's own background and upbringing, the film's intricate narrative and complex emotional allegiances make it her most personal and poignant work.

Yo, la peor de todas (1990) takes a big step further, both ideologically and in formal terms, Bemberg's search for new approaches to the depiction of women's predicament in a male-dominated society. Her sheer energy as a film-maker, a producer and a citizen have made María Luisa Bemberg a popular, controversial, truly unique figure in Argentine public life.

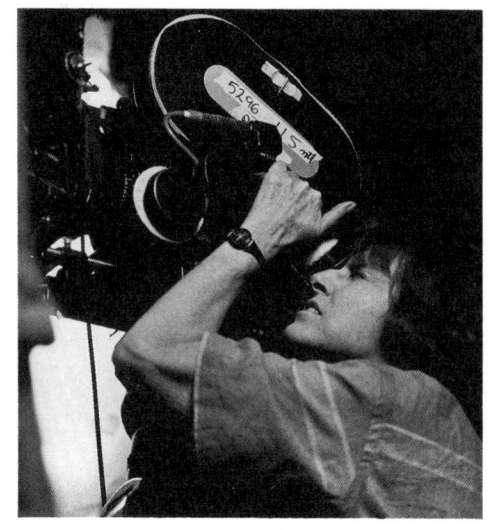

María Luisa Bemberg

Yo, la peor de todas (I, the Worst of All)

Direction: María Luisa Bemberg. Screenplay: M.L. Bemberg and Antonio Larreta, based on *The Pitfalls of Faith* by Octavio Paz. Photography: Félix Monti. Production Design: Voytek. Players: Assumpta Serna, Dominique Sanda, Héctor Alterio, Lautaro Murúa, Graciela Araujo, Alberto Segado, Gerardo Romano, Hugo Soto. Produced by Lita Stantic A Gea Cinematográfica Production.

Juana de Azbaje, born in 1641, the daughter of a peasant family in the Spanish colony of New Spain (today's Mexico), was to become, as Sister Juana Inés de la Cruz, one of the great Baroque poets in the Spanish language. Admitted to court at the age of 17, she later enters a convent as the only place where, at the time, a woman would be left in peace to read and study. A playwright and an astronomer, she is protected by the Spanish viceroy and, especially, by his wife María Luisa, with whom she develops a Platonic and literary romance. When the couple is called back to Spain, she becomes the prey of hateful and jealous superiors. After being exposed as the author of a would-be anonymous "Defence of Women," her books are burned and she defiantly conforms to the image others want to impose on her – becoming a devoted nurse during a plague, renouncing literature by breaking her glasses with her own hands and scribbling in her own blood "I, the Worst of All..." shortly before the plague kills her.

This historical character emerges from María Luisa Bemberg's treatment as something other than a feminist cult figure – an individual consumed by those appetites most intolerable to the society she lives in, namely for knowledge, for freedom, for truth. Definitely no "period piece," the film is totally shot in studio sets of ascetic austerity – the characters stand out against surfaces of light and shadow, a solitary tree and a wall represent a "cloister garden," props are chosen for their evocative power and not for documentary realism, while the sumptuous costumes summon up the social hierarchies of the times. Such a highly stylised approach is as unusual as the subject matter in Argentine cinema, and the film (as seen in a rough cut) is a very original, occasionally disturbing, intensely personal work.

Alberto Tabbia

ALBERTO TABBIA is an Argentine film critic and cultural journalist. He co-edited the film series Flashback *and is a regular contributor to the main Buenos Aires and Montevideo dailies, their literary supplements and other magazines as well.*

Flop

Screenplay and Direction: Eduardo Mignogna. Photography: Ricardo de Angelis. Art Direction: Jorge Ferrari. Editing: César d'Angiolillo. Music: Lito Nebbia. Players: Víctor Laplace, Leonor Manso, Dora Baret, Federico Luppi, Walter Santa Ana, Enrique Pinti, Lidia Catalano.

Florencio Parravicini was a mythical actor of the Argentine stage in the first decades of this century, who appeared only occasionally in some films of the 1930's. Mignogna has approached this larger-than-life character with a theatrical frame – a prologue, three acts and an epilogue, from childhood in a prison where his father was the director, though a theatrical career seen as a dialogue between the "real" and the "financial" selves of the actor, up to his suicide on stage, to the wild applause of the audience. Mignogna aims at an understanding of the reasons that made Parravicini into a legend, and of the society his outrageous personal behaviour shocked and titillated.

Alberto Tabbia

Other Films

Futbol Argentino (Argentine Soccer). Dir: Victor Dinenzon. Script: Osvaldo Bayer. Prod: Lita Stantic for Gea Cinematográfica. *The Argentine passion for soccer is at the basis of this feature-length documentary. Through archive material, interviews and film clips, it tries both to capture the feeling of mass enthusiasm and to delve into its mythology. Scriptwriter and director say their*

TOP GROSSING FILMS IN ARGENTINA: 1989

Rain Man
Twins
Mujeres al borde de un ataque de nervios (Women on the Verge of a Nervous Breakdown)
Working Girl
The Naked Gun

film is "as contradictory and full of passion" as soccer itself.
Pais cerrado, teatro abierto (Closed Country, Open Theatre). Dir: Arturo Balassa. Script: Arturo Balassa and Graciela Wegbrait. Phot: Diego Bonancina and Julio Lencina. A Siluetas Production. *A 16 mm documentary, the kind that in Europe would find its natural slot on cultural TV, about the informal "resistance" movement conducted by playwrights, actors and producers, many of them marginalised during the military régime, during the 1980 and 1981 seasons.*

Producers

Aries Cinematográfica Argentina
Lavalle 1860
Buenos Aires (1051)
Tel: 40–3430, 3438, 3439
Telex: 17227–ARIES–AR
Fax: (541) 11–1912

GEA Cinematográfica S.A.
Pacheco de Melo 2141
Buenos Aires (1126)
Tel: 803–7779, 3421
Telex: 19051 GEACI AR

Jorge Estrada Mora Producciones
Reconquista 609
Buenos Aires (1003)
Tel: 312–6539
Telex: 18783 TALA AR
Fax: (541) 311–4498

Argentina Sono Film, S.A.C.I.
Lavalle 1975
Buenos Aires (1051)
Tel: 49–0216/18
Cable: Mentasti Baires

Distributors

United International Pictures S.R.L.
Ayacucho 520
Buenos Aires (1026)
Tel: 49–0261/64
Telex: 9051
Fax: 54–1111303

Theatrical S.A.
Tucumán 1938
Buenos Aires (1050)
Tel: 45–6094/7, 953–7941
Telex: 27638 22–238
Fax: 953–7678

Transeuropa Cinematográfica, S.A.
Ayacucho 586
Buenos Aires (1026)
Tel: 49–3417, 49–2653
Telex: 17387 TRAFI AR
Fax: 541–111191

Faro Films
Ayacucho 595
Buenos Aires (1026)
Tel: 45–1739/9945, 47–4005
Telex: 17039 NORVI AR

Mundial Films
Ayacucho 595
Buenos Aires (1026)
Tel: 45–1739/9945, 47–4005
Telex: 17039 NORVI AR
Fax: 54–1–3256489

Useful Address

Instituto Nacional de Cinematografía
Lima 319
Buenos Aires (1073)
Tel: 37–9091
Telex: 21104 INCINE AR
Fax: (541) 11–2559

PALACE *Entertainment* CORPORATION

AUSTRALIA'S LEADING INDEPENDENT
FILM • VIDEO • TELEVISION DISTRIBUTION

Head Office: 233 Whitehorse Rd, Balwyn 3103, Australia. Ph: (03) 817 6421 Fax: (03) 817 4921 Telex: 36062

AUSTRALIA

by David Stratton

After a couple of difficult years, the future of the Australian film industry is, on one level at least, starting to look brighter. Now that the Film Finance Corporation is operating smoothly, feature film production is once more restored to a more reasonable level. In addition, progressive funding decisions by the Australian Film Commission and Film Victoria have meant that several low-budget features by up-and-coming directors have become a reality.

The problem now is one of confidence in local films. The period when Australian films could command a loyal local audience is long gone, and distributors are increasingly reluctant to take a risk in releasing films which don't attract audiences. Last year films like *Evil Angels* (*A Cry in the Dark*) and *Dead Calm* did well commercially, but they were large-scale, Hollywood-style productions. Jane Campion's *Sweetie* was a critical success and enjoyed excellent runs in major cities, but few other Australian films fared well – Ann Turner's *Celia*, for example, quickly came and went, despite its qualities.

1989–90 failed to produce a single

Chris Haywood and Gosia Dobrowolska in Paul Cox's *Golden Braid*

feature with the imagination and daring of *Sweetie*; but a talent like Campion doesn't emerge all that often. Characteristically, the director and her film were virtually ignored by the increasingly irrelevant Australian Film Awards, in which artistic contributions to the Australian cinema are supposedly judged by peer groups: Campion wasn't even nominated for best director, and *Sweetie* wasn't nominated for best film.

Cox Back on Form
Perhaps the most exciting new film this year is **Golden Braid**, a complete return to form for Paul Cox (who, with *Island* last year, disappointed some of his supporters). Loosely based on a Guy de Maupassant story, the film stars Chris Haywood who gives a remarkable performance as a middle-aged collector of clocks whose passionate affair with the wife (Gosia Dobrowolska) of a Salvation Army Major (Paul Chubb) is briefly sidetracked by his unaccountable passion for a hank of blonde hair he finds in an antique Venetian cabinet.

Cox brings out all the humour and poignancy of this bizarre situation, and is ably supported by his fine cast. Dobrowolska, as the woman with a most unusual rival, gives a glowingly sensual performance, and there's some very low-key comedy from Cox regular Norman Kaye as a different psychiatrist. The camerawork by Nino Martinetti is in itself a work of art.

Golden Braid was shot in only three weeks on an astonishingly tight budget, and the other revelation of the year, Ray Argall's **Return Home**, cost even less, proving once again that a big budget isn't necessary to make a fine movie. Argall, better known as the cinematographer for Ian Pringle (*Wrong World*, *The Prisoner of St. Petersburg*) scripted this drama about two brothers (Dennis Coard, Frankie J. Holden) reunited after ten years when Coard returns from his high-pressure job in Melbourne (and a broken marriage) to the Adelaide suburb where he grew up. Outstanding

Australian Film Commission

Fifteen year's commitment to script development, production investment, cultural policy and international marketing . . .

If you want to know about . . .

- film & television projects in development or production
- sales contacts
- industry trends
- co-productions and financing mechanisms

Contact us at the key international film and multi-media markets or at the AFC

Sydney 8 West Street North Sydney NSW 2060 Telephone 61·2·925 7333 Telex 25157 FICOM Facsimile 61·2·954 4001

London 2nd Floor Victory House 99-101 Regent Street London W1 Telephone 44·71·734 9383 Telex 51 28711 AUSFILMG Facsimile 44·71·434 0170

THE WESTERN AUSTRALIAN FILM COUNCIL

is proud to have contributed to the development of the following major film projects for release in 90/91

HAYDAZE — Barron Films
$2.4m 12 part Children's TV series

JACKAROO — Crawford Productions
$4.5m 4 part TV series

DINGO — Gevest Australia
$5.6m feature film

- PROJECT DEVELOPMENT -
- PACKAGING • MARKETING -

Westfilm

The Western Australian Film Council
Suite 8, 336 Churchill Ave, Subiaco, Western Australia 6008
Tel (09) 382 2500 Fax (09) 381 2848

---

performances from the two men, plus Ben Mendelsohn as a nervous employee in Holden's garage, enhance this deceptively simple, but extremely moving, story of family ties.

Mendelsohn plays the lead in **The Big Steal**, the new comedy from Nadia Tass and David Parker, the husband and wife team who made *Malcolm*. After a slow start, this engaging tale of a teenager with two dreams – to own a Jaguar and to date Joanna (Claudia Karvan) – builds into a frequently very funny comedy. Steve Bisley is particularly good as an odious car salesman who tries to cheat the young hero but who is thoroughly humiliated for his pains. There are a number of delightfully eccentric characters and situations in the film.

Larger Scale

These are all modest productions. On a larger scale there's **The Crossing**, the first film produced by the lively and enterprising Beyond International Group (BIG). Directed by George Ogilvie, this is a drama which unfolds in the space of less than 24 hours in a small country town some thirty years ago. Danielle Spencer plays a teenage girl torn between two lovers, one an ingenuous country boy, the other a budding artist who's moved to the city and wants her to join him. Handsomely shot (by Jeff Darling), the film builds on its central relationships with a fine attention to details and to minor characters, and it's most beautifully acted.

Another film with a similar theme is **The Delinquents**, which was conceived as a vehicle for *Neighbours* star Kylie Minogue. This melodrama about teenagers in love in the 1950's is crippled by the ludicrous mis-casting of American Charlie Schlatter as Kylie's small-town beau; Schlatter is out of his depth and out of place, and he drags the film, ponderously directed by Chris Thomson, down with him.

Frankie J. Holden and Dennis Coard in Ray Argall's *Return Home*

Two films this year have explored wartime atrocities. **Blood Oath** is set immediately after the Japanese surrender in 1945 on Ambon, an island where Australian prisoners of war were held captive. Bryan Brown gives one of his strongest performances as the officer given the task of prosecuting Japanese suspected of unlawful executions, and director Stephen Wallace handles the tension and moral ambiguities of the courtroom drama with great skill.

Father suffers, unfortunately, from its coincidental similarity to the Costa-Gavras film *Music Box*. In the Australian film, Max Von Sydow plays a German who's lived in Melbourne since the war, and who is suddenly accused of atrocities by an old woman (Julia Blake) from the Baltic states. John Power directs (his first film since *The Picture Show Man* in 1977) and Von Sydow makes his character intriguingly ambivalent.

Struck by Lightning, directed by Jerzy Domaradzki, tends to polarise audiences. The film centres around the efforts of a sports teacher to train a soccer team of physically disabled people, and it is, in a very real sense, a "feel good" movie; but some viewers find the treatment of the disabled characters (played by a mixture of actors and the genuinely disabled) demeaning. However, there's no denying Garry McDonald's splendidly funny/touching performance as the alcoholic, self-pitying school principal.

Comedy Efforts

One of the country's most skilful directors, Arch Nicholson, died during the year. His

Director George Ogilvie on the set of *The Crossing* with Robert Mammone and Danielle Spencer

last film was a comedy, **Weekend with Kate**, in which Colin Friels plays a husband with a mistress and Catherine McClements is wholly delightful as the wife who wins him back. The snappy pacing and sharp dialogue make this modest picture a minor delight.

Sadly, a more amitious comedy, **Wendy Cracked a Walnut**, remains stillborn. Rosanna Arquette was imported to play the lead, a wife who fantasises a dream lover (Hugo Weaving) to escape her dull life with salesman husband Bruce Spence. But the script is weak, and director Michael Pattinson (*Ground Zero*) shows no flair for comedy.

An unusually large number of thrillers winds up the year's productions. **Harbour Beat** is the best of them: it's a cop/buddy movie about a Glaswegian (John Hannah) posted to Sydney who helps local cop Steve Vidler crack a drug ring and, incidentally, get the goods on his former partner. Longtime producer David Elfick (*Newsfront*, *Starstruck*) turned director with this one, and combines suspense and comedy to good effect. Ellery Ryan's camerawork ensures that Sydney has rarely looked more handsome.

Another producer – Frank Howson – turned director with **Hunting**, an ambitious and nearly successful foray into David Lynch territory. John Savage plays a ruthless business tycoon who becomes involved with a married woman (Kerry Armstrong) and has his goons murder her husband. Howson uses the Scope format with confidence and delights in pushing the film further and further onto the wild side, culminating in a dinner party scene almost worthy of *The Cook, The Thief...*

In Too Deep, made by newcomers John Tatoulis and Colin South, is an erotic thriller seemingly influenced by French films of another era. Santha Press plays a provocative young blues singer who becomes involved with a gangster who also fancies her younger sister; John Flaus is excellent as the tired cop on the gangster's trail.

Strangers is, essentially, *Strangers on a Plane*, but director Craig Lahiff makes the most of John Emery's very derivative screenplay so that at least this thriller is fun to sit through. The same can't be said of **Sher Mountain Killings Mystery**, a lacklustre outdoor thriller about a ghostly avenger, or **Bloodmoon**, a singularly inept slasher pic (set in a girls' school) which the distributors attempted to enliven by means of a 'fright break,' a device that fooled no-one.

Finally, **Fatal Sky** is an oddity: director Frank Shields (*The Surfer*) made it in Yugoslavia, though it's supposedly set in Norway, with an international cast, and the intention seems to be to create a Hawksian

Anne Looby in Beyond International's *Strangers*

Brian Vriends and Garry McDonald in Beyond International's *Struck by Lightning*

adventure in which an intrepid woman is involved with rival males, journalists on the trail of a hot story about UFOs. The script and the cast are weak, and the settings utterly unconvincing; Shields deserves better material.

Distribution and Exhibition Flourishing
Apart from local productions, the Australian film distribution and exhibition industry continues to flourish. A significant number of well-equipped and comfortable multiplexes have opened in suburban sites in all major cities, and downtown cinemagoing is becoming more than ever a teenage pursuit while older audiences opt for the new sites. Foreign language films and "art house" fare are still popular, perhaps proportionately more than they are in some other countries. For example, Peter Greenaway's films have all had successful cinema releases, and *The Cook, The Thief. . .*, despite its R rating and some reactionary, pro-censorship nonsense in the press, was a considerable success.

The Sydney and Melbourne Film Festivals continue to attract very large audiences, and have some influence on cinemagoing habits. The hit of the 1989 festival, George Sluizer's Dutch thriller *The Vanishing*, was picked up by a small local distributor and enjoyed an exceptionally long and successful run.

Short Films
Short film production is also enjoying a boom – there were over 100 entries in the Sydney Film Festival's short film competition this year. For once, the Dendy Awards – or at least the Fiction Section – seemed to by-pass the more interesting entries, and the fiction winner, **Outside**

CAPRICORN
PICTURES

We are an Australian Distribution and Service company.
We specialise in Australian and other quality product.
Your picture will get tender loving care.
We're skilled at marketing
and
our principals have all had a lifetime in the film business.
If you want strong effective representation
...call CAPRICORN

Tony Malone   **Allana Burns**
Managing Director   Manager

CAPRICORN PICTURES PTY LIMITED
Level 11, 55 Lavender Street
MILSONS POINT NSW 2061
AUSTRALIA
ph: (612) 955 9734, (612) 954 5075
fx: (612) 959 5357

Looking In, by Brendan Duhigg, is a fairly routine exploration of puberty (despite a typically good performance from Chris Haywood as the family priest.) Two films in the General Category were better, including the winner, **Teenage Babylon**, an eerie recreation of teenage suicide scenes of thirty years ago, filmed in black-and-white, and with a series of plaintive blues songs accompanying the horrific, and totally convincing, visuals. Graeme Wood directed.

Belinda Chayko won the award of the foreign guests of the festival with **Swimming**, a narrative about a bereaved father (Steve Jacobs) as seen via his 12-year-old daughter's video camera. The result is powerful.

It was left to the Cannes festival to discover a potential new feature talent in Pauline Chan with her two extremely stylish exercises in erotic film noir, **The Space Between the Door and the Floor** and **Hang Up!**, the former about the fantasies of a repressed husband, the latter a little drama about the odder reaches of lust.

Polish-born theatre director Bogdan Koca's first film, **Shall We Dance**, explores, in a stylised way, the problems of Australian film funding and sponsorship as seen through the eyes of a puzzled 7-year-old (played by the director's daughter, Veronica Koca; the frustrated film-maker is played by Koca's wife, Gosia Dobrowolska). The child's-eye-view makes some tellingly amusing points.

The Australian film that competed in Cannes, aboriginal director Tracey Moffat's **Night Cries: A Rural Tragedy**, also uses stylisation to great effect. This exceptional film, with its insights into black-white relationships in outback Australia, lays claim to be the most impressive short film of the year.

DAVID STRATTON was Director of the Sydney Film Festival (1966–1983) and divides his time between writing for Variety, and presenting movies on the S.B.S. TV network in Australia.

Production Funding and the AFFC

In Australia, the government-backed Australian Film Finance Corporation (FFC) is the principal funding mechanism behind Australian production.

With an initial four year mandate, it has just under $A270-million to back films, TV drama, and documentaries on a commercial return basis through a variety of investment methods. As at presstime, films had to have at least 35% of their budget in place via private equity to qualify for investment. Market attachments, track record, creative elements, and other factors impacting on the projects' commerciality are then assessed before the FFC enters into negotiation on investment.

In 1990 the FFC also launched a $A20-million film fund to back five films without market attachments. The fund aims to stimulate private investment for production, although the FFC took up the lion's share of investment for the maiden fund (private equity raised accounted for around $A4.5-million, just over two thirds of what was sought). The first of this quintet began production from July 1990. Beyond Intl. is representing them internationally.

In the 1989/90 Australian fiscal year, ending June 30, the FFC committed $A84.72-million, underpinning $A163.78-million worth of production. For the previous year it committed SA83.04 million to underpin $A149.22-million worth of production. In 1989/90, features accounted for $A97.5 million, TV drama $A52.9, and documentaries $A13.35 million.

Overall figures for the FFC are as follows, but these include a number of projects in negotiation at the time of going to press. Based on these figures, FFC has entered into $A187.9-million of offers of negotiation since opening its doors in late 1988, representing $A334.6-million worth of production.

Blake Murdoch

AUSTRALIAN FILM FINANCE CORPORATION INVESTMENTS, 1988–1990

Number of features funded

1988/89: 14
1989/90: 19*

Number of TV dramas (minis, telepix) funded

1988/89: 12
1989/90: 14*

Number of documentaries funded

1988/89: 20
1989/90: 33

Total Budgets of FFC Approved Projects

	1988/89	($AUST, millions) 1989/90
Features	69.376	132.753
TV Drama	42.267	62.811
Documentaries	10.187	17.164
TOTAL	121.830	212.728

Total Amount of FFC Investment Approvals (offers to negotiate) ($AUST, millions)

	1988/89	1989/90
Features	43.346	70.279
TV Drama	24.004	34.404
Documentaries	6.085	9.781
TOTAL	73.435	114.464

* Includes approvals subject to contract.
Also includes official co-productions, of which there were six in 1989/90 collectively worth $A69.17- million, representing FFC investment of $A18.6-million.
Since October 1988, 10 projects together worth $A47.6-million have lapsed, representing lapsed FFC investment of $A21.84-million.
Source: FFC

Recent Films

Golden Braid. Script: Paul Cox, Barry Dickins. Dir: Paul Cox. Phot: Nino Martinetti. Players: Chris Haywood, Gosia Dobrowolska, Norman Kaye. Prod: Paul Cox, Paul Ammitzboll, Santhana K. Naidu, for Illumination Films.

Return Home. Script and Dir: Ray Argall. Phot: Mandy Walker. Players: Dennis Coard, Frankie J. Holden, Ben Mendelsohn. Prod: Cristina Pozzan, for Musical Films.

The Crossing. Script: Ranald Allan. Dir: George Ogilvie. Phot: Jeff Darling. Players: Danielle Spencer, Russell Crowe, Robert Mammone. Prod: Sue Seeary, for Beyond International.

The Big Steal. Script: David Parker. Dir: Nadia Tass. Phot: David Parker. Players: Ben Mendelsohn, Claudia Karvan, Steve Bisley. Prod: Nadia Tass, David Parker, for Cascade Films.

Blood Oath. Script: Denis Whitburn, Brian Williams. Dir: Stephen Wallace. Phot: Russell Boyd. Players: Bryan Brown, George Takei, Deborah Unger. Prod: Charles Waterstreet, Denis Whitburn, Brian Williams, for Blood Oath Productions.

Father. Script: Tony Cavanaugh, Graham Hartley. Dir: John Power. Phot: Dan Burstall. Players: Max von Sydow, Julia Blake, Carol Drinkwater. Prod: Damien Parer, Paul Barron for Transcontinental Films.

Struck by Lightning. Script: Trevor Farrant. Dir: Jerzy Domaradzki. Phot: Yuri Sokol. Players: Garry McDonald, Brian Vriends, Catherine McClements. Prod: Trevor Farrant for Dark Horse Pictures.

Harbour Beat. Script: Morris Gleitzman. Dir: David Elfick. Phot: Ellery Ryan. Players: John Hannah, Steven Vidler, Gary Day. Prod: David Elfick, Irene Dobson for Palm Beach Pictures.

Weekend with Kate. Script: Henry Tefay, Kee Young. Dir: Arch Nicholson. Phot: Dan Burstall. Players: Colin Friels, Catherine McClements, Jerome Ehlers. Prod: Phillip Emanuel for Phillip Emanuel Productions.

Wendy Cracked a Walnut. Script: Susanne Hawley. Dir: Michael Pattinson. Phot: Jeffrey Malouf. Players: Rosanna Arquette, Bruce Spence, Hugo Weaving. Prod: John Edwards for Xanadu-ABC.

Hunting. Script and Dir: Frank Howson. Phot: David Connell, Dan Burstall. Players: John

FINANCING AUSTRALIAN FILM

The Australian Film Finance Corporation has become the major source of funding for Australian-made feature films, mini-series, telemovies and documentaries.
If you'd like to discuss your project with us or receive a copy of our funding guidelines, application forms and other information, contact either our Sydney or Melbourne office.

AUSTRALIAN FILM FINANCE CORPORATION PTY. LIMITED

SYDNEY Level 6, 1 Pacific Hwy., NORTH SYDNEY 2060 Ph: (02) 956 2555 Fx: (02) 954 4253 Toll Free: (008) 25 1061
MELBOURNE Level 11, 432 St Kilda Rd., MELBOURNE 3004 Ph: (03) 823 4111 Fx: (03) 820 2663 Toll Free: (008) 33 3655

Savage, Kerry Armstrong, Jeffrey Thomas. Prod: Frank Howson for Boulevard Films.
The Delinquents. Script: Clayton Frohman, Mac Gudgeon. Dir: Chris Thomson. Phot: Andrew Lesnie. Players: Kylie Minogue, Charlie Schlatter, Angela Punch-McGregor. Prod: Alex Cutler, Michael Wilcox for Cutler-Wilcox Productions.
In Too Deep. [Formerly *Mack The Knife*]. Script: Deborah Parsons. Dirs: John Tatoulis, Colin South. Phot: Mark Gilfedder, Peter Zakharov. Players: Hugo Race, Santha Press, Rebekah Elmalogou. Prod: John Tatoulis, Colin South.
Sweethearts. Script and Dir: Colin Talbot. Phot: Terry Howells. Players: Christabel Wigley, John F. Howard, Richmond Clendinnen. Prod: Kim Lewis, Colin Talbot for Sweethearts Film Prod.
Jigsaw. Script: Marc Gracie, Chris Thompson. Dir: Marc Gracie. Phot: James Grant. Players: Rebecca Gibney, Dominic Sweeney, Gary Day. Prod: Rosa Colosimo for Rosa Colosimo Films.
Strangers. Script: John Healey, Anne Looby,

Melissa Docker. Prod: Craig Lahiff, Wayne Groom for Genesis Films.
Fatal Sky [formerly *No Cause for Alarm*]. Script: 'Anthony Able' [David Webb Peoples]. Dir: Frank Shields. Phot: Richard Michalak. Players: Michael Nouri, Darlanne Fluegel, Maxwell Caulfield. Prod: Antony I. Ginnane for International Film Entertainment.
Sher Mountain Killings Mystery. Script: Denis Whitburn. Dir: Vince Martin. Phot: Ray Henman. Players: Phil Avalon, Tom Richards, Abigail. Prod: Phil Avalon for Intertropic Films.
Bloodmoon. Script: Robert Brennan. Dir: Alec Mills. Phot: John Stokes. Players: Leon Lissek, Christine Amor, Helen Thomson. Prod: Stanley O'Toole for Village Roadshow Pictures.

Forthcoming Films

Flirting. Script and Dir: John Duigan. Phot: Geoff Burton. Players: Noah Taylor, Tandy

Newton, Nicole Kidman. Prod: Terry Hayes, Doug Mitchell, George Miller, for Kennedy-Miller. *A sequel to The Year My Voice Broke (1987); Danny is now at boarding school.*
Till There Was You. Script: Michael Thomas. Dir: John Seale. Phot: Geoffrey Simpson. Players: Mark Harmon, Deborah Unger, Jeroen Krabbe. Prod: Jim McElroy for Ayer Productions. *A triangular love story set on a Pacific island.*
Flynn. Script: Frank Howson, Alister Webb. Dir: Brian Kavanagh. Phot: John Wheeler. Players: Guy Pearce, Rebecca Rigg, Paul Cantoni. Prod: Frank Howson for Boulevard Films. *The wild exploits of the young Errol Flynn.*
Breakaway. Script: Jan Sardi. Dir: Don McLennan. Phot: Zbigniew Friedrich. Players: Bruce Boxleitner, Bruce Myles, Deborah Unger. Prod: Don McLennan for Breakaway Films-Ukiyo Films. *An escaped prisoner takes a mild-mannered accountant hostage.*
Quigley Down Under. Script: John Hill. Dir: Simon Wincer. Phot: David Eggby. Players: Tom Selleck, Laura San Giacomo, Alan Rickman. Prod: Stanley O'Toole, Alex Rose for Quigley Down Under Prods. *The adventures of an American cowboy in colonial Australia.*
Beyond My Reach. Script: Frank Howson, Philip Dalkin. Dir: Dan Burstall. Phot: Peter Bilcock. Players: Terri Garber, David Roberts, Alan Fletcher. Prod: Frank Howson for Boulevard Films. *The misadventures of Australian film-makers in Hollywood.*
A Kink in the Picasso. Script: Hugh Stuckey. Dir: Mark Gracie. Phot: James Grant. Players: Jane Menz, Jane Clifton, Jon Finlayson. Prod: Will Spencer for Rosa Colosimo Prods. *A comedy about a stolen Picasso.*
Aya. Script and Dir: Solrun Hoaas. Phot: Geoff Burton. Players: Eri Ishida, Nicholas Eadie, Chris Haywood. Prod: Denise Patience, Solrun Hoaas for Goshu Films. *An Australian soldier marries an Australian woman at the end of World War II and brings her home to Melbourne.*
Death in Brunswick. Script: John Ruane, Boyd Oxlade. Dir: John Ruane. Phot: Ellery Ryan. Players: Sam Neill, Zoe Carides, John Clarke. Prod: Timothy White for Meridian Films. *The chef in a seedy rock club has an affair with a voluptuous young woman.*
Waiting. Script and Dir: Jackie McKimmie. Phot: Steve Mason. Players: Noni Hazlehurst, John Hargreaves, Deborra-Lee Furness. Prod: Ross Matthews for Filmside Prods. *Old friends converge on an isolated farm to await the birth of a baby.*
Dead to the World. Script and Dir: Ross Gibson. Phot: Jane Castle. Players: Richard Roxburgh, Agnieszka Perepeczko, Noah Taylor. Prod: John Cruthers for Huzzah Prods. *A drama of revenge and corruption centring on a boxing gymnasium.*
Holidays on the River Yarra. Script and Dir: Leo Berkeley. Phot: Brendan Lavelle. Players: Craig Adams, Luke Elliot, Tahir Cambis. Prod: Fiona Cochrane for Jungle Pictures. *Out of work teenagers become involved with a gang of mercenaries.*
Dingo. Script: Marc Rosenberg. Dir: Rolf De Heer. Phot: Denis Lenoir. Players: Colin Friels, Miles Davis, Helen Buday. Prod: Marc Rosenberg, Rolf De Heer for Gevest (Australia)-AO Prods (France). *An Australian from the outback comes to Paris to play jazz.*
Dead Sleep. Script: Michael Rymer. Dir: Alec Mills. Phot: John Stokes. Players: Linda Blair, Tony Bonner, Christine Amor. Prod: Stanley O'Toole for Village Roadshow Pictures. *A thriller from the Bloodmoon team.*
Until the End of the World. Script: Wim Wenders, Peter Carey. Dir: Wim Wenders. Phot: Robby Muller. Players: William Hurt, Sam Neill, Jeanne Moreau, Max von Sydow. Prod: Jonathan Taplin for Road Movies-Trans Pacific. *The ultimate road movie.*

MADE IN AUSTRALIA

Feature length movies, mini series, tele-features, FILM AUSTRALIA documentaries, children's programmes. Over 2000 titles in all. For your free catalogue, contact Film Australia, Eton Road, Lindfield, NSW 2070. Phone (02) 413 8777, fax (02) 416 5672, telex 22734.

Australian Film Awards

1989

Best Film: *Evil Angels* [*A Cry in the Dark*] (Dir: Fred Schepisi)
Best Director: Fred Schepisi (*Evil Angels*)
Best Actor: Sam Neill (*Evil Angels*)
Best Actress: Meryl Streep (*Evil Angels*)
Best Supporting Actor: Chris Haywood (*Emerald City*)
Best Supporting Actress: Victoria Longley (*Celia*)
Best Photography: Dean Semler (*Dead Calm*)
Best Original Screenplay: Gerard Lee, Jane Campion (*Sweetie*)
Best Adapted Screenplay: Robert Caswell, Fred Schepisi (*Evil Angels*)
Best Editing: Richard Francis-Bruce (*Dead Calm*)

Best Music: Graeme Revill (*Dead Calm*)
Best Production Design: Chris Kennedy (*Ghosts...Of the Civil Dead*)
Best Sound: Ben Osmo, Lee Smith, Roger Savage (*Dead Calm*)
Best Documentary: *Joe Leahy's Neighbours* (Bob Connolly, Robyn Anderson)
Best Short Fiction: *Bonza* (David Swann)
Best Animation: *Still Flying*
Best Experimental: *Soul Mate*
Byron Kennedy Award: Jane Campion
Raymond Longford Award: John Meillon (posthumously)
AFI Members' Award: *Evil Angels*

TOP GROSSING FILMS IN AUSTRALIA: JULY 1989–JULY 1990

$AUST Gross

Pretty Woman (Touchstone)	17.09-million
Batman (WB)	13.17-million
Look Who's Talking (Tristar)	11.45-million
Back to the Future 2 (UIP)	9.07-million
The War of the Roses (Fox)	9.03-million
Lethal Weapon 2 (WB)	9.01-million
Honey I Shrunk The Kids (Disney)	6.08-million
The Hunt For Red October (UIP)	6.06-million
Bird on a Wire (UIP)	6.05-million
Dick Tracy (Touchstone)	5.09-million

(*Source: MPDAA*)

AUSTRIA
by Jack Kindred

Austria's feature film industry, long on talent but short on cash, failed to make substantial gains in 1989 over the past few years. Production was limited to around a dozen important films, most of them in the low budget class, and made far too cheaply to hold their own internationally. The industry's main production outlets concentrated on television product, TV spots and to some extent industrial films.

Unlike commercial filming, feature production in the Alpine country (population 7.5 million) is largely dependent on subsidy financing from the AFF (Federal Film Board) and the national public broadcaster ORF. Funding from private sources is limited. Under the AFF system, a total of 49,593,712 schillings ($4.3 million) was meted out for feature film projects in 1989, while the ORF upped its contribution (in return for broadcasting rights) to 34 million schillings ($2.25 million). To obtain AFF support, 30% of the budget must come from Austrian sources, which usually means insufficient funds for big productions. The risk factor also limits bank credits for film projects. With funds from the private sector as scarce as hen's teeth, there is hardly enough to finance even one major feature film production, judging by American standards.

Apart from a shortage of screenplay writers (many of the best work in television), Austria has no dearth of talent. Directors like Wolfram Paulus, Axel Corti, Milan Dor, Niki List, Maria Knilli, Peter Patzak and Kitty Kino have received recognition (and assignments) abroad, not to mention such notables as actor-director Klaus Maria Brandauer and director and cinematographer Xaver Schwarzenberger. Fledgling director Erhard Riedlsperger showed real promise in his first full-length feaure, *Tunnel Child*. Austria also enjoys a tradition of excellent stage and screen actors, who almost always turn out fine performances, given a reasonably good script and competent direction.

Joining EFDO
From 1990 on, Austria will be a full member of the European Community's "Low Budget Film Project" within the framework of the European Film Distribution Office (EFDO), which could facilitate distribution of Austrian movies in the European market and open up co-production possibilities.

Austria also has an incipient animated film industry with its own animated film and sound studio. Early works include Mara Mattuschka's *Loading Ludwig*, an experimental 60-minute animated cartoon, while Andi Karner and Hans Werner Poschauko collaborated on a 100-minute animated feature, *Rococo Comes to the Island of the Huzzis*. A 50-minute cartoon employing 30 graphic artists, painters and musicians, *Journey to a Planet* (working title), is planned for completion in mid-1990.

In 1988, the ORF rescued the Rosenhugel Studio complex from being razed to make way for development projects, and started a three-year trial plan to see whether the studio could eventually pay for itself through rentals of facilities. The project seems to have paid off, since a major, high budget international TV

Timothy Dalton in *The King's Whore*, directed by Axel Corti and released via J & M Entertainment

production, *The Strauss Dynasty*, was made there.

On the technical side, the Listo company was Vienna's only operating lab in 1989, meaning that film-makers had to farm out lab work to companies outside Austria.

The Vienna Film Festival, which dates back to 1959 when it was started as a "Festival of Comedy," skipped 1990 following the resignation of Viennale Chief Helmut Dimko. The non-competitive event is now scheduled for October 17–27 in October, 1991, and will be under the co-direction of noted German film-maker Werner Herzog and Reinhard Pyrker, long-standing director of the Austrian Film Days in Wels. The last Viennale in March, 1989, featured a New Spanish Film section, with Pedro Almodóvar's *Women on the Verge of a Nervous Breakdown* opening the festival, which attracted a record 25,000 patrons.

Little Presence Abroad

The Austrian film understandably had little presence abroad. Early in 1990, considering the industry's small output. At the Berlinale, Michael Kreihsl's **Idomeneo** film with music from the Mozart opera, was screened in the Panorama section as well as Paulus Manker's **Weiniger's Last Night**, an excellent screen version of Joshua Sobol's stage play. Erhard Riedlsperger's **Tunnel Child**, a timely story of the barriers between East and West at the height of the Cold War in 1969, was shown in the Children's section. At the Cannes festival, only Axel Corti's 17th Century melodrama, **The King's Whore**, a French-Austrian-British-Italian co-production, was entered in the competition. At the Karlovy Vary International Film Festival, **The Altar Boys** from Wolfram Paulus was selected for the competition and *Tunnel Child* for the official out-of-competition sections. Susanne Zanke's **The Scorpion Woman**, about a 44-year-old female judge's affair with a 23-year-old youth, competed in 1989 Rio de Janeiro festival.

Veit Heiduschka, head of Wega Film Productions, is one of the most active producers on the Vienna film scene, with four or five projects going at the same time. Among others, he produced *Weiniger's Last Night* and Kitty Kino's third feature, **True Love**, a stylish comic investigation of sexual confusion among smart-set yuppies in Vienna. Niki List, who directed Wega-Film's commercially successful *Müller's Büro* in 1986, also directed Heiduschka's last production, **Ach, Boris**, which *Variety* critic J.R. Keith Keller described as a "black comedy with a bleak, morbid style," lacking the elements of "madcap slapstick and human compassion that could have made it all really palatable." Heiduschka also has in the pipeline **Die Spitzen der Gesellschaft** (roughly translated *High Society*), a political thriller with humour directed by Franz Novotny, and Michael Pilz's **Weekend**, described as a film about work and love, what they have in common and what separates them.

August Zirner and Sabine Berg in Kitto Kino's Wahre Liebe

Austria has about 280 feature film releases annually. Attendance in 1989 totalled 10,256 million, up slightly from 10,234 million the previous year, but down a discouraging 37.5% from the 16 million cinemagoers in 1986. Perhaps the slump has bottomed out. In any case, hardly more than ten releases ever attract more than 500,000 visitors.

At the end of 1989, there were 290 houses with 399 screens, showing a slight improvement over the 345 screens extant in 1988. Houses, especially those in rural communities forced to wait from two to three months for a first-run print, are hardest hit by the prolonged decline. Ticket prices remained constant in 1989, ranging between 40 to 50 schillings ($3.00 to $3.85).

Recent and Forthcoming Films

Most of the films listed below are scheduled for completion in 1990.

Death of a Schoolboy. Director Peter Patzak collaborated with David Anthony in adapting the English-language script from Hans Konig's novel. The movie is a psychogramme of Gavrilo Princip, the assassin of Archduke Franz Ferdinand in Sarajevo, a deed that set off the chain of events in 1914 leading to the First World War and the end of old Europe.

Ferien mit Sylvester (*Vacation with Sylvester*). Bernd Neuburger is to direct this tender family film about two little girls who enter a shy old bachelor's life, whose hobby is astronomy, playing tricks on him and lending excitement to his dull existence.

Fleischwolf (*Meat-Grinder*). Iranian-born director Houchangk Allahyari also wrote the script for this grim Austrian prison tale of three young men serving time for minor misdemeanors, who come up against the prison's merciless subculture, a hierarchy characterised by violence and sexual suppression.

Der Nachbar (*The Neighbour*). Götz Spielmann, who also wrote the screenplay, directs this thriller about a seemingly harmless and polite elderly gentleman, known by everybody in a quiet Viennese suburb, none of whom suspect he is capable of murder.

Vagabund (*Vagabond*). Director Leopold Huber and Eva Krkyll wrote the screenplay about the ten-year-old Andreas, who after his grandmother dies puts a crucifix in his mouth and refuses to speak. Adult efforts to make a normal child out of him only cause him to flee deeper into his fantasy world of snow and a talking snowman, a vagabond who supplies the snowman's voice.

Wiener Bluuut (*Viennese Blood*). Director Helmut Berger and Nina Grosse scripted this bank robbery psycho thriller set against black snow and a grey sky in the midst of Vienna's carnival.

Zeit der Rache (*Time of Vengeance*). Cinematographer turned director, Anton Peschke, is at the helm of this story of Orphan, a ten-year-old Turkish boy from a village in Anatolia, who, armed with his grandfather's revolver, goes to Vienna intending to revenge the death of his father, who was killed in a car accident.

Vadim Glowna in Franz Novotny's Die Spitzen der Gesellschaft

TOP GROSSING FILMS IN AUSTRIA: 1989

	Admissions
Rain Man	430,673
A Fish Called Wanda	393,016
Otto – Der Ausserfriesische	369,705
The Bear	298,635
Cocktail	248,151
Indiana Jones and the Last Crusade	243,380
Twins	236,303
Licence to Kill	234,521
The Naked Gun	215,766
Batman	182,869

Producers

Satel Fernseh-und
Filmproduktionsgesellschaft
Kirchengasse 19
A 1070 Vienna
Tel: (222) 93–24–41
Fax: (222) 96–43–28

Schönbrunn Film
Neubaugasse 1
A 1070 Vienna
Tel: (222) 93–22–65
Fax: (222) 93–96–58

Wega
Filmproduktionsgesellschaft
Hagelingasse 13
A 1140 Vienna
Tel: (222) 923481/86
Fax: (222) 951211/220

Distributors

Centfox Film
Neubaugasse 35
A 1071 Vienna
Tel: (222) 93–26–29
Fax: (222) 96–72–97

Columbia – Tri-Star Film
Verlag
Waldgasse 21/1/1/9
A 1060 Vienna

Tel: (222) 597–15–15
Fax: (222) 597–15–16

Constantin Film
Siebensterngasse 37
A 1070 Vienna
Tel: (222) 93–13–53
Fax: (222) 93–14–02

Czerny Film
Neubaugasse 1
A 1070 Vienna
Tel: (222) 02–02–49
Fax: (222) 93–33–09

Fleur Film
Stadlgasse 1
A 4470 Enns
Tel: (7223) 2670
Fax: (222) 93–82–53 (Vienna Office)

Top Film
Lindengasse 56
A 1070 Vienna
Tel: (222) 96–19–19
Fax: (222) 96–19–18

UIP
Neubaugasse 1
A 1070 Vienna
Tel: (222) 93–46–31
Fax: (222) 96–75–48

Warner Brothers
Zieglergasse 10

A 1070 Vienna
Tel: (222) 93–86–26
Fax: (222) 93–94–62

Useful Addresses

Austrian Film Commission
Neubaugasse 36
A 1070 Vienna
Tel: (222) 96–33–23
Fax: (222) 93–34–36

Fachverband der
Audivisions und
Filmindustrie Österreichs
(Association of Audiovisual and
Film Industries)
Federal Chamber of
Commerce
Wiedner Hauptstr. 63
A 1045 Vienna
Tel: (222) 50105–3012
Fax: (222) 50206m 253 (Jointly
with Exhibitors Association)

Österreichischer
Filmförderungsfonds
(Austrian Film Fund)
Plunkergasse 3–5
A 1150 Vienna
Tel: (222) 92–56–01
Fax: (222) 92–01–63

BELGIUM

by Patrick Duynslaegher

With more than a dozen films released in 1989, for the first time in the history of Belgian cinema, there was a rich variety of movies on display in the theatres. This could give the misleading impression of a healthy situation for local film production: nothing is further from the truth. The fact that Belgian product had to line up to get in the theatres at the end of the year, did not mean there was suddenly a boost of continuous production; it's rather by coincidence that so many films hit the theatres around the same time.

Financing films remains difficult, with government help insufficient to help a weak – some would say non-existing – industry. Few films are in production right now and of the dozen directors who had a new film released during the season 1989–1990, probably no one will get a new project completed in the next two years.

Only three films were successful at the box office. **Koko Flanel**, the second effort by low brow comedian Urbanus, again won a warm response from the Flemish mass audience. Except for the financial beneficiaries, *Koko Flanel* offers a pretty discouraging experience, with Urbanus as a simpleton who becomes an idol in the fashion world. It's a shapeless, thoughtless mess of a comedy with easy laughs and no wit in sight. Director Stijn Coninx and Urbanus don't even succeed in satirising the fashion scene, and God knows they've really tried.

The two other hits were Robbe De Hert's **Blueberry Hill** (reviewed in last year's IFG) and Dominique Deruddere's **Wait Until Spring, Bandini**, based on the novel by recently rediscovered American writer John Fante about the immigrant experience in America. Jean-Jacques Andrien's ambitious co-production, **Australia** performed poorly at the box-office, while all the others simply bombed.

The talented young director Dominique Deruddere (*Crazy Love*) assembled an international cast for *Wait Until Spring, Bandini*, an Euro-(Belgium, France, Italy)-American co-production with Francis Coppola's Zoetrope, shot on location in Salt Lake City.

The movie takes place in a small town in Colorado during the winter of 1925 and the story is told through the eyes of the young boy Arturo Bandini (an astonishing fresh performance by newcomer Michael Bacall) who loves baseball, movies, a girl who doesn't return his love, and of course his family. While his mother, a devout Catholic (Ornella Muti), struggles to get food on the table, his father Svevo (Joe Mantegna) gambles away his savings at the local poolhall and doesn't mind getting seduced by the lonely widow (Faye Dunaway) for whom he fixes the fireplace. Soon, Svevo moves in with his new employer; for mother and children coming Christmas doesn't look very promising, but twelve-year-old Arturo uses all his childlike shrewdness to get his father back home.

All this could become unbearable melodramatic, but Deruddere gives his film a fairy tale quality. Everything is set in an imaginary, glowing past and the affectionate look at the Italian immigrants in the New World has also moments of gentle humour. Deruddere clearly projected the Catholic angst of his own childhood in a small Flemish city onto the emotional traumas of his young Italo-American hero. His direction of actors is very impressive and the whole movie is well crafted.

Australia is another proof of Jean-Jacques Andrien's powerful cinematic language and distinctive personality. Jeremy Irons and Fanny Ardant star in this Belgian-Franco-Swiss co-production. Edouard Pierson (Irons) has left the family wool business in the industrial city of Verviers (Belgium) to begin a new life in the adventurous land of Australia, just before the outbreak of the Second World War. It is now 1955 and Edouard is called back to Verviers by his brother to save the ailing family business. His homecoming is prolonged and complicated when he meets Jeanne (Ardant) and discovers he's still capable of falling in love. The protagonist is a man torn between two worlds: the stiff, old-world tradition in Belgium where people are slow to react to changing economic patterns, and the wild and rugged Australian continent. In a refined narrative structure, Andrien cuts back and forth between the horizontal, vast and sun-lit Australian spaces and the narrow Belgian environment. Andrien, who was born in Verbiers, observes the futile social activities of a provincial life style in a rigorously ritualistic mode. The typical Belgian greyness contrasts dramatically with the wide blue skies of South Australia; the cinematography of Angelopoulos' great Greek cameraman Yorgos Arvanitis is breathtaking. As always with Andrien, there's a complex soundtrack that adds immensely to the impact of the story.

Linguistic Problems

A third co-production, **Il Maestro**, directed by Marion Hänsel fared less well; it's a case in point of the linguistic problems facing this kind of Euro-pudding. The anecdotal story (based on a novella by Italian film-maker Mario Soldati) tells of a renowned conductor and a poseur and is mainly set

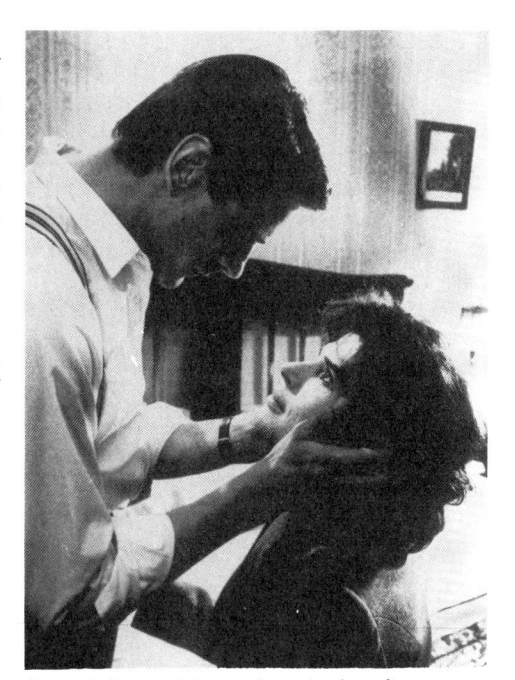

Fanny Ardant and Jeremy Irons in *Australia*

during the Second World War in Tuscany. Malcolm MacDowell and Charles Aznavour are starring as very unconvincing English-speaking Italians. The mixture of French, Italian, Belgian and American talent is miscalculated and finally deprives the movie of any identity.

Hugo Claus doesn't fall into this trap with **The Sacrament**. Based on his own 1963 novel (already adapted for the stage in 1971 as *Interieurs*) his material is as deeply rooted in the national soil as possible. The whole movie takes place in an archetypical Flemish village during the 1950's, where the Catholic church holds everyone firmly in her grip. The annual commemoration of the death of mother Heylen in the vicarage where Natalie Heylen (Ann Petersen) is priest Deedee's (Frank Aendenboom) housekeeper, reunites a bunch of petty bourgeois charactors. Over-generous eating and drinking lead to an explosion of latent grudges and hidden frustrations. *The Sacrament* is mostly played for laughs with

Faye Dunaway and Joe Mantegna in *Wait Until Spring, Bandini*

Claus looking down in contempt on a Flemish community where fear, hypocrisy and stupidity set the tone. Efforts to suddenly veer the satirical material in a heart-felt direction misfire. Even the acting is very uneven: ranging from the naturalistic to the amateurish.

Freddy Coppens' three-years-in-the-making **Dilemma**, set among the nouveaux riches in Antwerp, couldn't make up its mind what it really wanted to be: a psychological thriller, a family drama or a film about major social issues in a yuppie society.

The only nice thing to be said about **Cruel Horizon**, Guy Lee Thys's exploitation film about the fate of the boat people, is that it was the first Belgian film shot in the Philippines and released with a 70mm print.

Coming from the director of *Noce en Galilée*, **Cantique des pierres** was a major disappointment. Michel Khleifi, born in Nazareth and living in Brussels, mixes documentary footage of Palestinian life in the hills and villages of the occupied West Bank with a mannered love story that sounds sometimes like a bad parody of *Hiroshima mon amour*.

Another Belgian film that borrowed the premise from a classic of the French new wave, was **L'Air de rien**. Mary Jimenez starts more or less where Agnès Varda's *Cléo de cinq à sept* took off. Jessie expects a medical report which will confirm that her days are counted. Instead of waiting for the final results, she breaks with her bourgeois life style and enjoys the chance meetings of a bunch of colourful Brussels strangers. Despite Jessie's imminent death, the film is told as a lightweight fantasy, celebrating the vulnerability of life and the transience of happiness. Good intentions abound, but film remains remote and unengaging.

Marquis, the Belgian contribution to the Bicentennial of the French Revolution, was a bizarre technical experiment, with a cast of animals played by human performers who are wearing heavy masks designed by French screenwriter and caricaturist Roland Topor. The protagonist is an aristocratic dog, Marquis (de Sade of course), who is imprisoned in the Bastille and muses about the conflict between mind and instinct with his own phallus, named Colin and the only character with human features. The result is certainly thought-provoking, but the laborious technique of mask-wearing slows the film down and makes the proceedings extremely static.

One of the most noteworthy productions was a debut film by Paris-based Belgian writer Jean-Philippe Toussaint. The hero of **Monsieur** is an anonymous man who works in an insurance company and undergoes his daily routine with a surprising impassiveness. With the help of striking black-and-white photography, Toussaint creates a sarcastic and dark bureaucratic underworld, somewhere between Kafka and Magritte.

PATRICK DUYNSLAEGHER is film critic for the leading Belgian weekly magazine, Knack. His articles have appeared in Variety, Sight and Sound, and other periodicals. Co-author of a book on André Delvaux.

BOLIVIA

by Pedro Susz K.

Finally, after a long and tedious wait, Bolivian cinema seems to be recovering its zest. During 1989, not only was the first feature film in five years actually completed, but several new projects were launched, which one hopes will see the light of day before 1990 has come to an end.

The efforts to have a new Film Law enacted are still continuing, and there has even been a modest improvement in the attendance figures at Bolivian movie theatres. During 1989, there were 189 new releases (compared with the average of 2809 during the early 1980's). Of this total, 69.3% were U.S. productions, followed by 10% from Mexico. The European presence remains low, just 12.7%.

The big event of the year was undoubtedly the triumph of **The Hidden Nation** (*La Nación clandestina*) at the San Sebastian Festival. This seventh feature from Jorge Sanjinés – our major contemporary director – also won the "Glauber Rocha" award, given by the specialised press during the most recent Festival of New Latin American Cinema in Havana; the film also attracted good notices from its screening at the Forum of Young Cinema in Berlin.

La Nación clandestina tells the story of Sebastian, an Aymura peasant, who emigrates to the city, where he becomes involved in the toils of a repressive military dictatorship. He changes his name and abandons his identity. At a certain moment, Sebastian goes through a crisis, and decides to return to his community, to dance a ritual "Dance of the Dead" as a gift to his people. On his way home memories of his past return and he assesses his life, in the same way as the country itself is facing its immediate historical past. *La Nación clandestina* is a work of great formal beauty, marked by the long-shots that distinguish Sanjinés' cinema. It is a mature film, of tremendous force and emotional impact (particularly of Bolivian audiences).

Profile: Jorge Sanjinés

Born in la Paz in 1936, he studied film in Santiago (Chile). Returning to Bolivia in 1960, he joined Oscar Soria (the most important Bolivian screenwriter) and Ricardo Rada. In 1963 he made *Revolucion*, a short that took a prize at the Leipzig Festival. In 1965 he was named head of the Bolivian Film Institute. While there, he filmed *Ukamau* (1966), and his filmography also includes *Yawar Mallku* (1969), *El Coraje del pueblo* (1971), *Fuera de Aquí* (1974), *El Enemigo principal* (1977), and *Las Banderas del Amanecer* (1983). Sanjinés has won numerous international awards, among

Shooting *La Nación clandestina*

them the Critics' Prize at Cannes, a first prize at Venice, and also major awards at Karlovy Vary, Havana, and Figueira da Foz.

PEDRO SUSZ K. is a film critic for newspapers, TV channels and radio. Author of two books about Bolivian cinema. Director of the Bolivian Film Archive (Cinemateca Boliviana). Executive Director of the National Film Board.

TOP TEN GROSSING FILMS IN BOLIVIA: 1989
Batman
Indiana Jones and the Last Crusade
Licence to Kill
Rain Man
The Name of the Rose
Women on the Verge of a Nervous Breakdown
Salsa
Danko
Cocktail
Moonwalker

Producers

Ukamau Ltd
Casilla 2796
La Paz
Tel: 373377

Grupo Ukamau
Casilla 10373
La Paz
Tel: 354628

Centro Cine Video
Casilla 594
La Paz
Tel: 340990

Distributors

Pelmex
Casilla 2613
La Paz
Tel: 326863
Telex: 2525 Pelmex BV

Manfer
Casilla 4709
La Paz
Tel: 321041
Telex: 2650 Manfer BV

Anmdina
Casilla 2695
La Paz
Tel: 350122
Telex: 2657 Andina BV

Incofisa
Casilla 1475
La Paz
Tel: 342898

Corporacion Americana
Casilla 4802
La Paz
Tel: 325051
Cable: Cocinema

Pelinter
Casilla 7599
La Paz
Tel: 377262
Telex: 3399 Pelint BV

Useful Addresses

Consejo Nacional del Cine (Conacine)
Casilla 9933
La Paz
Tel: 325346
Telex: 3288 Cormesa BV

BRAZIL
by Luis Arbex

1989 marked the sharpest slump in the country's industry both in quality and quantity. Brazilian production remained unstable (only 25 films). The country's catastrophic economic situation struck hard at the cinema, along with the vicious inflationary spiral. The industry has now become the victim of severe retrenchment. Embrafilme, which sponsored most production, was closed by the new government in April 1990.

Attendances for Brazilian films dropped from 61,854,000 in 1978 to 23,987,000 in 1988. No improvement has been made to encourage people to go to the movies. Among the 134 movie houses existing in São Paulo only three show a high quality standard. The people's buying power dropped sharply as a consequence of this recession. None of the Brazilian projects in joint ventures with foreign producers has been completed or ready for screening. The only notable event of the year continues to be the São Paulo International Film Festival. This Mostra (in its fourteenth year) has been possible thanks to Leon Cakof whose patience and perseverance continue to make history here.

Recent and Forthcoming Films

ABC da Greve (Strike's ABC). Dir: Leon Hirszman. *Documentary.*
Amor Vagabundo (Vagabond Love). Dir: Hugo Carvana. Players: Marieta Severo, Nelson Xavier, Wilson Grey. *Comedy.*
Barrela. Dir: Marco Antônio Cury, from a play by Plínio Marcos. Players: Cláudio Mamberti, Marcos Palmeira, Paulo Cesar Pereio. *Drama.*
Beijo 23480/72 (Kiss 23480/72). Dir: Walter Rogério. *Drama.*
Brasil na Segunda Guerra (Brazil in the Second World War). Dir: Sílvio Back. *Documentary.*
Cem Anos de Abolição (The Emancipation Centennial). Dir: Eduardo Coutinho. *Documentary.*
O Corpo (The Body). Dir: José Antônio Garcia, based on a story by Clarice Lispector. Players: Antônio Fagundes, Marieta Severo.
Dias Melhores Virão (Better Days Will Come). Dir: Carlos Diegues. Script: Antônio Calmon, Vicente Pereira, Vinicius Vianna, Diegues. Phot: Lauro Escorel. Music: Rita Lee, Roberto de Carvalho. Players: Marília Pera, Paulo José, Zezé Motta, José Wilker, Rita Lee, Paulo Cesar Pereio. Jofre Soares, Patrício Bisso. *Comedy. Screened on TV only.*
O Escorpião Escarlate (The Scarlet Scorpion). Dir: Ivan Cardoso. Players: Andrea Beltrão, Nuno Leal Maia, Herson Capri. *Comedy.*
Forever. Dir: Walter Hugo Khoury. Players: Ben Gazzara, Eva Grimaldi, Vera Fischer, Cecil Thiré. *Drama.*
A Grande Arte (The Great Art). Dir: Walter Salles Jr., based on a novel by Rubem Fonseca. Players: Peter Coyote, Ruy Rezende, Giulia Gam. *Thriller.*
Manouche. Dir: Luiz Carlos Begazo. Music: Paco de Lucia. Players: Breno Moroni, Drica Morais, Lélia Abramo. *Drama.*
Natal da Portela (One-Armed Natal). Dir: Paulo Cesar Saraceni. Players: Milton Gonçalves, Almir Guinelo. *Documentary made in 1988 and never released theatrically.*
Real Desejo (Real Desire). Dir: Augusto Savá. Players: Ana Maria Magalhães. *Drama.*
Santa Dica do Sertão. Dir: Carlos Del Pino. Players: Denise Milfont, Tânia Alves, Fagner. *Drama.*
Stelinha. Dir: Miguel Faria. Script: Rubem

Marilia Pera in *Días melhores virão*

Fonseca. Players: Marcos Palmeira, Esther Goes, José Lewgoy. *Romance*.
Sermões (Sermons). Script and Dir: Júlio Bressane. Players: Othon Bastos, José Lewgoy, Ankito, Eduardo Tornoghi. Phot: José Tadeu Ribeiro. Music: Lívio Tragtemberg. *Released on TV only*.

Círculo de fogo (Circle of Fire). Dir: Geraldo Moraes. Players: Cristina Prochaska, Roberto Bonfim, Tonico Pereira. *Drama*.
Matou a família e foi ao cinema (He Killed His Family and Went to the Movies). Dir: Neville D'Almeida. *Drama*.

TOP TEN GROSSING FILMS IN BRAZIL: Jan–July 1989

	Admissions
Rain Man	2,337,993
Twins	1,908,793
Indiana Jones and the Last Crusade	1,408,627
Mississippi Burning	1,176,151
The Fly II	1,075,951
Nightmare on Elm Street IV	1,061,393
Moonwalker	966,800
Working Girl	923,496
Gorillas in the Mist	781,845
Cocktail	780,212

Producers

CDK-Produções Cinematográficas Ltda
c/o Carlos Diegues
Rua Miguel Pereira 62
22261 Rio de Janeiro.
Tel: (021) 266-7995

L.C. Barreto Produções Cinematográficas
c/o Luiz Carlos Barreto
Rua Visconde de Caravelas 28
22271 Rio de Janeiro
Tel: (021) 266-5561

Raiz Produções Cinematográficas
c/o João Batista de Andrade

Rua Epeira 59
05447 São Paulo
Tel: (011) 814-4491

Regina Films
c/o Nelson Pereira dos Santos
Rua Jornalista Orlando Dantas 1
Botafogo
Rio de Janeiro
Tel: (021) 552-3648

Distributors

Alvorada-Gaumont
Av. Ipiranga 318
São Paulo
Tel: 231-2361
Telex: 33221

Art Films
Av. Rio Branco 227/102
Rio de Janeiro
Tel: 210-1371
Telex: 30758

Bitelli International
Rua Traipu 210
São Paulo
Tel: 825-5599
Telex: 3255

CIC
Av. Rio Branco 245/28
Rio de Janeiro
Tel: 210-2400
Telex: 21202

Cinematografica Sul
(F.J. Lucas)
Av. São João 1588
São Paulo
Tel: 220-5622

Haway
Rua Turiassu 716
São Paulo
Tel: 864-7199
Telex: 82255

Paris Films
Av. Pacaembu 1702
São Paulo
Tel: 864-9111
Telex: 83505

Severiano Ribeiro
Praça Mahatma Gandhi 2
Rio de Janeiro
Tel: 240-4242

DR. LUIS ARBEX won a scholarship to the U.S. for postgraduate medical training and remained there for eight years. Now retired, he dedicates his time to cinema research and travelling as a genuine movie buff.

BULGARIA
by Ivan Stoyanovich

As Bulgaria joined in the fervent quest for democracy and higher living standards, highly controversial subjects and people who were blacklisted until recently have started appearing in the media. A wide range of political parties and movements has opened fire on the past and drawn up plans for the future. Meanwhile, an economic crisis has generated strong friction between stratified urban and rural communities. This article will appear after the general elections. Whatever their outcome, the country will face a vague future for quite some time. Understandably, this holds good for the film industry as well.

The present social upheaval has

Still from *The Camp*

predictably shifted the emphasis on documentaries and television. Since early 1990, a number of bold new releases have hit the screen along with documentaries shelved by the totalitarian regime. Here are several: Vassil Zhivkov's **Favourable Outcome**, Nevena Tosheva's **Krustyo Rakovski**, Ivan Rossenov's **Complaint**, Oleg Kovachev's **Run for Your Life**, Kristina Shopova's **Cadets**, Stanimir Trifonov's **Till Tomorrow**, Adela Peeva's **In the Name of Sport**, Eldora Traikova's **Black Chronicle** and Andrei Slabakov's **A Seabound Train**.

Bulgarian feature films have somewhat

Still from *Walks with the Angel*

lagged behind the times as a result of a longer production process; besides, scriptwriters have also been slower to adapt to the changes. However, the courage and ingenuity of certain film-makers who started work on their features before the fall of the dictatorship, have been richly rewarded these days. The first name to quote is established director Georgi Dyulgferov and **The Camp**, an ironic, psychological study of "voluntary" student work brigades in the totalitarian age and the crippling thirst for power. A shady and manipulated political career manipulates and kills love. *The Camp* and Nikolai Volev's **Margarit and Margarita** were screened with success at the Directors' Fortnight in Cannes.

Of the older generation, Plamen Maslarov made another interesting and sincere film which traced the downfall of the Bulgarian village under socialism over the past half century through the fate of a leader caught up in the whirlwind of history (**Mayor, Mayor**). Ivanka Grubcheva, best known for her films for children, screened a sci-fi satire with a political message: **The Carnival**.

Maturing Talents

As I noted in last year's IFG, however, eyes are on the newcomers. I cannot single out a leader, but the past year established Lyudmil Todorov (*Running Dogs*) as both scriptwriter and director with **The Love Summer of a Schlepp**, a modern, subtle analysis of free youth feelings and liaisons in contrast with the stagnation in social and family relations.

An original plot about gamblers which actually condemns the wild risks and corruption of socialist society is recounted in fledgling director Iskra Yossifova's **Cruel and Innocent**, a profound insight into yesterday's mandatory duplicity.

In **Shortage**, young director Haim Cohen (*Protect the Small Animals*) examines the bitter-sweet fruit of corruption cultivated by two women who love each other tenderly. Ivan Pavlov came back after a long break in his career with **A Walk with the Angel**, an essayistic philosophical fable.

In an effort to cope with the economic crisis brought on by universally condemned government policies, Bulgarian Cinematography has been seeking mutually beneficial co-operation in the West. It established numerous contacts, founded joint ventures and negotiated co-productions and production services, offering an appealing landscape, technical equipment and a wealth of actors, cameramen, designers, directors and technicians. The first Bulgarian–British joint venture in the cultural field, called Balkan Film Enterprises, has been launched by Bulgarian Cinematography, Pergamon Media, part of the Maxwell Entertainment Group, and the Elektronika Bank. Harrison Reader, President of the Los Angeles-based Longridge Films, is the partnership's North American representative. In a recent deal, Maxwell bought 70 Bulgarian films.

Screenings in the U.S.

Three of the 47 East European films run at the Los Angeles Festival were Bulgarian. **Monday Morning**, **Ivan and Alexandra** and **Time of Violence** fuelled interesting debates and got reviews in *Variety*, *The New York Times*, *The Los Angeles Times* and other papers. A Hollywood company signed contracts for co-productions. Two American sci-fi stories, *Destalker IV* and *The Queen of the Barbarians III* are currently being shot in Bulgaria. Concord President Roger Corman, director and producer, said he would consider shooting *all* his films in Bulgaria if these projects were successful. Bulgarian Cinematography President Lyudmil Staikov met ICN Vice President Peter Bowly to negotiate 40 to 50 minutes for Bulgaria in *Letters to America*, a co-production between the Los Angeles Public Television Company and Eastern Europe. Universal have sent Bulgarian

Still from *The Love Summer of a Schlepp*

Cinematography a script and the conditions for producing the film in this country. This autumn, a Bulgarian cinema season will run at Washington's Kennedy Center.

About 50 million tickets are sold in Bulgaria annually. The backbone of the local film repertoire comes from the "Panorama of World Cinema" which shows the year's international prize-winners and box-office hits in Sofia each November.

Closer ties with the Western market through a series of top international contracts will pave the way for the future of the Bulgarian film industry. A freely elected democratic Parliament and multi-party government on the basis of a market economy are expected to boost the industry.

IVAN STOYANOVICH has been a film critic and journalist for 35 years, and Editor of the magazine Bulgarian Films *since 1960. He has written several hundred film reviews, 12 books, plays, sketches, film and TV scripts, and lyrical essays. He also appears on radio and TV. Ivan Stoyanovich has never held any government or public office, nor has he ever been a member of any party.*

Recent and Forthcoming Films

Antrax (Anthrax). Script: Georgi Bogdanov. Dir: Stanislava Kalcheva. Phot: Alexander Ivanov. Player: Peter Slabakov.
Bashtata na yaitseto (The Father of the Egg).

TOP TEN GROSSING FILMS IN BULGARIA: 1989

Willow
Coming to America
A Fish Called Wanda
Margarit and Margarita (Bulgaria)
Adios, Rio (Bulgaria)
The Untouchables
Le Solitaire
Ne reveillez pas un flic qui dort
The Last Emperor
La Bamba

Script: Boris Hristov. Dir: Henri Koulev. Phot: Svetlana Ganeva. Players: Ivailo Hristov, Lyuben Chatalov, Konstantin Kotsev.
Lyubovta e nemirna ptitsa (Love Is a Wilful Bird). Script and Dir: Rangel Vulchanov. Phot: Emil Hristov. Players: Emilia Tsaneva, Itzhak Fintsi, Todor Kolev, Nikolai Binev.
Onova neshto (That Thing). Script: Hristo Boichev. Dir: Georgi Stoyanov. Phot: Krassimir Kostov. Players: Velko Kunev, Pavel Poppandov, Nahum Shopov.
Rezervat (Nature Reserve). Script: Eduard Zahariev and Plamen Maslarov. Dir: Eduard Zahariev. Phot: Radoslav Spassov. Players: Georgi Staikov, Evelina Pesheva, Itzhak Fintsi.
Sofiiska istoria (Sofia Story). Script: Lyuben Stanev. Dir: Nadya Staneva. Phot: Hristo Totev. Players: Svetla Todorova, Ilia Karaivanov, Stanislava Armoutlieva.
Sreburnata lisitsa (The Silver Fox): Script: Ivan Golev. Dir: Nikola Roudarov. Phot: Viktor Chouchov. Players: Georgi Staikov, Elena Boicheva, Aneta Sotirova.
Tishina (Silence). Script and Dir: Dimiter Petkov. Phot: Hristo Bakalov. Players: Hristo Gurbov, Peter Popyordanov, Zhoreta Nikolova.
Vse otlagam da te zabravya (I Still Put off Forgetting You). Script: Nikolai Nikiforov. Dir: Stefan Gurdev. Phot: Mircho Borissov. Players: Emil Djourov, Albena Chakurova-Djamdjieva, Yuliana Karanyotova.

Useful Addresses

Bulgarian Cinematography Corporation
President: Lyudmil Staikov
96 Rakovski St
Sofia
Tel: 87-66-11
Telegr: Bulgariafilm
Telex: 22-447
Fax: 88-24-31

Boyana Feature Film Studio
Director: Emil Angelov
Boyana 16 Film City
Sofia
Tel: 58-131
Telex: 22-376
Fax: 59-31-15

Vreme Popular Scientific and Documentary Film Studio
Director: Bozhidar Manov
9 Biryuzov Blvd
Sofia
Tel: 44-28-23
Telex: 23-010

Sofia Animated Film Studio
Director: Hristo Tsachev
Boyana 16 Film City
Tel: 58-131
Telex: 567

The Globus Team
Head: Hristo Kovachev

13 Moskovska St
Sofia
Tel: 87-87-28

Bulgariafilm
Import-Export
Director: Zdravko Vatev
96 Rakovski St
Tel: 87-66-11
Telegr. Bulgariafilm
Telex: 22-447
Fax: 88-24-31

Balkan Film Enterprises Bulgarian-British Joint Venture
75 Biryuzov St

Sofia
Tel: 470-91-28
Fax: 470-91-48

Film Distribution
Director: Bogomil Grozdanov
135A Rakovski St
Sofia
Tel: 88-12-91
Telegr: Bulgariafilm

Bulgarian Video
Director: Marcho Markov
60 Samokov Blvd
Sofia
Tel: 72-07-77
Telex: 22-812

Interfilm
The Sofia Press Agency
Director: Sashko Velichkov
113 Lenin Blvd
Sofia
Tel: 70-20-48

BURMA
by Fred Marshall

The oldest film business in Asia is once again flourishing under the new military regime, and will probably become even more active.

A leading actress and director, Wah Wah Win Shwe, and producer U Than Htut recently completed shooting on the first film to be made on location outside Burma. This production, **Mount Dar Tu Kalyar**, was made in Bangkok.

In addition to imported pictures, some 10 or 11 colour films have been produced this year in the country. The maximum playing time for a Burmese release is twice daily except at weekends. Admission charges run to around US$ 1.00, and each film must play two years to break even – and that is unlikely.

The import of foreign films is restricted to reissues. Hongkong actioners are brought into Burma by the Motion Picture Corporation. The Japanese and Soviets continue to donate films, dubbed into English, which are of course screened along with reissues of Indian and American pictures. New rules and regulations are said to be more liberal in tone and should allow private distributors to import films. Under martial law and curfew conditions, attendances at many cinemas have been poor, but there are signs of improvement.

Television in Burma is still controlled and its entertainment programming strictly limited. Videos operating on the PAL system are imported from Thailand and form the country's newest entertainment fad.

Kyaw Thu and Moe Moe Myint Aung, two of Burma's most popular screen stars

CAMBODIA

by Fred Marshall

Kampuchea is once again known as Cambodia, but the country's media situation remains difficult to disentangle. Festivals are screening the Czech-Cambodian film, *The Ninth Circle*, about a Czech doctor who falls in love with a resistance worker-cum- nursing sister from Cambodia. Barrandov Studios shot it here on location some years back and it offers magnificent images of the country's lakes, waterfalls, mountains and temples including Angkor Wat. In addition, visiting directors have made documentaries about recent Cambodian history.

It is hard to say when the minuscule Cambodian film industry will revive and rival the heady days when Prince Sihanouk devoted so much time and talent to film-making. Pnom Penh, the capital, has some six operating cinemas, which have monthly performances. They depend on outside assistance from other major countries with whom Cambodia enjoys good relations. As in Laos, French is understood better than English. Films are often screened in Vietnamese, Chinese, or Thai depending on where they are available. Outside the capital, in areas like Battabang and Siam Reap, there are outdoor cinemas for workers and soldiers.

Pnom Penh has a public TV outlet which operates daily for three hours between 6 PM and 9 PM. Video is still the big attraction and pirate videos in Thai and English which come from Bangkok are readily available and are shown in many hotels, restaurants and public halls.

CANADA

by Gerald Pratley

The past year has been exceptional. Most of the 40-odd films listed here are genuinely Canadian, most of them very good; too many still contain the seemingly-obligatory American references and players, and because few found their way into cinemas or received distribution and exhibition in the U.S. the cry persists that once again indigenous Canadian films have no international appeal. Telefilm, the federal film funding agency, is concerned over the short playing time given to those features which *do* get shown on the Famous Players and Cineplex–Odeon circuits, and has introduced a new policy to make sure that "films and television (films) will have a good chance of recouping their investment" and thus return more money to Telefilm.

Telefilm should not be put into a position of worrying over recouping its annual $145 million investment money. Films deserve to be subsidised just as much as oil, gas, wheat

Lothaire Bluteau in *Jesus of Montreal*

and manufacturing are worthy of government support. But under the Conservative government's objective of making "cultural agencies" pay their way, Telefilm is being forced to consider commercial arrangements which should play no part in its support of imaginative and indigenous film-making by creative individuals. The difficulties however, of getting films to audiences remain, and the solution would seem to be in following the pattern, established in Britain, in which Channel 4 and the BBC have brought British films not seen in cinemas to television audiences.

Many of the Canadian films now being made and not shown are more suitable (these days) for TV and video where they are more likely to find large and appreciative audiences who spend more time watching the home screen than going to cinemas. It now costs $7.50 to go to the movies in the larger cities. With parking and baby-minding fees, and perhaps dinner out, the cost of a night at the movies is fairly high. For the 18's to 30 year-old audience, which forms the mass of moviegoers, the price of a ticket requires instant assurance of sensational entertainment, not the quiet, intimate, reflective studies which characterise most small-budget domestic films.

Telefilm already advances money to distributors toward the cost of advertising the opening of a film, but these charges are enormous, growing larger, and are not always effective. American companies spend as much on opening a film as most producers here spend on making one. It would make more sense for Telefilm to buy network time from the commercially-minded CBC to run Canadian feature films every week, repeating them during the summer, free from commercials, and in this way, create a regular presence for film-makers, including the actors, among

NFB
sharing our vision

SHARING OUR VISION
The NFB has documented, dramatized and animated Canada and the world in more than 7,000 productions.

CELEBRATING CREATIVITY
From Cannes to Hollywood to Yorkton, Saskatchewan — NFB films and filmmakers have garnered more than 3,000 awards since 1939.

PROJECTING INNOVATION
NFB research and development advances the technology of cinema — watch for CINETEXT, the next generation of electronic film subtitling systems.

MONTRÉAL
C.P./P.O. Box 6100,
Succursale/Station A,
Montréal (Québec)
H3C 3H5

PARIS
15, rue de Berri
75008 Paris
France

NEW YORK
16th Floor
1251 Avenue of the Americas
New York, New York
USA 10020

LONDON
1 Grosvenor Square
London, England
W1X 0AB

DU CINÉMA À NOTRE IMAGE
L'ONF a dispensé au Canada et dans le monde plus de 7 000 productions, que ce soit des documentaires, des fictions ou des films d'animation.

UNE CRÉATIVITÉ RECONNUE
Du Festival des films de Cannes à Hollywood en passant par le Festival de Yorkton, Saskatchewan les films de l'ONF et ses cinéastes ont remportéplus de 3 000 prix depuis 1939.

TOURNÉ VERS L'INNOVATION
La recherche-développement à l'ONF permet de faire progresser la technologie cinématographique. À cet égard, surveillez CINÉTEXTE, la prochaine génération de sous-titrage électronique.

ONF
du cinéma à notre image

National Film Board of Canada
Office national du film du Canada

receptive audiences. Across this country may be found an enormous number of quiet Canadians living far from the few specialised cinemas which might show our films, longing for the opportunity to be a part of the growing film activity brought about by Telefilm, the OFDC, and other provincial bodies. "Telefilm Presents . . ." every week would fill the void.

Other Happenings . . .
On the government level, the watered-down film policy announced last year to satisfy Jack Valenti, and the new Television Bill devised to increase the amount of Canadian programming on CBC and private stations, have still not been passed by the House of Commons; the CBC has two new men at the helm, broadcaster-writer Patrick Watson and bureaucrat Gérard Veilleux, who have not yet managed to change its stripes; CTV has a new man in charge, John Cassady who comes from Campbell's Soup Co. and believes that television's only purpose is to sell advertising; the CRTC remains an ineffectual body; but thankfully, to all intents and purposes, the National Film Board (NFBC) seems to be holding its own and producing a steady stream of excellent work inspite of its budget problems (*Black Mother, Black Daughter, No Way, Not Me; Media in Society*). The tiresome parade of seminars and conferences for business men, "to examine the essential issues confronting the film and television industries in Canada today," from which nothing is learned, continued with seldom a film-maker in attendance; and on the co-production front there is a flurry of TV series for the Americans involving, principally, Alliance (Robert Lantos), Atlantis (Michael MacMillan) and Astral (Harold Greenberg and André Bureau) who lead the way – attempting the difficult task of performing a balancing act between making Canadian films and paying for them

Geneviève Bujold (right) in Michel Brault's *Les Noces de papier*, released through Films Transit

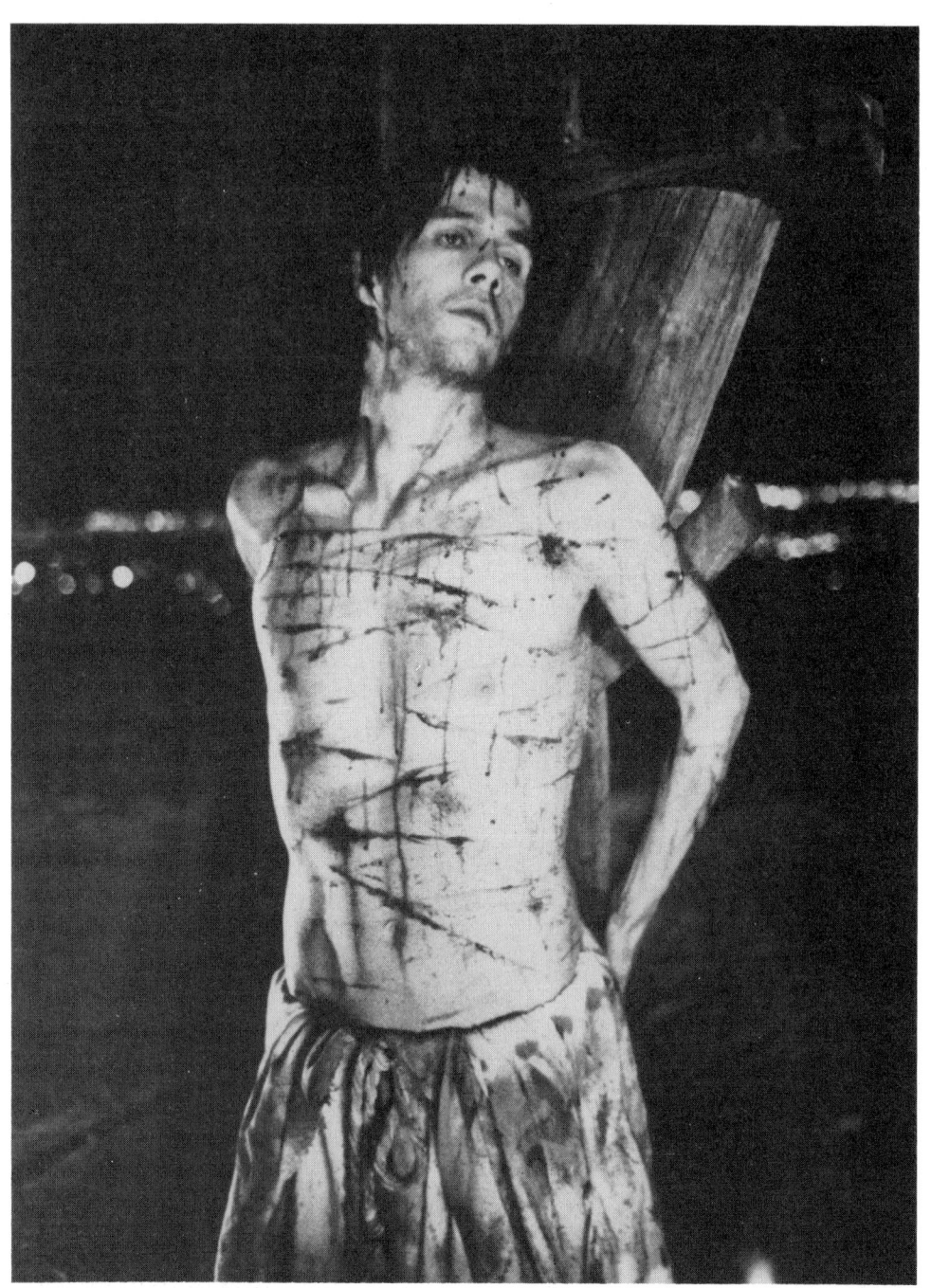

Lothaire Bluteau in *Jesus of Montreal*

through TV co-productions. The public is informed regularly through the media that Canadian films and TV programmes are selling well abroad, but what they are not told is that most of them cannot be identified as being Canadian. Most audiences think they are watching American programmes.

Sad Demise ...

The man who could have changed the pattern of English-language film-making, Garth Drabinsky, chose over the years not to do so and as a result the empire he built on the foundations of Rank's Odeon in this country, Cineplex–Odeon, came crashing down last year. Drabinsky was so determined to conquer the American market that he over-reached himself, lost the U.S. assets, and almost ruined the company in Canada, which is now falling more deeply into the MCA fold. Had his financial skills, his driving ambition, his interest in motion pictures, been directed into strengthening the Canadian film industry through his cinemas, distribution company, his technical services companies, and by financing a continuing programme of Canadian films instead of making American movies, the story of Cineplex and Drabinsky would have been entirely different. He could have accomplished for Canadian cinemas what J. Arthur Rank once did for British films under circumstances similar to those facing Drabinsky when he began his career. (He has now turned to the production of stage shows, the long-running *Phantom of the Opera*, and will be remembered for restoring the beautiful Imperial Cinema in Toronto – now the Pantages – for stage performances.) When Drabinsky opened the first of his multiplexes, with their small seating capacity and low overhead costs, he said this would mean longer runs for specialised films, giving them time to find their audiences. This has been true for many foreign-language films, but not for

The outstanding Canadian film of 1989: *Jesus of Montreal*

Canadian pictures – with one exception, *Jesus of Montreal*.

Man of the Year

Denys Arcand has become the first "celebrity" in Canadian film as a result of the great success of his *Jesus of Montreal*. It ran for over a year in a Cineplex cinema in Toronto and in its home province of Québec grossed over two million dollars; it received splendid reviews in the U.K. and Europe and has been sold successfully almost world-wide giving the lie to all the reasons advanced by the money-men why we should not make indigenous films. As with *The Decline of the American Empire* in 1988, *Jesus* didn't win the Academy Award as Best Foreign Language entry, but this did not distress Denys Arcand in the slightest: of his visit to Hollywood he said, "Tomorrow, important people who wanted to lunch with me yesterday won't even know me. I dream only of returning to my cottage in the Laurentians to settle down to writing my next scenario in peace."

While Arcand seeks peace, the industry on the whole is working itself into a frenzy over becoming partners in the perplexing, complicated, and costly business of co-productions for Europe 1992, for cinemas, TV and satellite broadcasting services.

Heaven knows what arrangements the businessmen and bureaucrats are making to gain entry into this baffling film and TV international market. British critics have already dubbed this kind of filmmaking, "Euro Pudding." Euro Stew would be more like it and we'll be there to help stir the pot – even if the servings are few!

In the final analysis the success of a nation's film production in both cultural and economic terms is measured by the impression it makes on its citizens watching these films in cinemas and on television; and in as much as they make them feel a part of their country sharing its concerns, pleasures and achievements and in creating a sense of recognition of belonging to a distinctive society. By these terms, Canadian English-track films have been little more than brief and passing glances over the years of what and where we are – and seldom seen at that. The encouraging number of indigenous films seen this year made possible by Telefilm, the OFDC, SOGIC and other provincial funding organisations, would appear to herald a long awaited turn for the better. The task now is to sustain it.

Notable Films

Les Noces de Papier (A Paper Wedding) (d. Michel Brault) Geneviève Bujold, who appeared in Brault's first feature film as a director, *Entre la mer et l'eau douce* in 1968 (and Denys Arcand's first screenplay), returns here to Montréal to play a solitary, 40-year-old university professor and mistress to a married Hungarian businessman, who finds her life lacking in any sense of purpose. To help her sister, a lawyer with a difficult immigration case, she reluctantly agrees to a marriage of convenience with a Chilean refugee to give him the right to live in Canada. It is purely a business matter, she doesn't even like him, and they will go their own way until a divorce can be arranged. But it turns out not to be as easy as this; they are watched by immigration officials, tested repeatedly on their knowledge of each other, and as a result of being thrown together, actually fall in love. This is to be expected; it is a familiar plot device, we have seen it before, yet it is utterly convincing and conveyed in subdued tones with a sense of grace, beauty and tenderness. Written by Jefferson Lewis and André Pelletier and photographed by Brault's son, Sylvain, with a wonderful feeling for atmosphere (on 16mm for Québec television) it is in every way a remarkable piece of cinema, with near perfect performances by all concerned. (Geneviève Bujold, Manuel Aranguiz, Dorothe Berryman, Gilbert Sicotte, Jean Mathieu. Les Productions du Verseau Inc./NFBC. 90 mins.)

Bye Bye Blues (d. Anne Wheeler) is her third and best film following the promising *Loyalties* and *Cowboys Don't Cry*, all set in Western Canada and conveying a marvellous, graphic sense of people and place. It starts in India, where Daisy Cooper's husband, a doctor with the British army, is transferred to Singapore. Daisy returns to her parents' home on the prairies with her two children, where she hears that Singapore has fallen to the Japanese and her husband is a prisoner-of-war. She must now find a way to earn a living; her gift for music prompts her to play and sing for a local dance band. Soon she is away from her family on tour where she meets a trombone player who falls in love with her. With no word from her husband or to his fate in prison, Daisy has her own war to contend with over her mixed emotions and sense of loyalty to her husband. Dismissed by several critics as being "another conventional film," *Bye Bye Blues* is much more than this, straightforward though it may be in narrative form; it consistently fills ordinary things with life and meaning. It is strikingly photographed by Vic Sarin, it captures the sense of wartime Canada, it has a lively, well-played jazz background, the characters are perfectly played, and Rebecca Jenkins as Daisy (herself a singer and musician) conveys a sense of decency and goodness without being either prim, dull or bland. (Rebecca Jenkins, Michael Ontkean, Luke Reilly, Robyn Stevan, Kate Reid, Sheila Moore, Wayne Robson. Festival Films Ltd., 118 mins.)

GERALD PRATLEY, *former CBC film critic and founder–director of the Ontario Film Institute, teaches film history at Ryerson Polytechnical Institute in Toronto.*

Other Films

American Boyfriends (d. Sandy Wilson) The disappointing sequel to the autobiographical *My American Cousin*, in which Sandy goes to her cousin's wedding in the US and seeks further adventures in California. (Margaret Langrick, John Wildman, Lilsa Repo-Martell. Alliance Releasing Co. 90 mins.)

Archangel (d. Guy Maddin) This is "more of the same" from the creator of *Tales from the Gimli Hospital*, a surreal comedy–tragedy of the Great War set in the Russian Arctic, sometimes clever, mostly confusing, often pointless, in which a Canadian officer goes on a mission to help the White Russians. (Kylie McCulloch, Kathy Marykuca. Cinephile Ltd., b/w. 90 mins.)

Barbar The Movie (d. Alan Bunce) A flat and ordinary animated film, mainly for children, based on the classic stories by Jean de Brunhoff. (Voices: Gordon Pinsent, Elizabeth Hanna, etc. Astral Films. 76 mins.)

Beautiful Dreamers (d. John Kent Harrison) Walt Whitman came to London, Ontario, in 1880 on a short visit to stay with Dr. Maurice Bucke and discuss the subjects of sex and mental illness. This first-feature is a picture postcard pastiche misrepresenting what actually took place. (Rip Torn, Colm Feore, Wendel Meldrum, Sheila McCarthy, Colin Fox. Cinexus– Famous Players. 108 mins.)

Bethune (d. Phillip Borsos) This long-delayed, over-budget, production-plagued film is not as bad as might have been expected, but falls far short of the greatness of treatment that Dr. Norman Bethune deserves. Screenplay by Ted Allan – rewritten by others. (Donald Sutherland, Helen Mirren, Helen Shaver, Colm Feore, Ronald Pickup, Guo Da, Anouk Aimée. Filmline International. 119 mins.)

Brown Bread Sandwiches (d. Carlo Liconti) A simple, noisy, tedious comedy–drama of immigrant Italian family life in Toronto in which Giancarlo Giannini, brought over specially from Italy, sits around with nothing to do. (Lina Sastri, Kim Cattrall. Cineplex–Odeon. 91 mins.)

Cold Comfort (d. Vic Sarin) The first feature from noted cinematographer, Vic Sarin, begins as a drama of prairie winter life only to turn into a somewhat unconvincing horror film for its last part. Expertly filmed and well-acted. (Margaret Langrick, Maury Chaykin, Paul Gross, Ted Follows. Norstar. 92 mins.)

Donald Sutherland in *Bethune*

Cruising Bar (Meet Market) (d. Robert Menard) In this very popular film in Québec, actor Michel Cote plays four different characters in four amusing stories; he is clever and convincing, but his material often lets him down (Michel Côte, Louise Marleau, Geneviève Rious. Malofilm. 96 mins.)

Erik (One Man Out) (d. Michael Kennedy) A U.S. mercenary and a journalist in South America. Lots of violence, not much sense. (Stephen McHattie, Deborah Van Valkenburgh. SC Entertainment. 90 mins.)

The First Season (d. Ralph Thomas, who had his name removed from the credits after a disagreement with the producers over the final version of the film). The story of a fisherman's widow left to fend for herself and daughter, and befriended by a former acquaintance who has become a drunken recluse, the film has much to recommend it with its fine acting performances and attractive British Columbia locations; but compromised it has been and it falls apart at the end. (R.H. Thomson, Kate Trotter. Thomas Howe Releasing Co. 96 mins.)

Foreign Nights (d. Izidore K. Musallam) Set in Toronto, this is the now familiar situation of an immigrant father who refuses to let his daughter live the life of their adopted country. Stodgy, but not without feeling and honesty. (Terri Hawkes, Dean Richards, Youssef Abed-Alnour, Mohammad Bacri. Norstar. 90 mins.)

Freakshow (d. Constantino Magnatta) An unconvincing horror story about an opportunistic TV reporter who finds herself in an Art Gallery filled with peculiar people and exhibits. Pointless. (Audry Landers, Dan Gallagher. Brightstar. 96 mins.)

George's Island (d. Paul Donovan) Set against attractive scenery in Nova Scotia, this is a broad comedy involving a young boy, a frustrated teacher, a weak bureaucrat, a crusty old sailor – and the ghost of Captain Kidd. They all have their moments! (Maury Chaykin, Sheila McCarthy, Ian Bannen, Astral Films. 90 mins.)

Glory Enough for All (d. Eric Till) A splendid biography of Drs. Frederick Banting and Charles Best (written by Grahame Woods) depicting their discovery of insulin. (R.H. Thomson, Robert Visden, John Woodbine, Martha Henry, Michael Zeiniker. Gemstone–Primedia. 200 mins.)

Justice Denied (d. Paul Cowan) This is a hard-hitting, convincing, sometimes flawed re-telling of the case of Donald Marshall, a 17-year-old Micmac Indian in Sydney, Nova Scotia, who was imprisoned for a murder he didn't commit – a shameful miscarriage of justice blinded by racism. (Thomas Peacocke, Peter MacNeil, Daniel MacIvor, Wayne Robson. NFBC. 97 mins.)

Kingsgate (d. Jack Darcus) Domestic warfare between the super-sophisticates: tired professor, cynical airline pilot, tipsy wife, supercilious writer, young student into affairs. They make a tiresome unfunny film. (Christopher Plummer, Roberta Maxwell, Duncan Fraser, Allan Scarfe. Thomas Howe Ltd. 110 mins.)

Lantern Hill (d. Kevin Sullivan, who is back in Lucy Maud Montgomery's *Anne of Green Gables'* country; this time with the simple drama of a daughter who discovers that her father, whom she thought dead, is alive and working as a writer on Prince Edward Island). Family fare for TV and good of its kind. (Mairon Bennett, Sam Waterston, Zoe Caldwell, Colleen Dewhurst. Sullivan Films. 109 mins.)

The Last Winter (d. Aaron Kim Johnston) Set in rural Manitoba in the mid-1950's, this is another sentimental family story in which a young boy is distressed by his father's plans to leave the country to seek a better life in the city.

Naturally and imaginatively told. (Gerard Parkes, David Ferry, Wanda Cannon. Brightstar. 104 mins.)

Long Road Home (d. William Johnston). An American who has received his draft notice for Vietnam comes north to Canada as a camp counsellor. He suffers a crisis of conscience in his political confrontations with his campers – obviously contrived and far-fetched. (Denis Forest, Gareth Bennett, Kelly Rowan, Cinephile Ltd. 95 mins.)

Manuel (Manuel le fils emprunté) (d. François Labonté) A 12-year-old Portuguese boy in Montréal runs away from his father and goes to live with an old man, a friend of the family, who had fought in the Spanish Civil War. The moral dilemma which his teachings create for the boy make for a thoughtful, sparing and entirely convincing study of immigrant life. (Nuno DaCosta, Francisco Rabal, Kim Yaroshevskaya. Films Transit. 80 mins.)

Matinee (d. Richard Martin) For once, a good horror story, set in a Vancouver cinema where the Horror Film Festival leads to murder most foul. All the usual suspects make this an exciting film. (Ron White, Gillian Barber, Jeff Schultz. Thomas Howe Ltd. 90 mins.)

Midday Sun (d. Lulu Keating) A well-intentioned but unconvincing account of a young Canadian woman on her first visit to a former British colony in Africa, whose naive perceptions of social habits and political ways land her in trouble with the authorities. (Isabelle Mejias, Robert Boackstael, Jackie Burroughs. Cinema Plus. 94 mins.)

Millennium (d. Michael Anderson) A small-scale, effective and original piece of science-fiction about a daring mission into Earth's past in order to save its future. (Kris Kristofferson, Cheryl Ladd, Victoria Snow, Daniel Travanti, Brent Carver. Gladden Entertainment. 110 mins.)

Mindfield (d. Jean-Claude Lord) Vaguely based on mind-control experiments carried out by the CIA in Montréal several years ago, attempts to make a *policier* out of the matter in which a detective and a lawyer "race against time" to expose the deadly cover-up. (Michael Ironside, Lisa Langlois, Christopher Plummer. Cinegem. 94 mins.)

Mob Story (d. Jancarlo Markiw and Gabriel Makiw) There is very little point or purpose to this Winnipeg-based story of mobsters and

Nuno Da Costa in François Labonté's *Manuel*

mayhem, set against winter snows, which strains credibility to the breaking point. (John Vernon, Kate Vernon, Margot Kidder. Brightstar. 103 mins.)

Office Party (d. George Mihalka) A mild mannered accountant takes his fellow workers hostage in an unnamed American city. Very soon all are quarrelling among themselves descending into a state of primitive violence. Unsavoury and predictable. (David Warner, Michael Ironside, John Vernon, Kate Vernon, Jayne Eastwood. SC Entertainment. 99 mins.)

Pas de reit pour Melanie (The Case of the Witch Who Wasn't) (d. Jean Beaudry) This is No. 10 in Rock Demers' long-running and successful family series, *Tales for All*, and concerns three children who help a lonely old lady find her way back into society by dint of many adventures. Sensible and appealing. (Marie Stefane Gaudry, Kesnamelly Neff, Vincent Bolduc, Madeleine Langlois. Productions La Fête/Astral Films. 95 mins.)

Portion d'éternité (Looking for Eternity) (d. Robert Favreau) starts out as an interesting story about a childless couple who try the new experiments in artificial insemination. The expensive clinic in which this takes place however, is not what it seems, and soon we are into the machinations of drug companies and scientists. The plot then becomes a cousin to Frankenstein- several times removed, and with a subsequent lack of realism. (Marc Messier, Danielle Droulx, Patricia Nolin, Paul Savoie. Prima Films. 96 mins.)

Prom Night III: The Last Kiss (d. Ron Oliver and Peter Simpson) The spirit of dead debutante Mary Lou Maloney returns to Hamilton High to continue her reign of terror. Feeble and forgettable. (Tim Conlon, Cyndy Preston. Norstar. 95 mins.)

Roadkill (d. Bruce McDonald) A "just for a lark" first film, free-wheeling and often foolish, but refreshing in its attempt to capture the flavour of pop-culture and its incoherent followers. A timid assistant goes out on the road for a rock promoter to find out what happened to one of his touring bands of musicians lost in the wilds of Ontario. Uneven, unfinished, but spontaneous. (Valerie Buhagiar, Gerry Quigley, Larry Hudson. Cinephile Films. 80 mins.)

Sous les draps, les étoiles (d. Jean-Pierre Gariepy) Love affairs in Québec movies are seldom free from all manner of uncertainties, frustrations, emotional turmoils, doubts and deceptions. So it is with Thomas, an astronomer returned from South America, and Sylvie, who wants to get away from Montréal. They fall passionately in love, but there is something about the past which makes it impossible to resolve the present. Stylish and fascinating, but in the end, not much of consequence. (Guy Thauvette, Marie-Josse Gauthier, Marcel Sabourin. Vision 4/NFBC. 90 mins.)

Termini Station (d. Allan King) is set in the bleak winter streets of Kirkland Lake, Ontario, where a young teenage prostitute, driven by family problems and social disadvantages, attempts to cope with her own life and that of her alcoholic mother. For the most part it is a riveting, accurately observed portrait of desperate people, marred at times by overtones of melodrama which tend to lessen the reality of the whole. (Megan Follows, Colleen Dewhurst, Gordon Pinsent, Gordon Clapp, Debra McGrath. Astral Films. 107 mins.)

The Top of His Head (d. Peter Mettler) This is the first feature film from cinematographer–experimentalist, Peter Mettler, a top-of-the-head excercise in *avant-garde* comedy about a satellite-dish salesman whose promising commercial future change into a different way of life when he meets a black-haired, blue-eyed, radical-social-activist beauty whose ideas of what life should be like change him into something other than what he once was. This makes a different, demanding excursion into existentialism. (Stephen Ouimette, Christie MacFadyen, Gary Reineke. Cinephile Films. 110 mins.)

The Traveller (d. Bruno Lazaro Pacheco) Once again we are into the dreams and torments of childhood and visions of images of the past, this time in the life of a successful international dealer of Pacific Northwest Indian masks. On a business trip, he is mysteriously lost in a landscape. There are times when it seems he might be better off not found. (R. Lewis Morrison, Ginette St-Denis, Denise Brillon. Cinephile Films. 96 mins.)

Trois pommes à côté du sommeil (d. Jacques Leduc) is an introspective study of a day in the life of a freelance journalist on his 40th birthday and his encounters with the three women who have influenced his past: in politics, passions and personal perceptions. If this were not enough, he has a friend with whom he questions the meaning of life and the cosmos. Heavy going. (Normand Chouinard, Paule Baillargeon, Paule Marier, Josée Chaboillez, Guy Nadon. Malofilm/NFBC. 91 mins.)

The Vacant Lot (d. William D. MacGillivray) is an all-female rock-band. The youngest member is 17-year-old Trudy, from a broken home, obsessed with memories of a father who abandoned her, who meets a 42-year-old rock guitarist whose career is at its end. He joins the band, and after further periods of despair, they manage to strike an harmonious note together. Interesting characterisation and Nova Scotian backgrounds put a new face on familiar material. (Trudi Petersen, Grant Fullerton. Cinephile Films. 103 mins.)

Vincent and Me (Vincent et moi) (d. Michael Rubbo) is No. 11 in the *Tales for All* series, and easily one of the best as it tells a charming story of Josephine, a 13-year-old-student of art, who admires the work of Van Gogh, becomes involved with forgers, and dreams of meeting him. (Nina Petronzio, Christopher Forrest, Tchecky Karyo. Productions La Fête/Astral Films. 95 mins.)

Welcome to Canada (d. John N. Smith) In 1987 a group of Tamils calling themselves refugees landed mysteriously on Canada's East Coast. They had been put ashore in small boats from the ship which had brought them illegally to Canada. But this film is only "inspired" by the incident and while looking like a documentary, it is not. It contains several natural character studies and conversations between Tamils and Newfoundlanders, which may or may not have taken place, but of the furor and controversy this incident created, the film has nothing to say. Without this there isn't much to relate. (Noreen Power, Brendan Foley, Madonna Hawkins. NFBC. 90 mins.)

Where the Spirit Lives (d. Bruce Pittman) During the 1930's native Indian children were taken away from their homes by Government decree and sent to Christian schools. They were treated badly and stripped of their cultural values. This film, a change of pace for its director, movingly recalls this awful period with the story of Amelia, a young Blackfoot girl, and her brother, who went through this chapter of intolerance. (Michelle St. John, Anne-Marie

Megan Follows and Colleen Dewhurst in Allan King's *Termini Station*

MacDonald, Heather Hess, Ron White. Atlantis Films. 97 mins.)
Whisper to a Scream (d. Robert Bergman) is an incomprehensible study, part horror part experimental, of a group of artists in turmoil seeking "perfection in their work." It hardly seems worth it! (Nadia Capone, Yaphet Kotto, Lawrence Bayne. Lightshow Communications & Inc. 96 mins.)

Experimental

Off Off Off ou sur le toit de Pablo Neruda (Off Off Off or On the Roof of Pablo Neruda) "A man searches for a woman he loved. But his language and methods are unsuited to a foreign country, and she's not there. He scans his memory but the memories have faded. Little by little he sinks in confusion and realises that even the image of the woman he loves has evaporated. Overcome by grief, he takes his life. But history doesn't stop the day he dies." Made by Jorge Fajardo, with Alberto Kurapel, Marie Yolaine Albert, Denis Dallaire, Marinea Mendez. 80 mins. Les Films de l'Insomniaque, Montréal.

Documentaries

Forcier: "en attendant..." (d. Marc André Berthiaume) A study of the work of artist Marc-André Forcier (Les Films du Crépuscule. 90 mins.) **Le Brande monde** (d. Marcel Simard) The treatment of mental patients. (Cinéma Libre. 76 mins.) **Le Tour du diable** (d. Richard

Maury Chaykin in Norstar Entertainment's *Cold Comfort*

Lavoie) Three miles of underground galleries are discovered under the city of Boischatel in Québec. (Films Crépuscule. 80 mins.) **Strand, Under the Dark Cloth** (d. John Walker) A splendid study of Paul Strand, his journeys and his work. (Creative Exposure. 81 mins.) **White Lake** (d. Colin Brown) A family reunion on a cattle ranch in British Columbia. (CFDC West. 80 mins.)

Short Documentaries

Forgotten Mother (d. Adrienne Amato) A personal exploration of the relationship between Alice, a black domestic worker in Zimbabwe, and Adrienne, the white child she raised. (Hand In Hand Films. 26 mins.) **L'Humeur à l'humour** (d. Michèle Perusse) A collage of well-known Québec Comediennes attempting to change preconceived ideas about women. (Vidéo Femmes. 48 mins.) **La Complainte du beluga** (d. Alain Belhumeur) Finding the means to protect the Beluga Whale from pollution in the St. Lawrence River. (Cinéma Libre. 51 mins.)

Reading Between the Lines (d. Martha Davis) Reading the replies to a personal ad she has placed, a woman imagines herself in relationships with three different men. (CFDC. 36 mins.) **Stunt People** (d. Lois Siegel) The Fournier family have performed stunts in over 200 feature films. (Lightscape. 48 mins.) **The Last Days of Contrition** (d. Richard Kerr) The director travels across America studying the political climate of the 1980's. (CFDC. 35 mins.) **Who Gets In?** (d. Barry Greenwald) Canada's immigration system and how it works. (NFBC 52 mins.)

Short Dramas

Alter Ego (d. Louise Lamarre) A pair of mirrored glasses shows a young woman a different aspect of herself. (Prima Film. 6 mins.) **Elle-vis** (d. Mary Holmes) Angela Barker, an Elvis impersonator, goes to the Amateur Elvis Contest in Memphis. (Hep. Films. 25 mins.) **Fat Man/ Thin Man** (d. Derek Rogers) A man struggles with his alter ego for possession of a refrigerator. (Hand in Hand Films. 21 mins.) **In Search of the Last Good Man** (d. Peg Campbell) Six girlfriends gather in an espresso bar, a stream of men arrive, and the search is on. (CFDC West. 10 mins.) **L'Aieule** (d. Claude Palardy) Members of a family drive their elders to a nursing home to the music of Purcell's aria *When I Am Laid in Earth*. (Prima Films. 8 mins.) **Mike** (d. M.B. Duggan) is released from a mental home and finds the world around him disintegrating. (Winnipeg Film Group. 24 mins.) **Monster in the Coal Bin** (d. Allen Schinkel) which arouses the subconscious fears of an imaginative eight- year-old boy. (Winnipeg Film Group. 24 mins.) **Multiple Choice** (d. Debbie McGee) A conflict develops between a man and a woman making a documentary on poverty. (Atlantic Independent Media. 23 mins.) **Odyssey in August** (d. Stephen Roscoe) A man is trapped in a long, slow queue in the passport office, giving him time to think about his place in the world. (Kaleidoscope Entertainment. 25 mins.) **Parable of the Leaven** (d. Gail Henley) A young girl and her ambivalent feelings about her mother. (CFDC 14 mins.) **Portfolio** (D. John Hopkins) An aspiring photographer and his race with Time. (CFDC 19 mins.) **Sortie 234** (d. Michel Langlois) Two men and a woman are in love with each other in different ways but cannot hope to consummate it. (J.A. Lapointe. 27 mins.) **Stealing Images** (d. Alan Zweig) A face in the crowd becomes involved in a new project relating to art and life. (Northern Outlaw Productions. 28 mins.) **The Black Veil** (d. Glenn Warner) A widow flees her rich in-laws and meets a lonely man. (Willy-Nilly Releasing. 16 mins.) **The Civil Servant** (d. John Detwiler) and his different world of inner thoughts and images. (LCA Productions. 27 mins.) **The Journey Home** (d. Marc Voizard) A wealthy 15-year-old girl discovers that life is not as simple as it seems. (Cinefort. 27 mins.) **The Light Brigade** (d. François Labonte) A gentle reminder about the magic of Christmas. (Cinefort. 25 mins.) **The Lost Salt: Gift of Blood** (d. Christian Fennell) A man returns a stranger to his home in Newfoundland. (Filmclips. 30 mins.)

Animation

Adam's Dream (d. Alan Pakarnyk. Winnipeg Film Group. 5 mins.) **In and Out** (d. Alison Snowden & David Fine. McNabb & Connolly Ltd. 10 mins.) **Juke Bar** (d. Martin Barry. NFBC. 11 mins.) **The Dingles** (d. Les Drew. NFBC. 8 mins.)

Rebecca Jenkins in *Bye Bye Blues*, directed by Anne Wheeler

Distributors

Alliance Releasing
920 Yonge Street
Suite 400
Toronto, Ontario
Tel: (416) 967–1174
Telex: 06–23776
Fax: (416) 960–0971

Alliance Vivafilm
355 Place Royale
3e étage
Montréal (Québec)
H2Y 2V3
Tel: (514) 844–3132
Telex: 05–25828
Fax: (514) 284–2340

Astral Films
175, boul. Montpellier
Bureau 600
Montréal (Québec)
H4N 2G5
Tel: (514) 748–6541
Telex: 05–826734
Fax: (514) 748–1348

720 King Street W.
Suite 600
Toronto, Ontario
M5V 2T3
Tel: (416) 364–3894
Telex: 06–22411
Fax: (416) 364–8565

Atlantis Releasing Inc.
Cinevillage
65 Heward Avenue
Toronto, Ontario
M4M 2T5
Tel: (416) 462–0016
Telex: 06–426129
Fax: (416) 462–0254

Brightstar Films Distribution Inc.
424 Adelaide Street E.
Toronto, Ontario
M5A 1N4
Tel: (416) 364–5144
Fax: (416) 364–5339

Canadian Filmmakers Distribution Centre
67A Portland Street
Toronto, Ontario
M5V 2M9
Tel: (416) 593–1808

Canadian Filmmakers Distribution West
1131 Howe Street
Suite 100
Vancouver, British Columbia
V6Z 2L7
Tel: (604) 684–3014

CBC Enterprises-TV Program Sales
415 Yonge Street
4th Floor
Toronto, Ontario
M5B 2E7
Telex: 06–218269
Fax: (416) 975–3482

P.O. Box 500, Stn A
Toronto, Ontario
M5W 1E6
Tel: (416) 975–3522

C/FP Distribution Inc.
8275, rue Mayrand
Montréal (Québec)
H4P 2C8
Tel: (514) 342–2340
Fax: (514) 342–1922

146 Bloor Street W.
3rd Floor
Toronto, Ontario
M5S 1P3
Tel: (416) 944–0104
Fax: (416) 964–3820

Cineplex Odeon Films Canada
1303 Yonge Street
Toronto, Ontario
M4T 2Y9
Tel: (416) 925–8246
Fax: (416) 324–5494

Cinéma Libre
3575, boul. Saint-Laurent
Bureau 704
Montréal (Québec)
H2X 2T7
Tel: (514) 849–7888
Fax: (514) 843–5681

Cinéma Plus Distribution Inc.
225, rue Roy E.
Bureau 204
Montréal (Québec)
H2W 1M5
Tel: (514) 848–0673
Telex: 05–267530
Fax: (514) 848–0714

131 Avenue Road
Suite 2
Toronto, Ontario
M5R 2H7
Tel: (416) 928–1044
Fax: (416) 924–6205

Ciné 360 Inc.
1590 avenue du Mont-Royal E.
Bureau 304
Montréal (Québec)
H2J 1Z2
Tel: (514) 521–4114
Fax: (514) 521–3166

Cinephile Limited
388 King St. W.
Suite 211
Toronto, Ontario
M5V 1K2
Tel: (416) 581–1251
Fax: (416) 581–1382

Cinévidéo Inc.
360, Place Royale
3e étage
Montréal (Québec)
H2Y 2V1
Tel: (514) 284–9354
Fax: (514) 284–6715

Creative Exposure Ltd.
2236 Queen Street E.
Toronto, Ontario
M4E 1G2
Tel: (416) 690–0775
Telex: 062–17622
Fax: (416) 690–0775

Ellis Enterprises
1231 Yonge Street
Suite 201
Toronto, Ontario
M4T 2T8
Tel: (416) 924–2186
Telex: 06–22435
Fax: (416) 924–6115

Festival Films Inc.
203–2105 West 38th Avenue
Vancouver, British Columbia
V6M 1R8
Tel: (604) 264–0070
Fax: (604) 264–0071

Films du Crépuscule Inc. (Les)
55, avenue du Mont-Royal O.
Bureau 302
Montréal (Québec)
H2T 2S5
Tel: (514) 849–2477
Fax: (514) 849–5859

Films Transit Inc.
402, rue Notre-Dame E.
3e étage
Montréal (Québec)
H2Y 1C8
Tel: (514) 844–3358
Telex: 055–60074 Fax: (514) 844–7298

Imax Systems Corporation
38 Isabella Street
Toronto, Ontario
M4Y 1N1
Tel: (416) 960–8509
Telex: 065–24664
Fax: (416) 960–8596

Lapointe Films International Inc.
3575, boul. Saint-Laurent
Bureau 108
Montréal (Québec)
H2X 2T7
Tel: (514) 844–6613
Telex: 055–62322
Fax: (514) 844–5197

Malofilm Distribution Inc.
1207, rue Saint-Andre
Montréal (Québec)
H2L 3S8
Tel: (514) 844–4555
Telex: 055–61301
Fax: (514) 844–1471

22 Davisville Avenue
Toronto, Ontario
M4S 1E8
Tel: (416) 480–0453
Telex: 065–24090
Fax: (416) 480–0501

Nelvana Enterprises
32 Atlantic Avenue
Toronto, Ontario
MGK 1X8
Tel: (416) 588–5571
Telex: 06–22803
Fax: (416) 588–5588

Norstar Releasing Inc.
86 Bloor Street W.
5th Floor
Toronto, Ontario
M5S 1M5
Tel: (416) 961–6278
Telex: 06–219870
Fax: (416) 961–5608

Prima Films Inc.
1594 boul. Saint-Joseph E.
Montréal (Québec)
H2J 1M7
Tel: (514) 521–1189
Fax: (514) 521–2918

Productions La Fête Inc.
225, rue Roy E.
Bureau 203
Montréal (Québec)
H2W 1M5
Tel: (514) 848–0417
Telex: 055–62385
Fax: (514) 848–0064

Sullivan Films Distribution Inc.
16 Clarence Square

Toronto, Ontario
M5V 1H1
Tel: (416) 597–0029
Telex: 06–218692
Fax: (416) 597–0320

Thomas Howe Associates Ltd.
1100 Homer Street
Vancouver, British Columbia
V6B 2X6
Tel: (604) 687–4215
Telex: 04–508654
Fax: (604) 688–8349

Vivafilm/Québec/Amérique Distribution Inc.
411, rue Saint-Jean-Baptiste
Montréal (Québec)
H2Y 2Z7
Tel: (514) 861–2400
Fax: (514) 398–0412

Winnipeg Film Group
304–100 Arthur Street
Winnipeg, Manitoba
R38 1H3
Tel: (204) 942–6795

Useful Addresses

Telefilm Canada
Tour de la Banque Nationale
600, rue de la Gauchetière Ouest
14 étage
Montréal (Québec)
H3B 4L2
Tel: (514) 283–6363
Telex: 055–60998
Fax: (514) 283–8212

2 Bloor Street West
22nd Floor
Toronto, Ontario
M4W 3E2
Tel: (416) 973–6436
Telex: 06–218344
Fax: (416) 973–8606

5525 Artillery Place
Suite 220
Halifax, Nova Scotia
B3J 1J2
Tel: (902) 426-8425
Fax: (902) 426-4445

350-375 Water Street
Vancouver, British Columbia
V6B 5C6
Tel: (604) 666-1566
Fax: (604) 666-7754

144 South Beverly Drive
Suite 400
Beverly Hills, California
U.S.A. 90212
Tel: (213) 859-0268
Fax: (213) 276-4741

15, rue de Berri
75008 Paris
France
Tel: (33-1) 45.63.70.45
Telex: 42-648082F
Fax: (33-1) 42.25.33.61

55/59 Oxford Street
Fourth Floor
London, England
W1R 1RD
Tel: (44-1) 437-8308
Telex: 923-753
Fax: (44-1) 734-8586

TRIBUTE TO ROCK DEMERS:
"Tales For All"

by Gerald Pratley

Rock Demers, founder of Productions La Fête and initiator of the *Tales for All* project, has worked in virtually every aspect of cinema, from production to distribution and programming. His production of Canadian family-oriented movies has earned him the respect of the film profession throughout Canada and around the world.

Not since the pioneer days of Mary Field's invaluable work in establishing the Children's Film Foundation in England during the 1950's has any producer other than Rock Demers devoted himself to the intelligent application of devising an entire, continuing series of family films for children and their parents. In 1984, motivated by the same sentiments which made Mary Field's work so exemplary, he began his 12-film programme, *La Fête (Tales for All)* with *The Dog Who Stopped the War*. Since then, the twelve films have been completed and as a result of their international success, both critically and commercially, Demers is considering extending the series of fifteen.

This is a remarkable achievement in many ways; and the odds against finding success with such an idealistic project designed primarily for cinema showings for young audiences in a cinematic age of violence, vulgarity and noise, were immense. Demers seemed to be flying in the face of both economic and artistic reasoning: while many parents bemoaned the lack of family films (they went out only for Disney) and usually ignored individual family films which have turned up over the years (usually from Britain, *Swallows and Amazons, Beatrix Potter*, etc.), most children watched television more than they went to the movies (Mary Field, at least, had the Odeon Saturday morning club showings to depend on) and what they saw ranged from the suitable (*Black Beauty, The Muppets*) to the awful (unpleasant cartoon characters. Their cinema outings embraced *Superman* and *Star Wars* and their derivations – all noise and violence.

In addition, Demers, a Québec producer,

The first "Tale for All": *The Dog Who Stopped the War*

was working in Canada, a country without a firmly based indigenous film industry to support him – although since he began Québec itself has become a remarkably lively and often self-sufficient market the success of which is due in no small measure to Demers's production activity. He was also faced with the additional burden of making his films in French and English (family audiences including young children can hardly be expected to read sub-titles); some have been shot in French and dubbed into English and vice versa.

In each case, the dubbing (which most true cinema-lovers cannot abide and will not accept) is carried out with such care and technical expertise that few audiences for these films would be aware of it. Dubbing could also be excused on the grounds that while all the young players give excellent performances, their voices are not such an integral part of their portrayals as would be the voices of accomplished actors in dramas and comedies. Yet, in spite of all these difficulties facing him, Demers, with the support of private investors, the federal government's funding agency, Telefilm, the provincial government's funding agency, SOGIC, and many other groups, has succeeded beyond his quiet yet determined expectations. His faith in his project and in his audiences has been justified by the international acclaim given these films and the fact that they have, in the long run and with their subsequent television showings (most films come around to the small screen in the end for their final income) and their video sales and rentals, recovered their costs.

Man with a Mission

Rock Demers, the force behind this series, now considered an epoch in Canadian film-making, is quite obviously a man with a mission. "There are not enough individuals concerned with developing the imagination of young people in the right way," he says. "I want to help children leave childhood and go into adulthood with certain values. This is the age when they will build the values they will carry with them for the rest of their lives."

Balding, rumpled and white-bearded, Rock Demers looks more like a friendly professor, a character out of one of his own movies, than a producer. After growing up on a farm in south eastern Québec (he was born in 1933) he trained to become a teacher at the University of Montréal. While studying for his teaching certificate in the 1950's, he became involved in the creation of numerous ciné-clubs for various academic institutions in Québec. Later, in collaboration with a few friends, he began the film magazine *Images*.

His interest in cinema led him to enrol at the Ecole Normale Supérieure de Saint-Cloud in Paris, where in 1958 he received a diploma in audio-visual technology, before undertaking research into cinema, television and children's theatre. During the following two years he travelled in Europe and Asia, all the while pursuing his interests in the communications media.

It was during these travels that Rock Demers made his first contact with Eastern European cinema, then in its burgeoning days in Czechoslovakia, Poland and Hungary. There he became familiar with new names, new stories and new ways of seeing the world through cinema. Among film-makers he met with Vojtech Jasny, Krzysztof Zanussi and Bretislav Pojar – the very same names that would, some 30 years later, become involved with *Tales for All*.

Upon his return to Canada in 1960, his passion for quality movies led him to join with colleagues who had just started the first Montréal International Film Festival, and from 1962–1967 he served as the festival's director general. The festival, the third of its kind in North America, invited the works of the very same new directors who had impressed Demers during his European travels.

Rock Demers left the Montréal Festival in 1968 to work full time on his company Faroun Films, first founded as a hobby in 1965. This company specialised in the import–export of movies, particularly those for young people, distributing films in

"Tale for All" #2: *The Peanut Butter Solution*

Mahée Paiement in "Tale for All" #3: *Bach and Broccoli*

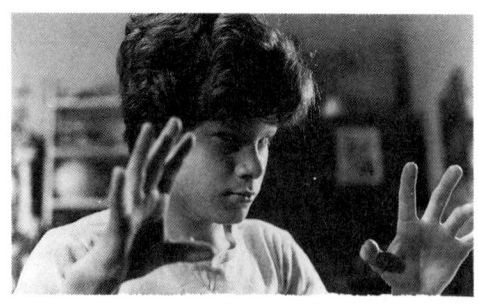

Rusty Jedwab in "Tale for All" #4: *The Young Magician*

Canada and selling to some 50 countries around the world. And among the titles Faroun distributed in North American was an early Márta Mészáros film *Riddance*.

It was in his capacity as President and Executive Director of Faroun Films that he came to production through investing in and distributing two films for young audiences, *The Christmas Martian*, directed by Bernard Gosselin, a science-fiction picture that preceded Spielberg's *E.T.*, and *Two Silent Friends*, the story of a dog who saves a drowning child, directed by Paul Fritz-Nemeth.

During its 13 years of existence, Faroun Films acquired the rights to more than 200 feature and short films from over 20 different countries. Having developed a relatively unique expertise as a programmer of quality pictures, Demers convinced Radio-Canada to include in its schedule a series of films directed to children. It proved to be successful and, in 1969, the CBC television network decided to start the "CBC Children's Film Festival," based on the many good films Demers had screened for them. It was equally well received by its young viewers. The French network, ORTF, was not far behind in seeing the potential of such a series, and each year it purchased up to six features for young people from Faroun Films.

From 1977 to 1979, Demers devoted most of his energy to the formation of the Institut Québecois du Cinéma, a government agency mandated to assist in the development of a private industry for the production, distribution, exhibition, research and conservation of cinema.

In 1978, he was awarded the Governor General's medal in recognition of his valuable contributions to the entire area of film. The London Film Festival, Ontario's Stratford Film Festival and the Canadian Film Institute, all paid homage to the work done by Rock Demers.

He was one of the co-founders of the Cinémathèque Québécoise and a member of the Consultation Committee on the establishment of a Canadian film policy established in 1973 by the then Secretary of State, Gérard Pelletier.

Rock Demers previously headed the Québec Association of Film Distributors and more recently, the Québec Film and Video Producers Association, where he continues to be an active member of the executive. He has served on numerous film festival juries and has taught cinema at the University of Québec at Montréal. In 1987 he was awarded the coveted Albert Tessier Prize by the Québec government for his lifelong contributions to cinema.

Long-Cherished Ambition

In 1980, Demers put all this behind him, withdrew from all his connections and activities, to carry out his long-cherished ambition to make films which truly seemed worthwhile to him; movies for children and families. And he did something no other Canadian producer has ever done – he laid down plans to make twelve films, faithfully carried out to this day against all the odds and realised without compromising his initial vision of quality entertainment in the form of "a learning experience of life for young people."

The project was so well-organised that he had commissioned scripts for eight of them before the first even started shooting. Unlike Disney films, the style varies from film to film, but they all conform to Demers' basic principles: the leading roles must be played by children 10 to 12 years old, the stories must appeal to audiences of all ages, and the scripts should avoid stereotyping characters as good or evil, that children of different races can live together, that boys and girls are equally adept at activities once thought of as being "girl's job" or "boy's job."

"My intuition is that the traditional concept of good versus evil told to children for generations has harmed humanity," thinks Rock Demers, "because it tells us unconsciously that the world is divided into two camps, like Protestant or Catholic, or Communist or Capitalist. I'm 57 and I've never met anyone who is all good or all bad. For this reason, my films usually have an affirmative and reconciliatory tone designed to bring children and adults together.

"I'm told that I'm old-fashioned, my films are whimsical, the moral values out-dated. I just know that with the audience I have attracted the identification process is so strong that it can heal wounds. Children have too much violence on TV, or unhappy

Michael J. Anderson in "Tale for All" #5: *The Great Land of Small*

Fanny Lauzier in "Tale for All" #6: *Tadpole and the Whale*

homes or school lives. They may be entertained by *Star Wars, Superman, Roger Rabbit*, but these will never bring them the peace and warmth that my films can bring to them."

Over the years, Demers' films have amassed an encouraging total of over 100 prizes from around the world since Tale #1, *The Dog Who Stopped the War* was released in late 1984. Directed by André Melançon, a part of the *Tales for All* creative team, this film literally came out of nowhere to not only win some 13 international prizes, but to become the highest grossing Canadian film of the year.

While the success of the first *Tale* might have been thought of as a "lucky break," the success of the second a "fluke," the third a "coincidence" and the fourth "good timing," it is clear that the appropriate response to the success of these films is to admire their originality, their spirit and, above all, their quality.

It was followed by *The Peanut Butter Solution* (1985), written and directed by Michael Rubbo, which has been released across Canada, the United States and the rest of the world, collecting its share of international prizes, among which are the Public's Choice Award at the Laon Film Festival and a Gold Medal at Italy's Giffoni Festival.

In 1986, Rock Demers re-teamed with director André Melançon on *Bach and Broccoli*, shot on location in Montréal and Québec City. A box office phenomenon in Québec, its uniformly excellent reviews in both English and French Canada assured it a long and prosperous future at home and abroad. It, too, received a Silver Medal at the 1987 Moscow Festival as well as two honours from the Festival's Youth Jury for its "warm-heartedness" and "fantasy." One month earlier, it swept the top four prizes at the First Algiers International Children's and Youth Film Festival in June of 1987. Its brilliant career reached new heights when it was awarded the top prize at the First International Francophone Film Festival held in 1987 in Martinique, where the jury chose it from among many worthy contenders. More recently, it was named the 1988 winner of the Parents' Choice Gold Medal Award. The Boston-based authority on a wide range of quality children's entertainment selected *Bach and Broccoli* over some of the world's best films for young children.

International Co-production

The fourth film in the series, *The Young Magician*, was the first of what was to become a familiar and important tenet of the *Tales for All*, an international co-production. Shot in Poland during the fall and winter of 1985–86, it has won a Silver Medal from the Official Competition Jury at the Moscow International Film Festival and the two top prizes at the Giffoni Film Festival in Italy from the children's jury and the Association of Italian Distributors. Two other Grand Prizes were awarded this film

Jill Stanley in "Tale for All" #7: *Tommy Tricker and the Stamp Traveller*

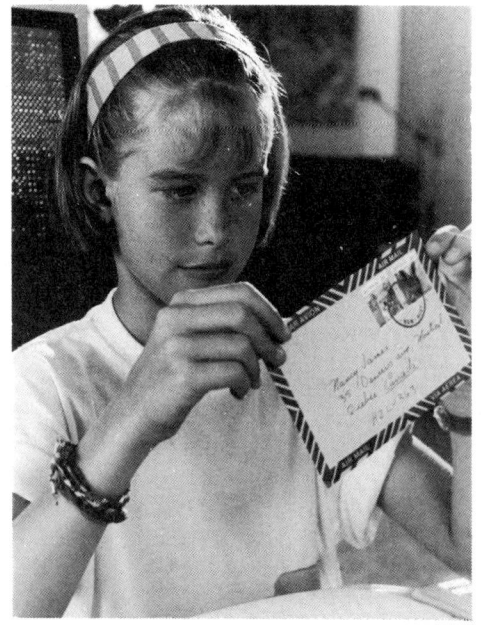

in Laon, France from the children and adult juries.

In 1988, Rock Demers produced three more *Tales for All*. *Tadpole and the Whale*, directed by Jean-Claude Lord and starring Fanny Lauzier, was shot on location on Québec's North Coast, as well as in Florida and the Virgin Islands; and *Tommy Tricker and the Stamp Traveller*, written and directed by Michael Rubbo, was shot on location in Montréal, Hangzhou, China and Sydney, Australia. *By-Bye Red Riding Hood*, directed by Márta Mészáros, is another co-production, this time with Hungary, in which the classic fable is brought into a contemporary setting.

Released in 1988 to considerable critical acclaim and box-office successes, *Tadpole and the Whale* was the Academy of Canadian Cinema and Television's Golden Reel Award as the highest grossing film of the year. *Tommy Tricker and the Stamp Traveller* led all films in Québec at the all important Christmas box-office season and has been hailed by philatelist organisations across the country for having created a new interest in the world of stamp collecting, most particularly among young people.

The 1989 release was *Summer of the Colt*, the first Canada– Argentina co-production, starring two of Argentina's most respected actors, Hector Alterio and China Zorrilla. It is the third collaboration between Demers and André Melançon.

1990: and Rock Demers, with three new films on his release schedule, shows no sign of letting down the pace that has marked his first decade. Joining the team for *The Case of the Witch Who Wasn't* is Jean Beaudry, talented director of *Jacques in November*, and set in rural Québec; Michael Rubbo returns for *Vincent and Me* (Demers' contribution to Van Gogh's 100th anniversary), the story of an art student and her love for the work of the artist; and a first co- production with strife-torn Romania, *The Champion*, directed by the noted maker of children's films, Elisabeta Bostan.

Juan de Benedictis and Mariano Bertolini in "Tale for All" #8: *Summer of the Colt*

One of the strengths of Demers' films is the charming and natural performances of the children, usually unknown, untrained youngsters who seem to take to film-making with the same joy and enthusiasm as ducks take to water.

Rock Demers comments: "I wouldn't feel at home making exploitation films. I feel much more comfortable with family films. Besides, it's easier to work with children 10 to 12 who are about to leave childhood, and not with too many professional actors. A child can accept doing 13 to 15 takes easier than an adult. However, I have never used children from one film in a following film. I would have trouble employing them again for similar roles. Children of this age change so fast; it takes two years from the start of filming to release and then they're teen-agers. I call my projects childhood films, not children's films. There are fewer directors gifted in working with children than with adults.

"I have a valuable backlog of good scripts. I could easily make two films in the series every year until the end of the century. I'm

Fanny Lauzier in "Tale for All" #9: *Bye Bye Red Riding Hood*

thinking of making films for older audiences, although I'm not sure how they would be different. It may be simply a case of the story being told from the point of view of an adult and not a child. Otherwise, they would still present the hopeful side of life as I see it.

"My films, I think, will become a library for the future. The subjects do not date, they would simply slip into period pieces. We don't make a lot of money in the short term, but in the long term we are building up quite a library to sell to video and TV. And every time a new film comes out there's more interest in the previous ones. My films show children that life is not easy to go through, that there are difficulties in relationships, in understanding other people, and in adjusting to conditions around us. But that, in the end, it's worthwhile. Although I employ fantasy, I want to portray reality as it is."

Keeping costs down is a problem. Starting with two-million dollar budgets, Demers now finds that he must spend around three million and more to maintain quality. As the producer, Demers spends much of his time on the set. He does not interfere with his directors, but he watches to make sure that his ideas and beliefs are never compromised. In an industry noted for its unprincipled producers, Demers lives up to his name by being a rock of honesty and dependability. André Melançon says of him: "Unlike so many producers, Rock does not act like a real-estate agent. He's a businessman, yes, but he has an artistic vision and a strong ethical code."

THE TALES FOR ALL . . .

1. *The Dog Who Stopped the War*
   (La guerre des tuques)
   Dir. André Melançon

2. *The Peanut Butter Solution*
   (Operation beurre de pinottes)
   Dir. Michael Rubbo

3. *Bach and Broccoli*
   (Bach et Bottine)
   Dir. André Melancon

4. *The Young Magician*
   (Le jeune magicien)
   Dir. Waldemar Dzki
   (co-production with Poland)

5. *The Great Land of Small*
   (C'est pas parce qu'on est petit qu'on peut pas etra grand!)
   Dir. Vojtech Jasny
   (co-production with Czechoslovakia)

6. *Tadpole and the Whale*
   (La Grenouille et la baleine)
   Dir. Jean-Claude Lord

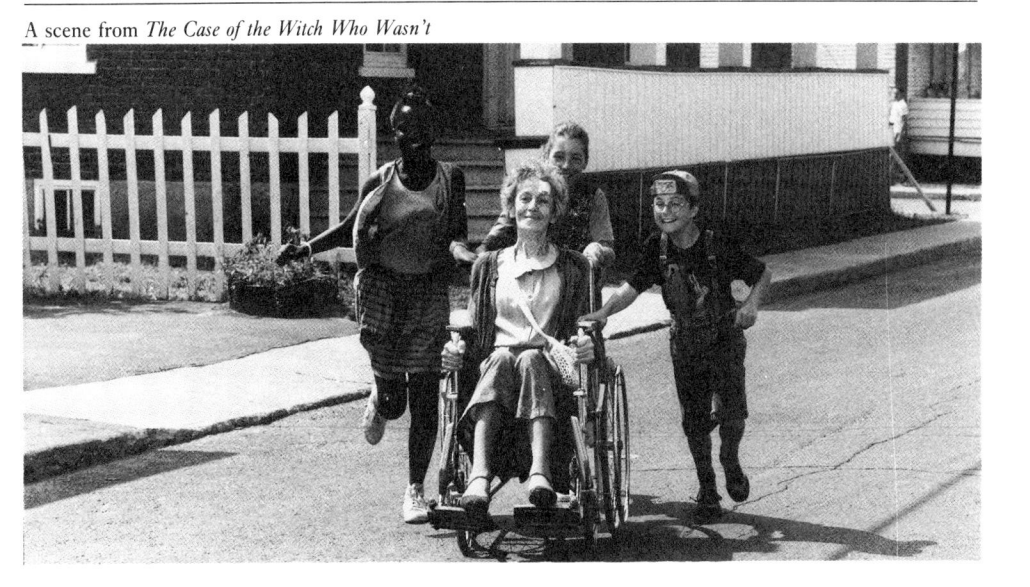

Marie-Stefane Gaudry, Kesnamelly Neff, and Vincent Bolduc in "Tale for All" #10: *The Case of the Witch Who Wasn't*

A scene from *The Case of the Witch Who Wasn't*

Tcheky Karyo and Nina Petronzio in "Tale for All" #11: *Vincent and Me*

Mircea Diacovu and Izabela Meldovan in "Tale for All" #12: *The Champion*

7. *Tommy Tricker and the Stamp Traveller*
   (Les aventuriers du timbre perdu)
   Dir. Michael Rubbo

8. *Summer of the Colt*
   (Fierro ou l'été des Secrets)
   Dir. André Melançon
   (co-production with Argentina)

9. *Bye Bye Red Riding Hood*
   (Bye Bye Chaperon Rouge)
   Dir. Marta Mészáros
   (co-production with Hungary)

10. *The Case of the Witch Who Wasn't*
    (Pas de répit pour Mélanie)
    Dir. Jean Beaudry

11. *Vincent and Me*
    (Vincent et moi)
    Dir. Michael Rubbo

12. *The Champion*
    Dir. Elisabeta Bostan (co-production with Romania)

CHILE

by Hans Ehrmann

The first presidential election in two decades, and the cautious recovery of the democracy were the main features of last year and early 1990. Several films were developed and shot during this period, are now in post production and will open later this year, but most of them appear to have little connection with recent history.

Only two films were actually finished and released. **All for Nothing** (*Todo por nada*), a first for television director Alfredo Lamadrid, received the worst critical drubbing seen in years. It had the look of a rather poor pilot for a *telenovela*, its plot suggesting that the way to the top for an aspiring actress in the TV genre means leapfrogging from bed to bed; steps on this ladder were an advertising executive, a fashion photographer, a TV director, a variety show host and the owner of a production company. Instead of interrupting for commercials as would be the case on the small screen, a series of products were blatantly promoted within the film.

Lizard Stories (*Historia de lagartos*), a deeply personal film written, photographed and directed by Juan Carlos Bustamante (who had previously made several documentaries with his brother Patricio) stands at the opposite end of the spectrum. In its three episodes, dialogue is reduced to a minimum and the story line, never explicit but only insinuated and sometimes cryptic, shows human beings integrated in the landscape with the Maule river as, perhaps, a sort of Tarkovsky–Taviani countryside. Within this context, the main themes are people fleeing and returning. By no means an easy film, even on a festival level this could well be the most personal voice to emerge in Chile since Ruiz.

The last film Raúl Ruiz shot in Chile before the 1973 coup was **White Dove** (*Palomita Blanca*), based on a bestselling novel by Enrique Lafourcade. This film was at a rough cut stage when the military took over Chile Films, the government-owned studio. Ruiz went into exile and, based in Paris, made a series of films, the best known of which may be *L'Hypothese du Tableau Volé* and *Les Trois Couronnes du Matelot* and acquired a considerable buff reputation. When he was first able to return to Chile, several years ago, he found that someone had edited the rough cut in a way that made the film's retrieval impossible and it was given up as lost.

Chile Films was privatized in 1988 and two years later, surprisingly, the negative of *Palomita Blanca* was found within its vaults. Ruiz returned briefly to edit and the film should be released in 1990, seventeen years after it was shot. The situation is in a way reminiscent of shelved films in the Socialist countries.

Ruiz was also the author of the screenplay of the only co-production shot in Chile during the period in review. **Amelia Lópes O'Neill** is the second feature directed by Valeria Sarmiento, who has also made *Notre Mariage* and several documentaries. Starring Laura del Sol and Franco Nero, it was shot in the director's native Valparaiso and the final version will be in French and play out here with subtitles.

Distribution and Exhibition

The largest force on the local scene is José Daire's Chile Films, which runs or owns

Chilean director Valeria Sarmiento
photo: Hans Ehrmann

with the U.S. majors and some independents providing the approximately 200 films that play each year. For these circuits it was business as usual, with one specific item differentiating them from their peers in other countries.

During the second semester of 1987, admissions were on a steady decline and fears of a serious crisis swept the film community. Out of this came the unanimous decision to cut Wednesday admission prices by 50%. This was at first thought of as a stopgap until the storm blew over and had in fact been tried before in Chile, Argentina and other countries. But what on those previous occasions was used as a short time miracle drug has now become a long term vaccine. 1989 ended on a dire note (with 10% less spectators than the previous year) but early 1990 once again saw an improvement. It is likely that the Wednesday crowds keep the filmgoing habit alive and generate word of mouth projected towards the weekend.

No changes have as yet been applied to the censorship system but a commission is presently studying changes in the law. They will probably suggest the elimination of the "over 21" rating, leaving "over 18" as the maximum and recommend the reconsideration of films rejected over the

eighteen of Santiago's fifty cinemas. There are two smaller circuits: Socine and Compañía Cinematográfica Nacional. All of these also have distribution branches which,

TOP TEN GROSSING FILMS IN CHILE: 1989

(Based on number of spectators at Santiago first run houses)

	Attendance
And God Created Woman	207,009
Who Framed Roger Rabbit	194,160
Rain Man	157,307
Moonwalker	137,949
Indiana Jones and the Last Crusade	131,584
Salsa	103,227
Twins	99,360
The Lady and the Tramp (reissue)	89,338
"Crocodile" Dundee 2	75,076
Dangerous Liaisons	74,404

last 16 years. These range all the way from *Fiddler on the Roof* and Fellini's *Casanova* to Oliver Stone's *Salvador*, *Last Tango in Paris*, *Emmanuelle*, *The Last Temptation of Christ* and the Chilean *Latent Image* (*Imagen Latente*). It will take some months for the commission's findings to be submitted, discussed and – hopefully – approved by the new Chilean parliament.

HANS EHRMANN *has been a film critic since 1957 and* Variety *correspondent since 1961. He is a critic and editor on a Chilean newsmagazine.*

CHINA
by Derek Elley

With a sullen calm settling over the country since the Tiananmen Massacre of June 4, 1989, China's film industry is more and more caught between a rock and a hard place. The economy continues to worsen as hardliners attempt to reimpose centralisation and western investment becomes thinner and thinner; inflation remains high, eating into living standards and budgets; and political jargon not heard for over a decade attacks anything that is "anti-socialist" or smells vaguely of western "pollution." More and more, as reported in previous IFGs, film-makers have had only one option – to grind out box-office fodder in the form of thrillers and martial arts movies.

By early 1990 even these were coming under attack from the ideologues. Film-makers were exhorted to apply the "two fors" ("for the people and for socialism") and the "double hundred" (Mao's old saying of "let a hundred flowers bloom and a hundred schools of thought contend"). Quite apart from the inherent contradiction in these two slogans, no one takes such pronouncements literally, especially considering the crackdown that took place after the original Hundred Flowers Movement in 1957. More seriously, nobody any longer takes any notice of what the politicians say. The government, which still controls the film industry, is as bankrupt of ideas as the economy is of credit.

Since the 1989 crackdown, hard statistics have once again become scarcer. Production during the year was at a record high (almost 200 features, compared with some 160 in 1988) but most failed to make a return on capital. Wang Jin's **Village of Widows** (*Guafu cun*), a co-production between Pearl River Studio and Hongkong's Mainland-funded Sil-Metropole, earned the dubious distinction of being China's first "X-rated" movie (a new category) and did major business as a result – 180 prints and takings of over 40 million yuan. (In unshockable Hongkong it only took some HK$4 million.) Shi Shujun's big-budget (1.2 million yuan) **Jiating shenshen**, the first Mainland movie based on Taiwan writer Ch'iung Yao's romances, was distributed in 150 copies.

With 1989 also being the 40th anniversary of the PRC, an expected number of political blockbusters also rolled off the production line. These included *The Birth of New China*, *The Kunlun Column*, *The Baise Uprising* and *The Republic Will Never Forget*. Audiences are now holding their breath for 1991, which marks the 70th anniversary of the founding of the Chinese Communist Party.

Directors Widely Scattered

On the artistic front, the era of the so-called Fifth Generation is now only a memory – battered by a combination of commerce and politics. Several of its members are scattered abroad: as of summer 1990 Chen Kaige and Wu Tianming were still in the US, the former preparing a foreign-funded feature to be shot in China, the latter still considering whether to return to his job at Xi'an Film Studio; Zhang Zeming was resident in the UK, working on several scripts. Of those in China, Tian Zhuangzhuang continued to alterate between varying genres, and in early 1990 started work on a big-budget period drama about the Empress Dowager's eunuch Li Lianying; and Wu Ziniu, following his two-parter *To Die Like a Man/Between Life and Death*, has shot the village ghost story *A Mysterious Woman*, co-produced with Sil-Metropole.

The highest profile, however, has been by former cameraman Zhang Yimou, working steadily with actress Gong Li. Following the slick thriller *Operation "Cougar"*, the pair acted in the Hongkong/Canadian co-production *A Terra-Cotta Warrior* (directed by Ching Siu-tung) before making **Judou** (*Judou*), first shown at Cannes in 1990. Funded with Japanese (300 million yen) and Mainland (3 million yuan) money, and with all post-production done in Tokyo, the film is a stunningly shot drama about a young wife (Gong Li, the "Chrysanthemum Bean" of the title) who takes a lover in the face of a cruel elder husband. To avoid political complications, and for extra atmosphere, Zhang transposed the original story's late 1940's/early 1950's northern setting to the 1920's and southern China, and has come up with a winner. As of mid-1990, however, there were doubts whether the film would ever be shown in China in its original form.

Zhang's high profile has allowed him considerable freedom in his career, despite being technically employed as a cameraman by Guangxi Film Studio on a measily salary of 160 yuan a month. He has repeatedly said he will remain based in China rather than fall into the trap of becoming a rootless emigre, and has so far managed to skirt political snares. In mid-1990 his plans included a project to be shot in China, with Taiwan's Hou Hsiao-hsien as associate producer (see Taiwan section).

The other major accomplishment of 1989/90 has been **Black Snow** (*Ben ming nian*), an impressively stark tale by Xie Fei, co-director of the atmospheric village drama *A Girl from Hunan* (1986). Featuring current male idol Jiang Wen (*Red Sorghum*, *Hibiscus Town*, *A Woman for Two*), the film strikingly captures the bleak side of modern Chinese urban society as an ex-convict tries to make a fresh start in an uncaring world.

The political antics which regularly surround China's two major awards ceremonies look like continuing. Following the debacle of the 1989 Golden Rooster/Hundred Flowers awards (see below), seven movies were prevented from taking part in the 1990 Hundred Flowers – including Xie Jin's *The Last Aristocrats* (from a short story by Taiwan writer Kenneth Pai), He Ping's *Yoshiko Kawashima* (about the Japanese transvestite female spy of the 1930's), Xia Gang's *Half Flame, Half Brine* (dissolute youth) and Zhang Liang's *A Woman's Street* (capitalistic youth).

After doubts about whether it would ever take place, the First Chinese Film Festival (actually the second if you count a dry run in 1987) was held in Peking during September 21–27, 1989, with much ceremony, little conviction, and several awards for reliable veterans. The following month saw the setting up of a China Film Fund headed by Yang Hansheng and Xia Yan, to "encourage the development of Chinese cinema." The year also saw the completion of a nationwide circuit of 11 "art-film cinemas" (against a total of some 10,000 movie houses) specialising in minority-appeal product.

None of this will do much to solve the problems affecting China's film industry. With ticket-prices still unrealistically low, capital scarce, self-censorship the name of the game, and a mass audience that prefers escapism above all, the country's industry is more than ever subject to the classic constraints of Third World film-making. The occasional jewel will continue to emerge; but the fine balancing act between art and commerce that Hongkong has mastered has yet to be learned on any major scale by its big brother.

DEREK ELLEY *is Consulting Editor of this book, and has been associated with it for more than 18 years. He is known as a specialist in Hungarian and Far East cinema, and is author of* The Epic Film: Myth and History *and consultant editor of* The Variety Movie Guide. *He is currently completing* A Handbook of Chinese Cinema: The Films and Film-Makers of Hongkong, China and Taiwan.

Recent and Forthcoming Films

Judou (Judou). Script: Zhang Yimou, Liu Heng, from the latter's novel. Dir: Zhang Yimou. Players: Gong Li, Li Wei, Li Baotian. Prod: Tokuma Communications (Japan)/China Film Export & Import, Xi'an Film Studio (China).
Ben ming nian (Black Snow). Script: Liu Heng. Dir: Xie Fei. Players: Jiang Wen, Cheng Lin, Cai Hongyu, Yue Hong. Prod: Peking Film Academy Youth Film Studio.
Damo fang (The Big Mill). Script: Qiao Liang, Wu Ziniu, from the novel by the former. Dir: Wu Ziniu. Players: Li Yusheng, Liu Zhongyuan, Shen Danping, Tao Zeru. Prod: Xiaoxiang (China)/Sil-Metropole (Hongkong).
Si shui wei lan (Ripples on Dead Water). Script: Han Lanfang, from the novel by Li Jieren. Dir: Ling Zifeng. Players: Jiang Wen, Liu Xiaoqing.
Feifa shengming. Dir: Tian Zhuangzhuang. Players: Xie Yuan, Shi Ke.
Datai Li Lianying. Dir: Tian Zhuangzhuang.

Players: Liu Xiaoqing, Jiang Wen. China/Hongkong co-prod.
Dunhuang ye tan. Dir: Li Han-hsiang. Cast: Pauline Wong, Pai Ying. China/Hongkong co-prod.
Hei shan lu. Dir: Zhou Xiaowen. Players: Xie Yuan. Prod: Xi'an.
Beijing, ni zao. Dir: Zhang Nuanxin. Players: Jia Hongshen, Ma Xiaoqing.

The 9th Golden Rooster Awards

After several delays and changes of locale, the awards were finally announced on August 10, 1989, in conjunction with the 12th Hundred Flowers Awards (voted by the readers of the monthly magazine *Popular Cinema*). In contrast to previous years the ceremony was small and low-key, shunted away from public gaze in a small screening room at the Chinese Filmmakers Association in Peking. There were no awards in six categories – Best Feature Film, Script, Supporting Actress, Music, Sound and First Work.

Best Director: Wu Ziniu (*Evening Bell*,* *To Die Like a Man* and *Between Life and Death*).
Best Actor: Tao Zeru (*Evening Bell*,* *To Die Like a Man* and *Between Life and Death*) and Xie Yuan (*Chess King* and *Out of Breath*).
Best Actress: Xu Shouli (*To Die Like a Man* and *Between Life and Death*).
Best Supporting Actor: Sun Min (*Evening Bell**).
Best Photography: Hou Yong (*Evening Bell**).
Best Art Direction: Shao Ruigang, Hu Hongyuan (*The Path Takes Me Home*).
Best Editing: Zhong Furong (*Obsession*).
Best Children's Film: *The Dreaming Age*.
Best Scientific/Educational Film: *Price of Increase – Population and Economy*.
Best Documentary: *Sonata of Shekou Special Economic Zone*.
Best Animated Film: *Landscapes*.

* Made in 1986, released in 1989

The 12th Hundred Flowers Awards

Best Feature Film: *A Woman for Two*, *Widow Village* and *The Republic Won't Forget*.

Best Actor: Jiang Wen (*A Woman for Two*).
Best Actress: Liu Xiaoqing (*A Woman for Two*).
Best Supporting Actor: Shen Junyi (*To Die Like a Man* and *Between Life and Death*).
Best Supporting Actress: Gong Li (*Code Name "Cougar"*).

Actress Gong Li in Zhang Yimou's *Judou*

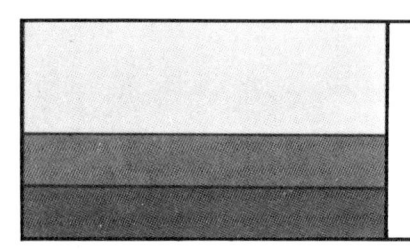

COLOMBIA
by Paul Lenti

Violence continues to intrude on Colombian reality. As a result of the murder of presidential candidate Luis Carlos Galán, the Colombian government declared open war on the drug cartels on August 18, 1989. The drug barons retaliated and the ensuing violence – mostly aimed at the citizenry and police – is proving disastrous for the national entertainment industry.

During the first year of the drug war, almost 300 bombs were detonated, mainly in Colombia's principal cities. (On November 25, 1989, 107 people were killed – including actor Gerardo Arellano – when an Aviance flight between Bogotá and Cali was bombed; and 68 people were killed and more than 650 wounded when a bomb went off in Bogotá on December 6, 1989.) Although there was a lull during the first quarter of 1990, as the result of a truce offered by the cocaine lords, the wave of bombings has resumed.

Although foreigners may come away with the impression that Colombians are living in a battle zone reminiscent of Beirut, the assaults are generally limited to urban centres and most Colombians are able to carry on their regular routines without overt fear.

Needless to say, Colombian exhibitors are major victims of the drug war. According to Iván Mcallister Braidy, vice president of Colombia's leading exhibition chain Cine Colombia, attendance has fallen drastically at national cinemas, as have most other night-time activities. Many restaurants, theatres, night-clubs and other after-dark entertainments have been put on hold by clients as citizens have sought the shelter of their homes. The bombing of the Esmeralda Cinema in Bogota only reinforced these stay-at-home sentiments and late-night screenings play to empty or near-empty houses.

The home video industry, plagued by rampant piracy and cheap contraband tapes smuggled from Venezuela or Panamá, has replaced the cinema-going tradition for many, although the majority of video profits – an estimated 70% – end up in the pockets of pirates and bootleggers.

While government agents fight drug

lords, Colombian film-makers are caught in the crossfire of another war: the long-standing statemate between the state production company Focine and national exhibitors, who have been withholding tax funds destined to domestic production. And, with bombs exploding in the streets, government efforts to crack down on exhibitors have low priority. Recent developments prompt many to suggest that the government is finally throwing in the towel.

The national production company Focine (Compañía de Fomento Cinematográfico) was founded by the federal Communications Ministry in 1978 to produce and promote national films. Funded by an 8.5% tax levied on cinema tickets, Focine began producing a regular slate of features, medium-length films and shorts.

In 1985, the government decided to up the tax a further 7.5% (specifically targeted at the production of short films), hoisting overall box-office tariffs for Focine to 16%. Exhibitors, reacting to a downward trend at the country's box-offices, protested. (National attendance declined from 49 million in 1986 to an estimated 37.5 million for 1990.) And, while Cine Colombia came to an agreement with the Fomento, last year the smaller exhibition chains – which make up approximately 50% of the nation's cinemas – have withheld the entire Focine quota and the debt now stands at about U.S. $6-million.

Soldiering On

Despite scant funds, Focine has managed to continue with limited production capabilities, mainly through co-productions with foreign or private producers: for example, with European TV Focine co-produced the one-hour social and ecological documentary *Law of the Jungle*, by Patricia Castaño and Adelaida Trujillo, which analyses the complex history of land reforms.

Still from *María Cano*, directed by Camila Loboguerrero

Focine also managed to finish post-production on Victor Gaviria's searing slice-of-life feature **Rodrigo D. – No Futuro**, originally shot in 1986. Filmed in Medellín, six of the nine non-professional actors in the film have been killed since production wrapped. Besides being included in the "From Magic to Realism" series at MoMA, the film went on to be the only Spanish-language movie to compete at Cannes.

The only 100% Focine venture, Camila Loboguerrero's two-hour filmed biography of *María Cano*, shot in 1988, waited almost two years for a final print that eventually premiered at the Cartagena Film Festival, winning the best photography prize.

In spite of international interest, last year Focine decided to get out of the production business. According to José Luis Reyes, the latest head of Focine, the government now plans to act as middleman between film-makers and producers by stimulating domestic production through private-sector interest.

This plan includes offering credits and low-interest loans, subsidising exhibition of Colombian films, promoting national cinema, marketing Colombian films abroad and granting cash prizes to films that have received awards at film festivals.

For a low-budget (U.S. $200,000) national film to recoup investment within the country, the picture needs approximately 1-million spectators at the average 500 pesos (U.S. $1) per ticket on initial release. (Mario Mitrotti's 1988 action film *Mujer de Fuego* was considered a commercial success, selling around 400,000 tickets; *Batman*, a national blockbuster, sold only 800,900 tickets.)

In order to make investment in film production a profitable venture, Focine proposes to grant credits for production coupled with a three-year low-interest loan to producers. (During the first year, nothing is owed on the principal. Interest rates are set at 16%, considerably lower than the 42-45% charged at private banks, due in part to the nation's approximate 25% annual devaluation of currency against the dollar, coupled with an equal rate of inflation – around 2% a month. Despite these figures, Colombia has one of the healthiest economies in Latin America.)

Focine is currently wrapping its final production, Sergio Cabrera's contemporary ensemble comedy **Snail's Strategy**, co-produced by Cabrera's company Producciones Fotograma and Crear TV. The film, which Cabrera describes as a "Chinese puzzle box," was shot in 1989 and is awaiting a final print.

Faced with official frustration, Colombian film-makers are tenacious and continue their efforts by following the only options left to them: while some have chosen to live and work abroad, others remain and manage to work using foreign co-production money. Still others have found employment working for national television.

Several directors avoid Focine's infrastructure altogether. For example, Francisco Norden, maker of the 1984 film *A Man of Principle*, shot the one-hour film *Kantus, the Final Voyage* for France's Antenne 2. Using Colombian locations, the post-production was completed in France.

A Study of Violence
Jaime Osorio's first feature film **Confession to Laura**, produced by Colombia's Méliès Productions in co-production with Televisión Espanola (TVE) and the Cuban Film Institute (ICAIC), was shot entirely in Havana in 1989-90. The film was produced under the auspices of the New Latin American Cinema Foundation and the Sundance Institute. The action takes place during the turbulence of the "Bogotazo," when widespread rioting erupted in the streets of the capital following the assassination of presidential candidate Jorge Eliecer Gaitán on April 9, 1948. Starring Vicky Hernández and Gustavo Londono, thhis intimate film offers a study of violence, noting that the violence between individuals is a metaphor for the unrest raging outside.

Rodrigo Castano Valencia is currently seeking foreign funding to finish his epic **The Night of All Saints** in co-production with the Colombian private companies Producciones Casablanca and Castano Valencia Cine y TV and Mexico's Producciones Rodar y Rodar and Fase Comunicaciones. Scheduled for release in 1992 to commemorate the 500th anniversary of the discovery of the Americas, the film will be issued in two separate formats: as a five-part miniseries and a 100-minute theatrical feature. To find production monies, Castano Valencia has produced a 20-minute pilot starring Spanish actor-singer Miguel Bosé as Hernán Cortés and Mexican Manuel Ojeda as the Aztec leader Montezuma.

A number of short films were also produced, using foreign capital. The documentary **Haddock with Arepa**, by Gustavo Fernández about street venders in Medellín, was co-produced with France; **Dokosvania** and **Nocturnal Sun** were both directed by Raúl García in Bulgaria; **María** and **Re-Encounters** were both filmed by Luisa Fernanda Espíndola in Romania, while the shorts **Snow** and **Morning** were made in New York by Felipe Paz, a graduate of the NYU film school.

Other shorts include **Monday Holiday**,

by María Regina Pérez and Juan Escobar, and **The Incredible and Sad Tale of Latin America and the Heartless Conquistadors**, by Ricardo Cabal.

Meanwhile, other noted Colombian film-makers have found a place working with national television producers, making series, miniseries and made-for-television movies shot on videotape.

The production company RCN Television hired Carlos Mayolo and Lisandro Duque, both internationally recognised film-makers. Mayolo is directing the highly rated on-going series **Sugar**, and original story of a family told over three generations written by Mauricio Navas Talero, while Duque both scripted and directed the 12-hour adaptation of **The Turmoil**, based on the well-known novel by José Eustasio Rivera and starring Frank Ramírez, Florina Lemaitre and Vicky Hernández.

Luis Fernando "Pacho" Botía, from Barranquilla, will direct **The White Piano**, based on a story by Alvaro Cepeda Samudio, a two-hour made-for-television feature for Caracol TV.

Long-running Festivals

Colombia boasts two annual film festivals. The 31st edition of the Cartegena Festival is slated for May 1991. Directed by Víctor Nieto, the Caribbean-based festival has a focus on new Latin American films. In the capital, the eighth edition of the Bogotá International Film Festival, headed by Henry Laguado, is scheduled for October 6–14, 1991. Besides the competitive international section, the theme will be a tribute to African cinema.

The Cinemateca Distrital de Bogotá also merged last year with the Fundación Patrimonio Filmico Colombiano (National Film Archives) in order to consolidate their collections and be better able to restore deteriorating copies of pioneer works. The 1928 venture *Dawn of Justice*, about the U.S. role in the succession of Panama, was restored in 1990 by New York's MoMA, while the Fundación Patrimonio is attempting to rescue *Manizales City* (1925), *Alma Provinciana* (1926), *Flores del Valle* (1941) and other works.

And, with a formal proposal in congress to create a national film council, similar to Brazil's Concine, coupled with the political appointment of María Emma Mejila – former head of Focine – into the new administration of President César Gaviria, film-makers are hopeful that official support will improve in the new decade.

PAUL LENTI is a freelance journlist specialising in Latin American cinema. In addition to working eight years as a film critic for the Mexico City News and seven years with the trade paper Variety, he more recently co-ordinated the film section of the 1990 New York Festival Latino.

Rodrigo D. – No Futuro (Rodrigo D. No Future)

Script: Vítor Gaviria, Luis Fernando Calderon. Angela Pérez, Juan Guillermo Arredondo. Direction: Víctor Gaviria. Photography: Rodrigo Lalinde. Music: Germán Arieta. Editing: Luis Alberto Restrepo. Players: Ramiro Meneses, Carlos Mario Restrepo, Jackson Idrián Gallego, Vilma Díaz, Juan Guillermo, Johana Hernández. Produced by Focine, Tiempos Modernos and Foto Club 76. 90 mins.

A first feature film by documentary and short-film director Víctor Gaviria, *Rodrigo D. – No Futuro* is a powerful exploration of the bleak and precarious lives of working-class street kids in Medellín. So dangerous is this world that six of the nine non-professional actors in the film have been killed violently since the production wrapped.

The naturalistic script, written in near-impenetrable Medellín street slang, won second place in Colombia's 1986 annual

Non-professional actor Ramiro Meneses as Rodrigo D, in Victor Gaviria's *Rodrigo D. – No Future*

screenplay competition. It was based on an article that appeared in the local newspaper "El Mundo," about a teenager, Rodrigo Alonso, who leaped from the top floor of a downtown building.

Rather than pursue a linear plot, the film presents a slice of life as we follow Rodrigo and his teenage friends over a several-day period, exploring their world as they live it as best they can.

Rodrigo (Ramiro Meneses) can't sleep at night. He has headaches and thinks about his mother, who died sometime previous to the story. He is also looking for a drum kit so he can start a punk band with his mates, who sell cocaine to school kids, steal cars, listen to raucous punk music or simply hang around.

Gaviria manages to capture the essence of this nether world through able camerawork and judicious selection of locations, the shanty towns that line the valley walls overlooking modern Medellín. The non-professional actors are always believable.

The story is unsettling, more often for things unsaid. Rodrigo's suicide becomes an existential decision in the face of a hopeless future.

Paul Lenti

Recent and Forthcoming Films

Maria Cano. Script: Camilia Loboguerrero, Luis González, Felipe Aljure. Dir: Camilia Loboguerrero. Phot: Carlos Sánchez. Music: Santiago Lanz K. Editing: Luis Alberto Restrepo, Gabriel González. Players: María Eugenia Dávila, Frank Ramírez, Jorge Herrera, Germán Escallón, Diego Vélez. Prod: Focine. 104 mins.

Confessión a Laura (Confession to Laura). Script: Alexandra Cardona Restrepo. Dir: Jamie Osorio. Phot: Adriano Moreno. Editing: Nelson

Rodríguez. Music: Gonzalo Rubalcabar. Players: Vicky Hernández, Gustavo Londoño, María Cristina Galvez. Prod: Melies Producciones (Colombia), in co-production with Televisión Española and ICAIC (Cuba). 90 mins.
Estrategia del Caracol (Snail's Strategy). Script: Humberto Dorado, based on a prized script by Sergio Cabrera and Ramón Jimeno. Dir: Sergio Cabrera. Phot: Carlos Congote. Editing: Manuel Navia. Music: Eduardo Carrisoza. Players: Frank Ramírez, Humberto Dorado, Florina Lemaitre, Gustavo Angarita. Prod: Focine, Crear T.V. and Producciones Fotograma. 100 mins.
Amor, Mujeres y Flores (Love, Women and Flowers). Script: Martha Rodríguez. Dir: Martha Rodríguez, Jorge Silva. Phot: Jorge Silva. Music: Iván Benavides. Editing: Jorge Echeverry (Bogotá), Esther Ronay (London). Prod: Fundación Cine Documental Investigación Social, in co-production with Sintrainpoagro (Colombia), Firefret Productions, La Fundación Interamericana, Swissaid, Agked, Channel 4 TV (London) 58 mins.
La Ley del Monte (Law of the Jungle). Script: Antonio Caballero. Dir: Patricia Castaño, Adelaida Trujillo. Phot: Fernando Vélez. Sound: Gustavo de la Hoz. Editing: Diego Ospina. Prod: Focine, in co-production with Citurna Ltd. for ZDF and TVE/UNEP. 52 mins.
Milagro en Roma (Miracle in Rome). Script: Lisandro Duque Naranjo, Gabriel García Márquez, based on the story "The Long Happy Life of Margarito Duarte." Dir: Lisandro Duque. Phot: Mario García Joya. Music: Blas Emilio Atehortua. Editing: Gabriel González. Players: Frank Ramírez, Gerardo Arellano, Amalia Duque Garcia, Santiago García, Humberto Dorado. Prod: Para Elsa Cinematográfica, in co-production with TVE (Spain) and the International Network Group (ING). 82 mins.
El Dia que Me Quieras (The Day You Love Me). Script: José Ignacio Cabrujas, Sergio Dow, Olinto Taverna, Jorge Goldenberg, based on the play by Cabrujas. Dir: Sergio Dow. Phot: Edward Lackman. Music: Luis María Serra. Editing: Sabine Mamou, Olinto Taverna. Players: María Eugenia Dávilla, Graciela Duffau, Fausto Verdial, Ulises Dumount, Claudio Berge. Prod: Productora Colombiana de Películas in co-production with Técnica de Venezuela. 76 mins.

Colombian actress Vicky Hernández in *Confession to Laura*

Useful Addresses

Focine
(Compañia de Fomento Cinematográfico)
Calle 35 No. 4–89
Bogotá
Tel: 288–4661, 288–4575, 288–4712
Fax: 285–5749

Fundación Patrimonio Colombiano
Carrera 13 No. 13–24, piso 9
Bogotá
Tel: 281–5241, 283–6495

Festival de Cine de Bogotá
Calle 26 No. 4–92
Bogotá
Tel: 282–5196
Fax: 283–0141

CUBA

by Tim Barnard

At this writing (summer 1990) there is no indication if, when or how the changes seen in Eastern Europe last fall will reach Cuba, although Havana is teeming with foreign press waiting for the big day. Cuba, meanwhile, is "fortifying its trenches," as the billboards say, for a long political and economic siege. And after a few years of gradually expanding cultural relations with other countries, even capitalist ones, a period of extreme cultural isolation seems to be on the horizon. Last fall, two popular Soviet magazines were banned and Cuban students were recalled en masse from Eastern Europe; film ties with the "formerly socialist countries" surely will not survive. This, coupled with large budget cuts to national production and reports of waning Spanish TV interest in Latin American co-productions spell trouble for Cuban film.

The paradox is that while the present government brings censorship and isolation to culture, it also brings stable, subsidised production and distribution and exhibition policies that serve the national, and not the multinationals', interest (see last year's IFG report for some of the forms this takes). Thus Cuba can now boast of something that much of Latin America and Eastern Europe for the moment cannot: a film industry.

What does that industry produce? Not much of interest. From **Coming Alive** (*Venir al mundo*), a feature-length soap opera, to **La Vie en Rose** (*La vida en rosa*), an insipid and garbled story of teenagers who meet incarnations of themselves 50 years hence, to **Under Pressure** (*Bajo presión*), a feeble working class milieu attempt at social criticism, it's clear that the goal of a "revolutionary" cinema has been long forgotten. More precisely: a politically or formally revolutionary cinema cannot be made or exhibited in Cuba today, nor is the cultural and intellectual climate condusive to producing directors capable of making such a cinema if they were allowed to. Scripts are either gutted by the bureaucracy or no good to start with, and the safest, and thus most used, themes are nostalgia pieces and/or literary adaptations with little relevance to present-day life.

Thus the most popular Cuban film of all time was this year's **The Belle of the Alhambra** (*La Bella del Alhambra*), a 1930's song-and-dance film set in the world of burlesque theatre. Its main claim to fame is that it is the Cuban film with spicy sex scenes, apart from Cuban pride in lavish production values that rival European standards. But it amounts to one big, inconsequential cliché.

Documentaries and Animation Clicking
The only hope for Cuban film remains that genre less subject to the political and economic restraints of feature production: the documentary short. Cuba is justifiably proud of its documentary heritage, and while the glory days are over, solid work is still being done, often by prominent feature directors in between films. Someone should organise a major retrospective solely of short Cuban films, especially since the features of the past ten years are such an embarrassment.

On the animation front, the Cuban–Argentine co-production **Martin Fierro**,

Still from *The Belle of the Alhambra*

based on the epic gaucho poem, was completed this year. It's a medium-length puppet film. The pre-eminent Cuban animator Juan Padron continues to churn out his Elpidio Valdés series, which is wearing a little thin, besides being of little interest to foreign audiences.

The annual Festival of New Latin American Cinema, held in December, ran into trouble this year as a result of budget cuts and a dearth of product in the region. Organisers are currently under a lot of pressure to make it a biennial, or at least to trim it down from its unwieldy 14 day length, especially now that guests are invited for only one week and not two.

As reported in last year's IFG, Havana this past year hosted the annual International Federation of Film Archives (FIAF) congress, bringing the world's film archive heads to Havana to discuss the problems of film preservation in the Third World. The Cuban Cinemateca organised a mammoth public exhibit of old Latin American films to accompany the event, as well as special symposia on film preservation in the Third World, with Third World archivists learning from Western archivists, and on the films of the 1930's, 1940's and 1950's in Latin America, a field of new theoretical interest. Unfortunately, the founding director of the Cuban Cinemateca and the man who had spent years organising all this, Héctor García Mesa, had a heart attack 10 weeks before it got under way and ten months before his own retirement. His interim replacement is Pastor Vega, head of the film festival and heir apparent to the film institute itself when Julio García Espinosa, now 64, steps down.

Last year's IFG also reported on the activities of the International Film and TV School located outside Havana. Run by Fernando Birri and presided over by Gabriel García Márquez, the school has troubles of its own. Financial and administrative problems prevented it from accepting new students last year, while it trimmed its programme from three years to two. Although a sound studio is being built

Still from *La Vie en rose*

and an ambitious programme of foreign shoots and international lecturers remains in place, serious financial problems loom. The school is under attack both within Cuba, by powerful interests who disapprove of Fidel Castro's hands-off promise to García, and abroad, for example by the once-liberal *New Republic* magazine as a front for the "International Communist Conspiracy" which uses personalities like Robert Redford, Francis Ford Coppola and George Lucas to "infiltrate" Hollywood, a scheme masterminded by Fidel Castro himself, of course.

On the subject of Cuban relations with Hollywood, a revision of the U.S. embargo now allows for limited payment for cultural goods by each country to the other. Cuba is keeping mum about whether it intends to start paying for U.S. films, which it presently pirates (this past year *The Last Emperor*, *Robocop*, *Radio Days*, *Who Framed Roger Rabbit*, *Lethal Weapon* and *Rain Man* were among those screened) from a very secret source (Panama? if so, we may soon see supply problems). Cuba desperately wants into the U.S. market, so it may have to play ball, but deteriorating relations may rule this out. Meanwhile, the U.S. has gone ahead with its universally condemned. "TV Martí" project, beamed into Cuba from Florida, and the U.S. Congress is expected to approve large sums of money for the station, despite the fact that the Cubans are successfully jamming it . . .

Thirty years after the revolution, with its sweeping and promising changes in the cultural field, we may have come full circle: U.S. films, especially action films, are again coming to dominate Cuban screens, alongside growing quantities of junk from China and North Korea, Cuba's only remaining allies. Revolutionary cinema indeed.

Recent Films

La Bella del Alhambra (The Belle of the Alhambra). Dir: Enrique Pineda Barnet. Script: Enrique Pineda, Miguel Barnet and Julio García Espinosa, based on the novel *Rachel's Song* by Miguel Barnet. Phot: Raúl Rodríguez Cabrera. Players: Beatriz Valdés, Omar Valdés, César Evora. Prod: ICAIC (Cuba)/Television Española (Spain).
Bajo presión (Under Pressure). Dir: Víctor Casaus. Script: Reinaldo Montero, based on the play *Accident* by Roberto Orihuela. Phot: Adriano Moreno. Players: René de la Cruz, Isabel Moreno. Prod: ICAIC.
Venir al mundo (Coming Alive). Script and Dir: Miguel Torres. Phot: Raúl Rodriguez. Players: Mario Balmaseda, Susana Pérez. Prod: ICAIC.
La vida en rosa (La Vie en rose). Script and Dir: Rolando Díaz. Phot: Roberto Fernández. Players: Manuel Porto, Tony Cortés. Prod: ICAIC.
Martin Fierro (*medium length animation*). Dir: Fernando Laverde. Script: Jorge Zuhair Jury, based on the epic poem by José Hernández. Puppetry: Fernando Laverde.

Useful Address

Instituto Cubano del Arte e Industria Cinematográficos (ICAIC)
Calle 23 #1155
La Habana
Tel: (53-7) 30-5041
Telex: 511419 ICAIC CU

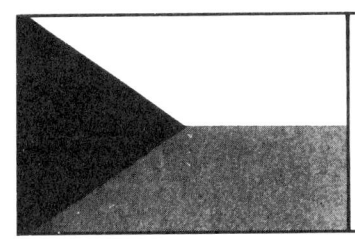

CZECHOSLOVAKIA
by Deborah Young

1990 will be remembered as one of the finest years in Czechoslovakian cinema: not for the pictures that were made, but for those that were shown. Twenty years of censorship came tumbling down with the rebirth of democracy and the election of playwright-president Václav Havel.

The 27th Karlovy Vary Film Festival, held July 7–19, was built around a programme of banned and blacklisted Czech and Slovak films, most made around 1969 and the Prague Spring. "The liberated festival," as interim fest chief Jiří Janousek and programmer Milan Hanuš dubbed the event, promised to throw off the restraints of "political manipulation" along with the "ideological criteria" by which films had been selected for competition. Representing production from the Slovak Republic was Juraj Jakubisko's **Birds, Orphans and Fools**, shot in 1969 but finished and released this year; and from the Czech Republic **Were We Really Like This?**, by Antonín Máša, called the first Czech film made freely after the "Velvet Revolution" of November 1989. Máša had been thrown out of Barrandov Studios in 1972 after some of his scripts were censored, and was forced to work in theatre until last year.

But Karlovy Vary's success was not based on current production, much less a disappointing competition section that failed to ignite enthusiasm from noticeably diminished audiences. Its glory lay in a superb retrospective featuring virtually all the films censored by Czech authorities over the last twenty years.

Whereas just a year ago it was a Herculean task to put together a reliable list of titles that had been banned or blacklisted shortly after release, at the festival it was possible to see the films themselves in excellent prints. Works like Vojtěch Jasný's **All My Good Countrymen** that had circulated in the West in bad prints and on cassettes received their just re-evaluation from delighted audiences. *All My Good Countrymen* reverberates with the tragic history of Moravian farmers forced to give up their rich lands in the state's short-sighted drive to collective farming. Jasny emigrated to the U.S. after the ban.

One of the finest discoveries was Zdenek Sirový's **Funeral Ceremonies**, a chilling modern version of the Antigone myth. Jiří Macháně's haunting black-and-white photography matches Jaroslava Tichá's stern-faced rigour as a widow determined to bury her husband in the family plot, against the will of local Communist authorities who had taken their farm away and let it rot during the period of forced collectivisation. The film was locked up shortly after it was finished and Sirovy was forced to leave Barrandov Studios. The film was screened at Montréal this year.

Karel Kachyňa's masterpiece of black tragicomedy, **The Ear**, got Czechoslovakia into competition at Cannes for the first time in 18 years. The ear in question is a listening device planted by a power that is both Kafkaesque and all too real. Radoslav Brzobohatý (the hero in *All My Good Countrymen*) and comedienne Jiřina Bohdalová are the bickering spouses who fear for their lives when they discover their villa has been bugged.

Top Award for Menzel
Berlin awarded a Golden Bear to Jiří

CZECHOSLOVAK FILMEXPORT

YOUR PARTNER TO SELL, BUY AND PRODUCE IN CZECHOSLOVAKIA

Václavské nám 28, 111 45 Praha 1
tel: 236 53 85–9   telefax: 235 84 32
telegrams: EXIMPFILMS   telex 122 259

Menzel this year for **Skylarks on a String**. This delightful, tender love story between two young people in a Communist labour camp is drenched in the deadpan black humour that is Menzel at his best. Story is based on tales by writer Bohumil Hrabal. It was also named best film of the year by the Czechoslovak Critics Association.

In Drahomíra Vihanová's striking first film, **Killing a Sunday**, an army lieutenant oppressed by the absurdity of his mechanical existence commits suicide. The film was forcibly pulled out of the vaults two years ago at Karlovy Vary by the active local chapter of Kino Women International (KIWI, an East-West association of women film-makers). But in the intervening 18 years, the talented Vihanová had been turned aside from feature film-making into a documentary career.

Another discovery was **The Seventh Day, the Eighth Night**, by Evald Schorm, who died in 1988, before events could vindicate his work. The film can be read as, among other things, an extraordinarily direct allegory about the Soviet invasion of Czechoslovakia. Even before prints could be made, the authorities locked the negative in a safe, where it remained for two decades, while director and scriptwriter Zdeněk Mahler were kept out of work. This parable shows how the inhabitants of an isolated town become paranoid over an unspecified, looming threat, and film's comic tone gradually turns to horror as savage instincts emerge.

In an excellent 23-minute student film, **The Uninvited Guest**, writer-director Vlastimil Venclík demonstrates his control over grotesque comic allegory. A married couple is shocked when a rough workman turns up on their doorstep to sleep in their bedroom and make hourly "reports" on them, but soon reconcile themselves when they see how much nastier their neighbours' "guests" are – things could be worse! Pavel Landovský and Jiří Hálek turn in fine performances. Venclík was thrown out of

Still from Jiří Menzel's award-winning *Larks on a String*

Still from Karel Kachyna's long-shelved and now successful *The Ear*

the Film and TV Faculty and charged with sedition in 1971.

More from the Blacklist

The other films on the blacklist – which has now taken on the sound of an honour roll – were Ivan Balad'a's **Ark of Fools**, based on Chekhov's story *Pavilion No. 6*, an allegory set in a madhouse, filmed in a distinctive avant-guarde style, too long, high-pitched and repetitive to make pleasant viewing, but full of interesting metaphors in its flood of images; Bulgarian director Rangel Vulchanov's **Aesop**, written by Angel Wagenstein, exuberantly combines a standard Roman historical film with an uninhibited political tract (including an unforgettable meeting between Aesop and Sappho); Vaclav Gajer's **Catherine and Her Children**, based on Jiří Křenek's novel, is a family saga centred around a proud country woman; in **Lilies of the Field**, the late director Elo Havetta showed veterans returning from a senseless First World War; Dušan Hanák's documentary **Images of an Old World**, which began winning prizes at international festivals in 1988, shows the dignity of old country folk who speak honestly about their dismal lives; Hynek Bočan's fine **Decoy** is one of the most chilling, and unredeemed, portraits of boys in reform school and their idealistic young teacher; the 38-minute, Kafkaesque short about a boy trying to return a "borrowed" cat, **A Statue to be Propped** by the late Pavel Juráček and Jan Schmidt, was screened in Oberhausen, Mannheim, and Cannes in 1965 before being blacklisted; and lastly, Jakubisko's **Bird, Orphans and Fools**, which he practically remade in 1989 as **Sitting On a Branch and I Feel Fine**.

Other banned and blacklisted shorts and documentaries were screened at Karlovy Vary, along with famous films from the 1960's Czech New Wave and films made by directors living in exile, like Miloš Forman, Ján Kadár, Jan Němec, and Ivan Passer.

Best of the new productions were a promising debut by Irena Pavlásková, **Time of the Servants**, depicting the rise of a ruthlessly manipulative woman in the Czech bourgeoisie; and Milan Steindler's bitter, demented comedy about a hapless sociologist engrossed in studying young people, **Ready for the Grave**.

Meanwhile, as far as the film industry goes, reorganisation is the order of the day. So far, however, no one knows exactly what the new face of Czecho-Slovak film will look like. The official body Czechoslovak Film was dissolved this year, leaving a void until a new film law gets passed.

Czechoslovak Filmexport director Jiří Janousek is well aware this is probably the last year his company will have a monopoly in buying foreign films and selling local ones. And the new manager of the Film Distribution Central Office, Jan Jira, doesn't know whether his organisation will become part of a larger body or an independent company, possibly with competitors. With fewer film-goers buying tickets and overhead costs on the rise, many film theatres are expected to close soon.

Vtáčkovia, siroty a blázni (Little Birds, Orphans and Fools)

Script: Juraj Jakubisko, Karol Sidon. Direction: Juraj Jakubisko. Photography: Igor Luther. Editing: Bob Wade. Music: Zdeněk Liška. Players: Philippe Avron, Jiří Sýkora, Magda Vašáryová, Francoise Goldité, Míla Beran, Mikuláš Ladižinský. Produced by Feature Film Studio (Bratislava)/Marenčin-Bakoš Production Group (Paris). 80 mins.

The similarity of story-line in Jakubisko's *Little Birds, Orphans and Fools* (shot in 1969 as a Slovak-French coproduction; released in 1990 after twenty years on the shelf) and the director's *Sitting on a Branch and I Feel Fine* (1989) is no accident. Fearing *Birds...* would never see the light of day, Slovakia's best known director decided to remake the earlier film.

But the abrupt revival of democracy in

Still from Juraj Jakubisko's *Little Birds, Fools and Orphans*

Czechoslovakia brought *Birds...* out of the freezer just a year later. The film is a wild, avant-garde work very much tied to the Czech New Wave of the 1960's, and made in the shadow of the Soviet invasion of 1968. It seems to say that reality is too absurd and terrible to be faced; each individual is responsible for carving out his own slice of happiness; but since all happiness is based on illusion, it can only end in tragedy.

Instead of talking about tanks and invaders, *Birds...* shows the involvement of two crazy pals, Yorick and Andrew, with a little Jewish waif, Martha. All three are war orphans; all three want to prove friendship is greater than selfish love. Both young men fall for Martha, however, and their moments of happiness are paid for with horror: Yorick lands in prison, then insanely murders Martha and their unborn child, and burns himself to death.

Instead of continuous narrative, Jakubisko adopts a rapid, episodic structure of scenes filmed on sets littered with surreal debris. Nothing makes much sense outside the logic of the film's thesis, but in its best moments, *Birds...* conveys the impossibility of reacting honestly in a world gone made, and at the same time, the futility of reacting madly, on the world's own terms.

Deborah Young

Byli jsme to my? (Were We Really Like This?)

Script and Direction: Antonín Máša. Photography: Ivan Šlapeta. Editing: Ivana Kačirková. Music: Svatopluk Havelka. Art direction: Jiří Hlupý. Players: Leoš Sucharípa, Peter Čepek, Táňa Fischerová, Tereza Brodská, Ladislav Frej, Jiří Zahajský, Ondřej Vetchý, Miloslav Štibich. Produced by Barrandov Dilm Studios/ Miloslav Vydra Production Group. 98 mins.

Dubbed the first Czech film to be made

after the "Velvet Revolution" of November 17, 1989, *Were We Really Like This?* is practically Antonín Máša's return to the screen since he was dismissed from Barrandov Studios in 1972. The director's interim work in the theatre offers a background for this film.

Leoš Suchařípa plays Jan Jonáš, a politically persecuted stage director whose attempts to circumvent party censorship bring on more than one heart attack. Before the final, fatal one that ends the film (a foregone conclusion), Jonáš rehearses a fiery production of *Othello*, while his cast's personal lives intertwine in a knot of backstage amours.

Actors are the real subject of *Were We Really Like This?*. The need for each to take a political and moral stance is strongly brought home. There are good guys, like Jonáš, his mistress, and his daughter, who strive for excellence; and bad guys, like the highly-paid actor who puts work last and is always ready to give a puffy speech at Party meetings. Máša's point is that truth on stage and truth in social and private matters are one and the same. In light of recent developments, film may be said to have a happy ending.

It is dedicated to the memory of Pavel Juráček and Evald Schorm, two long-banned film-makers who didn't live to see the old regime tumble.

Deborah Young

DEBORAH YOUNG is head of Variety's editorial bureau in Rome and specialises in Eastern European cinema.

Václav Havel (President of Czechoslovakia) with Miloš Forman, Theodor Pištěk, and Pavel Landovská at the Karlovy Vary Film Festival in July 1990

photo: Milos Fikejz

FINANCING PROMOTING PRESENTING DANISH FILMS

DANISH FILM INSTITUTE

THE DANISH FILM INSTITUTE
ST. SOENDERVOLDSTRAEDE
DK-1419 COPENHAGEN K
PHONE: +45 31 57 65 00
FAX: +45 31 57 67 00
TELEX: 31465 (dfilm dk)

»Babette's Feast« »Pelle the Conqueror«  »Pelle the Conqueror«

DENMARK

by Ebbe Iversen

Although Denmark did not manage to win a third consecutive American Academy Award, Kaspar Rostrup's *Waltzing Regitze* received an Academy Award nomination for Best Foreign Language Film in 1990 and thus upheld the recent international success for Danish films.

At home, however, the financial conditions for producing quality films deteriorated drastically due to the new film law which was introduced in 1989, the most important aspect of which was the establishment of the so-called fifty-fifty principle, which means that an independent producer is automatically granted state support via the Danish Film Institute (DFI) of 50% of his film's budget – up to a maximum of DKK 3.5 million – provided that he has secured the other half of the budget from private investors.

The legislators intended the fifty-fifty principle to support the production of more popular Danish films, thereby helping declining local cinema attendance to rise again. Some people feared, however, that the introduction of this principle might cause a decline in the over-all artistic quality of Danish films, and this fear has unfortunately proved to be justified. Whereas the past year has seen a number of rather primitive farces – strictly for the local market – being produced thanks to the fifty-fifty principle, the DFI is bitterly complaining that the amount of money left for supporting ambitious quality films is far from sufficient.

This is not only due to the fifty-fifty principle, but to a number of factors. As explained by Jørgen Kleener, who is the chairman of the board of the DFI, the Film Institute now has at its disposal a total annual amount of DKK 66 million (approx. US$ 10.5 million) for the support of film production. Out of this amount no less than DKK 41.2 million is earmarked for special purposes – DKK 1 million for producing more copies of popular films for local cinemas, DKK 970,000 for the European Co-production and Distribution Fund EURIMAGES (under the aegis of the European Council), DKK 3.2 million for the recently established Nordic Film and Television Fund – which is a kind of Scandinavian equivalent to EURIMAGES – DKK 18 million for the production of films for children and youngsters, and finally DKK 18 million for the fifty-fifty principle.

For the film consultant at the DFI, who allocates financial support to the production of quality films for grown-ups, there thus remains only DKK 24.8 million (approx. US$ 3.9 million), and as the average budget for a Danish feature film is DKK 9 million, out of which the DFI usually contributes DKK 7 million, the DFI is only able to support three and a half "serious" films a year. This is obviously far from enough to maintain the level of quality, which has resulted in two Academy Awards and one nomination in the past three consecutive years.

The situation can also be described from a different angle. If the DFI in a fiscal year takes part in one co-production with EURIMAGES, one with the Nordic Film and Television Fund and one with Danish television, it will tie up a total amount of DKK 15.5 million leaving DKK 8.5 million at the film consultant's disposal, which is

Still from Gabriel Axel's *Christian*, released worldwide via J & M Entertainment

only enough for the production of one strictly Danish feature film.

It is therefore being discussed, whether it is reasonable that some 25% of the total amount of DFI-money for film production is earmarked for the production of films for children and youngsters, and whether the fifty-fifty principle should be abolished. The general attitude of the legislators is that it would be premature to abolish the fifty-fifty principle this year, as more time is needed to see whether the system might eventually result in the production of films, which are both popular and of acceptable quality. The Ministry of Culture has recently agreed to a suggestion put forward by the DFI's board, whereby the fifty-fifty principle can also be used for co-productions.

The board has also put forward a budget suggestion for 1991 totalling DKK 75.4 million, which includes DKK 14 million earmarked for co-productions with the two national Danish TV stations.

Nordic Co-Production Year

The Film Institutes of Denmark, Sweden, Norway, Finland, and Iceland have decided to appoint 1991 The Nordic Co-production Year. A total amount of DKK 80 million has been allocated for the production of five co-productions, all of which are guaranteed distribution in the five Nordic countries. Among the projects chosen is Danish director Søren Kragh-Jacobsen's **The Boys from St. Petri** (*Drengene fra Sct. Petri*) with a budget of DKK 21.5 million.

In spite of the very limited financial resources, a number of interesting films have been made in Denmark during the past year. Apart from **Waltzing Regitze** one should mention the tough, satirical

> **TOP QUALITY FILMS WANTED !!!**
> for exhibition and distribution in Denmark
>
> **GRAND** 1:2:3:4:5:6   **CAMERA FILM**
> Leading Danish art cinema   Importer and distributor of
> in the heart of Copenhagen   quality films from all countries
>
> Write or phone:
> Peter Refn, 8 Mikkel Bryggersgade, DK–1460 Copenhagen K, Denmark. Tel: 45 33 13 61 12 · Telex: 19703 palace dk · Telefax: 45 33 15 08 82

Syrup by Helle Ryslinge, her second feature after *Cœurs Flambés*. Swedish-born director Åke Sandgren managed in **Miracle in Valby** (*Miraklet i Valby*) to tell a dramatic adventure story with a touch of Spielberg, and Leif Magnusson gave in **Another World** (*En verden til forskel*) a visually highly original description of a young boy's escape from Eastern Europe to his Polish father in Copenhagen.

A more or less similar theme was dealt with in Polish director Maciej Dejczer's **300 Miles to Heaven** (*300 mil til himlen*), which was a Polish–Danish–French coproduction – the film received a European Film Award as "Best Young European Film of the Year" in Paris last November – while Erik Clausen told a sweet and simple story, which pleased a lot of children, in **Tarzan Mama-Mia** (the curious title is the name of

Kirsten Lehfeldt in Helle Ryslinge's *Syrup*, produced by Per Holst Filmproduktion

Stine Bierlich in *Happiness Is a Curious Catch*, directed by Linda Wendel and produced by Metronome

a pony in the film). Also for children, but more mature, was **Let the Polar Bears Dance** (*Lad isbjørnene danse*) by the obviously talented new young director Birger Larsen.

Stefan Henszelman depicted without inhibitions the lives and loves of two free-spirited young women in **A Modern Woman** (*Dagens Donna*), and Tom Elling, who was the photographer of Lars von Trier's provocative *The Element of Crime*, tried his hand at directing with the experimental *Perfect World*, which turned out to be too self-consciously weird even for the most open-minded audiences. Linda Wendel described the strained relationship between a mother (played by Helle Ryslinge) and her rebellious daughter in the grimly realistic **Happiness Is a Curious Catch** (*Lykken er en underlig fisk*), and Oscar-winner Gabriel Axel (*Babette's Feast*) proved to be a rather naive romantic with the awkwardly directed **Christian**, concerning a young Danish criminal who finds love and happiness among warm-hearted Arabs in Northern Africa.

The films produced within the fifty-fifty principle are better left undescribed, but a few films with serious intentions are on their way to the screens. *The Man Who Would Be Guilty* by Ole Roos is based on a novel by Danish writer Henrik Stangerup and has the Danish–French actress Anna Karina in the female lead. *Dangerous Game* by first time director Preben Østerfelt is described as a very erotic love story, and *The Song About a Time of Cherries* by Irene Werner Stage should, if its style is similar to her previous short films, be a poetic and experimental modern fairy-tale.

Oscar-winner Bille August (*Pelle the Conqueror*) grew tired of the American company Warner's continual delaying of his planned film adaptation of Isabel Allende's acclaimed novel *House of the Spirits* and postponed the project himself in favour of directing *The Good Intention*, which has been shot in Sweden based on a script by none other than Ingmar Bergman. *The Good Intention* will be shown internationally as a major television series as well as two feature films for the cinemas. Bille August has not however given up his plans to shoot *House of the Spirits* sometime in the future, and he still holds the legal filming rights, given to him by Isabel Allende personally.

EBBE IVERSEN has been a professional journalist since 1966. He has been film critic of "Berlingske Tidende" since 1973, and is a former co-editor of the magazine, "Kosmorama."

Adam Kozlowski in *A World of Difference*, directed by Leif Magnusson

Ghita Nørby in *Waltzing Regitze*

photo: Rolf Konow

Dansen med Regitze (Waltzing Regitze)

Script and Direction: Kaspar Rostrup. Photography: Claus Loof. Editing: Grete Møldrup. Music: Fuzzy. Art Direction: Henning Bahs. Players: Ghita Nørby, Frits Helmuth, Rikke Bendsen, Michael Helmuth. Produced by Nordisk Film Production and The Danish Film Institute. 90 mins.

Based on a popular novel by Martha Christensen, this film tells the story of a very ordinary married couple, Regitze and Karl Aage – from their meeting as young people during the German occupation of Denmark to the present day, where the elderly Karl Aage during a midsummer party keeps drifting away into his memories. The reason for his reminiscing turns out to be the fact that his beloved Regitze is terminally ill, but apart from this somewhat melodramatic revelation – and in spite of the film's structure of continual flash-backs – *Waltzing Regitze* is a very gentle and straight-forward film, easy to understand and to appreciate.

Director Kaspar Rostrup, who usually works in the theatre, has not attempted to give his film a flashy style, but concentrates on carefully reconstructing the changing times in precise details and especially on giving a warm and loving picture of his two main characters, who are neither glamorous nor exceptionally bright, but plain people struggling bravely to be decent and to do the right things. Their fears and their hopes, their defeats and their small victories, are the unassuming core of the film, and by never being pretentious *Waltzing Regitze*

> **SFC**
>
> **DANISH SHORT FILMS AND DOCUMENTARIES**
>
> Please write:
>
> **Statens Filmcentral**
>
> 27, Vestergade,
> DK 1456 Copenhagen K.
> Denmark
> Tel: 33 13 26 86

makes their story utterly believable, funny and moving. Regitze and Karl Aage are wonderfully played by Ghita Nørby and Frits Helmuth, two of the top stars in Danish theatre and both blessed with the gift not to appear theatrical in front of the camera.

Ebbe Iversen

Sirup (Syrup)

Script and Direction: Helle Ryslinge. Photography: Dirk Brüel. Editing: Birger Møller Jensen. Music: Peer Raben. Players: Peter Hesse Overgaard, Kirsten Lehfeldt, Inger Hovmand. Aage Haugland. Produced by Per Holst Filmproduktion and The Danish Film Institute. 114 mins.

Helle Ryslinge's new film is a satirical portrait of a young man, Lasse, who wants to be liked and admired so desperately that his is quite willing to lie and steal in order to obtain this goal. He also yearns to be a progressive artist, but lacks true talent, so his life in self-absorbed semi-artistic circles in Copenhagen is full of deceit. Maybe this clever, but weak and insecure hustler even deludes himself, and for a time he certainly manages to hoodwink his girl-friend, who is a painter with all the talent he lacks himself. When everything else fails, he starts crying helplessly and thus has his way with her, until he is finally found out.

Syrup is tough on Lasse, and the film has offended quite a few male spectators in Denmark – whereas most women like it! – but his character is believable, and Helle Ryslinge does not describe him without a certain amount of sympathy. It's unpleasant to know him, but it's even more unpleasant to *be* him, and his surroundings are also far from perfect with their snobbish eagerness to be in vogue. People are not evil in this film, just scared not to appear smart and fashionable.

Peter Hesse Overgaard and Kirsten Lehfeldt – who both had important parts in Helle Ryslinge's first film, *Cœurs Flambés* – are very convincing as Lasse and his girl-friend, and stylistically *Syrup* is extremely dynamic and full of odd, amusing details. Copenhagen looks very exotic in *Syrup*, and its young and hopeful artists appear rather ridiculous, but also recognizable. So like *Cœurs Flambés*, this is a wild comedy with a sad and serious undertone.

Ebbe Iversen

Danish Producers

Columbus Film A/S
16–18 Islands Brygge
DK-2300 Copenhagen S
Tel: 31 57 81 20

Crone Film Production A/S
c/o The Danish Film Studio

Dagmar Filmproduktion A/S
c/o The Danish Film Studio

TOP TEN GROSSING FILMS IN DENMARK: 1989

Rain Man
A Fish Called Wanda
Licence To Kill
Indiana Jones and the Last Crusade
The Jut-Nuts (*Danish Comedy*)
Cocktail
Who Framed Roger Rabbit
Die Hard
Tarzan Mama-Mia (*Danish family film*)
Batman

Dansk Filmindustri A/S
1 Telegade
DK-2630 Tåstrup
Tel: 42 99 85 55
Fax: 42 99 47 77

(The Danish Film Studio)
52 Blomstervaenget
Dk-2800 Lyngby
Tel: 42 87 27 00
Fax: 42 87 27 05
Telex: 37798 (studio dk)

Film-Cooperativet Danmark 1983 ApS
3 Bymandsgade
DK-2791 Dragør
Tel: 31 53 56 31

Filmforsyningen ApS
24 Vesterbrogade
DK 1620 Copenhagen V
Tel: 31 23 44 84

Filmselskabet Danmark
16 Gasvaerksvej
DK-1656 Copenhagen V
Tel: 31 21 98 88

Palle Fogtdal Film
22 Østergade
DK-1100 Copenhagen K
Tel: 33 15 39 15

Fortuna Film
90 Vordingborgvej
DK-4681 Herfølge
Tel: 53 67 64 46

Per Holst Filmproduktion ApS
17 Livjaegergade
DK-2100 Copenhagen Ø
Tel: 31 26 42 00
Fax: 31 26 04 01
Telex: 19430 (kaerne dk)

Hanne Høyberg Filmproduktion
31 Vesterbrogade
DK 1620 Copenhagen V
Tel: 31 21 79 11

L & M Filmproduktion ApS
9 Holsteinsgade
DK-2100 Copenhagen Ø
Tel: 31 26 15 00

Still from Stefan Henszelman's *Donna of the Day*

Jakob Katz in Åke Sandgren's *Miracle in Valby*, a Danish–Swedish co-production

Jørgen Leth Productions
16–18 Islands Brygge
DK-2300 Copenhagen S
Tel: 31 57 77 00

Metronome Productions A/S
16 Søndermarkvej
DK-2500 Valby
Tel: 31 46 77 55
Fax: 36 44 06 04
Telex: 19497 (unique dk)

Nordisk Film Production AS
Mosedalvej
DK-2500 Valby
Tel: 31 30 10 33
Telex: 15286 (filmko dk)

Gunnar Obel Film
36A Toldbodgade
DK-1253 Copenhagen K
Tel: 33 13 75 38

Jens Ravn Film & TV Produktion ApS
31 Vesterbrogade
DK-1620 Copenhagen V
Tel: 31 23 00 62

Viktoria Film
c/o The Danish Film Studio

A/S Panorama Film International
59 Rådhuspladsen
DK-1550 Copenhagen V
Tel: 33 12 12 71

Regner Grasten Film
8 Axeltorv
DK-1609 Copenhagen V
Tel: 33 12 14 41

Pathé-Nordisk A/S
1 Skelbaekgade
DK-1717 Copenhagen V
Tel: 31 23 24 88
Fax: 31 23 04 88

Danish Distributors

AB Collection ApS
30 Reventlowsgade
DK-1651 Copenhagen V
Tel: 31 21 37 00

Bellevue Film
19 Kompagnistraede
DK-1208 Copenhagen K
Tel: 33 11 76 03

Camera Film
8 Mikkel Bryggersgade
DK-1460 Copenhagen K
Tel: 33 13 61 12

Carina Film
231 Alekistevej
DK-2720 Vanløse
Tel: 31 71 58 00

Cinnamon Film ApS
29 Pantheonsgade
DK-5000 Odense C
Tel: 66 12 17 16

Columbia-Fox
13 Hauchsvej
DK-1825 Copenhagen V
Tel: 31 23 22 66

Constantin Film ApS
50A Bülowsvej
DK-1870 Frederiksberg C
Tel: 35 37 81 11

Dan-Ina Film
147B Trekronergade
DK-2500 Valby
Tel: 31 16 61 66

Kaerne Filmstudier ApS
17 Livjaegergade
DK-2100 Copenhagen Ø
Tel: 31 26 42 00
Fax: 31 86 86 59

Dansk Filmindustri A/S
1 Telegade
DK-2630 Tåstrup
Tel: 42 99 85 55
Fax: 42 99 47 77

Egmont Film
71 Dortheavej
DK-2400 Copenhagen NV
Tel: 31 19 80 00
Fax: 38 88 22 30

Kaktus Film
15 Kultorvet
DK-1175 Copenhagen K
Tel: 33 13 40 38

Kommunefilm
143 Vestbuen
DK-2750 Ballerup
Tel: 42 65 62 62

Kaerne Film ApS
17 Livjaegergade
DK-2100 Copenhagen Ø
Tel: 31 26 42 00

Nordisk Film Distribution A/S
7 Axeltorv
DK-1609 Copenhagen V
Tel: 33 14 76 06

Saga Film International
3A Søndervang
DK-9800 Hjørring
Tel: 98 92 21 99

Scala Film
1 Gyldenbjergsvej
DK-5700 Svendborg
Tel: 62 21 88 66

Scanbox
3 Hirsemarken
DK-3520 Farum
Tel: 44 49 62 00
Fax: 42 95 17 86

United International Pictures
13 Hauchsvej
DK-1825 Copenhagen V
Tel: 31 31 23 30

Warner & Metronome ApS
16 Søndermarksvej
DK-2500 Valby
Tel: 31 46 88 22
Fax: 36 44 06 04

Useful Addresses

The Danish Film Institute
Store Søndervoldstraede 4
PO Box 2158
DK-1419 Copenhagen K
Tel: 31 57 65 00
Fax: 31 57 67 00
Telex: 31465

Ministry of Cultural Affairs
2 Nybrogade
DK-1203 Copenhagen K
Tel: 33 92 33 70

The Danish Film Workshop
24 Vesterbrogade
DK-1620 Copenhagen V
Tel: 21 24 16 24

The Danish Video Workshop
4 Lermbckesvej
DK-6100 Haderslev
Tel: 74 52 86 95
Fax: 74 53 24 61

The Association of Danish Cinemas
c/o The Danish Film Institute

The Danish Government Film Office (Statens Filmcentral)
27 Vestergade
DK-1456 Copenhagen K
Tel: 45 33 13 26 86
Fax: 33 13 12 03

The Association of Danish Film Distributors
and
The Association of Danish Video Distributors
14 Oslo Plads
DK-2100 Copenhagen Ø
Tel: 31 42 21 66

The Association of Danish Film Clubs
7 Skovvejen
DK-8000 Århus C
Tel: 86 13 31 01

The Association of Danish Children's Film Clubs
20 Niels Hemmingsensgade
DK-1153 Copenhagen K
Tel: 33 15 67 60

The Danish Film Academy
5 Vestagervej
DK-2100 Copenhagen Ø
Tel: 31 18 25 11

The Film Workers' Union
and
The Association of Danish Film Directors
21 Kongens Nytorv
DK-1050 Copenhagen K
Tel: 33 14 33 55

The Danish Film Studio
52 Blomstervaenget
DK-2800 Lyngby
Tel: 42 87 27 00
Fax: 42 87 27 05

Nordisk Film Production AS
Mosedalvej
DK-2500 Valby
Tel: 31 30 10 33
Fax: 31 16 85 02

Risby Studios
DK-2620 Albertslund
Tel: 42 64 96 46

EGYPT
by Fawzi Soliman

Egyptian cinema during the past year can be regarded in pessimistic terms. The number of cinemas has decreased from 240 in 1971 to a mere 168 in 1990. The quality of most local films has drastically deteriorated, made as they are for more profit through video (and distributed mainly in the Arab countries).

The star system remains supreme. A sizeable chunk of a film's budget goes to the stars – especially of comedy. American movies still dominate the market. To counter this problem, certain actors and film-makers have established a new company to handle production and distribution.

Nevertheless, several efforts have been made to produce high-level films. New names have been emerging. Adel Awad, for example, has shown promise in his debut, **The Scorpion**, and his second film, **Below Zero** (released before the first one). Alaa Karim also made his mark with **Suspicion**. Both directors are graduates of the Film

Still from Sherif Arafa's new film, *Silence!*

Institute here. Tarek El Erian made his debut with **The Emperor**, and has studied in the United States. Asma El Brakry made her first feature, **Beggars and Humiliated**, in co-production with France and comes from a background in documentary films.

The Cairo International Film Festival continues to attract entries from around 60 countries, while a "Cinema Palace" has been opened by the Ministry of Culture. There are screenings of 35mm and 16mm films, and a programme of lectures and a training programme for amateur filmmakers.

Recent Films

Iskendria Kaman Wakaman (Alexandria, More and More). Script and Dir: Youssef Chahine. Phot: Ramses Marzouk. Music: Mohamed Nouh. Players: Yousra, Youssef Chahine, Hussein Fahmy, Amr Abdel Gelil. Prod: Misr International Films (Cairo)/Classics Productions/Le Sept (Paris). *The third film in an autobiographical trilogy.*

Leil wa Khawana (Night and Traitors). Script: Ahmad Saleh, from a story by Naguib Mahfouz. Dir: Ashraf Fahmy. Music: Michel El Masri. Players: Nour El Sherif, Mahmoud Yasin, Safia El Emary-Shahira. *An up-to-date transcription of a story by the Nobel laureate about a young man's being duped by a ruthless businessman.*

El Beda Wa Elhagar (The Swindler). Script: Mahmoud Abou Zeid. Dir: Ali Abdel Khalik. Phot: Said Shimy. Music: Hassan Ab El Seoud. Players: Ahmad Zaki, Maali Zayed, Memdouh Wafy, Abdalla Moushref. Prod: Tamido (Medhat El Sherif). *An idealistic professor turns charlatan, with some astonishing results.*

Mawed Maa El Rais (Appointment with the President). Script: Ahmad El Khatib. Dir:

Mohamed Radi. Phot: Maher Radi. Music: Mustafa Nagui. Players: Kamal El Shenaoui, Ilham Chahine, Farouk El Fishaoui, Said Abdel Ghani, Sayed Radi. Prod: Sphinx Film. *A young woman member of the National Assembly uncovers some widespread corruption and seeks the President's aid.*

Samaa Houss! (Silence!). Script: Maher Awaad. Dir: Sherif Arafa. Phot: Mohsen Ahmad. Music: Moudy El Imam. Players: Leila Olwy, Mamdouh Abdel Alim, Hassan Kamy, Ahmad Bedeir. Prod: Try Production. *One of the best recent Egyptian films, tracing the fortunes of an itinerant song and dance duo.*

Kalb el Leil (Heart of the Night). Script: Mohsen Zayed, from a story by Naguib Mahfouz. Dir: Atef El Tayeb. Phot: Abdel Moneim Bahnasi. Music: Moudy El Imam. Players: Farid Shawki, Nour El Sherif, Hala Sidky, Mahmoud El Guindi, Mohseha Tawfik. Prod: El Shorouk (Motei Zayed). *Considered by the Egyptian Film Critics' Association as the best film of 1989. Reflects Mahfouz's yearning for social justice and man's relation to the world about him.*

El Mourshed (The Informer). Script and Dir: Ibrahim El Mougi. Phot: Mohsen Nasr. Music: Ammar El Shereie. Players: Farouk El Feshaoui, Sherihan, Mahmoud El Guindi, Afaf Shoeb. Prod: El Doha (Mahmoud El Guindi). *A first feature by the screenwriter Ibrahim El Mougi.*

El Moghtasiboun (The Rapists). Script and Dir: Said Marzouk. Phot: Tarek El Telmissany. Music: Mohamed El Sheikh. Players: Leila Olaoui, Hassan Hosni, Hamdi El Wazir. Prod: Yehia Shanab. *Authentic story about five young men raping a woman in front of her fiancé, and then being condemned to death.*

Still from Youssef Chahine's *Alexandria, More and More*

Still from *The Swindler*

Useful Addresses

Egyptian Film Centre
City of Arts
Gaza
Tel: 854707, 850897
Telex 21863 Egfic UN

Egyptian Film Fund
1 Behlar Street
Kasr El Nil
Tel: 393 7686
Telex 20382 pbgla UN

Egyptian Film Industry Chamber
Orabi Street
Cairo

National Centre for Film Culture
36 Sherif Street
Cairo
Tel: 392 7460

SAUNA, SISU AND SÄÄTIÖ*)
WHICH ONE IS UNFAMILIAR?

FINNISH FILM FOUNDATION (FFF) IS THE ANSWER

FFF FOR FINANCING FILMS

DOLLY AND HER LOVER / MATTI IJÄS
I HIRED A CONTRACT KILLER / AKI KAURISMÄKI
AMAZON / MIKA KAURISMÄKI
FRIENDS, COMRADES / RAUNI MOLLBERG

FFF FOR FINDING FILM FACTS FROM FINLAND

CINEMAS IN 1989: 344
ATTENDANCES: 6.7 MILLION
PREMIERES: 188
ASK FOR OUR ANNUAL CATALOGUE

FFF FOR FILMING FACILITIES

FILM HOUSE K13
SOUND TRANSFER UNIT,
AUDIO POST PRODUCTION UNIT, MIXING UNIT,
ANIMATION STUDIO, EDITING UNITS

FIND US, WE'LL FIND THE ANSWER

THE FINNISH FILM FOUNDATION, K13, KANAVAKATU 12, SF-00160 HELSINKI, FINLAND
PHONE INTERNATIONAL +358 0 177 727, TELEFAX +358 0 177 113, TELEX 125032 sesfi sf.
*) SÄÄTIÖ MEANS FOUNDATION

FINLAND

by Matti Apunen

The film business boom, begun 1988, continued in 1989. The year was marked by several foreign megahits plus one Finnish success story. When books were closed in December, total audiences had reached 7.3 million and the future looked good. (Unfortunately, the prognoses for 1990 have been somewhat gloomier.)

1989 was a year totally dominated by one film at the box-office: the 3½ hour spectacle **Winter War** by Pekka Parikka was an exceptional success. After enormous publicity it reached a domestic audience of more than 600,000.

Finland is a country of very few political passions or friction. The common historical and political myths are widely accepted, and among these the "miracle" of the Winter War is probably the most carefully guarded. *Winter War* did not rewrite the wartime Finnish mythology, but reinforced the myth of the heroism of a small and poorly equipped army fighting against overwhelming odds.

Hardly any film ever has had a more favourable reception than *Winter War*: national unanimity acquired the proportions of national hubris. Naturally, the film won most of the national Jussi Film Awards. *Winter War* represented Finland in Berlin but failed to impress the international audience.

The World According to Kaurismäki

Internationally, the director who stole the attention and publicity from Pekka Parikka was Aki Kaurismäki, of course. The screenings of Kaurismäki's two films in Berlin were happenings where Kaurismäki established his reputation as one of the wittiest and most original European film-makers. Kaurismäki's laconic and sarcastic style was accentuated in **Girl from the Match Factory**, widely recognised as his best and most solid performance so far.

In late 1989 Aki Kaurismäki moved to Portugal where he concentrated on winegrowing and scriptwriting. The shooting of Kaurismäki's latest film, **I Hired a Contract Killer** was completed in London in May 1990. The film stars the former favourite of François Truffaut, Jean-Pierre Léaud.

Aki's brother Mika was immersed in a big-budget action movie, **Amazon**. The film was shot in the Amazon jungle with an international cast and multinational financing. The largest of the individual investors was a Finnish Wall Street banker Pentti Kouri, who has shown some further interest in operating in the film business and film financing.

Last year the absence of one man was widely noticed: that most popular of Finnish comedians, Spede Pasanen, withdrew temporarily from film-making. Pasanen has made almost a dozen cheap and coarse comedies starring the same character called "Numbskull Emptybrook." Every one of these films has been in the Finnish "Top Ten" and some have been more popular than big Hollywood movies. In 1989, as a protest following an argument over distribution, Pasanen did not continue the production of his films. Anyway, in early 1990 he was reported to be active again.

Film distribution was still dominated by one big company, Finnkino, owned by its three top executives and relatively well protected against takeovers. Foreign movies provided some excellent results in 1989. Big international hits like *Licence to Kill*, *Indiana Jones and the Last Crusade*, *A Fish Called Wanda* and *The Bear* did not let the distributors down. The only major disappointment was the heavily marketed *Batman*, which was left far behind the real winners. One noteworthy Finnish phenomenon is the constant success of the *Police Academy* sequels; Part Six, like all its predecessors figured among ten of the most popular films in Finland.

In November 1989 the death was reported of Edvin Laine, a great actor and one of the most prominent film-makers of his generation. In his last years Laine was busily preparing a spectacular biographical film on the composer Jean Sibelius and the first shots were taken in early 1989. The project was closely connected to Laine and it has been suspended since his death, and its future looks very uncertain.

Harlin: a Success Story

The Finnish film community followed the rocketing career of their young compatriot Renny Harlin, who enjoyed an extraordinary success in Hollywood. After two minor productions Harlin directed the fourth episode in the *Nightmare on Elm Street* series for New Line, after which he made *Ford Fairlane* and *Die Hard 2* for 20th Century-Fox. In early 1990 Harlin signed a major contract with Carolco for a couple of major projects.

The most successful round of international film festivals was made by a first feature film, **Homebound**, by Ilkka Järvi-Laturi. In April 1990 his film was awarded the main prize at the Nordic film festival in Kristiansand, Norway. Järvi-Laturi is maybe the most promising young director in the "second wave", following the breakthrough of Aki and Mika Kaurismäki. Järvi-Laturi's style is less sardonic, less stylish and more straightforward, but strongly original and rooted in Finnish mentality.

WE DON'T EXIST WITHOUT LEAVING A TRACE

FINNKINO OY
Kaisaniemenkatu 2b 00100 HELSINKI
FINLAND
tel. 358-0-131 191 telefax 1311 9300

Mikk Mikiver and Stina Ekblad in Rauni Mollberg's *Friends, Comrades*

Donner Out, Mäkelä In

The most powerful man in Finnish cinema, managing director Jukka Mäkelä of Finnkino, was appointed chairman of the board at the Finnish Film Foundation, the most important official institution, financing and promoting Finnish film. Mäkelä succeeded Jörn Donner, film-maker, writer and MP who left FFF with some bitter remarks on the Finnish production system.

The Finnish Film Foundation and Finnish production companies made an effort to strengthen their foreign sales by founding a new sales organisation. The company was named "White and Blue Sales" and is headed by Anne Jokelainen. In an attempt to boost Finnish film-making, the Film Foundation declared a competition for screenwriters. The best original treatment will be awarded 100,000 Finnish Marks ($25,000).

Public money in Finland is channeled through the Finnish Film Foundation. In 1989 the total sum was about FIM 30 million ($7.5 million). The public support did grow a little in late 1980's but much slower than was intended (or what was expressed in official platforms). Characteristically, political ignorance reached its nadir in early 1989 when the Finnish Minister of Culture, who is also responsible for public film financing, admitted that she had not seen a single film in a cinema for 21 years. The last film she recalled she had seen was a Danish soft porn comedy.

Finns have not taken part in Nordic co-productions and they have not been able to share the extraordinary success of other Scandinavian countries, mainly Denmark. On the other hand Finnish production companies were the first to exploit the post-perestroika Soviet film market and production facilities, due to Finnish experience and traditions in Soviet trade.

A New Film Festival

Espoo, the neighbouring town of Helsinki, hosts the newest of international European film festivals. Cine Espoo is an annual event with the emphasis on Scandinavia, the Baltic countries (Estonia, Latvia and Lithuania as independently represented countries) and the Soviet Union, East and West Germany, Finland, Sweden, Norway, Denmark and Poland). The Baltic entries form a limited international competition, but the very core of the festival is non-competitive.

The first Espoo festival in August 1990 paid tribute to Charles Chaplin and arranged a retrospective of the career of Renny Harlin. The festival is headed by a pioneering figure in Finnish film culture and distribution, Aito Mäkinen, and Ilkka Kalliomäki, who was one of the founders of International Short Film Festival in Tampere.

The Tampere festival celebrated its 20th year with a special programme of French short films and with remarkable support from the public: this cosy but effective festival sold over 20,000 tickets in four days.

Tulitikkutehtaan tyttö (Girl from the Match Factory)

Script and Direction: Aki Kaurismäki. Photography: Timo Salminen. Players: Kati Outinen, Vesa Vierikko, Elina Salo, Esko Nikkari. Produced by Villealfa Filmproductions/Svenska Filminstitutet.

Girl from the Match Factory is the third and final part of Aki Kaurismäki's "low life trilogy." In its style and characterisation it continues the trail blazed by *Shadows in Paradise* (1986) and *Ariel* (1988).

The tone and setting are fully matured Kaurismäki. The film is a story of a reticent factory worker, a young girl looking for love and honesty in a cold world filled with

Kati Outinen in Aki Kaurismäki's *Girl from the Match Factory*

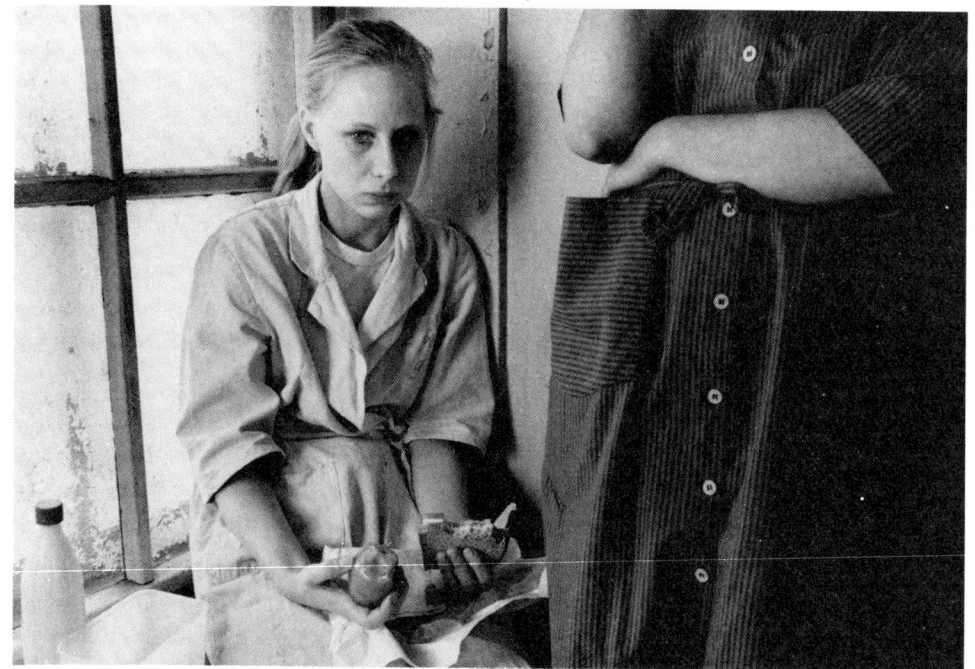

petty-bourgeois hate and egoism. She is exploited by her parents and men alike, and when she gets pregnant nobody seems to care enough to do anything else but despise the credulous girl. Finally, when she has lost practically everything, she fights back and her revenge is merciless.

The dialogue is carefully written to imitate the style of pulp fiction and old romantic novellas. It is contrasted by the almost expressionless and apathetic style of acting by Kati Outinen, one of the regular actresses in Kaurismäki's ensemble. The style of directing and cutting underlines the static state of things; the apparent impossibility of changing anything in this world, ruled by sheer greed and insensibility.

Girl from the Match Factory is more intense than *Shadows in Paradise* and it has the heart and soul that are missing from *Ariel*. Kaurismäki's strongly stylised cinematic style is now 100% waterproof; the atmosphere here has taken enough distance from realism and naturalism and remains unrepentant in its superb artificiality. Kaurismäki walks the thin line between melodramatic over-emotionalism and subtle irony. His comical intentions are barely to be recognized: the stronger the tragedy, the stronger the comedy.

Matti Apunen

Yksinteoin (Single-handed)

Script: Jussi Parviainen. Direction: Pekka Lehto. Photography: Kari Sohlberg. Editing: Olli Soinio. Monologue: Jussi Parviainen. Produced by: Kinofinlandia/Pekka Lehto.

Jussi Parviainen is one of the most contradictory young celebrities in Finland: a director, a playwright and an actor followed almost fanatically by cohorts of young actors and drama students. When Parviainen's marriage broke up in late 1989, evening papers and magazines were instantly filled with interviews with Parviainen, who amazingly seized control over the media and publicity. His agony could be seen everywhere: he became the Strindberg of the yellow press.

His wife had barely moved out from their apartment, when Parviainen got his cameras rolling. *Single-handed* is a 90-minute monologue by Parviainen, on the divorce of Parviainen, written and performed by Parviainen.

The film is a furious eruption of one man's primitive feelings. Parviainen does not analyse the reasons, he just lets go and creates a truly impulsive and intensive reckoning without parallel. *Single-handed* is a description of his jealousy, disappointment and anger that lead to regression and potential violence.

Parviainen phones his wife and her new lover and threatens to slit the man's throat with his jack-knife. There is no written dialogue in the film and every person speaking is real: the wife and the new man did not know their conversation was being taped and later used in the film.

The film provoked another scandal and a law suit. Parviainen was hated and despised and the making of the film was considered as a cheap revenge. Jussi Parviainen is a public person to the extent that it is impossible to separate the Private Parviainen from Public Parviainen: his marriage had been public from the beginning, so he decided that his divorce should be too. That is why *Single-handed* is not just an act of revenge or a one-sided pile of accusations; it is simply an excellent monologue that uses a different medium than Strindberg but with the same impact.

Matti Apunen

MATTI APUNEN is film critic for the Tampere-based morning newspaper, Aamulehti, *and also editor of a yearbook covering film, TV, and video in Finland.*

Raija Paalanen in *Dolly and Her Lover*

Recent and Forthcoming Films

Amazon. Dir: Mika Kaurismäki. Phot: Timo Salminen. Players: Kari Väänänen, Robert Davi, Rae Dawn Chong. *A big-budget action film, set in the jungles of Amazon. A bank manager in Helsinki embezzles some money and tries to flee with his family to the U.S., but soon they find themselves in Brazil, getting lost deeper and deeper in the jungle...*
Talvisota (The Winter War). Dir: Pekka Parikka. Phot: Kari Sohlberg. Players: Taneli Mäkelä, Vesa Vierikko, Konsta Mäkelä, Heikki Paavilainen. Prod: National Filmi/Marko Röhr. *"The battle of Finland": a spectacular recreation of the Winter War in 1939.*
Ameriikan raitti (Paradise America). Dir: Lauri Törhönen. Players: Kari Sorvali, Juha Järvimaa, Mari Rantasila, Åke Lindman. Phot: Esa Vuorinen. Prod: Jörn Donner Productions. *A group of Finns commit a tax fraud, make a new start in America and get involved in drug dealing.*
Räpsy ja Dolly (Dolly and Her Lover). Dir: Matti Ijäs. Phot: Tahvo Hirvonen. Players: Matti Pellonpää, Raija Paalanen, Pertti Sveholm. Prod: Filminor/Heikki Takkinen. *An ex-con tries to make a comeback to society.*
Porttikielto taivaaseen (Banned from Heaven). Dir: Tapio Suominen. Phot: Timo Heinanen. Players: Satu Silvo, Tapani Perttu, Nina Nurminen, Riikka Suikkari, Minna Aaltonen. Prod: National Filmi. *A melodramatic "true story," based on a recent scandal. The manager of one of the international hotels in Helsinki is also running a call girl business. One day, one of the girls is killed...*
Ystavat, toverit (Friends, Comrades). Dir: Rauni Mollberg. Players: Mikk Mikiver, Stina Ekblad. *An epic drama from the "Finnish Wild West": in 1939 several nations are struggling for control of the nickel ore deposits in northeastern Lappland.*
Kadunlakaisijat (Street-Sweepers). Dir: Olli Soinio. Player: Kari Sorvali. *A black, grotesque horror comedy: based on the characters created for The Moonlight Sonata (1988) by the same director.*
I Hired a Contract Killer. Dir: Aki Kaurismäki. Phot: Timo Salminen. Player: Jean-

TOP TEN GROSSING FILMS IN FINLAND: 1989

	Attendance
Indiana Jones and the Last Crusade	440,399
Rain Man	429,364
The Bear	377,613
Licence to Kill	377,328
The Winter War (from Nov 30)	334,172
A Fish Called Wanda	273,739
Batman	225,887
Who Framed Roger Rabbit (prem. Dec 1988)	195,935
Lethal Weapon II	193,397
Police Academy VI	192,124

Pierre Léaud. *A man tries to commit suicide but lacks the courage. He contacts a professional killer and hires him to do the job. Almost immediately he regrets his decision but he cannot reach the killer who is set on performing his part of the deal...*

Producers

Filmi-Molle Oy
Siltakatu 12 A 5
SF-33100 Tampere 10
Tel: (31) 12 64 65

Filminor
Laivastokatu 8–10 D
SF-00160 Helsinki
Tel: (0) 65 14 22
Fax: 17 68 60
Telex: 125032 sesti sf

Filmiryhmä Oy
Vyökatu 8
SF-00160 Helsinki
Tel: (0) 17 10 55
Fax: 66 26 02

Finnkino Oy
Kaisaniemenkatu 2 B
SF-00100 Helsinki
Tel: (0) 13 11 91
Telex: 100 1658
Fax: 13 11 93 00

Franck Films/Michael Franck Productions Oy
Iso Roobertinkatu 42 B
SF-00170 Helsinki
Tel: (0) 62 45 11
Fax: 62 40 04
Telex: 100 0566 forumsf

Giron Filmi Oy
c/o Jörn Donner Productions Oy
Pohjoisranta 12
SF-00170 Helsinki
Tel: (0) 1356060

Jörn Donner Productions
Pohjoisranta 12
SF-00170 Helsinki
Tel: (0) 1356060
Fax: (0) 1357568

Kinotuotanto Oy
Katajanokankatu 6
SF-00160 Helsinki
Tel: (0) 66 32 17

Matti Kassila Ky
Piikkikuja 6 A
SF-01650 Vantaa
Tel: (0) 66 32 17

National-Filmi Oy
Lönnrotinkatu 30 C
SF-00180 Helsinki
Tel: (0) 64 39 11
Fax: 13 11 93 75

Nelimarkka Riitta – Seeck Jaakko
Marjaniemenranta 4
SF-00930 Helsinki
Tel: (0) 33 12 29

Neofilmi
Pohjoisranta 8 B
SF-00170 Helsinki
Tel: (0) 63 67 23

Partanen & Rautoma
Pietarinkatu 12 B
SF-00140 Helsinki
Tel: (0) 66 99 56

Reppufilmi Oy
Johanneksentie 6 A
SF-00120 Helsinki
Tel: (0) 60 17 48
Fax: 61 21 031

Spede-yhtiöt
Ilmalankatu 2
SF-00240 Helsinki
Tel: (0) 14 16 33

Villealfa Filmproductions Oy
Väinämöisenkatu 19 A
SF-00100 Helsinki
Tel: (0) 49 83 66
Fax: 49 86 61

Distributors

Finnkino Oy
Kaisaniemenkatu 2 B
SF-00100 Helsinki
Tel: (0) 13 11 91
Telex: 1001658
Fax: 13 11 93 00

Gaudeamus Elokuva
Mannerheimintie 5 C
SF-00100 Helsinki
Tel: (0) 13 11 41
Telex: 121395 libacsf

Miofilm Oy
Torpantie 36
SF-90230 Oulu
Tel: (81) 22 86 60
Telex: 32300 urfil sf

Senso Films Oy
Väinämöisenkatu 19 A
SF-00100 Helsinki
Tel: (0) 49 83 66
Fax: 49 86 61

United Pictures Finland
Lastenkodinkuja 1
SF-00180 Helsinki
Tel: (0) 694 08 11
Telex: 121808 uip sf

Urania Film Oy/Ltd
Torpantie 36
SF-90230 Oulu
Tel: (81) 22 86 60

Walhalla ry
Kaisaniemenkatu 2 B
SF-00100 Helsinki
Tel: (0) 13 11 93 38

Warner Bros Finland Oy
Lastenkodinkuja 1
SF-00180 Helsinki
Tel: (0) 69 40 522
Telex: 122530

Useful Addresses

Central Organisation of Finnish Film Producers
Katajanokankatu 6
SF–00160 Helsinki
Tel: (0) 66 32 17

Finnish Film Foundation
Kanavakatu 12
SF–00160 Helsinki
Tel: (0) 17 77 27
Fax: 17 71 13
Telex: 125032

Federation of Finnish Film Societies
Annankatu 13 B
SF–00120 Helsinki
Tel: (0) 64 83 72

Finnish Cinema Association Finnish Film Chamber
Kaisaniemenkatu 3 B
SF–00100 Helsinki
Tel: (0) 63 55 06

Finnish Broadcasting Company (YLE)
TV Centre
SF–00240 Helsinki
Tel: (0) 41 88 11
Telex: 121055

FRANCE
by Michel Ciment

Despite government efforts to support French cinema, and a number of initiatives which have been pursued (reduced prices on Mondays, a cinema "celebration day" each year in June where for the price of one ticket you can see as many films as you want), the spiral of attendance continued downwards during the 1989 season: 118.8 million spectators as against 122.4 million in 1988 and 163.4 million in 1986! Among them, 33.8% went to see French productions (38.5% the year before), and 55.5% to American productions (45.9% in 1988).

Altogether the audience is focusing more and more on French and English-speaking films. Out of the top 63 films at the box-office in 1989, two Italian features and one Yugoslav represent the rest of the world! The same lack of variety is conspicuous on TV screens where out of 950 films programmed during the year (excluding cable TV), Eastern Europe, for example, was represented only by two Soviet pictures. Little by little one witnesses a uniformity of taste.

As a consequence of the fall in cinema attendances, less films were released (366 as against 431 in 1988), although their average cost has climbed (21 million francs as against 18.4 million) and only 66 enjoyed 100% state financing (93 in 1988). Italy has been the main partner for co-production (31) followed by West Germany (9), Switzerland, Belgium, and Canada (6). However, the shrinkage in the foreign markets for French film is particularly worrying and in sharp contrast with all the talk about a European cinema. Except in the U.K. (which has shown an increase of 7.8%), attendances for French film have been declining everywhere – and in Switzerland the fall was 63.3% compared to the previous year.

In a European perspective the Minister of Culture issued a decree in January 1990 which regulates the granting of official funds in very strict terms. Out of five main categories (scriptwriter, director, Star —1, star —2, technician), one non-European contribution is permitted. The announcement of this regulation was officially responsible for the withdrawal of French producer Anatole Dauman from Elia Kazan's project, *Beyond the Aegean*. With the same aim of strengthening European production, the French government – taking into account the huge transformation in the former "socialist" countries – has offered 10 million francs for co-productions with Eastern Europe, while enforcing the presence of 10% of European film on the various TV channels. In identical spirit, the Minister for Economy and Finance prevented the Italian businessman Giancarlo Parretti from buying a majority of shares in the Pathé company in order to defend national interests.

While obvious emphasis was given to Eastern Europe at the last Cannes Festival (a one-day symposium in the presence of Jack Lang, Minister of Culture, and Danièle Mitterand, plus 20 films selected in the various sections), the French producer-distributor UGC announced the opening of theatres in the U.S.S.R. and Marin Karmitz produced *Taxi Blues*, a first film by Pavel Longuine and a joint effort with Lenfilm.

New Initiatives

A month hardly goes by without evidence of a will to find new departures or some solutions to the current difficulties. One, for instance, is an initiative in the field of education. Some 60 film appreciation classes have been launched in French high schools, and people can now choose a "cinema" option for their *baccalauréat* exam. Similarly, 20 classes were created in elementary schools. At a higher level of education, Jean-Luc Godard was entrusted with responsibility for a "centre of research into cinema and the audiovisual" – a place for producing and experimenting with new techniques and which will closely relate to FEMIS, the national film school.

The *Avance sur recettes* commissions,

Gérard Depardieu in his award-winning role in *Cyrano de Bergerac*

Dirk Bogarde and Jane Birkin in *Daddy Nostalgie*

which give money to producers, have been divided into two sections, with one being devoted exclusively to features. The most spectacular event, which reveals both the cult of the *auteur* (to the point of absurdity) and the government's efforts to support what it considers "prestige" directors, has been the protracted production of *Les Amants du Pont Neuf*, the third film by Léos Carax, a promising director still in his twenties. The film was left stranded in August 1989, with its male star injured and 80 million francs already spent on a mere 30 minutes of film! In June this year it was confirmed that Christian Fechner had decided to take over the production and spend another 80 million francs on completing it.

Quality Not in Question
So France, despite having on average the highest per capita attendance in Western Europe, is still declining in film exhibition terms. Few would question, however, the quality of the films themselves. In Cannes both *Cyrano de Bergerac* and *Daddy Nostalgie* received excellent reviews from foreign and French journalists alike, as well as applause from the audience, but too many films are being produced and a number of those are not well enough prepared, especially where the screenplay is concerned. One reason may be that those participating in a production take fewer risks than before, being protected by advance sales, TV co-production money, and state grants. However, the first six months of 1990 witnessed some good results achieved by French films. Seven out of the top 20 box-office winners in Paris were French.

As usual, a great variety of directors from every generation has been active during the past year – old-timers like Chabrol, Deville, and Rohmer as well as 28 debutants, half of them made with the help of advance cash from the Centre National du Cinéma (CNC), some of them directed by actresses who tried their luck behind the camera such as Marie France Pisier (*Le Bal du Gouverneur*), Tonia Marshall (*Pentimento*), Brigitte Rouan (*Outremer*), and Nicole Garcia (*Un Week-end sur deux*).

The extraordinary popular and critical acclaim for **Cyrano de Bergerac** is certainly explained by the fame of Rostand's play and the charisma of Gérard Depardieu in the title role, but also by the fact that all too few French films show a sense of the spectacular, offer a broad canvas, and reveal a control of extras and crowd scenes. This is to the credit of Jean-Paul Rappeneau, a remarkable craftsman who has directed only five films in 25 years and who has now made what is undoubtedly his best work. This elegant and classical director does not belong to the New Wave but to the same generation. As does Michel Deville, who once again in **Nuit d'été en ville** has devoted himself to an exercise in style (in this respect he is one of the few courageous artists of our cinema) by opposing two excellent players (Marie Trintignant and Jean Hugues Anglade) who spend a night in bed and after spend a post-coital session discussing their past and present sexual and sentimental life. The film's preciousness might irritate some, but the tone recalls the libertine novellas of the 18th Century.

Another moralist is Eric Rohmer who has launched a series of four films named after the seasons of the year. **Conte de Printemps** combines the intellectual dialogue of the author's "Moral Tales" with the sense of improvisation of his "Comedies and Proverbs." There is much discussion of philosophy in this exceptional film, but there is also a daughter jealous of her father's girlfriend and other characters caught in their psychological games.

As faithful as Rohmer to his own original inspiration, Jean-Luc Godard celebrates in his own way three decades of New Wave

Marie Trintignant and Jean-Hugues Anglade in *Nuit d'été en ville*

cinema in his aptly-named **Nouvelle Vague**. It is a dazzling display of colours, framing, sound and editing with the same frustration for the audience in the end as with his other recent films. Godard is like a refined jeweller who cuts each stone immaculately but in the end somehow forgets to make a necklace. However, his latest effort, with Alain Delon used more as an icon than as an actor, is one of his best of the past decade, a love story that deals also with nature, business, and poetry.

Chabrol Off Form

Claude Chabrol, on the other hand, is now far removed from the New Wave and his own source of inspiration with the awkward international co-production, **Quiet Days in Clichy**. Henry Miller's world is hardly congenial to the Frenchman, who is ill at ease in rendering the Paris of the 1930's and the sexual goings-on of American expatriates. The best of Chabrol is rarely in period pieces, as his new film again demonstrates. As for Louis Malle, another contemporary of the New Wave, his **Milou en mai** is a social comedy set in the provinces while the May "events of '68" take place in Paris. With the help of

Alain Delon and Domiziana Giordano in *Nouvelle Vague*

Anne Teyssèdre and Florence Darel in *Conte de printemps*

Jean-Claude Carrière, Malle has staged a kind of boulevard romp, rather mechanical in its development, which has echoes of *La Règle du jeu* but which never really takes off. Michel Piccoli plays the lead in this satire, where every character represents a different social and political attitude on the French chessboard.

Claude Lelouch also deals with a host of actors but in a more freewheeling way in his

Michel Piccoli and crayfish in *Milou en mai*

Il y a des jours et des lunes, a kind of *Nashville* made in France (with all due respect to Robert Altman), where the full moon and the summer change of time play the role of the folk concert. People mix and separate. Lelouch plays with comedy and pathos, unashamedly sentimental as always but somehow invigorating in his joy in images and his talent for directing people.

Tavernier and Doillon Shine

The generation following the New Wave has also figured prominently in recent months, particularly Bertrand Tavernier who followed *La Vie et rien d'autre* with another success, **Daddy Nostalgie**. On a smaller canvas he achieves a genuine pitch of emotion through his portrayal of the relationship between a daughter (Jane Birkin) and her father (Dirk Bogard) in a Mediterranean setting. It is a more subdued version of *A Sunday in the Country*, with Tavernier revealing a delicacy of touch as persuasive as his more epic treatment of his previous two films (his medieval incest story, *La Passion Béatrice*, being worthy of rediscovery). Jacques Doillon's **La Vengeance d'une femme** could have been a remarkable film were its director not so self-indulgent. But the brilliance of the two actresses (Isabelle Huppert and Béatrice Dalle) and the power of the story (after the death of her husband, a woman intrudes into the life of his mistress and tortures her psychologically, with fatal consequences) lead to some rewarding scenes.

The same talent for psychology (which is at once the *forte* of the French cinema and also its limitation) is apparent in **La Désenchantée**, where Benoit Jacquot, after several films marked by a dry, cerebral approach, finally touches his audience with a portrait of a young girl involved with men of various generations. The spare idiom, reminiscent of Bresson's *Mouchette*, does not stifle the emotions. The same could be said of Bertrand van Effenterre, for long a prisoner of theoretical ambitions, who in

Isabelle Huppert and Béatrice Dalle in *La Vengeance d'une femme*

Tumultes gives way to a cool lyricism around the death of a young man, mourned by his family, which acts as a catalyst for the relationships between his father, his mother, and his three sisters. The acting, the maritime setting, and a kind of romantic atmosphere hark back to Gremillon and his poetic realism.

Also worth watching is Jean Claude Brisseau's **Noces blanches**, a passionate love story between a professor of philosophy (Bruno Cremer, also excellent in *Tumultes*) and his young pupil (the pop star Vanessa Paradis in a brilliant screen debut). A pure tragedy, the film dares to go to extremes – something quite rare in French cinema – and confirms Brisseau, a middle-aged director but rather a newcomer, as one of the strongest talents currently at work.

Disappointing Thriller

It's a pity that our few attempts to escape from time to time from the psychological realm turn out to be so disappointing. **Nikita**, for instance, by Luc Besson, is a spy thriller and a portrayal of a rebellious girl. It tries to create a visual style akin to the comic strip world but is ultimately flawed by sophomoric dialogue and incongruities of plot.

Arthur Joffé's second feature, **Alberto Express**, is a kind of nightmarish and humorous journey by a young man travelling from Paris to Rome to pay his debt to his father for his upbringing. The film never quite finds its balance between realism and fantasy. The French do not have the knack of creating an *After Hours*.

Nor do they often succeed where the historical pageant is concerned. Those who were supposed to celebrate the bicentennial of the French Revolution (ironically they were all strongly anti-revolutionary!) lacked visual invention, original ideas, and looked like routine TV miniseries (**Chouans!**; **Vent de Galerne**; **Les Années Lumière/ Les Années Terribles**; **L'Autrichienne**).

Comedy, another genre quite popular with audiences, also proved less than rewarding last year. **Ripoux contre Ripoux** by Claude Zidi, a sequel to his huge success, *Les Ripoux*, about corrupt cops, failed to match its predecessor. Nor did Etienne Chatiliez's **Tatie Danielle**, the study of an acerbic old woman, recapture the inventive and witty tone of *La Vie est un long fleuve tranquille*. Neither Gérard Oury, with **Vanille fraise**, nor Diane Kurys, with **La Baule les Pins**, proved successful despite their indisputable gift for comedy.

There were some oddities from eccentric directors. Otar Iosseliani, who is semi-resident in France, went to Africa to shoot a village fable (**Et la lumière fut**) which with its leisurely pace and deadpan humour looked curiously like his famous Georgian comedies. Andrzej Zulawski gave a frantic rendition (as might be expected) of Moussorgsky's **Boris Godounov** with lashings of visual splendour, a brilliant performance by Ruggero Raimondi, and some baroque irony (soldiers in modern Soviet uniforms lost in the corridors of the Tsar).

Raymond Depardon, a famous photo-journalist and documentarist, brought to his second feature, **La Captive du désert** (with Sandrine Bonnaire) a different style of direction. In filming the captivity of a young Frenchwoman held by a group of nomads in

Tsilia Chelton in Etienne Chatiliez's *Tatie Danielle*

the desert, he keeps the camera immobile to a point at which cinema merges with photography. The contemplative effect is either hypnotic or boring, depending on your disposition. As for Serge Gainsbourg, a famous poet and singer, he directed **Stan the Flasher**, in which Claude Berri, the well-known director and producer, plays an exhibitionist attracted by nymphets. The film contains a mood of anguish, a dark tone, and a distinctive style.

New Talents Surface

Finally, four films revealed new talents, affording at least some crumbs of comfort. Radovan Tadić's **Erreur de jeunesse**, shot in black-and-white, is close in spirit to the New Wave. It tells the story of a young man addicted to poetry, who lives under the roof of a Paris building next to a free-loving young woman. This charming film is made up of meetings and surprises. More classical, Nicole Garcia's **Un Week-end sur deux** follows the journey to Spain of a divorced woman (convincingly played by Nathalie Baye) and her two children. In the tradition of French psychological realism, the film holds promise with some original touches and genuine sensitivity. **Chine ma douleur** manages to recreate a Chinese concentration camp in the Pyrenees, no mean feat. The director, Daï Si-Jie, living in exile in France, portrays without pathos the

Sandrine Bonnaire in *La Captive du désert*

photo: Raymond Depardon

misfortunes of a young boy who has been punished for listening to modern music.

Printemps perdu takes the opposite line. It is a Chinese story too, but shot by a Frenchman in Mongolia. Alain Mazars takes a melodramatic subject – a man from a camp marries a young girl but lets her free when her former suitor, to whom she is tied by a promise of eternal love, returns from three years of military service – and deals with it at arm's length. The emotion is all the stronger and the counterpoint created by a Chinese opera directed by the now lonely husband achieves a palpably lyrical tone. Alain Mazars, both ambitious and artistically successful, demonstrates that it is still possible to break new ground in an art form more and more dominated by the formula approach.

Judith Godrich in *La Désenchantée*

MICHEL CIMENT is one of the key figures behind the well-known French magazine Positif, and the author of numerous books on film, including the award-winning studies of Kubrick, Losey, Rosi, Kazan, and Boorman.

Recent and Forthcoming Films

Alberto Express. Script: Arthur Joffé, Jean-Louis Benoit. Dir: Arthur Joffé. Phot: Philippe Welt. Players: Sergio Castellito, Eugenia Marruzzo, Marie Trintignant, Thomas Langmann, Nino Manfredi. Prod: AFC/Ciné Cinq/Gérard Mital Production/Christian Bourgois Production.
L'Amour. Script and Dir: Philippe Faucon. Phot: Bernard Tiphine. Players: Laurence Kertekian, Julie Japhet, Nicole Porte, Mathieu Bauer, Sylvain Cartigny. Prod: Paris Classics Cinéma.
L'Autre. Script and Dir: Bernard Giraudeau. Phot: Yorgos Arvianitis. Players: Francisco Rabal, Wadeck Stanczak, Smail Mekki, Julian Neguiesco. Prod: Carthago Films.
Baby Blood. Script: Alain Robak, Serge Cukier. Dir: Alain Robak. Players: Emanuelle Escourrrou, Jean Francois Gallotte, Christian Sinniger. Prod: Partner's Production/Exo 7.
Bienvenue à bord. Script and Dir: Jean-Louis Leconte. Phot: Charlie Vandamme. Players: Pierre Richard, Martin Lamotte, Evelyne Bouix. Prod: Blue Dahlia/Ciné-Cinq.
Le Brasier. Script: Eric and Jean-Pierre Barbier. Dir: Eric Barbier. Phot: Thierry Arbogast. Players: Maruschka Detmers, Jean-Marc Barre. Prod: Flach Film.
La Campagne de Ciceron. Script: Jacques Davila. Dir: Jacques Davila, Michel Hairet, Gérard Frot-Coutaz. Phot: Jean-Bernard Menoud. Players: Tonie Marshall, Sabine Haudepin, Jacques Bonnafé, Judith Magre. Prod: ACS/Films Aramis.
Chambre à part. Script: Serge Frydman, Jackie Cukier. Dir: Jackie Cukier. Phot: Yves Angelo. Players: Lio, Michel Blanc, Jacques Dutronc, Frances Barbier. Prod: Flach Film/Soius Production/TF1 Films Production.
Daddy Nostalgie. Script: Colo Tavernier O'Hagan. Dir: Bertrand Tavernier. Phot: Denis Lenoir. Players: Dirk Bogarde, Jane Birkin, Odette Laure. Prod: Cléa Productions/Little Bear/Solyfic.
Les Dames galantes. Script: Jean-Charles Tacchella and Jacques Emmanuel, based on the work by Brantôme. Phot: Dominique Le Rigoleur. Players: Richard Bohringer, Isabella Rossellini, Laura Betti, Robin Renucci, Marie-Christine Barrault. Prod: Gaumont/Cecchi Gori/Cinévideo.
Dancing Machine. Script: Marc Cerrone, Paul-Loup Sulitzer, Loup Durand, Didier Decoin. Dir: Gilles Béhat. Phot: Jose-Luis Alcaine. Players: Alain Delon, Patrick Dupond, Claude Brasseur. Prod: Cité Films/Leda Films.
Dédé. Script and Dir: Jean-Louis Benoit. Phot: Dominique Le Rigoleur. Players: Luc Thuillier, Didier Besace, Hélène Vincent, Yves Afonso. Prod: Septembre Productions.
Docteur M. Script: Sollace Mitchell, Thomas Bauermeister, Claude Chabrol. Dir: Claude Chabrol. Phot: Jean Rabnier. Players: Alan Bates, Jennifer Beals, Jan Nikias. Prod: Nef/Anthea/Clea Productions.
Docteur Petiot. Script: Dominique Garnier, Christian de Chalonge. Dir: Christian de Chalonge. Phot: Patrick Blossier. Players: Michel Serrault. Prod: Sara Films/Philippe Chapelier Degliame.
Farendj. Script: Sabine Prenczina, Barbara Jago. Dir: Sabine Prenczina. Phot: Elisabeth Provoost. Players: Tim Roth, Marie Matheron. Prod: Rivers Films.
Faux et usage de faux. Script: Jean-Marc Roberts, Christel Ega, Laurent Heynemann. Dir: Laurent Heynemann. Players: Philippe Noiret, Robin Ranucci, Laure Killing. Prod: Messine Productions/PCC/TF1 Films/ Ciné Cinq.
La Femme fardée. Script: José Pinheiro, Lou Inglebert, Jean-Jacques Pauvert, Frédéric Fajardie, based on the novel by Françoise Sagan. Dir: José Pinheiro. Phot: Raoul Coutard. Players: Anthony Delon, Jeanne Moreau, André Dussolier, Laura Morante, Jacqueline Maillan. Prod: ATC 3000.
La Fête des pères. Script: Joy Fleury, Pierre Grillet. Phot: Manuel Teran. Players: Thierry Lhermitte, Alain Souchon, Gunilla Karizen. Prod: GPFI/TF1 Films Production.
Feu sur le candidat. Script: Didier Van Cauwelaert. Dir: Agnès Delarive. Phot: Yves Rodallec. Players: Michel Galabru, Patrick Chesnais, Giuliana de Sio. Prod: Cité Film/Capac/Madeleine Films/Ciné Cinq/Clesi Cinematografica/Titanus Produzione.
La Fille des collines. Script: Patrick Laurent, Alain Le Henry, Robin Davis, from the novel "Hill Girl" by Charles Williams. Dir: Robin Davis. Phot: Michel Abramowicz. Players: Florent Pagny, Nathalie Cardone, Tcheky Karyo. Prod: Partner's Production/Hachette Première et Cie./Ciné Cinq/Nickelodeon.

AN AMERICAN IN PARIS

For representation in France and all international markets

THEATRICAL – TELEVISION – VIDEO

Contact BILL HARPER

American-European Entertainments, Inc., 18 Rue Beaujon, 75008 Paris
Tel: (33–1) 4256 4505   Fax: (33–1) 4256 1142

Il y des jours . . . et des lunes. Script and Dir: Claude Lelouch. Phot: Jean-Yves Le Mener. Players: Gérard Lanvin, Patrick Chesnais, Marie-Sophie L., Vincent Lindon, Philippe Léotard. Prod: Films 13/TF1 Films Production.
Isabelle Eberhardt. Script: Ian Pringle and Stephen Sewell. Dir: Ian Pringle. Phot: Manuel Teran. Players: Mathilda May, Tcheky Karyo, Peter O'Toole. Prod: Seon Films/Flach Films/Aramis.
Jean Galmot, aventurier. Script: Daniel Saint Hamon, Anne Théron, Santiago Amigorena, Alain Maline. Dir: Alain Maline. Phot: Walther Van Den Ende. Players: Christophe Malavoy, Belinda Goffe, Jean Michel Martlai, Vincent Martin. Prod: Partner's Production.
Le jeu du renard. Script and Dir: Anne Caprile. Phot: Daniel Gaudry. Players: Pauline Macia, Abel Jores, Bernard Malaterre. Prod: Archimède International Production.
Le Jour des rois. Script: Marie-Claude Treilhou, Noel Simsolo. Dir: Marie-Claude Treilhou. Phot: Jean-Bernard Menoud. Players: Danielle Darrieux, Micheline Presie, Paulette Dubost, Robert Lamoureux. Prod: Films du Losange. TF1.
La Baule les Pins. Script: Diane Kurys, Alain Le Henry. Phot: Giuseppe Lanci. Dir: Diane Kurys. Players: Nathalie Baye, Richard Berry, Zabou, Jean-Pierre Bacri. Prod: Alexandre Films/SGGC/Films A2.
Maman. Script: Simon Michael, Romain Goupil. Dir: Romain Goupil. Phot: Renan Polles. Players: Anémone. Prod: French Production/Générale d'Images/Planètes et Cie.
Le Marie de la coiffeuse. Script: Patrice Leconte and Claude Klotz. Dir: Patrice Leconte. Phot: Eduardo Serra. Players: Jean Rochefort, Anna Gallicna. Prod: Lambart Productions/TF1.

La Messe en si mineur. Script and Dir: Jean-Louis Guillermin. Phot: Jean Badal. Players: Margaux Hemingway, Denis Charvet, Denis Amoyal. Prod: Films de la Concorde.
Miss Missouri. Script: Elie Chouraqui and Fernand Moszkowitcz, freely based on the novel "Amours américaines" by Michel Boujout. Dir: Elie Chouraqui. Phot: Flore Thulliez. Players: Richard Anconina, Helen de Saint Père, Wendy Visser. Prod: Sept Films Cinéma.
Monsieur. Script and Dir: Jean-Philippe Toussaint, based on his novel. Phot: Jean-François Robin. Players: Dominique Gould, Wojtek Pszoniak, Eva Ionesco. Prod: Les Films des Tournelles/Les Films de l'Etang.
Montalvo et l'enfant. Script and Dir: Claude Mourieras, based on the choreographic work by Jean-Claude Gallotta. Phot: Walther Van Den Ende. Players: Mathilde Altaraz, Christophe Delachaux, Robert Seyfried, Jean-Claude Gallotta. Prod: C.D.N. Productions.
Noce blanche. Script and Dir: Jean-Claude Brisseau. Phot: Romain Winding. Players: Vanessa Paradis, Bruno Cremer, Ludmila Mikael, François Négret. Prod: Films du Losange/La Sorcière rouge.
Nuits d'été en ville. Script and Dir: Michel Deville. Phot: Bernard Lutic. Players: Marie Trintignant, Jean-Hugues Anglade. Prod: Elefilm/AAA Productions/Séléna Audiovisuel/Studios Eclair/TSF Productions.
Outremer. Script: Brigitte Rouan, Philippe Le Guay, Christian Rullier, Cédric-Emmanuel Kahn. Dir: Brigitte Rouan. Phot: Dominique Chapuis. Players: Nicole Garcia, Brigitte Rouan, Marianne Basler. Prod: Paradise Productions/Lira Films.
Pacific Palisades. Script: Marion Vernoux. Dir: Bernard Schmitt. Phot: Martial Barrault. Players: Sophie Marceau, Adam Coleman

Claude Berri in Serge Gainsbourg's *Stan the Flasher*

Howard. Prod: Sandor Productions/Bernard Verley Films/Films A2.
Passport. Script: Gueorgui Danelia, Revaz Gabriadze, Alexandre Khait, Constantin Alexandrov. Dir: Gueorgui Danelia. Phot: Vadim Youssov. Player: Gérard Darmon. Prod: Passport Productions.
Pentimento. Script: Tonie Marshall, Sylvie Granotier. Dir: Tonie Marshall. Phot: Pascal Lebègue. Players: Patricia Dinev, Antoine de Caunes, Magali Noel. Prod: Téléma/FR3 Films Production.
Plein fer. Script: Bernard Stora, Vincent Lambert, Mark Princi, from the novel by Serge Martinat. Dir: Josée Dayan. Phot: André Domage. Players: Serge Reggiani, François Négret, Jean-Pierre Bisson, Julien Guiomar, Patrick Bouchitey. Prod: Chrysalide Films.
Le Provincial. Script: Christian Gion, Jean-Louis Richard. Dir: Jean-Jacques Tarbès. Players: Roland Giraud, Gabrielle Lazure, Michel Galabru. Prod: Lapaca Productions.
Rendez-vous au tas de sable. Script: Richard Gotainer, Jean-Pierre Domboy. Dir: Didier Grousset. Phot: Yves Dahan. Players: Richard Gotainer, Thierry Fortineau, Jean-Claude Leguay. Prod: Gérard Mital Productions/Films A2.
Ripoux contre Ripoux. Script: Claude Zidi, Simon Michael, Didier Kaminka. Dir: Claude Zidi. Phot: Jean-Jacques Tarbès. Players: Philippe Noiret, Thierry Lhermitte, Grace de Capitani, Line Renaud. Prod: Films 7/Orly Films/ SEDIF/TF1 Films Production.
Rome-Roméo. Script: Alain Fleischer, Patrick Sandrin. Dir: Alain Fleischer. Phot: Alessandro Pesci. Players: John Hargreaves, Danièle Schirman, Yann Colette. Prod: Arion Productions.
S'en fout la mort. Script: Claire Denis, Jean-Pol Fargeau. Dir: Claire Denis. Phot: Pascal Marti. Players: Alex Descas, Isaach de Bankolé, Jean-Claude Brialy, Solveig Dommartin. Prod: Cinéa/Pyramide/Camera One.
Le Silence d'ailleurs. Script and Dir: Guy Mouyal. Phot: Alain Choquart. Players: Clémentine Célarié, Michel Galabru, Jean-Paul Lillienfeld, Daniel Olbrychski. Prod: Films du Rabb.
Suivez cette avion. Script: Patrice Ambard, Alain Estève. Dir: Patrice Ambard. Phot: François Amado. Players: Lambert Wilson, Isabelle Gélinas, Claude Piéplu. Prod: Top Films/ GPFI/Madeleine Films/Films A2/La Sept.

TOP GROSSING FILMS IN FRANCE: 1989

	Admissions
Rain Man	6,386,000
Indiana Jones and the Last Crusade	5,670,000
Le Grand Bleu	2,750,000
Twins	2,147,000
Batman	2,096,000
Licence to Kill	2,069,000
A Fish Called Wanda	2,048,000
Gorillas in the Mist	2,004,000
The Gods Must Be Crazy II	1,941,000
Trop belle pour toi	1,877,000

Tatie Danielle. Script: Florence Quentin. Dir: Etienne Chatiliez. Phot: Philippe Welt. Players: Tsilia Chelton, Catherine Jacob, Eric Prat, Isabelle Nanty. Prod: Téléma/FR3 Films/Productions du Champ Poirier.
Tom et Lola. Script: Bertrand Arthuys, Christian de Chalonge, Muriel Teodori, from story idea by Luc Goldenberg. Dir: Bertrand Arthuys. Phot: François Catonné. Players: Neil Stubbs, Melodie Collins. Prod: Cinemanuel/Cerito Films/Caroline Productions/EFVE/Orly Films/Zoom 24.
Transit. Script: René Allio, Jean Jourdheuil, from novel by Anna Seghers. Dir: René Allio. Phot: Richard Copans. Players: Sebastien Koch, Claudia Messner, Rüdiger Vogler. Prod: Paris Classics Production/Action Films/SFPC/FR 3/SEPT.
Tumultes. Script: Claire Alexandrakis, Bertrand Van Effenterre. Dir: Bertrand Van Effenterre. Phot: Yves Angelo. Players: Bruno Cremer, Nelly Bourgeaud, Julie Jezequel, Clotilde de Bayser, Laure Marsac. Prod: Mallia Films/Renn Productions/Paradise Films.
Un jeu d'enfant. Script and Dir: Pascal Kané. Phot: Romain Winding. Players: Paul Schmidt, Dominique Lavanant, Laura Morante, Jean Carmet. Prod: Titane Productions.

GERMANY

by Jack Kindred

Although 1990 marks the year that the two German states were united, film production, distribution and exhibition in 1989 and much of 1990 remained separate pending restructuring of the German Democratic Republic's centrally-directed economic system into a free market. While West German distributors and the branches of U.S. majors in the Federal Republic began distributing films in East Germany in July, 1990, other developments in production and exhibition depend on complex political and economic developments. Though restructuring may take place faster than expected, the East German film community still has a long way to go before revision of its system results in an integrated all-Germany film industry.

Any way you look at it, 1989 was a bad year for the German film. On the business side, the market share of German productions was a paltry 16.7%, down from 23.4% in 1988. Of the 79 films produced, only 29 actually appeared on the nation's screens and just six of these accounted for 86% of the market share. On the artistic side, the German film failed to live up to the past glories of the New German Cinema. At the 40th international Film Festival Berlin, the only kudos for Germany went to Michael Verhoeven as best director for his black comedy **The Nasty Girl** (*Das Schreckliche Mädchen*). And only Jörg Graser's grim aftermath of the Holocaust, **Abraham's Gold** in the Un Certain Regard section and Andrzej Wajda's film biography **Korczak** screened out of competition were selected for the 1990 Cannes festival.

The five most successful German films, those luring more than one million patrons through the wickets, were by and large pure entertainment, eschewing turgid political, social or philosophical themes designed to keep the public out of the theatres in droves. The third Otto Waalkes comedy, **Otto – Der Ausserfriesicher**, with 3,585,645 visitors was on a box-office par with the American blockbuster *A Fish Called Wanda*. **Asterix–Operation Finklestein**, a

Franco-German co-produced feature-length animated cartoon based on the popular comic strip, attracted some 2.2 million visitors. **Autumn Milk** (*Herbstmilch*), a "Heimat" film based on the true story of a young Bavarian woman forced to take over management of a farm during the Second World War, was a surprise hit, with more than two million admissions. The romantic comedy **With the Next Man Everything Will Be Different** (*Beim nächsten Mann wird alles anders*) pulled in slightly over a million patrons and the ballet film **Anna**, also topped the million mark.

Although not exactly a flop with 755,201 admissions, producer Bernd Eichinger's **Last Exit to Brooklyn**, whose production story was featured in last year's I.F.G., proved a disappointment. The $18 million film based on Hubert Selby Jr.'s brutal novel depicting the seamy side of life during the 1950's on the Brooklyn waterfront was originally shot in English with an eye on the global market. That the West German market is too small to recoup the production costs of a high-budget film is one of the facts confronting enterprising producers like Eichinger.

Taking a cue from Eichinger, who has produced such successful megabudget films as *The Neverending Story* and *The Name of the Rose*, another "think big" producer Dieter Geissler put the finishing touches on **The Neverending Story II** in autumn, 1989. Geissler initiated the $28 million budget special effects project based on Michael Ende's best-selling novel after Eichinger showed no interest in continuing the fantasy epic in celluloid form. Shot in English at Bavaria Film with an Oscar-winning crew handling special effects, production design and f/x animatronics, the dubbed German version is set for a fall release in 1990.

Producer-director Peter Fleischmann, whose real talent appears to be raising budget funds, took years to put together the $17 million French-Soviet-German co-production **Hard To Be a God** only to have it turn out to be the superflop of 1989. Based on the futurist novel by the Russian brothers Arkadi and Boris Strugatzki, it pulled a mere 116,521 people into the theatres. The science-fiction film was shot in English near Yalta in the Soviet Union with a German-Russian crew and an international cast.

The Adventures of Baron Munchausen, a German-financed film with a German producer Thomas Schühly, ranks seventh on the 1989 top ten box-office list of domestic films. Although it attracted more than 220,000 viewers, measured by its overrun budget of $50 million, *Munchausen* can also be relegated to the superflop category. Many Germans could not help comparing it negatively to the 1943 Ufa classic *Münchausen* starring Hamburg film idol Hans Albers, which has had repeated exposure on TV in recent years.

Local Film Awards

Perhaps the 1990 Deutsche Filmpreis (German Film Awards) shed some light on the abysmal state of the German film. At a June ceremony in Berlin, *Last Exit to Brooklyn* received the 1990 Golden Film Ribbon top prize, which carried with it a cash premium of $475,000, one of the ways in which the Bonn Federal government subsidises film projects. Actor-director Klaus Maria Brandauer's **Georg Elser – Einer aus Deutschland** and director Bernhard Wicki's **The Spider's Web** (*Das Spinnennetz*) received Silver Film Ribbons including cash prizes of $350,000. None was an out and out critical success and, with the possible exception of *Last Exit*, they fared poorly at the box-office.

Most of the films screened in the German section at the Cannes likewise made little impact on the German box-office scene, though some like *The Nasty Girl*, *Korczak* and Hark Bohm's *Crossing Borders* received critic's praise. The list of el floppos included Reinhard Hauff's *Blue Eyed*, Horant Hohlfeld's *Carmen on Ice*, and Peter Bringmann's *African Timber*. Though not screened at Cannes, Percy Adlon's latest comedy *Rosalie Goes Shopping* also failed to live up to the success of its predecessor, *Bagdad Café*, both shot in English in the U.S.A.

Despite some $60 million worth of production subsidies year after year from the Federal Film Board (FFA), television, the Bonn government and city and state film commissions, the malaise of the West German film is chronic. Apart from the financial aspects, even the erstwhile awards bestowed on the world's film festivals on such renowned New German Cinema directors as Volker Schlöndorff, Werner Herzog, Wim Wenders and the late Rainer Werner Fassbinder are a thing of the past.

While it is universally recognised that, like the French and Italian, the West German industry cannot survive without subsidies – among other factors, the domestic market is too small to recoup production and release costs of most film projects – it has become increasingly evident in recent years that the present subsidy system simply does not work.

In 1970, the market share of German films still amounted to 39.2%. A decade later it had dropped to an all-time low of 9.3%, and in the 1980's the average was 17.2%. In view of the hard facts, the failure of the system can hardly be refuted. Only true believers like directors Jeanine Meerapfel, who even calls for "complete subsidisation" (doubtless at taxpayers' expense), uphold the system. Support also comes from "vested interest" producers who make a good living through high salaries and lavish promotion costs, whose films never find a distributor and are never seen in the cinemas.

Heavy Subsidies

Since its inception in 1967 to rescue the film industry from the TV peril, the FFA

Oliver Stokowski in *Schatten der Wüste*, released through Filmverlag der Autoren

has meted out some $260 million in subsidies, largely for film production. The principal source of the FFA funds is a 3% levy on ticket sales and a smaller levy on video rentals and sales. There is a perennial hue and cry from a certain chauvinistic minority against films from the U.S. majors, on grounds that commercial Hollywood productions undermine the nation's cultural heritage. Ironically, however, the FFA tithe on admissions comes largely from American films, which in 1989 had a 62% share of the market.

Besides the FFA subsidies, West Germany's two public TV networks, the ARD and ZDF, have pumped more than $100 million into co-production financing, in return for broadcasting rights. On the surface, they appear to be helpmates for the production side of the industry. Hardly any films are made in Germany without TV participation. Nevertheless, the networks demand the rights in perpetuity. Financially hard-pressed producers have little choice but to accept the broadcasters' terms, which robs them of the important TV return market and potential financing for new film projects. As Bavaria Film production head Günter Rohrbach pointed out to a symposium, TV participation. Nevertheless, the networks demand the rights in perpetuity. Financially hard-pressed producers have little choice but to accept the broadcaster's terms, which robs them of the important TV rerun market and potential financing for new film projects. As Bavaria Film production head Günter Rohrbach pointed out at a symposium, TV representatives are on all-important committees approving projects for subsidies, meaning that the networks virtually decide what film projects are to materialise.

With the Filmförderungsgesetz (Film Aid Law) up for revision (new regulations on subsidies are to go into effect in 1993), reform proposals from diverse sources have already been put forth in the media. Herbert Strate, director of the Haubtverband Deutsche Filmtheater (The Association of German Film Theaters) and FFA board member, called for "a rethinking of the Filmförderungsgesetz." Rohrbach advocates fewer film projects with more substantial financing, since spreading funds available over 60 ro 70 productions results in lower budgets and in the end films with little prospects of box-office success. Bavaria Film's foreign sales executive Benno Nowotny says what the industry needs is a yearly production at most of 50 films and a 25% share of the market. Others like film-maker Hark Bohm and critic Wolf Donner, former head of Berlin's international Film Festival, have criticised the subsidy committees. The debate is bound to intensify as the various industrial executives, producers, distributors' and exhibitors' associations, individual film-makers and politicians meet to hammer out a new and hopefully more effective film aid law. Their recommendations will subsequently be submitted to the Interior Ministry in Bonn for approval and implementation.

Das Schreckliche Mädchen (The Nasty Girl)

Script and Direction: Michael Verhoeven. Photography: Axel de Roche. Editing: Barbara Hennings. Music: Mike Hertung, Elmar Schloter, Billy Gorlt, Lydie Auvray. Sound: Haymo H. Heyder. Art Direction: Hubert Popp. Costumes: Ute Truthmann. Players: Lena Stolze, Monika Baumgartner, Michael Gahr, Fred Stillkrauth, Elisabeth Bertram, Robert Giggenback, Michael Guillaume, Karen Thaler, Hans-Reinhard Müller, Barbara Gallauner. Produced by Sentana Filom Production. 92 mins.

Just in time for all the German reunification hoopla, along comes nasty old Michael Verhoeven with a viciously funny film accusing his fellow West Germans of being a bunch of incorrigible hypocrites who find no difficulty in being Nazi stooges yesterday, liberal-minded democrats today and God only knows what tomorrow.

This well-crafted picture promises to be a crowd-pleaser even on its home turf, brightened by the timeliness of Verhoeven's scathing examination of the Teutonic psyche. The world is asking whether the Germans have learned from two world wars. Verhoeven's answer: Don't count on it.

His plot is based on the true story of a teenage girl in Bavaria a few years back who wanted to write an essay on the Nazis' impact on her town. She quickly became the object of scorn from townspeople who had a surprising amount to conceal. Lena Stolze as the movie's "nasty girl" deftly handles her character's development from winsome girlhood to maturity. A strong supporting cast convinces the audience that loving friends can become bitter foes when cornered.

Verhoeven is an old hand at making his fellow Germans squirm. His 1970 anti-Vietnam film *O.K.* was rejected by the Berlin Film Festival jury as anti-American – blowing the Berlinale wide open. His 1982 movie about Nazi resistance fighters, *The White Rose (Die Weisse Rose)*, spawned a national debate over some wartime "treason" convictions that were never revoked.

Verhoeven makes it clear he wants his film to apply to any German town. To do that, he has departed from his usual straight-forward storytelling approach to create a surreal setting where living-room divans careen through a town market square, and the major's office doubles as a nursing home deathbed.

Ernest Gill

Herzlich Willkommen (Crossing Borders)

Script: Hark Bohm with Dorothée Schön from the novel by Walter Kempowski. Direction: Hark Bohm. Photography: Hermann Fahr. Music: Jens Peter Ostendorf. Sound: Richard Burowski. Art Direction: Christian Bussmann. Costumes: Birgit Missal. Players: Uwe Bohm, Barbara Auer, David Bohm, Hark Bohm, Anna Thalbach, Eva-Maria Hagen, Micheal Gwisdek, Peter Franke, Heinz Hoening. Produced by ZDF-TV and Hamburger Kinokompanie Production. 123 mins.

With this stark portrayal of postwar Germany, Hark Bohm puts himself at the lead of a new breed of West German directors trying to shake intellectual dust off film-making here and produce old-fashioned human-interest pictures. This latest film may not prove as popular at the box-office as his 1987 *Romeo and Juliet* takeoff, *Yasemin*, because it offers less sheer entertainment. But it is easily his most well-rounded film.

"Herzlich Willkommen" are the words that greet the film's protagonist (Bohm's

Barbara Auer and Uwe Bohm in *Herzlich Willkommen*

actor son Uwe) as he arrives in West Germany after fleeing the East in the mid-1950's. A former political prisoner in East Germany, the new arrival's first job is at a home for wayward children in a converted castle. The welcome is anything but cordial from the teenage thugs and the holdover Nazi who runs the joint. Our hero's efforts to save a difficult young boy from succumbing to the system, and a budding love affair with an attractive teacher, form the fulcrum for the plot.

On a deeper level, of course, West Germany itself is the bratty youth who secretly wants to be loved and to amount to something. Bohm skilfully develops this metaphor toward a baptism under fire – gunfire – along a river dividing the two Germanys.

The elements of humour which brightened *Yasemin* do not work this time around, and the occasional slapstick bit is distracting. The love interest and the relationship between the child and the young man are handled well. The musical soundtrack by Jens Peter Ostendorf gives the movie just the right touch for period and mood. The other Bohm son, young David, as the lovable brat, is the best of a strong crew of young thespians.

Ernest Gill

Crowds at the Filmfest München, with Sam Fuller (below) surrounded by German fans

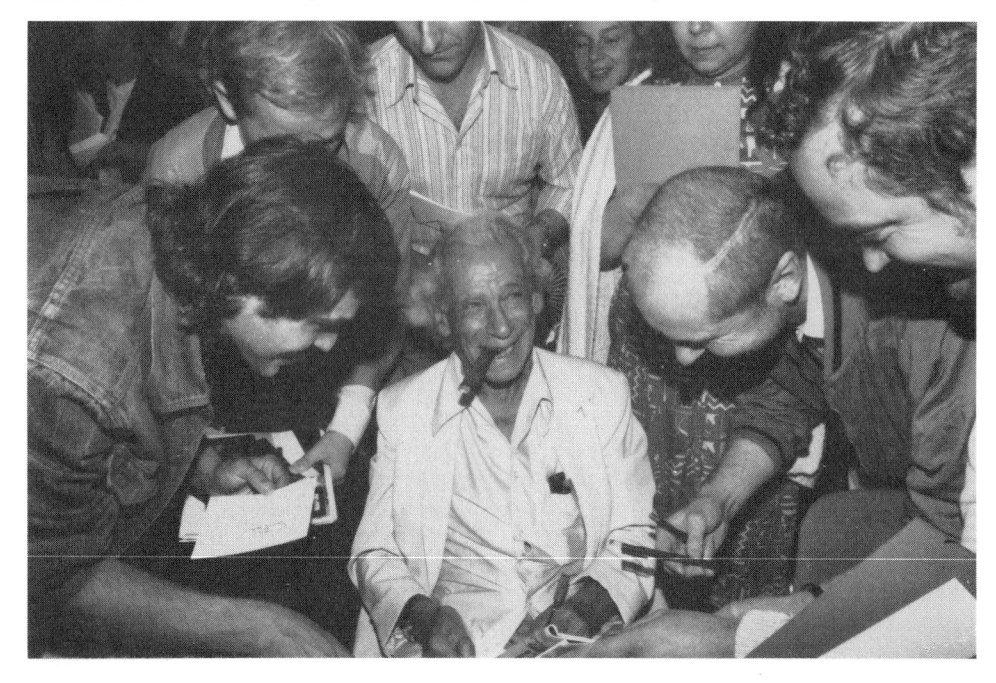

Last Exit to Brooklyn

Script: Desmond Nakano, from the novel by Hubert Selby Jr. Direction: Uli Edel. Photography: Stefan Czapsky. Editing: Peter Przygodda. Music: Mark Knopfler. Art Direction: David Chapman. Costumes: Carol Oditz. Sound: Danny Michael, Milan Bor. Makeup: Kathryn Bihr. Production manager: Dieter Meyer. Players: Stephen Lang, Jennifer Jason Leigh, Burt Young, Peter Dobson, Jerry Orbach, Stephen Baldwin, Alexis Arquette, Cameron Johann. Produced by Neue Constantin Film Production with Bavaria Film and Allied Filmmakers. 102 mins.

West Germany's latest slumming expedition into the hinterlands of American society, *Last Exit to Brooklyn* is a bleak tour of urban hell. Bernd Eichinger's $16 million production of Hubert Selby Jr.'s controversial 1964 novel seemed an unlikely choice for screen translation, although the story's dark, oppressive social vision must have struck a quasi-expressionist chord.

Eichinger, screenwriter Desmond Nakano and director Uli Edel have succeeded in presenting a conscientious illustration that is well acted and technically impeccable, but it doesn't hold a scalpel to the lacerating torrential prose that made the book so cringingly urgent.

For the spectator, the film's abiding obstacle is an unsavoury gallery of largely contemptible characters who are at best pitiable and at worst have not developed beyond Neanderthal awareness. Edel, whose international reputation was made on the 1980 teen drama *Christiane F.*, proves himself an accomplished professional ripe for Hollywood assignments.

Optioned by a number of film-makers since its publication (notably Stanley Kubrick and Brian De Palma), the novel was long regarded as unfilmable, in part because of its short-story structure and large cast of characters. This obstacle largely has been surmounted in Nakano's well-structured screenplay, which sets time and place, introduces the players and interweaves their destinies with economical story logic.

Action is set in a working-class section of Brooklyn in 1952, close by the Navy yards where young Americans are embarking for the Korean War. Residents, however, couldn't care less about happenings beyond their own back yards – many engaged in a bitter six-month strike against a local factory. A sense of stagnation intensifies personal and group discontents and passions. The film's spectacular centrepiece is a well-staged riot pitting strikers against police when factory management uses scab labour to break the picket lines.

Apart from the trite Christian symbolism, some heavy social satire and occasional portentous touches (such as smoking manholes à la Martin Scorsese), Edel's direction is relatively restrained. Stefan Czapsky's lensing makes evocative nocturnal use of the notorious Red Hook section of Brooklyn, where most of the exteriors were filmed at night in conditions just as dangerous as those in the book.

Edel is adept with his native American cast, notably Lang, Leigh and Arquette (whose screen time is unfortunately curtailed). Orbach is fine as the unscrupulous union leader, while Peter Dobson, Steve Baldwin and Cameron Johann are competent in supporting roles.

Lenny Borger

Jennifer Jason Leigh in *Last Exit to Brooklyn*

Otto Der Ausserfriesische

Script: Bernd Eilert, Robert Gernhardt, Peter Knorr, Otto Waalkes. Direction: Otto Waalkes, Marijan Vajda. Photography: Egon Werdin. Music: Thomas Kukuck, Christoph Leis-Bendorff. Players: Otto Waalkes, Barbara May, Volker Kleinert, Hans-Peter Hattwachs, Wolfgang Zerlett. Produced by Rialto/Russel Video & Audio Production. 92 mins.

This film is the third vehicle for West Germany's most popular standup comic, straw-haired beanpole Otto Waalkes. There's no good material in this movie, which attempts to be a spoof of well-known films and TV series. The title, itself, is a pun on the German version of *E.T. – The ExtraTerrestrial*, and translates very loosely as "Otto - the Far Out Frisian."

The film has little appeal for filmgoers outside Germany, due to its reliance on in-jokes stemming from regional German stereotypes. (Germans tell Frisian jokes the way the English tell Irish jokes or Americans Polish ones.) The threadbare plot involves a bumbling attempt by a yokel (Waalkes) to save his pastoral homeland from environmental destruction at the hands of the military industrial complex. His fumble-footed crusade takes him to Florida for an encounter on the set of *Miami Vice*. He winds up on a tennis court with Wimbledon champ Steffi Graf.

It is painfully obvious that Waalkes and his team of writers assumed that the star's mere presence would ensure laughs. They've skimped on the material, which is dated and often just dumb. Too bad, since Waalkes is a gifted comic who is capable of much more than what he delivers this time out.

Ernest Gill

Recent and Forthcoming Films

Abrahams Gold. Script: Jörg Graser. Dir: Graser. Phot: Henning Stegmüller. Players: Hanna Schygulla, Günther Maria Halmer, Daniela Schötz, H.C. Blech. Prod: Avista Film/Pro-ject/Adanos/ZDF.
Der Achte Tag (The Eighth Day). Script: Reinhard Münster. Dir: Münster. Phot: Axel Block. Players: Katharina Thalbach, Hans Christian Blech, Hannelore Elsner. Prod: Von Vietinghoff/WDR.
The Adventures of Pico and Columbus (Animation). Script: Scott Santoro. Dir: Michael Schoemann. Phot: Bernd Deventer, Günter Redl, Andre Katzenwadl, Lutz Gruenenwald. Prod: MS Film/ZDF/Bavaria/CineVox.
Anna Göldin – Letzte Hexe (Anna Göldin – Last Witch). Script: Gertrud Pinkus. Dir: Pinkus. Phot: Franz Rath. Players: Cornelia Kempers, R. Vogler, Dominique Horwitz, Ursula Andermatt. Prod: Alpha Film.
Bronsteins Kinder (Bronsteins Children). Script and Dir: Jerzy Kawalerowicz. Phot: Withold Sobocinski. Players: Maximilian Wigger, Mario Adorf, Lena Stolze, Hans Korte. Prod: Novafilm/ZDF.
Café de l'Union. Script: Dominikus Probst. Dir: Probst. Phot: Lutz Konermann. Players: Mercedes Echerer, Herbert Tratnigg, Marc Arn. Prod: Volcano M/BR/SWF.
Dr. M. Script: Thomas Bauermeister, Claude Chabrol. Dir: Claude Chabrol. Phot: Jean Ralbier. Players: Jan Niklas, Alan Bates, François Cluzet, Jean-Louis Trintignant, Jennifer Beals. Prod: NED/Roco/ZDF.
Eine Frau Namens Harry (Harry and Harriet). Script: Vivian Naefe. Dir: Cyril Frankel. Phot: Heinz Hölscher. Players: Thomas Gottschalk, Fiona Fullerton, Heinz Hönig. Prod: Lisa/Roxy/K.S. Film.
Erfolg (Success). Script and Dir: Franz Seitz from the book by Lion Feuchtwanger. Phot: Rudolf Blahacek. Players: Jan Niklas, Franziska Walser, Peter Simonischek, Martin Benrath, Ernst Jacobi, Mathieu Carrière. Prod: Franz Seitz Film Produktion.
Feuer, Eis und Dynamit (Fire, Ice and Dynamite). Script: Tony Williamson, Willy Bogner. Dir: Willy Bogner. Phot: Charlie Steinberger. Players: Roger Moore, Shari Belafonte, Uwe Ochsenknecht. Prod: Willy Bogner Film.
Gründ. Script: Mathias Wilfert. Dir: Wilfert. Phot: Ulrich Gambke. Players: Elisabeth Niederer, Werner Asam, Drago Ragotin, Olivia Grigolli. Prod: HFF/Salinas/Bloria Burkert.

Geliebte Milena (Beloved Milena). Script and Dir: Vera Belmont. Photo: Dietrich Lohmann. Players: Valery Kaprisky, Stacy Keach, Philip Anglim, Gudrun Landgrebe. Prod: Bavaria/Stephane Films/FR 3/BR.
Hallooh Sisters. Script: Richard Hey, Lisa Kristwaldt. Dir: Ottokar Runze. Phot: Michael Epp. Players: Gisela May, Ilse Werner, Harald Juhnke. Prod: Ottokar Runze/ZDF.
Hard Days – Hard Nights. Script and Dir: Horst Königstein. Phot: Klaus Brix. Players: Wigald Boning, Annette Hörmann, Roland Schäfer, Helmut Griem. Prod: Provobis/Project/NDR.
Korczak. Script: Agnieszka Holland. Dir: Andrzej Wajda. Phot: Robby Müller. Players: Wojciech Pszoniak, Ewa Dalkowska, Marzena Trybala. Prod: Regina Ziegler/Filmstudio Perspektywa/Telmar Film International/Erato.
Labyrint. Script: Hans Jörg Weyhmüller. Dir: Jaromil Jires. Phot: Igor Luther. Players: Maximilian Schell, Christopher Chaplin. Prod: Art Oko/SR/Barrandov.
Malina. Script: Elfriede Jelinek. Dir: Werner Schroeter. Phot: Elfie Mikesch. Players: Isabelle Huppert, Mathieu Carrière, Can Toquay. Prod: Kuchenreuther Filmproduktion/ZDF.
Die Ministraten (The Alter Boys). Script: Wolfram Paulus. Dir: Paulus. Phot: Volker Tittle. Players: Christoph Schnell, Gerald Bachler. Prod: Hermes/BR/Infratel.
Murder East/Murder West. Script: Ted Whitehead. Dir: Peter K. Smith. Phot: Thomas Mauch. Players: Jeroen Krabbé, Susannah Hamilton, Joanne Pearce.
Passagier Faber (Passenger Faber). Script: Rudi Wurlitzer, Volker Schlöndorff from the Max Frisch novel 'Homo Faber.' Dir: Volker Schlöndorff. Phot: Pierre Lhomme. Players: Sam Shepard, Barbara Sukowa, Julie Delpy. Prod: Bioskop/Argos/Hellas.
Rama Dama – Im Jahr der Trümmerfrau (In the Year of the Rubble-clearing Woman). Script: Martin Kluger, Joseph Vilsmaier. Dir: Joseph Vilsmaier. Phot: Joseph Vilsmaier. Players: Dana Vavrova, Werner Stocker, Renate Grosser, Hans Schuler.
Reise ohne Wiederkehr (Journey without Return). Script and Dir: Alexandra von Grote. Phot: Heinz Pehlke. Players: Gabriele Osburg, Mark McGann, Ulrich Matschoss, Bruce Payne, Mathew Burton.
Die Rückkehr (The Return). Script and Dir:

Margarethe von Trotta. Phot: Domino Tenicolli. Players: Agnes Fink, Barbara Sukowa, Stefania Sandrelli, Sami Frey.
Spieler (Gambler). Script: Christoph Fromm. Dir: Dominik Graf. Phot: Klaus Eichhammer. Players: Peter Lohmeyer, Hansa Czypionka, Anna Dobra, Joachim Kemmer, Anthony Dawson. Prod: Bavaria/ZDF.
Staub vor der Sonne (Dust in Front of the Sun). Script and Dir: Petra Katharina Wagner. Phot: Izzet Akay. Players: Eric Stappenbeck, Andreas Gülcke, Johanna Karl-Lory. M. Bohm. Prod: Lichtblick.
Super High Score. Script: Gustav Ehmck, Peter Lawrence. Dir: Gustav Ehmck. Phot: Gerard Vandenberg. Players: Gudrun Landgrebe, James Brolin.
Taxandria. Script: Alain Robbe-Grillet. Dir: Raoul Servais. Phot: Gilberto Azeudo. Players: Armin Mueller-Stahl, Elliot Speals, Katja Studt.
Prod: Bibo TV & Film Productions/Iblis/SPFC.
Tod Eines Schülers (Death of a Schoolboy). Script and Dir: Peter Patzak. Phot: Igor Luther. Players: Reuben Pillsbury, Christopher Chaplin.
Under Cover. Script: Günter Schütter. Dir: Dominik Graf. Phot: Klaus Eichhammer. Players: Heinz Hönig, Werner Stocker, Meg Tilly, Hannes Jaenicke. Prod: Janusch Kozminski Filmproduktion.
Until the End of the World. Script: Wim Wenders, Peter Carey. Dir: Wim Wenders: Phot: Robby Müller. Players: William Hurt, Max von Sydow, Solveig Dommartin, Jeanne Moreau, Rüdiger Vogler, Sam Neill, John Lurie, Chico. Prod: Road Movies/Argos Films.

JACK KINDRED is head of the Variety bureau in the Federal Republic of Germany, and bases in Munich.

TOP GROSSING FILMS IN THE F.R.G.: 1989

	Admissions
Rain Man	5,748,668
A Fish Called Wanda	3,637,106
Otto – Der Ausserfriesische	3,585,645
Indiana Jones and the Last Crusade	3,518,900
Licence to Kill	2,467,666
The Naked Gun	2,447,727
Cocktail	2,407,392
The Land Before Time	2,289,573
Asterix – Operation Hinkelstein	2,235,880
Herbstmilch	2,184,959

Producers

Allianz Filmproduktion GmbH
Leibnitzstr. 60
1000 Berlin 12
Tel: (30) 323 9011
Fax (30) 323 1693

Alcor film-und Fernseh-Produktions GmbH
Schweigerstr. 2
8000 Munich 90
Tel: (89) 66 1094-99
Fax (89) 651 7881

Anthea Film GmbH
Widenmayerstr. 4
8000 Munich 22
Tel: (89) 226 194
Fax (89) 221 251

Alpha Entertainment
Haselburg str. 14
8000 Munich 90
Tel: (89) 642 1588
Fax (89) 54 39 82

Bavaria Film GmbH
Bavariafilmplatz 7
8022 Geiselgastig/Munich

Tel: (89) 6499 2389
Fax (89) 649 2507

BioSkop-Film GmbH
Türkenstr. 91/111
8000 Munich 40
Tel: (89) 394 987
Fax (89) 396 820

CCC Filmkunst GmbH
Verlängerte Dammstr. 16
1000 Berlin 20
Tel: (30) 334 200–1
Fax (30) 334 0418

CineVox Film GmbH
Bavaria Filmplatz 7
8022 Geiselgasteig
Tel: (89) 649 541
Fax (89) 791 2164

Delta Film GmbH
Otto Suhr-Allee 59
1000 Berlin 10
Tel: (30) 342 4075
Fax (30) 342 5082

Manfred Durniok Produktion
Hausotterstr. 36
1000 Berlin 51
Tel: (30) 491 8045
Fax (30) 491 4066

Impuls Film
Grazerstr. 20
3000 Hanover 81
Tel: (511) 835 001
Fax (511) 838 6253

Hermes Film Gmbh
Kaiserplatz 7
8000 Munich 40
Tel: (89) 394 368

Lisa Film GmbH
Wildenmayerstr. 48
8000 Munich 22
Tel: (89) 227 195
Fax (89) 291 156

Mondada Film
Klausenerstr. 19
8000 Munich 90
Tel: (89) 692 5884
Fax (89) 691 6709

Neue Constantin Film GmbH
Kaiserstr. 39
8000 Munich 40
Tel: (89) 3860 9221/2
Fax (89) 38609 242

Oko-Film GmbH
Mauerkircherstr. 3
8000 Munich 80
Tel: (89) 987 666

Olga Film GmbH
Tengstr. 16
8000 Munich 40
Tel: (89) 271 2635
Fax (89) 272 5768

Primodessa Film GmbH
Cuvillierstr. 8
8000 Munich 40
Tel: (89) 982 568
Fax (89) 982 8506

Studio Hamburg
Tonndorfer Hauptstr. 90
2000 Hamburg 70
Tel: (40) 6688-0
Fax (40) 665 601, (40)6688 4370

Roxy-Film GmbH
Schützenstr. 1
8000 Munich 2
Tel: (89) 555 341

Rialto Film GmbH
Bismarckstr. 108
1000 Berlin 12
Tel: (30) 310 000-0

Tele-München GmbH
Kaufingerstr. 25
8000 Munich 2
Tel: (89) 296 661
Fax (89) 227 875

Vision Film GmbH
Kurfürstenplatz 4
8000 Munich 40
Tel: (89) 390 025
Fax (89) 395 569

Von Vietinghoff Filmproduktion
Potsdamerstr. 199
1000 Berlin 30
Tel: (30) 216 8931

Regina Ziegler Filmproduktion
Budapeststr. 35
1000 Berlin 30
Tel: (30) 261 8071
Fax (30) 262 8213

Distributors

Ascot Filmverleih GmbH
St. Annastr. 16
8000 Munich 22
Tel: (89) 29 69 95
Fax (89) 33 18 39

Columbia Tri-Star Filmgesellschaft mbH
Ickstattstr. 1
8000 Munich 5
Tel: (89) 23 69-0
Fax (89) 26 43 80

Concorde Filmverleih GmbH
Widenmayerstr. 5/6
8000 Munich 22
Tel: (89) 22 07 44
Fax (89) 29 64 50

Delta Filmverleih GmbH & Co KG
Rosenheimerstr. 2
8000 Munich 80
Tel: (89) 48 30 35-7
Fax (89) 48 36 52

FIFIGE Hamburgische Filmeikaufsgesellschaft GmbH-AG Kino
Allendeplatz 3
2000 Hamburg 13
Tel: (40) 44 40 06
Fax (89) 41 85 71

Futura/Filmverlag GmbH
Rambergstr. 5
8000 Munich 40
Tel: (89) 38 170-1
Fax (89) 38 17 00 20

Highlight Film Verleih GmbH
Herkomerplatz 2
8000 Munich 80
Tel: (89) 92 69 66 02
Fax (89) 98 15 43

Impuls Film
Grazerstr. 10
3000 Hanover 81

Tel: (0511) 83 50 01
Fax (0511) 838 6253

Jugend Verleih GmbH
Lietzenburgerstr. 44
D-1000 Berlin 30
Tel: (30) 219 9010
Fax (30) 219 90111

Metropol Filmverleih GmbH
Viktoriastr. 34
8000 Munich 40
Tel: (89) 39 30 96
Fax (89) 39 63 03

NEF 2 Filmverleih GmbH
Erhardtstr. 8
8000 Munich 40
Tel: (89) 201 1747
Fax (89) 201 1634

Neue Constantin Film GmbH & Co. Verleih KG
Kaiserstr. 39
8000 Munich 40
Tel: (89) 38 60 90
Fax (89) 38 60 92 42

Scotia International Filmverleih GmbH Deutschland
Possartsts. 14
8000 Munich 80
Tel: (89) 41 30 90–
Fax (89) 470 6320

Senator Film Verleih GmbH
Kaiserstr. 35
8000 Munich 40
Tel: (89) 381 9030
Fax (89) 3819 0326

Tobis Film Verleih GmbH
Bismarckstr. 108
1000 Berlin 12
Tel: (30) 310 0050
Fax (30) 3100 0559

Transit Film GmbH
Dachauer Str. 35
8000 Munich 2
Tel: (89) 55 52 61
Fax (89) 59 61 22

20th Century Fox of Germany GmbH
Hainer Weg 37–53
6000 Frankfurt
Tel: (69) 60 90 20
Fax (69) 62 77 16

Warner Bros. Film GmbH
Rosenheimerstr. 143b
8000 Munich 80
Tel: (89) 418 0090
Fax (89) 4180 0945

Useful Addresses

Verband der Filmverleiher e.V (VDF)
(*Assn. of Distributors*)
Langenbeckstr. 9
6200 Wiesbaden
Tel: (6121) 1405–0
Fax (6121) 140512

Hauptverband Deutscher Filmtheater e.V (HDF)
(*Assn of German Exhibitors*)
Langenbeckstr. 9
Postfach 2927
6200 Wiesbaden
Tel: (6121) 30 66 60
Fax (6121) 37 64 05

Spitzenorganisation der Filmwirtschaft e.V (SP10)
(*Film Industry Trade Organisation*)
Langenbeckstr. 9
6200 Wiesbaden
Tel: (6121) 1727–0
Fax (6121) 17 27 39

Filmförderungsanstalt (FFA)
(*Federal Film Board*)
Postfach 301808
1000 Berlin 301
Tel: (30) 261 6006
Fax (30) 262 8976

Export Union
Türkenstr. 93
8000 Munich 40
Tel: (89) 39 00 95
Fax (89) 39 52 23

GREECE

by B. Samantha Stenzel

The formation of a conservative administration after the April election ended eight years of socialist rule. After three elections in less than a year and a series of shaky coalition governments, the weary populace looked forward to a period of relative calm.

On the other hand, an austerity package was implemented immediately to help cut the 17% annual inflation rate (three times the EC average) and to reduce a current massive account deficit of over $1 billion. The grim economic situation does not seem to have greatly altered the life style or spending habits of the Greeks, perhaps due to a thriving 'black market economy.'

All forms of entertainment, including video, have suffered from competition from Hellenic Radio and Television (ERT), retransmission of satellite broadcasts, and more significantly by the launching of several private TV stations, signalling the end of the state monopoly. Distributors reported a 20–30% drop in ticket sales this season, following the pattern of previous years.

Hardest hit were cinemas which had not been renovated. 90% of central Athens cinemas have Dolby or an equivalent stereo system and most have been renovated. No multiplexes exist in Athens nor have plans for any been announced. A modern Greek tragedy struck Spantzos Film when its historical Ideal cinema was destroyed by fire at the beginning of the year, one year after a complete facelift. Original plans for a twin were scrapped because the cinema is too small. A new cinema is being built on the site at the cost of almost $1 million.

Overcoming the Slump

Distributors have attempted to overcome the slump with experimentation in booking. ELKE put *Dead Poets Society*, its biggest hit ever and possibly the biggest grosser in Greek history (over 300,000 tickets sold), into a continuous run for several cinemas for almost four months. "People are ready for the extended run, a system never used here before," said ELKE head George Michaelides. Spentzos Film releases *Cinema Paradiso* and *My Left Foot* also were held over.

The 100 or so open-air cinemas struggled for survival. Many came close to locking their doors due to extremely poor business during the World Cup matches. Theodore Rigas, president of the Open Air Exhibitors Union, is leading the lobby for government aid for the quaint establishments located in vacant lots or rooftops at which customers are usually seated on folding chairs. "They are an Athenian institution and need to be subsidised in order to continue," said Rigas.

In January a long-awaited law was passed returning up to 55% of the 12% tax on cinema tickets to exhibitors booking an agreed amount of Greek films. Domestic films fizzled at the box-office while American movies continued to top the charts. Cinema admission was raised to 600–700 drachmas ($3.80–$4.50).

B. SAMANTHA STENZEL is a Chicagoan who has resided in Athens for the past decade. She is the Variety Athens correspondent, Cinema Editor for The Athenian Magazine and organises seminars and film programmes at cultural centres and schools.

from FILMS GREECE

GREEK FILM CENTRE
10, Panepistimiou Avenue
106 71 Athens
Tel. 363.17.33 - 363.45.86
Telex: 222614 GFC
Fax: 361.43.36

Still from Nikos Antonakos's *Farther Right than the Right*

Production Declines

Local production level dropped and the Greek Film Centre (GFC) announced in spring that its board of directors was unable to proceed with all of the 23 films approved. Yiannis Tzannetakis, former Prime Minister recently appointed Minister of Culture, had not yet announced the new budget for 1990 at presstime, but it had dropped since the tenure of former actress Melina Marcouri as Minister of Culture. It is expected that another drop in the budget will occur.

In 1988, 530 million drachmas ($3.7 million) was allotted while in 1989 the sum had been reduced to 450 million drachmas ($2.8 million). The largest share of the funds are invested in financing films from 20-50% of each budget. Hellenic Radio and Television contributed over $1 million under a co-production agreement, with an average budget running about 50-60 million drachmas ($320-380,000).

Manos Zacharias, although of leftist orientation, had not been asked to resign as president of Board of Directors of the GFC under the New Democracy conservative government. It seems likely he will serve out the remainder of his term until June, 1991.

Zachorias has admitted to mistakes made by the GFC and has vowed to bridge the gap between "artistic and commercial films." The GFC commissioned a public opinion survey to gauge audience preferences and its results will be announced next spring.

Hellas Film was launched this year to promote Greek films abroad. George Kaloyeropoulos is the GFC representative in New York and Munich-based Export Films Bischoff handles worldwide sales. Voula Georgakakou, head of sales and promotion, continued to work tirelessly, maintaining a high profile at GFC stands in foreign festivals, especially Cannes and Berlin.

Top Prizes Abandoned

At the awards presentation of the 30th Thessaloniki Film Festival, the nine-member jury announced to a stunned audience that the three top prizes for Best Film, Best Director and Best Screenplay would not be awarded. Explaining this drastic departure from normal procedure, jury president Yiorgos Xourmouziadis referred to the crisis in Greek cinema characterised by the small yearly production (nine competing entries) and the weak scenarios of the entries.

Poor scripts seem to be a pan-European problem, one that has been the bugaboo of Greek cinema for many years. Efforts to overcome this flaw include funding from the GFC for scriptwriters and a workshop with international consultants sponsored by the Greek Film Directors Union.

Vassilis Kassissoglou's **The Wedding on the Fringe**, which captured the Best Actress Award for Alaka Paizi and a special Lifetime Achievement Award for Stavros Xenidis for his leading role in the film and his total contribution to Greek cinema was the sentimental favourite of foreign guests and the general audience. The warmhearted romantic comedy, laced with gentle parody and social comment, is about an elderly couple separated by a misunderstanding during the First World War but reunited decades later when they rekindle their relationship.

It seemed as though the jury had to dig deep to find suitable recipients for the awards that were given, with the result that some of them seemed gratuitous. For example, Menelaos Karamaggio's study of gypsy life, **Rom**, was given the Best Feature Documentary Award when it was the only documentary in competition. *Rom*, also winner of Best Editing Award, is visually appealing and well researched but so chock full of information about the history and customs of this much-aligned subculture that the narrative distracts from the visual aspect.

Kostas Ferris' musical parable **Oh Babylon** received the Technical Achievement Award for its use of Dolby stereo, which seemed facetious because, up till now, it is the only Greek film to use Dolby stereo. *Oh Babylon* is largely an inventive visual exercise, a modern adaption of *The Bacchae*, with an unintentionally funny script.

Oh Babylon ranges from a claustrophobic womb-coloured villa in which Penthaus, a dour writer, resists joining the lascivious games of his naughty mom and her playmates, to sweeping shots of Salvador Dali- inspired landscapes. Running through it all is an incongruous but rousing video clip featuring Reggae star Maxi Priest and a chorus of gyrating Rastafarians.

It is a case for subtitling as the proper British accent of actors used in dubbing seems stilted. Ferris cornered the technical awards, including Best Musical Score, Best Set Design and shared Best Cinematography with **Olga Robards**.

Christos Vakopoulos' *Olga Robards* epitomises the shortcomings of modern Greek films. It looks terrific, with razor-sharp cinematography and a visual style influenced by elegant French films with a hint of German expressionism. Suspense is created in the opening scenes in which an unknown assailant murders an Arab businessman. But the plot never coheres and the audience is left guessing just who Olga Robards was anyway.

Three awards went to Nikos Antonakos' political drama **Farther Right Than The Right**. The acting is solid, especially the performances of Gerasimos Skiadaressis, who won the award for best actor, and established actress Yiota Festa. The turgid handling of a group of people who express their differing political ideologies in the period following the junta, robs it of interest for a general audience.

Patrice Vivancos' road movie **Xenia**, winner of Best First Feature, shows promise. The photography is top-notch and Denis Podalidis is skilfully understated as Mathieu, a young French actor who pairs up with Xenia (Themia Bazaka), a pregnant

Greek woman who wants to get to Andalusia to give birth. Marvellously expressive Bazaka (*Stone Years*) unfortunately resorts to overacting in some scenes while remaining curiously aloof in others.

Dimitris Arvanitis' **Guilty Or Not Guilty** is a well-intentioned but overly dramatic made-for-TV movie about a real-life case in which a drifter is accused of attempted rape, sentenced and executed on the basis of circumstantial evidence. Another crudely made TV movie, Nikos Yannopoulos' **Television Close Circuit** is enlivened by good performances and an interesting premise about an estranged couple that uses a closed circuit camera in separate flats.

Kostas Zirinis' **The Last Bat** stars renowned Polish actor Daniel Olbrychsky and comely Katerina Hazolou in a muddled drama about a leftist who becomes a key suspect in a case involving a series of executions.

Vassilis Vafeas' **Red Daisy** features veteran comic Costas Voutsas, also star of Vafeas' **The Love of Ulysses**, as a middle-aged innocent who escapes from his job at a pharmaceutical company and joins an acting troupe as a stagehand. Voutsas' excellent comic timing and charming expression of his infatuation with a lively actress (Pemy Zouni) are not enough to compensate for inefficient plot development.

Two other films that premiered outside the Thessaloniki Festival are Vessiliki Iliopoulou's **The Crossing**, a drama with interesting psychological nuances about a murderer trying to escape from Greece and Panos Kokkinopoulos' **Scars of the Night**, an eye-appealing ethnic thriller that falls flat.

Animation Studio Opens

Although no artistic animated shorts were unveiled this year, the opening of Artoon in late 1989, was good news. Founded by Yiorgos Nikoloulias and Nikos Vergitsis, one of Greece's leading feature film-makers, Artoon is the first Greek animated studio to work only on TV series and spots rather than advertising.

As is so often the case when the leading figures of Greek cinema gather in Thessaloniki for the festival, verbal fireworks exploded onstage after the "non-Awards Presentation" at the 30th event. The announcement of the withholding of major prizes was soundly applauded by most of the general audience but provoked heated protests from many directors.

Many foreign guests found the exchange of outbursts more exciting and far more typical of the Greek character than the pretentious, detached posturing found in many of the films. Many wondered why so little of this passion had been transferred to the screen in recent years.

Production Companies

Dimitri Dimitriadis
9 Hadjiyanni Mexi Street
Athens 115 28
Tel: 721–4976
Fax: 724–8131

Gemini Film Productions
2 Therianou Street
Athens 114 73
Tel: 643–3626, 642–3103
Fax: 364–7608

Yannis Petropoulakis
13/14–16 Sissini Street
Athens 115 28
Tel: 722–3053, 722–8884

Stefi
4 Agelikara Street
Athens 117 42
Tel: 902–5560

Distributors

ELKE
96 Acadimias Street
Athens 106 77
Tel: 362–3801
Fax: 360–3611

Nea Kinisi
Motion Pictures Enterprises
9–13 Gravias Street
Athens 106 78

TOP GROSSING FILMS IN GREECE: OCTOBER 1989–MAY 1990

	Admissions
Dead Poets Society	330,000
Batman	175,000
Lethal Weapon 2	80,000
When Harry Met Sally	70,000
Lock Up	70,000
The Fabulous Baker Boys	65,000
Weekend at Bernie's	60,000
Honey, I Shrunk the Kids	60,000
Dead Ringers	60,000
Three Fugitives	55,000

Figures from statistics by ELKE.

Tel: 362–8454
Fax: 363–9008

Prooptiki
40–42 Koletti Street
Athens 106 82
Fax: 361–3762
Tel: 364–4541

Spentzos Film
9–13 Gravias Street
Athens 106 78
Tel: 362–956
Fax: 362–1438

UIP
4 Gambetta St.
Athens 106 78
Tel: 361–1472

Useful Addresses

Ministry of Culture
Aristidou 14
Athens 101 86
Tel: 322–4737

Greek Film Centre
Voula Georgakakou
Panepistimiou 10
Athens 106 71
Tel: 363–4586
Fax: 361–4336

Worldwide Sales
Exportfilm Bischoff & Co.
Isabellastr. 20
8000 München 40
Tel: 089/271–9940.
Telex 528290

Cinema and TV Technicians' Guild
Veltetsiou 25
Athens 106 80
Tel: 360–2379

Greek Directors' Guild
Tossitsas 11
Athens 106 73
Tel: 822–3205, 822–8936

Greek Actors' Guild
Kaningos 33
Athens 106 82
Tel: 363–3742, 361–7369

Assn. of Greek Motion Picture Video and TV Producers
Skalidi 16–18
Athens 115 25
Tel: 671–7297
Fax: 647–5057

Assn. of Open-Air Cinema Owners
Acadimies 95
Athens 106 77
Tel: 361–9239

Panhellenic Theatre Owners Assn.
Acadimias 96
Athens 106 77
Tel: 801–1045

HONGKONG

by Derek Elley

Although you would never guess it from the stream of energetic, confident movies that still pours out of the territory, Hongkong is passing through its most jittery period in more than 20 years. In an economy where market confidence is everything, the film industry seems more and more in the throes of a final wild party before the shutters come down in a few years' time.

The massive blow to Hongkong's collective psyche by the June 1989 Tiananmen Massacre was only a timely warning of what many already knew deep down: that with the takeover of the territory in mid-1997 by mainland China things will never be quite the same, and that the first real effects will start to be felt some time before that awesome date. In the film industry the nervousness is typically translating itself into a movie-making fever: stars' salaries have rocketed in the past couple of years (though temporarily peaking due to market demands), and the popular players are averaging 8–10 movies a year (male idol Andy Lau even managed 16 movies in 1989).

Film-makers have been quietly fixing their passports for some time. But with emigration from the territory now averaging 1,000 people a week, the topic is now openly discussed (and referred to in most movies as well). Canada is the favoured destination: any film-maker with sufficient capital to invest is virtually guaranteed a residency permit, and more and more are now taking the route pioneered several years ago by actor–director Sammo Hung. Film Workshop, run by director–producer Tsui Hark, is to link up in 1991 with Vancouver-based New Studio City (NSC), co-founded by Tsui's wife, Nansun Shi. NSC will also handle projects from Raymond Wong, one of the founders of the hugely successful Cinema City (itself undergoing restructuring).

Golden Harvest, still Hongkong's most profitable concern, has been playing its cards closer to its chest. But it already has a well-established international profile (especially with the runaway success of *Teenage Mutant Ninja Turtles*) and no binding ties to the territory (its studio complex and equipment is all leased). It has already set up a Toronto unit and is known to be looking, along with companies like Cinema City and Movie Impact, at possibilities in Singapore. (The latter has no native film industry but may prove too regulated for Hongkong's entrepreneurial talents.)

All this fever has lead to escalating budgets (now averaging HK$7.5 million) and consequently escalating box-office risks. The generally lacklustre results in the second half of 1989 worried many in the industry (see Facts and Figures). With most companies never publishing accounts, and money-laundering rife in some sectors of the industry, box-office figures are the only guide to "profitability." But the massive success of Wong Ching's slick action movie, *God of Gamblers*, in late 1989/early 1990 – plus titles like *Heart into Hearts, Shanghai, Shanghai, The Fortune Code* and *The Fun, the Luck & the Tycoon* – show that local audiences, despite the belated home video boom, will still turn out if the formula is right. For foreign films Hongkong remains one of the world's most difficult markets, although London-based UIP (grouping Paramount, Universal and MGM/UA) has been getting more screen time for its product since 1989 thanks to a tie-up with Golden Harvest's Panasia distribution division.

Rich Harvest

In terms of sheer spread and quality, 1989/90 was the richest year for a long time. Much critical attention was focused on Stanley Kwan's **Full Moon in New York** (*Yan tsoi Nau Yeuk*), teaming actresses Sylvia Chang, Maggie Cheung and Siqin Gaowa as three Chinese from Taiwan, Hongkong and mainland China respectively; but the film was a disappointment after his previous *Rouge*, with the designer look emphasising the shallowness of the script (much meaningful talk about identity, etc) and making the talented trio into little more than mannequins. As yet, Kwan is no Edward Yang.

Some of the same problems also afflicted Tony Au's **I Am Sorry** (*Sutfongdik nuiyan*), an off-the-wall slice of metaphysical cinema about young women "finding themselves" in colour-supplement relationships. But thanks to a lively performance by Carina Liu (now emerging as a considerable actress) and a generally lighter tone, the movie almost convinces that it is actually about something. At the very least, it is a complete original.

Much less ambitious, and all the better for it, was Jacob Cheung's **Beyond the Sunset** (*Feiyut wongfan*), a quiet, unflashy examination of a mother–daughter relationship patched up after a long separation. As the mother, Cantonese veteran Feng Po-po makes a remarkable return to the screen, with strong support from Cecilia Yip as the daughter from overseas and comedian Richard Ng reining himself back as Feng's middle-aged beau.

The movie was one of several that looked back to the gentler values of 1950's Hongkong cinema (the so-called *wen-yi pien*/emotional dramas). Johnny To's **All about Ah-long**, a modern remake of *The Champ* with Chow Yun-fat and Sylvia Chang, was flawed only by a melodramatic climax; others, like Jamie Luk's remake of the 1950's classic **Four Loves** (*Sei tsingam*), were undisguised (but fun) exercises in retro. Best of the bunch was **A Fishy Story** (*Battutmatdik yan*), classily directed by young actor Antony Chan. Stunningly shot, and revelling in its late 1960's setting, this romantic comedy–drama about an aspiring actress (Maggie Cheung) and penniless taxi-driver (Kenny Bee) proved to be one of the year's most delightful movies, with first-rate performances and a script to match.

Yuppie Romances

The growing body of yuppie romances over the past few years (a speciality of D&B Films) has now become an established genre, with some fine results and almost all showcasing the talents of actress Dodo Cheng. Prime mover Stephen Shin followed the excellent *Heart to Hearts* (see IFG 1990) with the sequel **Heart into Hearts** (*Samyan san seigai*), flawed only by a miscast Maggie Cheung as a film director, and **Happy Together** (*Seung gin ho*), with Kenny Bee and Cherie Chung as a virginal stockbroker and TV bachelor girl. He also produced Norman Chan's **The Nobles** (*Dansan gwaitsuk*), less confidently paced but with some pointed comedy between Dodo Cheng as a yuppie designer and Jacky Cheung as a working-class decorator.

Other notable entrants were first-timer Gordon Chan's **The Yuppie Fantasia** (*Siu namyan tsaugei*) and Chan Kwok-san's **Perfect Match** (*Tsuigai nampangyau*), both with excellent playing (again) by Cheng. These movies, though almost indistinguishable from each other, are Hongkong's closest equivalent to Hollywood comedies of the 1930's; and beneath the gloss they often express the territory's personality more acutely than many more self-conscious movies.

Fast-paced Violence

The other genre that Hongkong has honed to a fine art since the mid-1980's is the action movie, which now equals anything Hollywood can produce. John Woo's **The Killer** (*Diphut yinghung*), with Chow Yun-fat and Danny Lee, was a slick example of routine fast-pacing and cartoon violence. Tsui Hark's **A Better Tomorrow III** (*Yinghung bunsik III – tsikyeungtsi go*), a prequel to the smash series partly shot in Vietnam, was somewhat uneven, despite some impressive set-pieces and a gun-toting Anita Mui. More of a piece was Taylor Wong's **Triads – The Inside Story** (*Ngo tsoi haksewui dik yattsi*), with Chow Yun-fat as an overseas son unwillingly taking on his dead father's mantle. But the most substantial of all, and marking a change of direction for Ringo Lam, was **Wild Search** (*Bun ngo tsong tinngai*), with Chow as a disillusioned cop falling for a simple New Territories girl (Cherie Chung). The action sequences for once enhance the central relationship, which is drawn with considerable sensitivity by both players.

Other titles of note during 1989/90 include Jackie Chan's latest blockbuster, **Mr Canton and Lady Rose** (*Keitsik* – also known as **Miracle**), a remake of Capra's *Pocketful of Miracles* transposed to 1930's Hongkong that featured less action than usual and more storyline. Mabel Cheung's **Eight Taels of Gold** (*Bat leung gam*), a sensitive romance between a New York cabbie (Sammo Hung) and Chinese girl (Sylvia Chang) shot in mainland China. Lawrence Ah Mon's self-consciously talky prostitute drama **Queen of Temple Street** (*Miugai wonghau*), with Sylvia Chang. Raymond Leung's violent women's-prison drama **The First Time Is the Last Time** (*Daiyat gan*), let down only by a trashy script. Fok Yiu-leung's **The Iceman Cometh** (*Gapdung keihap*), a gleeful rip-off of *Highlander* with action star Yuen Biao and (a marvellous) Maggie Cheung as a loud-mouthed modern hooker. Ching Siu-tung's big-budget period adventure, **A Terra-Cotta Warrior** (*Tseun yung*), shot in China with actor Zhang Yimou and actress Gong Li. And, last but not least, the long-awaited **Swordsman** by "King Hu" (see below).

Hidden amongst such high-paced stuff, it remains to note two other productions. Allen Fong's **Dancing Bull** (*Mou ngau*), with Cora Miao trying to make a go of a modern dance troupe as her personal life crumbles, is uneven overall, more a series of conversation pieces than a dramatic unity; and the attempt to interweave the events of June 1989 is clumsy. Far better at drawing a portrait of the territory in the light of recent events was critic/film-maker Shu Kei's Japanese-funded documentary **Sunless Days**, a highly personal record of his family and friends' response to Tiananmen that reaches out to touch wider matters like Chinese identity and history. Immensely moving and brave by turns (the scenes of street battles with police have been censored from the Hongkong print) it deserves the widest possible showings, not least for its striking absence of easy anger.

Samuel Hui and Cecilia Yip in *Swordsman*

Casebook: Swordsman

The troubled history of **Swordsman** (*Siu ngou gongwu*), the first film by King Hu since 1983, has been touched on in IFG 1989 and 1990. Its final appearance in February 1990, earning a very respectable HK$16 million-plus, finally brought the three-year saga to a close. Based on a mammoth swordplay novel by Louis Cha (Chin Yung), it was originally budgeted by Tsui Hark's Film Workshop at HK$15 million; the final cost was double that amount, with some HK$1.5 million wasted on unused sets and actors in Taiwan.

After extensive pre-production and slow script development (partly caused by having to compress a complex novel into one feature film), the movie eventually began shooting in Hongkong in autumn 1988 and subsequently in Taiwan. For two months three directors (King Hu, Ann Hui and Ching Siu-tung) worked simultaneously on the movie. But after "differences of opinion" with Tsui Hark, King Hu left the project and the script was re-jigged. Three more directors (Tsui Hark, Li Hui-min and Kam Yeung-wah) completed the film. Actress Sally Yeh shot for half a day and was replaced by up-and-coming Chang Min; three Taiwan actors (Li Chih-hsi, Chang Fu-chien and Chin Yu-lan) were completely edited out. Production stopped completely for several months during summer 1989.

The finished result (with a "director" credit to King Hu and "line director" credit to Tsui Hark and Ching Siu-tung) is surprisingly cohesive, with traces of Hu's style in between the snappier style favoured by Tsui Hark. The set pieces are among the best in swordplay cinema (a fight on a boat, and several sequences in a dying factory) and the film captures some of the insouciant tone of the original novel. As of summer 1990 Tsui Hark was already planning a sequel, to star Taiwan actress Lin Ch'ing-hsia whom he worked with in *Peking Opera Blues*.

Recent and Forthcoming Films

Nau Yeuk hak (Farewell China). Dir: Clara Law. Players: Maggie Cheung. Prod: Golden Harvest.

Hoyat gwan tsoi lei. Dir: Tony Au. Players: Anita Mui, Leung Kar-fai, Carrie Ng, Tsui Siu-keung. Shot in Shanghai, Hongkong and Japan.

Tsuk fuk. Dir: Yang Fan. Phot: Ch'en K'un-hou. Players: Dodo Cheng, Ch'in Han, Elsie Chan.

A-fei tsingchun. Dir: Wong Ka-wai. Players: Maggie Cheung, Andy Lau, Leslie Cheung, Tony Leung, Carina Liu, Jacky Cheung.

Lunghing fudai tsuktsap (The Armour of God 2: Operation Eagle). Dir: Frankie Chan. Players: Jackie Chan, Dodo Cheng. Prod: Golden Harvest.

Moutoi tsemui. Dir: Wu Ma. Players: Wai Ying-hung, Chan Yuk-lin, Jackie Chan. Prod: Golden Harvest.

Chundou Fongtsi. Script: Lei Bik-wa. Dir: Eddie Fong. Players: Anita Mui, Andy Lau, Hsieh Hsien, Yee Tung-shing. Prod: Golden Harvest. Shot in Changchun, Harbin, Peking, Tianjin, Shanghai, Japan and Macau.

Yangan dou. Dir: Ching Siu-tung. Players: Leslie Cheung, Joey Wang, Jacky Cheung. Prod: Film Workshop. Sequel to *A Chinese Ghost Story*.

Biutse, nei hou ye!. Script and Dir: Alfred Cheung. Players: Dodo Cheng, Leung Kar-fai, Alfred Cheung. Prod: Golden Harvest.

TOP TEN GROSSING LOCAL FILMS IN HONGKONG: 1989

	Rentals (HK$)
Mr Canton and Lady Rose (Jackie Chan)	34.0 million
Mr Coconut (Clifton Ko)	31.2 million
All about Ah-long (Johnny To)	30.9 million
God of Gamblers (Wong Ching)*	28.9 million
Casino Raiders (Wong Ching)	23.1 million
Aces Go Places V: The Terracotta Hit (Lau Kar-leung)	20.0 million
A Better Tomorrow III (Tsui Hark)	18.5 million
The Killer (John Woo)	18.3 million
The Inspector Wears Skirts II (Wellson Chin)	18.1 million
The Crazy Companies II (Wong Ching)**	16.9 million

* 1989 gross only; total gross HK$36.9 million
** Total gross, including end-1988

George Lam and Maggie Cheung in *Heart into Heart*

Ninth Hongkong Film Awards

The awards for 1989, announced in mid-April 1989, were:
Best Film: *Beyond the Sunset*.
Best Director: John Woo (*The Killer*).
Best Script: Jacob Cheung, Chan Kam-cheung (*Beyond the Sunset*).
Best Actor: Chow Yun-fat (*All about Ah-long*).
Best Actress: Maggie Cheung (*A Fishy Story*).
Best Supporting Actor: Tony Leung (*My Heart Is That Eternal Love*).
Best Supporting Actress: Cecilia Yip (*Beyond the Sunset*).
Best Photography: Pau Hei-ming (*A Fishy Story*).
Best Editing: Fan Kung-wing (*The Killer*).
Best Art Direction: Sitou Wai-yung (*A Fishy Story*).
Best Martial Arts/Action Choreography: Jackie Chan's Martial Arts Group (*Mr Canton and Lady Rose*).
Best Music: Lo Ta-yu, Lu Shih-chieh (*Eight Taels of Gold*).
Best Song: sung by Julie Sue (*Pedicab Driver*).
Best Technical Award: *Mr Canton and Lady Rose*.
Life Achievement Award: Tsu Yat-hung.

DEREK ELLEY *is Consulting Editor of this book, and has been associated with it for more than 18 years. He is known as a specialist in Hungarian and Far East cinema, and is author of* The Epic Film: Myth and History *and consultant editor of* The Variety Movie Guide. *He is currently completing A* Handbook of Chinese Cinema: The Films and Film-Makers of Hongkong, China and Taiwan.

Facts and Figures

Total 1989 box-office receipts in Hongkong were HK$1,290 million, down by 6% on 1988's HK$1,370 million. Ticket prices rose by some 14%. The strongest period was January–July; the second half of the year was generally lacklustre, with a last-minute rally thanks to *God of Gamblers* (released in mid-December). By early 1990 this film had grossed HK$36.97 million, just beating the all-time local box-office record set in 1988 by Johnny To's *Eighth Happiness* (HK$36.51 million). The highest-grossing foreign film in 1989 was *Indiana Jones and the Last Crusade* (HK$24.1 million), followed by *Rain Man* (HK$12.7 million). Foreign films' share of the box-office fell to 22%. Some 114 Hongkong productions were released in the territory in 1989, about the same as the previous year; the percentage of comedies fell fractionally (to around 20%) but the amount of action/crime movies (almost 40%) virtually doubled.

Useful Addresses

Golden Harvest (HK)
8 Hammer Hill Rd
Ngau Chi Wan
Kowloon
Tel: 352–8222
Fax: 351–1683

Golden Way Films
Office B, Basement
154 Waterloo Rd
Kowloon
Tel: 794–0388

Cinema City Co.
12/F, Pioneer Bldg
748a Nathan Rd
Kowloon
Tel: 391–5368

Film Workshop Co.
Room 1103–1107
11/F, Pioneer Bldg
748a Nathan Road
Kowloon
Tel: 395–0125
Fax: 789–1685

D&B Films
5 Kent Rd
Kowloon Tong
Kowloon
Tel: 338–7888

Sil-Metropole Organisation
15/F, Sunbeam Commercial Bldg
469 Nathan Rd
Kowloon
Tel: 780–5355
Fax: 780–0719

Molesworth
Unit A, 4/F, Ka Cheong Bldg
2–4 Sunning Rd
Causeway Bay
Tel: 577–6255
Fax: 895–4104

Southern Film Corporation
19/F, Dominion Centre
37–59 Queen's Road East
Hongkong
Tel: 527–7284

HK-TVB
77 Broadcast Drive
Kowloon
Tel: 338–0222
Fax: 338–6690

Asia Television (ATV)
81 Broadcast Drive
Kowloon
Tel: 389–0111

HUNGARY

by Derek Elley

The only certainty about Hungary's film industry of the future is that it will bear little resemblance to anything of the past 40 years. Gone for ever seem the days when the country turned out a neat package of some 20 features, immaculately balanced in content, seasoned with political irony, and assured of festival exposure. The smooth-running machine that made Hungarian cinema the envy of many enters the 1990's almost at a standstill.

That is not to say that the industry is dead. But after three years of momentous change the time has come when the system that served it for four decades is past the point of more repairs. The irony is that the surface consensus that kept Hungary's cinema free from the upheavals of other East European industries is now making the passage to devolution much more traumatic. The consensus extended into all areas of intellectual life and made the country's cinema very different from that in, say, Poland, whose film-making more closely paralleled social and political changes. The struggle now is how to maintain in a market economy a cinema industry that is not used to volatility.

The pressures are immense. Although there were signs in the first half of 1990 that the economy was slowly pulling out of its trough, it is still far from healthy (inflation around 25% and unemployment nearing 10% of the working population). With massive state-industry debt on their books, local banks are in no mood to lend; as a result, foreign capital is the only solution – and has led to anything in the country that is saleable being touted to foreign investors. The unseemly rush to mammon has led many to worry about the future consequences of selling off the country's silver.

The parallel in the film industry has been the opening up of the distribution side to the U.S. majors. By 1990 there were three main distributors, all co-ventures: Danube Film, an alliance between Budapest Film (one of the four main studios, and owner of most of the capital's cinemas) and UIP (the foreign distributor of Paramount, Universal and MGM/UA product); Intercom,

---

HUNGAROFILM

-festival activities - (36 1) 112-5425
-import,distribution
  in Hungary   - (36 1) 132-8684
-production,dubbing,
  laboratory services,
  coproductions   - (36 1) 153-4153

H-1054 Budapest, Báthori u. 10.
Cables: Hungarofilm, Budapest
Telex: 22-5768
Telefax: (36 1) 153-1850

CINEMAGYAR Sales and distribution of
Hungarian films
coproductions

H-1054 Budapest
Báthori u. 10
Telex: 22-5768
Phone: (36 1) 111-4614
Telefax: (36 1) 153-1317

grouping Mafilm (the state studio complex), Hungarofilm and Carolco, handling Carolco, Warners, Disney/Touchstone, Columbia and Tri-Star product; and Saturnus Film, handling releases of product by Orion and smaller US companies. Even Mokép (which previously handled foreign imports) was setting up a venture with IFEX and (possibly) 20th Century-Fox.

Such ventures have meant that since spring 1989 Hungarian audiences have been able to see the latest U.S. movies as fast as anyone else in Europe. And the result, predictably enough, has been dire for home-grown product. The only thing that seems to be holding Hollywood up from completely swamping the country is the shortage of cinemas and their generally poor condition. Budapest Film, which has a virtual monopoly over the country's houses, reckons the capital has only about 15 decent cinemas and conversions/upgrading can only proceed at about four to five a year. The only way to move faster is either to show even more box-office blockbusters or to invite foreign investment.

Either way, local-made movies get squeezed. Foreign co-productions are nothing new in Hungarian cinema and, with inflation eating into state studio budgets, have become increasingly necessary. But relatively few have been artistically successful: the country's fiercely individual culture (one of its great strengths) does not adapt easily to the blander demands of internationalism. To add to the industry's woes, video is now starting to get a grip on the market (with concomitant direct-to-video movies) and the long-simmering debate between the older and younger generation of film-makers has finally broken into the open. There were even rumours in early 1990 that Mafilm, the country's state studio/services complex, was about to be hocked off to French interests on an exclusive European basis.

Turbulent Week
All these tensions were in evidence at the 22nd Hungarian Film Week in early February 1990. With the country's first free elections for over 40 years due in March

Still from *On Death Row*

and April, no one was taking any major decisions about the industry's future. But younger film-makers (following a street demo on February 4) held a press conference accusing their elders of making closed-door plans; calmer heads called for moderation in the form of a National Film Foundation (to include all sectors of the industry) to decide what to do and how to distribute available state funds. With the lowish number of features (16) and high number of documentaries (27) on show, some called for the Film Week to be divided in future years. But with few features in production during the summer of 1990 there were doubts whether the annual event would be held at all in 1991.

The miracle amidst all this activity — further evident in the spawning of small production units and film services companies — was that there were still some fine movies on show. The problem is not one of lack of talent, only of capital and a proper structure in which it can flourish. Two of the most impressive productions showed a return to "traditional" forms — strong scripts, structured mise-en-scene, and narrative drive. János Zsombolyai's **On Death Row** (*A halálraítélt*) seems on the surface like just another film based around the 1956 uprising; but it soon develops into an astute blend of human perfidy and romantic love, as a young engineer reminisces on events that brought him to the condemned cell. The uprising itself is for the first time portrayed as an improvised, chaotic affair, the principals swept along by events they respond to purely emotionally (parallels with Romania are not avoided). Only afterwards are political scores settled, and personal ties betrayed. The direction by Zsombolyai (best-known for *Duty-Free Marriage*, 1980) is taught in the dramatic scenes and warmly romantic during the personal moments; and the photography (Gábor Szabó) and acting (Péter Malcsiner, Barbara Hegyi and, as the ruthless security officer, István Bubik) are first class.

The same "classical" approach also informs an impressive feature debut by Krisztina Deák (b. 1953) — **The Book of Esther** (*Eszterkönyv*). Hardly surprisingly for a film from Objektiv Studio, it shows more than echo of István Szabó's style, cleanly shot by Iván Márk and with the accent on strong performances. Based on the book "Éva Heyman's Diaries," it deals on the surface with a Jewish woman's search for the daughter she abandoned during the Nazi occupation; on a secondary level it confronts the woman's guilt as she becomes obsessed with a diary which may or may not have been written by the daughter. Thanks to striking playing by Eszter Nagy-Kálóczy (a cross between Jessica Lange and Kristin Scott-Thomas) and a convincingly mellow András Bálint (Deák's real-life husband), it reaches a powerful climax that mitigates some of its more obscure moments.

Both these films, however, were the exception rather than the rule in last year's production. The dominant tone, reflecting the social upheavals in the country, was of anger, confusion and despair. It was no accident that the vast majority of films were from younger directors, with almost nothing from the older figureheads of the industry (Szabó, Makk, Kovács, Bacsó, Mészáros, Jancsó etc). One exception was Ferenc Kardos with **Truants** (*Iskolakerülők*), a poorly constructed light drama set in a country boarding school with Károly Eperjes (Hungary's Depardieu) as a teacher trying to reform a troublesome boy pupil. Muddled and loosely paced, it fails on all levels.

Several of the works by younger talents were not much more successful. András M. Monory's **Meteo** may look progressive to Hungarian eyes; but by international standards it is a feeble parable of cupidity, avarice and greed grafted on to a futuristic thriller plot. All that can be said for this Ridley Scott lookalike is that it accurately reflects a certain section of Hungary's contemporary youth. Less pop video and

Still from *The Book of Esther*

more grounded in reality is **Shooting Range** (*Céllövölde*), the first feature of Árpád Sopsits (b. 1952). Semi-vérité in style, and with tinted photography varying from ochre to green, it attempts to draw a psychological portrait of a teenager who one day shoots his father for no apparent reason. The problem is that the movie is as sulky and confused as the central character; with no apparent point-of-view it soon becomes tiresome.

Nihilism and escape are also the dominant themes in Sándor Sőth's **Stowaways** (*Potyautasok*), based on a true story about a group of youths who set out in 1982 for Sweden via Poland by train. For much of its length it is an impressive variation on a familiar theme, thanks to Sőth's striking visuals (the train scenes; a Kafkaesque sequence in an embassy) and a dark, propulsive musical score. But the intriguing idea of a group of young Hungarians lost in a foreign society collapses as soon as they reach the Polish seaboard: the characters have little depth beyond their rebelliousness and their internal squabbles seem of little interest.

Also ploughing the same furrow is **Don't Disturb!** (*Szédülés*), the feature debut of János Szász (b. 1958). But the approach is entirely different – an allegorical drama, entirely set in a crumbling apartment block, that looks like a cross between Pál Sándor and Léos Carax. The characters have no names and are bound together in a hellish world of private neuroses and sexual tensions, the latter satisfied by a beautiful girl (Andrea Kiss) who offers the only chance for escape. With minimalist dialogue and a constantly mobile camera, the movie is almost pure mise-en-scène; but its teasing obscurity, reminiscent of earlier Hungarian political allegories, holds the attention, even if the dénouement is equally nihilistic.

Similarly offbeat is Péter Gárdos' **Just for Kicks** (*A hecc*), an allegorical fantasy with traces of his first feature, *The*

Philadelphia Attraction, but much more wacky. The plot, about an ordinary man who finds himself progressively threatened by a gang of thugs for an unnamed offence, is typically Central European in its out-of-sync atmosphere. But given the recent changes in Hungary, it seems curiously old-fashioned: this kind of film belongs to an earlier age, when obliqueness was a necessary virtue and "Kafkaesque" a regular term of description.

More sanguine – and overall funnier – is the energetic **Cotton Chicken** (*Vattatyúk*), a satire of talking-heads documentaries, officialese and sloganeering originally shot in six days on 8mm by independent filmmakers Gábor Ferenczi, Mária Dobos and András Szőke. The wacky humour is untranslatable, and the film is as rough as its dialogue and direction. But it accurately reflects the mood of its time, and will be seen as a pure work of its time in years to come. Its packed screening at the Hungarian Film Week brought the house down.

Spirited and Accessible

The only established director who manages to combine the spirit of the age with more accessible technique is the maverick middle-generation director György Szomjas. As well as making a joyous, *Woodstock*-like documentary on Transylvanian folk music, **Days of Peace and Music** (*Mulatság*), shot on video in two days, Szomjas finally shot another long-planned project, **Fast & Loose** (*Könnyűvér*). Co-scripted with regular associates Ibolya Fekete and Ferenc Grunwalsky, from the true experiences of two hookers, it has all of the anarchic comedy–drama of his previous *Light Physical Injuries* and *The Wall-Driller* (with which it completes a loose trilogy). Part dime-novel thriller, part camera confessional, and with eye-opening playing by the actual women in question (Margó Kiwán and Ildikó Deim), it will delight Szomjas enthusiasts and further annoy his detractors.

Grunwalsky himself fared less well. After

Still from *Don't Disturb*

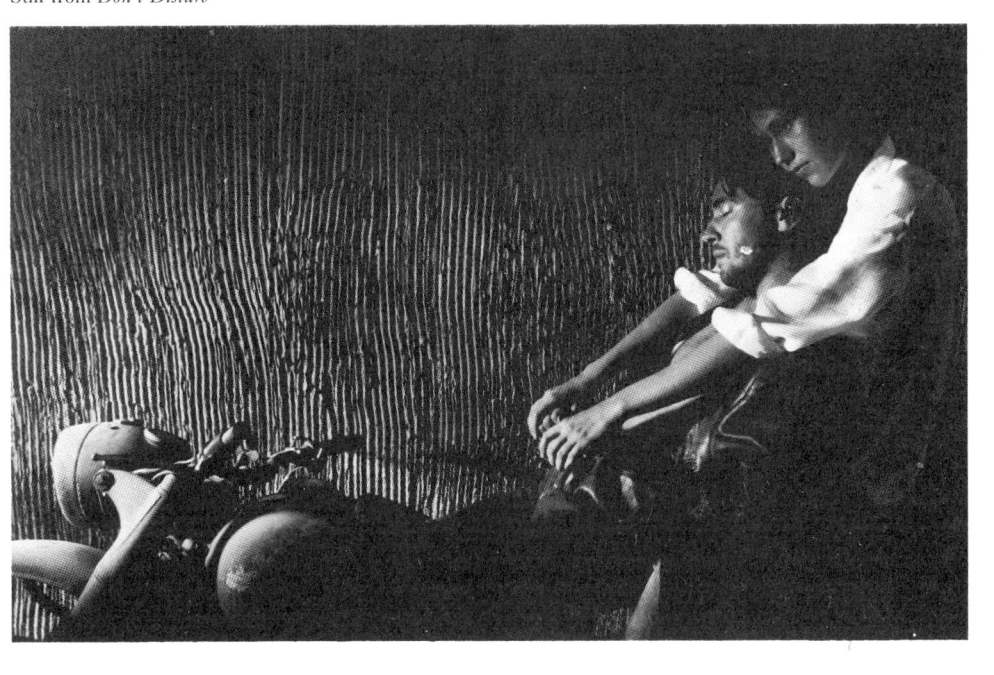

his completely off-the-wall *A Full Day* (IFG 1989), his latest movie, **Little but Tough** (*Kicsi, de nagyon erős*), comes as a disappointment. Again set among marginal working-class characters (here an unreformed burglar), the film lacks Grunwalsky's usual irony and makes little impression. The same can also be said for the work of a young director at the other end of the scale – **Leave Robinson Alone!** (*Hagyjátok Robinsont*) by Péter Timár. The sole work of the year from Dialóg Studio, and co-produced with Cuba's ICAIC, this self-indulgent, incredibly unfunny comedy about a drunken sailor who recounts his shipwrecked fantasies to Daniel Defoe is a major disappointment after Timar's other works. A farrago of mad missionaries, natives and sexual antics, it deserves quiet oblivion.

So, too, does Judit Elek's much-hyped Franco-Hungarian co-production **Memoirs of a River** (*Tutajosok*), inexplicably chosen as the Film Week's opening movie. Based on a true event (Jewish oppression in a remote corner of the Austro-Hungarian Empire in the 1880's), this two-and-a-half hour haul through interminable courtroom scenes and static exteriors may look better on TV. Elek's direction is worthy and unimaginative, her use of the stunning landscapes disappointing. For a story and theme of this magnitude there is a fatal absence of vision.

Two other very different films are worth noting. György Fehér's **Twilight** (*Szürkület*) may be tough viewing but it can never be faulted for a lack of vision. Somewhat reminiscent of Béla Tarr's *Damnation* (IFG 1989) in its highly stylised monochrome images, it takes a murder case involving young girls and imposes a bleak, hypnotic view of the universe that keeps the viewer guessing all the way. At the other extreme is a short, 45-minute piece of absurdist cinema that promises great things for its creators – Péter Kornai and Frigyes Gödrös' **Da Capo**. Co-produced by Hunnia Studio and Béla Balázs Studio (whose early 1960's shorts it recalls in spirit), it deals with a child's anarchic dreams, deliriously mingling elements of *Brazil* and early Dick Lester in a comedy that never outstays its welcome. It was one of the pure, most unalloyed delights of the past year.

22nd Hungarian Film Week Awards

The following were the main prizes on February 8, 1990, at the close of the 22nd Hungarian Film Week:
Grand Prix: no award.
Best Feature Film: *On Death Row* (János Zsombolyai)
Best Director: György Szomjas (*Fast and Loose*)
Best Actor: Sándor Gáspár (*Little but Tough* and *Memoirs of a River*)
Best Actress: no award
Best Photography: Gábor Szabó (*On Death Row* and *Meteo*)
Best Music: Zygmund Konieczky (*Stowaways*)
Best Art Direction: László Zsótér (*Meteo*)
Best Documentary: *With Blood and Rope* (Dezső Zsigmond, János Erdélyi)
Best First Film: *The Book of Esther* (Krisztina Deák)
Special Prizes (feature films): *Shooting Range* (Árpád Sopsits), *Twilight* (György Fehér)
Special Jury Prize: *Portrait of Béla Balázs by His Followers* (István Tényi)
Gene Moskowitz Award (voted by foreign critics): *Shooting Range* (Árpád Sopsits)

DEREK ELLEY is Consulting Editor of this book, and has been associated with it for more than 18 years. He is known as a specialist in Hungarian and Far East cinema, and is author of The Epic Film: Myth and History *and consultant editor of* The Variety Movie Guide, *to be published in 1991. He is currently completing A* Handbook of Chinese Cinema: The Films and Film-Makers of Hongkong, China and Taiwan.

Recent and Forthcoming Films

Napló apámnak, anyámnak (Diary for My Father and Mother). Script: Márta Mészáros, Éva Pataki. Dir: Márta Mészáros. Phot: Nyika Jancsó. Edit: Éva Kármentő. Music: Zsolt Döme. Players: Zsuzsa Czinkóczi, Jan Nowicki, Mari Törőcsik, Ildikó Bánsági, Anna Polony. Prod: Budapest Studio, Hungarofilm. 93 mins.

A távollét hercege (The Prince of Absence). Script: Sándor Schulz, Hilda Hársing. Dir: Tamás Tolmár. Phot: Gábor Halász. Music: Csaba Vedres. Players: Péter Vallai, Juli Básti, Géza Balkay, Pál Mihály, Piroska Molnár, Györgyi Kari. Prod: Dialog Studio.

Árnyék a havon (Shadow on the Snow – working title). Script: Attila Janisch, Antal Forgách. Dir: Attila Janisch. Phot: Tamás Sas. Players: Miroslaw Baka, Zsófia Baji, Joanne Kreft-Baka, János Kovács, Dénes Ujlaky. Prod: Budapest Studio.

Itt a szabadsag! (Here's Freedom! – working title). Script: Péter Vajda, András Salamon. Dir: Péter Vajda. Phot: Sándor Kardos. Players: Péter Andorai, Sándor Fábry, Károly Lőwy, Sándor Varga, Ágnes Szirtes. Prod: Hunnia Studio.

Szoba kiáltással (Room with Cry – working title). Script: Sándor Schulz, János Xantus. Dir: János Xantus. Phot: Tibor Klöpfler. Players: Anikő Für, Ferenc Andrzej, Zofia Rysiowna. Prod: Objektiv Studio.

Still from *Fast and Loose*

Hungarian Requiem. Script: Mihály Kornis, Károly Makk. Dir: Károly Makk. Players: Hans Christian Blech, Mathieu Carrière, György Cserhalmi, Károly Eperjes, Timea Raba. Prod: Transatlantic Media Associates.

Facts and Figures: 1989

Feature film production totalled some 16 works (about the same as in 1988), plus about 28 full-length documentaries (more than double the previous year). Cinema attendances continued to fall, to 45.8 million from 50.7 million in 1988 (down by 10%), with a 30% drop for Hungarian

TOP GROSSING FILMS IN HUNGARY: 1989

	Admissions
Rain Man	933,000
Twins	858,000
Red Heat	803,000
"Crocodile" Dundee II	789,000
Cocktail	726,000
Crime Busters (Italy)	640,000
Indiana Jones and the Last Crusade	629,000
Highlander	564,000
Les fugitifs (France)	564,000
Piedone in Hong Kong (reissue; Italy)	516,000

The three top-grossing Hungarian films were: *Willy, the Sparrow* (József Gémes; 248,000), *Pros. . . 2: A Film about Prostitution – Ladies of the Night* (György Dobray; 233,000), and *The Midas Touch* (Géza Bereményi; 190,000).

films within those totals (to 6.2 million from 8.9 million). The number of cinemas also fell, to 925 35mm houses (down by 12%) and 1,255 16mm houses (down by 34%).

Including re-issues, a total of 237 feature films (35 Hungarian plus 202 foreign) were shown during the year, compared with 224 (35 plus 189) in 1988.

Useful Addresses

Hunnia Film Studio
Lumumba utca 174
H-1145 Budapest
Tel: 183-3187, 184-0417
Telex: 22-6860

Dialóg Film Studio
(same address)
Tel: 183-4744
Telex: 22-6860

Budapest Film Studio
(same adress)
Tel: 163-1062
Telex: 22-6860
Fax: 183-5905

Objektiv Film Studio
(same address)
Tel: 183-3123
Telex: 22-6860

Mozgókép Innovációs Társulás & Alapítvány (MIT)
(same address)
Tel: 183-2571, 183-3599
Telex: 22-6860
Fax: 183-0377

Pannonia Film Studio
Vörös Hadsereg útja 64
H-1021 Budapest
Tel: 176-7091
Telex: 22-6823

Hungarian Film Institute
Népstadion út. 97
H-1143 Budapest
Tel: 142-9599

Béla Balázs Studio
Pasaréti út. 122
H-1026 Budapest
Tel: 176-7988

Hungarofilm/CineMagyar
(festivals, foreign sales)
Báthori utca 10
H-1054 Budapest
Tel: 153-1317, 112-5425
Telex: 22-5768
Fax: 153-1850

Reflex Film
Tel: 115-6900, 176-4903
Fax: 168-7918

Fórum Film Studio
(documentaries)
Könyves Kálmán körút 13-15
H-1097 Budapest
Tel: 134-3745

Novofilm (services)
Mészáros utca 18
H-1016 Budapest
Tel: 175-0858, 175-2575
Fax: 175-2764

FMS Studio
(Young Artists' Studio)
Hungarian Television
Szabadság tér 18
Budapest
Tel: 132-9526, 111-9093
Fax: 132-8514, 153-0874

ICELAND

by Arnaldur Indridason

Iceland is fast becoming Paradise Gained for TV addicts. After more than 20 years of state monopoly, the two recently-merged private TV stations, Channel 2 and the new Channel 7, promise the viewer an endless flow of foreign entertainment mostly from the United States and ranging from soap operas like *Dallas* and *Santa Barbara* to talkshows, miniseries and feature films.

At the same time movie theatres in Reykjavík are brimming with the latest and the best, again usually from America, and with video rentals on every street corner as well as a growing number of satellite TV-viewers Iceland, with a population of just 250,000, may be melting down into cultural oblivion.

Gone are the innocent days when the state-run television ruled the waves and exercised the now mind-boggling policy of never broadcasting on Thursdays, and never in July. The Icelandic film industry, still in its infancy, can by no means resist this invasion, and in fact the more we buy of foreign entertainment the less we produce in terms of feature films with probably only one movie due for theatrical release this year – **Rust** (*Ryd*), by one of our foremost directors, Lárus Ýmir Óskarsson, and one children's film edited from the TV series **Paper – Peter** (*Pappírs-Pési*).

In 1985, there were six new movies!

The new and larger Channel 2 will soon be broadcasting on two channels but due to financial difficulties it has cut down on domestic entertainment and leaves the old state-run station alone to produce homespun programmes such as plays, documentaries, and shorter films. This it does adequately despite a tighter budget this past year driven by the overwhelming threat to our language and nationality from foreign programmes.

It is in part this threat along with an effort to boost film-making that has prompted the government to issue a bill whereby the Icelandic Film Institute will take over the mantle of the Film Fund (which has put money into every feature film produced here since 1980). But Icelandic film-makers do not think they will gain much from this new organisation. They say that the money supposed to go to film-making will be less than it is now and as they see it, it has hit rock bottom already.

Declining Interest in Local Fare

All Icelandic films are low-budget, at an average cost of no more than $650,000, but no one can afford to make them without substantial contributions from the Film Fund. During the first few years after 1980, when continuous film-making began in Iceland, directors could rely on retrieving their money at the box-office and continuing to make films. But in recent years moviegoers have not shown such interest in local features as they used to, and so directors risk going bankrupt every time they make a film.

There are of course exceptions, notably the only Icelandic feature – Thráinn Bertelsson's black comedy **Magnús** – to open between June 1989 and June 1990. It turned out to be very successful, finishing Number One on the top grossing films list in Iceland. Thráinn's humour, well to the fore in his comedies *New Life, Country Life*, and *Cop's Life*, along with an excellent cast involving some of the best and funniest

ICELANDIC FILMS

A survey of the Icelandic Cinema between 1979 and 1989 with excerpts from 24 films.

Available on VHS from:
THE ICELANDIC FILM FUND
Laugavegur 24, P.O.Box 320
121 Reykjavik, Iceland
Tel.: 354-1-623580
Telefax: 354-1-627171

actors in the country, seemed to strike a nerve in the Icelandic audience. Both film and screenplay were nominated for the new European Felix awards. In addition, a short film by the promising young debutant Óskar Jónasson, entitled **The Squad Team**, was screened in Reykjavík and created something of a cult following with its dark humour in a story about the training of a homemade Icelandic group of would-be Rambo youngsters.

The funny thing is that in spite of the gloomy atmosphere in the Icelandic film "industry," there has never been so much interest in film-making. Applications for grants from the Film Fund have reached an all-time high and although there is only enough money to produce one film per year, smaller grants get people started on scripts that may, one day, lead to a finished movie. Thus Hilmar Oddson (*The Beast*) is working on a screenplay based on the hugely successful book *Kaldaljós* by author Vigdís Grímsdóttir; Sveinbjörn I. Baldvinsson (*Foxtrot*) is writing a script called *Jupiter* about a tragedy on board an Icelandic fishing-boat and director Gudný Halldórsdóttir (*Beneath the Glacier*) is at work on a comedy about a local choir touring overseas.

The big money this year went to director-scriptwriter Fridrik Thór Fridriksson to produce in the summer of 1990 a film he has written in co-operation with Einar Már Gudmundson called **Children of Nature**, about an old couple leaving the city to travel to their birthplace. It won additional backing from a production company in Germany, but Fridrik Thór describes it as a road movie, but with old folks in place of the usual youngsters.

Working Abroad

Icelandic directors have also been making films and TV programmes abroad with Hrafn Gunnlaugsson, known for his powerful Viking films, now preparing a Scandinavian co-production called **The White Viking**, and Ágúst Gudmundsson doing a series for Britain's Thames Television. But the major news came from Cannes. When David Lynch's *Wild at Heart* won the Palme d'Or it made front page news here, because Sigurjón Sighvatsson's independent production company, Propaganda Films, based in Los Angeles, produced the movie. Propaganda Films, owned by Sigurjón and his partner Steve Golin is "the most successful music-video company in the business" according to *Premiere* magazine, with an annual gross of around $50 million. It also makes commercials for such major accounts as Pepsi and Nike and has been getting into the movie business with productions like *Kill Me Again, Daddy's Dyin'* . . . *Who's Got the Will?*, *Wild at Heart* and the pilot of Lynch's TV series, *Twin Peaks*.

The first film produced by Sigurjón in Iceland is Óskarsson's **Rust**. It is a personal venture, with no money stemming from Propaganda and is scheduled for release in

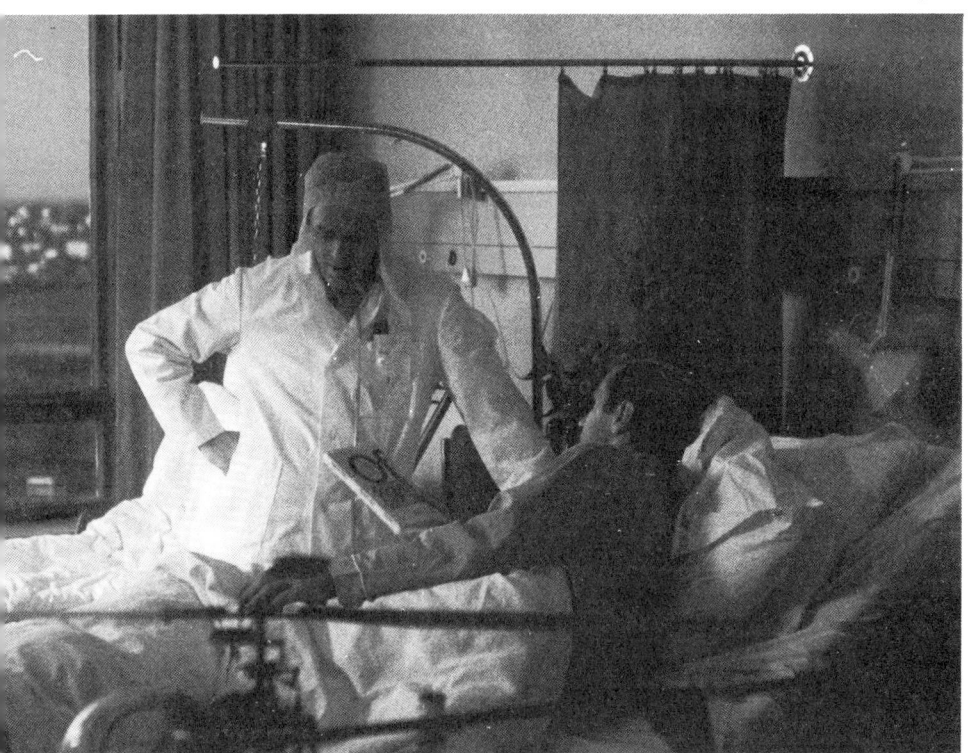

Still from the award-winning *Magnús*

autumn 1990. It is a psychological thriller based on the play *Baddi's Garage* by Ólafur Haukur Símonarson, and takes place in a run-down garage in the countryside where crimes surge up from the past to haunt people in the present. Lárus Ýmir's earlier films *The Second Dance* and *The Frozen Leopard* were made in Sweden.

So on the whole some interesting things are happening on the Icelandic scene and although there has been a decrease in film production these past few years, we are moving in the right direction, fighting that TV, video, and satellite "invasion."

ARNALDUR INDRIDASON is a film critic for the daily Morgunbladid.

Magnús

Script and Direction: Thráinn Bertelsson. Photography: Ari Kristinsson. Music: Sigurdur Rúnar Jónsson. Players: Egill Ólafsson, Thórhallur Sigurdsson, Gudrun Gísladóttir, Jón Sigurbjörnsson. Produced by Thráinn Bertelsson for New Life.

At the start of *Magnús*, Thráinn Bertelsson's black comedy, the title character (well played by pop star Egill Ólafsson) finds out from his doctor that he may have cancer and thus only a short time to live. This triggers a soul-searching personal drama mixed with a broad canvas of comic characters representing some of the funnier elements in the life and loves of an Icelander.

Thráinn's cast is excellent with many of the country's best actors in minor roles. The scene-stealer is Iceland's most popular comedian, Thórhallur Sigurdsson, who plays a taxi-driver and a friend of Magnús. Thráinn, well-known for his comedies, is at his best when writing witty dialogue but when he tries to blend it with the more sombre tones of a potential tragedy it does not quite work. Still, it is always amusing to watch and constitutes Thráinn's best film to date.

Arnaldur Indridason

TOP GROSSING FILMS IN ICELAND: 1989

	Admissions
Magnús	46,000
Rain Man	44,900
Licence to Kill	44,500
Indiana Jones and the Last Crusade	40,000
Lethal Weapon 2	36,000
A Fish Called Wanda	34,500
Batman	32,000
The Naked Gun	32,000
Twins	27,250
Cocktail	26,500
Beneath the Glacier	26,500

Useful Addresses

The Icelandic Film Fund
Chairman: Knútur Hallsson
Director: Thorsteinn Jónsson
Laugavegur 24
P.O. Box 320
121 Reykjavík
Tel: (1) 623580
Fax: (1) 623068

The Association of Icelandic Film Producers
Chairman: Ágúst Gudmundsson
Laugavegur 120
P.O. Box 7103
107 Reykjavík

The Icelandic Film-Makers' Association
Chairman: Thorsteinn Jónsson
Laugavegur 24
P.O. Box 320
121 Reykjavík

Association of Film Distributors in Iceland
Chairman: Fridbert Pálsson
Háskólabíó
Hagatorg
107 Reykjavík
Tel: (1) 611212
Fax: (1) 27135

Icelandic Film Sales
Hafnarstraeti 19
101 Reykjavík
Tel: (1) 17270

The Ministry of Culture and Education
Hverfisgötu 4–6
101 Reykjavík
Tel: (1) 25000
Fax: (1) 623068

INDIA
by Uma da Cunha

It seemed that at long last happy days were back for the world's most prolific begetter of films. The change of government towards end-1989 augured well for the industry, both in terms of granting it respect and status on a national scale, and providing badly needed relief from taxes and constraints.

Outwardly, the film industry basked in its new-found glory. Inwardly, it grew still weaker from factional bickering and disunity on the one side, and on the other, losing its potential and popularity to home video, cable video and TV.

Artistically, 1990 promised changes for the better. The government hiked the rates offered by TV for screening of feature films, with award-winning titles benefitting the most. It also planned to host bi-annual regional film festivals all over the country. The 1990 First International Festival of Documentary and Short Film held in Bombay gave the documentary movement the impetus it can look forward to annually.

The new National Front government paid serious attention to the industry's problems. The most concrete example of its sympathetic leanings was manifest in the 1990–91 Finance Budget. It scrapped the high excise duty that had to be paid on release prints, a long-standing demand of the film industry.

In response to agitated appeals, the government set up high level review meetings and committees. It actively supported the State Ministers' recommendation that individual States should reduce their exorbitant Entertainment Tax and abolish the additional Show Tax being levied on film screenings. It recommended that some of the revenue from Entertainment Tax should be ploughed back to develop the regional film industry.

Due regard for the industry was expressed in other ways. When the hue and cry over obscene film publicity, particularly on billboards, reached a crescendo, the government allowed the industry to deal with the problem by appointing its own regulatory committees.

The government also gave in to pressure from the film industry to withdraw the proposal to set up a statutory National Film Council to supervise and regulate the making and showing of films. The Council would not only perform the functions of consultancy and co-ordination on behalf of government but also take collective decisions on film trade.

For some years, the film industry was part of the opposition to incentives given for the import of films made and funded by non-resident Indians. The general consensus was that these films were vulgar and exploitative in content. The new government announced that it was taking measures to stop such imports altogether.

New Personalities Take Over

The value of film stars and the film community in electioneering was amply proven – and rewarded. Prominent producer D.V.S. Raju replaced film journalist–writer B.K. Karanjia as Chairman of the National Film Development Corporation. The new NFDC board includes leading representatives of mainstream cinema. Actress-social activist Shabana Azmi took over as Chairperson of

Barry John and Aneeta Kanwar in Arun Sachdev's *A Woman*

the Children's Film Society, replacing actress Jaya Bhaduri, wife of actor/ Congress-I supporter Amitabh Bachchan. Bhaduri resigned soon after the new government took over. Producer/ director Atmaram, actors Shatrughan Sinha and Raj Babbar gained high-profile favour. On the Film Festival front, assurances were issued that the prestigious National Awards would soon cover mainstream cinema. To date, the Awards have been restricted to the more serious, low-budget film.

Strict censoring of sex and violence held up a host of blockbusters. As many as 28 films were banned in 1989, 17 Indian and 11 foreign films. Recourse to the Appellate Tribunal provided relief, at least in two celebrated cases. The Tribunal passed Chandrashekhar Gowda's *Ekhaney Aamar Swarga* with a U certificate. The second instance concerned the successful video magazine called *Newstrack*. It had had to cancel its April release because a story on the police forcibly "rescuing" a prostitute's children was censored. The Appellate body passed it without any cuts. The government raised the price of black-and-white raw stock manufactured by yet another pet hate of the film industry, the public sector Hindustan Photo Films. Immediate and large-scale protest led to a government reconsidering the issue, but no reprieve was forthcoming. The import and export of feature and video films remained "canalised" through the public sector NFDC.

The film business, however, had more cause to look inwards for remedial action. The self-regulatory body set up a year ago the Film Makers' Combine, the apex film body of producers, introduced a ceiling on the number of assignments (not more than

12 at one time) on film stars, and on shifts (one per day). Although not enforceable and greeted with skepticism, the move was hailed as a laudable effort. On the issue of curbing video piracy, the Film-Makers' Combine clashed headlong with the Film Distributors' Council. The latter announced that the theatrical rights of films launched on or after April 15, 1989 would be bought by distributors along with the film's home video, commercial video and cable TV rights (causing a mad rush in film studios to commence shooting prior to that D-Day). This unilateral directive abrogated the Combine's existing arrangement where home video and TV rights belonged to the producers and only commercial video rights to the distributors.

The impasse threatened an all-out war for supremacy, which could involve an embargo by producers on supplying prints to distributors. The in-fighting was on, inflicting fresh wounds when the need was to heal those that were festering.

Buyers in Scant Supply

The film industry was in doldrums anyway. The production sector faced its biggest crisis ever, with no buyers for as many as 158 films that were in the pipeline. Fifteen completed films with stars had no takers. Money was scarce in a market where for two consecutive years 95% of films had failed. Star power sold but was dicey. Three films with Amitabh Bachchan, the biggest draw, back-fired in a row.

Of the 182 Hindi films released in 1988, 162 failed to recover even their production costs. Just six years ago, 60% of films were hits. From mid-1989 to mid-1990, only two or three films really clicked at the box-office. There was Rajiv Rai's **Tridev** and Yash Chopra's **Chandni**.

One film, made by the cautious Barjatiyas, **I Fell in Love** suddenly hit the jackpot to the delirium of downcast film traders. It has scored as one of seven all-time hits in India.

However, India stubbornly continued to record the top tally in number of films produced. The country delivered 781 films in 1989, on par with the previous year (773). Hindi, the national and most widely understood language, dominated with 176 films. Colour scored overwhelmingly, with only seven films made in black-and-white. Southern languages grouped in strength thereafter: Telugu (152), Tamil (148), Malayalam (96) and Kannada (75). Marathi followed with 30 films. Then came Oriya (13), Bhojpuri (10), Gujarati (9), Rajasthani (7), Assamese (4), Punjabi (2), English (3), Haryanvi (3), Sambalpuri, Karbi and Tulu (one each).

In terms of favoured themes, *I Fell in Love* confirmed that films presenting young, rebellious, "clean-cut" love was the rage. Cuteness is in. The words, "I Love You," in waves of accented English, hit the ear drums in every film, in song, in dialogue, even in a hit commercial with a child cooing the words to a tangy soft drink. The next in line as crowd grabbers are melody and song, moulded to the rhythm and body language of today. *I Fell in Love* and *Chandni* had clap-tapping music that the movie public adored, with song-and-dance numbers linking the narrative sequences.

1990 will surely be marked by fresh young faces serving as star couples, flaunting a *nouvelle vogue* fitness and fashion. Music makers will be in luck, thriving as never before. Sooraj Bharjatiya, the 24-year-old director of *I Fell in Love*, spent the greater part of his budget on songs, lyrics and their filmed choreography and presentation. The spin-off in terms of audio cassettes of the film's songs and dialogue made even sweeter commercial music.

No Room for Commitment

Socially involved film-makers working with low budgets are drawing blanks in the distribution game. There are no art theatres for their kind of films. For the "thinking" cinema, Doordarshan (Indian television) offers a practical outlet. Doordarshan is sponsoring its own tele-films and co-producing films with NFDC. Doordarshan films (e.g. *Salaam Bombay*, which it co-produced) are winning an increasing number of awards and festival viewings. The Indian entries at Cannes (Budhadeb Dasgupta's **Bagh Bahadur**) and Venice (Adoor Gopalakrishnan's **Mathilukal**) are both Doordarshan films. Among the new Doordarshan films is *enfant terrible* Mahesh Bhatt's **Daddy**, starring his winsome teenaged daughter, in a family tear-jerker about an illegitimate child who reforms her drunkard father.

Many of India's leading film-makers are making feature-length films on India's tradition of classical music and the arts. Among these are Mani Kaul's **Siddheshwari**, on the acclaimed singer (which inaugurated the Cinéma du Réel festival held early 1990 at the Pompidou Centre in Paris), Gautam Ghose's **Meeting a Milestone** on the distinguished instrumentalist Bismillah Khan (which had a special screening at the 1990 Cannes festival), and Kumar's Shahani's **Khayal Gatha** (produced by the Madhya Pradesh government, on the history of a musical genre, featured in Pesaro's XXV Mostra Internazionale del Nuovo Cinema held in June 1989). Girish Karnad has just finished his documentary on the Sufi tradition in Islam.

Tele-films are under production on Indian nationalists. Mid-1990, Gautam Ghose was busy researching a film on freedom fighter Sarojini Naidu.

Adoor Gopalakrishnan leads the way in redeeming the fate of the quality film in India. His latest, **The Walls**, a sharply etched and absorbing account of a writer's stay in prison, not only won India's highest award for direction but, before that, was invited to compete in Venice. The film has run to packed houses in eleven leading cinemas in his home State.

Satyajit Ray's new feature film, **Family Reunion**, the Indo–French production that owes its making largely to Daniel Toscan du Plantier and Gérard Depardieu of Errato Films. The film is due to inaugurate the 1990 Venice Film Festival.

The outlook appears better this year for the independent film-maker. Those in line to present their films are Sai Paranjpye, with **Disha**, made under her own banner; newcomer Arun Sachdev with his first feature film, **A Woman**, shot in English; and Girish Karnad, embarking on Chandeshekhar Kambar's Kannada play **Jokumaraswamy**, backed by Maharaja Movies of Bangalore.

Activity Abroad

Channel 4 is fast becoming a tangible mascot for the unconventional Indian film, thanks to Farrokh Dhondy's perspicacity. It will back Pradip Krishen's new English-language film, **An Electric Moon**, scripted by Arundhati Roy. Pratap Sharma's 13 episode tele-serial **The British Raj through Indian Eyes**, presenting unusual facets about India's Independence, is a Channel 4 project.

Co-productions are under way. They include the filming of Anita Desai's novel **In Custody**, which will mark Ismail Merchant's first feature film as a director. Another is on Rudyard Kipling's **The Light that Failed** directed by V.V. Hsu, and produced by Omar Kaszmarczyk of Los Angeles. The Canada-based Indian, Shreenivas, has in mind a co-production to be shot in India entitled **Masala** which will star Saeed Jaffrey.

Ashok Amritraj, in Los Angeles, has made a film directed by Dr. Jugmohan Mundhra called **Night Eyes**, starring Tanya Roberts and Andrew Stevens. Producer Trilok Malik, in New York, completed a feature in English, the comedy **Lonely in America**.

An epic film 17 years in preparation by film-maker/producer O.P. Ralhan is **Ashoka the Great**, coming together towards the end of 1990 with the help of Washington-based co-producers, The Unit Trust Industrial Corporation.

Two major film projects will use India as locations. One is Roland Joffé's **City of Joy**, poised in Calcutta for take-off after many a false start. The second is Bernardo Bertolucci's **The Buddha**, being kept under wraps, and scheduled to shoot November 1990.

New and Forthcoming Films

Sakha Prasakha (Family Reunion). Lang: Bengali. Script/Music/Dir: Satyajit Ray. Phot: Sandip Ray. Players: Ajit Banerjee, Haradhan Bandopadhyay, Soumitra Chatterjee, Dipankar De, Ranjit Mullick, Lily Chakraborty and Mamata Shankar. Prod: Errato Films, France/Ray Productions, India. *The film is based on a story by Ray that appeared in "Akshan" magazine about three decades ago, subsequently published by Ananda Publishers under the title Pikur Diary O Annanya. Set in Hazaribagh, Bihar, during the year 1900, the film depicts the clash of conflicting values among three generations in a family who spend a week in their ancestral home. They are gathered together to be with their patriarchal head, who has suffered a heart attack.*

Goopy Bagha Phire Elo (The Return of Goopy and Bhaga). Lang: Bengali. Dir: Sandip Ray. Script/Music/Lyrics: Satyajit Ray. Phot: Barun Raha. Players: Tapan Benerjee, Robi Ghosh, Haradhan Bannerjee. Prod: Satyajit Ray Productions/West Bengal Government. *Completing a trilogy with Satyajit Ray's two earlier, highly entertaining musical fantasies, Goopy Gyen Bagha Byne (1969) and Hirok Rajar Deshe (1980). This film marks the return of the two heroes Goopy and Bagha to their absorbing exploits in the pursuit of justice. The film contains ten songs written and composed by Ray.*

A Woman. Lang: English. Script and Dir: Arun Sachdev. Phot: Najeeb Khan. Music: Louis Banks. Players: Aneeta Kanwar, Barry John, Jayant Kripalani, Wincent Creado, Protap Roy, Roger Periera. Prod: Magnum Opus. *India, 1989. Different attitudes reflecting upon the life and politics of the times are conveyed through the relationships that develop around a zealous and*

Nana Patekar and Rajashree Sawant in Sai Parajpye's *Disha*

troubled woman journalist. A first film by journalist/writer Sachdev.

Electric Moon. Lang: English. Dir: Pradip Krishen. Script: Arundhati Roy. Players: Gerson da Cunha, Madhur Jaffrey, Raghubir Yadhav, Naseerudhin Shah. Prod: Film Four International/Channel 4/and an Indian co-producer. *This is a film about Extinction and Marketing. The extinction of Tigers, Jungles, Maharajas and the Oriental Mystique and the marketing of Tigers, Jungles, Maharajas and the Oriental Mystique!*

Disha (The Uprooted). Lang: Hindi. Dir/Script/Lyrics: Sai Parajpye. Phot: Madhu Ambat. Music: Anand Modak. Players: Nana Patekar, Om Puri, Raghubir Yadav, Nilu Phule, Rajashree Sawant and Shabana Azmi. Prod: Sai Paranjpye Films Private Limited. *Two friends leave their village to seek employment in teeming Bombay. Vasant, newly married, longs for his home, while Soma adapts to the demands of the dreaded city. The sad irony is that Vasant is forced to remain while Soma returns. A film on migration, village to city and vice-versa.*

Sardar Patel. Lang: Hindi. Dir: Ketan Mehta. Script: Vijay Tendulkar. Phot: Manmohan Singh. Music: Vanraj Bhatia. Players: Paresh Rawal, Urmi Jevekar, Benjamin Gillani, Tom Alter. Prod: The Foundation for Films on India's War of Independence. *A feature film retracing the life of the patriot-statesman Sardar Vallabhai Patel, looking at his pivotal role in gaining India's independence from the British.*

Aadi haqeeqat aadha fasana (Children of the Silver Screen). Lang: Hindi. Dir: Dilip Ghosh. Script: Jill Misquita. Camera: K.U. Mohanan.

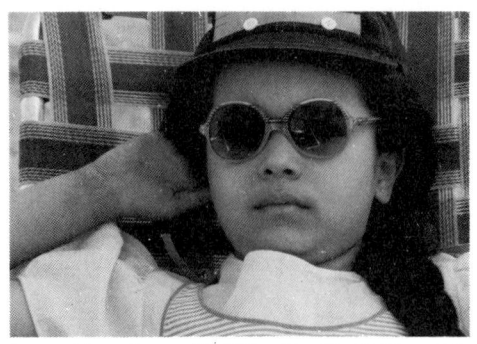

Actress Naaz, featured in Dilip Ghosh's *Children of the Silver Screen*

Music: Rajat Dholakia. Players: child actors, of the past and present, with supporting film excerpts, and members of the film industry. Prod: NFDC. *A journey into the world of child actors and how they are manipulated and forced to serve the ambition, folly and dreams of their elders. Despite the examples of and warnings given by child artistes of yesteryear, their mistakes are being repeated today. This is the first feature by Ghosh, a Pune Film Institute alumnus.*

Ek Doctor ki maut (Death of a Doctor). Lang: Hindi. Dir/Script/Music: Tapan Sinha. Phot: Soumendu Roy. Players: Shabana Azmi, Irfan Khan, Pankaj Kapoor, Deepa Sahi, Vijayendra Ghatge. Prod: NFDC. *A doctor makes it his sole mission to discover a life-saving medicine, only to find that his years of toil and self-sacrifice are nullified. His discovery is attributed to someone else. The intensity of his anguish and frustration leads him to seek another life elsewhere.*

Drishti (Vision). Lang: Hindi. Dir and Phot: Govind Nihalani. Script: Sashi Deshpande, Govind Nihalani. Music: Shantanu Mohapatra. Players: Madhusudhan Kar, Jayaswami, Raicharan Das, Duhiram Swain, Mihir Das, Sarat Pujari. Prod: NFDC. *A film made up of twelve scenes, each exploring a significant moment spread over three years in the life of a particular urban, professional couple. The time gaps are conveyed through visual images supported by classical singer Kishori Amonkar's voice and compositions.*

Moonamathoral (The Third One). Lang: Malayalam. Script and Dir: Kallikadu Ramachandran. Phot: Shaji. Music: G. Aravindan. Players: Archana, Screenivasan, Nedumudi Venu, Sreeram, Rajan Pothuval. Prod: NFDC. *Sankarankutty is an engineer living in Trivandrum. His beloved wife Devi has died two weeks earlier. He travels with his seven-year-old son to his home-town, Palghat, to tell Devi's parents that he has decided to marry again. During the visit, however, memories overwhelm him and cloud his decision.*

Aparanham. Dir: M.P. Sukumaran Nair. Phot: Ashwini Kaul. Music: Jerry Amaldev. Players: Babu Namboodiri, Murali, Babu Antony, M. Chandran Nair, Parvati, Kaviyoor Ponnamma. Prod: NFDC. *Brilliant student Nandkumar, now in his mid-twenties, joins the subversive Naxalites, is arrested and imprisoned. He is acquitted but kept under police surveillance. He meets divorcee Lalitha, a college friend, who has a daughter. She asks him to live with her. He returns instead to his village to work as a teacher.*

Nazar (Eye). Lang: Hindi. Script: Kamal Swaroop, Mani Kaul, Rajan Khosla, Cyrus Merchant, based on a story by Dostoievsky. Dir: Mani Kaul. Phot: Piyush Shah. Music: Rajat Dholakia. Players: Shekhar Kapoor, Shambhavi, Pervez Merchant, Vaishavi. Prod: NFDC/Doordarshan so-production. *An interpretation of relationships within a particular marriage, in which a girl of seventeen is the wife of a much older man. The husband runs a fashionable antique shop. The wife comes from a middle-class Bombay area firmly rooted to its culture. The two live in a well appointed, sophisticated apartment. The three locations express inherent contradictions.*

Eye of Stone. Lang: Hindi/Mewari. Dir: Nilita Vachani. Phot: Vangelis Kalambakas. Music: local folk songs. Players: the local people of Asind, Bhilwara district, Rajasthan. Prod: Film Sixteen. *A feature-length documentary about women and the ritual of spirit possession and healing in Rajasthan. A look at a young woman's interior and social worlds through her ongoing battle against the spirits, against the confines of daily existence.*

Phiringoti (The Sparks). Lang: Assamese. Script and Dir: Jahnu Barua. Phot: Anoop Jotwani. Music: Satya Baruah. Players: Malaya, Sujit, Ainu, Hemen, Bijoy. Prod: Patkai Pictures. *The distressed, newly widowed Ritu is advised by the Dept. of Public Instruction to apply for the job of a school teacher in remote village Puronipam. On reaching there, Ritu finds that no such school exists. Her dilemma is whether to introduce a formal education by starting her own school, or whether it is*

better for the oral, traditional folklore of the village to be left intact, without exposing it to a Westernized, structured method of learning.
Mathilukal (The Walls). Lang: Malayalam. Script and Dir: Adoor Gopalakrishnan. Phot: Ravi Varma. Music: Vijaya Bhaskar. Players: Mammooty, Thilakan, Murali, Ravi Vallathol. Prod: Doordarshan. *Based on the famed writer Valkom Muhammad Basheer's novel. During the freedom struggle of the early 1940's, a well-known writer is jailed for a lengthy unspecified term because of his avowed nationalism. The film deals with the writer's life in prison, conveying the free spirit of his mind, and how his creativity copes with his confinement.*

UMA DA CUNHA is based in Bombay and has acted in a promotional and executive capacity on several Indian films.

Specialist Producers

National Film Development Corporation Ltd
Discovery of India Building,
Nehru Centre
Dr Annie Besant Road
Worli
Bombay 400018
Tel: 4949856/7
Telex: 011–73489 NFDC In
Cable: Filmfinans
Fax: 4949751

Doordarshan
Mandi House
Copernicus Marg
New Delhi 110001
Tel: 382094
Telex: 3166413
Cable: TV GENERAL

Children's Film Society
c/o Film Bhavan
24 Peddar Road
Bombay 400026
Tel: 577080
Telex: FD/001–6433

Films Division
Film Bhavan
24 Peddar Road
Bombay 400026
Tel: 364633/361461
Telex: 011–6433 FD IN

INDONESIA

by Frank Segers

What is going on in Indonesia? Film production is up – way up – and there seems no accounting for the sharp increase. Americans look on from afar with a certain commercial envy.

This past summer, the big Hollywood studio members of the Motion Picture Export of America gathered in Bangkok to discuss ways of combating video piracy. Specifically, piracy in Indonesia, which is rampant. The subtext was clear – how to get a handle on this huge nation either in terms of feature films or homevideo.

The big American companies say they are shut out of Indonesia, commercially blindsided by a government-sanctioned oligopoly – as in South Korea in the bad, pre-1988 days – that controls distribution throughout Indonesia. Sure, the Americans want to control piracy, but mainly, their intent is to gain profitable access to a country of 180-million, the largest in Asia outside of China and India.

Indonesian film-makers, meanwhile, ignore – or do they? – American manoeuvres to concentrate on increasing the production rate. In 1989, Indonesia produced 104 films, 21 more than were produced the year before. And through August, 74 films were produced, 17 more than were sponsored in the prior year's comparable period.

The reasons for the increases are conjectural. Are Indonesian film-makers, feeling american commercial pressure, grinding out more films to gamble on bigger profits? Is it a case of make it while you can before the big Hollywood studios arrive to sell films on a royalty basis directly?

There's always the possibility, of course, that domestic demand is heavier from the ground up. General economic conditions in Indonesia are sound. The national economy grew by some 5% in 1989, after a 4.8% growth rate the year before. Indonesia is oil rich at a time when petroleum capacity takes on special economic lustre.

Big Stars Satisfy Home Demand

In terms of pure film content, *plus ça change* is the order of the day in Jakarta and other key film locales. That is, comedies, action films, and costume dramas are the order of the day – as usual, Indonesia's biggest stars have names like Ongky Alaxander, Doyok, Kadir and, of course, the ever popular and ever sensual siren, Meriam Bellina.

1989's biggest hits included **Saur Sepuh**, a costume with action, and a trio of comedies: **Catatan Si Boy**, **Kanan Kiri O.K.** and **Si Kebayan**. The current year brought to Indonesia's some 2,200 theatres more of the same in another trio of comedy hits, **Sabur Dulu Dong**, **Dorce Sok Akrab** and **Makelar Kodok**.

Indonesia like the Philippines is a familiar locale for obscure Western performers seeking a quick job. Cynthia Rothrock, an action heroine who's popular in other Far East territories including Hong Kong, will be toplined in Rapi Films' production of *Triple Cross*, an unusually expensive $3-million outing with some location shooting in the U.S. A more typical budget is 300-million rupiahs, less than $200,000. Rapi is grinding out 10 productions in 1990 – another company caught up in Indonesia's current production frenzy.

IRAN

by Jamal Omid

In spite of its 60-year-old history, Iranian cinema emerged as an artistically and culturally independent film industry only in the past five years. The major objectives of liberating local film art from western domination, reconstructing the industry's economic and financial underpinnings, attracting new talents to cinema and promoting an intellectual inter-relationship between film-makers and the young audiences (which make up the greatest portion of Iranian population) were finally brought to fruition after years of planning, policy formulations and revisions. For the first time film-makers have found it possible to conceive of their works without being paralysed by fear of box-office failure. They can now freely engage in creating works of art that derive directly from the traditional Iranian culture, and in fact many of their pictures are met with enthusiastic reception on the international film scene. In 1989, **Where Is the Friend's Home?** and **Nar-o-Nay** were screened in over ten international festivals and brought home a number of prizes.

Despite the general qualitative and even quantitative improvement, film industry in Iran (as in many other countries) has not yet achieved a dynamic and viable economic status. And despite efforts to effect a co-ordinated system of cost control, many film projects have turned out to be financial flops. As a matter of fact ticket prices are still too low to cover production costs (despite a moderate increase at the beginning of current year) and the Iranian film industry requires basic reconsiderations to attain economic self-sufficiency. The existing screening capacity (number of movie theatres) is disproportionately low in view of the rising annual production and the country's population. To overcome this deficiency, a number of surveys are being conducted to construct new screening halls and cinema complexes. The country's film industry is in urgent need of such remedial measures in order to weather the present crisis, which would otherwise take on catastrophic proportions.

Animation Comes Out Tops

The most successful film of the year at the box-office was **Golnar**, a live-action puppet animation directed by K. Partovi and aimed at children up to the age of ten. As might have been expected the commercial success of *Golnar* prompted a row of similar film projects aimed at the same vulnerable age groups. Another film directed by Partovi, **The Fish**, was awarded the prize of best film for children at the 1990 Berlin Festival.

Other successful films of the year were **The Horizon**, an adventure film directed by R. Mollagholipoor, and two comedies, **Grand Day** by Kianoush Ayyari and **Hey, Joe** by M. Asgarinassab. All four films managed to cover their production costs on first release in Tehran. Also all of these films were the type of pictures that appealed mostly to younger audiences and drew the greatest number of children to the movies.

In general the Iranian people, specially the lower age groups, are great film fans, and cinema is still the most popular form of entertainment in the capital and the provinces. All this points to the possibility of increasing local production above the present level of 50 to 60 films a year,

Farabi Cinema Foundation
Cinema is our middle name

Farabi Cinema Foundation
NO 55 SIE-TIR AVE TEHRAN 11358/IR IRAN
TELEX 214283FCF TEL 678545/678156
FAX 678155

Still from Dariush Mehrjui's *Hamoon*

provided the programme of adding the screening capacity is followed up in earnest.

Debutants Make a Splash

As a result of the policy of promoting the production of more valuable films (adopted since several years ago), a number of remarkable films were created in 1989. Interestingly some of the best pictures produced in the past two or three years were first features by newcomers, many of whom have by now successfully produced their second and third films. In recent years the ambition of making artistically respectable films and achieving international recognition at major international festivals has been a great incentive for Iranian directors and, encouraged by local support and the success of their peers, many of the artists plan their pictures with the ultimate goal of showing them at festivals abroad. This trend, which in some cases is coupled with genuine creative abilities, results each year in a number of outstanding releases.

Hamoon

Script and Direction: Dariush Mehrjui. Photography: Turaj Mansuri. Editing: Hassan Hassandoost. Music: Naser Cheshmazar. Players: Khosro Shakibai, Ezzatollah Entezami, Hossein Sarshar, Bita Farrahi, Turan Mehrzad, Jalal Moghaddam. Produced by D. Mehrjui, Pakhshiran Co.

Mehrjui is among the forerunners of Iranian serious film-makers and his latest picture is a philosophical exploration into spirituality and truth. Faced by the unbearable complications of daily life, the hero of the film finds spiritual support in his untiring quest for the meaning of existence.

In effect Mehrjui's film is a portrayal of modern man's alienation from his true self. And considering Mehrjui's past work, he seems to be treading new ground in this film. But he handles the story with ease and assurance. He portrays the complexity of the human psyche with strong *mise en scène* and a tightly edited overall structure. Over the years Mehrjui has acquired a maturity in his directorial style and a mastery over his performers which had already been promised in *The Cow* – the picture Mehrjui directed in 1969.

Jamal Omid

JAMAL OMID has been writing film reviews since 1966. He has been the editor of several film magazines and has written a four-volume history of Iranian cinema of which three volumes have already appeared. Omid has been a member of the organising committee of the Tehran International Film Festival and the Fajr International Film Festival.

Close-Up

Script, Direction and Editing: Abbas Kiarostami. Photography: Alireza Zarrindast. Players: Ali Sabzian, Hassan Farazmand, Abolfazl Ahankhah, Mohsen Makhmalbaf. Produced by A. Kiarostami, Institute for the Intellectual Development of Children and Young Adults.

Close-Up is among the few Kiarostami films which do not concern the problems of children. It is based on a real incident of one man impersonating another – which is not an uncommon subject in cinema. What attracted Kiarostami to the incident, however, was the fact that the impostor was a film buff who introduced himself as Mohsen Makhmalbaf, the celebrated

Still from Ebrahim Hatamikia's *The Immigrant*

Iranian film director. *Close-Up* is part documentary, part reconstructed and it is characterised by Kiarostami's realistic approach and his gentle humour. One shouldn't be searching in this film for the poetic allusions which gave *Where Is the Friend's Home?* its subtle resonances, although *Close-Up* is crafted with the same awareness of the complexity of social and human issues.

Jamal Omid

The Immigrant

Script and Direction: Ebrahim Hatamikia. Photography: Mohammad Taghi Paksima. Editing: Hossein Zandbaf. Music: Karim Gugerdchi. Players: Alireza Khatami, Ebrahim Asgharzadeh, Asghar Naghizadeh, Alireza Heidari. Produced by: Organization for the Propagation of Islamic Thought.

Having started his film career with short documentaries on the Iran-Iraq war, Hatamikia possesses a profound understanding of the emotional, human aspects of battle-front life. He has so far made three feature films on the subject of war which reveal the director's gradual progress in his mastery over the film medium. In *Immigrant*, Hatamikia presents a lyrical expression of the mystic experiences and feelings of the combatants. He has in effect created a new type of war film in which the war is used as a means of revealing the ingenuousness and the ideological aspirations of those engaged in the battle.

Jamal Omid

Profile: Ebrahim Hatamikia

The new Iranian cinema, in direct contrast with the pre-revolution methods, provides exceptional possibilities for the emergence of new talents. Last year Saeed Ebrahimifar rose to international fame with his debut film, *Nar-o-nay*, and the discovery of the 1990's is undoubtedly Ebrahim Hatamikia, who shows great promise in becoming one of Iran's foremost directors. Born in 1961, Hatamikia is a student of the Faculty of the Fine Arts of Tehran University. He began his film career by making war documentaries in 1980 and made his debut feature *The Identity* in 1986. His other films are *The Scout* (1988) and *The Immigrant* (1990).

Ebrahim Hatamikia

Recent Films

O Iran. Script and Dir: Nasser Taghvai. Phot: Mahmud Kalari. Players: Akbar Abdi, Hossein Sarshar, Hamid Jebeli, Soraya Hekmat, Kamran Fiuzat.
Snake Fang. Script and Dir: Masud Kimia'ie. Phot: Iraj Sadeghpoor. Players: Faramarz Sedighi, Ahmad Najafi, Golchehreh Sajjadieh, Jalal Moghaddam, Fariba Kosari.

Homework. Script and Dir: Abbas Kiarostami. Phot: Iraj Safavi.
Mother. Script and Dir: Ali Hatami. Phot: Mahmud Kalari. Players: Roghayeh Chehreh-Azad, Mohammad Ali Keshavarz, Farima Farjami, Amin Tarokh, Akbar Abdi, Hamid Jebeli.
Foreign Currency. Dir: Rakhshan Bani-etemad. Script: F. Mostafavi. D. Moadiyan. Phot: Hassan Gholizaedh. Players: Ali Nasirian Mahtaj Nojumi, Mohammad Ali Keshavarz.
All the Temptations of the Earth. Script and Dir: Hamid Samandarrian. Phot: M.R. Sharifian. Players: Homa Rousta, Jamal Ejlali, Reza Kianian.
Children of Divorce. Script and Dir: Tahmineh Milani. Phot: Reza Banki, Players: Mahshid Afsharzadeh, Faramarz Sedighi.
Lost Time. Script and Dir: Puran Derakhshandeh. Phot: Hossein Jafarian. Players: Sanaz Sehati, Faramarz Sedighi, Tania Johari, Shahla Riahi.
My Daughter, Sahar. Dir: Majid Gharizadeh. Script: S. Bazarjani, M. Gharizadeh. Phot: Ataollah Hayati. Players: Reza Ruygari, Mahshid Afsharzadeh, Sara Torabi.
Passing through Mist. Dir: Puran Derakhshandeh. Script: K. Ghadakchian, P. Derakhshandeh. Phot: M.R. Sharifi. Players: Khosro Shakibai, Mahnaz Afzali, Afsar Asadi.
Reyhaneh. Script and Dir: Alireza Raissian. Phot: Mahmud Kalari. Players: Fatemeh Motamed-Aria, Majid Mozaffari, Akbar Abdi, Hamid Jebeli, Hossein Mahjub.
Savalan. Dir: Yadollah Samadi. Script: B. Reypoor, J. Omid, H. Hedayat, Y. Samadi. Phot: Hassan Gholizadeh. Players: Majid Majidi, Ataollah Salmanian, Nilufar Mahmudi.
Fifth of June Flight. Script and Dir: Alireza Samiazar. Phot: Jamshid Alvandi> Players: Majid Jafari, Nasser Aghai, Atila Pasiyani, Tania Johari.
The Seeker. Dir: Mohammad Motevaselani. Script: E. Khalaj. M. Bahrami, M. Motavaselani. Phot: Maziar Partov. Players: Amin Tarokh, Dariush Arjomand. M.A. Keshavarz, Fatemeh Noori.
Swimming in Winter. Script and Dir: Mohammad Kasebi. Phot: Iraj Sadeghpoor Players: Majid Majidi, Masud Rahmani, Davud Ghanbari.
The Wage. Script and Dir: Majid Javanmard. Phot: Gholamreza Azadi. Players: Mohammad Saleh-Ala, Mehdi Fathe, Farzaneh Kaboli, Ahmad Hashemi.
Under the Roofs of the City. Dir: Asghar Hashemi. Script: E. Jeirani, A. Hashemi. Phot: Asghar Rafi'ie-Jam. Players: Iraj Tahmasb, Alireza Khamseh, Jamshid Esmail-khani, Mahvash Afshar-Panah.
Up to the Visit. Dir: Hossein Ghasemi Jami. Script: Ali Akbar Saghafi. Phot: Kamal Tabrizi. Players: Majid Majidi, Hedayatollah Navid, Jalil Farjad.
Dolls' Thief. Script and Dir: Mohammad Reza Honarman. Phot: Nemat Haghighi. Players: Akbar Abdi, Azita Hajian, Shirin Nafafian.
Kakoli. Dir: Ferial Behzad. Script: Hushang Moradi Kermani. Phot: Gholamreza Azadi. Players: Mehdi Fathi, Farzaneh Kaboli, Amir Sheisi, Mahmud Ahmadi.
Small Wishes. Dir: Masud Karamati. Script: R. Kianian, M. Sajjadechi. Phot: Azim Javanruh. Players: Reza Kianian, Mansureh Shadmanesh, Ahmad Aghaloo, Fariba Jedikar.
Courtship. Script and Dir: Mehdi Fakhimzadeh. Phot: Ali Akbar Mazinani. Players: Hadki Eslami, Soraya Ghasemi, Esmail Mehrabi.
Death of the Leopard. Dir: Fariborz Saleh. Script: K. Nasimi. F. Saleh. Phot: Faraj Heidari. Players: Faramarz Gharibian, Shahla Riahi, Fariba Kosari, Kazem Afrandnia.
Delnamak. Dir: Amir Ghavidel. Script: Ensieh Shahosseini. Phot: Reza Banki. Players: Hadi Eslami, Khosro Shojazadeh, Anushiravan Arjmand.
Do Not Muddy the Water. Dir: Shahriar Bahrani. Script: Ensieh Shah-hosseini. Phot: Homayoun Pievar. Players: Roya Nonahali, Behruz Razavi, Zohreh Sarmadi.

Forthcoming Films

The Sergeant. Dir: Masud Kimia'ie.
Time of Love. Dir: Mohsen Makhmalbaf.
City of Ashes. Dir: Hassan Hedayat.
Third Line. Dir: Amir Ghavidel.
Search in the Island. Dir: Mehdi Sabbaghzadeh.
The Wedding. Dir: Behzad Afkhami.
Homecoming. Dir: Hassan Majdzadeh.
The Call of the Sea. Dir: Rahman Rezai.
Renault, Tehran 28. Dir: Siamak Shayeghi.
Kokab's Secret. Dir: Kazem Masumi.

TOP GROSSING FILMS IN IRAN: 1989

	Rentals
Golnar (K. Partovi)	US $400,000
Horizon (R. Mollagholipoor)	387,500
Grand Day (K. Ayari)	330,000
Hey, Joe (M. Asgarinasab)	325,000
The Cyclist (M. Makhmalbaf)	255,000
In the Wind's Eye (M. Jafari Jozani)	242,000
The Ship Angelica (M.R. Bozorgnia)	230,000
Marriage of the Blessed (M. Makhmalbaf)	225,000
Canary Yellow (Rakhshan Bani-etemad)	175,000
The Lead (M. Kimia'ie)	170,000

Figures include first run in Tehran with an average ticket price of 40¢

Silent Hunt. Dir: Kiumars Poorahmad.
Love and Death. Dir: M.R. Alami.
Little Girl by the Lagoon. Dir: Ali Zhekan.
Summer of 58. Dir: Mojtaba Rai.
The Hidden Fire. Dir: Habib Kavosh.
Silence. Dir: Ali Sajjadi Hosseini.
Light and Shadow. Dir: Shapoor Gharib.

Shadow of Dream. Dir: Hossein Delir.
Light on the Horizon. Dir: Yusef Sedigh.
Chasing the Shadows. Dir: Alishah Hatami.
Last Act. Dir: Varuzh Karim Masihi.
Action. Dir: Dariush Farhang.
The Blood Crystal. Dir: Jamshid Andlibi.

Distributors

Tehran Group of United Cinemas
Nader Cinema
Barbad Alley
Lalehzar Street
Tehran. Tel: 314795.

Hedayat Film
25 Loghman Adham Street
Jomhuri Junction
Vali-e Asr Ave.
Tehran.
Tel: 3851962.

Laleh Film Production and Distribution Co-operative
72 Lalehzar Street
Tehran.
Tel: 3852954.

Iran Film Co-operative
7th of Tir Sq.
Tehran.
Tel: 824432.

Novin Film
15 Jomhuri Ave.
Tehran.
Tel: 6403697.

Khaneh Film Iran
Tavakol Building
Jomhuri Ave.
Tehran.
Tel: 671247.

Arman Film
26 Razi Street
Jomhuri Ave.
Tehran.
Tel: 675418.

Iranmilad Film Production and Distribution
186 Shiraz Street
Bahar Ave.
Tehran.
Tel: 755674.

Roshan Film
97 Arbab Jamshid Alley

Kushk Street
Tehran.
Tel: 3852975.

Film-Makers' Co-operative
9 Atarod Alley
Mofatteh Street
Tehran.
Tel: 821409.

Sepahan Cinema Company
126 Razi Street
Jomhuri Ave.
Tehran.
Tel: 676268.

Mahab Film
224 Gharanay Ave.
Tehran.
Tel: 897219.

Milad Film Production and Distribution
224 Iranshahr Street
Karimkhan Ave.
Tehran.
Tel: 828319.

Pakhshiran Company
8 Somayeh Street
Bahar Ave.
Tehran.
Tel: 824052.

Fajr Film Production and Distribution
7 Saadi Ave.
Tehran.
Tel: 391580.

Farabi Cinema Foundation
55 Sie-Tir Ave.
Tehran.
Tel: 671010.

Cinematic Affairs of Janbazan Foundation
Vali-e Asr Junction
Beheshti Ave.
Tehran.
Tel: 623536.

Arts Bureau of the Organization for the Propagation of Islamic Thought
213 Somayeh Street
Tehran.
Tel: 820023-9.

Islamic Republic of Iran Broadcasting
Jaam-e Jam
Vali-Asr Ave.
Tehran.
Tel: 832527.

Purika Film
119 Forsat Street
Taleghani Ave.
Tehran.
Tel: 828442.

Shiraz Film Production and Distribution

1/56 Neaufle-Le Château Street
Tehran.
Tel: 677952.

Filmiran
Central Cinema
Enghelab Square
Tehran.
Tel: 929436.

Farhang Film
Air France Building
Enghelab Ave.
Tehran.
Tel: 672340.

Hamrah Film Production and Distribution
Universal Cinema
Enghelab Square
Tehran.
Tel: 923854.

Useful Addresses

Arts Bureau
Intersection of Somayeh & Hafez
Tehran.
Tel: 820654.

Cinematographic Affairs Centre for the Intellectual Development of Children and Young Adults
Motahari Ave. No. 37
Jam St.

Tehran.
Tel: 836065-7.

Department of Photography and Film Production, Ministry of Culture and Islamic Guidance
Baharestan Sq.
Tehran.
Tel: 391333.

Farabi Cinema Foundation
55 Sie-Tir Ave.

Tehran.
Tel: 671010.
Telex: 214283 FCF IR.
Fax: 678155

Mostazafan and Janbazan Cinema Foundation
343 Shahid Beheshti Ave.
Tehran.
Tel: 623303, 627824/5
Telex: 213427.

IRELAND

by Michael Dwyer

Irish cinema over the past 18 months has been dominated by the remarkable critical and commercial success of **My Left Foot** both at home and abroad. Made on a modest budget in the region of three million dollars by a producer, Noel Pearson, and a director, Jim Sheridan, neither of whom had ever before worked on a feature film, this moving and uplifting picture of the disabled Irish artist, Christy Brown, has become the outstanding success of the indigenous Irish film industry.

Following excellent reviews and solid box-office business in Ireland, *My Left Foot* was rejected by the Cannes selectors in 1989 and despite three nominations, failed to take any prizes in the 1989 European Film Awards. Across the Atlantic, however, it was a very different story. The film first made its mark in North America with extremely well-received screenings at the New York, Telluride, Montréal and Toronto festivals. Daniel Day Lewis, who played Christy Brown in the film, received the best actor award at Montréal, and again at year's end from both the New York and Los Angeles film critics' circles. Brenda Fricker, who played his mother in the film, also received best supporting actress from the L.A. critics.

When it came to the announcement of the Oscar nominees in February, *My Left Foot* earned five principal nominations, including best picture, director, actor, supporting actress and screenplay; only *Driving Miss Daisy* and *Born on the Fourth of July* had more nominations. On Oscar night at the end of March, the film took half the Academy's acting awards, with victory going to both Day Lewis and Fricker.

Its U.S. commercial success already boosted by the best film award from the New York critics and by rave reviews, *My Left Foot* went on wide release after the Oscars and racked up a very impressive $15 million at the box-office, going on to perform very successfully on video release. The film also fared very well on its European release and, especially, in Australia.

These have been remarkable achievements for a low-budget film made in Ireland by an entirely Irish cast and crew – Day Lewis holds an Irish passport. However, given the perpetually underfunded status of the Irish film industry, most of the budget came from outside the country, principally from Granada in England.

Even before the end of 1989, the Pearson-Sheridan team had completed principal photography on their second feature film, *The Field*, a rural drama set in 1930's Ireland starring Richard Harris, Tom Berenger, John Hurst and Brenda Fricker. Pearson and Sheridan recently signed a three-picture deal with Universal Pictures and they are considering a wide range of possible prospects for their first Hollywood-backed productions.

Ironically, the *My Left Foot* team received a hero's welcome home from the Oscar ceremony from none other than the Taoiseach (the Irish prime minister), Charles Haughey, who in 1987 made the decision to close down the Irish Film Board, just as it was becoming established. Unwilling to admit he made a mistake, Haughey has refused persistent demands to re-establish the board in one form or

Brenda Fricker and Hugh O'Conor in the acclaimed Irish production, *My Left Foot*

another, and funding for film in Ireland remains difficult and precarious.

Apart from *My Left Foot*, the only other Irish film to open at Irish cinemas in 1989, from a total of 159 new releases, was Ronan O'Leary's **Fragments of Isabella**, adapted from a book by Auschwitz survivor Isabella Leitner, who was played in the film's solo performance by Gabrielle Reidy. Both Reidy and lighting cameraman Walter Lassally were highly praised for their work on the film. Finding an audience for a one-person show on film was not easy; the film had a short run in Dublin and seems likely to attract its biggest audience on TV.

Attendances Up Up and Away

The upswing in attendances at Irish cinemas, which began in the late 1980's, continued apace into the new decade, particularly in Dublin, the capital, where the 20 first-run city-centre screens again found themselves with too much popular product and not enough seats. The pressure on the city-centre cinemas is unlikely to be eased by the arrival of the multiplexes – two UCI complexes, a 12-screen and a 10-screen cinema, due to open in outer suburban Dublin in November 1990 and March 1991, respectively.

As ever, precise attendance figures and box-office receipts are not made available on the Irish market, even though it is controlled almost entirely from the head offices of the majors in London. Consequently, the accompanying chart of 1989 box-office hits had to be compiled from a consensus survey of Irish distribution managers and exhibitors.

The box-office leaders in the first half of 1990 have been *Pretty Woman, Look Who's Talking, Honey I Shrunk the Kids, When Harry Met Sally, Parenthood, Born on the Fourth of July* and *The War of the Roses*. The biggest recent art-house hits have been *The Cook, The Thief, His Wife and Her Lover, sex, lies and videotape*, *Cinema Paradiso* and *Trop Belle pour toi!*

A new film festival in Galway, in the west of Ireland, joined the established festivals in Cork and Dublin. Cork's October 1989 festival opened on a high note with *Jesus of Montreal*, attended by its star, Lothaire Bluteau, and featured the world premiere of Ronan O'Leary's *Fragments of Isabella*, and a retrospective of the Irish documentarist, John Davis.

The Dublin Film Festival, smoothly settled into its new spring dates, opened in February 1990 with the world premiere of Thaddeus O'Sullivan's *December Bride*, reviewed below and closed with another Irish director's work, the European premiere of Neil Jordan's *We're No Angels*, which went on to fare very well on Irish cinema release, in contrast to its reception in the US and Britain. Over the summer, the prolific Jordan shot his sixth feature film, *The Miracle*, on location outside Dublin – his first film in Ireland since he made his debut with *Angel*.

The Galway festival kicked off its second outing in July 1990 with the Irish premiere of Ken Loach's controversial *Hidden Agenda* and attracted guests from Gillo Pontecorvo to Oliver Reed. The programme showcased recent African cinema and the work of the Dublin-born director, Rex Ingram, who made his mark in Hollywood in the era of silent cinema.

Meanwhile, observers of Irish film censorship history are bemused by the number of movies given an X rating in the U.S. and passed without cuts in Ireland. The progressive policies of Irish censor Sheamus Smith have seen no notable films banned or cut in recent years. In fact, the main problems faced by his office have been those of certification. Columbia Tri-Star Films successfully appealed against his "over 15" certificates for both *The Karate Kid III* and *Look Who's Talking*, while an appeal by Warner Bros to reduce the same certificate on *Gremlins 2* failed.

Saskia Reeves in *December Bride*
photo: Simon Mein

December Bride

Script: David Rudkin. Director: Thaddeus O'Sullivan. Photography: Bruno de Keyser. Editing: Rodney Holland. Music: Jurgen Kneiper. Production Design: Adrian Smith. Players: Donal McCann, Saskia Reeves, Ciaran Hinds, Patrick Malahide. Produced by Little Bird Productions for Film Four International, CTE and British Screen. 87 mins.

Given its world premiere at the 1990 Dublin Film Festival and selected for the Directors' Fortnight at Cannes, this impressive period picture marks a notable debut as a director of feature films for Thaddeus O'Sullivan, the Irish film-maker who also directed the 1985 short film, *The Woman Who Married Clark Gable*, but has been best known for his work as director of photography on films such as *On the Black Hill*, *The Love Child*, *Rocinante* and *Ladder of Swords*.

Adapted by David Rudkin from the novel

by Sam Hanna Bell, *December Bride* begins at the turn of the century in a rural peninsula in the north of Ireland. The central character, Sarah, played by Saskia Reeves, is a strong-willed young servant employed by a farmer and his two sons. After the father dies in a boating accident, Sarah goes against her mother's advice and stays on the farm with the two sons, played by Donal McCann and Ciaran Hinds. When she becomes sexually involved with each of the two men, they are ostracised by the conservative local community.

This sombre, low-key drama simmers in the exposition of the characters, their plight and their fate. It is a thoughtful, well-observed and compelling picture, memorably acted by a strong cast, notably McCann, Hinds and the very expressive Reeves in the central roles. Their lives are set against a rugged, bleakly beautiful landscape indelibly captured in the images of the gifted French lighting cameraman, Bruno de Keyser – an inspired choice by O'Sullivan, the lighting cameraman turning director. The convincing look of the film is enhanced by the work of production designer Adrian Smith and costume designer Consolata Boyle.

This assured production marks an auspicious start for O'Sullivan in features, which he hopes to follow with a film of the award-winning John Banville novel, *The Book of Evidence*.

Michael Dwyer

Julie Christie and Sean McClory in *Fools of Fortune*

Fools of Fortune

Script: Michael Hirst. Direction: Pat O'Connor. Photography: Jerzy Zielinski. Editing: Michael Bradsell. Music: Hans Zimmer. Production Design: Jamie Leonard. Players: Iain Glen, Mary Elizabeth Mastrantonio, Julie Christie, Michael Kitchen, Niamh Cusack, Tom Hickey. Produced by Working Title. 109 mins.

Working in his native Ireland for the first time since he made his cinema debut with *Cal* in 1984, director Pat O'Connor returns to the work of author William Trevor with *Fools of Fortune* following his deservedly acclaimed television films of Trevor's *The Ballroom of Romance* and *One of Ourselves*, which led to his cinema career. *Fools of Fortune* is O'Connor's best work since his second feature, *A Month in the Country*, and a true return to form after his American films, *Stars and Bars* and *The January Man*.

The central character in *Fools of Fortune* is a traumatised recluse (Iain Glen) haunted by horrific memories of his past which are outlined in a skilfully structured series of extended flashbacks, beginning in 1920, when he was 11. Then, his well-appointed family home was razed to the ground in a vicious act of retribution by an English sergeant, killing his father and his young sisters and leading to the total disintegration of his despairing mother (Julie Christie).

This engrossing drama, which builds in power, follows the snowballing events as it observes the legacy of tragedy as it is passed down through the different generations of the family and the past exerts its hold on their ruined lives. The victims struggle through it, trying to understand it all.

In a good cast, Julie Christie is outstanding and her performance perfectly captures her character's transition from a contented woman full of the joys of life to a nervy, distraught alcoholic retreating from the world.

Michael Dwyer

TOP GROSSING FILMS IN IRELAND: 1989

Batman
Indiana Jones and the Last Crusade
Who Framed Roger Rabbit
Rain Man
Dead Poets Society
The Accused
Twins
Licence to Kill
The Naked Gun
Cocktail

Recent and Forthcoming Films

The Commitments. Dir: Alan Parker. Prod: Roger Randall-Cutler and Lynda Myles. Script: Dick Clement and Ian La Fresnais, from the novel by Roddy Doyle. Prod: Beacon Communications.
The Field. Script and Dir: Jim Sheridan, from the play by John B. Keane. Phot: Jack Conroy. Players: Richard Harris, Tom Berenger, John Hurt, Brenda Fricker, Sean Bean, Frances Tomelty. Prod: Noel Pearson.
The Miracle. Script and Dir: Neil Jordan. Players: Beverly D'Angelo, Donal McCann. Prod: Palace Pictures.
The Playboys. Script: Shane Connaughton. Dir: Terry Jones. Prod: Simon Perry, Umbrella Films.
Rock-a-Doodle. Script: David N. Weiss. Dir: Don Bluth. Voices: Glen Campbell, Sandy Duncan, Christopher Plummer, Ellen Greene.

MICHAEL DWYER is Film Correspondent of The Irish Times and the producer-presenter of the RTE Television series, Freeze Frame. He has been Programme Director of the Dublin Film Festival since he co-founded it in 1985.

Producers

City Vision
23 Carleton Road
Marino
Dublin 3
Tel: 331645

Emdee Productions
22–24 Upper Sheriff Street
Dublin 1
Tel: 741954

Emerald City Productions
1 Harbour Road
Dun Laoghaire
Co. Dublin
Tel: 804044

Gandon Productions
27 Harcourt Street
Dublin 2
Tel: 784399

Little Bird Productions
122 Lower Baggot Street
Dublin 2
Tel: 614245

Mirror Films
44 Nassau Street
Dublin 2
Tel: 795202

Murakami Wolf
Bell House
Montague Street
Dublin 2
Tel: 783199

Poolbeg Productions
10 Hagan Court, Lad Lane
Dublin 2
Tel: 618631

Pearson Productions
27 Dawson Street
Dublin 2
Tel: 772951

Sullivan Bluth Studios (Ireland)
Phoenix House
Conyngham Road
Dublin 8
Tel: 795099

Tara Productions
Ardmore Studios

Bray, Co. Wicklow
Tel: 862971

Windmill Lane Productions
4 Windmill Lane
Dublin 2
Tel: 713444

Yellow Asylum Films
6 Montague Street
Dublin 2
Tel: 781016

Distributors

Abbey Films
35 Upper Abbey Street
Dublin 1
Tel: 723922
Fax: 723687

Columbia Tri-Star Films
Merchant's Court
24 Merchant's Quay
Dublin 8
Tel: 798234

Dublin Film Distributors
53 Middle Abbey Street
Dublin 1
Tel: 748214

20th Century-Fox Film Co.
5 Upper O'Connell Street
Dublin 2
Tel: 743068

Warner Bros
Russell House
Stokes Place
St. Stephen's Green
Dublin 2
Tel: 784000
Fax: 784572

United International Pictures
D'Olier Chambers
D'Olier Street
Dublin 2
Tel: 792433

Useful Addresses

The Arts Council
70 Merrion Square
Dublin 2
Tel: 61140

Film Makers Ireland
1 Fitzwilliam Square
Dublin 2
Tel: 614399
Fax: 611397

Irish Film Institute
6 Eustace Street
Dublin 2
Tel: 795744

Irish Film and Television Guild
c/o Royal Marine Hotel
Dun Laoghaire
Co. Dublin
Tel: 803050/607753

ISRAEL

by Dan Fainaru

All things considered, this has been a very strange year indeed. A year in which practically nothing happened except promises, mergers, more promises and more mergers. Theoretically, it should be much easier nowadays to make an Israeli film. In practice, it looks like the same old obstacles which prevented the Iraeli cinema from breaking through in the past, are still very much in evidence. They may have changed aspect here and there, but not the essence.

First, the money. The perennial lack of it is still here. Sure, things have happened. The Ministry of Industry and Culture, once the sole supporter of the Fund for the Promotion of Quality Films, has joined forces with the Ministry of Industry and Commerce, and now every project can get twice the amount of money it did in the past, up to $250,000. The Israeli Broadcasting Authority (operating the First and for the time being the only official TV Channel), opposed in the past to any direct participation in feature film projects, is now willing to advance up to $100,000 per title. Not a bad start.

But, once you start talking with producers and particularly with directors, you find out that first, this money is not as readily available as it might look at first glance, second, it barely covers 60% but certainly not more of a very modest production, and third, finding the rest of the money has become even more difficult than it was in the past. What's more, the decision of the Quality Fund to comply with the demands of its new partner, Industry and Commerce, and take into consideration not only the artistic quality of a project but also its commercial potential (without specifying exactly how it should be assessed), has diverted part of the already modest budget available for purposes that are, to say the least, debatable. Take for instance, the contribution to *The Skipper 2*, a straightforward, simplistic, unpretentious Mediterranean soap opera, a vehicle for producer-star Yehuda Barkan, which obtained the Fund's support for reasons that no one could truly fathom.

Disasters and Embarrassments

Even statistics, a science that bends any way you want it to, confirm that last year was a very bad one. Instead of the average annual 15 features' production, this year's crop, if indeed all the films will get a release before the end of the year, will be less than ten. And this includes a disastrous candid camera comedy, *Flat on your Face (Al Hapanim)*, a well intentioned but awkwardly amateurish home movie made by director Jonathan Paz, *The Valley Train (Rakevet Ha 'Emek)*, and the embarrassing English-speaking *Road to Ein Harod*, produced and directed by Doron Eran from a futuristic political fantasy by Amos Kenan, a hopelessly botched affair with vain international pretensions.

If there is any hope of a professionally sound cinema, with a potential for commercial rentability, it still lies with people like Uri Barbash. After the unhappy experience of *The Dreamers*, Barbash is back on familiar grond with **One of Us**. His new film may have some structural problems, but it proves beyond doubt that he can still produce tight, effective drama, with strong political undertones, as long as he deals with topical problems he has intimate knowledge of, such as the moral aspects of being an Israeli soldier serving today on the West Bank.

The good news from the past year is that two veterans, generally considered among the top talent available in the country, Avraham Heffner and Daniel Wachsman, have new films out. Heffner, a highly respected writer whose film activity is getting scarcer all the time, had to wait ten years before shooting **The Last Love of Laura Adler**, a sad, gentle requiem to the Yiddish theatre and the people working in it. As for Wachsman, it took him eight years to come out with **The Appointed**, which discusses love, religion and faith (should be but are not always the same thing at all), using for inspiration some easily identifiable occurrences at rabbinical courts in the Galilee. Whatever reservations one might have about both films, there is no doubt that denying people like Heffner and Wachsman a chance to work for such a long time, is sheer waste, something the Israeli cinema can't really afford.

Is it going to be any better, in future? Neither one of these two directors, both drained by the films they have just finished, seems to think so and said that much in recent interviews. Still, new possibilities are opening up on several levels. A second TV Channel has been voted in and will start operating properly on a full time basis, next year. Cable TV is spreading all over the country, and this time, it's the legitimate version, aspiring to replace the pirates. In both cases, their licence requires they devote part of their budget and air time to local productions. If they comply with the regulations, there should be a lot more money for production, but it still remains to be seen what kind of production these people have in mind. The Film Institute is energetically pushing Israel film weeks abroad, maybe not always the best possible programmes, but at least the presence of Israeli cinema is being felt more now than it used to be, a couple of years ago.

Also, after a serious slump in the first

IT IS OUR BUSINESS

to pave the way for smooth production work in Israel and assist with advice, contacts and financial incentives.

Israel Film Centre

Ministry of Industry and Trade, P.O.Box 299, Jerusalem, Israel.
Tel: 210433, 210297. Telex: 25211; Fax: 245110

---

year of the *intifada*, it seems now that many international productions are willing to come back and shoot films here once again. Being the only natural place to shoot Middle Eastern subjects, particularly the kind that aren't entirely complimentary to their Arab revolution and the terrorist movement, Israel will have some ten such productions using its local facilities before the year is out, bringing into the industry some badly needed foreign currency. Maybe, as this is being written, things are once again beginning to pick up. Judging by precedents, they have to. Troubles on a national scale have always spelled good times for show business, and God knows there is trouble enough in this part of the world.

DAN FAINARU is an Israeli film critic and journalist who has written regularly for "Variety", and has been correspondent for I.F.G. for several years. He is a familiar face at the world's major and minor festivals alike.

One of Us

Script: Benny Barbash, adapted from his own play. Director: Uri Barbash. Photography: Amnon Salomon. Editing: Tova Asher. Music: Ilan Virtzberg. Art Direction: Eytan Levy. Players: Sharon Alexander, Alon Aboutboul, Dan Toren, Arnon Tzadok, Dahlia Shimko, Shaul Mizrahi, Alon Neuman, Eli Yatzpan. Produced by Zwi Spielman and Shlomo Mograbi for Israfilm.

An Army investigator, Rafa, is dispatched to look into the death of an Arab, shot by Israeli combat officers during interrogation. The action takes place in the Occupied Territories, and the officers accused of taking the law into their own hands turn out to be the investigator's intimate friends from way back.

Now Rafa faces several dilemmas. First of all, can he pry into the deeds of his former mates and eventually charge them, thus betraying the spirit of comradeship in which they have all been brought up together? Second, is he going to exploit the opportunity offered to him in order to get even with certain persons who have let him down in the past? And third, is he willing to endanger the safety of his own people and eventually of the entire nation, for the sake of an abstract notion such as justice?

A tight military drama with political undertones, well shot, each scene squeezed for maximum effect, this film shows Barbash back in top form. Sharon Alexander as the investigator and Alon Aboutboul as his pal who refuses to believe a friend will turn against him, deliver strong performances, backed by the solid, reliable presence of Arnon Tzadok and Dan Toren. The film's problems are mostly in the script, requiring a very long flashback at an early stage which almost becomes a separate film on Army training camps. The characterisation, while effective, remains within the stereotype of the genre, and the ambivalent ending lacks the bitter edge of the original stage play. Still, there is no doubt about Barbash condemning the political situation which imposes on immature young men "life or death" decisions, their own and that of others, that are beyond their capacity to reach.

Dan Fainaru

Yaakov Shapira, Rita Zohar, and Menashe Washavski in *The Last Love of Laura Adler*

The Last Love of Laura Adler

Script and Direction: Avraham Heffner. Photography: David Gurfinkel. Editor: Lina Kadish. Art Director: Uriel Roshko. Music: Shemtov Levi. Players: Rita Zohar, Shulamit Adar, Menashe Warshavski, Avraham Mor, Yaakov Shapira, Sally Anne Friedland, Menorah Zahav, Bela Luciano. Produced by Marek Rosenbaum.

It took Avraham Heffner ten years to get this film on the way, and even then, he had to compromise largely before he could finish it. It is a subdued, gentle and affecting tribute to the Yiddish theatre, a dying species about to be relegated to the Archeological Museums. The story follows an actress, Laura Adler, who is no longer young, through her last romantic fling, her last professional hopes and her last role on stage. Laura's talent is evidently wasted on the traditional tearjerkers she stars in, she performs for a geriatric audience in a language that less and less people speak currently but she had resigned herself to her fate long ago when a young American film director – fascinated by her potential – offers her the lead in a new picture. For a few weeks, as she is preparing another Yiddish show, indistinguishable from those she did before, it seems like Laura might have a chance to break away from her lot after all. But, as it inevitably happens in Heffner's pictures, promises are illusory and clouds have no silver linings.

Rita Zohar, as Laura, manages to convey the level-headed character of a handsome, mature woman, who will not allow herself to be deluded by false hopes but doesn't have the heart to reject them altogether. What she lacks is that certain spark that will make audiences believe she is different, not only as a person, but as an artist too. And Heffner, who has always believed that in films less is more, cannot help in this instance. With admirable restraint he observes her without interfering, draws many faceted characters around her, recreates the backstage atmosphere of an expiring theatrical tradition, but keeps at a respectful distance from it all, as if once he

Still from *The Appointed*

has created the characters and the situation and put them on the right track, he has no right to meddle with their affairs any more, the most he can do it catch their movements with a camera. It is a pity he lacked the means to explore both sides of the limelights, the actors and their audiences too, for the audiences of the Yiddish theatre are no less interesting than its performers.

Dan Fainaru

The Appointed

Script: Daniel Wachsman, Shmuel Haspari, Razi Levines. Direction: Daniel Wachsman. Photography: Ilan Rosenberg. Editing: Zohar Sela. Art Director: Avi & Anath Avivi. Costumes: Rona Doron. Music: Uri Vidislavsky. Players: Shuli Rand, Zwi Shissel, Ronit Alkabetz, Shabtai Konorti. Produced by Enrique Rottenberg and Ehud Bleiberg. World distribution: 21st Century.

Another script with a long history, variously discussed as a possible international production with imported stars, to be shot in English, or as a local production with local stars to be shot in Hebrew and dubbed. The subject, everybody agreed, was dynamite, so much so, that many of the potential producers got cold feet on the eve of committing themselves.

No wonder, for the story of a rabbi's son who leaves his father's court and becomes a magician, only to return home later and take over the leadership left vacant by his father's death, has evident parallels in real life that could generate political troubles. And Wachsman's astute observations on the conduct of religious zealots who will take dogma over gospel any day of the week, only aggravated the case.

After many disappointments, Wachsman's patience finally paid off. He made his film the way he wanted it, his only concession being to shoot every scene twice, once in Hebrew and once in English, for the international version. This does not appear to have hindered him, for the final result is a complex reflection on faith, love and religion. His hero, as portrayed by Shuli Rand, is nothing more than a second-rate ham, either as an entertainer or as a religious leader, and only the presence of a silent, mysterious girl inspires him to greatness, literally ignites the fire in him. This can be interpreted as a sublime love story, but also as the allegory of a man who will not transcend his natural condition except in a state of grace, which, in this film, is represented by the visual contact between the two protagonists.

Using landscapes practically never seen in Israeli pictures, all of them remarkably shot by Ilan Rosenberg, and helped by a suggestive, haunting soundtrack, Wachsman maintains a sober approach all through and does not succumb to the tempting scandalous insinuations this type of story would almost naturally generate. He refers to, but never elaborates on the strict hierarchical structures of the religious establishment and on its exploitation of ignorant innocents. He preserves a mystical atmosphere without ever falling into the exotic, and hints that both religion and art are only a conjurer's trick, of one kind or another, as long as they are not touched by a sublime dimension – call it love, faith or grace.

Dan Fainaru

Useful Addresses

Israel Film Centre
Ministry of Industry & Trade
P.O. Box 299
94190 Jerusalem
Tel: (972) 210433, 210297
Fax: (972) 245110

Israel Film & TV Producers Association
P.O. Box 22372
Tel Aviv
Fax: (972) 3–346122

ITALY

by Lorenzo Codelli

Is it right to define last season as "The Waterloo of the Italian Cinema" (a sensational full-page heading used by the serious daily *La Stampa*)? Well, production decreased to around 80 released features (–20%); they took just 20.7% of the gross (–4,7%); only two titles made the Top Ten list (–1), and none of them got near half the total rentals of the former season's phenomenon, Roberto Benigni's *Il piccolo diavolo*.

To exorcise this Waterloo syndrome somebody could object that dozens more "invisible" pictures were generated and then aborted by distributors and exhibitors (both scorning Italian products actually much more than their audience!), or shown only at specialised festivals, or awaiting a limited video circulation. Months after his **Buon Natale, Buon anno** was abruptly withdrawn from public screenings, the well-known director Luigi Comencini bought bitterly ironic ads in a daily to announce that his much-praised picture was "to be seen in no nearby theatre."

This crisis was worsened by the threat of a new (15 years in the making) law finally regulating the anarchic television field and its main coin sources, commercials and sponsors. As a result Berlusconi blocked

Still from *Il sole anche di notte*, directed by Paolo and Vittorio Taviani
photo: Umberto Montiroli

most of his Reteitalia film investments, and the already financially drained Rai was facing a troubled restructuring.

In fact the battalion of Italian pictures that invaded all sections of the Cannes Festival was assembled as a kind of offshore counter-attack in the face of the disasters at home, as well as to demonstrate that Italian producers – particularly Angelo Rizzoli – have originated prestigious international ventures assigned to Axel Corti, Gleb Panfilov, Vasily Pichul, and Paul Schrader.

Season for Connoisseurs

Anyway the connoisseurs will remember the 1989–1990 season as a gratifying one indeed, during which almost all major film-makers were active – even Michelangelo Antonioni who directed the contemplative short **Roma**, for the city portraits series commissioned by the Soccer World Cup. **La voce della luna** was Federico Fellini's first sleeper in many moons, attracting an audience of nearly 750,000 (and reaching third place among Italian hits). Thanks of course to his two stars, Roberto Benigni and Paolo Villaggio, but especially thanks to the omnipotent producers/distributors Mario and Vittorio Cecchi Gori, the only team that during the lucrative Christmas season could fight the stronger American blockbusters with a blanket release of their low-budget comedies **Willy Signori e vengo da lontano** and **Ho vinto la lotteria di Capodanno** – in which Francesco Nuti and Paolo Villaggio respectively recapped their slapstick routines.

Other popular comedians proved less profitable, like Carlo Verdone's childish vehicle **Il bambino e il poliziotto**; or Alberto Sordi in **L'avaro**, freely inspired by Molière; or Jerry Calà, Massimo Boldi and Christian De Sica in the portmanteau farce **Fratelli d'Italia**. Massimo Troisi's charismatic humour was underplayed by Ettore Scola in **Che ora è**, a placid father-and-son reunion based on Silvia (daughter of Ettore) Scola's verbose screenplay, and co-starring Marcello Mastroianni. The same Mastroianni returned grotesquely aged as the Sicilian grandfather who travels along the peninsula to meet his deceiving children in Giuseppe Tornatore's **Stanno tutti bene**; an ambitious odyssey swamped by sententious rhetoric and cheap sentimentality.

Three actors directed their first film. Monica Vitti stole some ideas from *sex, lies and videotape* in conceiving her **Scandalo segreto**, a lame variation on voyeurism. Michele Placido immersed his **Pummarò** in a vague Neorealist tradition, in order to condemn the current wave of racism against Third World emigrants. Ben Gazzara's **Oltre l'oceano** dealt in a pleasant way with the existential dilemmas of an American executive relaxing in the paradise of Bali.

TV Influence

Too many film-makers appeared more and more TV-oriented. Gianni Amelio in his solemn adaptation of Leonardo Sciascia's thrilling novel **Porte aperte**, for instance, despite Gian Maria Volonté's vehement performance. Or Nanni Loy in his Neapolitan musical **Scugnizzi**. Or Carlo Vanzina in his journalist whodunit **Tre colonne in cronaca**, impressively played again by Volonté. Similarly Dario Argento and George Romero in their two soporific horror episodes of **Due occhi diabolici**.

Not to forget Lina Wertmüller's ludicrous, pseudo-debate on Aids, **In una notte di chiaro di luna**. The Taviani brothers opted instead for a mystic and calligraphic disquisition on sanctity, **Il sole anche di notte**.

Mario Brenta's **Maicol**, Giacomo Campiotti's **Corsa di primavera** and Franco Piavoli's **Nostos** adhered brightly and sometimes lyrically to the documentary principles of their master Ermanno Olmi.

There were a few promising works by young directors: **Musica per vecchi animali** by Stefano Benni and Umberto Angelucci, a bizarre satire starring the wild marionette Dario Fo; **Il prete bello**, Carlo Mazzacurati's second effort, a droll memento of a childhood during Fascism; **Turné** by Gabriele Salvatores, a fresh account of two rival travelling actors; **Evelina e i suoi figli** by Livia Giampalmo, starring the ever seductive Stefania Sandrelli as a typical contemporary mamma.

Still from Nanni Loy's *Scugnizzi*

New books analysing Italian cinema include *Alessandro Blasetti*, by Luca Verdone, and *Stelle d'Italia*, a pictorial revival of lost divas by Stefano Masi and Enrico Lancia (Gremese Editore, Rome); the lively collection by the Province of Mantua, publishing recent, classic and un-produced screenplays; the bilingual *1990 Yearbook of Italian Cameramen* (A.I.C.,

The whole cast of Pupi Avati's *Storia di ragazzi e di ragazze*

Cinecittà); *Neorealismo, 1945–1949*, edited by Alberto Farassino, an informative catalogue of the Cinema Giovani Festival retrospective (E.D.T., Turin); the gorgeous megatome from the Lanterna Magica Institute of L'Aquila, *Costumisti e scenografi del cinema italiano*, by Stefano Masi, about great art directors and costume designers.

camera literally waltzes up in the air), Mafia symbols, crimes and truths, irrevocably hidden. This neat parable, adapted from portions of a French bestseller by Edmonde Charles-Roux, embodies Rosi's disenchantment with any rational intervention to heal the spongy immobility of his country.

Lorenzo Codelli

Dimenticare Palermo (To Forget Palermo)

Script: Francesco Rosi, Gore Vidal, Tonino Guerra, from Edmonde Charles-Roux's novel. Direction: Francesco Rosi. Photography: Pasqualino De Santis. Editing: Ruggero Mastroianni. Production Design: Andrea Crisanti, Stephen Graham. Music: Ennio Morricone. Players: James Belushi, Mimi Rogers, Joss Ackland, Philippe Noiret, Vittorio Gassman, Carolina Rosi, Harry Davis, Marco Leonardi, Ronald Yamamoto, Tiziana Stella. Produced by Mario and Vittorio Cecchi Gori for Cecchi Gori Group, Reteitalia (Rome)/ Gaumont Production (Paris). 100 mins.

Rejected at the last moment by an embarrassed Rai, but finally saved by Berlusconi's finances, *Dimenticare Palermo* had the bad luck to open right in the midst of the vehement parliamentary debate about the introduction of tougher laws against drug trafficking. Mistaken for a one-sided pamphlet to legalise drugs, the film was boycotted by most official media. Nothing new for a perennial non-conformist like Francesco Rosi, even if his political thesis this time goes against the line of his Socialist Party, and even if he intended to encompass a broader series of problems.

This is more than a revisit to Sicily – or what remains of the once magnificent island – as seen through the innocent eyes of an Italian–American from New York. It is also an extraordinarily impressionistic and sensual travelogue among irretrievable miseries, crumbling palaces (including that of Visconti's *Leopard*, in which the

Il male oscuro (The Dark Illness)

Script: Suso Cecchi d'Amico, Tonino Guerra, from Giuseppe Berto's novel. Direction: Mario Monicelli. Photography: Carlo Tafani. Production Design: Franco Velchi. Editing: Ruggero Mastroianni. Music: Nicola Piovani. Players: Giancarlo Giannini, Emmanuelle Seigner, Vittorio Caprioli, Stefania Sandrelli, Antonello Fassari, Elisa Mainardi. Produced by Giovanni Di Clemente for Clemi Cinematografica. 114 mins.

A neurotic screenwriter – Giancarlo Giannini at the top of his form – asks the

Emmanuelle Seigner and Giancarlo Giannini in Mario Monicelli's *Il male oscuro*

help of a Freudian psychoanalyst – the late Vittorio Caprioli, a glory of the Italian stage – to initiate a painful liberation from his memories: a bitter conflict with his father, an unhappy marriage to a gorgeous teenager – Emmanuelle Seigner, Polanski's discovery – followed by more big and small failures. The famous autobiographical novel by Giuseppe Berto maintains its 1960's flavour through this faithful adaptation.

Other film-makers would have transformed the same story into a Bergman-like drama, whereas Mario Monicelli – back at work after a serious car accident – uses his typical irony to paint the tics and contradictions of this troubled character, and makes us laugh frequently at the surrealistic situations. During his old age retirement in a lonely mountain cabin overlooking the sea, the protagonist finds at last a kind of inner peace, perhaps a new childhood. The unexpected ending lyrically reaffirms Monicelli's Virgilian optimism.

Lorenzo Codelli

Palombella rossa (Little Red Dove)

Script and Direction: Nanni Moretti. Photography: Giuseppe Lanci. Music: Nicola Piovani. Editing: Mirco Garrone. Production Design: Giancarlo Basili, Leonardo Scarpa. Players: Nanni Moretti, Silvio Orlando, Mariella Valentini, Alfonso Santagata, Claudio Morganti, Asia Argento, Giovanni Buttafava, Raoul Ruiz. Produced by Angelo Barbagallo and Nanni Moretti for Sacher Film, Nella Banfi-Palmyre Film, Rai 1 (Rome)/So.Fin.A. (Paris).

After dealing with the decay of the Catholic Church in his former film *La messa è finita*, now Nanni Moretti impiously attacks the other Italian sacred institution, the Communist Party. Playing a Communist leader who has suddenly lost his memory, he also pokes fun at the fall of dogmas and ideals. The whole picture is set during a water-polo match that his character desperately tries to win while at the same time he remembers distorted fragments from his past.

Opening the narrative frame of this multi-edged crisis – à la $8^{1}/_{2}$ – Moretti gives one of the most sophisticated chapters of his ongoing self-analysis (incidentally, he was a professional water-polo player!). Superbly funny cameos brighten this satire: a leftist female journalist talking in clichés, a couple of unctuous party activists, a mindless guru of the religious revival (Raoul Ruiz), neo-romantic young fans of Lean's *Zhivago*... Moretti's humorous irreverence seems to stem from his early years, because in the final scene he shows his child alter-ego bursting into laughter in front of a huge Socialist Sun sign being erected on the top of a hill.

Lorenzo Codelli

Storia di ragazzi e di ragazze (Story of Boys and Girls)

Script and Direction: Pupi Avati. Photography (black-and-white): Pasquale Rachini. Production Design: Daria Ganassini, Giovanna Zighetti. Editing: Amedeo Salfa. Music: Riz Ortolani. Players: Felice Andreasi, Angiola Baggi, Anna Bonaiuto, Claudio Botosso, Alessandro Haber, Lucrezia Lante della Rovere, Susanna Marcomeni, Enrica Maria Modugno, Roberta Paladini. Produced by Antonio Avati for Duea Film, Unione Cinematografica, Rai 1, Provincia di Bologna, Terme di Porretta. 89 mins.

Around an engagement feast involving two large families and held in the countryside near Bologna in February 1936, Pupi Avati depicts an exquisite fresco in delicate shades of 1930's black-and-white, grey and silver. This "special day" alters the destinies of thirty people, all of them captured as distinctive individuals. From the personal memories of his old aunt, Avati resuscitates the ordinary grievances and social disparities of the Fascist era.

An impeccable ensemble of players –

mostly regular members of Avati's enterprises – sparkle throughout this tender but unsentimental ode to a forgotten past. *Storia di ragazzi e di ragazze* marks the twentieth anniversary of ex-jazzman Pupi Avati's – and his brother–producer Antonio's – eccentric film career, full of impressive achievements. Note: some foreign distributors are releasing a colour version of the film which was not conceived by the director.

Lorenzo Codelli

La voce della luna (The Voice of the Moon)

Script: Federico Fellini, Tullio Pinelli, Ermanno Cavazzoni, from Cavazzoni's novel *Il poema dei lunatici*. Direction: Federico Fellini. Photography: Tonino Delli Colli. Music: Nicola Piovani. Production Design: Dante Ferretti. Editing: Nino Baragli. Players: Roberto Benigni, Paolo Villaggio, Susy Blady, Sim, Angelo Orlando, Nadia Ottaviani, Marisa Tommasi, Dominique Chevalier, Nigel Harris, Eraldo Turra, Uta Schmidt. Produced by Mario and Vittorio Cecchi Gori for Cecchi Gori Group Tiger Cinematografica, Rai 1 (Rome)/Cinemax, Films A2, La Sept (Paris). 118 mins.

Adapting for the first time a novel by a living writer – the folksy and rather "Fellinesque" *Poem of Lunatics* (1987) by Ermanno Cavazzoni, a debutant from Reggio Emilia, Fellini has exhumed some ideas about folly. He focuses on two quite contrasting crazy guys: the white clown Ivo Salvini (Roberto Benigni), an instinctive Candide with echoes of Pinnocchio and the poet Leopardi; and the gloomy, manically persecuted Prefect Gonnella (Paolo Villaggio). Their misadventures in a rural wasteland, which never began and will certainly never end like an ancient legend, were invented freely day after day by the director, following the "method" already employed in *Intervista*. The decline of TV consumerist aberration, and above all a cacophony of jarring noises have doomed the moon-less earth. His obsessive nightmare is fertilised by the creative vigour of Benigni and Villaggio, two incomparable comedians giving the performances of their career. And around them a batch of minor but much-liked funny men from the small screen, who reinforce our pleasure in watching a deranged representation of familiar shows.

Lorenzo Codelli

LORENZO CODELLI is a regular contributor to Positif *and other magazines, and one of the organisers of the Silent Film Festival in Pordenone.*

Recent Films

L'avaro (The Miser). Script: Tonino Cervi, Cesare Frugoni, Rodolfo Sonego, Alberto Sordi, from Molière's play. Dir: Tonino Cervi. Phot: Armando Nannuzzi. Players: Alberto Sordi, Laura Antonelli, Christopher Lee. Prod: Splendida Film, Rai 1, Cinecittà, Carthago Film (France)/Velarde Film (Spain). *Comedy.*

Il bambino e il poliziotto (The Child and the Cop). Script: Leo Benvenuti, Piero De Bernardi, Carlo Verdone. Dir: Carlo Verdone. Phot: Danilo Desideri. Players: Carlo Verdone, Federico Rizzo, Barbara Cupisti. Prod: Cecchi Gori Group Tiger Cinematografica, Reteitalia, Penta. *Comedy.*

Barbablu Barbablu. Script and Dir: Fabio Carpi. Phot: José Luis Alcaine. Players: John Gielgud, Susannah York, Hector Alterio. Prod: Rai. *Drama.*

Buon Natale, Buon anno (Merry Christmas, Happy New Year). Script: Luigi Comencini, Cristina Comencini, Raffaele Festa Campanile, from Pasquale Festa Campanile's novel. Dir: Luigi Comencini. Phot: Armando Nannuzzi. Players: Virna Lisi, Michel Serrault. Prod: Titanus. *Drama.*

Che ora è? (What Time Is It?). Script: Ettore Scola, Silvia Scola, Beatrice Ravaglioli. Dir: Ettore Scola. Phot: Luciano Tovoli. Players: Marcello Mastroianni, Massimo Troisi, Anne Parillaud. Prod: Cecchi Gori Group Tiger Cinematografica, Studio EL (Rome)/Gaumont (Paris). *Drama.*

Corsa di primavera (Springtime Race). Script: Giacomo Campiotti, Lucia Maria Zei. Dir: Giacomo Campiotti. Phot: Carlo Tafani. Players: Giusi Cataldo, Roberto Citran, Alessandro Borrelli. Prod: Clemi Cinematografica. *Drama.*

Due occhi diabolici (Two Evil Eyes). Script: George Romero, Dario Argento, Franco Ferrini, from two Edgar Allan Poe stories. Dir: George Romero, Dario Argento. Players: Adrienne Barbeau, Harvey Keitel, Martin Balsam. Prod: Gruppo Bema, A.D.C. *Horror.*

Evelina e i suoi figli (Evelina and Her Children). Script and Dir: Livia Giampalmo. Phot: Maurizio Dell'Orco. Players: Stefania Sandrelli, Maurizio Donadoni, Pamela Villoresi. Prod: Aura Film, Penta. *Drama.*

Fratelli d'Italia (Italian Brothers). Script: Carlo Vanzina, Enrico Vanzina. Dir: Neri Parenti. Phot: Roberto Gerardi. Players: Christian De Sica, Jerry Calà, Massimo Boldi, Sabrina Salerno. Prod: Gruppo Bema. *Farce.*

Gioco al massacro (Massacre Play). Script: Damiano Damiani, Raffaele La Capria. Dir: Damiano Damiani. Phot: Gianfranco Transunto. Players: Elliott Gould, Tomas Milian, Nathalie Baye. Prod: Istituto Luce Italnoleggio. *Drama.*

Ho vinto la lotteria di Capodanno (I Won the New Year Lottery). Script: Leo Benvenuti, Piero De Bernardi, Alessandro Bencivenni, Domenico Saverini, Neri Parenti. Dir: Neri Parenti. Players: Paolo Villaggio, Antonio Allocca. Prod: Cecchi Gori Group Tiger Cinematografica, Reteitalia, Maura International Film. *Farce.*

Indio. Script: Peter Gonzales. Dir: Anthony M. Dawson (Antonio Margheriti). Phot: Sergio D'Offizi. Players: Marvin Hagler, Francesco Quinn, Brian Dennehy. Prod: Filmauro, R.P.A. International, Reteitalia. *Adventures.*

In una notte di chiaro di luna (In a Full Moon Night). Script and Dir: Lina Wertmüller. Phot: Carlo Tafani. Players: Rutger Hauer, Nastassja Kinski, Peter O'Toole. Prod: I.I.F., Istituto Luce Italnoleggio, Rai 2 (Rome)/Carthago Films (Paris). *Drama.*

Lambada. Script and Dir: Giandomenico Curi. Phot: Gianlorenzo Battaglia. Players: Vya Negromonte, Andrew J. Forrest. Prod: Artisti Associati International. *Erotic drama.*

Maicol. Script: Angela Cervi, Francesca Marciano, Roberta Mazzoni. Dir: Mario Brenta.

Roberto Benigni and Susy Blady in Fellini's *La voce della luna*

Phot: Fabrizio Borelli. Players: Sabina Regazzi, Simone Tessarolo. Prod: Ipotesi Cinema Bassano, Rai 1. *Drama.*
Mio caro Dottor Gräsler (My Dear Doctor Gräsler). Script: Ennio De Concini, Roberto Faenza, Hugh Fleetwood, from Arthur Schnitzler's novel. Dir: Roberto Faenza. Phot: Giuseppe Rotunno. Players: Keith Carradine, Miranda Richardson, Max von Sydow. Prod: Eidoscope International, Reteitalia (Rome)/Mediapark (Budapest). *Drama.*
Musica per animali (Music for Old Animals). Script and Dir: Stefano Benni, Umberto Angelucci. Phot: Pasqualino De Santis. Players: Dario Fo, Paolo Rossi. Prod: Unione Cinematografica. *Comedy.*
Nostos – Il ritorno (Nostos – The Homecoming). Script, Dir and Phot: Franco Piavoli. Players: Luigi Mezzanotte, Branca de Camargo. Prod: Zefiro Film, Immaginazione. *Drama.*
Oltre l'oceano (Beyond the Ocean). Script: Anthony Foutz, Ben Gazzara. Dir: Ben Gazzara. Phot: Franco Di Giacomo. Players: Ben Gazzara, Rebecca Glenn, Treat Williams, Prod: Scena International, Reteitalia. *Drama.*
La più bella del reame (The Most Beautiful Girl in the Kingdom). Script: Enrico Vanzina, Cesare Ferrario, from Marina Ripa di Meana's novel. Dir: Cesare Ferrario. Phot: Cristiano Pogany. Players: Carol Alt, Jon Finch. Prod: Numero Uno International, Reteitalia. *Erotic comedy.*
Porte aperte (Open Doors). Script: Gianni Amelio, Vincenzo Cerami, from Leonardo Sciascia's novel. Dir: Gianni Amelio. Phot: Tonino Nardi. Players: Gian Maria Volonté, Ennio Fantrastichini, Renzo Giovanpietro. Prod: Erre Produzioni, Istituto Luce, Urania Film, Rai 2. *Drama.*
Il prete bello (The Handsome Priest). Script: Franco Bernini, Carlo Mazzacurati, Enzo Monteleone, from Goffredo Parise's novel. Dir: Carlo Mazzacurati. Phot: Giuseppe Lanci. Players: Roberto Citran, Massimo Santelia, Jessica Forde. Prod: Nickelodeon, Rai 3 (Rome)/Partner's Production (Paris). *Drama.*
Pummarò. Script: Sandro Petraglia, Stefano Rulli, Michele Placido. Dir: Michele Placido. Phot: Vilko Filac. Players: Thwill Abraham Kwaku Amenya, Pamela Villoresi, Franco Interlenghi. Prod: Numero Uno International, Cineuropa 92, Rai 2. *Drama.*

Scandalo segreto (Secret Scandal). Script: Monica Vitti, Roberto Russo. Dir: Monica Vitti. Phot: Luigi Kuveiller. Players: Monica Vitti, Catherine Spaak. Prod: Komika Film, Reteitalia. *Comedy.*
Scugnizzi (Neapolitan Boys). Script: Nanni Loy, Elvio Porta. Dir: Nanni Loy. Phot: Claudio Cirillo. Players: Leo Gullotta, Claudio Muzii, Piero Pepe. Prod: Clemi Cinematografica. *Musical drama.*
Il segreto (The Secret). Script and Dir: Francesco Maselli. Phot: Pierluigi Santi. Players: Nastassja Kinski, Stefano Dionisi, Franco Citti. Prod: Penta Film. *Drama.*
Il sole anche di notte (Sunshine Even by Night). Script: Paolo and Vittorio Taviani, Tonino Guerra, from Tolstoi's *Father Sergius*. Phot: Giuseppe Lanci. Players: Julian Sands, Charlotte Gainsbourg, Patricia Millardet. Prod: Filmtre, Rai 1, Capoul, Interpool (Rome)/Sara Film (Paris)/Direkt Film (F.R.G.). *Drama.*
Stanno tutti bene (They're All Fine). Script and Dir: Giuseppe Tornatore. Phot: Blasco Giurato. Players: Marcello Mastroianni, Michèle Morgan, Valeria Cavalli. Prod: Erre Produzioni (Rome)/Les Films Ariane, TF1 (Paris). *Drama.*
Tempo di uccidere (Time to Kill). Script: Furio Scarpelli, Paolo Virzi, Giacomo Scarpelli, Giuliano Montaldo, from Ennio Flaiano's novel. Dir: Giuliano Montaldo. Phot: Blasco Giurato. Players: Nicolas Cage, Ricky Tognazzi. Prod: Ellepi Film, Dania Film, Surf Film, Reteitalia (Rome)/Italfrance (Paris). *Drama.*
Tre colonne in cronaca (Three Columns on the Crime Page). Script: Enrico and Carlo Vanzina. Dir: Carlo Vanzina. Phot: Luigi Kuveiller. Players: Gian Maria Volonté, Massimo Dapporto, Sergio Castellitto. Prod: Cecchi Gori Group Tiger Cinematografica, Reteitalia, Pixit. *Thriller.*
Turné (Tournée). Script: Francesca Marciano, Fabrizio Bentivoglio, Gabriele Salvatores. Dir: Gabriele Salvatores. Phot: Italo Petriccione. Players: Diego Abatantuono, Fabrizio Bentivoglio, Laura Morante. Prod: A.M.A. Film, Cecchi Gori Group Tiger Cinematografica, Reteitalia. *Comedy.*
Volevo i pantaloni (I Wanted the Trousers). Script: Leo Benvenuti, Piero De Bernardi, Bruno Garbuglia, Roberto Ivan Orano, Maurizio Ponzi, from Lara Cardella's novel. Dir: Maurizio Ponzi. Phot: Maurizio Calvesi. Players: Giulia Fossà, Lucia Bosè, Angela Molina. Prod: Cecchi

Gori Group Tiger Cinematografica, Maura International Film, Reteitalia. *Drama.*

Willy Signori e vengo da lontano (Willy Signori and I Am Coming from Afar). Script: Giovanni Veronesi, Francesco Nuti. Dir: Francesco Nuti. Phot: Gianlorenzo Battaglia. Players: Francesco Nuti, Isabella Ferrari. Prod: Union P.N., Cecchi Gori Group Tiger Cinematografica. *Comedy.*

Lo zio indegno (The Disreputable Uncle). Script: Leo Benvenuti, Piero De Bernardi, Franco Brusati. Dir: Franco Brusati. Phot: Romano Albani. Players: Vittorio Gassman, Giancarlo Giannini, Andrea Ferréol. Prod: Ellepi Film, D.M.V., Dania Film, Surf Film, Reteitalia. *Drama.*

Nanni Moretti and Asia Argento in Moretti's *Palombella rossa*

TOP GROSSING FILMS IN ITALY: AUGUST 1, 1989–JULY 1, 1990

	Rentals
Indiana Jones and the Last Crusade	$14,729,554
Dead Poets' Society	$14,500,647
Batman	$11,194,325
Look Who's Talking	$11,187,501
Back to the Future 2	$10,844,543
Willy Signori (Italian)	$8,127,008
War of the Roses	$7,498,352
Lock Up	$6,967,337
Born on the Fourth of July	$6,765,646
Honey, I Shrunk the Kids	$5,479,143

Producers

A M A Film SRL
Via Pierluigi da Palestrina 48
00193 Roma
Tel: 321.1143
Fax: 322.0364

Aura Film SRL
Lungotevere
Flaminio 26
00196 Roma
Tel: 360.5295
Fax: 361.9489

Cecchi Gori Group
Via Barnaba Oriani 91
00197 Roma
Tel: 887.0961
Fax: 887.0378
Telex: 624656

Clemi Cinematografica SRL
Via Salaria 292
00199 Roma
Tel: 884.0274
Fax: 844.9749
Telex: 625485

Clesi Cinematografica
Via Francesco Carrara 24
00196 Roma
Tel: 361.3771
Fax: 361.0854
Telex: 614576

Cristaldi Film
Via V. Mangili 5
00197 Roma
Tel: 321.5010
Fax: 322.1036

Dania/DMV
Via Monti Parioli 40
00197 Roma
Tel: 361.0541
Fax: 361.2107

Dean Film
Vindei Tre
Orologi 10/e
00197 Roma
Tel: 805500
Fax: 802823

Ellepi Film SRL
Via dei Banchi Vecchi 61
00186 Roma
Tel: 687.5349
Fax: 654.8747
Telex: 6020238

Erre Produzioni SRL
Viale Bruno
Buozzi 60
00197 Roma
Tel: 872225
Fax: 877009
Telex: 625545

Filmauro SRL
Via della Vasca Navale 58
00146 Roma
Tel: 5560788
Fax: 5590670

Istituto Luce
Via Tuscolana 1055
00173 Roma
Tel: 722931
Fax: 722.2090
Telex: 620478

Italian International Film SRL
Via degli Scialoja 18
00196 Roma
Tel: 361.1377
Fax: 679.9149
Telex: 626117

Numero Uno
Via Kircher 20
00197 Roma
Tel: 877.686

Fax: 802.755
Telex: 626089

RAI
Viale Mazzini 14
00195 Roma
Tel: 3878
Fax: 361.9595
Telex: 614432

Reteitalia
Viale Mazzini 9/11
00195 Roma
Tel: 316.541
Fax: 679.9755
Telex: 623681

Scena International
Via Archimede 144
00197 Roma
Tel: 872562
Fax: 887.0258

Titanus Produzione SPA
Via Sommacampagna 28
00185 Roma
Tel: 495.7341
Telex: 612173

Unione Cinematografica
Via Giovanni Nicotera 29
00195 Roma
Tel: 358.1694
Fax: 312315
Telex: 628557

Distributors

Columbia Tri-Star Italia
Via Palestro 24
00185 Roma
Tel: 494.1966
Fax: 494.1594

United International Pictures
Via Bissolati 20
00187 Roma
Tel: 482.0626
Fax: 494.1231
Telex: 610544

Warner Bros Italia
Via Varese 16/b
00185 Roma
Tel: 493.191
Fax: 675.1022
Telex: 622421

Medusa Distribuzione
Via Barnaba Oriani 22
00197 Roma
Tel: 804.651
Fax: 874.325
Telex: 612093

CDI
Largo Ponchielli 6
00198 Roma
Tel: 884.8632
Fax: 884.5710
Telex: 612302

20th Century-Fox
Via Palestro 24
00185 Roma
Tel: 404.0525
Fax: 404.0391
Telex: 610204

Pentafilm
Via Barnaba Oriani 91
00197 Roma
Tel: 887.0861
Fax: 887.0378
Telex: 624656

Titanus Distribuzione
Largo Chigi 19
00187 Roma
Tel: 67031
Fax: 679.7507
Telex: 62663

Academy Pictures
Via Fratelli Ruspoli 8
00198 Roma
Tel: 884.0424
Fax: 857.043
Telex: 621595

Artisti Associati
Via E. Gianturco 6
00196 Roma

Tel: 360.1903
Fax: 361.0725

Mikado
Lungotevere Flaminio 26
00196 Roma
Tel: 360.8649
Fax: 361.9489
Telex: 613092

DLF
Via degli Scialoia 18
00196 Roma
Tel: 361.2109
Fax: 679.9149

Useful Addresses

Anica
(*Italian Motion Picture Assn.*)
Viale Regina Margherita 286
00198 Roma

Tel: 884.1271
Fax: 884.8789
Telex: 624659

Ministerio del Turisino e dello Spettacolo
(*State Ministry for Show Business*)
Via della Ferratella in Laterano 45–51
00184 Roma
Tel: 7732

Unefa (*Italian Exporters Assn.*)
Via Regina Margherita 286
00198 Roma
Tel: 884.1271
Fax: 884.8789
Telex: 624659

EAGC (*Ente Autonomo Gestione per Il Cinema – Public film group parent of Cinecittà and Istituto Luce/Italnoleggio*)
Via Tuscolana 1055
00173 Roma
Tel: 722.2141
Fax: 722.2362

SACIS
(*Exporter of RAI and EAGC Group*)
Via Tomacelli 139
Roma
Tel: 396841
Fax: 687.8824
Telex: 624487

IVORY COAST

by Roy Armes

The Ivory Coast, until recently one of the stablest as well as wealthiest of African states, has a film history which encapsulates the whole range of problems facing African film-making. While the comparative wealth of Abidjan has been used in the music industry to attract talented performers from elsewhere rather than to promote local talent (prompting Manu Dibango's jibe that the Ivory Coast has many good musicians but no music), there has been at least minimal support over the years for film making. Film distribution has remained in private hands and, though the pattern is that customary throughout Africa (a few first-run theatres showing recent European and U.S releases to the well-to-do, while the mass of movie theatres show the lowest common denominator of commercial pap), the occasional African films which have received a showing have found an enthusiastic audience. Among these are Gaston Kaboré's *Wend Kuuni* from Burkina Faso and Souleymane Cissé's *Yeelen* from Mali, as well as locally made recent films by Désiré Ecaré and Henri Duparc.

These two, along with Timité Bassori, were among the intellectuals from the Ivory

Coast who studied in Paris during the 1960's. All three graduated from the Institut des Hautes Etudes Cinématographiques and their early films ranked them among the most talented of the pioneers of African cinema. None of them was, however, able to sustain a satisfying career through the 1970's. Désiré Ecaré made two striking studies of exile communities in Paris during the late 1960's and then abandoned the cinema for 15 years. Timité Bassori returned to the Ivory Coast to make two studies of cultural alienation which received little local showing and then turned more to literature and administration, making no more than the occasional documentary. Only Henri Duparc struggled on through the 1970's and into the 1980's – *Mouna ou la rêve d'un artiste* (1969), *Abusan/ La famille* (1972), *L'Herbe sauvage* (1977) – but his efforts to find an authentic African style failed and he too was condemned to ten years of silence.

The problems of these pioneers were more than matched by those of their younger compatriots who began their careers in the early 1980's. A number of newcomers – Mory Traore, Jean-Louis Koula, Moussa Dosso, Yeo Kozola, and the very gifted Kramo Fadika Lancine (writer-director of the splendidly realised *Djeli*) all made a first feature, but none has been able to move on to direct a second. In the Ivory Coast as elsewhere in Africa a very high proportion of the films produced are first features and comparatively few directors are able to profit from their initial experience of production or go on to refine and develop their vision of Africa. The only one of this group to go on to make a second feature was the writer Kitia Touré, who followed his first study of the clash of cultures, *Comédie exotique* (1984) with a film for children, warning them of the dangers of modern urban life (electricity, high windows, medicines etc), *The Ten Commandments* (1988).

But the late 1980's saw the return of the veterans with works which enjoyed striking successes with the popular audience. Désiré Ecaré's return after 15 years was signalled by *Visages de femmes* (1985), a forceful study of the situation of women in African society which proved a sensation with African audiences wherever it was shown, largely because of its trenchant views and its (in African terms) unprecedented display of nudity. Similarly Henri Duparc's *Bal poussière* (1988), a truculent comic study of polygamy, is also liberally spiced with nudity and benefits from an uninhibited performance by the attractive young lead artist Tchelley Hanny, as well as a bright musical score (by Boncana Naiga). The film tells the story of a rich villager, popularly known as Demi- Dieu (because after God he is the most important man in the community) who incautiously takes a sixth wife. The scheme has a neat logic (a wife for each of the first six days of the week, with Sunday reserved for the one who has given most pleasure), but within a short while Binta has wrought chaos in the household, confronted Demi- Dieu with the limits of his capacities as a husband, and run off with her musician lover. But the end of the film shows Demi-Dieu contemplating a (still younger) replacement . . .

Notable New Talents

Since the mid 1980's there have also been two notable film debuts. Mbala Roger Gnoan, who studied at the Conservatoire Indépendent du Cinéma Francais in Paris and subsequently in Sweden, began his career with a number of shorts and made his first, TV-funded feature, *Le Chapeau* in 1976. He re-emerged in the mid-1980's with the satirical comedy, *Ablakon* (1985) and, more recently, **Bouka** (1988). Adapted from a story by Timité Bassori and funded by the Ivory Coast Ministry of Information and the French Ministry of Cooperation *Bouka* is a powerful drama, shot with a local crew and with music by the locally born (but Paris-based) composer, Martial Anney.

Another newcomer to directing is Sijiri Bakaba, one of Africa's most charismatic and best known actors, who recently made a powerful impression as the tormented Pays in Sembene and Sow's *Camp de Thiaroye* (see Senegal entry). Bakaba's *Aduefue, The Lords of the Street (Les Guérisseurs* 1988) typifies of a distinctively African form of film narrative. It offers a nightmare vision of a sprawling African metropolis (Abidjan masquerading as Katakata) which recaptures perfectly the impact the city made on Bakaba when he first visited it as a teenager from a remote rural community. The plot is derisory and the actions of the characters follow without logic or pattern, because this is a world in which events can not be told, cannot make up a coherent logical chain. The contradictions of contemporary Africa which, like the moon, is always changing yet always remains the same, cannot be encompassed in a western-style narrative, but they can be experienced visually and above all heard through the bewildering array of songs (by Salif Keita, Nyanka Bell, Alphonse Bondy and many others) which mix tradition and modernity in vibrant but astonishing ways.

JAPAN
by Frank Segers

Keeping abreast of Japan's film-related developments more often these days requires a look at the financial pages rather than the arts and entertainment section. Cinema and finance are increasingly intermeshed, especially in relation to Japan's bold moves in Hollywood over the last year.

The reasons for this are complex but essentially boil down to Japan's having the financial wherewithal to invest abroad and the U.S. harbouring the knowhow to make commercial films of universal appeal – a skill the Japanese seem congenitally to lack.

What joins the two is the Japanese sense that the "information" business is the wave of the economic future fueled by what's termed in Tokyo as the "media mix" – the coming profusion of entertainment choices provided by cable and direct broadcast satellite. Japan investors wishing to get in on the ground floor were increasingly willing to co-invest in film production, to control subsequent theatrical and auxiliary rights – from the very beginning – at the source.

That's not to suggest Japan as a cinema nation was completely absorbed in Western-oriented finance over the last year. in 1989 and through the summer of this year, things perked nicely along the artistic home front.

1989 saw in early fall the third edition of the Tokyo International Film Festival, an event that has been held every two years since 1985. The venue was a spankingly new ultramodern skyscraper, dubbed the Bunkamura, in the crowded Shibuya section, not an ideal locale for a festival but one that is a fixture as long as one of the Festival's key backers – which has department stores in the area – remains on the scene.

The festival competition jury included a range of personalities from Yves Montand to Korean actress Kang Soo-yeon through *Los Angeles Times* film critic Kevin Thomas.

Films unspooled in the main section covered an equally broad range of fresh American and foreign films ranging from Jean-Jacques Beineix' *Rosalyne and the Lions* to Soviet director Pyotr Todorovsky's *Intergirl* to Ron Howard's *Parenthood*. The festival's other sections included the young cinema sidebar for first-time directors and a highly popular fantastic film festival.

The festival's grand prize in the competitive section went to Yugoslav helmer Rajko Grlíc's *That Summer of White Roses*. Best actor nod went to Marlon Brando for his role in *A Dry White Season*; best actress citation went to Elena Yakovleva for her remarkable performance as an opportunistic prostitute in *Intergirl*. The Tokyo event is one of the world's costliest festivals, and was largely supported by no fewer than 15 major Japanese industrial concerns.

The death on July 19 of 72-year-old Tatsuro Ishida, a powerful media mogul in Japan who was an artful fundraiser on the Festival's behalf, was a big blow especially since the event has never enjoyed the wholehearted support of the Japanese film industry. (Ishida worked for the Fujisankei Communications conglomerate, which operates TV network and a homevideo units, among others. Although a successful feature film producer, Fujisankei is not considered a part of the traditional film establishment.) The Tokyo Festival will be held again in 1991, but after that, the future is somewhat clouded by Ishida's loss.

A permanent fixture of the Tokyo Festival is an appearance at a formal press conference from director Akira Kurosawa. He discussed his latest completed feature, **Dreams**, which opened the Cannes Festival this year – to a largely lukewarm reception – and went on to play a so-so commercial run in Japan. At 80, Kurosawa seems more energetic than ever, plunging full-speed ahead on another project, **Rhapsody in August**, backed entirely by Shochiku Co., the first time a Japanese film company entirely on its own has produced a Kurosawa film in 20 years.

Rhapsody is based on Kiyoko Murata's Akutagawa Prize-winning novel, *Nabe no Naka* (*Inside the Pot*), about a family's summer vacation at their grandmother's farmhouse. None other than actor Richard Gere, the lone American in a key role, plays a visiting Japanese-American son of the grandmother's brother who had emigrated to Hawaii after the bombing of Nagasaki. Kurosawa says the film will deal in large measures with Japan-U.S. relations: the former coming to grips with Pearl Harbour, the latter with the atomic bombing of two Japanese cities.

Colours Flying at Cannes
Japan was noticeably represented at the Cannes Festival. Independent film distributor Hayao Shibata was a jury member, perhaps a frustrating role since he couldn't bid on the films in the main competition that he was called upon to adjudicate. A hardcharging husband-and-wife team, Fran and Kaz Kuzui, heads of another specialty film concern, decamped with the Japan rights to Palme d'or winner, director David Lynch's *Wild at Heart*.

Entered by Shochiku into the official Cannes competition was director Kohei Oguri's **Sting of Death**, a rigorous examination of a thirtysomething postwar couple's emotional grappling with the husband's infidelity. The film caught the fancy of European *cinéastes* particularly the French, and walked off with grand prix (formerly the jury prize) and the FIPRESCI international critics' prize.

Japan and the Shibata distribution company were represented with stylish quirkiness with **Homemade Movie**, Fumiki Watanabe's tale of a school tutor's affair – infidelity seemed to be a popular subject with Japanese film-makers over the last year – with the mother of a pupil. The film, in which Watanabe's own family was

Sachiko Murase (centre) in Akira Kurosawa's *Rhapsody in August*, produced by Shochiku

prominently featured, played at the Director's Fortnight, drawing more walkouts than raves.

Director Shohei Imamura, a Cannes regular, engaged himself over the course of the year in a TV documentary project. But director-producer Juzo Itami, who recently set up an office in Hollywood, came up with **Ageman**, a comedy that had a fairly successful run in Japan and was invited to the Venice Festival.

Attendances Hit Rock-bottom

On the film trade side, the picture in 1989 in Japan was bleak. Film attendance hits its lowest level since the end of the Second World War. The American distribution companies, particularly U.I.P., rolled up strong earnings, taking market share from the Japanese independents. Foreign films, mostly from the U.S., took the lion's share of the film audience, with Japanese films dealing with a smaller share (46.6%) of a shrinking pie. Film theatres closed while those that remained raised admission prices. It costs nearly $12 per ticket at many Tokyo first-run theatres.

To compensate, the big Japanese studios – Shochiku, Toho and Toei – are seeking well-heeled partners to co-finance features and pre-sell them in Japan via the time-honoured advance ticket concept. This involves big companies forcing suppliers to sell advance seating at a discount. By the summer, four major films from the Japanese side were sold in this fashion.

Toei combined with TV Asahi, a commercial network, on **Under Aurora**, a Japanese-Russian project. Toho blended with Fuji TV, another commercial network, on **Tasmania Story**, a save-the-earth themed project set Down Under. And

> **SHIBATA ORGANIZATION INC.**
>
> **Distributes in Japan**
>
> the films by
> Wenders, Jarmusch
> Angelopoulos, Erice
> Godard, Renoir
> Hou Hsiou-hsien
>
> **Exports to the World**
>
> the films by
> Oshima, Yanagimachi
> Oguri, Hayashi
>
> ■
>
> 2-10-8, Ginza, Chuo-ku, Tokyo
> Tel:(03)545-3411 ● Fax:(03)545-3519

Shochiku's Shochiku-Fuji unit distributed an American-made **Solar Crisis**, a clunky, sci-fi offering with Jack Palance, Charlton Heston and Tim Matheson aboard. This curious bit of filmic cross-fertilization was the combined product of NHK, Japan's public broadcaster, and Gakken, a major publishing company.

The summer's biggest hit, **Heaven and Earth**, came from producer-director Haruki Kadokawa, a major force in Japan since he also runs a highly successful publishing company. Kadokawa's costume drama, about the lifelong battling between two samurai, was turned down as a Cannes entry, but nonetheless a big hit in Japan – thanks to advance ticket sales. Kadokawa says his latest feature will be his last, thus ringing down the curtain on the career of one of Japan's most successful and stubborn independents.

There's little doubt that the last year in Japan's film life was dominated by headlines in the U.S. There was the JVC $100-million investment in Hollywood producer Larry Gordon's Largo Entertainment. Then there was the spectacular Sony acquisition of Columbia Pictures for a mammoth $3.4-billion. This was followed by Pioneer Laserdisc's 10% equity purchase of high-flying American independent, Carolco Pictures.

The motivation in all of this was the same – to control software at the source. At presstime, NHK along with two banks and the giant Seiyu Ltd. conglomerate plus the C. Itoh trading company joined forces to form Media International Corp., a consortium intent on acquiring software from outside Japan. The formation of Media horrified commercial broadcasters in Japan, who complained that NHK was unfairly entering the commercial arena. Hollywood cheered, however.

Cinema in all of this commercial pushing and hauling was reduced to yet one more unit of software. Perhaps this, more than declining attendance and shuttered theatres, was the last year's most enervating reality.

FRANK SEGERS writes for Variety and specialises in Far Eastern entertainment issues.

Bengal (left) and Masako Motai in Nobuhiko Obayashi's *Beijing*

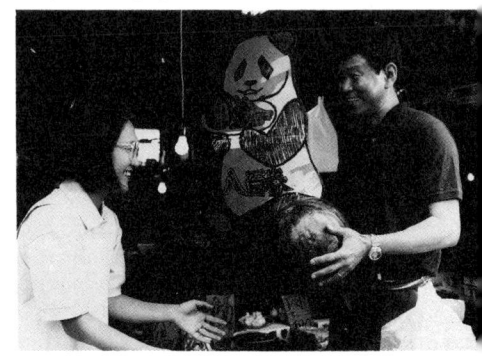

TOP GROSSING FILMS IN JAPAN: 1989

	Rentals (millions of yen)
Indiana Jones and the Last Crusade	4,400
Rain Man	3,300
Cocktail	1,750
Who Framed Roger Rabbit	1,446
Black Rain	1,350
Twins	1,240
Coming to America	1,210
Die Hard	1,150
Major League	900
The Bear	760

Statistics

Figures for the period, January–December 1989, with previous year's figures in brackets.

Number of cinemas:
total	1,912	(2,005)
for domestic films only	630	(715)
for foreign films exclusively	755	(747)
for both categories	527	(543)

Number of films released:
total	(777)	(750)
domestic films	255	(265)
foreign films	522	(485)

Box-office:
annual attendance 143,573,000* (144,825,000)
gross theatre receipts 166,681 million yen (161,921 million yen)
average admission fee (without tax) 1,161 yen (1,118 yen)

*Of this total, the attendance for foreign films was 76,668,000 or 53.4% of the total in 1989. Attendance for Japanese films was 66,905,000 or 46.6% of the total.

SOUTH KOREA
by Frank Segers

If art is the byproduct of widespread social, political and commercial upheaval, South Korean cinema is currently enjoying an aesthetic boom of considerable proportion. Few other of the world's film territories have been shaken by so much change so quickly.

In barely three years, Korea shifted from military dictatorship to genuine democracy, and its populace – and its politicians – lived to tell about it. Relations both artistic and social are warming considerably with once-despised Japan, which occupied the peninsula for more than three decades until the end of the Second World War.

And, incredibly, the anti-communist Zietgeist of Eastern Europe is resonating to some extent in Seoul and Pyongyang in the North. On the occasion in August of the 45th anniversary of the restoration of independence to Korea, the North and the South surprised one another by opening the barbed-wire border at the 38th parallel just a crack, enough to convince sceptics that despite considerable hurdles, reunification is not beyond imagining.

No wonder then that South Korea remains a favourite of cinophiles and festival fans, a preference that seems to have outlasted the "flavour of the month" attitude that European cineastes often adopt when assessing Asian film-making.

There are signs that the entry of the American major film distributors into South Korea in the fall of 1988 is actually benefitting local film-makers. United International Pictures set up shop first with the release of *Fatal Attraction*, an event that provoked mayhem complete with demonstrations, threats, firebombings and the unleashing of snakes in theatres.

The brouhaha, complete with international headlines, resulted because the American partnership which handles the films of Paramount, Universal and MGM/UA directly confronted a cozy – and profitable – oligopoly of Korean distributors who through various sorts of government protection were able to buy outright the distribution rights to even the biggest American hits, distribute the films themselves and pocket all the royalties. This arrangement had side benefits for Korean film-makers since to get an import licence, favoured distributors had to put up money to produce a homegrown feature. Many cheaply made sex movies, one of the charms of Korea's eclectic cinema mix, resulted, but so did some artistically audacious efforts.

At presstime, the American presence on a direct distribution basis in Korea is accepted as *fait accompli*. Not only UIP is currently represented in the market but also Twentieth Century Fox, Warner Bros., Orion Pictures and, very soon, Columbia Pictures. The U.S. presence has to some extent strengthened the resolve of Korean directors – freshly praised at international festivals and cinema events – to compete with the best commercial films from Hollywood.

The government-backed Motion Picture Promotion Corp. has set up a fund to be ploughed into production of quality films. Film departments at universities and colleges around the country have become increasingly popular and well-attended. The official promotion board is also planning to open in 1995 what it describes as a "film studio of international scale" in a suburb outside Seoul.

Kwon-teek Emerges

Perhaps most indicative of a cinema on the rise is the emergence of a star director, a commanding figure at home who draws widespread notice beyond national borders. Im Kwon-teek is just such a director, as important to his national cinema as Bergman, Fellini and Kurosawa are to theirs – although Im's work is far more commercially popular at home.

Born 54 years ago in a rural province in southern Korea, Im was the oldest of seven children, forced to support his family in the absence of an itinerant father. Im was emotionally scarred by the violence and personal loss of friends and relatives during the Korean War Period (1950–53), experiences, he says, that are reflected in his some 90 features since 1962.

Im disowns most of his work prior to *Weeds* in 1973 – he was a poor man who had to make a living, after all, by making flimsy commercial projects. His later work, especially the 1980's films, are something quite else again. **Come, Come to a Higher**

continued on p. 498

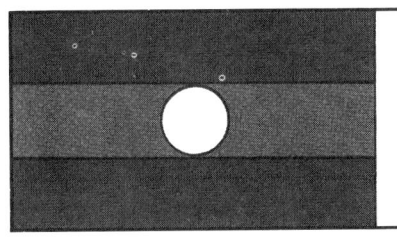

LAOS

by Fred Marshall

This tiny Buddhist kingdom of 4 million people adjoining Thailand relies on motion pictures as a form of entertainment and, like Thailand, draws upon numerous resources. The language is Lao (similar to Thai). There are a dozen movie theatres and many outdoor situations where films are screened to audiences composed of farmers and manual workers who sit on wooden benches.

Films shown are usually Chinese, Thai or Indian, dubbed in Thai and imported from Bangkok for a maximum of $1,000 (licence and print). There are no associations or companies, as motion pictures come under the aegis of the Ministry of Information and Culture; the officer in charge is Khammon Soapuonc.

Previously the movie theatres showed films from Eastern Europe, Cuba, and the U.S.S.R. with Vietnamese subtitles (which were none too popular). The country remains too small to support a film industry and since Thai is understood and relations

Burmese actor and director Ko Myint filming *Soul of the Mekong* in Laos

with Thailand are good, there is no need for prints to be subtitled. Television is received clearly from Thailand, and Laotians can see three channels from their neighbouring country. They also have their own Central TV which transmits three hours nightly, mostly informational news and cultural programmes. All five cities in Laos have access to LCTV, which is PAL Secam standard. Thailand supplies Laos with the latest video titles which are widely distributed throughout the country.

Many towns in Laos provide evening programmes only in cinemas (and Vientiane, for example, has just four halls). One of last year's biggest films was *Air America*, with Mel Gibson, about the CIA's covert activities in Laos during the Vietnam War. The famous Chiang Mai, where a set was designed, and the landmark "White Rose Café" was photographed in Thailand's Chiangmai. The Lao airports were shot in another province, Mae Hong Son.

An independent Hongkong production company entered Laos last year to shoot a one-hour TV film entitled *Soul of the Mekong*, which was shot with a Thai and Burmese crew. The many beautiful locations, jungles, mountains, lakes, waterfalls, and natural flora and fauna have never been seen before on film.

Useful Address

State Film and Video Company
P.O. Box 1624
Vientiane

LUXEMBOURG
by Jean-Pierre Thilges

Things must be looking up when location managers step on each other's toes while scouting around for shooting locations in tiny Luxembourg. With the tax shelter laws having recently come into full effect, a minor stampede of foreign producers seems to have engulfed the country, where the likes of Frank Agrama of Harmony Gold or U.S.-based former Australian distributor Andrew Gaty are setting up shop and announcing multimillion co-production agreements. Together with the local Ficomedia Group, Andrew Gaty Productions are planning construction of a $30 million studio facility and have announced, for 1991-92, production of four films in Luxembourg at an average cost of $15 million. International film and television crews are increasingly seen in the streets of Luxembourg. Thus, a Canadian crew spent the whole summer of 1990 in and around the country's medieval castles to shoot the pilot film and 20 episodes of the forthcoming *Dracula - The Series*.

Tax incentives certainly share responsibility for the recent boom, but the possibility of European television quotas still lurking on the horizon also seems to play a major part in the increasing interest in U.S.- European co-productions. Needless to stress the fact that the fledgling Luxembourg film-makers and craftsmen welcome the occasion to gather international experience and improve their skills while working on these productions as assistants. With the international response to the new audiovisual laws at an alltime high, the Luxembourg government has taken further steps to support and increase the creative output by local talent. In setting up the "Fonds de Soutien à l'Audiovisuel," they created a government and privately sponsored fund to subsidise new film projects. The fund is managed by a board of six governors appointed by the Minister of Culture and took up work during the summer of 1990.

For all the above reasons, 1990 has been the most exciting year as far as film-making in Luxembourg is concerned. Over the last 12 months, no less than four new features were completed or released to great public response, short and feature films were presented at festivals in Munich and Berlin, at the New York Museum of Modern Art, in Washington, in Los Angeles and in Melbourne. Andy Bausch's *A Wopbopaloobop a Lopbamboom* was nominated twice at the 1989 European Film Awards, for best supporting actress and best music score. And yes, even *Variety* started reviewing (and panning) films from Luxembourg.

A Wopbapaloopbop a Lopbamboom was reviewed here last year – it was seen by approximately 9,000 patrons during its initial run at a Luxembourg cinema and subsequently, by several million TV viewers when aired by its co-producer, West Germany's ZDF, in November 1989. With their musical comedy **Mumm Sweet Mumm**, directed by Paul Scheuer attracting well over 15,000 at the wickets, AFO Films brought home a major hit for the producer, the Luxembourg Ministry of Culture. The 16mm feature film, yet again shot for an abysmal amount (less than $150,000), looked like a million dollar feature on the screen. The convoluted story of this acerbically funny (but dramatically overlong) film meanders around a rich American who returns to his native Luxembourg, where he wants to trace the origins of a song from an operetta, which his

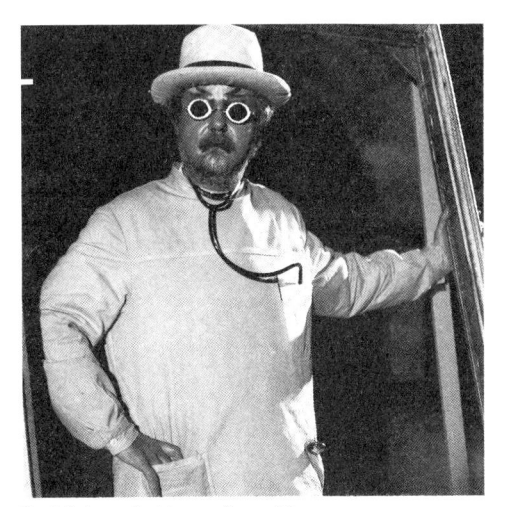

Paul Scheuer's *Mumm Sweet Mumm*
photo: Georges Fautsch

mother used to sing to him. As his quest is met with total disinterest by the natives, he triggers off a major contest, thus inviting local theatre honchos to stage modern productions of the dusty play. Intended as a sort of roundup of Luxembourg's stage scene, the film takes a devilish pleasure in poking fun at the country's "intelligentsia," including its film critics, who were rounded up and seen biting the dust in some very forgettable cameo appearances. Several musical production numbers in the film are excellent.

On a more serious note, **The Traitor** (*De Falschen Hond*) co-directed by Menn Bodson, Gast Rollinger and Marc Olinger (for RTL Television) takes a trip down memory lane on the occasion of the 150th anniversary of the country's independence from its warmongering neighbours. The central character of the story which takes place in 1830, the rather simple-minded clerk Matthias Brëcker (played by André Jung) finds himself in strong opposition with his fellow countrymen, when he spreads the idea that the country should be neither Belgian nor German, but should remain Luxembourgish. His (then progressive)

C.N.A. DEALS WITH ANY QUESTION ON CINEMA IN LUXEMBOURG
Ministere des Affaires Culturelles
For information on production, distribution and festival participation, please contact: Centre National de l'Audiovisuel 5, Route de Zoufftgen L-3598 dudelange (Gr. Duchy of Luxembourg) Telephone: (352) 51 93 44 Fax: (352) 52 06 55
Centre National de l'Audiovisuel

ideas force him to flee the country. Later, he drowns in his attempt to return from exile, just a few years before his country gains independence at the "Treaty of London Conference" in 1839 ... Obviously, this adaptation of a patriotic novel by Nikolaus Hein strikes an overly melodramatic note, but the lavish historical reconstruction and the excellent actors compensate for any shortcomings in Henri Losch's expert but sometimes literary script. The synthetised score by Jacques Neuen tends to overemphasise several well staged crowd scenes.

Another literary adaptation, and the first feature from Luxembourg to be shot in 35mm, **Schacko Klak**, directed by Paul Kieffer and Frank Feitler (Samsa Films)

from a popular novel by local scribe Roger Manderscheid, was being rushed for completion at press time for a September release. Again centred on the country's strong wish for independence, this one tells the Second World War adventures of a young country boy, Chrëscht Knapp, who comes of age by witnessing the war crimes inflicted to the population by the Nazi oppressors ... The script for *Schacko Klak* won a 1989 screenwriting contest, organised by the Minister of Culture, who contributed some $500,000 to the film's $1 million budget.

Forthcoming projects from Luxembourg's very own Andy Bausch include a programme of short features called **Short Movies, right?**, a screwball

TOP GROSSING FILMS IN LUXEMBOURG: 1989

(*Alphabetical Order*)

Batman
Dangerous Liaisons
A Fish Called Wanda
Indiana Jones and the Last Crusade
Lethal Weapon 2
Licence to Kill
Mumm Sweet Mumm
Oliver and Company
Rain Man
Sex, Lies and Videotape
When Harry Met Sally
Working Girl

comedy entitled **Three Shake-a-Leg Steps to Heaven**, which should start rolling in early 1991 and finally, **El Loco**, a rather ambitious modern day western taking place in a derelict movie theatre in an Indian reservation, to be shot entirely in the United States...

JEAN-PIERRE THILGES earns a living in banking; as a film critic, he has been fighting for the survival of the art of cinema in Luxembourg since 1972; a witness to the birth of the ongoing Luxembourg film boom, he has run his own cinema multiplex together with equally filmstruck friends since 1989; and was recently appointed to the board of governors of the "Fonds d'Aide à l'Audiovisuel".

Useful Addresses

Centre National de l'Audiovisuel
5 route de Zoufftgen
L-3598 Dudelange
Gr. Duchy of Luxembourg
Tel: (352) 51 93 44

Service des Médias et de l'Audiovisuel Ministère d'Etat
5 rue Large
L-1917 Luxembourg-City
Gr. Duchy of Luxembourg
Tel: (352) 47 81
Fax: (352) 46 17 20

Ficomedia Group
18 rue de l'Eau
L-1499 Luxembourg-City
Gr. Duchy of Luxembourg
Tel: (352) 46 12 20

MALAYSIA

by Baharudin A. Latif

A.R. Badul, the toothy comedian whose slapstick comedies are habitually regarded with disdain by intellectuals but are the rage of the non-discriminating filmgoers here, achieved a rare accomplishment at the 8th Malaysian Film Festival (held in September 1989), which silenced his critics forever. He won awards for Best Actor and Best Director for **Guru Badul** and **Oh Fatimah** respectively, a coup equalled previously only by veteran Jins Shamsuddin. At his acceptance speech, Badul cynically remarked that he was elated to be finally "in" after 15 years of toil. His films have kept producers' coffers swelling and he continues to be the busiest actor, director and scriptwriter multiple-threat around.

His comedies are mercilessly torn apart by the critics which is a pity, for Badul has made a number of durable and genuinely humorous films which can one day attain cult status. One, **Hantu Siang**, about a womanising chauffeur who uses his employer's premises and facilities to lure his prey, is seriously adult in content and reminiscent of the Cary Grant/Katharine Hepburn classics. It is not preposterous to hope that one day Badul's status as a genuine comedian will spark the same heated interest and achieve similar appreciation and idolatry accorded comic Jerry Lewis by French intellectuals.

In a less than sober time when films about do-gooders dressed up in bat costumes or turtle casings go round delivering mayhem to criminals and make millions at the box-office, Badul's comedies are a kind of antidote to remind all and sundry that life has its lighter side and exhilarating moments too.

Promising Crop Ahead

The current year looks promising after two years of dismal showing by local films. At the time of writing, **Fenomena**, an excellent tear-jerker that Joan Crawford or Bette Davis in their younger days would have given anything to get their hands on, is set to be a box-office winner. Effectively acted by a well-chosen cast, this is the kind of polished production that revives one's interest in a declining cinema. Aziz M. Osman, making his directorial debut, has provided a visual treat in a stirring drama about a dying girl with Ramana Rahman perfect in her first big role.

Over the past year, three other young directors also made their debuts – Raja Ahmad Alauddin with **Hati Bukan Kristal**, Anwardi Jamil with **Tuah** and Zarul Shahrin Al-Bakri with **Mat Gelap**. These films, rewarded with varying degrees of critical and financial success, have heralded a new era for the local industry. Critics and film buffs have welcomed the predominance of new blood and are hoping for a radical change in the overall presentation of future productions.

Another encouraging development is the emergence of the cineplexes, with the two major exhibition companies, Golden Communications and The Cathay Organisation, vying for prime location areas in the Federal Capital and other key towns. The latter has gained an edge with the setting up of two multiplexes at The Cultural Square, one of the city's most popular tourist areas.

But whether cinema patrons are willing to adjust their spending habits and dish out more money to see movies at multiplexes

Aziz M. Osman directing Ramona Rahman in *Phenomenon*

photo: Aziz Md. Ali

TOP GROSSING FILMS IN MALAYSIA: 1989

	Gross
Licence to Kill	M$3.6 Million (US$1.4M)
Indiana Jones and the Last Crusade	M$3.4 Million (US$1.3M)
The Miracle (Hongkong)	M$3.3 Million (US$1.2M)
God of Gamblers (Hongkong)	M$2 Million (US$800,000)
Mr Coconut (Hongkong)	M$2 Million (US$800,000)
Rambo III (from 1988)	M$2 Million (US$800,000)
Peacock King (Hongkong)	M$1.7 Million (US$700,000)
Pedicab Driver (Hongkong)	M$1.6 Million (US$650,000)
Kickboxer	M$1.4 Million (US$600,000)
Batman	M$1.3 Million (US$550,000)

Note: other than those marked as Hongkong imports, all films are English-language.

while other prints are simultaneously showing at regular prices in other theatres is obviously the big question mark. It would be a good business move to adopt a limited release pattern for multiplexes before films are generally released elsewhere.

Ominous Overtones

Another development with slightly ominous overtones is the intended take-over by Perlis Plantations Bhd. (PPB) of Borneo Film Organisation Sdn. Bhd. (BFO) which in turn owns 66% interest in Cathay Organisation, one of the two major distribution and exhibition circuits, for some M$60 million (US$25 million).

PPB already owns Golden Communications, the other top distribution and exhibition circuit. Each circuit has 33 cinemas and PPB stands to become the sole monopoly giant when the deal goes through. However, approval from the Foreign Investment Committee is pending.

PPB's rationale for the sale is that GC was running at a consistent loss prior to its take-over and the expert management it had pumped in since had resulted in a complete turn-around. Its beefed-up position had given GC more clout in obtaining better foreign films.

It is difficult to argue against facts, and facts have shown GC's remarkable recovery from the doldrums over the past two years. 1989 was its boom year and GC is set for another one. PPB hopes to do the same for Cathay, presently incurring big losses. Why Cathay has been running downhill is a mystery when it had a big hit like **Rambo III**, which it exhibited but did not purchase.

Meanwhile, local productions still average 12 a year, with most ending up as losses. However, 1990 looks bright with **Fenomena** leading the way. It earned M$1 million (US$300,000) in 29 days and most likely will double that when the film finishes its first run.

Fenomena (Phenomenon)

Script: Zain Mahmud. Direction: Aziz M. Osman. Photographer: Badaruddin Hj. Azmi. Editing: Ibrahim Ahmad. Production Manager: Aziz Md. Ali. Executive Producers: Zahari Zain & Alias Omar. Produced by Teletrade Sdn. Bhd. 115 mins.

Isabella, an English girl suffering from a terminal illness, comes back to Malaysia to get a traditional cure from a medicine man (*bomoh*) who had once cured her as a child. Meeting up with him in Terengganu, where her English father and Malay mother had lived previously, she finds Pak Labib himself burdened with a host of problems. He has to cope with a reclusive son-in-law, Azlan, and a grand-daughter with a defective heart. Moved by sympathy, Isabella succeeds in getting Azlan out of his shell and stages a fund-raising concert for the toddler. In the process, she finds inner tranquillity. However, on the day the little girl is due to leave for overseas treatment, Isabella herself succumbs to another coma. Does she live?

Thousands have flocked to the theatre to find out the answer, but the firm has a cliff-hanger for a climax. Just right for a sequel but, like *E.T.*, it has exhausted itself artistically and creatively. Nonetheless, what could have been a routine soap opera has been transformed into an enthralling and gripping drama, and credit for this must go to the excellent dialogue and intelligent directing.

Baharudin A. Latif

Profile: Aziz M. Osman

Aziz M. Osman's directional debut film *Fenomena* is presently riding a wave of critical and financial success, highly likely to end up as the most profitable film over the past few years. A mere 28-year-old, Aziz comes from a show business family and started acting at age one. At 14, he won the "Twin Lion Award" for Best Child Actor at the 21st Asian Film Festival for *Sayang Anakku Sayang*.

Besides acting, he has tried his hand at comic strip drawing, feature and scriptwriting, photography and numerous behind the camera chores.

In 1985, after a spell as assistant producer at Radio Television Malaysia, the Government-owned agency, he directed his first television move, *Mawas*, about a man with a werewolf personality. He came into prominence with outstandingly directed television movies like *Ubi, Kaki Monyet, Time Bomb, Alina* and the four-part mini-series *Primadona*. The last was sold to Indonesia and telecast to overwhelming response.

Baharudin A. Latif

New and Forthcoming Films

Driving School. Dir: Othman Hafsham. Script: Othman Hj. Zainuddin. Phot: Zainal Othman. Music: Manan Ngah. Players: Azmil Mustafa, Ziela Jalil, Julis Rais, Yusuf Haslam, Imuda. Prod: Julie Dahlan for J.D. Productions. 100 mins.

Hati Bukan Kristal (The Ear Is Not a Crystal). Dir: Raja Ahmad Alauddin. Script: Habsah Hassan. Phot: Badaruddin Hj. Azmi. Music: Ooi Eow Jin. Players: Redzuan Hasham, Erma Fatimah, Julia Rais, Zaiton Sameon, Shah Rezza, Imuda, Adibah Amin. Prod: Habsah Hassan and Rahimah Rahim for Director's Team.

Main-Main Hantu (Ghost Story). Dir: Tommy Chung, Junaidi Dahalan. Script: Bing Bing. Phot: Lee Keng Hong. Music: Azman Abu Hassan. Players: Hamid Gurkha, Nancie Foo, Melissa Saila, Alice Voon. Prod: Tan Sri Dato' Mohd and Ghazali Seth for Solid Gold Studio.

Mat Gelap (The Zany Cartoonist). Dir: Zarul Shahrin Al-Bakri. Script: Liz Tajuddin. Phot: Zainal Othman. Music: Roslan Aziz, Mac Chew. Players: Imuda, Liza Othman, Mano Maniam, Apen Mahidin, Jit Murad, Sri Ratu. Prod: Mohd, and Shafek Isa for ZSA Productions.

Rentak Desa (Country Frolic). Dir: Rahim Razali. Script: Rahim Razali. Phot: Zainal Othman. Music: Adnan Abu Hassan, Susan Goh. Players: Fauziah Ahmad Daud, Eman Manan, Ebby Saiful, Ziela Jalil, Zulkarnain Ramli, Abmad Tarmimi Siregar, Abu Baker Omar. Prod: Wan Rohani Zin for ASA XX.

Producers (West Malaysia)

Kay Films
16th Floor, Menara Apera/ULG
84 Jalan Raja Chulan
50200 Kuala Lumpur
Federal Territory
Tel: (03) 261-8455

Pengedar Utama
9173-A, Jalan Negara
Taman Melawati, Hulu Kelang
53100 Selangor Darul Ehsan
Tel: (03) 407-4537, 408-2082

Studio Jalan Ampas
25A, 1st Floor
Jalan Bandar 12, Metro II
Taman Melawati, Hulo Kelang
51300 Selangor Darul Ehsan
Tel: (03) 407-4786

Teletrade Sdn. Bhd
24, 2nd & 3rd Floor
Jalan SS 15/8, Subang Jaya
47500 Petaling Jaya
Selangor Darul Ehsan
Tel: (03) 733-3377

ZSA Holdings
11th Floor, South Block
Wisma Selangor Dredging
142-A Jalan Ampang
50450 Kuala Lumpur
Federal Territory
Tel: (03) 261-0742

Fuego Enterprises
22-2, 2nd Floor, Jalan 1/82B
Bangsar Utama
59000 Kuala Lumpur
Federal Territory
Tel: (03) 232-7850

ASA XX
71, Jalan SS 15/4B
Subang Jaya
47500 Petaling Jaya
Selangor Darul Ehsan
Tel: (03) 733-8520, 733-8522

Distributors (West Malaysia)

Cathay Film Distributors (M)
No. 1, Jalan SS 22/19
Damansara Jaya
47400 Petaling Jaya
Selangor Darul Ehsan
Tel: (03) 719-5666

Golden Communications (M)
Lot 11, Jalan 13/6
46000 Petaling Jaya
Selangor Darul Ehsan
Tel: (03) 241-2077, 756-7911

U.I.P.
B-4, Khoon Lin Court
Jalan Yew Pasar
Kuala Lumpur
Federal Territory
Tel: (03) 984-7884, 241-528

Sunny Film Productions
60-B, 1st Floor, Jalan Desa Bakti
Taman Desa Town Centre
58100 Kuala Lumpur
Federal Territory
Tel: (03) 78 3-9018

Karyamas Sdn. Bhd.
253, 2nd Floor, Hotel Merlin
No. 2, Jalan Sultan Ismail
50250 Kuala Lumpur
Federal Territory
Tel: (03) 248-0033, 242-0033

Juita-Viden
21-01, 21st Floor
Menara MPPJ, New Town Centre
46200 Petaling Ehsan
Selangor Darul Ehsan
Tel: (03) 757-5061

Studios

Asia Pacific Videolab
52, Jalan Dungun, Damansara Heights
50490 Kuala Lumpur
Federal Territory
Tel: (03) 255-3188

Addaudio
6, Jalan 17/54
46400 Petaling Ehsan
Tel: (03) 756-0600, 756-4166

Studio 3
Lot 1045, 71/2 Mile
Jalan Hulu Kelang
68000 Selangor Darul Ehsan
Tel: (03) 408-2525

BAHARUDIN A. LATIF is currently Publications and Public Affairs Assistant Director at FINAS, the National Film Development Corporation of Malaysia. He has written more than 2,000 articles on films for domestic and international publications including The Asia Magazine, Asiaweek and Dewan Budaya.

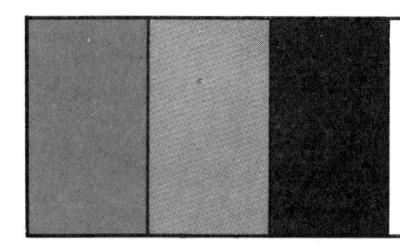

MALI

by Roy Armes

In the 1960's and early 1970's French influence on the emergent Malian cinema was strong, with the personal impact of the ethnographer Jean Rouch, an interesting, French-guided experiment in collective film-making at a ciné-club in Bamako, a number of fictional and documentary films made in the French language and quite outside the commercial system by the writer Alkaly Kaba, who trained in Canada, and especially with the two feature films – *Fate* (*Mogho Dakan*, 1976) and *The Prisoner* (*Kasso den*, 1978) made by a director who studied in Paris, Sega Coulibaly. But since then Mali has been the West African state whose cinema has had the closest links with the U.S.S.R. and the then communist governments of Eastern Europe. The new generation of Malian film-makers have all been trained in the socialist world, but most of them have made only one feature. In 1980, for instance, the East German trained Falaba Issa Traore made *An Be Nodo/We Are All Guilty* and the Moscow-trained Kalifa Dienta completed *A Banna/It's All Over*

As elsewhere in West Africa a number of successive organisations have been set up to control distribution and to foster production, but with little tangible result. By the end of the 1980's these national corporations (OCINAM, CNPC etc) had been enforced to inactivity and what little help was given to film-makers came directly from government ministries. Nevertheless there was a little burst of film making in the mid-1980's. Falaba Issa Traore was able to complete a second feature, *Duel on the Cliffs*, after a break of six years, and a young newcomer, Cheikh Oumar Sissoko, shot two features in quick succession. The first was *Lessons from the Garbage/Nyamanton* (1986), a charming tale of small children maintaining their humour and dignity though compelled to work on the streets collecting garbage in order to pay for their lessons. This film was widely shown and well received, but Sissoko was less successful with his second effort, *Finzan* (1988), a rather disjointed study of woman's place in society.

A third member of the 1970's Soviet trained group also re-emerged in the late 1980's. Djibril Kouyate – in fact the first of them to return from study in Moscow – had made a number of shorts in the late 1960's, a short financial film, *The Return of Tieman*, in 1970 and a 30 minute documentary, co-ordinated with the Yugoslav Branco Segović, *Mali Today*, in 1978. But he had to wait a further ten years for his first fictional feature film assignment, *Falato/The Orphan* (1988) and even this is claimed in the credits by its producer-screenwriter as "un film de Mamo Cisse." The film was sponsored by the Ministry of Co-operation and Development and the Ministry of Culture and Communication and has the basically optimistic stance common to films with this kind of production backing. A governor on the point of retirement remembers his own childhood and expresses his thanks to those who helped him, an orphan, to rise to influence. The strength of the film lies in its portrayal of a deprived and disjointed childhood, filmed with feeling and a telling simplicity.

Cisse the Towering Figure

Towering above his Malian contemporaries is Souleymane Cisse, another Moscow-trained director and a major figure in black African film-making. In thirty years of activity since his return to Mali, Cisse has been able to make a handful of commissioned documentaries, one fictional short, *Five Days of a Life* (1971), and just four features of steadily increasing force and authority. After a simple black-and-white study of a young woman trapped by social contradictions, *Den Muso/The Girl* (1975), Cisse moved on to study the African urban working class in *Baara/Work* (1979) and the structures of power in a society caught between tradition and modernity in *Finye/ The Wind* (1982). Built around a student revolt against military dictatorship, this latter film examines a whole range of social issues (drug-taking, polygamy, authoritarian rule, traditional values), mixing this analysis effortlessly with dream sequences and passages of unreality. Cisse's most recent work, **The Light** (*Yeelen*, 1987) is again a new departure, a timeless fable drawing on the Bambara tradition of oral storytelling and set in an African rural landscape. Basically it is a story of the clash between an evil father who misuses his magical powers and his idealistically minded son. The young hero may be tempted into sin and be in need of ritual purification, but he faces his fate resolutely. In the climactic confrontation, father and son destroy each other, but hope for the future remains in the figure of the hero's young son, whom the camera follows in the film's final images. Subtly directed and with some striking sound and visual effects, *Yeelen* is a major statement about African tradition and values. Cisse has completed nothing since *Yeelen*, but, at the 1989 FESPACO at Ouagadougou, Mali was represented by one of the most applauded films in the festival, the short puppet film, *Le geste de Segou*, intended by its director, Mambaye Coulibaly, as the first of a series of ten 13-minute episodes for African TV.

MEXICO
by Tomás Pérez Turrent and Gillian Turner

Although notwithstanding the crisis, 112 films were produced in Mexico in 1988, this being the highest number since 1958, in 1989 production decreased to 76. In 1990 even fewer films will probably be produced, as up until May only 27 features were being made. As has been the case since the 1970's, for the greater part production is directed towards the Mexican market, the so-called "Hispanic" market of the United States – more and more restricted as days go by – and that of some Central American countries.

Faced with the continuing reduction of markets, commercial film producers making films based on popular or spectacular themes cannot invest large amounts of money on their products, the average cost of which fluctuates between 400 and 850 million pesos (about $160,000 to $310,000) to the detriment of the films' technical quality. The members of the Film Producers' Association, besides being severely limited by the difficulties of the market, seem incapable of finding either new working methods or new and more interesting themes for their films. However, it is fair to point out that when they do dare to experiment with some new theme they usually find themselves faced with some new kind of restriction, as is the case of the film of political fiction: **Will the President Betray Us?** (*¿Nos traicionará el Presidente?*), produced and directed by Fernando Pérez Galvan, the showing of which has been forbidden ever since 1988.

Worth noting is the success of the group of folk singers **The Tigers of the North** (*Los Tigres del Norte*), whose films are extremely popular in the interior of the Republic and especially in the North. The three films produced by this group to date: **The Black Door** (*La puerta Negra*, 1989), **The Three Roosters** (*Los tres gallos*, 1989) and **The Grey Van** (*La camioneta gris*, 1990) stand out for their production values not customary in this sort of film, well constructed scripts (by Xavier Robles) and professional direction with a good sense of action (by José Luis Urquieta).

As usual, the few films with some minimum ambition with regard to theme and expression are those produced or co-produced by the State via the Mexican Film Institute (IMCINE), produced or co-produced by the "Fund for the Promotion of Quality", by some small independent companies and the co-operatives. The IMCINE, which had announced very ambitious plans in 1989, is presently finishing its first two films: **The Legend of the Masked Angel** (*La leyenda del angéel enmascarado*) by José Buil, and **Lumber Town** (*Pueblo de madera*) by Juan Antonio de la Riva. It has participated in several co-productions.

In accordance with its general policy the state has been gradually retreating from the field of cinema. In March 1990 the state film production companies Conacine and Conacite disappeared, together with the distributing companies Continental de Peliculas and Nueva distribuidora de Películas and the film advertising company called Publicidad Cuauhtemoc. Still under study is the sale of Operadora de Teatros, grouping together the greatest number of movie theatres in the country (IMCINE would keep only about twenty screens for the showing of quality films), and the sale of the America Film Studios. Churubusco, the most important film studios, will continue under state management.

Attendances Still on Slide

Up to December 31, 1989 there were 1,765 film screens in the Mexican Republic. That same year 500 screens were closed down in the entire territory, contrasting with 220 which had been closed between 1986 and 1988. On the other hand, the number of TV sets has increased to 21,000,000 (15,000,000 in 1980) and VCRs to 3,500,000 (150,000 in 1980). Thus in Mexico, as in the rest of the world, the number of filmgoers decreases steadily. In the case of Mexico, to this should be added the fact of the low entry price, state controlled, which varies from $850 to $2,400 Mexican Pesos (approximately US$0.30 to US$0.90), which makes it impossible for the theatres to be properly maintained and to offer film projection of good technical quality both in image and sound.

Altogether 328 films were shown in 1989 in Mexico City. Of these, 158, or 58% were American. 68, or 27% were of Mexican production, and the remaining 25% was composed of films from the U.K., France, Italy, Spain, Germany, U.S.S.R., Poland, Hongkong, Australia, Canada, Argentina, Brazil, Cuba, Venezuela, India. Only 3% of these films were from Latin America. The market in Mexico, as in other countries, greatly favours production from the United States.

The major American distribution companies operate in Mexico, including Columbia Pictures, 20th Century-Fox, United International Pictures, and Warners. United International Pictures shows its

Still from *Goitia – A God unto Himself*

material via the state chain of theatres, Operadora de Teatros; Fox and Columbia in "Cadena Ramirez," the most important of the independent chains; Warner uses both outlets. The most important national distributor, Arte Cinema de México, distributes mainly American films together with some European material and oriental "karate" style films.

With regard to the distribution of Mexican cinema, Películas Mexicanas, the company which traditionally held first place, has lost its foothold not in the number of films distributed but in profit margins. The leader is now Videocine, an affiliate of Televisa, the huge television conglomerate, whose films occupy first place in profits, thanks to their constant TV advertising and to the fact that they generally illustrate values made popular by television itself. Unfortunately, this company is not interested in distributing quality cinema, but its example demonstrates that in the future cinema will depend more and more on an ever closer collaboration with television.

Goitia, un dios para si mismo (Goitia, a God unto Himself)

Script: Diego Lopez, Jorge Gonzalez de Leon, Javier Sicilia, Enrique Vargas, Raúl Zermeño. Direction: Diego Lopez. Photography: Arturo de la Rosa. Music: Amparo Rubin. Editing: Sigfrido Garcia. Players: Jose Carlos Ruiz, Patricia Reyes Espindola, Alejandro Parodi, Ana Ofelia Murguia, Alonso Echanove, Angelica Aragon. Produced by Imaginaria, S.A., IMCINE, Fondo de Fomento a la Calidad Cinematografica.

For his third film – his first made fully within the industrial system – Diego Lopez has chosen the life of an unusual Mexican painter who died in 1960: Francisco Goitia. This is not, however, a biographical film in the traditional sense. He prefers to present aspects of the painter's life partially and in fragments, concentrating more on the interior rather than the exterior of his character: his spiritual search, his internal conflicts, his obsessions, the importance of his repressed sexuality. Using a perspective very far from the folkloric, Lopez constructs a kind of mystical documentary which is very close to the attitude and outlook of the character himself.

Diego Lopez moves freely from one time to another, from one dimension to another, without following any preconceived order. With the excellent photography of Arturo de la Rosa, which reproduces faithfully the colours and textures of the painter's work, the film oscillates between bitterness, an exalted illumination, and outright sarcasm. There are several ruptures in tone which achieve the required break with realism.

Tomás Pérez Turrent

Intimidades en un cuarto de bano (Intimacy in a Bathroom)

Script and Direction: Jaime Humberto Hermosillo. Photography: Guillermo Navarro. Music: Rockdrigo Gonzalez. Editing: Jaime Humberto Hermosillo. Art Direction: Leticia Venzor. Players: Gabriela Roel, Alvaro Guerrero, Martha Navarro, Emilio Echeverria, Maria Rojo. Produced by Profesionales, S.A., Sociedad Cooperativa de Producciones Cinematograficas Jose Revueltas.

This marks one step further in Jaime Humberto Hermosillo's search for alternatives with regard to film production and creative independence. The result is Mexican cinema's first real answer to the crisis: five actors, one photographer, one set, six days of rehearsal and four days of filming, just 10,000 feet of film, meaning that only two scenes had to be repeated. All the action occurs in a bathroom and the camera remains in one position only, equivalent to the point of view of the bathroom mirror.

The film offers a response to Mexico's economic crisis but also to the aesthetic crisis of Mexican cinema. Its technical simplicity and the extreme paucity of movement, lending greater emphasis to the film's narrative, its *mise en scène* and the director's work with his actors, all this is no mere display of virtuosity. In the reduced space of a bathroom, for a period of 24 hours, the four members of a family (the fifth character is alien to the drama and serves as a counterpoint) destroy each other and themselves, reflected by the mirror, and this reflection is in turn caught by the camera. Thus, the film is the reflection of a reflection, and the result is exceptional.

Tomás Pérez Turrent

Intimidad (Intimacy)

Script: Leonardo García Tsao, based on the stage play "Intimidad" by Hugo Hiriart. Direction: Dana Rotberg. Photography: Carlos Marcovich. Music: Gerardo Batiz. Editing: Oscar Figueroa. Players: Emilio Echeverria, Lisa Owen, Angeles Gonzalez, Alvaro Guerrero, Juan Jose Nebreda, Ana Ofelia Murguia, Agustín Silva. Produced by Leon Constantiner, Producciones Metropolis.

This is the first full-length film and professional debut of the young film-maker Dana Rotberg whose career up until now has been a noteworthy one in the field of the documentary. In this case it should be recognised that this is not a personal project but one commissioned by a producer who had already acquired the rights to the stage play, and that Dana Rotberg was required only to make the film. However, the result is a decorous one. Without any pretension of having made "the film of her life," this is a well-made, well-told story, with a fine feeling for image and rhythm. She has accomplished what she set out to do, and has shown herself to be a film-maker with a promising future.

Still from *Intimacy*

Using García Tsao's very free adaptation, Dana Rotberg's theme is that of the couple and the erosion of its relationship, illustrated by the experience of a professor of literature and frustrated writer who has reached the age of 50 and accumulated 30 years of marriage, in the same tedious and useless existence. What begins as a mere act of voyeurism develops into the passion of his life with one of his neighbours, a young married girl of 25. Successfully maintaining a tone of cruel comedy although never losing a certain ambiguity, Dana Rotberg leads her characters up a blind alley where love and liberation are mere utopias. On the other hand, it is curious to find that a film made by a woman should give such a negative portrait of women in general.

Tomás Pérez Turrent

Profile: Juan Antonio de la Riva

Juan Antonio was born in San Miguel de Cruces, Durango in 1957, in the projection room of a cinema. He studied cinema at the CUEC (University Center for Film Studies) and at the CCC (Centre for Cinematographic Capacitation). The film he presented for his thesis **Dust, Victor over the Sun** (*Polvo vencedor del sol*) won a prize as the best fiction short film at the Festival of Lille, France in 1979. His first documentary film was **Wandering Lives** (*Vidas errantes*) in 1983, which won him a prize as the best Opera Prima at San Sebastian, in 1984. His second film was **Obdulia** in 1986. Since then he has made four programmes in the television series on "gothic" themes: **The Right Time** (*La hora marcada*), together with many other film-makers of his generation. He has just finished his third full-length film: **Lumber Town** (*Pueblo de madera*).

Juan Antonio de la Riva's father first travelled with a portable cinema, then bought a film theatre in the small lumber town of San Miguel de Cruces, Durango, in the mountains of Northern Mexico, and that is why Juan Antonio was born in the projection room. He has devoted the greater part of his film production to life in that town. *Polvo vencedor del sol* is concerned with its daily life devoid of horizons. *Vidas errantes* is the story of a travelling film showman, in homage to his father and the popular Mexican cinema that formed him. *Obdulia* differs in surroundings but not in style: a way of seeing people and their relationships tinted with tenderness and human warmth. With *Pueblo de madero* he returns to life on the mountain, without losing his former qualities, but instead gaining in maturity and professionalism. De la Riva is one of the most promising film-makers of the new generation.

TOMÁS PÉREZ TURRENT has published several books on the cinema since 1963. He has also written numerous film scripts. He is a graduate of UNAM (National Autonomous University of Mexico) in Philosophy.

Recent and Forthcoming Films

La camioneta gris (The Grey Van). Script: Xavier Robies. Dir: José Luis Urquieta. Phot: Agustin Lara. Players: Mario Almada, Fernando Almada, "Los Tigres del Norte," Blanca Rosa Torres. Phot: José Ortiz Ramos. Prod: Carlos Moreno, José Luis Orduña, STYM, Los Tigres del Norte.

Casas grandes: una aproximación a la gran Chichimeca (Casas Grandes: An Approach to the Great "Chichimeca"). Script: Oscar Montero. Dir: Rafael Montero. Phot: Mario Luna. Prod: Archivo Etnográfico Audiovisual INI.

Historias de ciudad (City Stories): Alguien se acerca (Someone's Coming). Script and Dir: Ramón Cervantes. Phot: José Barajas. Players: Ramón Huerta, Patricia Calzado, Margarita Isabel, Fausto Retes. Prod: DIAC-UNAM.

Viajeros (Travellers). Script: Rafael Montero. Oscar Montero. Dir: Rafael Montero. Phot: Juan Carlos Martin. Players: Agustin Pimentel, Mónica Cadena, Raquel Cruz, Gilberto Chávez. Prod: DIAC-UNAM.

Lili (Lily). Script and Dir: Gerardo Lara. Phot: Juan Carlos Martin. Players: Estela Flores Ocampo, Delfina Careaga, Javier Torres, Hector Sánchez. Prod: DIAC-UNAM.

Azul celeste (Sky Blue). Script: Beatriz Novaro, Maria Novaro. Dir: Maria Novaro. Phot: Santiago Navarrete. Players: Gabriela Roel, Carlos Chávez, Cheli Godinez, Gina Morett. Prod: DIAC-UNAM.

Lola. Script: Beatriz Novaro, Maria Novaro. Dir: Maria Novaro. Phot: Rodrigo Garcia. Players: Leticia Huijara, Martha Navarro, Roberto Sosa, Alejandra Vargas. Prod: Macondo Cine-Video, Conacite II, Cooperative José Revueltas Television Espãnola.

Maten a Chinto (Kill Chinto). Script and Dir: Alberto Isaac. Phot: Jorge Stahl. Players: Pedro Armendáriz, Hector Ortega, Patricia Páramo, Gerardo Quiroz, Eduardo López Rojas. Prod: Conacine – Estudios Churubusco.

Morir en el golfo (Dying in the Gulf). Script: Victor Hugo Rascón, Alejandro Pelayo. Dir: Alejandro Pelayo. Phot: Guillermo Navarro. Players: Enrique Rocha, Blanca Guerra. Alejandro Parodi, Carlos Cardán, Emilio Echeverria. Prod: Tabasco Films, Cooperativa José Revueltas, IMCINE.

El otro crimen (The Other Crime). Script: Carlos González Morantes, Ruben Torres, Tomás Pérez Turrent. Dir: Carlos González Morantes. Phot: Jack Lach. Players: Enrique Rocha, Elizabeth Aguilar, Maria Rojo, Claudio Obregón, Xavier Marc. Prod: DIAC-UNAM.

Un lugar en el sol (A Place in the Sun). Script and Dir: Arturo Velazco. Phot: Alex Phillips Jr. Players: Manuel Ojeda, Blanca Sánchez, Odiseo Vichir, Rolando de Castro, Sergio Sánchez, Claudia Sánchez. Prod: Fondo de Fomento a la Calidad Cinematrográfica/Imcine.

Una moneda en el aire (To Spin a Coin). Script: Hugo Bonaldi. Ariel Zúñiga. Dir: Ariel Zúñiga. Phot: Guillermo Navarro. Players: Arturo Beristain, Isabel Benet, Jorge Martinez de Hoyos, Delia Casanova, Andrea Ferrari. Prod: Sinc S.A., Cooperativa José Revueltas.

TOP TEN GROSSING FILMS IN MEXICO: 1989*

	Rentals
Batman	9,500 million pesos**
The Karate Kid III	3,500 " "
Indiana Jones and the Last Crusade	3,400 " "
Die Hard	3,318 " "
Escapate conmigo	2,500 " "
My Stepmother Is an Alien	2,480 " "
Rain Man	2,450 " "
Sueltate el pelo	2,448 " "
Vacaciones del terror	2,446 " "
Three Fugitives	2,300 " "

* Statistics refer to the Metropolitan Area (including Mexico City) only. Population 20 million, 25% of the national population. Statistics referring to the rest of the country are not accurate.

** Exchange rate (as of December 31, 1989) $2,649 pesos per U.S. dollar.

MONGOLIA

by Fred Marshall

The capital of Ulan Bator is the centre of film activity in Mongolia, and of course the "industry", such as it is, depends upon government subsidies. For the most part the output consists of local material, and imports are composed almost entirely of Soviet pictures. One of the biggest films ever produced in the country was last year's epic adventure, **Mandhkai**.

Screened at the Tokyo International Film Festival in 1989, the film boasts a cast of thousands. It is a Genghis Khan adventure in scope and colour, and it was sold for theatrical release to Japan and Hongkong, as well as to Soviet TV. This historical drama takes its audience back to the time when Mongolia was a mighty empire of fierce warriors. Its budget was approximately twenty times as much as the average Mongolian feature. Its battle sequences are impressive considering the limitations of the local film facilities.

Useful Address

General Department of
Mongolian Cinematography
P.O. Box 490
Ulan Bator 13

NEPAL

by Kalendra Shahi

The emergence of Tulshi Ghimiray as a significant director here in Nepal has marked the past year. Ghimiray studied first in India and entered the industry in Bombay in 1974. Since then he has edited more than 50 feature films in different languages. He made his directing debut in 1979 with *Bansuri*, produced by Sai Nath Productions. His second film was *The Waiting (Jagwal)*, the first-ever Gadwali feature, written, directed and edited by Tulshi Ghimiray. Five years later Ghimiray attracted wide audiences for *Kushume Rumal*, a full-fledged Nepali feature again written and edited by the director himself.

Lahurey (1989) is probably the best film to have been made in Nepal. It traces the story of a courageous Gurkha soldier, whose fiancé kills a man who tries to rape her. She goes into hiding, but gives birth to the Gurkha's child, only to find that she cannot contact him until it is too late... There is a strong emphasis on the patriotic traditions of the Gurkha. Tulshi Ghimiray makes a creditable debut as an actor in *Lahurey*.

Forthcoming films include Ghimiray's **Annyaya**, produced by Bishwa, and **Kosheli**, again directed by Ghimiray, this time for Ajambari.

Tulshi Ghimiray in *Lahurey*

To mark the Silver Jubilee of the Filmmakers' Association of Nepal, a festival was organised in 1989 at which all 18 feature films of the past decade were screened. Ravindra Khadka took Best Actor prize for *Mayapriti*, Sharmila Shah the Best Actress for *Kanchi*, and Prakesh Thapa was singled out as Best Director for *Santan*.

Tulshi Ghimiray

Other Recent Films

Behuli (Bride). Dir Shambhu Pradhan. Players: Prakash Adhikan, Sunita, Ishwan. Prod: Premkaji Gurung and Shambhu Pradhan.
Mayapriti (Beloved). Dir: B.S. Thapa. Players: Ravindra Khadka, Sharmila Shah, Krishna Malla.

Useful Address

Kanchanjanga Films
P.O. Box 3311
Kathmandu
Tel: (2) 24407, (4) 10795

and

Second floor, Kalpavrikhsa
13/18th Road Junction
Khar - West
Bombay 400052
India

NETHERLANDS
by Pieter van Lierop

Cinema attendances in the Netherlands are on the increase again. A total of 15,614,812 tickets were sold in 1989, which is 5.2% more than in 1988, when sales were down 5% compared with 1987. Box-office takings totalled 174,000,000 guilders, as compared with 165,700,000 in 1988 and 165,800,000 in 1987.

The non-commercial cinemas belonging to the Association of Dutch Film Theatres sold 557,542 in 1989, and seven new cinemas joined the Association. Taking only the twenty members in 1988, the increase is 14.6%: from 446,782 tickets sold in 1988 to 511,982 in 1989. Nevertheless, art houses are not doing as well as these figures might suggest. They are showing more and more films obtained from commercial distributors, thus undermining the market for subsidised distributors offering more demanding films.

The rise in attendances might seem to justify cautious optimism about the Dutch public's interest in film, but other figures show that by international standards the situation in the Netherlands is not in fact very encouraging. Interest in film turns out to be lower in the Netherlands than in any other country in Europe. Belgium has about five million fewer inhabitants than the Netherlands, but each year about five million more cinema tickets are sold. On average the Dutch go to a film once a year, as opposed to an average of twice a year for cinemagoers in France, Denmark, Spain, Sweden, Switzerland, Ireland and the U.K. In Eastern Europe the average is much higher. One particularly disturbing aspect is how little interest the Dutch show in the products of their own film industry, except for highly commercial popular hits. In 1989 Dutch films drew only 4.2% of total cinema audiences. This is the lowest figure since 1985. The most successful Dutch film in 1989 was *Theo & Thea*, which got to number 17 in the top 50. Lower down were *Lily was Here* (*De Kassière*) at 18, *Tough* (*Jan Rap en zijn Maat*) at 37 and *Evenings* (*De Avonden*) at 40.

Improved quality

These low ratings are not a fair reflection of artistic quality, since this has improved over the last twelve months. **Evenings**, for example, is a highly skilful adaptation of the classic novel by Gerard Reve, regarded by most insiders as impossible to film. Set in 1947, it concerns a young clerk, paralysed by a fear of life who observes his parents' narrow-mindedness and vulgarity with cynical humour, veering all the time between disgust and fond affection. Under Rudolf van den Berg's direction, Thom Hoffman in the leading role proves that he is currently the best Dutch film actor.

No less impressive is **Polonaise** (*Leedvermaak*), Frans Weisz's film version of a play by Judith Herzberg. In the course of elaborate wedding celebrations, various illusions about marital bliss are painfully dispelled. The difficulty young people have in sustaining relationships is explained in terms of their parents' traumatic wartime experiences. Excellent acting together with Frans Weisz's ingenious direction and the compelling subject matter form the main strengths of this film, although it sometimes reflects its theatrical origins.

HOLLAND FILM PROMOTION

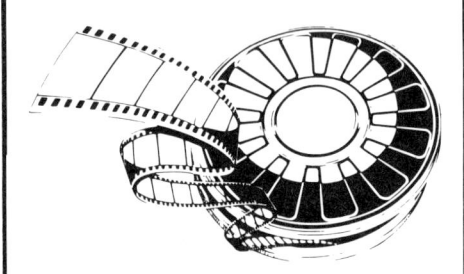

P O BOX 5048,
1007 AA AMSTERDAM,
THE NETHERLANDS
Tel: (31) 20 799261
Tel: (31) 20 750398
Telex: 12151

Thom Hoffman and Marion van Thijn in *Lily Was Here*

Lily Was Here (*De Kassière*) is a disappointing melodrama about a pregnant girl who runs away from home and ends up carrying out robberies in the big city to avoid resorting to prostitution. Thom Hoffman gives another fine performance as Lily's protector, and director Ben Verbong again shows that he is a gifted stylist, but their talents are largely wasted on such trite material. Nonetheless the film proved quite a success with teenage audiences. Karst van der Meulen, a specialist in children's films, was not at his best in **At Stalling Speed** (*Kunst en Vliegwerk*), but the Berlin Festival jury for the children's section decided this was the best film in the programme.

The biggest commercial success of the year was the farce **Theo & Thea**, based on a refreshingly irreverent children's TV series. Arjan Ederveen and Tosca Niterink's cabaret-style humour at the expense of various peculiarities of the Dutch (not excluding the Royal Family) proved to be so deadly accurate that it raised as many laughs from parents as from their offspring, and the film did good business at late night showings.

Debut Films
There were two interesting debuts: **Wings of Fame** by Otakar Votocek and **Romeo** by Rita Horst. The range of Dutch films on offer was also enlivened by Eric de Kuyper's

Arjan Ederveen and Tosca Niterink in *Theo & Thea*

Pink Ulysses, a wildly extravagant, collage-like treatment of Homer, and by two new "minimal moves" from Pim de la Parra. **Max and Laura and Henk and Willie** was made in twelve days for $30,000. Using more or less the same group of high-spirited pals, De la Parra went on to make **Night of the Wild Donkeys** (*De Nacht van de Wilde Ezels*) for next to nothing. This is a satire on the way films are made in the Netherlands and focuses on the discouraging process by which film-makers are forced to find their way, script in hand, through a labyrinth of production funds, TV organisations and other potential sources of funds. The granting of a subsidy by one body is often dependent on funds being obtained from another, so a Dutch producer may find he

Kenneth Herdigein and Liz Snoyink in *The Night of the Wild Donkeys*

CITY LIFE FOUNDATION - THE NETHERLANDS PRESENTS

The first international episode film

Initiated and compiled by

Rijneke & Van Leeuwaarden

CITY LIFE

with

Krzysztof Kieślowski
WARSAW

Dick Rijneke
Mildred van Leeuwaarden
ROTTERDAM

Alejandro Agresti
BUENOS AIRES

José Luis Guerin
BARCELONA

Gabor Altorjay
HAMBURG

Clemens Klopfenstein
BEVAGNA

Carlos Reichenbach
SAO PAULO

Tato Kotetishvili
TBLISI / USSR

Eagle Pennell
HOUSTON / USA

Ousmane William
DAKAR

Béla Tarr
BUDAPEST

Mrinal Sen
CALCUTTA

Information
City Life Foundation / Rotterdam Films
Provenierssingel 33, 3033 EG Rotterdam, The Netherlands
Tel. (10) 465 85 65 - Fax (10) 465 83 92 - Telex 26401 INTX NL

WORLD SALES - METROPOLIS FILM
Josefstrasse 106, CH - 8031 ZÜRICH
Tel. (1) 271 89 39 - Fax (1) 271 33 50 Tlx (1) 823 530 JOSF CH

has cleared the first four hurdles only to fall at the fifth. To begin with, there is the Production Fund, with an annual budget of 7,070,000 guilders. Provided it approves the script and a distributor has already shown an interest, the Fund can meet up to 60% of the costs of a film. Then there is the Film Fund, which only supports shorts, documenaries and features of particular artistic significance. The maximum it can grant is a million guilders (about half a million dollars), but its total annual budget is only 5,380,000 guilders.

There are also ten broadcasting organisations which can participate in film productions and are eligible for funds from the Co-Production Fund and the Fund for Promoting Dutch Cultural Broadcast Productions, provided the project is of cultural value. This complicated situation is enough to drive any film-maker with artistic aspiratitons to despair. On the other hand, a shrewd producer who knows the way round this labyrinth and also knows how to tap the various European sources can obtain up to 100% financing.

International Markets

Dutch producers can afford to take few risks because even successful films cannot recover their costs from the domestic market, and there is little chance of selling a thoroughly Dutch film to other countries. So several enterprising producers are setting their sights on the international scene. Ludi Boeken and Jacques Fansten of Belbo Films (aiming mainly at the TV market) produced the Van Gogh series *Vincent and Theo* directed by Robert Altman, of which there is also a cinema version. Kees Kasander and Denis Wigman of Allarts Films combine purely Dutch projects with international co-productions. They have recently had great success with Peter Greenaway's *The Cook, the Thief, His Wife and Her Lover* and Alejandro Agresti's *Secret Wedding*. Laurens Geels and Dick Maas of First Floor Features work with Dutch directors and international casts. The first result of this approach is Otakar Votocek's *Wings of Fame*, soon to be followed by *The Last Island* by Marleen Gorris. First Floor Features have recently built their own studios in Almere with floor space of 2,500 square metres and a backlot of 30,000 metres. From 1991 these facilities will be available to other producers. Dick Maas is to shoot *The Missing Diaries* there, and Alex van Warmerdam will make *The Northerners* (*De Noorderlingen*). Other productions planned by First Floor Features include *My Blue Heaven* by Ronald Beer and *Oh Boy* by Orlow Seunke.

In the field of animation, a Dutch speciality, Paul Driessen was again in characteristically witty form in **Uncles and Aunts**. Other films worthy of mention were the almost abstract **Fire** by Martin Keppy and the amusing **Musca** by Mark Reijnders. But the most pleasant surprise came from Maarten Koopman and his one-minute tribute to Van Gogh. In this piece we see furniture and objects being moved around a room until they finally produce the composition which has become world famous as Van Gogh's painting of his bedroom at Arles. Koopman's film won the special Jury Prize at the Cannes Festival.

Another maker of animated films, Gerrit van Dijk, has brought together colleagues from nine countries in a joint project which is intended for a wide audience and will be called **The Seven Deadly Sins**. A somewhat similar project has been realised by the Rotterdam film-makers Mildred van Leeuwaarden and Dick Rijneke. They invited eleven colleagues from other countries to contribute to a film in twelve episodes, each portraying the city with which the director felt the closest links. Mildred van Leeuwaarden and Dick Rijneke made the Dutch contribution and also supervised this very complicated production together with Jan Heijs. The other contributors were Tato Kotetishvili (Tbilisi), Carlos Reichenbach (São Paulo),

Scene from *Warsaw*, Krsysztof Kieślowski's contribution to the episode film, *City Life*

Eagle Pennell (Houston), Krzysztof Kieślowski (Warsaw), Alejandro Agresti (Buenos Aires), Gabor Altorjay (Hamburg), José Luis Guerín (Barcelona), Ousmane William M'Baye (Dakar), Clemens Klopfenstein (Bevagna) and Mrinal Sen (Calcutta). The result, entitled **City Life**, was shown at the opening of the nineteenth Rotterdam Film Festival, which is where all the contributors had originally met.

Festivals

City Life is dedicated to the late Huub Bals. The appointment of the Italian Marco Mueller to succeed him as festival director was initially greeted with some scepticism, but Mueller had proved remarkably successful in adapting to the Dutch situation and organised a festival in keeping with the tradition that Bals had established. The nineteenth Rotterdam Film Festival presented 240 films, with a heavy emphasis on work from Eastern Europe and Asia. There were 175,000 visitors (15,000 more than in 1989) and box-office takings increased by 7.5%.

There was some concern about the CineMart, which attracted many sellers but very few buyers. Rotterdam's first FIPRESCI jury awarded its prize to Kumar Shahani for *Khayal Gatha*, while the Dutch critics gave their annual prize to *Life is Cheap* by Wayne Wang.

Our national festival, the Dutch Film Days, went through a major administrative crisis as a result of the controversial appointment of a new director. In the aftermath of this affair the new director and several members of the board resigned. Despite this, the festival held in September 1989 was more than usually colourful and lively. The number of visitors to this relatively small-scale event, held annually in Utrecht, was 24,786 (over 8,000 more than in 1988) and audiences averaged 66% of capacity. As the Dutch contribution to films made in other countries steadily increases, the Film Days are becoming more international and the work of Dutch film-makers and actors abroad is followed with keen interest. This is in line with the views of Jacques van Heijningen, who was appointed the festival's supervisor in the spring of 1990.

The national film prizes, the Golden Calves, were presented during the closing ceremony. The award for best film went to *Secret Wedding*, which was made for the Dutch producers Kees Kasander and Denis Wigman by the Argentinian director Alejandro Agresti, who now lives in the Netherlands. Best director: Frans Weisz for *Polonaise*. Best actor: Pierre Bokma for *Polonaise*. Best Actress: Annet Nieuwenhuijzen for *Polonaise*. Special Jury Prize: Anneke Blok for her performance in *Your Opinion Please* (*Uw Mening Graag*). Best short: *Alaska* by Mike van Diem. Best documentary: *Beeld van een Kind* by Albert Vanderwildt. The Cultural Prize went to Ellen Waller, the doyenne of Dutch film critics. A special prize was awarded to Gerard Soeteman for his work in general, which includes the screenplays for the films with which Paul Verhoeven and Fons Rademakers made their international breakthroughs.

Wings of Fame

Script: Otakar Votocek and Herman Koch. Direction: Otakar Votocek. Photography: Alex Thomson. Editing: Hans van Dongen. Players: Peter O'Toole, Colin Firth, Marie Trintignant, Andréa Ferréol, Ellen Umlauf, Maria Becker, Robert Stephens, Walter Gotell, Michiel Romeyn. Produced by Laurens Geels and Dick Maas for First Floor Features.

Otakar Votocek, who earlier won a Golden Calf for his short *Turkish Video*, has made a dream debut with his first full-length feature *Wings of Fame*. The highly successful team of producers Laurens Geels and Dick Maas assembled an international cast for *Wings of Fame* based on a story about immortality, written by this Czech-born Dutchman. The cast is led by Peter O'Toole and Colin Firth.

According to Otakar Votocek the hereafter is a misty sea, in which dead spirits bob about groaning. However, those who live on in the memories of living people – a chosen few – inhabit a grandiose, mausoleum-like five-star hotel on a subtropical island. There is a kind of hierarchy among the VIPs and changes are possible in the meantime.

Peter O'Toole is the perfect embodiment of the actor Cesar Valentin, a spoilt, vain and arrogant man. We meet him at a film festival where one Brian Smith is vainly trying to get in touch with him. After yet another humiliating brush-off, Smith grabs a pistol in a burst of fury and fatally shoots the actor. By an unlucky chance, Smith also dies on the spot. The two men meet again in Charon's boat while on their way to the island of the immortals. At the hotel their roles are reversed. Valentin constantly tries to find his murderer because he is obsessed by the question of why on earth Smith shot him. It turns out that writer's frustration lies behind it all and the plagiarism is involved. This material may well have been too insubstantial to produce a really compelling drama. Most of us are unlikely to feel very involved with the problems of being famous and wanting to remain so. But Votocek presents a lively portrayal of relationships in Valhalla and adds to the interest by introducing a love story involving Marie Trintignant as a rock starlet killed in an accident. She arouses the interest of both Smith and Valentin.

Wings of Fame is undoubtedly a stylish film. The acting is good and it is directed with remarkable assurance and breadth of vision. The film is composed, attractive and intelligently made. Without reaching for the skies, Votocek has certainly turned in an impressive performance.

Pieter van Lierop

Colin Firth and Peter O'Toole in *Wings of Fame*

Pink Ulysses

Script and Direction: Eric De Kuyper. Photograph: Stef Tijdink. Editing: Ton de Graaff. Players: José Teunissen, Jos IJland, Dolf Wilkens, Maarten Almekinders. With film clips from *La Caduta di Troia* (by Piero Fosco), *The Good Hope* (by Maurits Binger), *Battleship Potemkin* and *Strike* (by Sergei Eisenstein), and the *Sleeping Beauty* performed by the National Ballet in Amsterdam. Produced by Suzanne van Voorst for Yuca Film.

After *Casta Diva*, *Naughty Boys* and *A Strange Love Affair*, the deputy director of the Film Museum in Amsterdam, Eric De Kuyper, has made *Pink Ulysses*, a work no less extravagant than its predecessors. In a refreshing blend of seriousness and humour, De Kuyper explores the boundaries between art and kitsch, and it is hard to imagine a more whimsical view of the Odyssey. He combines quotes from ancient costume films, baroque opera excerpts, photos of swimming clubs and other visual material featuring scantily clad male bodies. To this De Kuyper adds various scenes of his own. Odysseus lashes himself to the mast of his ship to resist the seductive call of the Sirens, while the heavy-breathing camera caresses the body-builder's torso straining against the ropes. Meanwhile Penelope is languishing in Ithaca trying to control her impatience and lusting after the splendid body of her errant hero. An otherwise unexplained present-day gentleman is preoccupied with his own physical charms and reaches a climax in a close-up with a mirror.

It becomes abundantly clear what the art of film means to Eric De Kuyper. French chansons and German schmaltz alternate cheerfully with Tchaikovsky, Stravinsky, Monteverdi, Ravel and Prokofiev. With the same sense of irony, Penelope is shown in

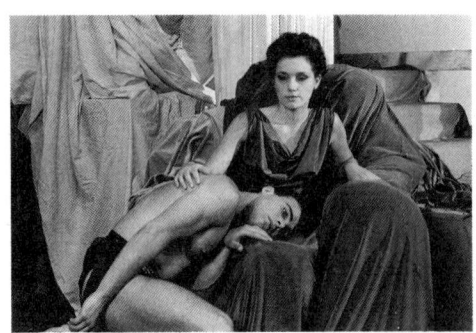

José Teunissen and Jos Ijland in a scene from *Pink Ulysses*

her cardboard boudoir, with a gilt handbag and a red plastic washing bowl. At a certain point we see the classical hero leave Circe's cave sporting a jaunty little rucksack. De Kuyper's highly personal wet dream, which has all the breathtakingly lurid kitsch of cheap devotional pictures, is preoccupied with male muscle-flexing, yearning, languorous desire and aesthetically pleasing death. It ends with a descent from the Cross which is full of pathos and requires the use of stepladders. It seems as if Homer rather than Jesus Christ has been crucified.

Rarely has a film maker displayed his cultural stock-in-trade as flirtatiously as De Kuyper in *Pink Ulysses*. But at the same time it is hard to think of anyone else who could provide such a frank, uninhibited and self-mocking picture of the gaudy scrapbook of his own soul.

Pieter van Lierop

Romeo

Script and Direction: Rita Horst. Photography: Theo Bierkens. Editing: Ot Louw. Players: Monique van de Ven, Johan Leysen, Ottolien Boeschoten, Pieter de Wijn, Peter Bolhuis, Hans Croiset. Produced by Frans Rasker for Horizon Film Productions.

Romeo is a drama about a woman and a man who love each other deeply but are driven apart by their different ways of coping with the loss of their baby. Anne (an illustrator) and Mathijs (an actor) are looking forward to the birth of their first child. A medical examination reveals that the baby will not survive because of stones in its kidneys. It is decided to induce labour prematurely. The baby is born that same night, but has only a few hours to live. The parents are given an hour in which they can play with the baby on a hospital bed as if they were a normal family. In that period joy at the birth and grief at the child's imminent death become incongruously entwined.

The idea of making a film about this subject is unlikely to occur to someone who has not had a similar experience. It happened to Rita Horst and her husband, the actor Johan Leysen, two years ago. Under his wife's direction Leysen relives his own experience as Mathijs in the film. The role of Anne is played by Monique van de Ven. Both give outstanding performances.

Rita Horst's debut is more than an autobiographical docudrama for use in counselling sessions. What makes *Romeo* interesting is the way in which she has taken a tragic case as the starting point for a psychological drama with wide appeal. She explores the husband's efforts to come to

Monique van de Ven and Johan Leysen in *Romeo*

terms with the death by removing all trace of it, by negating what has happened. But Anne takes the opposite course in attempting to deal with her grief. She tries to resign herself to the baby's death by cultivating the memory and giving it meaning in her present and future life. Inevitably this leads to a clash between husband and wife. He accuses her of wallowing in misery, while she finds him insensitive. In fact, these are different ways of coping with the same pain, and once they realise that the worst is over.

A film on this subject could go wrong in any number of ways. There is the danger of exhibitionism, which would make the audience feel uncomfortably like voyeurs. Rita Horst has managed to avoid this completely. The film might also have turned out unbearably tragic and lachrymose, but this too has been avoided. The scenes are so structured as to make them recognisable and effective rather than highly dramatic. The same is true of the dialogue, which excels in its transparent directness.

Pieter van Lierop

Profile: Alejandro Agresti

The most talented young film-maker now working in the Netherlands seems to be the Argentinian Alejandro Agresti (born in 1964). At the 1988 Dutch Film Days he won the Special Jury Prize for *Love Is a Fat Woman*, and in 1989 the Golden Calf for the best Dutch film of the year with *Secret Wedding*. The awards caused some surprise as both films were made in Spanish and shot in Argentina. But they were accepted for the Dutch Film Days because the co-producers Kees Kasander and Denis Wigman were Dutch and because Agresti himself has been living in the Netherlands with his wife and child for some years.

Alejandro Agresti worked as a cameraman in Argentina. He came to Europe at the age of 22 and ended up in the Netherlands. He was hoping to get financial backing for the post-production work on *El Hombre que gano la razon*, the first film he had made. Kees Kasander arranged the funding and had the film launched at the Rotterdam Film Festival. He also became the producer of Agresti's subsequent films. Agresti writes his own screenplays and so far all his films have been about the sense of disorientation and continuing despair of post-junta Argentina. *Love Is a Fat Woman* is a more or less autobiographical story about a man who continues to hope against his better judgement for the return of the woman he loves after her disappearance in the "dirty war".

Secret Wedding is about two lovers who do come together again but find each other changed beyond recognition as a result of the torments they have suffered. Agresti's first two films, shot in black and white, are charged with emotion and a sense of agitation. He often works on the principle of the "subjective camera", for example in *Love Is a Fat Woman* where many of the scenes are shot from a high vantage point, as

Alejandro Agresti

though seen through the eyes of the lover who is spiritually but not physically present. *Secret Wedding* was shot in colour because this tragedy is set in the countryside rather than in the grey metropolis of Buenos Aires which was the setting of his earlier film. However, the city is shown in colour in Agresti's contribution to *City Life*, a Dutch production with episodes by different directors. Agresti's part, *A Short Film about Nothing*, is a witty contrast between the adventures a young Argentinian claims to have had during a day in the big city and the prosaic, unvarnished truth. Agresti is now working on his first film to be shot in the Netherlands, *Luba*, which is about a political refugee who finds shelter with a prostitute and spends a dramatic night with her. Meanwhile Agresti has worked as a cameraman on Erik van Zuylen's experimental film *Alicia in Concert* and Pim de la Parra's *Night of the Wild Donkeys*, in which he also acts. It is clear that, while Alejandro Agresti cannot perhaps be counted a Dutch film-maker, he has been taken up by the Dutch film world and is making a growing contribution to it.

Pieter van Lierop

Yolanda Entius and Joan Nederlof in *Crocodiles in Amsterdam*

PIETER VAN LIEROP *was born in Tilburg in 1945. He studied Dutch Language and Literature and became an arts correspondent with the* Utrechts Nieuwsblad *in 1968. He was appointed the paper's film editor in 1974, a position he still holds. He was one of the founders of the Dutch Film Critics Circle, serving as its secretary for four years and chairman for three years, and has been the Dutch correspondent of the International Film Guide since 1981.*

Recent and Forthcoming Films

City Life. Episode film based on an idea and compiled by Dick Rijneke and Mildred van Leeuwaarden. Dir: Rijneke & van Leeuwaarden. (Randstad, Tato Kotetisvhili (Tbilisi), Carlos Reichenbach (Sao Paulo, Eagle Pennell (Houston), Krzysztof Kieślowski (Warsaw), Alejandro Agresti (Buenos Aires), Bela Tarr (Budapest), Gabor Altorjay (Hamburg), José Luis Guerín (Barcelona), Ousmane William M'Baye (Dakar), Clemens Klopfenstein (Bevagna), and Mrinal Sen (Calcutta). General editor: Mario Steenbergen. Prod: Dick Rijneke, Mildred van Leeuwaarden and Jan Heijs for Rotterdam Films. 240 mins.

Krokodillen in Amsterdam (Crocodiles in Amsterdam). Script: Yolanda Entius, Annette Apon and Henriëtte Remmers. Dir: Annette Apon. Phot: Bernd Wouthusen. Players: Yolanda Entius, Joan Nederlof. Prod: Rolf Orthel for Orthel Filmproducties.

Max & Laura & Henk & Willie. Script: Pim de la Parra, Paul Ruven, Sabine van den Eynden. Dir: Paul Ruven. Phot: Frans Bromet. Players: Marina de Graaf, Pim de la Parra, Manouk van der Meulen, Jake Kruyer, Gerardjan Reijnders, Wim Verstappen, Marleen Stoltz. Prod: Hermann Pohle and Frank Lucas for Fly By Night Film Productions.

De Nacht van de Wilde Ezels (The Night of the Wild Donkeys). Script: Pim de la Parra, Paul Ruven and Steven van Galen. Dir: Pim de la Parra. Players: Pim de la Parra, Liz Snoyink, Camilla Braaksma, Hans Dagelet, Kenneth Herdigein, Manouk van der Meulen, Jake Kruyer, Marian Moree. Prod: Emjay Rechsteiner for Wild Donkey Films.

Theo & Thea en de Ontmaskering van het Tenenkaas Imperium (Theo & Thea and The Seven Dwarfs). Script: Arjan Ederveen and Tosca Niterink. Dir: Pieter Kramer. Phot: Erik Zuyderhof. Players: Arjan Ederveen, Tosca Niterink, Marco Bakker, Adele Bloemendaal. Prod: Kees Kasander for Van Den Beginne B.V.

Ava and Gabriel. Script: Felix de Rooy and Norman de Palm. Dir: Felix de Rooy. Phot: Ernest Dickerson. Players: Nashaira Desbarida, Cliff San-A-Jong, Carol Brown Winkel, Theu Boermans, Dolf de Vries, Geert de Jong, Edmond Classen, Frederik de Groot. Prod: Felix de Rooy for Cosmic Illusion Productions. **My Blue Heaven.** Script and Dir: Ronald Beer. Phot: Marc Felperlaan. Players: Bo Bojo, Ruud de Wolff, Ivon Pelasula, Angelique Corneille, Michel Sorbach, Leen Jongewaard, Edda Barends, Remco Djojosepoetro. Prod: Laurens Geels and Dick Maas for First Floor Features. **The Last Island.** Script and Dir: Marleen Gorris. Phot: Marc Felperlaan. Players: Paul Freeman, Shelagh McLeod, Patricia Hayes, Marc Berman, Ian Tracey. Prod: Laurens Geels & Dick Maas for First Floor Features.

TOP GROSSING FILMS IN THE NETHERLANDS: 1989

	Admissions
Licence To Kill	1,314,831
Rain Man	1,140,811
Indiana Jones and the Last Crusade	912,718
A Fish Called Wanda	798,893
Cocktail	773,555
Twins	704,104
Roadhouse	601,281
The Naked Gun	483,821
Who Framed Roger Rabbit	438,748
(already no. 8 in 1988 with 440,676 admissions)	
Lethal Weapon 2	385,166

Producers

Added Films Holland BV
Paul Voorthuysen
Herenstraat 64A
1406 PH Bussum
Tel: (2159) 35908
Fax: (2159) 38808

Allarts BV
Denis Wigman
Kees Kassander
Sarphatistraat 117
1018 GB Amsterdam
Tel: (20) 384866
Fax: (20) 207254

Annette Apon Prods.
Annette Apon
Binnenkant 24-III
1011 BH Amsterdam
Tel: (20) 267856

Cannon City Prods. BV
J. Bruinstroop
Nieuwe Spaarpotsteeg 1–2
1012 TG Amsterdam
Tel: (20) 5751751
Fax: (20) 6622085

Casa Film
Rosemarie Blank
Prinsengracht 151
1015 DR Amsterdam
Tel: (20) 265550

Castor Films
Karst van der Meulen
Hoofdstraat 94
9968 AG Pieterburen
Tel: (5952) 422
Fax: (5952) 446

Cinété Film Prods.
willem Thijssen/Hans Otten

Elisabeth Wolffstraat 45
1053 TR Amsterdam
Tel: (20) 167719
Fax: (20) 891594

Cine Ventura
Ruud den Drijver/
Dorna van Rouveroy
Allard Piersonstraat 6
1053 ZZ Amsterdam
Tel: (20) 837439

Cine/Vista BV
Gerrit Visscher
Prinses Marielaan 8
3743 JA Baarn
Tel: (2154) 23720
Fax: (2154) 23736

Commercial Artists
Fransjoris de Graaf
Leeuwenwerf 77

1018 KA Amsterdam
Tel: (20) 271045

Cosmic Illusion Prods.
Brigitta Gadella
P.O. Box 11582
1001 GN Amsterdam
Tel: (20) 237234
Fax: (20) 247922

Nico Crama Films
Nico Crama
Stevinstraat 261
2587 EJ Den Haag
Tel: (70) 3544964

**Roy Dames Film-
productions**
Roy Dames
Sumatrastraat 225 d
1092 PH Amsterdam
Tel: (20) 925479
Fax: (20) 6658423

Stichting DD Film Prods.
Phil van der Linden
Entrepôtdok 66
1018 AD Amsterdam
Tel: (20) 381327
Fax: (20) 209857

Dessafilms B.V.
René van Nie
O.Z. Voorburgwal 219
1012 EX Amsterdam
Tel: (20) 250093/245602

Cilia van Dijk
Ged. Voldersgracht 20
2011 WD Haarlem
Tel: (23) 314213
Fax: (23) 314213

Ecco Films
Orlow Seunke
P.O. Box 53223
1007 RE Amsterdam
Tel: (20) 239457

**First Amsterdam Film
Association**
(Eerste Amsterdamse Film
Associatie)

Eddy Wijngaarde/
Leon de Winter
Leliegracht 25
1016 GR Amsterdam
Tel: (20) 265613
Fax: (20) 228753

First Floor Features
Laurens Geels/Dick Maas
P.O. Box 53221
1007 RE Amsterdam
Tel: (20) 6647471
Fax: (20) 794040
Telex: 12027 basic nl

Fly by Night Film Prod.
Hermann Pohle/Frank Lukas
Saksenburgerstraat 10-III
1054 KP Amsterdam
Tel: (20) 222200/229283

Frank Fehmers Prods. BV
Frank Fehmers
Prins Hendrikkade 161 b
1011 TB Amsterdam
Tel: (20) 238766/235863
Fax: (20) 246262
Telex: 11802 Inter

Filmwerk
Hans de Ridder
Vasteland 447
3011 BJ Rotterdam
Tel: (10) 4116385

Grace Films BV
Ank Muller
Van Eeghenstraat 109
1071 EZ Amsterdam
Tel: (20) 753671
Fax: (20) 753671

Haagse Filmstichting
Denis Wigman
Denneweg 56
2514 CH Den Haag
Tel: (70) 3459900
Fax: (70) 3657666

Bert Haanstra Films BV
Bert Haanstra
Verlengde Engweg 5
1251 GM Laren (NH)

Tel: (2153) 82428
Fax: (2153) 82428

**Holland Animation
Foundation**
Nico Crama
Stevinstraat 261
2587 EJ Den Haag
Tel: (70) 544964

Horizon Film Prods. BV
Frans Rasker
Nieuwe Keizersgracht 58
1018 DT Amsterdam
Tel: (20) 258817
Fax: (20) 200226

**Roeland Kerbosch Film
Prods. BV**
Roeland Kerbosch
Keizersgracht 678
1017 ET Amsterdam
Tel: (20) 230390
Fax: (20) 279879

Linden Film BV
Jos van der Linden
Chopinstraat 25
1077 GM Amsterdam
Tel: (20) 793128
Fax: (20) 797209

**Filmproduktie
'De Maatschap'**
Jonne Severijn
Nieuwe Uilenburgerstr. 110
1011 LX Amsterdam
Tel: (20) 234628
Fax: (20) 253729

Olga Madsen BV
Olga Madsen
Marnixstraat 356
1016 XV Amsterdam
Tel: (20) 266295

Meatball Film en Televisie
Rien Hagen/Cesar
Messemaker
Oranjestraat 3
2514 JB Den Haag
Tel: (70) 646915
Fax: (70) 3562282

MGS Film Amsterdam BV
Golden Egg Film
George Sluizer/Anne Lordon
Singel 64
1015 AC Amsterdam
Tel: (20) 131593/6629960
Fax: (20) 243181
Telex: 41275 MayD NL

Movies Film Productions
Chris Brouwer/Haig Balian
Prinsengracht 546
1017 KK Amsterdam
Tel: (20) 275636
Fax: (20) 252981

Open Studio Productions
Lily van den Bergh
Herengracht 156
1016 BN Amsterdam
Tel: (20) 223661
Fax: (20) 275090

Oranda Films B.V.
Henk Bos
De Lairessestraat 111–115
1075 HH Amsterdam
Tel: (20) 5751751
Fax: (20) 6622085

Rolf Orthel Film Prods.
Rolf Orthel/Evelyn Voortman
Lauriergracht 123 II
1016 RK Amsterdam
Tel: (20) 220255
Fax: (20) 261885

Praxino Pictures BV
René Solleveld
Keizersgracht 60
1015 CS Amsterdam
Tel: (20) 266355
Fax: (20) 201059
Telex: 16183 Euroc NL

Pretty Pictures
Ruud van Hemert
Stadhouderskade 104 III
1073 AX Amsterdam
Tel: (20) 730297
Fax: (20) 892635

Fons Rademakers Prods. BV
Fons Rademakers
Prinsengracht 685
1017 JT Amsterdam
Tel: (20) 221298

Riverside Pictures
Gijs Versluys
P.O. Box 190
1430 AD Aalsmeer
Tel: (2977) 54452/51711
Fax: (2977) 45106

Rotterdam Film City Life Foundation
Dick Rijneke
Provenierssingel 33
3033 EG Rotterdam
Tel: (10) 4658565
Fax: (10) 4658392

Scorpio Verstappen Films BV
Wim Verstappen
P.O. Box 245
1000 AE Amsterdam
Tel: (20) 225552
Fax: (20) 208660

Shooting Star Filmcompany B.V.
Hans Pos, Dave Schram, Maria Peters, José Steen
Keizersgracht 651
1017 DT Amsterdam
Tel: (20) 247272
Fax: (20) 236301

Sigma Film Productions B.V.
Matthijs van Heijningen
Bolensteinweg 3
3603 CP Maarssen
Tel: (3465) 70430/70341
Fax: (3465) 69764

Sol Film Prods. v.o.f.
Bob Entrop
P.O. Box 1032
4801 BA Breda
Tel: (76) 220080
Fax: (76) 229359

Spectrum Film
Louis van Gasteren
Kloveniersburg 46
1011 JX Amsterdam
Tel: (20) 241921

Van de Staak Film Prods.
Frans van de Staak
Jacob Oliepad 2
1013 DP Amsterdam
Tel: (20) 260634

Staccato Films
Emjay Rechsteiner, Herman Pohle
De Ruyterweg 37
1057 JV Amsterdam
Tel: (20) 168641/222200
Fax: (20) 892929

Jos Stelling Film Prods. BV
Jos Stelling
Springweg 50–52
3511 VS Utrecht
Tel: (30) 313789
Fax: (30) 310968

Studio Nieuwe Gronden
René Scholten
Van Hallstraat 52
1051 HH Amsterdam
Tel: (20) 867837
Fax: (20) 824367
Telex: 12682 sngfp

Theorema Films
Frank Bak
Van Hallstraat 52
1051 HH Amsterdam
Tel: (20) 881843
Fax: (20) 863574

Three Lines Productions BV
Otto Wobma
Soesterdijkerstraatweg 58
1213 XD Hilversum
Tel: (35) 833815
Fax: (35) 857696

Topaz Pictures
Tom Burghard
St. Antoniesbreestraat 69

1011 HB Amsterdam
Tel: (20) 226345
Fax: (20) 242536

United Dutch Film Company
(Verenigde Nederlandse Film Compagnie BV)
Rob Houwer
Singel 440
1017 AV Amsterdam
Tel: (20) 273631
Fax: (20) 249277

Jan Vrijman Cineproductie
Vondelstraat 51
1054 GJ Amsterdam
Tel: (20) 187943/124423
Fax: (20) 854491

Yuca Film
Suzanne van Voorst
P.O. Box 1379
1000 BJ Amsterdam
Tel: (20) 270274
Fax: (20) 380149

Zigzag Film BV
Jane Waltman
W.G. Plein 467
1054 SH Amsterdam
Tel: (20) 168911
Fax: (20) 853716

Distributors

Actueel Film BV
Co Bremanlaan 29
1251 HT Laren (NH)
Tel: (2153) 89230

Stichting Animated People
Cilia van Dijk
Ged. Voldersgracht 20
2011 WD Haarlem
Tel: (23) 314273

Argus Film BV
Rob Langestraat
P.O. Box 18269
1001 ZD Amsterdam
Tel: (20) 254585
Fax: (20) 272925
Telex: 11084 argus nl

Cannon City Film Distribution BV
De Lairessestraat 111–115
1075 HH Amsterdam
Tel: (20) 5751751
Fax: (20) 6622085

Cannon Nova Film BV
De Lairessestraat 111–115
1075 HH Amsterdam
Tel: (20) 5751751
Fax: (20) 6622085

Cannon Tuschinski Film Distribution BV
de Lairessestraat 111–115
1075 HH Amsterdam
Tel: (20) 5751751
Fax: (20) 6622085

Cinetrust
Soestdijkerstraatweg 58
1213 XD Hilversum
Tel: (35) 833815
Fax: (35) 857696

C.N.R. Film & Video
Franciscusweg 249
1216 SG Hilversum
Tel: (35) 255680
Fax: (35) 236292
Telex: 43013

Columbia/Tri-Star Films (Holland) BV
P.O. Box 533
1000 AM Amsterdam
Tel: (20) 5737655
Fax: (20) 5737656

Concorde Film
R. Wijsmuller
Lange Voorhout 35
2514 EC Den Haag
Tel: (70) 3605810/3924571
Fax: (70) 3604925
Telex: 34568 cofil nl

Cor Koppies Filmdistribution BV
P.O. Box 5242
1007 AE Amsterdam
Tel: (20) 767841
Fax: (20) 714968

Express Film
Heemraadschapslaan 11–13
1181 TZ Amsterdam
Tel: (20) 412331

Film Entertainment Group BV
Beijersweg 18
1093 KR Amsterdam
Tel: (20) 6652335/6651798
Fax: (20) 923667

Filmtrust BV
Molenkade 57A
1115 AC Duivendrecht
Tel: (20) 957719/955503
Fax: (20) 956625

Gofilex Film BV
P.O. Box 334
3430 AH Nieuwegein
Tel: (3402) 70922
Fax: (3402) 70283

Hafbo BV
P.O. Box 424
3740 AK Baarn
Tel: (2154) 13213
Fax: (2154) 13213

Holland Film Releasing BV
De Lairessestraat 111–115
1075 HH Amsterdam
Tel: (20) 5751751
Fax: (20) 6622085

Hungry Eye Pictures BV
K. Meerburg
Prinsengracht 452
1017 KE Amsterdam
Tel: (20) 223187
Fax: (20) 268978
Telex: 39345

**Vereniging Onderlinge
Studenten Steun 'Kriterion'**
Roeterstraat 170
1018 WE Amsterdam
Tel: (20) 231709

Melior Films BV
Menno van der Molen
Steynlaan 8
1217 JS Hilversum
Tel: (35) 45542
Fax: (35) 235906

Meteor Film BV
Prinsengracht 546
1017 KK Amsterdam
Tel: (20) 233858
Fax: (20) 252981

Motion Picture Group BV
Beijersweg 18
1093 KR Amsterdam
Tel: (20) 6684866
Fax: (20) 923667

The Movies BV
Haarlemmerdijk 161
1013 KH Amsterdam
Tel: (20) 245790

**BV Netherlands Fox Film
Corp.**
De Lairessestraat 111–115
1075 HH Amsterdam
Tel: (20) 5751751
Fax: (20) 6622085

**NIS Film Distribution
Holland**
Anna Paulownastraat 76
2518 BJ Den Haag
Tel: 31 (70) 3564205
Fax: 31 (70) 3564681
Telex: 33159

Profile Films BV
Beijersweg 18
1093 KR Amsterdam
Tel: (20) 6652335/6651798
Fax: (20) 923667

**UIP United International
Pictures (Netherlands) BV**

Still from Marleen Gorris's *The Last Island*

Willemsparkweg 112
1071 HN Amsterdam
Tel: (20) 6622991
Fax: (20) 6623240

**Verenigde Nederlandsche
Filmcompagnie BV**
't Witte Huys
Singel 440
1017 AV Amsterdam
Tel: (20) 273631
Fax: (20) 249277

Warner Bros (Holland) BV
De Boelelaan 16–III
1083 HJ Amsterdam
Tel: (20) 464766
Fax: (20) 449001

Cinemien
Entrepôtdok 66
1018 AD Amsterdam
Tel: (20) 279501/238152/
258357
Fax: (20) 209857

International Art Film
Rieks Hadders
Vondelpark 3
1071 AA Amsterdam
Tel: (20) 5891400
Fax: (20) 833401

Notorious Film
Van Diemenstraat 410–412
1013 CK Amsterdam
Tel: (20) 252423

Useful Addresses

**Ministry of Welfare, Health
and Cultural Affairs**
PO Box 5406
2280 HK Rijswijk
Tel: (70) 406143/406128
Fax: (70) 201703

**Ministry of Foreign Affairs
Audio Visual Section**
PO Box 20061
EB Den Haag
Tel: (70) 485004/484120

**Netherlands Information
Service**
PO Box 20006
2500 EA Den Haag
Tel: (70) 614181
Fax: (70) 463585

Dutch Film Fund
PO Box 15693
100 ND Amsterdam
Tel: (20) 6647838

Holland Film Promotion
PO Box 5048
1007 AA Amsterdam
Tel: (20) 799261
Fax: (20) 750398

Dutch Cinema Association
Jan Luykenstraat 2
1071 CM Amsterdam
Tel: (20) 799261

NOW – IT'S TIME TO SEE N.Z. MOVIES!

ALL PROUDLY SUPPORTED BY THE

NEW ZEALAND FILM COMMISSION

Lindsay Shelton, Marketing Director. Rhys Kelly, Marketing Manager.
P.O. Box 11-546, Wellington, New Zealand. FAX 64 4 849-719.

NEW ZEALAND
by Mike Nicolaidi

Television deregulation has introduced fierce competitiveness to the small screens of this country of only 3.3 million people – and impacted strongly upon the theatrical movie business.

A ratings war, using block-buster movies and major mini-series as the weapons, raged between the state-owned, two-channel network and the new independent web, TV3, during the early months of 1990. Then, a movies-only pay-TV channel was launched in Auckland, the prime local market.

In the first five months of 1990, the gross box-office for all N.Z. cinemas plummeted 20%. Timothy Ord, managing director of UIP (NZ) Ltd., and current president of the local chapter of the Motion Picture Distributors' Association, said the battle of the airwaves was largely to blame – but not the only reason.

Ord has campaigned long and loud against the practice of local exhibitors of interrupting movies half-way through to sell icecreams, candy and soft drinks, claiming it turns-off modern day audiences. He has also castigated the industry over its sluggishness in developing multiplexes.

One of the two major chains, Hoyts Group, which has 33 screens nationwide, rewarded his persistence in June by scrapping all intermissions in its cinemas. The other circuit – Pacer Kerridge (26 screens) – announced it would hold fast to intervals in the meantime. Ord trumpeted that PK was now the only film exhibition circuit in the English speaking world to maintain such a policy.

Tony Watts, brought over from the U.K. last year to acquire and programme feature films on Television New Zealand's two-channel state network, was more scathing. He maintained the fall in admissions was mainly due to the cinema business being at least 15 years out of date.

"With few exceptions cinemas are poorly kitted out. Sound is bad, the seats are poor. Like the anachronism of intermissions this is not conducive to a good cinema-going experience."

Watts saw the overall problem as being a lack of investment in cinema infrastructure and poor advertising and promotion of shows and facilities.

As with all industries in New Zealand, the cinema business is forced to confront the economic constraints imposed by a country of small and (with the exception of the Auckland conurbation) scattered population, an economy in the doldrums and little investment money making its way into property development.

There is private money about. But the wily burghers are placing it on fixed deposit for high interest rather than investing in new development. In 1990 this was the continuing legacy of the crash of '87 and subsequent collapse of several high-flying N.Z.-based entrepreneurial companies.

John Barnett, managing director of one of the country's very few locally-based film and video distribution companies, Endeavour Entertainment, believes the film theatrical situation has also been aggravated by the failure of exhibitors to adopt the more aggressive retailing stance taken by other leisure activities over recent times. "Equally, we are desperate for new cinemas, because they should help the box-office and enhance downstream activities."

Film, TV & Video Production

THE NATIONAL FILM UNIT OF NEW ZEALAND IS NOW PART OF AVALON TELEVISION CENTRE

Film & Video Production • Opticals & Special Effects • Full Laboratory Services • Equipped Editing Rooms • Broadcast Quality Video • Design & Animation • Stock Shot Library • Sound Recording • Mixing Facilities • Equipment Hire • Post Production • Office Space • Sound Stages • TV & Video Production, MakeUp, Catering, Wardrobe, Mobiles, Graphics, Design & Set Construction.

OUR COMBINED RESOURCES OFFER PRODUCERS IN TV & FILM WORLDWIDE:

THE LARGEST AND MOST COMPREHENSIVELY EQUIPPED FACILITIES IN AUSTRALASIA

AVALON
INCORPORATING NFU NATIONAL FILM UNIT

FOR INFORMATION CONTACT: **MARKETING: AVALON TELEVISION CENTRE:** PO BOX 31-444, LOWER HUTT, WELLINGTON, NEW ZEALAND, PHONE (04) 6190-600 OR 666-969, FAX (04) 674-411

A Television New Zealand Subsidiary

Multiplex Launch

Given the snail's pace approach towards creating a new cinema-going experience for New Zealanders, a great deal is hanging on the projected opening of the country's first true multiplex in Palmerston North in August. If it is a success, the on-again off-again plans for others around the country – West Auckland, Whangarei, Hamilton, Nelson – could be placed on fast track.

What the six-screen plex in the southern North Island provincial city (pop. 63,000, with teacher training college, and university) has to prove is that it can regularly attract much larger cinema audiences than are currently enticed into the city's three outdated movie barns.

As with cinema development, so too the local feature film industry. The N.Z. Film Commission, backed to the extent of $NZ 10,000,000 in 1990–91 by the government and N.Z. Lottery Board, remains the predominant force and the major source of investment funds. Private investors are rare birds indeed and a recent imaginative bid by the Commission to sell a film investment bond scheme to major institutions, like insurance companies, failed to wring coin. But the body is continually seeking ways to smooth the production path, and at this year's Cannes Festival, David Gascoigne, Commission chairman, and Judith McCann, executive director, were active in opening up new avenues for co-production.

A major development was the formation of the Commonwealth Co-production League, linking film agencies and production companies in four countries – the U.K., Australia, N.Z., and Canada. It intends to make four features a year over the next three years and brings together U.K. companies, Zenith and Film Four International, Canadian company, Sunrise Films, and the New Zealand and Australian Film Commissions.

Each country will be responsible for

Vanessa Rare in *Ruby and Rata*
photo: Geoff Short

financing one film with distribution guaranteed in each territory. The scheme should reduce dependence on the American market in putting feature film projects together. Gascoigne and McCann also believe that as well as allowing each country to work with a level of quality film that normally would not attract U.S. presales, potential new sources of private equity will be located.

After the most arid of production years in 1988–89, N.Z. feature production (as distinct from off-shore productions locating on facility deals) could now be settling down at about five to six annually. The commission's current funding policy precludes any 100% underwriting with unconfirmed overseas market interest – other than low budget first features.

The highlight of 1989–90 was the return home of Jane Campion (*Sweetie*) to make **An Angel at My Table**, a miniseries based on the three-part autobiography of novelist Janet Frame.

Although Campion did not favour theatrical release, such was the pressure applied by offshore distributors and sales' agents – at Cannes and elsewhere – that she eventually agreed. It was selected for main

TOP GROSSING FILMS IN NEW ZEALAND: YEAR TO MARCH 31, 1990

	(N.Z.$)
Batman	2,176,000
Back to the Future 2	1,800,000
Indiana Jones and the Last Crusade	1,735,000
Rain Man	1,700,000
Young Einstein	1,250,000
Twins	1,230,000
Ghostbusters 2	970,000
Honey, I Shrunk the Kids	970,000
Dirty Rotten Scoundrels	912,000
Lethal Weapon 2	900,000

competition at the Venice Film Festival in September.

Campion and Vincent Ward (*The Navigator, Vigil*) are two of the country's most exacting and accomplished talents. They probe the idiosyncratic, austere emotional landscape of the European New Zealander in ways that reveal and entertain. *An Angel at My Table* is stunning for the detail and exceptional craft Campion brings to unravelling the awful joys of Frame's early life, and the performance she extracts from actress Kerry Fox.

Another woman director to impress is Gaylene Preston with **Ruby and Rata**, a neighbourhood film that gently unfolds a tale of loneliness and mutual dependency in the suburbs with surprising ultimate impact.

Peter Jackson's adult fantasy puppet movie, **Meet the Feebles**, carries on from where *Bad Taste* left off and confirms his inventiveness and skill in handling bizarre X-rated material. Gregor Nicholas's **User Friendly** is a first feature and harbinger of better things to come from a young director of much promise, while Martyn Sanderson's **Flying Fox in a Freedom Tree** is a mostly affecting, if at times too-slow- moving story of a young Samoan's rite of passage.

Recent and Forthcoming Films

Ruby and Rata. Script: Graeme Tetley. Dir: Gaylene Preston. Players: Yvonne Lawley, Vanessa Rare, Lee Mete-Kingi, Simon Barnett. Prod: Robin Laing (Preston Laing Productions).
An Angel at My Table. Script: Laura Jones. Dir: Jane Campion. Players: Kerry Fox, Karen Fergusson, Alexia Keogh, Prod: Bridget Ikin (Hibiscus Films Ltd).
The Returning. Script: Arthur Baysting, John Day. Dir: John Day. Players: Phillip Gordon, Alison Routledge, Max Cullen, Jim Moriarty. Prod: Trishia Downie (Echo Pictures).
Te Rua. Script: Barry Barclay. Dir: Barry Barclay. Players: Wi Kuki Kaa, Peter Kaa, Stuart Devenie, Donna Akersten. Prod: John O'Shea (Pacific Films Productions).
Flying Fox in a Freedom Tree. Script: Albert Wendt, Martyn Sanderson. Dir: Martyn Sanderson. Players: Junior Amigo, Richard von Sturmer, Afatia Aloese. Prod: Grahame McLean (Grahame McLean Associates).
User Friendly. Script: Frank Stark, Gregor Nicholas, Norelle Scott. Dir: Gregor Nicholas. Players: William Brandt, Alison Bruce, Judith Gibson, Joan Reid.

Prod: Trevor Haysom, Frank Stark (Film Konstruktion).
Meet the Feebles. Script: Peter Jackson, Stephen Sinclair, Danny Mulheron. Dir: Peter Jackson. Puppeteers: Jonathan Acorn, Danny Mulheron, Eleanor Atkin, George Port. Prod: Jim Booth, Peter Jackson (Wingnut Films).

MIKE NICOLAIDI was London correspondent for the New Zealand Press Association 1965–68, and has been New Zealand correspondent for "Variety" since 1978.

Lee Mete-Kingi in *Ruby and Rata*
photo: Geoff Short

Joan Reid administering the experimental serum in Gregor Nicholas's *User Friendly*

Representing
NORWAY
Worldwide

+ **FESTIVALS** + **MARKETS** + **FILM WEEKS** + **ARCHIVES** +
IN NORWAY: **Cinemateque. Library. Home Video Register and Guarantees for Feature Film Production**

NORSK FILMINSTITUTT

Membre de la Fédération Internationale des Archives du Film (FIAF)

**PO Box 482 Sentrum, 0105 Oslo 1, Norway
Tel: **47-2-428740. Fax: **47-2-332277**

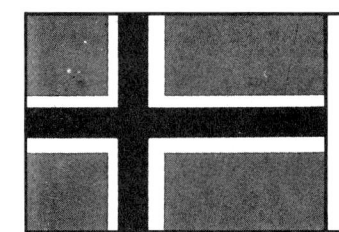

NORWAY

by J.R. Keith Keller

Norway has an incredibly forceful feature film production scene. Incredible considering the smallness of the nation (pop. 4.2 million) and also in view of the fact that this social welfare Kingdom allots less subsidy money (under 1% of the fiscal budget) to cultural enterprises in general.

About 20 full-length films are currently shooting or committed to roll before the end of 1991. This happens in spite of the Norse right-wing government's abrupt snatching away of 30% of the film subsidising coin earmarked for feature production in 1990.

There is a hope, if only a faint one, that the full subsidy budget of 36-million Kroner/$5.5 million will be restored in the nation's next fiscal budget. How Norwegian producers cope is a matter of expert juggling with existing subsidies and an additional 20 million Kroner/$3.07 million coming from a special Film & TV Fund.

More juggling can be done with whatever share Norway will get in 1991 from the new Nordic Film & TV Co-Production Fund, which dispenses an annual 45 million Kroner/$7 million. Not having access to any kind of European Economic Community funding, Norwegian film-makers have sometimes been enlisting support from British or U.S. film enterprises (e.g. *Håkon Håkonsen*, a co-production with Buena Vista).

At home, the public subsidy funding is given to individual producers (20-million Kroner/$3.07 million plus 13 million Kroner/$2 million by the production committee of the Norwegian Film Institute and directly to Norsk Film, the state-owned production and studio facility (16 million Kroner/$5.5 million plus 7 million Kroner/$1.07 million).

Norsk Film, a dominating force in Norse production, had reigned more or less supreme before the Norwegian Film Institute was finally, in 1990, given the nod to expand into a major film activities agency with Jan-Erik Holst at the helm. At Norsk Film, Terje Bogen, called in as trouble-shooter, reorganised the company, added a distribution division and left at year's end after having seen Denmark's multi-talented filmed media executive Esben Højlund Carlsen, appointed to take over the reins.

Talent Recognised

If Norse producers are displaying guts in face of meagre fundings, film-maker talent abounds. Only by an exceptional stroke of bad luck (it was held up in the customs by mistake) did Martin Asphaug's **A Handful of Time** (see review below) fail to make it to the 1990 Berlin festival's competition programme and since its producer had opted for Berlin, the film never stood a chance of being accepted at Cannes.

Still, *A Handful of Time* is now doing well in foreign sales. The film exemplifies the high level, artistic as well as technical, of today's Norwegian film production output. New films by established helmers like Anja Breien (*Twice Upon a Time*) and Erik Gustavson (*Herman*) and by younger experimenters like Oddvar Einarson (*Rising Tide*), and Vibeke Løkkeberg (*Seagulls*) plus big-format ace Nils Gaup (*Håkon Håkonsen*) all seem assured of exposure beyond their home territory.

Sven Wollter and Kjersti Holmen in *Twice upon a Time*

On their own shores, Norwegians still flock to their cinemas in larger numbers than in any other Nordic land. The nation's municipalities have a virtual monopoly on exhibition and seem to handle that responsibility in a tough-minded way that includes major marketing efforts like the annual Haugesund International Film Festival in August, the largest event of its kind north of Berlin. When a so-called art item (*Jesus of Montreal* would qualify for this description) gets a local pick-up, it usually does business comparable to a Stallone or Schwarzenegger item.

Distribution, which has remained in private hands, has, however, recently neglected art fare to the dismay of fastidious exhibition chieftains in Oslo and Norway's other major cities. The new pan-Scandinavian distribution companies (Denmark's Pathé-Nordisk and Metronome, Sweden's SF and Sandrews) have caused the demise of many a Norse outlet with art on its programme.

The hope today is that Norsk Film's new distribution division, set up as a joint venture with Sandrews and Metronome, will find the art gap. Furthermore, the Norwegian Film & Cinema Foundation has encouraged small film clubs with restricted funds to venture into regular theatrical distribution of items like Terence Davies's *Distant Voices, Still Lives* which proceeded to make it as a near-top grosser at a midtown Oslo cinema.

J.R. KEITH KELLER is a veteran Danish journalist who for the past five years has headed Variety's Scandinavian bureau in Copenhagen.

En håndfull tid
(A Handful of Time)

Script: Erik Borge. Direction: Martin Asphaug. Photography: Philip Øgård. Players: Espen Skjønberg, Nicolay Lange-Nielsen, Camilla Strøm Henriksen, Per Jansen, Minken Fosheim, Björn Sundquist, Susannah York, Nigel Hawthorne. Produced by Harald Ohrvik for Norsk Film. 95 mins.

Of *A Handful of Time* you would like to say that this feature by first-time director Martin Asphaug has everything: sit-up-and-gasp suspense, romantic-cum-Gothic atmosphere, emotional substance and gorgeous cinematography achieved in settings of voluptuous natural scenery. The story is a terrific one, too. Erik Borge's original screenplay recounts an old man's struggle to come to terms with certain sins of omission of his youth. This calls for lots of flashbacks, normally a device to stop the action. Asphaug still manages to maintain the impetus from beginning to end.

Old Martin heeds the voice of Anna, who calls him back to the mountain cabin where he had once been forced to leave her. While he was away, she died giving birth to their surviving son. Prior to this, Martin had killed Anna's father, a notorious pervert. This happens in the rugged Norwegian outback, where Martin hopes to make his fortune as a horse trader. Wandering west, the young people had found love. they had also experienced a strong social bonding with another couple, and together they had met, and survived, harsh psychological challenges.

Throughout the travels and travails of young and old, past and present, both story and camera move naturally to create a seamless drama. Violent action is most often seen with awesome nature as a direct participant. The film is spiced, too, with compassionate and witty observations of wilderness people. Every character in *A Handful of Time* is fully-fleshed and nuanced. In the role of the older Martin, Espen Skjønberg gives a performance that was to win him last year's Amanda Film Award as Best Actor. Maybe there is a slight excess of blood in evidence, and some plot contrivances might well have been pruned without deterring from the essential drama. The cameo performances of two leading British actors (Susannah York and Nigel Hawthorne as a couple of angels) constitute silly and unnecessary comedy relief.

None of this detracts seriously from the joy and almost physical pleasure of watching a strong and beautiful film move to its inevitable conclusion.

J.R. Keith Keller

Til en ukjent
(To a Stranger)

Script and Direction: Unni Straume. Photography: Harald Paalgard. Players: Hilde Aarø, Harald Heide-Steen Jr., Toril Brevik. Produced by Bente Erichsen for Magdalena Film in association with Norsk Film. 82 mins.

Solid entertainment fare, often of international scope (such as *The Dive*,

Hilde Aarø and Harald Heide-Steen Jr. in *To a Stranger*

photo: Carle Lange

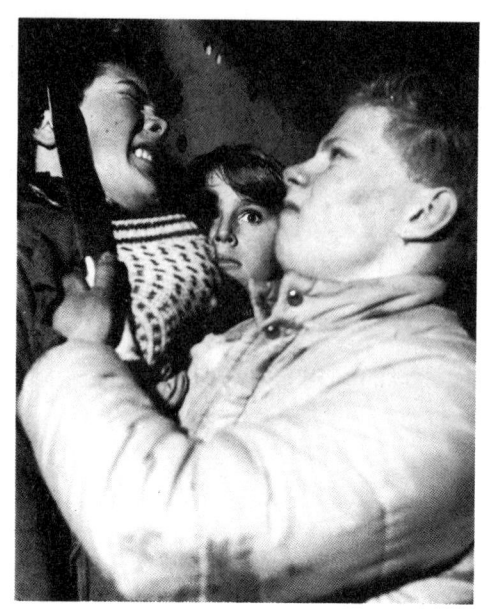

Still from *Death at Oslo C.*

directed by England's Tristan de Vere Cole), comes out of Norway with regular intervals. Unni Straume, too, has had her sights set on faraway shores, yet her first-time writer- director's effort, *To a Stranger*, is a different matter entirely.

Straume's film never leaves home, even when it draws strong inspiration from the works of the late Andrey Tarkovski. *To a Stranger* is a thoroughbred art film. It has exquisite artistic control in its highly personal rendition of a young woman's search for catharsis by reliving childhood events as she goes back to the village-by-the-sea where she was brought up by sternly religious parents. It does not seem that the girl suffered any of the injustices traditionally blamed for causing mental anguish up through the years. She just needs to take stock before proceeding with her Big City life. She has, however, been suppressing the memory of a sister who dies in a fire. She once found a bottle by the sea and has kept it ever since. It contains fragments of thoughts penned in Russian (Nezna komunu = to a stranger).

To a Stranger (and any viewer may take that as a personal dedication) is done 99% in black-and-white. Little dialogue is used. Instead, a lot of inner-voice poetic-existentialist (or is it Zen?) musing is heard, sometimes coming dangerously close to droning. At the end, the woman lies down, at peace with herself and the world, and leaves the bottle to roll into the sea, presumably bringing its message forward to other finders and audiences.

Fresh-faced Hilde Aarø plays the film's dominating lead and really does not have too much to do except for moving in rhythm with the flow of proceedings in general. En route, she meets an elderly man who teaches her that even the footfall of an ant has a sound worth listening to. While there is a little of Tarkovski's dramatic thunder in evidence, his Norse pupil is deft in emulating the master's particular obsessions with fire and water. Cinematographer Harald Paalgard works in total harmony with the director's subdued moods. His lighting adds depth and shadings to shots that hold both grace and suspense even when moving at their slowest pace.

J.R. Keith Keller

Recent and Forthcoming Films

Døden på Oslo S (Death at Oslo C). Script: Axel Helstenius, based on novel by Ingvar Ambjørnsen. Dir: Eva Isaksen. Phot: Philip Øgaard. Players: Håvard Bakke, Tommy Karlsen, Helle Figenschow. Prod: Norsk Film (Harald Ohrvik).

For dagene er onde (Because These Are Evil Days). Script: Eldar Einarson, based on novel by Anne Karin Elstad. Dir: Eldar Einarson. Phot: Bjørn Jegerstedt. Players: Anne Krigsvoll, Björn Sundquist, Pål Skjønberg. Prod: Norsk Film (Hilde Berg).

Smykketyven (Twice upon a Time). Script: Anja Breien and Carl Martin Borgen. Dir: Anja Breien. Photo: Philip Øgaard. Players: Sven

Wollter, Kjersti Holmen, Ghita Nørby. Prod: Norsk Film (Gunnar Svensrud).
Den lange veien hjem (The Long Way Home) Script: Leidulv Risan and Arthur Johansen. Dir: Leidulv Risan. Phot: Harald Paalgard. Players: (shooting start Feb. 1991, cast not confirmed). Prod: Norsk Film (Elin Erichsen).
Håkon Håkonsen (Håkon Håkonsen – English title subject to change). Script: Nils Gaup, Bob Foss, Greg Dinner, Nick Thiel. Dir: Nils Gaup. Phot: Erling Thurmann-Andersen. Players: Gabriel Byrne, Stian Smestad, T.P. Munch, Louisa Haigh. Prod: Filmkammeraterne (John Jacobsen) with Buena Vista (L.A.).
Sensommer – gult og sort (Summer's Ending). Script and Dir: Roar Skolmen. Phot: Svein Krøvel. Players: Bjørn Andresen, Anniken Korgstad, Jan Clemens, Astrid Follstad. Prod: Atomfilm (Odd G. Iversen, Road Skolmen).
Herman (Herman). Script: Lars Saabye Christensen. Dir: Erik Gustavson. Phot: Kjell Vassdal. Players: Anders Danielsen Lie, Bjørn Floberg, Elisabeth Sand, Harald Heide-Steen Jr, Jarl Kulle, Linn Aronsen. Prod: Filmeffekt (Petter Borgli).
Svampe. Script: Elisabeth Young. Dir: Martin Asphaug. Phot: Philip Øgaard. Players: Martin Bliksrud, Espen Skjønberg, Karl Sundby, Brit Elisabeth Haagensti. Prod: Filmeffekt (Dag Alveberg).
Havet stiger (tentative English title: **Rising Tide**). Script and Dir: Oddvar Einarson. Phot: Svein Krøvel. Players: Gard Eidsvold, Petronella Barker, Darota Stalinska, Marek Walezewski, Maciej Orlos, Jerzy Kryszak, Anna Romantowska. Prod: Oslo Film (Aamund Johannesen).
Måker (Seagulls). Script and Dir: Vibeke Løkkeberg. Phot: Paul René Roestad. Players: Vibeke Løkkeberg, Helge Jordal, Tonje Kristiansen, Julie Marie Kristiansen, Elisabeth Grannemann, Klaus Hagerup. Prod: The Norway Film Development Co (Terje Kristiansen).
Buicken og reisverket (The Buick and the Monument). Script and Dir: Hans Otto Nicolayssen. Phot: Kjell Vassdal. Players: Anne-Marie Ottersen, Helge Jordal, Lasse Lindtner. Prod: Motlys (Sigve Endresen).
Bak sju hav (Beyond the Seven Seas). Script and Dir: Espen Thorstensson. Phot: Halvor Næss. Prod: Aprilfilm.

Petronella Barker in Oddvar Einarson's *Rising Tide*

Håvard Bakke and Helle Figenschow in *Death at Oslo C.*

Trond Peter Stamsø Munch and Helge Jordal in *The Wanderers*
photo: Rolv Haan

TOP GROSSING FILMS IN NORWAY: 1989

	Admissions
Rain Man	521,068
Licence To Kill	500,478
A Fish Called Wanda	357,037
Indiana Jones and the Last Crusade	318,478
Who Framed Roger Rabbit	276,244
Lethal Weapon	223,170
The Bear	216,369
The Wedding Party (Norway)	168,758
S.O.S. Swedes at Sea (Sweden)	149,263
Twins	127,504

(Note: Report covers only major cities and townships, i.e. 90% of the market. Final tally for last five items incomplete at press time).

Producers

Aprilfilm A/S
Langes gt. 11
N–0165 Oslo 1
Tel: (2) 20 60 68

Filmeffekt A/S
Sørkedalsvn. 10 A
N–0369 Oslo 3.
Tel: (2) 69 03 78.
Telex: 742700

Filmkameratene A/S
Stortingsgt. 16
N–0161 Oslo 1.
Tel: (2) 33 27 84
Fax: (2) 33 27 97

Mediagjøglerne A/S
St. Olavs pl. 2
N–0165 Oslo 1.
Tel: (2) 42 56 33.

A/S Mefistofilm
Gyldenløvesgt. 41
N–0260 Oslo 2.
Tel: (2) 43 82 60.
Fax: (2) 55 77 77.

Norsk Film A/S
Wedel Jarlsbergsvei 36
N–1342 Jar.
Tel: (2) 12 10 70.
Fax: (2) 59 13 70
Telex: 77337.

NorWay Film Development Company
P.O. Box 57
N–1430 Ås.
Tel: (9) 94 29 38
Fax: (9) 94 10 61

Penelopefilm A/S
Kongensgt. 4B
N–4600 Kristiansand S.
Tel: (42) 70 040.

Regional Film A/S
Øvre Langgt. 40
N–3100 Tønsberg.
Tel: (33) 14 151.

Teamfilm A/S
Keysersgt. 1
N–0165 Oslo 1.
Tel: (2) 20 70 72.
Telex: 19294.

Vikingfilm A/S
Sørkedalsvn. 10 A
N–0369 Oslo 3.
Tel: (2) 60 10 55.
Telex: 78642.

Distributors

Cinefilm
Kirkegt. 34
N–0153 Oslo 1.
Tel: (2) 33 47 50.
Fax: (2) 42 72 93.
Telex: 79464

Europafilm A/S
Stortingsgt. 30
N–0161 Oslo 1.
Tel: (2) 83 42 90
Fax: (2) 83 41 51
Telex: 71033

Fram Film A/S
Colbjørnsensgt. 2
N–0256 Oslo 2
Tel: (2) 55 15 20

Kommunenes Filmcentral A/S
Nedre Vollgt. 9
N–0158 Oslo 1.
Tel: (2) 41 43 25.
Fax: (2) 42 14 69
Telex: 72767

Helge Jordal and Tonje Kristiansen in Vibeke Løkkeberg's new film, *Seagulls*

Norena Film A/S
Stortingsgt. 12
N–0161 Oslo 1.
Tel: (2) 42 71 45.

Norsk Filmindustri A/S
Teglverksgt. 7D
N–0533 Oslo 5
Tel: (2) 37 68 90
Fax: (2) 37 61 70
Telex: 78451

Norsk Film Distribution
P.O. Box 4
N–1342 Jar.
Tel: (2) 12 10 70.

Norsk Filmklubbforbund
Teatergt 3
N–0180 Oslo 1.
Tel: (2) 11 42 17.
Fax: (2) 20 79 81

Royal Film A/S
P.O. Box 6296 Etterstad
N–0658 Oslo 6.
Tel: (2) 68 51 40.

SF Norge A/S
Stortingsgt 16
N–0161 Oslo 1
Tel: (2) 42 01 65
Fax: (2) 33 27 97

Syncron-Film A/S
Kirkegt. 34B
N–0153 Oslo 1
Tel: (2) 41 07 90
Fax: (2) 42 72 93

T & O Film A/S
Vålerenggt 47
N–0658 Oslo 6
Tel: (2) 67 31 31
Fax: (2) 67 30 05

United International Pictures A/S
Hegdehaugsvn. 27
N–0352 Oslo 3
Tel: (2) 56 61 15
Fax: (2) 56 71 81
Telex: 19057

VCM Film A/S
Kristian Augustsgt. 11
N–0164 Oslo 1.
Tel: (2) 20 06 84.
Fax: (2) 20 31 54

Warner Bros (Norway) A/S
P.O. Box 7053 Homansbyen
N–0306 Oslo 3.
Tel: (2) 43 18 00
Fax: (2) 55 46 83
Telex: 78356

Useful Addresses

Norwegian Cinema and Film Foundation
Stortingsgt. 16
N–0161 Oslo 1
Tel: (2) 42 89 49

Norwegian Film Institute
Grev Wedels Plass 1
N–0105 Oslo 1
Tel: (2) 42 87 40
Fax: (2) 33 22 77

National Association of Municipal Cinemas
Stortingsgt. 16
N–0161 Oslo 1
Tel: (2) 33 05 30
Fax: (2) 42 89 49

Norwegian Film Distribution Association
Nedre Vollgt. 9
N–0158 Oslo 1
Tel: (2) 42 48 44
Fax: (2) 42 30 93

PAKISTAN
by Aijaz Gul

The state of cinema in Pakistan was not very healthy during 1989–90. Urdu films continued to face a production decline, foreign illegal video and video piracy of local films prospered, and action movies with a liberal dosage of sex and vulgarity reigned supreme at the box-office during this period. Meaningful films with themes relevant to life and its current issues were just not present.

101 titles opened in 1989 (42 Punjabi, 28 Pushto, 22 Urdu, 9 Sindhi). Similarly, 40 titles were released in the period January–June 1990, and the list was again headed by Punjabi films. The box-office has been often mean and cruel to the producers. The bankable superstars like Anjuman, Sultan Rahi, Nadira, Neeli and Nadeem could not save most of their vehicles from total disaster. On the aesthetic level, these artists were not equipped to give us real feelings and emotions and the kind of performance which could move the audiences to tears and laughter. They merely go through the motions without integrating essence of life.

Director Mumtaz Ali Khan, still remembered for his notorious, sexy and now de-certified hit *One Night Bride* from the mid-1970's, made an astonishing comeback last year with the low-budget high-actioner, **Hell to Hell**, released in three versions (Urdu–Pushto–Punjabi), with a new cast. This film introduced among others, Ajam Gul, who rose to stardom overnight. There were handsome dividends for everyone in spite of the picture's modest production values and below-average technical effects.

Director Hussnain's Urdu hit, **Enemy**, which opened in February 1990, became the most successful film in the last five years. The film owed its remarkable success not only to gripping direction, quickfire dialogue and action and impressive production values but also to popular songs and a multiple cast of superstars (Nadeem, Neeli, Sultan Rahi, Afzal and Abid Ali). The highlight of *Enemy* was Anjuman, the heart-throb of Punjabi films who was seen here (without romancing, singing or dancing) as a leader of a criminal gang, mean, cruel and ruthless. *Enemy* has not only helped in advancing the dwindling career of its cast and crew but has also modestly opened the way for more Urdu films. The film is one man's battle against greed, corruption, moral decay, drugs and crime and in this eternal battle between the clean hero and the dirty villains, the good obviously prevails over the evil.

The other box-office winners from 1990 included director Jan Mohammad's **International Gorilley** and the late Haider Chaudhry's **Smart**. *Gorilley*, filmed in the Far East, exploited Muslim sentiments to the hilt against "infamous" Salman Rushdie. The villain, played by Afzal, controls his drugs empire from the Far East (obviously a stupid replacement for London). A group of patriots from Pakistan is determined to teach him a lesson. However, the lesson comes from the pages of Holy Quran and the villain is burnt alive in its mysterious flames (remember *Raiders of the Lost Ark*!). Audiences applaud this movie magic. Praise the Lord.

NAFDEC (National Film Development Corporation) organised successful film festivals from Poland, China, France, Britain and Iran. USIS held fascinating events in three cities, focused on James Ivory–Ismail Merchant and their memorable films. *Slaves of New York, A Room with a View, The Bostonians* and *Bombay Talkie* unspooled to enthusiastic crowds. The major hits at the Pakistan box-office included *Cobra, In the Line of Duty* Part III, IV, and *Cyborg*.

Video Piracy Unchecked

An illegal, uncensored and smuggled video trade prospered nationwide, notwithstanding minor protests from conservative political groups against porno video. The Government continued to propose legislation which includes amendments in the Copyright Act. The video piracy of local films was so outrageous that pirated copies were seen on the video shelves simultaneously with the theatrical release. The producer seemed helpless except for raiding the video shops with the police. And since the police remained on the sidelines in Karachi and Hyderabad, there was nothing the film trade could do to stop the piracy menace.

Kavita in *Decait*, a big money-winner in Pakistan

The notable directors in the limelight this year included Hussnain, Jan Mohammad, Masood Butt, Yonus Malik and the late Haider Chaudhry (who died last May from kidney failure). Women directors Shamim Ara (*Lady Commando*) and Sangeeta (*Acid*) performed poorly with lacklustre work.

Recent and Forthcoming Films

Aasman (Sky). Script: M. Kalim. Dir: Husnain. Phot: Babra Bilal. Music: Kamal Ahmad. Players: Nadeem, Yousaf Khan, Babra Sharif.
Laila (Love). Script: Bashir Niaz. Dir: Nazaral

Islam. Music: Wajahat Attrey. Players: Izhar Qazi, Nadira, Kavita.
Loha (Steel). Dir: Waheed Dar. Music: M. Ashraf. Players: Anjuman, Sultan Rahi.

AIJAZ GUL earned his A.B. and M.A. in Cinema from University of Southern California, Los Angeles. Now Head of Export and Film Promotion, National Film Development Corporation Limited. Also Director, Shabistan Cinema, Rawalpindi.

TOP TEN GROSSING FILMS IN PAKISTAN: 1989

Kalka (Shahid Rana)
Rangiley Jasoos (Iqbal Kashmiri)
Bilawal (Kaifi)
Madam Bavri (Nazaral Islam)
Qiamat Sey Qiamat Tak (Mumtaz Ali Khan)
Decait (Jehangir Qaiser)
Nagin Jogi (Mahmood Butt)
Achoo 302 (Altaf Hussain)
Manila Key Janbaz (Jan Mohammad)
Zakhmi Aurat (Iqbal Kashmiri)

Producers, Distributors and Exporters

Evernew Pictures
2 Abbot Road
Lahore
Tel: 52088, 58563
Telex: 44960 EVNEW PK

Eveready Pictures
Mawlai Mansion
M.A. Jinnah Road
Karachi
Tel: 215293, 215273
Fax: (9221) 737843 Karachi

Kashif Limited
Kashif Center
Main Sharah Faisal
Karachi
Tel: 526002, 521584, 521565
Telex: 24273 KASHIF PK

A & S Films
10, Amrat Park
Abdul Karim Road
Lahore
Tel: 223359, 311732

Rizwan Traders
36-G (Ground Floor)
Sharah Quid-e-Azam
Lahore
Tel: 303094

Shama Parvana Pictures
Royal Park
Lahore
Tel: 222284

Andata Pictures
Nazir Mansion
Royal Park
Lahore
Tel: 222549

Arian Pictures
Jabbar Building
Royal Park
Lahore
Tel: 226912

Al-Farooq Movies
Nazir Mansion
Royal Park
Lahore
Tel: 222549

Useful Addresses

National Film Development Corporation
56-F, Blue Area
Islamabad
Tel: 823148
Telex: 5789 NAFDC PK
Fax: 817323

Ministry of Culture
Block "D"
Pak Secretariat
Islamabad
Tel: 821790, 821301
Fax: 817323

Central Board of Film Censors
Street No. 55
F-6/4
Islamabad
Tel: 824393

16-D, Bambino Chambers
Garden Road
Karachi
Tel: 729497

Pakistan Film Distributors
Association
Sheikh Chambers (2nd Floor)
Near Light House Cinema
M.A. Jinnah Road
Karachi
Tel: 216378

18, Geeta Bhawan Building
McLeod Road
Lahore
Tel: 58785

Pakistan Film Exhibitors
Association
Lyrie Cinema Building
Garden Road
Karachi
Tel: 727764

Nadeem and Anjuman in *Enemy*

Prince Cinema Building
Mahmud Ghaznavi Road
Lahore
Tel: 227047, 52119

PHILIPPINES
by Agustin Sotto

Despite staff competition from television and video and the failure of the campaign to repeal the onerous tax laws, Philippine cinema continues to flourish with high box-office returns and a growing cultural influence. In 1989, it produced 162 films – a slight increase over last year's. Thirty theatres of 700–1400 seats each are being constructed in Metro-Manila; adding to the already staggering number of 220 cinemas. The close identification of the masses with movie stars has elicited rumours of possible presidential candidates from their ranks in the 1992 elections.

Leading the 1989–1990 box-office is the record-breaking **Even Just a Glance Suffices** grossing a phenomenal $2 million in just one week's screening. It starred the two top stars of the season: Fernando Poe Jr. and Sharon Cuneta. Several other movies did exceptionally well: *Last Two Minutes, Starzan, Barbi, Oras-Oras, Araw-Araw, Kailan Mahuhugasan ang Kasalanan, Joe Pring, Kapag Puno na ang Salop Part II*. Action films, superstar melodramas, and toilet humour dominated the box-office, beating the surprisingly feeble Hollywood product. (Only Sylvester Stallone with *Tango and Cash* and *Lock-Up* made it to the top.)

With commercial film-making in the pink, quality film production continues to languish without government support. Lino Brocka's **Fight for Us/Les Insoumis**, produced by Pathé, provoked a controversy from the day of its premiere in Cannes 1989 to its private screenings in Manila. Its outspoken director engaged the chief censor, Manuel Morato, in a heated exchange of views over the interpretation of the freedom of cultural expression guaranteed by the Aquino constitution. Morato countered with personal attacks. Although he reportedly approved the film for public screening, he has delayed issuing a permit pending the submission of official documents.

The film describes the post-Marcos era – assassinations, ambushes, kidnappings. Nothing much has changed. An ex-priest and ex-political prisoner (Phillip Salvador) investigates the killings being perpetrated by a para-military religious cult, *Ora Pro Nobis*. Based on real incidents, the film has been hailed by critics as ironically the most important film of the Aquino era.

Another film of interest is Ishmael Bernal's **Lend Me a Morning**, a look into the last six months of a cancer victim (Vilma Santos). She tries to patch up differences with her family and surrenders her son to her ex-boyfriend. The political instability and the economic crunch permeate the atmosphere as multinationals eat up the business opportunities and family fortunes collapse.

Elwood Perez's **Count the Stars in the Heavens** marked the comeback of superstar Nora Aunor who won several Best Actress trophies for her twin role as vengeful mother and conciliatory daughter. A baroque melodrama spanning two generations, the film centres on the revenge exacted by a former tenant on her erstwhile landlord.

Augusto Salvador's **Joe Pring** was the surprise of the season: a well-crafted police story full of action and suspense. Phillip Salvador plays Joe Pring whose relentless hunt for killers and dope dealers leads to his mistress' death. The minor characters are well written and lift the genre concerns a notch higher.

Two films were produced on the question of the American bases: **In the Claws of the Eagle** starring Senator Joseph Estrada, and **To Die for the Country**. Both films are largely anti-American, depicting the G.I.s as dope addicts, sex perverts, AIDS carriers, and personae non grata, wreaking havoc on the Philippines through their ignorance of cultural traditions and ther "everybody's for sale" mentality. Both films aim to alert the masses to the ills inflicted by the presence of the American bases. Presently, a new bases treaty is under negotiation.

POLAND

by Wanda Wertenstein

To say that life in postcommunist Poland is not easy is an understatement. Peaceful transition from communist regime to budding democracy may be seen as a near miracle but above all it is a long and difficult process. Nearly a year after the Solidarity activist, and Catholic journalist Tadeusz Mazowiecki formed the first non-Communist government since 1945 it became more and more evident how enormous was the damage to national economy, environment and above all to human minds and morale that the 45 years of the regime had brought about. Changes have to be made in all fields of life – as deep and rapid as the people's patience and purse can support. Still many cannot understand that what is happening here (and in Czechoslovakia and Hungary) is something never seen before in world history: we've known capitalism or, say, free market destroyed by various marxist regimes but nobody tried to reinstate capitalism and free market in a country where 80% of industry was in the hands of the State and all fields of social, cultural, political and economic activity controlled by the ruling party and its bureaucracy. Even if the spirit of the nation was never totally cramped as may be proved by many works of artists and scientists and above all by Solidarity itself; by the recurring upheavals of 1956, 1968, 1970, 1980 and the organised resistance to Martial Law of 1981; by secret recording of events on film and video and by huge underground production of newspapers, reviews and books – the scale of the task of transforming the country's economy into something normal, in Western sense of the word, is gigantic.

1990 began with dramatic economic reforms known as "Balcerowicz plan" consisting of drastic rises in bank interest, cuts in State subsidies, high price rises, practical freezing of salaries etc – all of which led to effective curbing down of superinflation and – with the necessary legal regulations – to the convertibility of Polish zloty. This meant considerable recession in industrial production and about 30% fall in the standard of living. Of course, in the circumstances, culture had to suffer, people had less money to spend on books, theatre, films etc. If a film like Stephen Frears's *Dangerous Liaisons* ran in Warsaw in June-July 1990 to an audience of 20% – this could give an idea of the situation.

Along with the national economy the system of Polish film industry is in transition. From October 1, 1989, the existing Film Units or Groups were transformed into independent Studios with full rights to decide on their production and finance and – for the transition period – supported with a State subsidy but free to enter into co-productions and other arrangements with foreign companies, to sell their films independently of existing state or private (now about 20) distributors and use the money they earn for their own purposes. The studios own a new limited company, the "Agency of Polish Film Producers", with more or less the same tasks and activities as the former Film Producers' Corporation "Zespoly Filmowe." The state distribution company was dissolved, seven independent distributing agencies in the seven biggest cities created, and private or foreign distributors allowed to operate. Over 6,000 private firms selling and renting video-cassettes were registered. Movie theatres are turning private or, if owned by local communities, are mostly emploited by privates on a lease basis. Nevertheless the whole system is still very fluid and the first version of a new law on cinema was firmly rejected by leading film-makers like Wajda and Zanussi.

With soaring production costs, no Polish film can recoup its expenses on the home market, not to mention making profit. One of the best production groups TOR (Krzysztof Zanussi) now renamed Film Studio TOR, calculates that a film which in the late 1970's could cover its cost on the home market – now with the same number of spectators could do it only at a level of ticket prices that would be prohibitive. Of course, the chances are much better if a film gets sold abroad. And so two films released in 1987, Andrzej Zaorski's *Mother of Kings* and Krzysztof Kieślowski's *Chance* were responsible for respectively 20 and 25% of the whole revenue of Film Polski for exports of feature films. And in 1988 two of Kieślowski's *Decalogue* films, **Short Film About Killing** and **Short Film About Love** brought in exports over 70% of those revenues.

Today the studios are free to sell their films directly to foreign distributors or through foreign agents and don't have to do it through the once obligatory State company Film Polski so they can get a higher share in the monies earned abroad but still the costs of production can be recouped in rare cases. The best-run studios either co-produce films with foreign companies or earn the means to produce their films by selling facilities and services to foreign productions shooting in Poland.

If there is still much uncertainty concerning the forms and practices of the new system of Polish film industry or the reasonable balance to be achieved between independence, privatisation and the inevitable subsidising of production – one fundamental development of 1990 is a certainty: the abolition of censorship voted by the Parliament in May. Since that date films are a matter of conscience and responsibility of their makers and producers.

1990 began with no more films withheld or shelved. The last and best known was Ryszard Bugajski's **Interrogation** made in Wajda's Unit "X" in 1982. The film – describing the arbitrary arrest, torture and suffering of a woman, an actress, in the Stalinist era – was presented at 1990 Cannes Festival and won its star Krystyna Janda the Best Actress Award. Earlier, in August 1989 another banned theatrical feature was released – the first film by Krzysztof Tchórzewski **Inner State** (1983), modest but interesting in its well-observed image of behaviour and reactions among a group of young people from Gdańsk at the moment of, and during the first days after the declaration of martial law in December 1989.

Of the films of 1989, **Lava or a Tale of Adam Mickiewicz's Forefathers**, adapted from the national romantic drama of 1822–32 and directed by Tadeusz Konwicki, was the most impressive and prestigious. Beautifully acted and staged, faithful to the original text, it reads for the Polish viewer as a comment on much more recent history. Spoken in verse, rich in associations and references only generations brought up on Mickiewicz's work can understand, it is a difficult, nearly incomprehensible film for foreign public. This was clear from the film's reception at the Moscow 1989 Film Festival. The situation is completely different with Maciej Dejczer's first film **300 Miles to Heaven**, written by the director together with Cezary Harasimowicz, which won the European Film Award 1989 as the "Young European Film of the Year." The delicate, subtle story of two small boys fleeing to Denmark under a hugh TIR lorry was inspired by a real event and showed talent and sensitivity. Another worthy comment on the recent past is Madgalena Lazarkiewicz's **The Last Schoolbell** – a story of young protesters in a repressive school near Gdańsk in the 1980's: a good professional job with some truly revealing insights. Krzysztof Zanussi's **Inventory**, starring Krystyna Janda and Maja Komorowska and excellent newcomer Arthur Zmijewski (also brilliant in **Lava**) shows the director at his cruel best – portraying two women, the elder a merciless prig, the younger desperately lost and hysterical in her incapability to cope with her life – both in different ways exploiting the kind, unselfish and sensitive boy who tries to help the younger and comply to the standards of the older, his mother. A great Zanussi film yet again.

Some of the films which may have seemed revelatory before the votes of June 1989 ring stale and second-hand when viewed today, like Janusz Kijowski's **State of Terror** or Waldemar Krzystek's **The Last Ferry**: both deal with human problems under martial law. But Radoslaw Piwowarski's **March Almonds**, showing a group of teenagers in a small provincial town faced with their Jewish class mate's forced emigration in 1968, is an honourable and moving effort.

In spite of all the difficulties, 28 theatrical features were made in 1989 as well as films for television, TV series, documentaries and shorts. The production of 1990 will probably be 28 features again.

Recent and Forthcoming Films

Po Upadku (After the Fall). Script: Andrzej Trzos-Rastawiecki, Tadeusz Siejak and Maciej Krasicki. Dir: Andrzej Trzos-Rastawiecki. Phot: Krzysztof Tusiewicz. Players: Zbigniew Zapasiewicz, Kazimierz Kaczor, Marek Kondrat, Barbara Soltysik, Anna Nehrebecka. Prod: Film Studio "Kadr", 1989.
Seszele (Seychelles). Script: Cezary Harasimowicz. Dir: Boguslaw Linda. Phot: Jaroslaw Szoda. Players: Zbigniew Zamachowski, Tadeusz Szymkow. Prod: Film Studio "Zebra", 1990.
Zabic na Koncu (Kill at the End). Script and Dir: Wojciech Wójcik. Phot: Jacek Mieroslawski. Players: Wojciech Malajkat, Piotr Siwkiewicz-Shivak. Prod: Film Studio "Zodiak", 1990.
Swinka (Pig's Gate). Script: Marcin Wolski and Krzysztof Magowski. Dir: Krzysztof Magowski. Phot: Wlodek Glodek. Players: Tadeusz Huk, Ewa Skibińska, Henryk Talar. Prod: Film Studio "Dom", 1990.
Niemoralna Historia (Immoral Story). Script and Dir: Barbara Sass. Phot: Wieslaw Zdort. Players: Dorota Stalińska, Teresa Budzisz-Krzyzanowska, Michal Bajor, Olaf Lubaszenko,

---

TOP GROSSING FILMS IN POLAND: 1989
Soccer Poker (Janusz Zaorski)
The Art of Love (Jacek Bromski)
What Tigers Like Best (Krzysztof Nowak)
Interrogation (Ryszard Bugajski)
Citizen P. (Andrzej Kotkowski)

TOP GROSSING FILMS: JANUARY–MARCH 1990
Porno (Marek Koterski)
Interrogation (Ryszard Bugajski)
Hotch-Potch (Roman Zaluski)
300 Miles to Heaven (Maciej Dejczer)
March Almonds (Radoslaw Piwowarski)

Henryk Bista. Prod: Film Studio "Kadr", 1990.
Kramarz (Peddler). Script and Dir: Andrzej Baranski. Phot: Driusz Kuc. Players: Roman Klosowski, Bozena Adamek, Artur Barciś. Prod: Film Studio "Oko" and Polish TV, 1990.
Pozegnanie Jesieni (Farewell Autumn). Script: Wojciech Nowak, Janusz Wroblewski, Mariusz Treliński, from the novel by S.I. Witkiewicz: Dir: Mariusz Treliński. Phot: Jaroslaw Zamojda, Players: Jan Frycz, Maria Pakulnis, Jan Peszek, Grazyna Trela. Prod: Karol Irzykowski Film Studio, 1990.
Pogrzeb Kartofla (Burying the Potato). Script and Dir: Jan Jakub Kolski. Phot: Wojciech Todorow. Players: Franciszek Pieczka, Adam Ferency, Grazyna Blecka-Kolska. Prod: Karol Irzykowski Film Studio, 1990.
Powrot Wilczycy (Return of the She-Wolf). Script: Wojciech Jedrkiewicz, Wojciech Nizynski, Jerzy Siewierski. Dir: Marek Piestrak. Phot: Janusz Pawlowski. Players: Jerzy Zelnik, Grazyna Trela-Stawska, Leon Niemczyk. Prod: Film Studio "Oko", 1990.
Superwizja (Super Vision). Script: Ewaryst Izewski and Robert Gliński. Dir: Robert Gliński. Phot: Krzysztof Ptak. Players: Jan Nowicki, Jan Englert, Malgorzata Piorun, Marian Opania. Prod: Film Studio "Dom".
Panny I Wdowy (Spinsters and Widows). Script: Maria Nurowska, Dir: Janusz Zaorski. Phot: Witold Adamek, Players: Maja Komorowska, Katarzyna Figura, Joanna Szczepkowska, Piotr Machalica. Prod: Film Studio "Dom"
Zycie za Zycie (Life for Life). Script: Jan Józef Szczepański. Dir: Krzysztof Zanussi. Phot: Slawomir Idziak. Players: Franciszek Pieczka, Andrzej Szczepkowski, Edward Zentara, Christopher Waltz. Prod: Film Studio "Tor" IFAGE Film Produktion (FRG).
Kuchnia Polska (Polish Cuisine). Script and Dir: Jacek Bromski. Phot: Edward Klosinski, Janusz Gauer. Players: Krystyna Janda, Marek Kondrat, Krzysztof Kolberger. Prod: Film Studio "Zebra".
Drapiezcy (Beasts of Prey). Script: Krystyna Kofta. Dir: Piotr Szulkin. Phot: Dariusz Kuc. Players: Hanna Dumowska, Ewa Salacka, Marcin Tronski, Krzysztof Bauman. Prod: Film Studio "Perspektywa".
Zakiad (Reformatory). Script: Andrzej Dziurawiec. Dir: Teresa Kotlarczyk. Phot: Piotr Wojtowicz. Players: Jan Peszek, Krzysztof Kolberger, Pawel Królikowski. Prod: Karol Irzykowski Film Studio.
Smierc Dziecioroba (Death of a Kidmaker). Script and Dir: Wojciech Nowak. Phot: Jaroslaw Szoda. Players: Anna Majcher, Marek Kasprzyk, Beata Tyszkiewicz, Henryk Bista. Prod: Karol Irzykowski Film Studio.
Mow mi Rockefeller (Call Me Rockefeller). Script: Ryszard Nyczka, Waldemar Szarek. Dir: Waldemar Szarak. Phot: Janusz Gauer. Players: Kamil Gewratowski, Malgorzata Markiewicz, Marek Barbasiewicz, Magdalena Zawadzka. Prod: Film Studio "Zebra", 1990.
Ferdydurke. Script: from the novel by Witold Gombrowicz. Dir: Jerzy Skolimowski. Phot: Witold Adamek.

PORTUGAL

by Peter Besas

Starting with the films made by pioneer Aurelio Da Paz dos Reis in 1896, Portugal has produced some five or six films a year for a market that contains only about 400 cinemas, showing mostly foreign films subtitled in Portuguese. Due to the limited audience within Portugal, the government has been subsidising local films since 1948, based on a 15% of box-office tax and another on distribution.

Certainly, the best-known Portuguese director is Manoel de Oliveira, who made his first film, *Douro, Faina Fluvial* in 1931. Since then he has shot over a dozen films. The most recent was that shown in Cannes in 1990, **No, Or The Vain Glory of Command**, a pensive dissertation on war and Portugal's history. Two years earlier, Oliveira presented in Cannes a strange operatic film, *The Cannibals (Os Canibais)*, which divided the opinion of film critics.

Other Portuguese film-makers who have made a mark over the past few years are José Fonseca e Costa (*Coracâo partido*), Antonio de Macedo (*A Maldicao de Marialva*), Joaquim Pinto (*Onde bate o sol*), João Mario Grilo (*O Proceso do Rei*), João Cesar Monteiro (*Recordacões da casa Amarela*) and Pedro Costa (*O Sangue*).

Portugal has a limited film infrastructure,

Still from *No, or the Vain Glory of Command*

though it does possess a lab (Tobis Portuguesa), various equipment rental outfits, and numerous technicians and crews. Producers such as Paulo Branco and José Luis Vasconcelos have sought to solve financing problems by making co-productions with other countries, or attracting foreign films to use Portuguese locations.

In 1990, Portugal's MGN Films co-produced **A Winter in Lisbon** with Spain and France. The film was directed by Spaniard José Zorrilla and starred Dizzy Gillespie.

Portugal also plays host to various film festivals. Oldest is that held in Figueira da Foz, a seaside resort north of Lisbon, specialising in experimental and art films. In northern Porto, the Fantasporto Festival each February draws large crowds of sci-fi and fantasy film buffs. And in June, the Troia Film Festival, south of Lisbon, set in a recreational development, plays host to an occasional celebrity and filmgoing guests who also enjoy the sun and sea.

PETER BESAS has lived in Madrid since the mid-1960's and is chief of Variety's bureau there. He has written various books, including a history of Spanish cinema.

Useful Addresses

Portuguese Film Institute
Rua San Pedro de Alcántara 45
Lisbon 1200
Tel: (3511) 346-7395
Fax: (3511) 372-777

Cinemateca Portuguesa
Rua Barata Sigueiro 39
Lisbon
Tel: (3511) 546-279

Producers/Distributors

Filmargem
Rua Padre Antonio Vieira 17
Lisbon 1000
Tel: 692-571

Camara 2000
Rua Gorgel do Amarel 5
Lisbon 1200
Tel: 693-200

Films Castello Lópes
Praça Marqués de Pombal 6
Lisbon 1288
Tel: 563-366

Lisboa Filmes
Praça Bernardino Machado
Lisbon 1700
Tel: 759-1063

Filmes Luso Mundo
Praça de Alegria 22
Lisbon 1200
Tel: 370-964

Opus Filmes
Rua de Oliveira ao Carmo 24
Lisbon 1200
Tel: 373010

Uniportugal
Avda. Duque de Loulé 79
Lisbon 1000
Tel: 520339

PUERTO RICO

by José Artemio Torres

In terms of output, film production in Puerto Rico for the year 1989–90 followed the same pattern that we have reported earlier in IFG: one or two features every other year, a few documentaries, maybe one short animation film and a lot of TV commercials. But this period, as we will see later, brought the added bonus of an increasing recognition of Puerto Rican films abroad.

Two feature films were released in the second half of 1989: **What Happened to Santiago** (*Lo que le pasó a Santiago*), written and directed by Jacobo Morales, and **Abelardo's Short Stories** (*Los cuentos de Abelardo*), directed by Luis Molina.

Santiago . . . is the third feature of writer, actor and director Jacobo Morales. It tells the story of Santiago, a widowed accountant who soon after retirement meets a younger, beautiful and mysterious woman with whom he has a love affair that ends happily. The film has the best production values of all the films Morales has made, including the fact that it was shot in original 35mm. The natural acting of long-time comedian and TV producer Tommy Muñiz as Santiago, the tenderness of the love story and certain observations of Puerto Rican contemporary life contributed to the appeal of a film that has been a big local hit.

But the film did much more than that. It went on to acquire a nomination for a Hollywood Oscar as Best Foreign Language Film, the first Puerto Rican film and one of the few Latin American films to win such recognition. It lost to Italy's *Cinema Paradiso*, a formidable competitor.

The success of *What Happened to Santiago* has strengthened the faith in Puerto Rican films, both in the film-makers and the general public. It also has triggered again the question of film production financing, both official and private, something that doesn't have any structure at all.

Luis Molina financed his film *Abelardo's Short Stories* through corporate sponsorships and the backing of the Institute of Puerto Rican Culture. Made as an educational project, the film, although shot in 35mm, hasn't had a cinema run yet. It translates to the screen three classic short stories by Abelardo Dîaz Alfaro, one of Puerto Rico's most noted writers. They were published in 1947, within the book *Terrazo*, a standard school text now. The stories, set in the countryside, deal with a professional mourner, a reluctant English teacher and an unemployed sugar cane worker. The film suffers from over-dramatisation and it doesn't attain the intended pathos of the original stories. So far, it has been shown in some universities.

Strangely enough, no documentary of note was released in this time period. On the other hand, the only animation film released, **The Plumage of the Owl** (*Las plumas del múcaro*) by Paco López, won the prizes for Best Animation Film and Best Script at the 1989 New Latin American Film Festival in Havana.

Talking about festivals, a small group of Puerto Rican features (*La gran fiesta*, *Los peloteros* and *Lo que le pasó a Santiago*) had a successful screening in November 1989 at the Festival des 3 Continents in Nantes, France. Also, a delegation of Puerto Rican film-makers participated in a symposium about Caribbean Cinema held at the Festival.

Tommy Muñiz and Gladys Rodriguez in the Academy Award nominee, *What Happened to Santiago*

New Festival Launched

Puerto Rico also had its own film festival, a new one, although the Cinemafest, held in October 1989, was more a "Mostra" of recent international films than a real festival. A group of film-makers from Argentina, Canada, France, México, Spain and the U.S.A. visited the island for the occasion and some symposiums and lectures took place. The organisers want to repeat it, so there will be two festivals at the end of 1990: the Cinemafest and, in its second edition, the Cine San Juan (Caribbean) Film and Video Festival.

The second half of 1989 witnessed some intense activity in the filming of outside productions, exclusively from the U.S. Some well-known directors like Sidney Lumet and Adrian Lyne shot some scenes of the later films *Q & A* and *Jacob's Ladder*, respectively. Also Bruno Barreto shot in its entirety *A Show of Force*, a film about the political murder of two pro-independence Puerto Rican fighters. In the fiscal year of 1988–89, according to the Film and TV Institute, outside production (including features, documentaries and commercials) contributed $3,596,446 to the local economy. In 1990, up to the month of May, no outside feature film production has landed on these shores.

Surprisingly, TV drama production increased in 1989 although the surge has been short lived. **In a Day** (*En un día*), **Every Day Is Christmas** (*Todo el año es Navidad*) and **Unusual** (*Insólito*) lasted more than a season but are now defunct. Occasionally, a TV mini-series, here a shorter version of the popular soap operas, appears to relieve the drought of employment for Puerto Rican actors.

The second half of 1990 will surely see a TV movie from Zaga Films titled **On the**

TOP GROSSING FILMS IN PUERTO RICO: 1989

	Rentals
Batman	$1,200,000
Indiana Jones and the Last Crusade	$970,000
Ghostbusters II	$950,000
Twins	$837,000
The Karate Kid II	$650,000
Honey, I Shrunk the Kids	$557,000
Lethal Weapon 2	$550,000
Look Who's Talking	$475,000
Rain Man	$450,000
Licence to Kill	$450,000
Lo que le pasó a Santiago	$393,000

(List compiled by Pedro Zervigón of *El Nuevo Día* daily)

Surface of the Skin (*A flor de piel*), about women's abuse. Some feature film projects have been announced. Maybe one of them will come out before the end of the year to break the pattern of production of one or two features every other year.

Useful Address

Puerto Rican Institute of Film and TV Arts and Industries
Administration of Economic Development
Government of Puerto Rico
PO Box 2350
San Juan
Puerto Rico 00936
Tel: (809) 754–7110
     (809) 758–4747
Fax: (809) 754–9645

SENEGAL
by Roy Armes

Senegal has the richest body of film-making of any French West African state, but its progress through the 1980's has been at best hesitant. Ousmane Sembene has finally been able to return to the cameras with a major feature after a break of over ten years and that most elusive of Senegalese directors, Djibril Diop-Mambety (author of *Touki-Bouki* in 1973), has at least made a tentative reappearance with *Parlons Grandmère*, a documentary study of the making of *Yaaba*. But to set against this progress, two other pioneer film-makers have gone through the past decade without a single feature – Mahama Johnson Traore and Safi Faye – and neither of the two newcomers who surfaced briefly in the early 1980's – Ben Diogaye Beye and Cheikh N'Gaido Ba – has made a second film. Moreover, 1987 saw the deaths of two of the great pioneers of Senegalese (and African) cinema: Paulin Soumanou Vieyra, documentarist, tireless historian of African cinema and author of a single feature, *Under House Arrest* (*En Résidence surveillée* 1981) and Ababacar Samb-Makharam, whose two feature films, *Kodou* (1971) and *Jom* (1981), span the decade of major Senegalese filmic achievement.

There was some progress in the late 1980's, however, Mansour Sora Wade made a short drama, *Fary l'Anesse* (1987) which received wide praise and it is to be hoped that his career fares better than those of the two very talented newcomers who made their short film debuts at the end of the 1970's, Ousmane William Mbaye and Félix Samba Ndiaye, neither of whom has been able to make a feature. Moussa Bathily, a former assistant of Ousmane Sembene, who began as a documentarist and then moved on to make a striking feature-length debut with *Circumcision* (*Tiyabu Biru*, 1978), was able to make a second, fully fictional feature some ten years later. But *Petits blancs au manioc et à la souce gombos* (1987) is a slight work, a not-too-successful comedy of the misadventures of an international aid team and the villagers who befriend them and act as their hosts.

In 1988 two brothers each succeeded in making a feature film debut with German financial backing. Pape Badara Seck, who had earlier studied at the Institut des Hautes Etudes Cinématographiques in Paris and made a couple of shorts, directed *Africa on the Rhine*, a curious tale of the cultural disorientation and subsequent politicisation of an African in Europe, using characters who shift unexpectedly from a human plane to a mythical dimension. His brother, Amadou Saaloum Seck, who carried out his film studies in Munich, followed the reverse trajectory, taking a largely German crew to Senegal to film a tale of the culture shock experienced by an African returning to his birth place after 17 years in Europe. In many ways the film is a throw-back to an earlier generation – the drama of the returnee, the "been-to" – but told with great technical assurance and a very westernised sense of drama and individuality.

But the major Senegalese work of the decade is **Camp de Thiarroye** (1988), co-directed by Ousmane Sembene and Thierno Faty Sow. Sow, who studied at the Conservatoire Indépendent du Cinéma Français in Paris and worked for five years as an assistant at ORTF, returned to Senegal to work as a director in television and in documentary film production. He made two independent features in the 1970's, *L'Option* (1974) and *L'Oeil* (1979). For Sembene the 1980's were barren filmically until he co-directed this 140-minute feature, though he continued publishing, with the novel *The Last of the Empire* and the stories *Niwam* and *Taaw*. The new film, *Camp de Thiarroye*, is a striking and impassioned piece of anti-colonial history. A group of *tirailleurs* (black infantrymen), repatriated to Dakar in 1944 after long years of military service in Europe, are not allowed to return to their local communities but incarcerated in a transit camp. There they are cheated out of their money and deprived of the U.S. uniforms which symbolise their distance from the old colonial world, and their new state of (non-colonised) selfhood. But the efforts of the French to push them back into their subservient role are relentless and in response they go so far as to kidnap a white general. The outcome is predictable. Despite his word of honour as a French officer that there will be no reprisals, at 3 A.M. on December 1 1944 the camp is razed to the ground and all its inhabitants slaughtered. This is a true story, though one omitted from French histories of colonial Africa, and it is told with passion and commitment, making this one of the most forceful denunciations of the French presence in Africa. Significantly, all the finance was raised in Africa, with SNPC in Senegal, SATPEC in Tunisia and ENAPROC in Algeria putting up the money for a production realised through the co-directors' own personal production companies.

SOUTH AFRICA

by Martin Botha and William Pretorius

Since 1986 (the last entry on this country in IFG), South African cinema has produced two, opposing types of film: mainstream commercial and, of necessity, progressive political films.

Both types of films are largely unknown locally. A small percentage of the commercial pictures – over 80 were made in 1988 alone – is released by the chief distributors, Ster-Kinekor, United International Pictures (UIP) and Nu-Metro. Their inferior quality too, has restricted many of them to release on video only. Censorship has made sure that the political films have remained mostly unseen.

The commercial industry was made possible by tax concessions and loopholes whereby films could turn out outrageous profits, often without ever being shown. Various local firms that had nothing to do with film and that wanted a tax write-off began investing in productions for the international market. American production companies could also make cheap, non-union films here.

Local production companies and film-makers like Dirk de Villiers, Elmo de Witt and Jan Scholtz who made chiefly Afrikaans films, also turned to international production, causing that indigenous branch of the industry to die out. The Afrikaans industry revived with director and producer Katinka Heyns's *Fiela se Kind*, based on the best-selling book by Dalene Mathee. An English version, re-edited by the British editor Terry Rawlings, was prepared for the foreign market. At present, a local television network M-Net has financed for four Afrikaans films that are in pre-production.

Films in the mainstream commercial industry fall into five categories: indigenous films with regional themes like **Fiela's Child**; local movies such as Regardt van den Bergh's **Circles in a Forest** (based on another bestseller by Dalene Mathee) that Americanise indigenous themes; films like **Paradise Road, The Emissary, Panga, Reason to Die**, and **Brutal Glory** that imitate American genre movies; American genre movies that use South Africa as an African background (*Ten Little Indians, Diamonds High*); and American genre movies that use South Africa as Vietnam (*Platoon Leader*), Cambodia (*American Eagle*) or South America (*River of Death*).

Several of the American genre movies were made by American production companies working in South Africa. The cultural boycott has ensured that this industry is, to an extent, clandestine. The films are often released internationally as having been made in Zimbabwe.

The international industry locally came to an end in 1989 when tax incentives were stopped, and the industry reverted to a governmental subsidy system that doesn't provide developmental money and that pays the subsidy on box-office profits. This has put film-making into the hands of a few established local companies who are interested only in commercial films. There's no place within these firms for new, experimental or "risky" work. And a movie with a political theme is an anathema. Jamie Uys, when promoting *The Gods Must be Crazy II* on local TV, said he would not make political films as there was no audience demand for them.

Subsidy Abuse

The subsidy system is open to abuse. For example, the local distributors Ster-Kinekor and Nu-Metro are themselves involved in film production. There is no law to prevent them from crippling a picture from other producers by rejecting their films outright or giving them a limited release in a small cinema. Before subsidy is paid, the films have to be seen by a minimum number of local viewers. Scripts also had to be submitted in advance, as the subsidy would not pay out on any film "likely to be banned," meaning, of course, political films that criticised the government.

Talks have been held between filmmakers and government representatives, but no agreement has been reached, leaving very few films in production and numerous technicians unemployed. There is also dissatisfaction with the Task Force the government has set up to investigate local films and the subsidy system. The Force was not elected by members of the film industry and is, therefore, not a representative body. A local TV programme was made attacking the industry and the local subsidy system, but this was never shown as the South African Broadcasting Corporation (SABC) suppressed it as "lacking quality." Sources within the industry feel, however, that the documentary was deliberately stifled because of the criticism it leveled against the subsidy system and the Task Force. The SABC is represented on the Force.

However, it is possible to by-pass governmental financing systems. The progressive group, Free Filmmakers, found financing for an anti-apartheid television series on the magazine "Drum" overseas when the British production company Chrysalis bought the option on the script written by Michele Rowe and Roger Smith. Free Filmmakers are also developing a local soap-opera set in Soweto and a political exile who returns to South Africa – a project made possible by equipment received from Sweden.

Socio-political Themes

Local Films with socio-political themes received an important input in the late 1980's with Darrell Roodt's **Jobman** and **The Stick**, dealing with racism and the border war in Angola; Francis Gerard's **A Private Life** based on a true story of the marriage between a white policeman and a so-called "coloured" woman; David Wicht's **Windprints** about the rent boycotts in black townships; Manie van Rensburg's **The Native Who Caused All the Trouble**, a satire on the Land Act that prevents blacks from owning land; and John Smallcombe's **An African Dream**, a neo-colonial film about relations across the so-called race barrier.

TOP GROSSING FILMS IN SOUTH AFRICA: 1989

The Gods Must Be Crazy II
A Fish Called Wanda
Skin Deep
Licence To Kill
Rain Man
Mississippi Burning
Dirty Rotten Scoundrels
Cocktail
My Stepmother Is an Alien
Working Girl

Mapantsula and *The Stick* were banned, but granted special showings at local festivals. The ban has been lifted on the films, and they are due for release by mainstream distributors. *Native, Life* and *Dream* have been seen locally, but the distributors, Ster-Kinekor, rejected *Jobman* outright, claiming the film as being more suitable for festivals. The film, however, has become highly popular on the alternative circuit (festivals etc.) and would no doubt also be a commercial hit.

Jobman has suffered an unlucky history. As part of the Weekly Mail Film Festival, "Cinema Under Siege," organised by the progressive newspaper, the film was condemned by the equally progressive, leftwing organisation, Film and Allied Workers (FAWO), as "racist." This decision was quickly rescinded.

In spite of this slip, FAWO has an important role to play in stimulating production by local, independent and anti-apartheid film- makers. They also promote film-making in the "black" townships. Their role will no doubt become even more central now that, under President F.W de Klerk, the ANC, PAC and other political organisations have been recognised.

Progressive documentaries, promoted by FAWO, exploring the political situation in this country, form a lively, but little seen, local industry. This aspect of the industry, including trade union and community videos, has suffered under censorship. The police, for example, confiscated Kevin Harris's documentary **Namibia: No Easy Road to Freedom** from his editing table.

Stricter Censorship Forecast

Censorship remains a problem. Although the country has seen radical change under President de Klerk, the entire state machinery of censorship remains almost intact. In fact, recent developments suggest that censorship will become stricter. With Professor Kobus van Rooyen as head of the Appeal Board, censorship saw a period of comparative leniency. After he released Richard Attenborough's film on Steve Biko, *Cry Freedom*, his house was burned down. The film was also seized by the police. Under the new political dispensation, the film was re-released without any problems and had a lukewarm reception at the box-office, partly because the Mass Democratic Movement was negative about the film, seeing it as a Hollywood bastardisation of an important "black" figure, and as placing a misleading emphasis on the role of Donald Woods. All cinemas in South Africa, it should also be noted, are now multi-racial.

Professor van Rooyen has retired, although reliable sources suggest he was ousted. His successor would have been Piet Oosthuizen, vice-chancellor of the University of Pretoria and one of the architects of the infamous Terrorism Act, but he was dropped after an outcry in the local newspapers. Louis Pienaar, ex-Administrator General of Namibia, was appointed Head of the Appeal Board. Current indications are that political material will no longer be banned, but that sex and violence will again come under strict control. *The Punisher*, for example, has been banned as violent. Films like *A Dry White Season* and *A World Apart* are

Johan Blignaut, prominent director–producer, talks to well-known South African poet Adam Small

unbanned but, at the time of writing, not distributed.

It is difficult to predict future developments in the industry. Progressive film-makers are managing, to an extent, to break the mainstream, establishment stranglehold on local film. At present, the future lies with the progressives rather than the commercial industry that has been weakened and made irrelevant by the subsidy system.

Recent and Forthcoming Films

A Private Life. Script: Andrew Davies. Dir: Francis Gerard. Players: Bill Flynn, Jana Cilliers, Ian Roberts, Kevin Smith. Prod: Totem Productions.
AWOL (The Quarry). Script: Neil Sonnekus, Roy McGregor. Dir: Neil Sonnekus. Players: Danny Keogh, Joanna Weinberg, Ramaloa Makhena. Prod: Everis Films.
An African Dream. Script: John Smallcombe, Nodi Murphy. Dir: John Smallcombe. Players: Kitty Aldridge, John Kani, Dominic Jephcott, Richard Haines. Prod: Jonoma Film Productions.
Brutal Glory. Script: Tinus Grobler. Dir: Koos Roets. Players: Robert Vaughn, Leah King Pinsent, Timothy Brantley, James Ryan. Prod: Phil Pieterse Productions.
Circles in a Forest. Script: Fabrice Ziolkowski, Lulu Barzman. Dir: Regardt van den Bergh. Players: Christo Niehaus, Arnold Vosloo, Joe Stewardson. Prod: Philo Pieterse Productions.
Fjela's Child (International version). Script: Chris Barnard. Dir: Katinka Heyns. Players: Shaleen Surtie-Richards, Andre Rossouw, Lida Botha, David Minnaar. Prod: Starcorp International Pictures, Starnet, Toron, Sonneblom Films.
Final Cut. Script: Emil Kolbe. Dir: Frans Nel. Players: John Barrett, Elizabeth Meyer, Matthew Stewardson. Prod: The Image Factory.
Have You Seen Drum Recently? Dir: Jurgen Schadeberg. Prod: Baily's African Photo Archives.
Hellgate. Script: Michael O'Rourke. Dir: William A. Levey. Players: Ron Palillo, Abigail Wolcott, Carel Trichardt. Prod: Ghost Town Film Management, Distant Horizon and Anant Singh.
Hold My Hand I'm Dying. Script: Mark Ezra. Dir: Terence Ryan. Players: Christopher Cazanove, Edita Brychta, Patrick Shai, Henry Cele, Oliver Reed. Prod: Burlington Enterprises.
Impact. Script: Jeno Hodi, Al Cheli, Juan Shambul Alam. Dir: Frans Nel. Players: Janine Denison, Tony Caprari, Wilson Dunster.
Jobman. Script: Darrell Roodt, Greg Latter. Dir: Darrell Roodt. Players: Kevin Smith, Tertius Meintjies, Lynn Gaines, Marcel van Heerden. Prod: Blue Rock Films.
Killer Instinct. Dir: David Lister. Players: David Dukes, Susan Anspach, Dustin Montgomery. Prod: Marton BV.
Let the Music Be. Script: Emil Kolbe. Dir: Frans Nel. Players: Ginger Lynn Allen, John Barrett, Michael Huff. Prod: Promotion Films.
Long Journey of Poppie Nongena. Dir: Koos Roets. Players: Nomsa Nene, Peter Sepuma. Prod: Movieworld.
Mapantsula. Script: Thomas Mogotlane. Dir: Oliver Schmitz. Players: Thomas Mogotlane, Gabriel Dichabe, Thembi Mtshali, Dolly Rathebe. Prod: Haverbeam Productions.
Operation Weissdorn-The Fourth Reich. Dir: Manie van Rensburg. Players: Marius Weyers, Grethe Fox, Ryno Hattingh, Elize Cawood, Louis van Niekerk, Ian Roberts. Prod: Zastron Films.
Panga. Script: John Hunt. Dir: Sean Barton. Players: Christopher Lee, Jenilee Harrison, Henry Cele, Andre Jacobs. Prod: Blue Rock Films.
Paradise Road. Script: Jan Scholtz. Dir: Jan Scholtz. Players: Jeff Weston, Susan Danford, Andre Jacobs, Greg Latter. Prod: Overseas Film Communication Ltd.
Reason to Die. Script: Aubrey Rettan. Dir: Tim Spring. Players: Wings Hauser, Arnold Vosloo, Anneline Kriel. Prod: SCY Productions.
Rhino. Script: George Canes, Heather Capon. Dir: Ronnie Isaacs. Players: Deon Stewardson, Maurice Mtshali, Lee van Zyl, Zamokhule Ndamane. Prod: Kevron Entertainment.
River of Diamonds. Script: Hans Kuhle, Ian Yule, Dir: Robert J. Smawley. Players: Dack Rambo, Angela O'Neill, Ferdinand Mayne. Prod: Karat Film International.
Run to Freedom. Script: Thomas Witt, Fred Lange. Dir: Laurens Bernard. Players: Bill Boy Dalada, Thomas Witt, Thys du Plooy, Phillip

Notununu, Matthew Monika. Prod: Focus Film Productions.
Schweitzer. Script: Michael Potts. Dir: Gray Hofmeyr. Players: Malcolm McDowell, Susan Strasberg, Andrew Davis, Patrick Shai, Henry Cele. Prod: Amritraj International.
Shotdown. Script: Rick Shaw. Dir: Andrew Worsdale. Players: Robert Colman, Megan Kruskal, Maruso Tshabalala. Prod: Jeremy Nathan.
Sweet Murder. Script: Percival Rubens. Players: Helene Udy, Russell Todd, Embeth Davidtz, Danny Keogh. Prod: Movieworld.
That Englishwoman. Script: Roy L. Allen, Paul C. Venter, Trix Pienaar. Dir: Dirk de Villiers. Players: Veronica Lang, Terence Alexander, Harvey Ashby, Jenny Runacre. Prod: C. Films.
The Endangered. Dir: Mark Engels. Players: Dominic Lee, Bernard Schiller, Tsepho Mathanda. Prod: HMC Productions.
The Gods Must Be Crazy II. Script: Jamie Uys. Dir: Jamie Uys. Players: Nixau, Lena Farugia, Hans Strydom, Eiros, Nadies. Prod: Elrina Investment Corporation.
The Great Pretender. Script: Hans Webb. Dir: Hans Webb. Players: Helen Sebedi, Joe Mynhardt, Boke Nxumalo, Matthew Oates. Prod: Videovision.
The Last Warrior. Script: Martin Wragge. Dir: Martin Wragge. Players: Gary Graham, Maria Holvoë, Cary-Hiroyuki Tagawa. Prod: ITC Entertainment Group.
The Native Who Caused All the Trouble. Play written by Danny Keogh, Vanessa Cooke, Nicholas Haysom. Dir: Manie van Rensburg. Players: John Kani, Vanessa Cooke, Graham Hopkins, Kurt Egelhof, Frantz Dobrowsky, Eric Nobs. Prod: The Film Theatre Institute.
The Sandgrass People. Script: Gerry O'Hara. Dir: Koos Roets. Players: Lena Farugia, Jamie Bartlett. Prod: Philo Pieterse Productions.
The Stick. Script: Darrell Roodt, Carole Shaw. Dir: Darrell Roodt. Players: Sean Taylor, Frantz Dobrowsky, James Whyle, Gys de Villiers, Greg Latter. Prod: Distant Horizon, Artistic Film Production Co.
Tyger Tyger Burning Bright. Script: Corrado J. Boccia. Dir: Neil Sundström. Players: Kitty Aldridge, Michael McCabe, Lynne White. Prod: Kevron Entertainment.
Voice in the Dark. Script: Rod Willis. Dir: Vincent Cox. Players: John Savage, Lucky Dube, Ken Gampu. Prod: Unital.
Windprints. Script: David Wicht. Dir: David Wicht. Players: John Hurt, Sean Bean, Marius Weyers, Eric Nobs, Lesley Fong. Prod: Film Afrika.

South African Film Awards 1989 (AA Life/ M-Net)

Best Film: *Mapantsula*.
Best Performance by a Lead Actor: Thomas Mogotlane (*Mapantsula*).
Best Performance by a Lead Actress: Jana Cilliers (*A Private Life*).
Best Performance in a Supporting Role (male): Graham Hopkins (*The Native Who Caused All the Trouble*) and Tertius Meintjies (*Jobman*).
Best Performance in a Supporting Role (female): Josephine Liedman (*Jobman*) and Dolly Rathebe (*Mapantsula*).
Best Direction: Darrell Roodt (*Jobman*) and Oliver Schmitz (*Mapantsula*).
Best Script: Thomas Mogotlane, Oliver Schmitz (*Mapantsula*).
Best Original Music Score: The Ouens (*Mapantsula*).
Best Sound: Alan Gerhardt, Darryl Martin, Nicky de Beer (*Mapantsula*).
Best Art Direction: Mark Wilby (*A Private Life*).
Best Editing: David Heitner (*The Stick*).
Best Cinematography: Paul Witte (*Jobman*).

MARTIN BOTHA is a film and television researcher. He has written more than 50 publications on film, television, radio and newspapers in South Africa. He has a special interest in Third Cinema.
WILLIAM PRETORIUS is a veteran film critic. He has served on the panels for the South African film awards (the "Rapport Oscars" and "AA Vita Film Awards") since the 1970's and has written numerous essays on South African cinema.

CINE ESPAÑOL PARA EL MUNDO
SPANISH CINEMA FOR THE WORLD

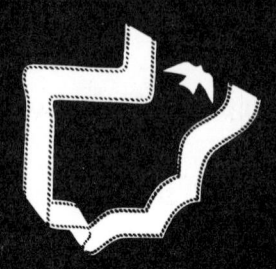

The SPANISH FILM INSTITUTE

MINISTERIO DE CULTURA
Instituto de Cine (ICAA)

is proud to have helped promote films from Spain at leading international film festivals throughout 1989

Among competing films were:

BERLIN	"Atame" (Tie Me Up, Tie Me Down) by Pedro Almodóvar.
CANNES	"Pont De Varsovia" (Warsaw Bridge) by Pere Portabella. "Innisfree" by José Luis Guerín
KARLOVY VARY	"Pont De Varsovia" (Warsaw Bridge) by Pere Portabella "Atame" (Tie Me Up, Tie Me Down) by Pedro Almodóvar
MONTREAL	"Ay, Carmela" by Carlos Saura "Don Juan, Mi Querido Fantasma" (Don Juan, My Dear Ghost) by Antonio Mercero "Sandino" by Miguel Littín "Pont De Varsovia" by Pere Portabella "Siempe Xonxa" by Chano Piñeiro
VENICE	"Boom Boom" by Rosa Vergés
SAN SEBASTIAN	"Las Cartas de Alou" (Letters From Alou) by Montxo Armendáriz "Contra El Viento" (Against The Wind) by Francisco Periñán

SPAIN

by Peter Besas

The advent of three new private TV networks in Spain has taken a heavy toll on the already ailing Spanish film industry. Due to the stepped-up competition, the State-run network, Radiotelevisión Española, has siphoned off talent, including actors and directors.

Top producers such as Emiliano Piedra, Elías Querejeta and directors like Mario Camus, Manuel Gutiérrez Aragón, José Luis Garci, Víctor Erice, Antonio Mercero and many others have been enticed to the safer and economically more lucrative TV medium.

Spanish feature production in 1989 was down to 47 and the 1990 crop is not expected to be greater. This despite a more conciliatory attitude from the Culture Ministry, substantial new subsidies to producers, and a pact with Spanish Television for the national web to help in the financing of Spanish features.

While the general box-office scene in Spain improved in 1989, with attendance finally up after over 25 years of decline, the share culled by Spanish films fell to an all-time low of only 7.60%.

With a few exceptions, Spanish films failed to attract local audiences, who preferred to see Anglo-American pictures. Nonetheless, some producers, realising that Spanish films must prove more entertaining in order to win back local audiences, came up with various films of both commercial and artistic clout.

The much-awaited new film by Pedro Almodóvar, **Tie Me Up! Tie Me Down!** (*Atame*) pulled in big crowds, but less than its predecessor, *Women on the Verge of a Nervous Breakdown*. The film nonetheless reaffirmed Almodóvar's talent and inventiveness.

Also popular was **Fond Things** (*Las Cosas Del Querer*), directed by Jaime Chávarri, a tale set in the postwar era, which relied heavily upon its catchy musical numbers. Similarly availing himself of a strong dose of oldtime song was Carlos Saura, who, after many years of sagging fortunes, came up with **Ay, Carmela!** Reverting to the period closest to his heart (the Civil War and the Franco era), Saura co-scripted with veteran writer Rafael Azcona a story about a group of three actors who, after entertaining Republican troops, unwittingly wander into a Nationalist camp and after almost being shot, are recruited to put on a musical show for the fascist troops.

Saura deftly handles both the comical and tragic situations in the story, which is gingerly paced and buoyantly played by Carmen Maura, stand-up comic Andrés Pajares and a new talent, Gabino Diego. All the former vigour of Saura's direction is back, and despite the downbeat ending, the film proved a critical success and a crowd-pleaser as well.

Another notable film in 1990 was Fernando Trueba's **The Mad Monkey** (*El Sueño del mono loco*), shot in English, with American actor Jeff Goldblum playing the lead. This quirky film falls somewhere between the "commercial" and "art" categories, but was offbeat enough for it to catch the eye of Spanish audiences. It also swept the yearly "Goya" awards, the Spanish counterpart of the Oscars, which are presented by the Spanish Academy in

IBEROAMERICANA FILMS

IBEROAMERICANA FILMS • Velázquez, 12 - 28001 Madrid. SPAIN • Tels.: (91) 431 42 46 - 431 42 73 • Telex: 45753 CINE E • Fax: 435 59 94

THE BEST OF SPANISH CINEMA :

ALMODOVAR
 BARDEM
  BIGAS LUNA
   BUÑUEL
    CHAVARRI
     COLOMO
      FERNAN GOMEZ
       GARCIA BERLANGA
        SAURA
         SUAREZ
          TRUEBA

... and many others in our 300 hundred-title catalogue!

Andrès Pajares and Carmen Maura in Carlos Saura's *Ay, Carmela!*, released through Iberoamericana Films

New Directors Disappoint

There were numerous attempts by new film-makers, mostly using shoestring budgets, to garner success, but most did not succeed in arousing much enthusiasm. Among the more interesting efforts were Antonio Ezeiza's **Days of Smoke** (*Días de humo*) which touched upon the Basque terrorist problem; Vicente Aranda's **If They Tell You I Fell** (*Si te dicen que caí*), a film whose complexity and involved plot put off many viewers; and **Tarantos y Montoyas**, a remake of *Los Tarantos* by Vicente Escrivá, telling a kind of Romeo and Juliet story with a flamenco background.

Catalans Bid for Attention

In Barcelona, the Catalans came up with several films which were selected for film festivals. Pere Portabella, one of the founders of the Barcelona School in the 1960's reappeared with **Warsaw Bridge** (*Pont de Varsovie*), a difficult film to follow which unfolded a collage of personal impressions. The production was selected for both the Cannes and Karlovy Vary festivals. Another Catalan film that made a bid for attention was an idiosyncratic documentary, **Innisfree**, shot in Ireland in English. Directed by José Luis Guerín, it offered the director's impressions of the village where *The Quiet Man* was shot.

At mid-1990, a number of new projects were shaping up. Probably the most controversial will be Bigas Luna's **The Ages of Lulu** (*Las edades de Lulú*), the lead part for which was turned down by various actresses, including Angela Molina, due to the sex scenes required.

Also expected to be an eye-catcher is **Alone, Or In the Company of Others** (*Sólo o en compañía de otros*) based on the

El Deseo S.A. Presents:

3 from ALMODOVAR

La Ley del DESEO
(Law of desire)

MUJERES al borde de un ataque de NERVIOS
(Women on the verge of a nervous breakdown)

ATAME!
(Tie me up / Tie me down)

Contact in Spain:
Agustín Almodóvar   Enrique Posner
El Deseo, S.A.   Ruiz Perelló, 15 - 1.º D   28028 Madrid - España
Tel.: (1) 355 83 71   Fax: (1) 355 74 67   Télex: 22034 - coim e

Antonio Banderas and Victoria Abril in Almodóvar's *Tie Me Up! Tie Me Down!*, an El Deseo production

much-publicised assassination of the Marqueses of Urquijo. The film is directed by Santiago de San Miguel, and is produced by Multivideo, who also did *El Lute, The Almeria Case* and other topical films.

In the fall of 1990, Spain's wiz kid Pedro Almodóvar is expected to roll a new film, the title of which was still undetermined at press time. Also on the roster is a new effort by Josefina Molina called **The Most Natural Thing** (*Lo más natural*). Molina made the successful historical film *Esquilache* in 1989.

Scheduled to shoot a new film, **The Letters of Alou**, is Basque director Montxo Armendáriz, which will be produced by Elías Querejeta. Armendáriz earlier made *Tasio*, much commented upon both in and out of Spain. Other projects are being prepared by directors such as José Luis Cuerda, José Luis Garcia Sánchez, Antonio Giménez Rico and Fernando Fernán Gómez, as well as a new group of yet-unknown tyro film-makers.

On the more commercial side, producer Emiliano Piedra was preparing **A Fallen Angel** to be directed by Roberto Bodegas, with an international cast. Producer-director Juan Piquer was planning a new film based on a Lovecraft story, following his two earlier films, **The Rift** and **Slugs**.

Spanish film-makers are now clearly trying to cover a wide range of subjects. Although such local problems as the Basque separatist question and the Franco era (one project is called *The Year Franco Died*) are still drawn upon for source material, many directors and writers are trying to range farther afield from "typical" Spanish subjects and social realism. It is surely significant that the most successful Spanish director, Almodóvar, shuns historical and political subjects and prefers to treat up-to-date subjects that are meaningful to modern

CATALAN FILMS &TV

CATALONIA is a country of six million inhabitants. Our film production consists of an average of 15-20 feature films per year. In its production Barcelona has technical film and video infrastructure of
- film studios and video editing
- processing laboratories
- sound, dubbing and subtitling laboratories

In the video sectors the production, design and technical services companies have an advanced technology which covers all video-engineering possibilities from HB production to video-animation, etc.

There are two important film events held in Catalonia:
- THE SITGES INTERNATIONAL FANTASY FILM FESTIVAL which is held in October.
- THE BARCELONA FILM FESTIVAL (FILMS & DIRECTORS), which is held in November.

If you need any more information about our cinema, our video production, production companies and our professionals get in touch with the CATALAN FILMS booth at the following markets: Berlin Filmesse, MIP-TV, Cannes Film Market. MIPCOM and MIFED, or write to our head office in Barcelona.

HEAD OFFICE
Diputació, 279-283
08007 Barcelona
Ph: (3) 317 35 85
Tx: 53916 TRPW E (ATT. GENERALITAT/CODE 836)
Fax: (3) 301 22 47

USEFUL ADDRESSES
SITGES INTERNATIONAL FANTASY FILM FESTIVAL
Diputació, 279-283
08007 BARCELONA
Ph: (3) 317 35 85
Fax: (3) 301 22 47

BARCELONA FILM FESTIVAL
Films & Directors
Lluria, 67
08009 BARCELONA
Ph: (3) 487 15 41
Fax: (3) 487 02 64

AGRUPACIÓ CATALANA DE PRODUCTORS CINEMATOGRÀFICS
Floridablanca, 135
08011 BARCELONA
Ph: (3) 423 24 55
Fax: (3) 423 06 22

ASSOCIACIÓ CATALANA DE CRÍTICS I ESCRIPTORS DE CINEMA
Valencia, 248
08007 BARCELONA
Ph: (3) 215 94 79

ANDICCA (ASSOCIACIÓ NACIONAL DE DISTRIBUIDORS CINEMATOGRÀFICS DE CATALUNYA)
Rambla de Catalunya, 47 1°.
08007 BARCELONA
Ph: (3) 301 57 40

ASSOCIACIÓ PROFESSIONAL DE DIRECTORS DE CINEMA DE CATALUNYA
Mestre Nicolau, 19
08021 BARCELONA
Ph: (3) 201 30 22

TV3 TELEVISIÓ DE CATALUNYA
Jacint Verdaguer s/n.
08970 SANT JOAN DESPÍ (Barcelona)
Ph: (3) 473 03 33
Tx: 97990 TVCT E
Fax: (3) 473 15 63

Generalitat de Catalunya
Departament de Cultura

audiences. Film-makers dwelling upon intimist films generally fare poorly at the box-office. However, the continued power of the Civil War as a subject was shown by the success of Saura's *Ay, Carmela*, although the musical numbers and comic asides in the film certainly contributed to making it a his.

A good local comedy can still bring in audiences as well, as was the case with *Aquí huele a muerto* and to a lesser extent *Disparate Nacional*. Both, however, were pooh-poohed by local critics as being commercial film-fodder.

A number of recent "discoveries," such as directors Agustín Villaronga (*Moonchild*) and Rafael Moleón (*Baton Rouge*) are busy writing screenplays, and new efforts can be expected from them over the coming year.

With more backing promised from the Spanish Culture Ministry, a new crop of striking films can be expected to appear in the future.

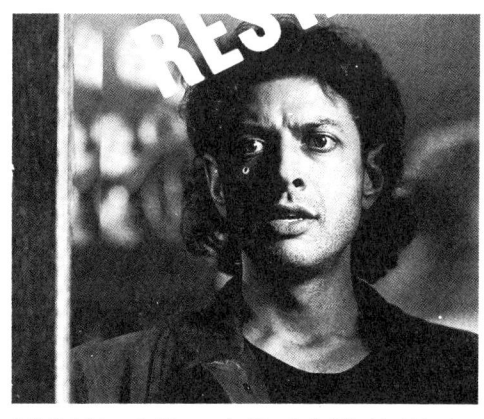

Jeff Goldblum in Fernando Trueba's *The Mad Monkey*, produced by Iberoamericana Films

PETER BESAS has lived in Madrid since the mid-1960's and is chief of Variety's bureau there. He has written various books, including a history of Spanish cinema.

Producers

Iberoamericana Films
Velázquez 12
Madrid 28001
Tel: 4314246

José Frade P.C.
Gran Via 70
Madrid 28013
Tel: 2487144

El Deseo S.A.
Ruiz Perelló 15
Madrid 28028
Tel: 2550285

Multivideo S.A.
Luna 15
Madrid 28004
Tel: 5229347

Luis Megino P.C.
Castellana 114
Madrid 28016
Tel: 2615077

Jet Films
Manuel Montilla 1
Madrid 28016
Tel: 2506200

Elías Querejeta
Maestro Lasalle 21
28006 Madrid
Tel: 2592322

Lauren Films
Balmes 73
Barcelona 08007
Tel: 3235400

Emiliano Piedra P.C.
San Bernardo 38
Madrid 28008
Tel: 5317884

Opalo Films
Consell de Cent 303
Barcelona 08007
Tel: 2549506

Dister Films
Caídos de la División
Azul 22–B
Madrid 28016
Tel: 2503900

Distributors

United International Pictures
Plaza del Callao 4
Madrid 28013
Tel: 5227261

Warner Bros/Columbia
Manuel Montilla 1
Madrid 28016
Tel: 2506200

Lauren Films
Balmes 73
Barcelona 08007
(*In Madrid*: Tetuán 29

Madrid 28013)
Tel: 3235400 (Barcelona)
5218285 (Madrid)

Araba Films
San Prudencio 13
Vitoria 01005
Tel: 140126

C.B. Films
Diagonal 407
Barcelona 08008
Tel: 2179354

Izaro Films
Raimundo Fernández
Villaverde 65
Madrid
Tel: 4558041

Iberoamericana Films
Velázquez 12
Madrid 28001
Tel: 4314246

Musidora Films
Princesa 5
Madrid 28008
Tel: 2487233

Manuel Salvador/20th Century-Fox
Callao 4
Madrid 28013
Tel: 5329320

Prime Films
Clara del Rey 17
Madrid 28002
Tel: 5190181

Alta Films
Martin de los Heros 12
Madrid 28008
Tel: 5422702

Alas Films
Maestro Guerrero 2
Madrid 28008
Tel: 2476585

Ivex Films
Pasco San Gervasio 16
Barcelona 08022
Tel: 4184858

Golem Distribution S.A.
Avda. de Bayona 52
Pamplona 31008
Tel: (948) 260243

Surf Films
Zurbano 74
Madrid 28010
Tel: 4422944

Useful Addresses

Spanish Culture Ministry (Film Institute)
San Marcos 40
Madrid 28004
Tel: 532–5089

Unión de Productores de Cine y TV (Film & TV Producers Union)
Caños de Peral 2
Madrid 28013
Tel: 2470086

Fedicine (Distributors' Association)
Velázquez 10
Madrid 28001
Tel: 2769511

Federación de Exhibidores (Exhibitors' Association)
Velázquez 10
Madrid 28001
Tel: 2762774

Servei de Cine Catalan
Diputación 279
Barcelona 08007
Tel: 3173585

Basque Film Producers Association
Reina Regente
San Sebastian 20003
Tel: 422944

Quinto Centenario
Avda. Reyes Católicos 4
Madrid 28040
Tel: 5931992

Academia de las Artes y las Ciencas Cinematograficas de España
General Oraa 68
Madrid 28006
Tel: 5633341

SRI LANKA
by Amarnath Jayatilaka

The year 1990 dawned with the ending of violence that engulfed the country for the last many years. Last year was the worst affected by the terrorist activities. It was also the most tragic year for the national cinema due to the acute and near anarchic situation created by terrorism. Frequent curfews and other disruptions severely harmed the exhibition sector.

At the height of the terrorist activities, around August 1989, Mr. K. Gunaratnam, Head of Cinemas Ltd., was gunned down by unknown assailants. He was one of the leading pioneers of the Sinhala cinema who had produced more than 25 films and owned a film studio and a chain of movie theatres. His company was one of the three giants of the film industry prior to the setting up of the State Film Corporation in 1972 which took over the import and distribution of films within the country.

All-time Low Output

Only 11 Sinhala films were released in the year 1989, the lowest recorded in the last decade. Among them two films were big box-office hits, others had average runs. Anoja Weerasinghe, who won the Best Actress award in the International Film Festival of India in 1987, starred in six of these films which belong to the popular mainstream cinema. She is one of the leading movie stars of the Sinhala cinema and was the first Sri Lankan actress to get a big break in an English movie when she was cast as one of the three leading female artistes in Paul Cox's film, *Island*. She is now pursuing an advanced course in Acting at the Academy of Music and Drama in London.

Over the past year no major American movie was released in Sri Lanka owing to a stalemate created by the National Film Corporation (NFC) with the companies that import and exhibit MPEAA movies in this country. According to the exhibitor group the dispute arose due to the NFC insisting on a higher percentage from the collections, which was not acceptable to the companies.

As the new hierarchy at the NFC does not have any experienced, able or knowledgeable people in the varied area of the film trade, they have not yet been able to lift the Film Corporation out of the financial doldrums into which it was put by the previous administration headed by Anton Wickremasinghe. Neither were they able to formulate and implement new plans of action to develop the national cinema. According to a series of questions raised by an opposition member in Parliament, it was revealed that the acts perpetrated by the former Head of the NFC had the deliberate intention of destroying the growth and development of a national cinema. In the absence of any programme to resuscitate the NFC and to help promote the production of artistically good movies, it is left to the creative film-maker himself to search for financial backing which is now a scarce resource within the present context of the film trade in this country.

With the withdrawal of the Indian Armed Forces from the North Eastern part of the country and the peace initiatives forged with the most powerful militant group there, the country has begun to enjoy normal peace and stability once again. Within this encouraging background a new company named Eastern Moonlight Movies has been

Geetha Kumarasinghe, a top star in Sri Lanka, in *Under the Bridge*, produced by herself and directed by H.D. Premaratna

established to go into the production of English- language movies based on subjects specially written to suit the fantastic locations of this beautiful land, which is famous for its unique low-cost facilities. The company has imported the latest equipment and has negotiated with few leading Hollywood production/distribution companies to launch several American film projects in the latter part of this year.

Profile: D.B. Nihalsingha

One of the "Ten Best Film Directors" voted by the film critics in Sri Lanka. He was honoured this year by several important film and cultural organisations for his contribution to cinema during the last 25 years. He started as an experimental film-maker in his student days; he won a Commonwealth Film Award held in Cardiff 25 years ago. He was later to be appointed as the Director of the Govt. Film Unit in Sri Lanka where he pioneered a New Image for the weekly Newsreel and for documentary film- making. He was the first General Manager and the Chief Executive of the State Film Corporation set up in 1972. During his five-year administration Sinhala cinema developed into a very viable enterprise and the groundwork was laid for its creative and artistic development. After the introduction of TV into the country, Nihalsingha started his own outfit, Telecine Ltd., and became the most powerful force in video production in the country. Filmography: *Welikatara* (1971), *Ridi Nimnaya* (1978), *Maldeniye Simion* (1986), *Keli Mandala* (1990).

Useful Addresses

Eastern Moonlight Movies
16/3, Rotunda Gardens
Colombo – 3
Tel: 695088
Telex: 22676 SHIPCO–CE
Fax: 574871–C/o.SMA

Filmvision
(*Production Consultants*)
165/2, Castle Street
Borella
Colombo 8
Tel: 695040

SWEDEN

by Peter Cowie

The past year might well have been regarded as the most depressing of recent times for the Swedish film, had it not been for the welcome success of Suzanne Osten's **The Guardian Angel** (*Skyddsängeln*) at the Cannes Festival in May 1990.

If one subtracts from the list of Swedish productions those being directed by non-Swedes, there is precious little remaining to excite the interest even of art houses abroad.

Ten years ago in these columns, I wrote that Swedish cinema was "passing through the valley of the Shadow." It may have emerged into the sunlight for brief intervals since then, but all too few new talents have grown to world stature. Suzanne Osten is established, Carl-Gustaf Nykvist made an exciting debut, and Agneta Elers-Järleman may be a name to conjure with.

Suzanne Osten's *The Guardian Angel* won selection for the Directors' Fortnight in Cannes and impressed everyone with its adroit blend of suspense and period detail. One of the strengths of Osten's work is her use of a regular troupe of colleagues, including Etienne Glaser and Malin Ek.

Per Åhlin's **Voyage to Melonia**, after years in gestation, finally appeared in September 1989, and was given a non-competing slot at the Berlinale two months later. This inventive animated feature is based literally on Shakespeare's *The Tempest*.

In the rites-of-passage stakes, **The Hero** harks back to the 1960's and the teenage experiences of its director, Agneta Fagerström-Olsson (played on screen by Lena Carlsson). Unusually, the setting is upper-class, which makes the rebellious mood of the decade seem even more threatening.

Two aspects of film life in Sweden hold promise for the future, however. One is the sustained technical quality of the country's films. Ulf Brantås, Sten Holmberg, Göran Nilsson, Jens Fischer, Peter Fischer, and Per Källberg have continued the exciting tradition of Swedish cinematography, investing their films with subtleties of light and shade, crispness and clarity, worthy of Julius Jaenzon and Sven Nykvist.

The other positive factor concerns attendances. The number of tickets sold at the Swedish box-office rose by 10% over 1988 (19,205,236 compared with 17,502,596), while that less reliable

Lena Carlsson in *The Hero*

The Swedish Film Institute

occupies a central position in Swedish film life

supporting
producing
selling
buying
distributing
exhibiting
collecting
preserving
publishing
informing

We also have our own studios, sound department and access to a full service laboratory for film.

Whatever your needs, get in touch with us.

Swedish Film Institute
P.O. Box 27126, S-102 52 Stockholm, Sweden.
Phone Int.: +46 8-665 11 00,
Telex: 13326 FILMINS S,
Telefax: 08-661 18 20

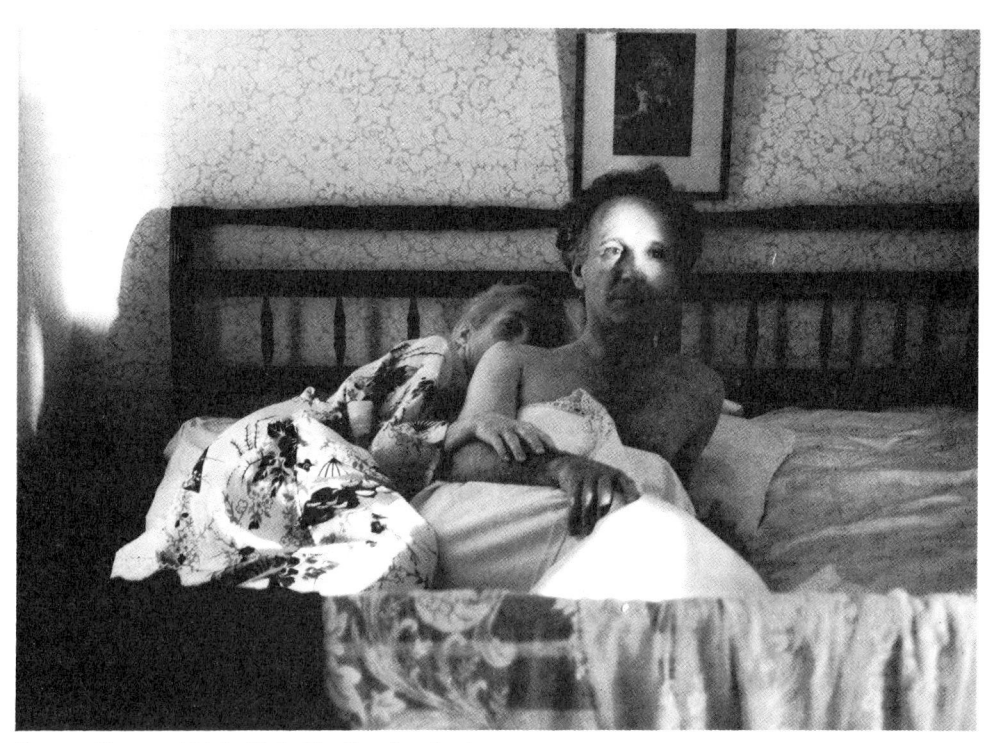

Etienne Glaser and Malin Ek in *The Guardian Angel*

barometer, gross receipts, increased by a formidable 23%. Although the first half of 1990 showed a decline, these are statistics that France, Germany, and Italy must regard with envy.

The Nordic Links

It would be unfair to brand the Swedish Film Institute for any shortcomings in the domestic film industry. Thanks to Klas Olofsson and his successor as Managing Director, Ingrid Edström, the Institute has wholeheartedly backed the "Nordification" process whereby each of the five Nordic countries seeks to collaborate with one or more of the others to produce quality films.

The appointment of Bengt Forslund as head of the Nordic Film and TV Fund should be saluted also. Forslund's own creative background as a screenwriter, allied to his experience as a producer at Svensk Filmindustri and the Film Institute, should serve as a guarantee of intelligent funding. A sum of approximately $7.5 million will be available to the Fund, which will help to promote Nordic film in the widest sense and capacity. Its primary remit is to encourage co-productions between Nordic countries.

Sweden has long believed in the principle of inter-Scandinavian co-operation, and Swedish investment may be found in several of the best Nordic films of recent years: *Hip Hip Hurrah, Katinka, Pelle the Conqueror, Leningrad Cowboys Go America...* This year, the Swedish Film Institute has put money into Anja Breien's new Norwegian comedy, *Twice upon a Time*, Martin Asphaug's impressive Norwegian drama, *A Handful of Time*, and the Finnish master Rauni Mollberg's epic of wartime greed, *Friends, Comrades*.

Recent and Forthcoming Films

Angel (Angel). Script and Dir: Stig Larsson. Phot: Gunnar Källström, Lennart Peters, Lil Trulsson. Players: Kim Kuusisto, Leif Andrée, Stig Larsson, Sissela Kyle. Prod: Golden Films/Omega Film/Swedish Film Institute.
Jönssonligan på Mallorca (The Jönsson Gang on Majorca). Script: Rolf Börjlind, Gösta Ekman, Mikael Ekman. Dir: Mikael Ekman. Phot: Dan Myhrman. Players: Gösta Ekman, Ulf Brunnberg, Björn Gustafson, Birgitta Andersson. Prod: Cinema Art/Svensk Filmindustri.
Brev till paradiset (Letter to Paradise). Script and Dir: Mikael Wiström. Phot: Peter Östlund. Players: Maud Nycander, Håkan Welff, Peter Torbjörnsson, Margareta Wase. Prod: FilmStallet/ Swedish Film Institute/Swedish TV1/Månharen.
Hajen som visste för mycket (The Shark Who Knew Too Much). Script: Dan Myhrman. Players: Anders Eriksson, Claes Eriksson, Kerstin Granlund, Per Fritzell. Prod: Svensk Filmindustri/Kulturtuben/Filmhuset.
S/Y Glädjen (S/Y Joy). Script: Göran du Rées, Inger Alfvén (from the latter's novel). Dir: Göran du Rées. Phot: Henrik Paersch. Players: Lena Olin, Stellan Skarsgård, Viveka Seldahl, Hans Mosesson. Prod: FilmStallet/Exat AB & Co KB/Swedish Film Institute/Hagafilm.
Resan till Melonia (Voyage to Melonia). Script: Per Åhlin, Karl Rasmussen. Dir: Per Åhlin. *Animated fantasy.*
Agnes Cecilia. Dir: Anders Grönros. Players: Gloria Tapia, Ron Elfors, Stina Ekblad, Allan Svensson, Mimi Pollak. Prod: Svensk Filmindustri.
Gränslots (The Border Plot). Dir: Lars-Göran Pettersson. Players: Anton Hjärtmyr, Line Storesund, Helge Jordal, Bjorn Sundquist. Prod: Public Motion Picture AB/Swedish Film Institute/Sandrew Film & Teater/FilmTeknik/Swedish TV2.
Dockpojken (Boy-Doll). Dir: Hilda Hellwig. Players: Sven Wollter, Lena Granhagen, Hampus Petterson, Thomas Antoni. Prod: Swedish Film Institute/Swedish TV1.
Wallenberg (Good Evening, Mr Wallenberg). Script and Dir: Kjell Grede. Phot: Esa Vuorinen. Players: Stellan Skarsgård, Katharina Thalbach, Erland Josephson, Percy Brandt. Prod: Swedish Film Institute/Sandrew Film & Teater AB/Swedish TV2.
Jag skall bli Sveriges Rembrandt – eller dö! (I Want To Be Sweden's Rembrandt – or Die!). Dir: Göran Gunér. Players: Magnus Nilsson, Kenneth Söderman, Per Bodner, Kim Haugen, Ulf Friberg. Prod: Athenafilm/ABF/Swedish Film Institute/Swedish TV1.
Kaninmannen (The Rabbit Man). Dir: Stig Larsson. Players: Börje Ahlstedt, Leif Andrée, Stina Ekblad, Björn Gedda, Eva Engström. Prod: Golden Films International/Swedish Film Institute/ Swedish TV1.

Documentaries

The Swedish Institute (PO Box 7434, S-103 91 Stockholm) maintains an expanding library of films on 16mm and videocassette. Recent titles of interest to readers of IFG include Nils Petter Sundgren's imaginative evocation of his country's movies in recent years, *Nordic Lives – Swedish Cinema in the Eighties*, and Gosta Werner's *Mauritz Stiller*, which includes clips from most of the silent master's feature films.

Other documentaries dealing with the cinema, and available via the Institute, include portraits of *Victor Sjöström* and *Bo Widerberg*, and various studies of Ingmar Bergman, including the excellent *Quiet Please! Stand By to Shoot The Magic Flute!* Even more enticing is the catalogue of Swedish feature films available via the Institute. This list covers the entire history of Swedish cinema, but this non-commercial service is intended primarily for countries that show very few, if any, Swedish films.

Peter Öberg and Susanne Björklund in *The Secret*

Sweden on Film

Apart from a world-wide non-commercial distribution of short films, the Swedish Institute organizes film weeks abroad together with film clubs, universities, etc., **and is also the contact organization in Sweden for international cultural film festivals.** *Order our film catalogues!*

THE SWEDISH INSTITUTE
P.O. Box 7434, S-103 91 Stockholm, Sweden
Telephone: + 46 8 789 20 00
Telex: 10025 swedin s
Telefax: + 46 8 20 72 48

TOP GROSSING FILMS IN SWEDEN: 1989

	Attendance
S.O.S. Swedes at Sea (Sweden)	1,301,382
Rain Man	1,018,647
A Fish Called Wanda	936,597
Licence To Kill	932,276
Lethal Weapon 2	798,072
The Jönsson Gang on Majorca (Sweden)	722,314
Indiana Jones and the Last Crusade	617,266
Cocktail	464,292
The Shark Who Knew Too Much (Sweden)	452,472
The Naked Gun	445,154

Producers

AB Artistfilm
Skötskär Torö
S-149 00 Nynäshamn
Tel: (752) 311–60

Athena Film
Hjortstigen 3
S-181–43 Lidingö
Tel: (8) 765–07–10

Bold Productions AB
P.O. Box 125
S-230–22 Smygehamn
Tel: (410) 243–11

Boomerangfilm
Artillerigatan 83
S-115–30 Stockholm
Tel: (8) 664–64–01

Cinema Art Productions
Danderyds Krog
S-182–36 Danderyd
Tel: (8) 753–10–40
Fax: (8) 753–49–21

Devkino
P.O. Box 43–073
S-100-72 Stockholm
Tel: (8) 19–31–89

Eden Film
S Brobänken Hus 30
S-111–49 Stockholm
Tel: (8) 20–94–03

EXAT AB & Co KB
Riddargatan 12 A
S-114–35 Stockholm
Tel: (8) 24–62–45

Facta & Fiction AB
Tantogatan 49
S-117–42 Stockholm
Tel: (8) 669–09–75

Filmarken AB
Rörstrandsgatan 40
Tel: (8) 31–55–99

Hagafilm AB
St Paulsgatan 34
S-116–48 Stockholm
Tel: (8) 58–44–46

Hinden HB
Humlegårdsgatan 13
S-114–46 Stockholm
Tel: (8) 663–12–10

MovieMakers Sweden AB
Djursholmsvägen 35
S-183–50 Taby
Tel: (8) 756–85–40

Nordisk Tonefilm International AB
Kungsklippan 7
S-112–25 Stockholm
Tel: (8) 54–20–65
Fax: (8) 54–46–67

Omega Film AB
Oxenstiernsgatan 33
S-113–27 Stockholm
Tel: (8) 662–0390
Fax: (8) 663–3313

Pennfilm
Bruksvägen 9B
Hököpinge
S-235–00 Vellinge
Tel: (40) 46–67–84

Pica-film
Östergatan 12
S-230–11 Falsterbo
Tel: (40) 47–16–43

Public Motion Picture AB
Karlbergsvägen 65
S-113–35 Stockholm
Tel: (8) 31–08–80

Sandrew Film & Teater AB
P.O. Box 5612
S-114–86 Stockholm
Tel: (8) 23–47–00
Fax: (8) 10–38–50

Sonet Media AB
P.O. Box 20–105
Tel: (8) 764–77–00
Fax: (8) 29–90–91

Spice Filmproduction AB
Banérgatan 55
S-115–26 Stockholm
Tel: (8) 663–05–55

AB SF-Produktion
S-117–88 Stockholm
Tel: (8) 58–75–00
Fax: (8) 669–37–78

Swedish Film Institute
P.O. Box 27–126
S-102–52 Stockholm
Tel: (8) 665–11–00
Fax: (8) 661–18–20

Viking Film AB
Humlegårdsgatan 22
S-114–46 Stockholm
Tel: (8) 661–33–10
Fax: (8) 662–55–77

Distributors

Columbia Film AB
P.O. Box 9501
S-102–74 Stockholm
Tel: (8) 58–11–40
Fax: (8) 84–12–04

Walt Disney Sweden AB
P.O. Box 9503
S-102–74 Stockholm
Tel: (8) 58–10–50

Esselte Entertainment
P.O. Box 9006
S-102–71 Stockholm
Tel: (8) 772–25–00
Fax: (8) 666–90–98

Folkets Bio
P.O. Box 2068
S-103–12 Stockholm
Tel: (8) 20–30–59

Plånborg Film AB
P.O. Box 4083
S-182–02 Enebyberg
Tel: (8) 758–04–30
Fax: (8) 768–72–76

Polfilm
Norrtullsgatan 29
S-113–27 Stockholm
Tel: (8) 34–22–92
also
Östra Rönneholmsvägen 4
S-211–47 Malmö
Tel: (40) 12–40–44

Sandrew Film & Teater AB
P.O. Box 5612
S-114–86 Stockholm
Tel: (8) 23–47–00
Fax: (8) 10–38–50

Sonet Film AB
P.O. Box 20–105
S-161–20 Bromma
Tel: (8) 764–77–00
Fax: (8) 29–90–91

Succéfilm AB
Klippvägen 3
S-181–31 Lidingö
Tel: (8) 765–26–10
Fax: (8) 767–61–40

AB Svensk Filmindustri
S-117–88 Stockholm
Tel: (8) 58–75–00
Fax: (8) 668–50–70

Swedish Film Institute
P.O. Box 27–126
S-102–52 Stockholm
Tel: (8) 665–11–00
Fax: (8) 661–18–20

Triangelfilm
P.O. Box 17156
S-200–10 Malmö
Tel: (40) 12–55–47

United Artists AB
P.O. Box 9502
S-102–74 Stockholm
Tel: (8) 58–10–40

United International Pictures AB
P.O. Box 9502
S-102–74 Stockholm
Tel: (8) 58–10–40
Fax: (8) 84–38–70

Warner Bros Sweden AB
P.O. Box 9503
S-102–74 Stockholm
Tel: (8) 58–10–50

PETER COWIE is Editor of this book, which he launched in 1963. He has written numerous studies of film, including biographies of Bergman and Coppola. His most recent work is Le Cinéma des Pays Nordiques, published by the Centre Georges Pompidou. He is European Publishing Director of Variety newspaper.

SWITZERLAND
by Christoph Egger

A mere 15.18 million people bought tickets to watch two thousand films in Swiss cinemas during 1987. 10.8 million (71%) chose U.S. productions, which accounted for the thirteen most successful films of the year. France came second in the rankings with 1.96 million, followed by the Federal Republic of Germany with 725,000 cinemagoers. In contrast to the American leader, the public tended to opt for more low-key entertainment in this case: *Astérix et le coup du menhir* (182,000) and *Otto der Ausserfriesische* (199,000 attendance taking it to 14th place). Switzerland came in at fourth place with 411,000 visitors, although an increasing number of co-productions often make a cut-off point impossible. The other places were taken up by Italy (387,000), the U.K. (350,000), Spain (121,000), U.S.S.R. (99,000), India (the entire 72,000 being for *Salaam Bombay*) and Denmark in tenth place (68,000).

Once again the Swiss feature film industry cannot report any great success stories: in neither commercial nor artistic terms. The topical theme of a Swiss man marrying an exotic foreigner came up three times. In **Happiness for Sale** (*Gekauftes Glück*), his second feature film, Urs Odermatt attempts a blunt and stark exposure of the mountain people's xenophobia, but achieves little more than a caricature.. Alain Tanner's **The Woman of Rose Hill** (*La femme de Rose Hill*) is veiled in wonderful images (cameraman Hugues Ryffel) but remains superficial in its portrayal of the characters, and makes occasional unqualified criticism of Switzerland's policy on the granting of political asylum. Meanwhile Rolf Lyssy has attained a measure of success with his comedy **Leo Sonnyboy**, the story of a train driver who is a confirmed batchelor but unexpectedly finds himself married to a Thai girl. The first two thirds of this film can unashamedly be compared with *Die Schweizermacher*. Markus Imboden has done well with his charming first film, **Bingo**, where veteran actor, Ruedi Walter, and Mathias Gnädinger portray a touching gangster duo. Apart from having a role in *Gekauftes Glück*, having the lead in *Leo Sonnyboy*, playing the inspector in **The Howald Case** (*Howalds Fall*), the follow up to the German detective series *Tatort*, produced by Urs Eggers for Swiss television – Gnädinger also plays the lead part in Markus Imhoof's new film **The Mountain** (*Der Berg*) based on a story by the dramatist Thomas Hürlimann, which is to be released this autumn.

Mixed Fortunes for Debutants

Beat Lottaz also presents a very appealing first film: **Silent Betrayal** (*Stille Betrüger*), completed while studying at the German Film and Television Academy in Berlin. Less convincing is Jacob Berger's ambitious first film, **Angels**, an English language Swiss-French-Spanish-Belgian co-production which focuses on street urchins in Barcelona. Christoph Schaub presents his second full-length feature film, **Thirty Years** (*Dreissig Jahre*), which comes across as a variation on *Wendel* which preceded it. Ueli Mamin's **Johnny Sturmgewehr**, also his second feature film, is little more than a mundane rehash of *The Black Pearl*. **The Husband** (*Der Gatte*) by Mark M. Rissi marks an unsuccessful attempt to recreate a current political situation inspired by the events surrounding leading parliamentarian Kopp and her husband, which forced her to step down. Two new productions by Beat Kuert are equally unconvincing: **L'Assassina** and **A Wife for Alfie** (*Eine Frau für Alfie*). Nicolas Gessner made his competent thriller **Tennessee Nights** for Condor in the United States with Julian Sands, Ned Beatty and, in a minor supporting role, Rod Steiger. Jean-Luc Godard continues to avoid all things Swiss, preferring to allow his work to create its own personal world; **Nouvelle Vague** contributes to this in the form of a fascinating multi-layered essay on identity and reality in film.

Documentaries on Target

Once again the documentary films have turned out more interesting than the feature films. In **Green Mountain** (*Der grüne Berg*) Fredi M. Murer presents a painstakingly beautiful study of the human, political and economic aspects of the project to build a depot for radioactive waste near a mountain community. In **Lynx**, Franz Reichle has achieved a fascinating and oppressive portrayal of the problems of reintroducing the lynx to Switzerland. **Duende** by Jean-Blaise Junod offers a meticulous and poetic insight into the tradition of bullfighting in Andalusia. **Step Across the Border** by Nicolas Humbert and Werner Penzel manages to transform a portrayal of the English musician Fred Frith and his music into a lyrical and expressive image of his life as a journey. The Arabic lovesong of the *zajal* serves in Beni Müller's **Levante** as a binding link in the form of a song, which rids the people and lands of Israel, Lebanon and Palestine of all borders.

Things To Come

Of the federal grants during 1989, a good 400,000 Swiss Francs was contributed towards film scripts, almost 6 million Swiss Francs went to production costs and

SWISS FILMS

Swiss Film Center – Schweizerisches Filmzentrum
Centre Suisse du Cinéma – Centro Svizzero del Cinema
Münstergasse 18, CH-8001 Zürich, Tel. 01/261 28 60, Tlx. 817226 SFZZ CH
Fax 01/262 11 32

roughly one million Swiss Francs to the development of film studies. Among those films recently finished or nearing completion are new productions from Daniel Schmid (*Der Tee der drei alten Damen*, based on the thriller by Friedrich Glauser), Thomas Koerfer (*Exit Genua*), Xavier Koller (*Journey of Hope*), Bernhard Giger (*Under One Roof*), Léa Pool (*La demoiselle sauvage*) and Gerhard Pinkus (*Anna Göldin – the last witch*). In the field of documentaries we are still waiting for Alexander J. Seiler's *Palaver, Palaver* (based on the play by Max Frisch) and above all for Richard Dindo's *Arthur Rimbaud, une biographie*.

Changes within the Industry

The changes taking place in the European film and media scene are also being reflected in Switzerland. Despite the fact that Switzerland is not an EEC member, there is a desire to take an active part in all initiatives and programmes for film production and distribution organised by the European Community and the Council of Europe.

Swiss film distribution has also picked up, especially the independent companies which are not controlled by the Americans. In 1988 Rex, Monopol and Cactus merged to a single distribution group and then proceeded to join forces with Rialto. The driving force behind this enterprise is Jürg Judin from Zürich. The only remaining independent companies are Sadfi in Geneva, the Zürich Film Cooperative and Columbus Film in Zürich which was sold to three shareholders by its founder, Rudolf Hoch, who continues as managing director.

The news from the Swiss Film Centre is that Alfredo Knuchel, director since 1987, will give up his duties at the end of this year. He has confirmed his intention to stay in office until the new organisational structure is running smoothly. In order to express this solid work in consolidated form, the Film Centre published a comprehensive new index to Swiss cinema which gives information on rights, distribution and copying of 500 films made between 1972 and 1990 of a length greater than 60 minutes. This index, which was presented at the Locarno Festival, may be seen as a farewell gesture. In future the "Swiss Film Centre's Newcomer Award" will be distributed twice yearly in Locarno and Solothurn as a successor to the newcomer's incentive of the "Swiss Film Campaign." The Lucerne Film and Video Festival, Viper, has meanwhile established itself well, taking place in 1989 for the tenth time and has become a particularly important forum for the presentation of experimental video work. The event "Stars de demain" will take place this year for the third time in Geneva, and will now be known as "Festival de Genève." The selection of films lies in the hands of Beki Probst, who already directs the Film Market at the Berlin International Film Festival.

The active Cinema Section in the official Pro Helvetia foundation is planning a major series of Swiss films for screening across the United States in 1991.

CHRISTOPH EGGER is responsible for cinema in the media section of the Neue Zürcher Zeitung, for which he has been writing since 1978. He is also a member of the Swiss Jury for quality awards.

Recent and Forthcoming Films

Les Anges (Angels). Script and Dir: Jacob Berger. Phot: Emmanuel Machuel. Players: Steven Weber, Belinda Becker, Justin Williams, José Esteban Jr. Prod: CAB Productions (Lausanne)/Marea Films (Madrid)/Cadrage S.A. (Paris)/K2 Film Production (Brussels).
Tennessee Nights. Script: Nicolas Gessner, Laird König. Dir: Nicolas Gessner. Phot: Pio Corradi. Players: Julian Sands, Stacey Dash, Ned Beatty, Ed Lauter, Rod Steiger. Prod: Condor Productions AG (Zürich)/Bernard Lang AG (Zürich)/Allianz Film-Intermonda AG/WDR.

Nouvelle Vague (New Wave). Script and Dir: Jean-Luc Godard. Phot: William Lubtchansky. Players: Alain Delon, Domiziana Giordano, Roland Amstutz. Prod: Vega Film (Zürich)/Sara Films (Paris).
Zürich-Bern-Basel. Script: Thomas Imbach, Peter Liechti. Dir: Thomas Imbach. Phot: Peter Liechti. Players: Christine Lauterburg, Roger Nydegger, Sylvia Wetz. Prod: Filmkollektiv Zürich AG.
Bingo. Script: Philipp Engelmann, Markus Imboden, Thomas Tanner. Dir: Markus Imboden. Phot: Martin Fuhrer. Players: Ruedi Walter, Mathias Gnädinger, Robert Hunger-Bühler. Prod: Vega Film AG (Zürich).
Duende. Script: Jean-Blaise Junod, Vincent Adatte. Dir: Jean-Blaise Junod. Prod: Hugues Ryffel. Players: Carmelo, José Martinez "Limeño", Concha Ahumada Vasquez. Prod: Strada Films SA (Geneva)/Les Films du Phare (Paris)/TSR/CNC (Paris).
Exit Genua (The Genoa Exit). Script: Thomas Koerfer, Joachim Haman, Bernard Stora. Dir: Thomas Koerfer. Phot: Lukas Strebel. Players: Dexter Fletcher, Fabienne Babe, Uwe Ochsenknecht. Prod: Thomas Koerfer Film AG (Zürich/ Adliswil/Crocodile Productions (Paris)/Stella Film GmbH (Munich).
Die Zukünftigen Glückseligkeiten (Future Felicities). Script and Dir: Fred van der Kooji. Phot: Fritz Beckhoff, Dragan Rogulj, Hansueli Schenkel. Players: Isolde Barth, Wolf-Dietrich Berg, Tilo Prückner, Ben Becker. Prod: Fama Film AG (Bern)/Promedia Film GmbH (Munich).
Reise der Hoffnung (Journey of Hope). Script: Xavier Koller, Feride Cicekoglu. Dir: Xavier Koller. Phot: Elemer Ragalyi. Players: Mathias Gnädinger. Prod: Catpics AG (Zürich)/Condor Features (Zürich)/Enzo Porcelli (Rome)/Dewe Hellthaler International (Stuttgart).
L'Assassina. Script and Dir: Beat Kuert. Phot: Reinhard Schatzmann. Players: Margaret Mazzantini, Vadim Glowna, Elena Sofia Ricci. Prod: Al Castello SA (Arzo).
Stille Betrüger (Sleepy Betrayers). Script and Dir: Beat Lottaz. Phot: Rainer Meissle. Players: Muzzu Muzzulini, Annemarie Knaak, Andreas Schmidt, Jale Arikan. Prod: Deutsche Film- und Fernsehakademie (Berlin)/Image Film (Zürich).
Leo Sonnyboy. Script and Dir: Rolf Lyssy. Phot: Hans Liechti. Players: Mathias Gnädinger, Christian Kohlund, Ankie Beilke-Lau, Stephanie Glaser. Prod: Edi Hubschmid AG (Zürich)/Rolf Lyssy/Walter Schoch/Herbert Lips/Werner Merzbacher/Ulrich D. Bär/Central-Film Cefi AG (Zürich)/Fernsehen DRS/SWF.
Johnny Sturmgewehr. Script and Dir: Ueli Mamin. Phot: Martin Gressmann. Players: Katharina Rupp, Stefan Witschi. Prod: Fama Film AG (Bern)/Ueli Mamin.
Der Gatte (The Husband). Script: Mathias von Wartau, Theodore Wilden, Mark M. Rissi. Dir: Mark M. Rissi. Phot: Werner Schneider. Players: Giulio Ricciarelli, Wolfgang Hepp, Eva-Maria Hoffman, Ernst Theo Richter. Prod: Pica-Film AG/Mark M. Rissi/Nicolas Reiniger.
Dreissig Jahre (Thirty Years). Script: Martin Witz, Christoph Schaub. Dir: Christoph Schaub. Phot: Patrick Lindenmaier. Players: Joey Zimmermann, László I. Kish, Stefan Gubser, Alfred Meier. Prod: Dschoint Ventschr (Zürich)/Videoladan Zürich.
Controtempi. Script: Silvio Soldini, Robert Tiraboschi. Dir: Silvio Soldini. Phot: Luca Bigazzi. Players: Fabrizio Bentivoglio, Antonella Fattori, Ivano Marescotti, Patrizia Piccinini. Prod: Pic Film S.A. (Massagno)/Monogatari SRL (Milan).
Maxanito. Script: Rudolph Straub, Martin Hueber. Dir: Rudolph Straub. Phot: Odd Geir Seather. Players: Anders Oehrn, Martin Hueber, Alexandra Prusa, Mario Adorf. Prod: Yo-Yo Production (Zürich).
La Femme de Rose Hill. Script and Dir: Alain Tanner. Phot: Hugues Ryffel. Players: Marie Gaydu, Jean-Phillipe Ecoffey, Denise Peron, Roger Jendly. Prod: Filmograph SA (Geneva)/CAB Productions (Lausanne)/Gemini Films (Paris).
Jeu de Mains, Jeu de Vilains. Script: Bertrand Theubet, Vince Fasciani, Pedro Campos, adapted from "L'année des treize lunes" by Alexandre Voisard. Phot: Jean-Bernard Menoud. Players: Andrea Ferreol, Juliette Brach, Yannis Schweri, Anouk Grinberg. Prod: Vega Film (Zürich)/Les Films Plain-Chant (Paris)/TSR.
Der Schweizer Film (Switzerland and the Silver Screen). Episode film, produced by Freddy Buache. Prod: Limbo Film AG (Zürich)/Film & Vidéo Productions (Lausanne)/Cinémathèque Suisse/SRG.
Chartres. Script and Dir: Heinz Bütler. Phot: Manfred Eicher, Hansueli Schenkel. Players: Paul Giger. Prod: Al Castello SA (Arzo).

TOP GROSSING FILMS IN SWITZERLAND: 1989

	Admissions
Rain Man	1,008,238
Indiana Jones and the Last Crusade	692,719
Licence To Kill	521,796
A Fish Called Wanda	511,252
When Harry Met Sally	373,963
Twins	313,466
Cocktail	268,506
Gorillas in the Mist	263,934
The Accused	247,764
Batman	232,627

Arthur Rimbaud, une Biographie (Arthur Rimbaud, a Biography). Script and Dir: Richard Dindo. Phot: Pio Corradi. Prod: Robert Boner, Ciné Manufacture (Lausanne)/Les Films d'ici (Richard Copans). *Documentary*.

Unter einer Decke (Accomplices). Script: Bernhard Giger, Karsten Witte (consulting). Dir: Bernhard Giger. Phot: Pio Corradi. Players: Heiner Lauterbach, Dietmar Schönherr, Brigitte Karner. Prod: Limbo Film AG (Zürich).

En Voyage avec Jean Mohr. Dir: Villi Hermann. Phot: Hans Stürm. Prod: Imagofilm SA (Lugano). (*Documentary*).

Der Berg (The Mountain). Script: Thomas Hürlimann, Markus Imhoof. Dir: Markus Imhoof. Phot: Lukas Strebel. Players: Susanne Lothar, Mathias Gnädinger, Peter Simonischeck. Prod: Bernard Lang AG (Zürich).

Anna Göldin-Letzte Hexe (Anna Göldin-The Last Witch). Script: Gertrud Pinkus, Eveline Hasler (collaboration), from the novel of the same name by E. Hasler. Dir: Gertrud Pinkus, Stephan Portmann (collaboration). Phot: Franz Rath. Players: Cornelia Kempers, Rüdiger Vogler, Ursula Andermatt, Dimitri and Pinkas Braun Prod: Alpha Film (Munich)/P&P Film AG (Solothurn)/Hexatel (Paris)/SRG/BR.

La Demoiselle Sauvage. Script: Léa Pool, Michel Langlois. Dir: Léa Pool. Prod: Limbo Film AG (Zürich)/Cinémaginaire Inc. (Montréal).

Himmel und Erde (Heaven and Earth). Script: Samir, Martin Witz. Dir: Samir. Phot: Samir, René Baumann. Players: Nicole Ansari, Oliver Broumis. Prod: Dschoint Ventschr (Zürich).

Hinter Verschlossenen Türen (Behind Locked Doors). Script and Dir: Anka Schmid. Phot: Ciro Cappellari. Players: Walter Pfeil, Susanne Lüperz, Hans Madin, Maria Fitzi. Prod: DFFB (Berlin)/Mano-Produktion (Langnau).

Der Tee der Drei Alten Damen (Tea with Three Old Ladies). Script: Martin Suter, Daniel Schmid (collaboration). Dir: Daniel Schmid. Phot: Renato Berta. Prod: Limbo Film AG (Zürich)/Metropolis Filmproduktion (Berlin)/Pierre Grise Productions (Paris).

Producers

Al Castello SA
CH-6864 Arzo
Tel: (91) 46–85–43
Fax: (91) 46–31–65

Balsli Res & Cie
Hauptstrasse 33
CH-2560 Nidau
Tel: (32) 51–75–10

Catpios AG
Theaterstrasse 10
Postfach
CH-8024 Zürich
Tel: (1) 262–42–22
Fax: (1) 262–45–14

Filmograph SA
12, Chemin du Point du Jour
CH-1202 Genève
Tel: (22) 733–16–53

The Film Department of PRO HELVETIA Arts Council of Switzerland

promotes Swiss cinema. We arrange and coordinate seasons, retrospectives and other special film events around the world. We specialize in bilateral exchange with film archives, universities, arthouses, ministries of culture, etc.

Hirschengraben 22, P.O. Box, CH-8024 Zurich
Phone: ++41 (1) 251 96 00, Fax: ++41 (1) 251 96 06, Telex: 817599

Boa Filmproduktion AG
Klosbachstr. 141
CH Zürich 8032
Tel: (1) 252–20–38
Fax: (1) 251–02–38

CAB Productions SA
Rue du Port-Franc 17
CH-1003 Lausanne
Tel: (21) 312–80–56
Fax: (21) 312–80–64

Cactus Film AG
PO Box 299
CH-8021 Zürich
Tel: (1) 272–87–11
Fax: (1) 271–26–16

Cinov AG
PO Box 22
CH-3000 Bern 13
Tel: (31) 22–40–39

Arthur Cohn
Gellerstr. 18
CH-4052 Basel
Tel: (61) 42–12–42
Fax: (61) 42–02–17
Telex: 962261

Condor Productions AG
Restelbergstr. 107
CH-8044 Zürich
Tel: (1) 361–9612
Fax: (1) 361–95–75
Telex: 817032

Elite-Film AG
Molkenstr. 21
CH-8026 Zürich
Tel: (1) 242–8822
Fax: (1) 241–2123
Telex: 812381

Fama Film AG
Bathasarstr. 11
CH-3027 Bern
Tel: (31) 56–44–10
Fax: (31) 56–64–04

Filmkollektiv Zürich AG
Turnerstr. 26
CH-8006 Zürich
Tel: (1) 362–4644

Hubschmid Edi AG Filmproduktion
Zimmergasse 8
CH-8008 Zürich
Tel: (1) 252–27–27
Fax: (1) 252–92–05

Imagofilm SA
4 via le Cassarate
CH-6900 Lugano
Tel: (91) 22–68–31
Fax: (91) 23–16–16

Thomas Koerfer Film AG
Rütistrasse 4
CH-8134 Adliswil
Tel: (1) 710–8541

Limbo Film AG
PO Box 258
CH-8031 Zürich

Tel: (1) 271–8881
Fax: (1) 271–3350
Telex: 823530

Praesens-Film AG
PO Box 322
CH-8034 Zürich
Tel: (1) 55–38–32
Fax: (1) 55–37–93

Strada Films
11 rue de Conseil-Général
CH-1205 Geneva
Tel: (22) 29–35–10
Telex: 429157
Fax: (22) 20–41–14

T & C Film AG
Seestr. 41A
CH-8002 Zürich
Tel: (1) 202–3622
Telex: 817–639 tc
Fax: (1) 202–30–05

Vega Film AG
Carmenstr. 25
CH-8032 Zürich
Tel: (1) 252–6000
Fax: (1) 252–66–35

Cinefilm AG
Gladbachstrasse 83
CH-8044 Zürich
Tel: (1) 252–72–66

Les Productions J.M.H. SA
PO Box
Rue de l'Ale 38

CH-1000 Lausanne 9
Tel: (21)–312–99–33
Fax: (21) 312–99–34

Pic Film SA
Via G. Lepori 16
CH-6900 Lugano-Massagno
Tel: (91) 5638–71
Fax: (91) 56–38–72

Jacques Sandoz Film Productions SA
20, rue Micheli-du-Crest
CH-1205 Genève
Tel: (22) 20–46–36
Fax: (22) 20–46–49

Thelma Film AG
Josefstrasse 106
PO Box 258
CH-8031 Zürich
Tel: (1) 271–88–81
Fax: (1) 271–33–50

Bernard Lang AG
Kirchgasse 26
CH-8001 Zürich
Tel: (1) 252–6444
Telex: 58378
Fax: (1) 252–77–29

Distributors

Alpha Film SA
4, place du Cirque
PO Box 233
CH-1211 Genève 11
Tel: (22) 28–02–12
Fax: (22) 781–06–76

Citel Films Distribution SA
6 rue du Prince
CH-1204 Geneva
Tel: (22) 21–93–22
Telex: 421241
Fax: (22) 21–93–15

Columbus Films
Steinstr. 21
CH-8036 Zürich
Tel: (1) 462–7366
Telex: 813322
Fax: (1) 462–01–12

Elite Film AG
Molkenstrasse 21
CH-8026 Zürich
Tel: (1) 242–8822
Fax: (1) 242–8822
Telex: 812381

Filmcooperative ZH
PO Box 172
CH-8031 Zürich
Tel: (1) 271–8800
Telex: 817565
Fax: (1) 271–80–38

Monopole Pathé Films SA
PO Box Neugasse 6
CH-8031 Zürich 5
Tel: (1) 271–1003
Fax: (1) 271–5643
Telex: 823104

Neue Cactus Film AG
PO Box 299
CH-8021 Zürich
Tel: (1) 272–8712
Fax: (1) 271–2616
Telex: 822843

Regina Films SA
4 rue de Rive
CH-1204 Geneva
Tel: (22) 28–81–36
Telex: 429465

Rialto Film AG *(including Neue Cactus, Rex, Monopol)*
PO Box 347
CH-8034 Zürich
Tel: (1) 55–38–31
Fax: (1) 55–54–85
Telex: 816923

Sadfi Films SA
8 rue de Hesse
CH-1211 Geneva
Tel: (22) 21–77–67
Telex: 428657
Fax: (22) 781–31–19

Septima Film SA
13 rue Louis Favre
PO Box 67
CH-1211 Geneva 7
Tel: (22) 34–97–80

Idéal Film SA
PO Box 162
CH-1000 Lausanne 9
Tel: (21) 312–99–33
Fax: (21) 312–99–34

Impérial Film SA
17, av. de la Gare
CH-1002 Lausanne
Tel. (21) 20–24–61

Look now!
PO Box 3172
CH-8031 Zürich
Tel: (1) 272–03–60

Trigon-Film, Filmverleih Dritte Welt
Rösmattstrasse 6
CH-4118 Rodersdorf
Tel: (61) 75–15–15

Twentieth Century-Fox Film Corp
PO Box 33
CH-1211 Geneva 26
Tel: (22) 43–33–15
Fax: (22) 43–92–55
Telex: 428689

United International Pictures (Schweiz) GmbH
Signaustr. 6
CH-8032 Zürich
Tel: (1) 383–85–50
Fax: (1) 383–61–12
Telex: 816462

Warner Bros. Inc.
Studerweg 3
Postfach
CH-8802 Kilchberg
Tel: (1) 715–50–11
Fax: (1) 715–34–51
Telex: 812480

TAIWAN

by Derek Elley

Taiwan cinema had one of its most schizophrenic years yet during 1989-90. On the one hand, the industry gained international prestige from Hou Hsiao-hsien winning the Golden Lion at Venice in September 1989 with *A City of Sadness*; on the other, its endemic problems gradually worsened.

The industry's split personality seemed summed up by the rows surrounding the December 1989 Golden Horse Awards (which also made a misguided attempt to launch an "international film festival" in parallel): Hou's film copped only two awards, while no less than seven went to Stanley Kwan's glossy but vacuous Hongkong production, *Full Moon in New York*. This not only provoked the usual complaints that Hongkong again dominated the awards but also set off a full-scale war in the press between Hou's supporters (who claimed the film had been sidelined for political reasons) and other elements who claimed it was not as good as many made out. The whole affair was reminiscent of the war between conservative and progressive factions in 1983 when New Taiwan Cinema first burst on the scene. Hou himself was so upset that he refused to talk at all to Taiwan journalists.

The truth of the Hongkong debate is that Taiwan movies still show no signs of breaking the stranglehold on their own market of productions from across the water. In 1989 seven of the top 10 box-office films were Hongkong-made (see below), with Jackie Chan's latest heading the list and running in Taipei for a whole month. For the first time in his career, Hou enjoyed local success as well as international prestige, with *A City of Sadness* running for a record length of two months and taking a record NT$70 million – partly thanks to the producer deciding to open it *after* the Venice festival (and gambling it would win an award), partly due to its cachet of being the first film to deal in any way with the notorious "28 February Incident" (previously a banned topic).

A City of Sadness (*Pei-ch'ing ch'eng-shih*) is certainly an impressive work; but it is also far too self-conscious for its own good, needlessly abstruse (withholding information from the viewer), and often annoyingly slow. The 28 February Incident, when KMT forces bloodily suppressed anti-government demonstrations in 1947, forms only a tiny part of the action; the majority concerns the travails of a Taiwan family during 1945-49 as the island passed from Japanese to Chinese (KMT) rule. Hongkong heart-throb Tony Leung is cannily cast as a deaf-mute photographer and gives a striking performance of wordless impotence as history unfolds around him. But the movie belongs to actor Ch'en Sung-yung, as his vociferous elder brother – an earthy performance that well-deserved its award (since launching the actor into the big-time), and which gives a glimpse of the more affecting work that *City* could have been.

Taiwan movies' long-standing weakness in the Hongkong market was painfully underlined when *City* was released there a few months later, taking only HK$1 million. Such is the relationship between the two "offshore" Chinese industries (and their differing tastes) that Taiwan actors are forced to move to Hongkong to become big names and Taiwan companies to co-produce with Hongkong ones to see sizable returns. Firms like Lung Hsiang, Scholar Films, New Ship and Hong Tai are now looking to invest even more in this way; the KMT-funded Central Motion Picture Corporation (CMPC) has already been pursuing this route for some years. No one has yet solved the conundrum of why Taiwan, with a population three times greater than Hongkong, still plays second fiddle in movie-making. (The situation has several parallels with the relationship between the U.K. and U.S. industries.)

One other fact is also very clear: New Taiwan Cinema as a cohesive concept is dead and buried. Just as in mainland China *Red Sorghum* marked the end of an era, so *A City of Sadness* seems to wrap up a decade of vital, exciting change. New Taiwan Cinema actually peaked around 1985 but its effect lingered on for several years; in the 1990's Chinese cinema as a whole looks like gradually becoming a much more free-range animal, with crossovers between its three centres and (in Taiwan) less distinction between "new wave" and "commercial" film-makers. Many factors have combined to shake up the easy divisions of previous years: the turbulence in Hongkong as 1997 approaches, the Tiananmen Massacre of June 1989 (both of which have created an unofficial film-making diaspora) and Taiwan's gradual political "liberalisation."

The most notable sign of this in 1990 has been the stampede by Taiwan film-makers to shoot on the Mainland, following the relaxation of government restrictions in April 1989 (see IFG 1990). Hou Hsiao-hsien was one of the first, shooting a few scenes for *A City of Sadness*; he also plans to return there in the second half of 1990 for his next feature (about the life of Li T'ien-lu, a famous hand-puppeteer who has appeared in several of his recent films) and to discuss a film to be directed by Zhang Yimou on which he will be associate producer (from a novel by Mainland author Su Tong).

Full-Scale Flotilla
The first full-scale feature to be shot on the Mainland was Chu Yen-p'ing's comedy **Dumb Dragons Go to Sea** (*Sha lung ch'un-hai*). Since then a full-scale flotilla has been launched. NYU film school graduate Huang Yü-shan, who debuted in 1988 with *The Cave of Desire* (IFG 1989), has shot a novel by Mainland writer Lu Zhaohuan in Fujian; veteran Pai Ching-jui made yet another film on Empress Dowager Tzu Hsi, in Peking, starring actress Siqin Gaowa; Richard Chen shot part of his latest movie, with actresses Lu Hsiao-fen and Hongkong's Cora Miao, from a novel by authoress Hua Yen (whose *Diary of Di-di* he filmed 12 years ago); and young director Yeh Hung-wei was planning in summer 1990 to shoot a novel by Mainland writer Yeh Yinlin in Shaanxi. Even CMPC has followed suit with a couple of productions, and Taiwan money (and stars) were behind Yim Ho's latest movie, about a 1930s woman writer's love life, shot in Harbin and Changchun.

Some restrictions still apply – there must be no Mainland investment or leading players – but it can only be a matter of time before film-makers achieve the freedoms that are already enjoyed by Taiwan's businessmen. There are also ways round the problem, either by setting up a company in Hongkong or using actors who are now domiciled outside the Mainland, such as Siqin Gaowa (Switzerland) or Joan Chen (U.S.). The latter has already starred in a drama series for Taiwan TV.

The crossover situation was clearly evident in one of the best Taiwan movies of the year, **Song of the Exile** – funded by Taiwan's COS Group and CMPC, written and directed by Hongkong's Ann Hui, starring Taiwan's Lu Hsiao-fen and

Hongkong's ubiquitous Maggie Cheung, and shot in London, China, Hongkong, Macau and Japan. Despite a few early failings, it is Hui's best film since *Love in a Fallen City*, a measured version of her own childhood years and the troubled relationship between herself (Cheung) and her mother (Lu). With its wide-ranging locations, the revelation that Hui's mother was in fact Japanese (making a mockery of her sense of "Chinese-ness"), and its sense of permanent exile, the film is a well-timed exploration of identity and roots. (New force COS is planning a further project with Hui, based around the Tiananmen incident, and a film by Stanley Kwan from an Eileen Chang story.)

Of other recent productions, Wang T'ung returned to the earthy comedy style of his Strawman with **Banana Paradise** (*Hsiang-chiao t'ien-t'ang*); former critic Ch'en Kuo-fu debuted with the glossy **Highschool Girls** (*Kuo-chung nü-sheng*); Yeh Hung-wei followed his impressive debut, *Never-Ending Memory* (IFG 1990), with **Curses of the Knife** (*Tao wen*), about a young couple pursued by establishment forces; and Yang Li-kuo bounced back with the quietly charming, pastoral **Rough Ice Flower** (*Lu-ping hua*), which made an instant star of kid actor Huang K'un-hsüan.

From other quarters it has been a quiet year. Edward Yang has still to get a project going in three years, despite several false starts; Wan Jen has been planning a black comedy on Taiwan's political–social changes; and Ch'en K'un-hou, after a spell in TV, recently worked as cameraman on a Hongkong production by Yang Fen. The past year also claimed a young victim – director Fred Tan, 35, who died on March 7, 1990 in Taipei of AIDS-related acute hepatitis. U.S.-based Tan had directed three features – *Dark Night*, *Split of the Spirit* and *Rouge of the North*.

DEREK ELLEY is Consulting Editor of this book, and has been associated with it for more than 18 years. He is known as a specialist in Hungarian and Far East cinema. He is currently completing A Handbook of Chinese Cinema: The Films and Film-Makers of Hongkong, China and Taiwan.

Recent and Forthcoming Films

Ming-yüeh chi-shih yüan. Dir: Richard Chen, from the novel by Hua Yen. Players: Lu Hsiao-fen, Cora Miao.
Kun-kun hung-ch'en. Dir: Yim Ho. Players: Ch'in Han, Lin Ch'ing-hsia, Maggie Cheung. Prod: TomSon.
Fan-mu an-k'ao. Dir: Terry Tong. Players: Lu Hsiao-fen, Wang Ye, Ch'en Sung-yung, Siqin Gaowa, Chang Kuo-kuei. Prod: CMPC.
Chia tao kung-li-te nan-jen. Dir: Pai Ching-jui. Player: Siqin Gaowa.
Shuang cho. Dir: Huang Yü-shan. Player: Ch'en Te-jung.
Wu-ko nü-tzu yü yi-ken sheng. Dir: Yeh Hung-wei. Players: Yang Chieh-mei, Chang T'ing, Lu Yüan-ch'i. Prod: TomSon.
Ti-hsia t'ung-tao. Dir: Michael Mak. Player: Wu Hsüeh-wen.
Wo-te erh-tzu shih t'ien-ts'ai. Dir: Yang Li-kuo. Player: Huang Kun-hsüan.

The 25th Golden Horse Awards (1989)

The 25th Golden Horse Awards, announced on December 9, 1989, were:
Best Feature Film: *Full Moon in New York*.*
Best Director: Hou Hsiao-hsien (*A City of Sadness*).
Best Original Script: Chiu Tai An-ping (*Full Moon in New York*).*
Best Actor: Ch'en Sung-yung (*A City of Sadness*).
Best Actress: Maggie Cheung (*Full Moon in New York*).*
Best Supporting Actor: Chang Shih (*Banana Paradise*).
Best Supporting Actress: Li Shu-chen (*Rough Ice Flower*).
Best Photography: Bill Wong (*Full Moon in New York*).*

Best Art Direction: Richard Chen, Chang Chi-p'ing, Li Pao-lin, Li T'ung (*Spring Swallow*).
Best Original Music: Peter Chang (*Full Moon in New York*).*
Best Song: Ch'en Yang, Yao Ch'ien (*Rough Ice Flower*).
Best Editing: Steve Wang, Chow Cheung-kan (*Full Moon in New York*).*
Best Sound: Yeung Wai-keung (*Full Moon in New York*).*
Best Costumes: Pan Lai (*Full Moon in New York*).*

* Hongkong production

Top 10 Local* Films: 1989

Mr Canton and Lady Rose* (NT$85 million)
A City of Sadness (NT$70 million)
The Iceman Cometh*
Casino Raiders*
A Better Tomorrow III*; 7 Wolves
The Killer*
Crocodile Hunter*
Private across the River*
The Crazy Companies II*

* includes Hongkong productions

Useful Addresses

Government Information Office
Dept. of Motion Picture Affairs
15/F. No. 17, Hau Chang Street
Taipei
Tel: 3318390, 3318351
Telex 11636 inform

Film Library
4/F, No. 7 Ching Tao East Road
Taipei
Tel: 3924243, 3923540
Fax 3926359
Telex 11636 inform

Central Motion Picture Corporation
116 Han Chung Street
Taipei
Tel: 3715191

Cinevidco Ltd.

Attention Film Buffs & Collectors

Asia's most active library of 16mm film classics. Non-commercial exhibition of the world's greatest motion pictures. Serving film clubs, libraries, universities and cinematheques. For additional inquiries, list or information about titles, rentals and acquisition: Cinevidco Ltd, P O Box 30510, Causeway Bay, Hong Kong, Fax: (662) 253 9184.
Attn Fred Marshall

THAILAND
by Fred Marshall

Thai cinema saw the return to form in 1990 of HRH Prince Chatri Yukol with two fine works. **Centre of the Nation** is an autobiographical documentary on Thailand's popular monarch King Bhumidol. The film, which took almost four years to make, was given a nationwide release and circulated to all Thai embassies as the official biography of the King.

The Prince also found time to complete his long-awaited film about the timber-logging problem, entitled **The Elephant Keeper**. It too enjoyed reasonable success and should do well abroad. Jazz Siam, another prominent director, did not fare so well at the box-office with his romantic drama.

Chalong Pakdeevichit, one of Thailand's action film specialists, released **In Gold We Trust**, which attracted big audiences and was one of the few Thai films to be exported in another language. Film-making in Thailand is usually restricted to simplistic comedies, exploitation dramas, and good actioners. Between 50 and 60 films are shot each year.

The import of films to Thailand is controlled by the major companies and there is a 200% tax on imported prints. Only in Bangkok can audiences see the original version; all films are dubbed into Thai for release outside the capital. Small-budget films are rarely imported and those releases that score the biggest success are the American pictures backed up by heavy expenditure on advertising and promotion.

The industry desperately needs to be recognised in toto by the government. One of the main advantages of this would be the government's ability to bring in equipment from overseas without paying import taxes. "Thai movie producers and directors have been complaining for decades that we lack modern equipment with which to upgrade the quality of our films," says Manop Udomdej, a "new wave" director, at a seminar held by the National Film Association.

Sorapong Chatri in *The Elephant Keeper*, produced by Manfred Durniok Filmproduktion

Bodin Duke and Siriam Pakdeedumrongrit in *Junkie*

Recent and Forthcoming Films

Life's Little Big man (Seven Ladies). Script and Dir: Toranong Srichuae. Phot: Pipat Payaka-Manu Wannayok. Players: Darin Kornsakun, Toranong Srichuae. Prod: Exit Film Production. *Tough, raunchy gangster thriller.*
In Gold We Trust. Script and Dir: Chalong Pakdeevichit. Players: Jan Michael Vincent, Sam Jones, Sorapong Chatri, Lek Isun. Prod: Chalong Pakdeevichit for Apex Pyramid Films. *Thriller.*
Kho Chue Suthee Sam See Chat. Dir: J.D. Supakanj, Kriangkrai Amatyakul, Kiat Kicharoen, Vachara Pun-iom. Prod: Five Star. *Comedy in five parts based on the best-seller by Prapass Chonsaranon.*
Twilight in Tokyo. Script and Dir: Thoranong Srichua. Players: Likhit Ekmongkhol, Darin Kornsakul, Rapheephan Kornsakul. *Romantic drama.*
Hope for Tomorrow (Chilli and Ham). Script and Dir: Somohing Srisuparb. Phot: Siripen Usomboon. Players: Kajornsak Rattananissai, Chanjira Choojang, Mayura Thanabutra. Prod: Tai Entertainment. *Comedy drama for young people.*
Young Blood. Dir: Monoo Wannayok. Phot: Wanchai Leng. Players: Samart Payakaroon, Kampanat Ungsungnern, Pathsorn Boonyakiat. Prod: Coliseum Group Co. *Police adventure drama.*
Wai Dip (Junkie). Dir: Chao Mikunsoot. Player: Bodin Duke. Prod: Saha Mongkol. *Actioner.*
Khomsan (Holy Spirits). Dir: Jazz Siam. Player: Santisuk Promsiri. Prod: Five Star Films. *About the "Messengers of God" phenomenon in Thailand.*
The Elephant Keeper. Script, Dir and Phot: Chatri Chalerm Yukol. Players: Sorapong Chatri, Doungduen Chathjaisong, Rhone Rhitchai. Prod: Prommitri Production (Bangkok)/ Manfred Durniok Produktion (Berlin). *Adventure thriller involving police corruption and timber-logging.*

TURKEY

by B. Samantha Stenzel

Turkey is grappling with deep-seated economic problems, including a staggering annual inflation rate of at least 70%. This situation has been reflected in cinema production, reduced in the last few years from about 200 films annually to about 100.

On the other hand, ticket sales in 1989–90 rose an estimated 20% compared to 1988–89. "A huge change has occurred in the Turkish market profile," according to UIP g.m. Mehmet Özduygu. "An audience hungry for quality films has existed for many years but we didn't have the product." Warner Bros. was the first American major to establish itself in Turkey in 1987. It concentrated on video distribution until

May, 1989. UIP was the first American major to launch theatrical distribution in March, 1989.

According to Özduygu of UIP, "We have not used block-booking nor will we have a need for it." He admits the local industry has had an adverse reaction to the launching of majors in Istanbul, fearing an unfair domination by American product.

Pressure was put on the Ministry of Culture to draft a law calling for a 25% quota of Turkish films shown in cinemas. The bill is planned to come before the National Assembly in October. According to well-respected Istanbul Festival executive director Hülya Ucansu, "This is a necessary measure to preserve our national cinema so that it isn't overlooked in favour of the more glamourous foreign pictures."

"It's not necessary," said Özduygu in reference to the quota, "It is best to let the audience be the judge. Good Turkish films such as Livanelli's *The Fog* and Tunc Baseran's *Don't Let Them Shoot the Kite*, attract customers."

New Promotional Organisation
TürkFilm, the first serious promotion by the Turkish State, made its official bow at the Berlin Fest. Modelled after Unifrance and funded by the Turkish Ministry of Culture, it is designed to help the Turkish film industry regain its vitality. TürkFilm's budget was about $300,000 its first year and the Ministry of Culture allotted other funds to construct studios and fund films.

In its short nine year history, the Istanbul Film Festival is rapidly establishing a reputation as a rich panorama of world cinema (largely due to the efforts of peripatetic programme director Vecdi Sayar), as well as presenting current Turkish features.

This year's festival was its most ambitious yet. Over the course of 16 days, 182 films were screened. Although the consensus of opinion from festival guests was favourable, there are some indications that the event is becoming unmanagable. According to festival director Ucansu, "I will recommend we shorten the festival next year."

Under the guidance of Ucansu, the festival has unflaggingly campaigned for the total abolishment of censorship. It has finally been successful in having a "hands-off" policy implemented in the international competition but not in the domestic section.

The battle continued this year, successfully waged to prevent cutting or banning of Yusuf Kurcenli's powerful drama **Blackout Nights**. Loosely based on the novel of the same name by prolific Rifat Ilgaz, the film recreates the poet's arrest as a suspected communist at the end of the Second World War and his subsequent period of hiding from the law.

The lead of *Blackout Nights*, handsome one-time matinee idol Tarik Akan, has matured into a fine actor. Much of the film's appeal comes from his interaction with those who befriend him during this period. The sombre tone is lightened with humorous touches and the cafés and their inhabitants are suitably colourful.

Torture in prison is not avoided nor overly emphasised. Although the topic of man's cruelty to man in the struggle for control is underlying, the film ultimately is optimistic, a paean to the durability of the human spirit. The cast, especially Nurseli Idiz as Ilgaz's wife, is excellent.

Blackout Nights' approval came just a few days before its premiere and it triumphantly captured the award for Best Turkish Film of the year and a sum of about $8,000. It was also an entry in the Venice Festival.

A similar focus on political imprisonment also figured strongly in the plot of Mamduh Ün's **All the Doors Were Closed**, which like *Blackout Nights* demonstrates a greater maturity than the socio-political films of previous years.

In *All the Doors Were Closed*, glimpses are given of torture endured by a young student Nil (Asli Altan), in her six years of

Poetic imagery in *A Ay*, directed by Reha Erdem

incarceration for political reasons. But the emphasis is on the psychological wounds and prejudice that taint her life upon release, preventing her from being able to develop a full relationship with a kindly architect (Uğar Polat). The visually appealing film especially struck a sympathetic chord with young audiences whose lives have been touched by the continuing imprisonment of young dissidents.

Political Films Prized
Politically-oriented films have dominated the festival awards in recent years. According to Atilla Dorsay, well-respected film critic and author, "Turks have been unable to deal with current events until the last couple of years because of censorship. It is natural they are doing so now.

"Producers, however, rate a film according to its commercial possibilities and most felt political films would never be popular," explained Dorsay. This has been proven incorrect by recent box-office figures which show well-made films with political overtones such as *Blackout Nights* and *Don't Let Them Shoot the Kite* scoring solid successes. Both deal with prison life, a seemingly endless source for plot material.

Other festival entries praised by viewers include Yavuz Turgul's **The Unforgettable Director of Hollywood Movies** and Raha Erdem's **A Ay**. *The Unforgettable Director of Hollywood Movies* would have scored at the box-office just from the name of Sener Sen, a beloved comic often cast as a rural aga and last year a lovestruck serf in the huge hit *Arabesque*. Sen displays new depth as a has-been director of popular romances who attempts a comeback in a timely "meaningful" film about social problems.

Scoffed at by backers, his former wife and his stunning lead actress (Pitircik Akerman), in one especially memorable scene, the defeated and embittered director attempts suicide. In a suitably symbolic fashion he ravels a reel of film about his neck and tries to ignite it. His fumbled attempts highlight Sen's excellent timing and convey a striking blend of humour and pathos.

Another festival triumph shown out of competition was Füruzan and Gülsün Karamustapha's debut film *My Cinemas*. The touching portrait of a young woman who escapes from her harsh family life through the cinema, eventually turning to prostitution as a means of buying nice clothes, is distinguished by insightful touches. Popular lead Hülya Avsar, a striking beauty with red hair and green eyes, is currently in vogue. *My Cinemas* was presented in the Cannes' Directors' Fortnight.

The French training of director Raha Erdem is evident in *A Ay*, a striking luminescent tone poem, a startling departure from traditional Turkish cinema. The dialogue is sparse and a moody atmosphere prevails, accented by cello and string quartet music, in this tale of Yakta (Yesim Tozan), a young orphan who lives with her grandmother in a wildly beautiful area of the Dosphorus. Yekta develops a communication with her dead mother who appears to her on a boat passing her window, although her elders assume she is going through a phase.

Baris Pirhasan's **A Fable on Little Fishes**, in the national competition and Yavuz Özkan's **The Film Is Over**, in the international competition, deal with the disintegration of romantic relationships during marriage, a timely topic in modern Turkey, in which divorce is not uncommon. Both are technically adept and have some moments of truth. But they suffer from meandering plots that don't give the necessary character development and motivation to make the triangular relationships plausible or interesting.

Halit Refiğ's **Women's Ward**, is another prison drama that captured the public's interest and was one of the year's most popular films. *Women's Ward* is an adaptation of Kemal Tahir's novel in which Murat, a sensitive journalist, buoys the spirits of his fellow inmates through his support and wit. A fascinating tapestry is woven through the character portrayals, giving a glimpse of life in the early 1940's.

Active Old Guard

Refiğ, along with Atif Yilmaz (*A Dead Sea*) and Serif Gören (*One Weird Movie*), represents the old guard of Turkish cinema, prolific veterans who continue to make relevant and popular films. Gören's **One Weird Movie** is an uneven comedy about a peasant who inherits a fortune and Atif Yilmaz turns to the unleashing of full sexuality in an affair between two middle-aged professionals in *A Dead Sea*.

One seasoned director absent from the current cinema scene is Ali Özgentürk, whose supposed "dream prize" from the Tokyo International Film Festival for his film *The Horse* turned out to be "a burden instead of a blessing." According to Özgentürk, his chaotic and prolonged negotiations with the Japanese to obtain the money to fund his next feature *Water Also Burns*, "have destroyed my love for filmmaking." *Water Also Burns*, ironically about a director's domestic and legal hassles while making a film about a dissident poet put him in debt, was banned and seized in Turkey and nearly landed him in prison.

Normally summer is a dead season for cinemas but according to Mehmet Özduygu of UIP, "a number of central cinemas have invested in air-conditioning and remain open in the summer, to pick up the slack created by the closing of the majority of open-air cinemas.

"It's amazing to see a rejuvenation, old cinemas being refurbished and new ones opening," said Özduygu. The Fitas and Beyoğlu have been renovated and divided into duoplexes. Fitas partner Abdullah Tüze owns the Metropol in Ankara, an upscale duo-screen complex with café, restaurant and nightclub which has had a huge increase in business since the change.

Recent Films

Tidal Views. Script: Neslihan Eyüboğlu, Mahinur Ergun. Dir: Mahinur Ergun. Players: Kadir Inanir, Zuhal Olcay, Yilmaz Zafer. Prod: Erka Film.
From Canto to Tango. Script: Ziya Özten, Tomris Giritioğlu. Dir: Tomris Giritioglu. Players: Aytac Arman, Serap Aksay, Tarik Ünlüoğlu, Pitircik. Prod: Vehbi Okur/Dunya Haklari Export.
The Lighthouse of Ponente. Script: Zeynep Avci, Isil Kasapoğlu. Dir: Sahin Gök. Players: Hülya Kocypiğit, Hakan Balamir, Arzu Aydin, Mine Cayiroğly. Prod: Hakan Balamir.
Blackout Nights. Script: Yusuf Kurcanli, based on the novel "Karatma Geceleri" by Rifat Ilgaz. Dir: Yusuf Kurcenli. Players: Tarik Akan, Nurseli Idiz, Bülent Bilgic, Deniz Kurtoğlu. Prod: Senar Film.
Great Solitude. Script and Dir: Yavuz Özkan. Players: Sezen Aksu, Ferhan Sensoy. Prod: Z Film Ltd.
A Fable on Little Fishes. Script and Dir: Baris Pirhasan. Players: Hale Soygazi, Nihat Ileri, Derya Köroğlu, Yasemin Alkaya. Prod: Baris Pirhasan, Kedi Film.
Women's Ward. Script: Halit Rafiğ based on the novel "Karilar Koğusu" by Kemal Tahir. Dir: Helit Refiğ. Players: Kadir Inanir, Perihan Savas, Hülya Kocyiğit, Tuncer Necmioğlu. Prod: Türker Inanoğlu.
Fazilet. Script: Gülin Tokat, Gökay Özgüc. Dir: Irfan Tözüm. Players: Hülya Avsar, Yaman Okay, Ihsan Yüce, Marih Akalin, Engin Inal. Prod: Feridun Kate.
Double Games. Script: Bilgesu Erenue. Dir: Irfan Tözüm. Players: Tarik Akan, Zeliha Berksoy, Erol Demiröz. Prod: Muhtesem Film.
The Unforgettable Director of Hollywood Movies. Script and Dir: Yavuz Turgul. Players: Sener San, Pitircik Akkerman, Yavuzer Centinkays, Gül Onat. Prod: Türker Inanoğlu.
All the Doors Were Closed. Script: Süheyla Acar Kalyoncu. Dir: Memduh Ün. Players: Asli Altan, Uğur Polat, Nalan Örgüt, Metin Belgin. Prod: Uğur Film.
The Silent Tempest. Script: A. Giray Karanlik. Dir: Oğuz Yalcin. Players: Fikret Hakan, Sahika Tekend, Engin Inal, Deniz Erkanat. Prod: Taner Askin.
One Weird Movie. Script: Ibrahim Gündüz. Dir: Serif Gören. Players: Kemal Sunal, Siva Gerede, Murat Ilker, Perin Aytac. Prod: Turgay Aksoy.

B. SAMANTHA STENZEL, a frequent visitor in Turkey, has reported on Turkish cinema for years. She covers the Istanbul Festival for The Athenian Magazine, Variety and other publications.

Producers

Alfa Film
Ömer Kavur
Ahududu sok. 21/3 Beyoğlu
Istanbul.
Tel: 1453108.

Eks Yapim
Eriş Akman
Erol Dernek solk. 11/4
Beyoğlu
Istanbul.
Tel: 1452187.

Erler Film
Türker Inanoğlu
Kodaman cad. 108 Nisantaşi,
Istanbul.
Tel: 1411358.

Gülşah Film
Selim Soydan
Siraselviler cad. 27/14 Taksim
Istanbul.
Tel: 1493585.

Hakan Film
Hakan Balamir Ömer Avni
Mah
Emekar sok. 26/4 Gümüşsuyu
Istanbul.
Tel: 1499101.

Istanbul Film
Osman Kavala
Rihtim cad. 207 Nesli han
Karakoy
Istanbul.
Tel: 1514103.
Tlx: 24073.
Fax: 1450793.

TOP GROSSING DOMESTIC FILMS IN TURKEY: 1989-90

Blackout Nights
The Lady
Don't Let Them Shoot the Kite
The Mist
The Unforgettable Director of Hollywood Movies
The Women's Ward
A Fable on Little Fishes
The Third Eye
My Cinemas
All the Doors Were Closed

Konsept Film
Onat Kutlar
Etiler sok. 12 Etiler
Istanbul.
Tel: 1577440.
Fax: 1635240.

Magnum Film
Tunc Başaran
Pitrak sok. 7/4 Yeşilköy
Istanbul.
Tel: 5732879.
Fax: 5737343.

Mine Film
Kadri Yurdatap
Kuloğlu sok. Girkik han 28/5
Beyoğlu
Istanbul.
Tel: 1430200.

STM Yapim
Cemal Sener
Koresehitleri cad. 48/2
Zincirlikuyu
Istanbul.
Tel: 1664747.
Tlx: 27157.
Fax: 1743773.

Seref Film
Seref Gür
Erol dernek solk. Erman han
Beyoğlu

Istanbul.
Tel: 1432792.

Distributors

Erler Film
Türker Inanoğlu
Kodaman cad. 108 Nisantas
Istanbul.
Tel: 1411358.
Fax: 1474740.

Filmcenter
Ugur Terzioğlu
Erol Dernek sok. 16 Beyoğlu
Istanbul.
Tel: 1433397.
Tlx: 24298.

Fono Film
Tuncan Okan
Yeşilçam sok. 5/2 Beyoğlu
Istanbul.
Tel: 1445655.

Istanbul Film
Osman Kavala
Rihtim cad. 207 Nesli Han
Karaköy
Istanbul.
Tel: 1514103.
Tlx: 24073.
Fax: 1450793.

Met Film
Erol Özpecen
Başağa Ceşme sok. 9 Beyoğlu
Istanbul.
Tel: 1499275.

Özen Film
Mehmet Soyarslan
Sakizagaci sok. 21 Beyoğlu
Istanbul.
Tel: 1437070.
Tlx: 25462.

Pop Film
Ismet Kazancioğlu
Erol Dernek sok
Dalyan apt. 15/2 Beyoğlu
Istanbul.
Tel: 1457585.

Standard Film
Metin Arcan
Ayhan Isik sok. 16 Beyoğlu
Istanbul.
Tel: 1431774. Tlx: 24298
Fax: 1436520.

Sener Film
Mahmut Saracer
Ipek sok
Ipek han
Beyoğlu
Istanbul.
Tel: 1458018.

UIP
Memmet Özduygu
Eytam cad.
Acikhava apt. 16/16 Macka
Istanbul.
Tel: 1528621.
Fax: 1528432.

Warner Bros
Mim Kemal öke cad. 16
Nisantaşi
Istanbul.
Tel: 1312569
Fax: 1317070.

Useful Addresses

Istanbul Kültür ve Sanat Vakfi (Istanbul Foundation for Culture and Arts)
Besiktas, Istanbul.
Tel: 1609072.
Tlx: 26687.
Fax: 1618823.

SESAM
(Turkish Film Producers Organisation)
Istikal Cad. 122/4A
Beyoğlu
Istanbul.
Tel: 1454645, 1499626
Fax: 1452848

Front row left to right: Animator Bill Plympton, MTV Executive Peter Dougherty, Festival Chairman Terry Thoren and MTV Executive Abby Terkhule, at the Los Angeles International Animation Celebration

UNITED KINGDOM
by Mark Le Fanu

British audiences are continuing to come back to the cinema. Admissions for 1989 were 87.9 million, calculated on theatres taking advertising, 96.4 million including regional film theatres and other non-advertising taking venues. This was the sixth consecutive rise in as many years. The big question for exhibitors is whether 1990 will see the magical 100 million mark being broken (which, however, would only return the position to what it was in 1980). It is very probable.

After the nadir of the mid-1980's, cinemas have become more comfortable and agreeable places to visit – better staffed and equipped. The American multiplexes, UCI and National Amusements, have made a big output here: clean, use-friendly places that have succeeded beyond expectation in wooing back the female audience and the older viewer, previously sometimes scared to go out at night. Admissions to multiplex screens jumped from 3.5 million in 1988 to 12.6 million in 1989, and are set to continue the same large percentage leap in 1990.

Of course it is the worldwide success of current Hollywood product that is filling the cinema. The national craze for *Batman* during July and August of 1989, for example, resulted in four million more admissions than in the corresponding period of 1988. With American films in general dominating admissions, it is growing harder for domestic independent distributors to place thoughtful and interesting European (including British) films in cinemas of their choice, or, once there, to keep them in place for any length of time. There is a need for more art houses and flexible small exhibition outlets, especially in London.

On the production side events are much gloomier. It is doubtful whether the total number of films made in the U.K. in 1990 will equal last year's 38 – itself an all-time low. Why is this? An obvious matter for concern is the continuing low level of state subsidy. While the West German film industry receives grants and exemptions worth £40 million per annum, and the French industry up to £50 million, Britain, through its agency British Screen receives a mere £1.5 million – a considerable disparity.

In general the British film industry is finance starved. The withdrawing in 1987 of tax incentives by the Inland Revenue was a crucial blow, as the investment figures for the years 1987–89 clearly attest: in 1987 £200 million was invested in British feature films; in 1988, £126 million; in 1989 only £55 million. The figure for 1990 is not available at the time of writing, but it is likely to be lower than last year's.

With the decline in investment, there has followed a decline in the fortunes of the studios, most of which survive on an exclusive diet of television series. At Pinewood in 1990 only three major productions are slated. Elstree, owned by the reconstituted Goldcrest (itself controlled by Brent Walker and nothing to do with the original company of that name) has sold off more than half of its studio space to the grocery chain Tesco, which is planning to build a superstore on the site. There is a real crisis here. Many of Britain's highly skilled film technicians (who in the mid-1980's helped craft Spielberg movies

SHELL Film and Video Unit

For further details, contact
your local Shell Company, or
Shell International Petroleum Co. Ltd.,
PAC/231, Shell Centre, London SE1 7NA.

A COLLECTION of **IMAGES** *by SHELL FILM & VIDEO UNIT '89*

and other super-productions) are for the first time languishing unemployed.

English Euromovies in Store?
Is the prospect one of unrelieved gloom? Not everyone thinks so. The coming of the integrated European market in 1992, if handled properly, could bring the British film industry new opportunities in the shape of funds for large "Euro-movies" – made in the English language, appealing equally to the North American market (220 millions) and to the western European (325 millions). The model for such productions might be such highly successful past European co-productions as *The Bear* and *The Name of the Rose*.

The Americans themselves seem to be anticipating some such shifting of markets. At the time of writing MCA Universal in partnership with Rank is considering setting up a $1.7 billion combined studio and theme park in Rainham Marshes in Essex (if this falls through, though, the project will go to France). Meanwhile three major British-based film personalities – David Puttnam, Jake Eberts and Roland Joffé – find themselves under contract to Warners, charged among other things with setting up specifically English industry based projects.

The beneficial knock-on effect of television, video and satellite should not be ignored as cinema has for a long time been linked to them symbiotically. Taken together, the exhibition window these outlets provide for feature films generates considerably more income than does theatrical release (in the case of video, three times as much). The question is whether the combined media can be persuaded not merely to purchase the end product (often in the past far too cheaply) but to invest seriously in production.

Sensing that the new European climate offers chances to be taken, Margaret Thatcher – not previously noted for her interest in the film industry – convened a special meeting at Downing Street with leading film personalities on June 15, out of which have emerged a number of interesting initiatives. The government pledged first of all an immediate £5 million to explore the possibility of more vigorous co-productions with the United Kingdom's continental partners. In addition, three potentially important committees were set up in order to look into (a) the renewal of tax incentives, (b) the structure of the industry and (c) the industry's overall funding arrangements. Sir Richard Attenborough (one of the participants) expressed himself delighted with the outcome. More cynical industry-watchers from the press urged the withholding of judgement until concrete results are discernible.

Fair to Middling
After all that, what kind of a year has it been for quality British movies? Fair to middling, perhaps. *My Left Foot* (technically British though shot in Ireland) picked up two Oscars in the face of strongish opposition. *The Adventures of Baron Munchausen*, which might legitimately have expected an Oscar for its art direction, conceded that prize to the dyspeptic urban vision of *Batman*.

Kenneth Branagh's *Henry V* was a fine success with the critics, though it did less well than might be expected at the box-office (but in the States it attracted more than $10 million). There was a somewhat disappointing dearth of British entries at Cannes in 1990 – only one film in the official selection, Ken Loach's controversial but flat movie about Northern Ireland, *Hidden Agenda*. Another controversial film politically was Paul Greengrass's *Resurrected*, an unheroic glimpse of the 1982 Falklands War, told from the point of view of an army private devastated by his injuries.

Comedy produced low par offerings; for example, Michael Tucker's *Wilt*, from the novel Tom Sharpe; Terry Jones's only intermittently zany *Erik the Viking*; and *Nuns on the Run*, a disappointingly dreary film-

Brian Cox and Frances McDormand in Ken Loach's *Hidden Agenda*

debut by Jonathan Lynn (the suave author of television's *Yes, Minister*).

Two films continued the vein of sociological interest in Britain's past (especially the sleazier aspects) which one finds in recent movies like *Scandal, Personal Services* and *Prick Up Your Ears*. These were *Chicago Joe and the Showgirl*, directed by Bernard Rose; and *The Krays*, directed by Peter Medak from a script by Philip Ridley.

Other films to notice included a strong Greenaway, not to everyone's taste: *The Cook, The Thief, His Wife and Her Lover*; also *Fellow Traveller*, directed by Philip Saville from an ingenious script by Mick Eaton about an American writer persecuted under McCarthyism; *In Fading Light*, a fine naturalistic drama about North East fisher folk; *Venus Peter*, a debutant effort directed by Ian Sellar, set in the Orkneys and beautifully photographed by Gabriel Beristain; and *The Wolves of Willoughby Chase*, an Anglo-Czech fantasy for children with first rate atmospheric art direction.

Jeremy Cooper in *The Reflecting Skin*

The Cook, the Thief, His Wife & Her Lover

Script and Direction: Peter Greenaway. Photography: Sacha Vierny. Production Design: Ben Van Os, Jan Roelfs. Scenic Artists: Michael de Graaf, Weiger de Jong. Music: Michael Nyman. Players: Richard Bohringer, Michael Gambon, Helen Mirren, Alan Howard, Tim Roth, Ciaran Hinds, Gary Olsen. Produced by Allarts Cook (London)/Erato Films/Films Inc. (Paris). 124 mins.

Any film by Peter Greenaway guarantees a feast of visual delights: along with Wim Wenders he is perhaps the most painterly of modern film-makers, with a particular appreciation for the richness of 16th and 17th century Dutch art. In *The Cook, the Thief, His Wife & Her Lover* the visual tone is set by the huge Frans Hals-style reproductions that decorate the sumptuous constructed restaurant in which most of the action takes place. Sacha Vierny, as ever, is Greenaway's cameraman charged with evoking magical richnesses of colour: deep reds, mysterious sables, odd, decadent greens – hues that require the big screen for their full effectiveness.

It is tempting to talk about Greenaway in purely formal terms. Yet movies – even the most avant-garde – suffer if they lack a story and a minimum amount of psychological verisimilitude. *The Cook, the Thief* centres its attention on the riotous behaviour of the owner of the plush restaurant, an overbearing Italian gangster, played with malevolent gusto by Michael Gambon. Greenaway remarks somewhere in an interview that he was intending in this film

---

Still from *The Cook, the Thief, His Wife and Her Lover*

to dramatise "pure evil," but the viewer is left feeling he hasn't quite succeeded. As portrayed by Gambon, the character lacks subtlety and nuance. Compared to the great Jacobean stage villains whom Greenaway admires, what strikes us most is a poverty of spoken dialogue – a crucial failure of eloquence needed to prevent the drama becoming merely sordid.

The film is indeed strong meat, kept alive by its constant visual inventiveness. The camera restlessly tracks backwards and forwards on a single long rail between the restaurant itself and the behind-the-scenes activities in the kitchens. Lots of deep focus; excellent visualisation of space (elegantly aided by production designers Ben Van Os and Jan Roelfs); some remarkable scenes of nudity (particularly in the Renaissance-style tableau where Alan Howard and Helen Mirren are hidden in a frozen meat compartment – you really feel how vulnerable their bodies are.) Whatever else it is, a film by Greenaway is an event. His fascination with death and decadence continues to issue in highly unusual works of cinema.

Mark Le Fanu

Fellow Traveller

Script: Michael Eaton, Direction: Philip Saville. Photography: John Kenway. Editing: Greg Miller. Design: Gavin Davies. Players: Ron Silver, Imogen Stubbs, Hart Bochner, Daniel J. Travanti, Katherine Borowitz, Julian Fellowes.

Set in the mid-1950's, *Fellow Traveller* tells the story of Hollywood scriptwriter Asa (played by Ron Silver and loosely based on the real life figure of Ring Lardner Jnr) who is hounded by McCarthyism and takes refuge in England, where he finds work of sorts composing hack episodes for the new television serial "Robin Hood."

Back in Hollywood, meanwhile, his friend the actor Clifford, having decided to "name" his fellow left-wing sympathisers at the HUAC hearings, commits suicide, shocking everyone who knew him. In fact, a theme of psychoanalysis runs through either man's destiny; both Asa and Clifford have been seeing a sinister psychiatrist, Leavy who, it turns out, has been betraying them to the American authorities. The scriptwriter has a wife, still living in the States; while the actor has (or had) a girlfriend, now in England – both pretty. The fact that the women are in the wrong place at the right time, so to speak, gives rise to further complications – scope for infidelity, or its temptation.

Fellow Traveller is a co-production between the BBC, the British Film Institute and the American company Home Box Office. In the past, BFI input has often led to films that are top-heavy in ideas, low on characterisation. There is a certain sense in which this is still true here: the political theme of McCarthyism is firmly in the foreground, where other films might have been content to leave it more in the background in order to concentrate on the characters' private relationships, in which cinema is usually strongest.

The film is genuinely subtle, even ingenious, in tying up the private and the public aspects of its characters' anxieties – the Freudian and the Marxian, if you like. Nor does the hero get off scot-free, though he is on the whole sympathetically treated (a nice performance by Ron Silver). Mick Eaton, the film's English scriptwriter, has an excellent ear for American dialogue, putting consistently believable words in the actors' mouths. The film is wittier and sharper than one was led to expect.

Philip Saville directs proceedings skilfully, without quite managing to solve certain problems of transition (in the movement between the film's present, 1954, and its flashback past, 1943, the characters don't appear to have aged). A particularly effective aspect of the film are the pastiche Robin Hood episodes: hilarious in their own

The late Ray McAnally in *Venus Peter*

way, but not over-caricatured, and in the closing reels meshing nicely into the general theme of liberty and conscience which the rest of the film is exploring.

Mark Le Fanu

Venus Peter

Script: Christopher Rush. Direction: Ian Sellar. Photography: Gabriel Beristain. Editing: David Spiers. Design: Andy Harris. Music: Jonathan Dove. Players: Ray McAnally, David Hayman, Sinead Cusack, Gordon R. Strachan, Caroline Paterson, Emma Dingwall, Louise Breslin, Juliet Cadzow, Sheila Keith. Produced by British Film Institute/Channel 4/The Scottish Film Production Fund/Orkney Islands Council/British Screen. 94 mins.

Memory, fantasy, childhood: these are not specifically British themes of course, but the British seem to do them very well. *Venus Peter* joins a group of thoughtful, poetic films of recent years that includes *The Kitchen Toto*, *The Magic Toyshop*, *A World Apart*, *Hope and Glory*, the Bill Douglas *Trilogy* and (going further back) *The Go-Between*: stories of childhood, and its connection to the fatal falling away of innocence.

Our hero, a small boy, is brought up in the lonely Orkneys, different from other children in that he is more sensitive and poetry-loving (oddly enough, one doesn't feel he'll grow up to be a poet). The father is away somewhere unexplained – the child thinks he is in the navy but it turns out he is only a prosaic businessman. Home, meantime, is run by the womenfolk who can be cruel and careless to a youngster's feelings. Only the old grandfather trawler captain (nicely played by Ray McAnally in his last performance) seems to be on the boy's spiritual wavelength.

Set in the late 1940's and early 1950's, the film convincingly conjures up a lost era, a period before modern amenities became available. Wood and stone are still the dominant materials of people's lives, rather than plastic. We are in the epoch before television, and story-telling is a real part of the community. A lovely scene shows the boy asleep by the hearth while, as the family mend their nets, the old grandfather spins a yarn about being swallowed by a whale. The substantial pleasures of the film are visual. Gabriel Beristain, the young cameraman (like the movie's director, a recent graduate of the National Film and Television School) manages to bathe his locations in beautiful, eerie, end-of-the-world colours – not the usual muted grays and blues one expects from a northern atmosphere. (In fact the original tale was set in Fife, on Scotland's lower East coast, but the transposition to the Orkneys works well.) There are lovely seascapes and landscapes resembling a pre-Raphaelite painting – by Holman Hunt, say, or William Dyce.

One strange omission: in a story so much about the sea, it is odd that we never venture onto the sea itself. The waves are always viewed from the shoreline. This is a pity: you feel that the film would have had a greater poetry if its climax had taken a plunge into the unknown.

Mark Le Fanu

MARK LE FANU is a freelance film critic who writes for most of the major British newspapers and magazines. He is the author of a study on Tarkovsky and a forthcoming book about Mizoguchi.

Recent and Forthcoming Films

American Friends. Script: Michael Palin. Dir: Tristram Powell. Phot: Phiip Bonham-Carter. Players: Michael Palin, Connie Booth, Trini Alvarado, Alfred Molina. Prod: Prominent Features Ltd.

The Big Man. Script: Don MacPherson. Dir: David Leland. Players: Ian Bannen, Joanne Whalley-Kilmer, Ian Bannen, Billy Connolly. Prod: Palace/Miramax/British Screen.

Buddy's Song. Script: Nigel Hinton. Dir: Claude Whatham. Phot: John Hooper. Players: Roger Daltrey, Michael Elphick, Chesney Hawkes, Sharon Duce. Prod: Corbishley-Baird Enterprises.

Bullseye. Script: Leslie Bricusse. Dir: Michael Winner. Phot: Alan Jones. Players: Michael Caine, Roger Moore, Sally Kirkland, Deborah Barrymore. Prod: Golan/Winner/21st Century Film Corporation (UK).

Centrepoint. Script: Nigel Williams. Dir: Piers Haggard. Phot: Richard Greatrex. Players: Jonathan Firth, Murray Head, Cheryl Campbell, John Shrapnel, Bob Peck, Veronica Quilligan. Prod: Rosso Productions for Channel Four.

Dear Rosie. Script: Peter Morgan, Mark Wadlow. Dir: Peter Cattano. Phot: Clive Tickner. Players: Fiona Victory, Terence Wilton, Roger Hammond, Su Elliot, Belinda Mayne, Remy Beard. Prod: World's End/Film Four International/British Screen.

Devices and Desires. Script: Thomas Ellice (from the P.D. James novel). Dir: John Davies. Players: Roy Marsden, Susannah York, James Faulkner, Gemma Jones. Prod: Anglia Films (John Rosenberg).

Diamond Skulls. Script: Tim Rose Price. Dir: Nick Broomfield. Phot: Michael Coulter. Players: Gabriel Byrne, Amanda Donohue, Michael Hordern, Judy Parfitt, Douglas Hodge. Prod: Working Title/British Screen/Channel Four.

Father Jim. Script and dir: Terry Green. Phot: Dusty Miller. Players: Dennis Waterman, Roger Daltrey, Ron Dean, Penelope Milford. Prod: East End Films.

Frankenstein's Baby. Script: Emma Tennant. Dir: Robert Bierman. Players: Nigel Planer, Kate Buffery, Yvonne Bryceland, Sian Thomas, William Armstrong. Prod: BBC Television/BBC Enterprises.

Hidden Agenda. Script: Jim Allen. Dir: Ken

Loach. Phot: Clive Tickner. Players: Brian Cox, Frances McDormand, Brad Dourif, Mai Zetterling, Jim Norton. Prod: Hemdale.
Hallelujah Anyhow. Script: Jean "Binta" Breeze, Matthew Jacobs. Dir: Matthew Jacobs. Phot: Remi Adefarasin. Players: Dona Croll, Keith David, George Harris, Valeria Buchanan. Prod: BBC Screen Two.
Hamlet. Script: Chris De Vore, from Shakespeare. Dir: Franco Zeffirelli. Phot: David Watkin. Des: Dante Ferretti. Players: Mel Gibson, Glenn Close, Alan Bates, Paul Schofield, Ian Holm, Helena Bonham-Carter, Trevor Peacock. Prod: Marquis Productions.
The Garden. Script and Dir: Derek Jarman. Phot: Christopher Hughes. Players: Tilda Swinton, Pete Lee Wilson, Jessica Martin. Prod: Basilisk.
In Fading Light. Script and dir: Murray Martin and Amber Films Collective. Phot: Tom Hadaway. Players: Joe Caffrey, Maureen Harold, Dave Hill, Brian Hogg, Sammy Johnson, Joanna Ripley, Amber Styles. Prod: Amber Films.

The Krays. Script: Philip Ridley. Dir: Peter Medak. Phot: Alex Thomson. Players: Billie Whitelaw, Tom Bell, Gary Kemp, Martin Kemp, Susan Fleetwood, Charlotte Cornwell, Steven Berkoff, Jimmy Jewel, Victor Spinetti, Barbara Ferris. Prod: Fugitive Features/Parkfield.
Looking for Langston. Script and Dir: Isaac Julien. Ph: Nina Kellgren. Players: Ben Ellison, Matthew Baidoo, Akim Mogaji, John Wilson, Dencil Williams. Prod: Sankofa Film and Video.
Madly in Love. Script: Sandy Welsh. Dir: Ross Devenish. Phot: Mick Coulter. Players: Penelope Wilton, Samantha Bond, Martin Wener, Caroline Goodall, Anna Healy, Gordon Reid. Prod: Shaker Films/Channel Four.
Memphis Belle. Script: Monte Merrick. Dir: Michael Caton-Jones. Phot: David Watkin. Players: Matthew Modine, Eric Stolz, D.B. Sweeney, Tate Donovan, Sean Astin, Billy Zane, Jane Horrocks. Prod: Warner Bros/Enigma.
The Miracle. Script and Dir: Neil Jordan. Phot: Philippe Rousselot. Players: Beverley D'Angelo, Donal McCann, Niall Byrne, Lorraine Pilkington, Mikkel Gaup, Tom Hickey, Stephen

A wounded Eric Stoltz in *Memphis Belle*

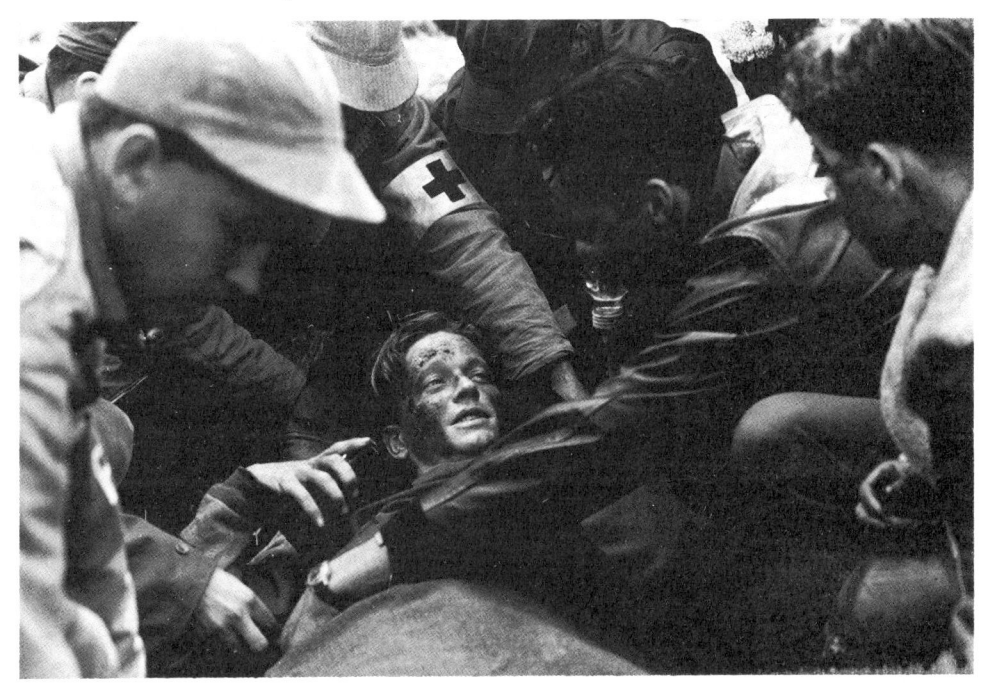

Martin and Gary Kemp in *The Krays*, released via United Media Film Sales

photo: Richard Blanshard

Brennan. Prod: Palace/Film Four International/British Screen.
The Monk. Script and Dir: Paco Lara. Phot: Angel Luis Fernandez. Players: Paul McGann, Sophie Ward, Isla Blair, Freda Dowie, Aitana Sanchez Gijon. Prod: Celtic/Mediterranean/Target International.
Never Come Back. Script: David Pirie. Dir: Ben Bolt. Phot: John McGlashan. Players: James Fox, Nathaniel Parker, Suzanna Hamilton, Martin Clunes. Prod: BBC.
Newshounds. Script and Dir: Les Blair. Phot: Remi Adefarasin. Players: Alison Steadman, Judith Scott, Adrian Edmondson, Paul Kember, Antony Marsh, Christopher Fulford. Prod: BBC/Working Title.
The Object of Beauty. Script and Dir: Michael Lindsay-Hogg. Phot: Chris Seager. Players: John Malkovich, Andie McDowell, Peter Riegert, Rudi Davies, Joss Ackland, Bill Paterson. Prod: Avenue Pictures/BBC.
A Perfect Hero. Script: Allan Prior. Dir: James Cellan Jones. Phot: Ernest Vincze. Players: Nigel Havers, James Fox, Bernard Hepton, Barbara Leigh-Hunt, Patrick Ryecart, Nicholas Pritchard. Prod: Havahall/LWT.
Prospero's Books. Script and Dir: Peter Greenaway, based on Shakespeare's *The Tempest*. Phot: Sacha Vierny. Players: John Gielgud, Isabel Pasco, Mark Rylance, Tom Bell, Michel Blanc. Prod: Allarts.
The Reflecting Skin. Script and Dir: Philip Ridley. Phot: Dick Pope. Players: Viggo Mortensen, Lindsay Duncan, Jeremy Cooper. Prod: Fugitive Films.
Rosencrantz and Guildenstern Are Dead. Script and Dir: Tom Stoppard. Phot: Peter Biziou. Players: Richard Dreyfuss, Tim Roth, Gary Oldman, Iain Glen, Ian Richardson. Prod: Brandenberg Productions.
The Runner. Script and editing: Mark Talbot-Butler. Dir: Chris Jones. Players: Terence Ford, Paris Jefferson, Andrew Mitchell, Raymond Johnson, Ivan Rogers. Prod: Living Spirit Pictures.
The Russia House. Script: Tom Stoppard

based on John Le Carré. Dir: Fred Schepesi. Phot: Ian Baker. Players: Sean Connery, Michelle Pfeiffer, Roy Scheider, James Fox, John Mahoney, Klaus Maria Brandauer. Prod: Pathe Entertainment-Schepesi Films.
The Sheltering Sky. Script: Mark Peploe from the novel by Paul Bowles. Dir: Bernardo Bertolucci. Phot: Vittorio Storaro. Players: Debra Winger, John Malkovich, Campbell Scott, Jill Bennett, Timothy Spall, Eric Vu An. Prod: The Sahara Company/Jeremy Thomas.
Silent Scream. Script: Bill Beech. Dir: David Hayman. Phot: Denis Crossan. Players: Iain Glen, Ann Kristen, Tom Watson, David McKail. Prod: BFI/Film Four International/Scottish Film Production Fund/Antonine.
Untitled 90. Script and Dir: Mike Leigh. Phot. Dick Pope. Players: Moya Brady, Jim Broadbent, Jane Horrocks, Stephen Rea, Claire Skinner, Timothy Spall, Alison Steadman, David Thewlis. Prod: Thin Man Films/Film Four International/British Screen.
When Love Dies. Script: Nigel Moffat. Dir: Horace Ove. Phot: Sean Van Hales. Players: Josette Simon, Brian Bovell, Norman Beaton, Stefan Kalipha, Mona Hammond, Calvin Simpson, Leila Marr. Prod: Picture Palace/Channel Four.
Young Soul Rebels. Dir: Isaac Julien. Prod: BFI/Channel Four Television.

British Production Companies

Allied Vision
360 Oxford Street
London W1N 9HA
Tel: (1) 409 1984

British Film Institute Production
21 Stephen Street
London W1.
Tel: (1) 255 1444

Boyd's Co. Film Prod
9 Great Newport Street
London WC2H 7JA
Tel: (1) 836 5601

British Lion
Pinewood Studios
Bucks
Tel: (753) 651700

Burrill Productions
51 Lansdowne Road
London W11 2LG
Tel: (1) 727 1442

Centre Films
7 Imperial Road
London SW6 2AG
Tel: (1) 731 6151

Cinema Verity
Goldcrest Elstree Studios
Borehamwood
Herts WDG 1JG
Tel: (1) 953 1600

Crossbow Films
42 Connaught Square
London W2 2HD
Tel: (1) 724 6966

Enigma Productions
13–15 Queens Gate Place Mews
London
SW7 5BG
Tel: (1) 581 0238

Euston Films
365 Euston Road
London NW1 3AR
Tel: (1) 387 0911

Enterprise Pictures
113 Wardour Street
London W1V 3TD
Tel: (1) 734 3372

Flamingo Pictures
47 Lonsdale Square
London N1 1EW
Tel: (1) 607 9958

Mark Forstater Productions
8A Trebeck Street
London W1Y 7RL
Tel: (1) 408 0733

Goldcrest Films and Television
36/44 Brewer Street
London W1R 3HP
Tel: (1) 437 8696

Greenpoint Films
5a Noel Street
London W1V 3RB
Tel: (1) 437 6492

HandMade Films
26 Cadogan Square
London SW1X 0JP
Tel: (1) 584 8345

Initial Films and Television
22 Golden Square
London W1R 3PA
Tel: (1) 439 8994

Little Bird
8 West Street
London WC2H 9NG
Tel: (1) 836 2112

Euan Lloyd Productions
Pinewood Studios
Bucks
Tel: (1) 753 651700

Merchant Ivory Productions
46 Lexington Street
London W1P 3LH
Tel: (1) 437 1200

NFH
37 Ovington Square
London SW3
Tel: (1) 584 7561

Palace Productions
16–17 Wardour Mews
London W1V 3FF
Tel: (1) 734 7060

Prominent Features
68A Delancey Street
London NW1 7RY
Tel: (1) 284 0242

Recorded Picture Company
8–12 Broadwick Street
London W1
Tel: (1) 439 0607

Red Rooster Film
11–13 Macklin Street
London WC2B 5NH

Sands Films
119 Rotherhithe Street
London SE16 4NF
Tel: (1) 231 2209

Umbrella Films
Twickenham Studios
London TW1 2AW
Tel: (1) 892 4477

Michael White
13 Duke Street
London SW1Y 6DB
Tel: (1) 839 3971

Working Title
10 Livonoa Street
London W1V 3PH
Tel: (1) 439 2424

Zenith Productions
15 St. George Street
London W1R 9DE
Tel: (1) 499 8006

Distributors

Majors

United International Pictures (U.I.P)
Mortimer House
37–41 Mortimer Street
London W1A 2JL
Tel: (1) 636 1655

Warner Brothers
135 Wardour Street
London W1V 4AP
Tel: (1) 734 8400

Columbia/Tri-Star Film Distributors
19–23 Wells Street
London W1P 3FP
Tel: (1) 580 2090

Twentieth Century-Fox
20th Century House
31–32 Soho Square
London W1V 6AP
Tel: (1) 437 7766

Rank Film Distributors
127 Wardour Street
London W1V 4AD
Tel: (1) 437 9020

Independents and Art-Houses

Artificial Eye Film Co.
211 Camden High Street
London NW1
Tel: (1) 267 6036

Blue Dolphin Films
15 Old Compton Street
London W1
Tel: (1) 439 9511

British Film Institute
21 Stephen Street
London W1
Tel: (1) 255 1444

Cinema of Women
27 Clerkenwell Close
London EC1
Tel: (1) 251 4978

Contemporary Films
24 Southwood Lawn Road
London N6 5SF
Tel: (1) 340 5715

Electric Pictures
22 Carol Street
London NW1 OHU
Tel: (1) 284 0524

Enterprise Pictures
113 Wardour Street
London W1V 3TD
Tel: (1) 734 3372

Entertainment Film Distributors
27 Soho Square
London W1V 6AX
Tel: 439 1606

Guild Film Distribution
Evelyn House
62 Oxford Street
London W1N 9LD
Tel: (1) 631 0240

Hobo Film Enterprises
9 St. Martins Court
London WC2N 4A7
Tel: (1) 895 0328

ICA Projects
12 Carlton House Terrace
London SW1
Tel: (1) 930 0493

Mainline Pictures
37 Museum Street

Useful Addresses

London WC1A 1LP
Tel: (1) 242 5523

Medusa Pictures
41–42 Berners Street
London W1P 3AA
Tel: (1) 255 2200

New Realm Film Distributors
Townsend House
22–25 Dean Street
London W1
Tel: (1) 427 0143

The Other Cinema
79 Wardour Street
London W1V 3TH
Tel: (1) 734 8508

Palace Pictures
16–17 Wardour Mews
London W1V 3FF
Tel: (1) 734 7060

Pathe Releasing
76 Hammersmith Road
London W14 8YR
Tel: (1) 603 4555

Premier Releasing
360 Oxford Street
London W1N 9HA
Tel: (1) 493 0440

Recorded Releasing
66–68 Margaret Street
London W1N 7FL
Tel: (1) 734 7477

Vestron Film Distributors (U.K.)
69 New Oxford Street
London WC1A 1DG
Tel: (1) 379 0406

Virgin Film Distributors
5 Gt. Chapel Street
London W1V 2AG
Tel: (1) 494 3756

Association of Independent Producers (AIP)
17 Great Pulteney Street
London W1
Tel: (1) 434 0181

British Academy of Film and Television Arts (BAFTA)
195 Piccadilly
London W1V 9LG
Tel: (1) 734 0022

British Board of Film Classification (BBFC)
3 Soho Square
London W1V 5DE
Tel: (1) 439 7961

British Equity
8 Harley Street
London W1N 2AB
Tel: (1) 636 6367

British Film and Television Producers' Association (BFTPA)
Paramount House
162–170 Wardour Street
London W1V 4LA
Tel: (1) 437 7700

British Screen
38–39 Oxford Street
London W1
Tel: (1) 434 0291

Cinematograph Exhibitors' Association (CEA)
22–25 Dean Street
London W1V 6HQ
Tel: (1) 734 9551

Directors' Guild of Great Britain
Lyndhurst Road
London NW3 5NG
Tel: (1) 431 1800

Federation Against Copyright Theft (FACT)
7 Victory Business Centre
Isleworth
Middlesex TW7 6ER
Tel: (1) 568 6646

Film Four International
60 Charlotte Street
London W1
Tel: (1) 631 4444

Independent Programme Producers' Association (IPPA)
50–51 Berwick Street
London W1V 4RD
Tel: (1) 439 7034

Society of Film Distributors (SFD)
72–73 Dean Street
London W1V 5HB
Tel: (1) 437 4383

Writers' Guild of Great Britain
430 Edgware Road
London W2 1EH
Tel: (1) 723 8074

The American Film Institute European Community Film Festival

June 1991

New York
Washington, D.C.
Los Angeles
Minneapolis

Now in its seventh year

"This event gives me particular pleasure because of its richness and symbolism. It emphasizes the already close ties between Europeans and Americans—namely a mutual respect for each others' cultures and talents—and it opens the way for even greater professional, economic and artistic dialogue."
—Simone Veil

Presented in cooperation with The European Community

The American Film Institute National Exhibition Programs
Ken Wlaschin, Director

AFI/L.A. FilmFest
FIAPF accredited, held annually in mid-April. Largest, most diverse film festival in the U.S. Non-competitive. International and U.S. features, shorts, documentaries.

The American Film Institute, Manor House
2021 N. Western Ave., Los Angeles CA 90027
Telephone (213)856-7707
Telex 3729910 FILM LSA
Fax (213)462-4049

AFI National Film Theater
Year-round programs at the Kennedy Center. *Preview* magazine issued bi-monthly. International and U.S. features, shorts, documentaries, video.

The American Film Institute
The John F. Kennedy Center for the Performing Arts
Washington, D.C. 20566
Telephone (202)828-4028
Telex 9102409077 AFI UQ
Fax (202) 659-1970

AFI National Video Festival
Founded in 1981; America's leading showcase for television and video art. Tours nationally.

The American Film Institute,
Manor House 2021 N. Western Ave.,
Los Angeles CA 90027
Telephone (213)856-7707
Telex 3729910 FILM LSA
Fax (213)462-4049

U.S.A.
by William Wolf

The world of movies in America grew more schizoid than ever as Hollywood further narrowed its aim for blockbusters, while movies with creativity as a greater priority still managed to break through despite the tightening crunch and the steeper odds. The cost of making films continued to soar in a new era of free-spending befitting the blockbuster mentality.

The talk of the industry was **Teenage Mutant Ninja Turtles**, New Line Cinema's bonanza that brought parents to theatres dragged by their hype-conditioned children, and that racked up nearly $115 million at the box-office in the first 52 days of the film's release. **Pretty Woman**, Disney's fluff teaming Richard Gere as a business tycoon and Julia Roberts as the hooker he falls for, grossed some $110 million in its first 59 days. Paramount's action sea drama **The Hunt for Red October** climbed well above the $100 million mark, as did the more intimate Oscar-winner **Driving Miss Daisy**, the race relations drama that had been widely turned down before Warner Bros. decided to release it. The $100 million gross status was becoming ever more attainable.

The blockbuster game was evident in the type of expensive pictures scheduled for 1990 summer release, with the list including *Dick Tracy*, starring Warren Beatty and Madonna (estimated to cost $25–$30 million), *Back to the Future III* (cost $40 million), *Another 48 Hours* (cost $40 million), *Total Recall* (cost $50 million), and *Die Hard II* (cost $55–60 million). Sequels to past winners were favourite gambles; Francis Ford Coppola began production on *The Godfather Part III* with an expected cost of at least $51 million. Among the top ten grossers of 1989, when moviegoers spent a record $5 billion at the box-office, four were sequels – *Indiana Jones and the Last Crusade* (2nd place behind *Batman*), *Lethal Weapon 2* (3rd place), *Back to the Future, Part II* (6th), and *Ghostbusters II* (7th). Only two films in the 1989 top ten aimed at what might be termed mature concerns – *Rain Man* (5th) and *Dead Poets Society* (10th).

Leading the big-spender tone in Hollywood was the Jon Peters-Peter Guber phenomenon. Demands for executive salaries rose in light of the $2.75 million a year, plus bonuses, each was assured as co-chairmen of Columbia after the company

Stanley Donen won the Golden Sheaf award at Spain's Valladolid Festival in 1989

From the classics to the cutting edge the American Cinematheque celebrates the world of the Moving Picture in the film capital of the world.

American Cinematheque
1717 Highland Avenue #814
Hollywood USA 90028
213.461.9622

Gary Essert, Artistic Director

Warren Beatty in his starring vehicle, *Dick Tracy*, which brought in more than $100 million at the U.S. box-office
photo: Peter Sorel

was bought by Sony, and the $500 million in assets Sony had to give Warner Bros. to acquire the duo. Excelling even that was the new trend created by the high prices Peters and Guber began paying for scripts, such as the $1.25 million in commitments for a screenplay called *Radio Flyer*.

Correspondingly agents began increasing demands for their writer clients. Meanwhile, the price for superstars continued to soar. Estimates were that Jack Nicholson, whose own much-delayed *The Two Jakes* was finally released, would reap $40 million from *Batman*. Increasingly hot Bruce Willis, who provided only the voice of a baby in the surprise success *Look Who's Talking*, was expected to earn $10 million as his profit share. That's not to mention such money-machines as Arnold Schwarzenegger and Sylvester Stallone.

Still Room for Quality
The artistic miracle in this high-rolling atmosphere was that creative, worthwhile films continued to surface. Oliver Stone's **Born on the Fourth of July** struck another blow for dealing with the lingering pain and shame of the Vietnam War. The AIDS crisis was dramatised in the director Norman René's independently-made **Longtime Companion**, which won acclaim for its candour and sensitivity. Joel and Ethan Coen did an entertaining, clever take on the gangster movie with **Miller's Crossing**. The highly unusual **Metropolitan**, a critical view of the young socialite crowd in New York, heralded the arrival of talented new director Whit Stillman. John McNaughton's **Henry: Portrait of a Serial Killer** won attention as a chilling drama about random violence.

Michael Moore's controversial pseudo-documentary **Roger and Me** hilariously attacked General Motors for policies that the film charged created misery in Flint, Mich. It was significant that a major

Michelle Pfeiffer delighted audiences everywhere with her interpretation of Susie Diamond in *The Fabulous Baker Boys*
photo: Lorey Sebastian/Fox

the screen based on the 1950's cult book by Hubert Selby, Jr.; Percy Adlon's **Rosalie Goes Shopping**, a satirical treatment of America's consumerism; Sandra Bernhard's funny and funky performance film **Without You I'm Nothing**; John Waters's teenage sendup **Cry Baby**, not as good as **Hairspray**, but still possessing the offbeat Waters brand of outrageous humour, and Gus Van Sant Jr.'s unsettling **Drugstore Cowboy**, a prime showcase for Matt Dillon. Michael Caine gave one of his superior performances as a vengeful executive bypassed for promotion in **A Shock to the System**, and Danny De Vito, Michael Douglas and Kathleen Turner teamed entertainingly in **The War of the Roses**, a comic if nasty film about divorce carried to extremes.

Rising Reputations

Director David Lynch, who conquered

Lena Olin in *Enemies, a Love Story*, based on the book by Isaac Bashevis Singer
photo: Takashi Sida

company, Warner Bros., distributed the film. Woody Allen's **Crimes and Misdemeanors** probed important moral issues confronting contemporary society in his comedy–drama about a man who has his mistress killed to save his position in life and gets away with it. **Glory**, directed by Edward Zwick, powerfully recalled the true story of a black regiment that fought in America's Civil War. **Enemies, a Love Story**, a Paul Mazursky film based on a work by Isaac Bashevis Singer, dealt with the effect of the Holocaust on post-Second World War immigrants to America. Sidney Lumet's **Q and A**, although saddled with a contrived love story, dug sharply into police and political corruption in New York.

Other noteworthy films included **Last Exit to Brooklyn**, the raw drama which German director Uli Edel finally brought to

Bruce Willis in *Die Hard 2*, directed by the 31-year-old Finn, Renny Harlin

television with his high-rated *Twin Peaks* series and is still praised for *Blue Velvet*, added to his laurels by snaring the top Cannes Film Festival prize for **Wild at Heart**. Amy Heckerling made a big leap in cracking Hollywood's coolness toward women directors when her **Look Who's Talking** became a huge hit. Although **Blue Steel** met a barrage of criticism, director Karen Bigelow gained in demonstrating that a woman could make a violent thriller, as did Jamie Lee Curtis in playing a tough cop in the film.

Among performers, Alec Baldwin was definitely the strong new male star on the block, as evidenced in *Miami Blues* and *The Hunt for Red October*. Julia Roberts became the sought-after new woman star, thanks to her performances in *Steel Magnolias* and *Pretty Woman*, a film which also spelled a comeback for Richard Gere. Michelle Pfeiffer, who had previously shown her versatility in *Dangerous Liaisons*, smouldered as a night club singer in *The Fabulous Baker Boys*. The career of Denzel Washington, winning a best supporting actor Oscar for *Glory*, was also taking off, as was that of Morgan Freeman, who gave such a fine performance in *Driving Miss Daisy* and landed a key role in *Bonfire of the Vanities*.

Controversy

New criticism of the Motion Picture Association of America's movie rating system erupted over the branding of several prominent films with an X rating. When *Tie Me Up! Tie Me Down!*, *The Cook, The Thief, His Wife and Her Lover*, and *Henry: Portrait of a Serial Killer* were slapped with X's, the distributors decided to open them without a rating rather than accept the X rating, which the public perceives as indicating pornography. Miramax began a legal action in the case of *Tie Me Up! Tie Me Down!*, and another suit was filed on behalf of *Henry*. As debate over the X heated up, influential television critics Gene Siskel and Roger Ebert proposed an A for adult rating that

Clint Eastwood starring in *White Hunter, Black Heart*
photo: Warner Bros.

wouldn't have the stigma of the X, a solution others have also been advocating.

In a move against the practice of presenting commercials in movie theatres, both the Disney Co. and Warner Bros. announced that they would not permit their films to be shown where commercials would also be exhibited. The practice, long accepted in many other countries, drew increased audience criticism in the United States, where some 6,000 theatres were showing advertisements on screen.

The most juicy legal battle in Hollywood that many were gleefully watching was columnist Art Buchwald's suit against Paramount claiming the idea for the film *Coming to America* was stolen from him. A court awarded $250,000 to Buchwald and 19% of the film's profits. But despite a world-wide rental gross of $125 million, Paramount claimed a loss of $18 million. The next step was a battle over the accounting. The fight delighted insiders long critical of studio accounting and occasioned a barrage of jokes.

The cinema suffered the loss of three legendary stars with the deaths of Bette Davis at 81, Greta Garbo at 84, and Laurence Olivier at 82. Other deaths included Hollywood star Paulette Goddard, 84, actor and song and dance man Sammy Davis, Jr., 64, and Jim Henson, 53, creator of the internationally adored Muppets, and Mel Blanc, 81, who provided the great variety of voices for characters in some 3,000 animated cartoons.

Miller's Crossing

Script: Joel and Ethan Coen. Direction: Joel Coen. Photography: Barry Sonnenfeld. Editing: Michael Miller. Music: Carter Burwell. Production Design: Dennis Gassner. Players: Gabriel Byrne, Albert Finney, Marcia Gay Harden, John Turturro, Jon Polito, J.E. Freeman. Produced by Ethan Coen. A Ted and Jim Pedas/Ben Barenholtz/Bill Durkin Production for Circle Films. A 20th Century-Fox release. 115 mins.

Brothers Joel and Ethan Coen, who scored with *Blood Simple* and *Raising Arizona*, have yet another winner in their quirky, stylised gangster spoof *Miller's Crossing*. Told straight, without the actors giving any indication that they think they're playing comedy, the film is a lively blend of suspense, humour, and incisive characterisation that is a distinctive variation on the gangster genre. The closest to it is *Prizzi's Honor*, but the Coens (both wrote it; Joel directed) are on a wavelength of their own.

The setting is an Eastern American city during prohibition. It is thoroughly corrupt, with mobsters controlling compromised politicians. The crooked deals are played out as if they're on a grand scale even though they are small potatoes, like a fixed fight between palookas. Gabriel Byrne is first-rate as a hood who is the protégé of a tough Irish gang boss, played by Albert

Gabriel Byrne and Albert Finney in *Miller's Crossing*

photo: Patti Perret/Fox

Finney in one of his memorable performances. Father-and-son type dynamics are at work in their relationship, which explodes over a woman, played toughly with inner- pain and outer cool by fascinating and sexy Marcia Gay Harden. Other entertaining character performances include John Turturro's effeminate, conniving hood Bernie.

Much but not all of the violence is played for laughs, with machine-guns riddling targets with overkill. The plot, also deliberately guilty of excess, is filled with so much double-dealing you could use a scorecard. We see nothing of the city beyond the mob milieu, which helps make the picture effectively single-minded in creating a bizarre little world of corruption, love, ambition, and betrayal depicted with visual panache, witty screenwriting, and refreshing talent.

William Wolf

Metropolitan

Script and Direction: Whit Stillman. Photography: John Thomas. Editing: Christopher Tellefsen. Music: Mark Suozzo, Tom Judson. Players: Edward Clements, Christopher Eigman, Carolyn Farina, Taylor Nichols, Isabel Gillies, Elizabeth Thompson, Will Kempe. Produced by Stillman for Westerly Films and Allagash Films. A New Line Cinema release. 98 mins.

American films, whether studio projects or independent efforts like *Metropolitan*, are rarely steeped in virtual non-stop conversation, as in the manner of the French *My Night at Maud's*. The producer–writer– director of *Metropolitan* has provided a delightful exception. Imagine going to a Hollywood story conference and trying to sell an executive on the idea of a film about young college-age socialites on New York's posh East Side who go to

Young socialites play strip poker in *Metropolitan*

debutant balls and meet to talk about their lives. Stillman creates a bit of tension in what passes for a plot with the arrival of a decidedly less affluent young man from the less fashionable West Side. He fancies himself a radical, but he, too, is mostly talk, and is accepted only because the women don't have enough escorts.

With this mix Stillman, making his first feature, deftly shows the utter emptiness of the daily social whirl among this declining breed while making them amusing to watch. He twits them without being condescending. He also develops a delicate romance between the shy group member Audrey, charmingly portrayed by Carolyn Farina, and Tom Townsend as the outsider, understandingly played by Edward Clements. An undercurrent of loneliness and unhappiness runs beneath the pretence, snobbery, and surface glitter that masks a decadent preppie lifestyle and the potential for inflicting hurt without any conflict of conscience. The acting is uniformly excellent, and the faces are new and fresh.

Any writer–director who can make such an unusual and polished film on such a difficult subject and manage to keep it both entertaining and insightful must be judged a promising talent. *Metropolitan* presents problem for foreign-language subtitlers since it is so talky, but nevertheless is so skilfully drawn that it can communicate universal truths about its special environment in the way that films of Eric Rohmer do.

William Wolf

WILLIAM WOLF is a veteran American film critic and journalist whose work has appeared in Cue, New York Magazine, *Gannett publications, and a variety of leading newspapers, magazines, and journals. He teaches at New York University and is the author of* Landmark Films: The Cinema and Our Century.

Henry: Portrait of a Serial Killer

Script: Richard Fire and John McNaughton. Direction: McNaughton. Photography: Charlie Lieberman. Editing: Elena Maganini. Music: Robert McNaughton with Ken Hale and Stephen A. Jones. Players: Michael Rooker, Tow Towles, Tracy Arnold. Produced by John McNaughton, Hale, and Jones. A Greycat Films release. 90 mins.

After a nearly four-year delay in getting released and advance talk about its level of violence, *Henry: Portrait of a Serial Killer* emerged as a serious and chilling depiction of cold-blooded, often random violence that plagues America and makes for upsetting newspaper headlines. Michael Rooker plays the killer Henry with blood-curdling naturalness as he assaults and viciously murders an assortment of victims. The film neither exploits the violence nor probes the psychology of Henry. He exists and he kills – that's it. Soon his buddy (Tom Towles) becomes his partner in aggression, while Otis's sister Becky, a victim of sexual abuse by her father and played with understated sensitivity by Tracy Arnold, becomes enamoured of Henry despite knowing he was imprisoned for killing his mother.

Director John McNaughton keeps amazing control of the film's low-key tone, and the bursts of brutality emphasise the contrast between the banality of Henry and Otis and the horror of their casually committed crimes. The drama, based on a real-life Texas murderer, has a purity of style and content that elevates it above other crime spree stories. It forces an audience to look at nightmarish behaviour behind the every-day headlines and confront a type of killer without speculating about sociological and psychiatric explanations. The lack of any rational motive makes the viewing experience all the more terrifying. McNaughton has created an unusual work that is powerful in its simplicity and may become a cult classic.

William Wolf

Patrick Cassidy in Longtime Companion
photo: Gabor Szitanyi/Samuel Goldwyn

Longtime Companion

Script: Craig Lucas. Direction: Norman René. Photography: Tony Jannelli. Editing: Katherine Wenning. Music: Greg DeBelles. Production Design: Andrew Jackness. Players: Stephen Caffrey, Patrick Cassidy, Bruce Davison, Mary-Louise Parker. Produced for American Playhouse by Stan Wlodkowski. A Samuel Goldwyn release. 96 mins.

When the first article about a mysterious new illness called AIDS appeared in the *New York Times* in 1981 the danger seemed remote to homosexuals merely preoccupied with the everyday problems of being gay. *Longtime Companion*, one of the best films ever made with homosexuals as the focal point, shows how one group of friends faced the AIDS crisis that developed in the ensuing years. Although emotionally wrenching, the film's strength derives from its avoidance of self-pity and the brave manner in which the men struggle to cope with tragedy as one after another falls victim.

Instead of becoming maudlin, *Longtime Companion*, a title taken from the way survivors are described in homosexual obituaries, is an inspirational depiction of trapped individuals summoning the best within themselves to face adversity. The acting is compelling but understated, with the most powerful performance given by Bruce Davison, who tends the slow death of his lover. Mary-Louise Parker is excellent as the woman friend in the group, a character played without the camp often assigned female pals of gays.

The script by Craig Lucas is warm and sensitive, although leavened by occasional humour, and it neither condescends toward its characters nor attempts to elevate them to a pedestal. They are New York middle-class homosexuals shown in their milieu, and the film doesn't proselytise for their life-style, but asks that they be accepted as human beings who love, suffer, and face the AIDS scourge with courage. Norman René's direction knowingly reflects this approach. The film merits special international interest as a worthy example of American independent film-making.

William Wolf

Dick Tracy

Script: Jim Cash and Jack Epps, Jr. Direction: Warren Beatty. Photography: Vittorio Storaro. Editing: Richard Marks. Music: Danny Elfman; original songs by Stephen Sondheim. Production Design: Richard Sylbert. Players: Warren Beatty, Madonna, Glenne Headly, Al Pacino, Dustin Hoffman, Charlie Korsmo. Produced by Warren Beatty for Touchstone. 120 mins.

A triumph in the visual department, *Dick Tracy* recaptures the essence of the renowned comic strip with style and integrity. To the credit of producer–director–star Warren Beatty, the film avoids the trend toward excessive violence and mindless blockbuster effects programmed for what studios think the youth audience demands. Instead the concentration is on an affectionate, nostalgic recreation of Tracy and the entourage of characters in the Chester Gould strip. That is both the picture's strength and what may have led to some early caution about the film's box-office potential as inevitably compared to *Batman*.

Beatty makes a fine Tracy, but adds a human touch to the square-jawed, one-dimensional character. Madonna is delightfully sultry as the vamp Breathless Mahoney, and she gets to sing several breathy songs by Stephen Sondheim. Glenne Headley is amusing and even touching as Tracy's ever-loyal Tess Trueheart. Al Pacino, wearing make-up that makes him almost unrecognisable, all but steals the picture as the villainous Big Boy Caprice. Dustin Hoffman hilariously mutters incomprehensibly as Mumbles. Kid, the abused boy who attaches himself to Tracy, is entertainingly played by Charlie Korsmo without the excessive cuteness that often plagues child actors.

The script, with its depiction of the hero bashing crime and fending off Mahoney's advances, is on the tame side, but the strip itself is hardly inspiration for a screenwriting masterpiece. What consistently shines through is the film's overall design, which provides obviously fake backgrounds for the reality of the story and action. Richard Marks, the production designer, and Vittorio Storaro, the cinematographer, have done superb work, with important visual effect contributions from Michael Lloyd and Harrison Ellenshaw, on-target costuming by Milena Canonero, and droll makeup creativity by John Caglione, Jr. and Doug Drexler. *Dick Tracy* is intelligent entertainment that deserves to be taken on its own terms.

William Wolf

House Party

Script and Direction: Reginald Hudlin. Photography: Peter Deming. Editing: Earl Watson. Music: Marcus Miller. Production Design: Bryan Jones. Players: Christopher Reid, Robin Harris, Christopher Martin, Tisha Campbell. Produced by Warrington Hudlin. A New Line Cinema release. 96 mins.

House Party is reminiscent of many teen pictures of various decades. The difference here is that the teenagers are Afro-Americans, and that's a big difference. The conventional white middle-class scene in middle America is replaced by black middle-class student life, and while the hell-raising is similar, these teenagers are defined by their own culture, sensational dance movements, rap, slangy ethnic talk, profanity galore, and music almost loud enough to blow the roof off the house in which the students are partying.

The story hangs loosely on the exploits of one youth named Kid and his pals. Kid is played by multi-talented Christopher Reid, whose "in" flatop hairstyle adds about six inches to his height. Problems with girls, disciplinarian parents, school routines, and general growing pains permeate the exuberant movie that is packed with good cheer and nose-thumbing humor. It's the sort of movie that can send older, conservative audiences into culture shock, but it's a "right-on" film for a younger generation, black, white, or whatever.

The actors are extremely likeable types, and the film has bounce from start to finish. There is also occasional sweetness, exemplified by a boy–girl scene involving sensitivity about the need for safe sex. For all their smart talk and bluster, these are basically nice kids out for a good time, which is what writer–director Reginald Hudlin gives his audience. His older brother, Warrington Hudlin, produced the film, the younger Hudlin's first feature, and it's evident that there is bright new talent at work. *House Party* raises teen films to a new level and shows a different corner of contemporary America.

William Wolf

Christopher Reid and A.J. Johnson in *House Party*
photo: Bill Nation/New Line Cinema

Focus on a Producer: Arnon Milchan

Arnon Milchan's name on the credits usually indicates provocative material and highly creative talent but two of his most recent films demonstrate that he's also no box-office slouch. The dark comedy of *War of the Roses* didn't mark it as a likely hit and Milchan recalls the former Fox topper Alan Hirschfield comparing it to another Milchan release, saying "This makes *The King of Comedy* look like a Cinderella story." From the outset Milchan said he was going with a grim ending but this didn't stop the film from reaping $33 million in rentals in its first month.

When he first heard the synopsis to *Pretty Woman*, however, he preferred a Cinderella ending to the original and so appropriately went to Disney for distribution. The domestic grosses for that film as of July 4 were just under $150 million. In both instances Milchan disavows any box-office prescience but cites his tastes in looking for extremes and stories about obsession.

Born in 1944 he took over his family firm in his native Israel after his education at the London School of Economics and the University of Geneva and multiplied it into other businesses in chemical, agricultural, and aerospace industries. This amassed him a fortune, giving him the independence to pursue film projects because they interested him and not to earn a living. He began with involvement in local productions including the film *Neither by Day Nor by Night*. Containing one of Edward G. Robinson's last screen appearances, the movie was never released although shown at the Berlin Film Festival in 1972. A partnership with producer Elliot Kastner brought Milchan into the international scene. Their 1977 *Black Joy* was the British entry at Cannes that year and followed by the release of the under- appreciated horror film *The Medusa Touch* directed by Jack Gold and produced by Milchan and Kastner with Lord Lew Grade.

The 1980's marked the period of Milchan's real ascension. Not everything he produced was golden, and only staunch John Candy fans my wish to recall *Who's Harry Crumb?* while Ridley Scott's *Legend* was a more respectable misfire. But in this period Milchan produced Martin Scorsese's *King of Comedy*, Sergio Leone's *Once upon a Time in America* and Terry Gilliam's *Brazil* – all highly dissonant works in an era of increasing conformity and all including Robert DeNiro. All three are stirring executions of manic and grandiose visions geared for an actor of DeNiro's intensity. Milchan also tried to finance what might have been a fourth addition to this pantheon but the production of Orson Welles's *Big Brass Ring* fell just short of fruition.

Milchan also produced the acclaimed TV miniseries *Masada*, and has been active in theatre, producing on Broadway *Ipi Tombi* and *It's So Nice To Be Civilized*. He produced a Paris production of Peter Shaffer's *Amadeus* directed by and starring Roman Polanski.

Milchan describes the Italian maverick Leone as "a charming and manipulative man who could talk you into doing anything." He maintains that while shooting on *Once Upon* went over schedule the film exceeded budget by only 5%. The real problem was in convincing the distributor into accepting its three hour plus length after a disastrous Boston preview. With partner Alan Ladd Jr.'s company crumbling and Leone in Europe Milchan concedes he gave in to pressure and accepted a cut version of the film that he considered "ridiculous." (He notes that on cassette the original version totally outpaced the edited one in sales.)

Sounding more like a director Milchan said that this experience left him with a determination to fight next time. A memorable fight did ensue when Universal threatened to cut and dragged its heels in releasing Gilliam's *Brazil*. The PR guerilla tactics used by Gilliam and backed by Milchan and chronicled in Jack Mathews' book *The Battle of Brazil* resulted in the L.A. Film Critics awarding *Brazil* the best picture and best director prizes even though it had been shown only in sneak screenings.

Another legacy of *Once Upon* is Milchan's only screen appearance when DeNiro suggested he play the chauffeur when DeNiro's character rapes his girlfriend in the limousine.

The earlier (1983) *King of Comedy* did not originate with the director but curiously began when DeNiro was being considered to play the lead in a film bio of Israeli Defence Minister Moishe Dayan. DeNiro suggested a Paul Zimmerman story and Milchan, deciding that DeNiro was unsuitable to play Dayan, plunged into that project instead. The choice of director passed from Miloš Forman to Michael Cimino before Milchan realized that Martin Scorsese was available although DeNiro hadn't thought of mentioning him. The resulting film was more serious than Milchan had originally envisioned and he acknowledges that the title and marketing campaign were inappropriate. But *The King of Comedy* is his personal favourite and Milchan sees something of a professional credo in its protagonist's mad obsession to get into show business.

Of the aborted Welles project he confirms the Henry Jaglom story that things floundered when Welles failed to get any star to agree to play the lead for the $2 million allotted by the budget. Asked why he wasn't scared off by reports of Welles' uncompleted films Milchan replied that he hadn't been frightened of other "difficult" directors and advises the industry not to go against its giants.

On his more recent movies Milchan is proud of *Q & A* despite its flop. He is involved in the upcoming films *Switch*, written and directed by Blake Edwards, and *Turtle Beach*, a film about the boat people starring Greta Scacchi and Joan Chen. But his most cherished current project is *Fear No Evil*, a drama of the McCarthyist period marking the directorial debut of Irwin Winkler. Perhaps not surprisingly, DeNiro is the star.

Fred Lombardi

Focus on a Director: KATT SHEA RUBEN

A reviewer for the *Tulsa World* wrote that Katt Shea Ruben's *Stripped to Kill Part 2* "many times gives the feeling of an art film ... Imagine Ingmar Bergman choreographing a stripper's routine and you'll get an idea of what the dream sequences are like." And this is what most people regard as her weakest film!

Katt Shea Ruben is still largely unknown except to trade reviewers and B film enthusiasts. But working for Roger Corman's Concorde Pictures she and her producer/co-writer husband Andy have fashioned four distinctly stylish genre pieces. Now, like other Corman alumni, Francis Coppola, Martin Scorsese and Jack Nicholson the team is leaving Corman's outfit for more upscale offerings.

Katt Shea was born in Detroit of Irish-German ancestry and after graduating from the University of Michigan spent six months teaching blind children. Although she had not acted since the age of 16 in her backyard theatre group she went to California to launch an acting career. She won a part in a TV pilot and within a couple of years was working for Corman.

At this time Katt Shea began to take films more seriously and used the desultory periods in shooting to question D.P.'s while also taking film-making courses at UCLA. She had also met and married Andy Ruben an NBC-TV writer. While acting in a Corman film, *The Destroyers*, in the Philippines she did second unit directing and with Andy co-wrote their first project, *The Patriot*. Their lack of satisfaction with the resulting film led them into directing and producing.

Katt Shea's first film as director, *Stripped to Kill* (1987), was an above-average thriller that had police undercover woman Kay Lenz pose as a stripper to catch a killer. Highly atmospheric it entered the dancers' milieu without ever lapsing into the sordid as the strippers (who were professionals) demonstrated even kabuki images of style.

Ruben's next film, *Dance of the Damned*, was selected for the A.F.I. Fest of Independent U.S. Cinema and New York's Museum of Modern Art is now interested in screening the film. Its nocturnal coupling of a suicidal stripper and a vampire might be interestingly compared to another stylish vampire film, Kathryn Bigelow's *Near Dark*. Both films exploit the genre's visual conflict between light and dark but where Bigelow inflates the action into the folkloric violence of the American heartland Ruben's "horror" film is her least violent movie and a poetic chamber piece.

Although she has made only one bona fide vampire film many of both Ruben's victims and villains are lost children of the night. Like Scorsese and Errol Morris, Ruben has turned out her own distinctive film noir without duplicating past forms.

Her latest film, *Streets*, contains more daytime sequences than any of her other films but with the help of cinematographer Phedon Papamichael even these scenes have a stylised look and its tale of a teenage streetwalker and middle-class boy pursued by a psycho cop manages to be both searing and sensitive. The Rubens have left Concorde's sub million dollar budgets and Katt Shea's next film at New Line is set to cost $5–6 million. At the very least she has demonstrated that at a time when action megahits have robotic hulks meting out mechanical massacres even poverty row genre films can still be made with grit, feeling and style.

Fred Lombardi

Focus on an Actor: JOE MANTEGNA

Joe Mantegna first burst into real prominence in 1984 with his Tony-award winning performance on Broadway in David Mamet's play *Glengary Glen Ross*. Mamet won a Pulitzer prize for his depiction of a group of hustling real estate salesmen and their relentless drive to close deals.

Three years later Mantegna appeared in *House of Games*, playwright Mamet's debut as a film director, along with other members of the *Glengary* cast including Mike Nussbaum, J.T. Walsh and Jack Wallace. But it was Mantegna who dominated the film as a seductive con man leading co-star Lindsay Crouse into a fascinating labyrinth of sophisticated shell games.

The following year Mamet directed Mantegna and his other "regulars" in *Things Change*. They were joined by star Don Ameche and another noted *Glengary* veteran, Robert Prosky. In this film Ameche is an innocent shoe repairman who agrees to plead guilty to a gangland murder in exchange for mob money to buy a fishing boat after serving a perfunctory sentence. Mantegna is the small-time hood sent to guard him until his surrender and who instead takes him on a last fling in Las Vegas where all kinds of comic complications ensue.

In *House of Games* Mantegna's expert con man ultimately revealed a vulnerable integrity but he is especially affecting here as he becomes touched by his companion's old time values. Ameche and Mantegna jointly won the Venice Fest Award for best actor – an especially pleasurable coup for Mantegna who traces his roots on both parental sides to Italian soil.

In retrospect while they touch on universal traits Mamet's pieces and especially *Glengary* and *House* are memorable artifacts of America in the

Joe Mantegna

1980's. As Mantegna acknowledges the spirit is, "I want mine whatever it takes. It seems like we're now getting a slight shift back to what the 1960's were about with a little bit more social consciousness."

Mantegna, who was born in Chicago in 1947, is indeed familiar with the spirit of the 1960's. After attending the Goodman School of Drama he appeared in the national companies of *Hair* and *Godspell*. He veered away from the musical path after he joined the now legendary Organic Theatre Company headed by future film director Stuart Gordon. He credits the group with teaching its members to do practically everything and while there co-authored a play he appeared in, *Bleacher Bums*, which as a TV production later won him an Emmy.

After his success in *Glengary*, Mantegna won film roles in *Compromising Positions, The Money Pit, Three Amigos, Critical Condition,* and *Suspect*. In John Hancock's film *Weeds* he rejoined an ensemble theatre group as he joined a company of ex-cons putting on a play of their expeiences. Mantegna also returned to the stage for Mamet's *Speed the Plow* and narrated an Oscar nominated documentary, *Crack U.S.A.: Country Under Siege*.

Mantegna is in fine form in *Wait Until Spring, Bandini*, his first film since *Things Change*, but as often in his work this drama of an errant immigrant husband is a lovely ensemble piece boasting winning performances from Faye Dunaway, Ornella Muti and particularly child actor Michael Bacall. Tentatively scheduled for release in early 1991 is *Queens Logic* co-starring Jamie Lee Curtis and John Malkovich and directed by Steve Rash.

Another barometer of Mantegna's talent is that he was tapped by both Woody Allen and Francis Coppola in the same year for roles in *Alice* and *The Godfather Part III*. Mantegna considered the experience both gratifying and a bit overwhelming. He found the Allen film "low key, intimate...almost like making a home movie" while comparing *Godfather III* to "Italian opera...monumental." Mantegna is scheduled to return to Mamet's direction in a police thriller entitled *Homicide*, to be shot this fall.

Among other directors he'd like to receive calls from, Mantegna cites Sidney Lumet, Martin Scorsese and Ridley Scott but points out that actors should be willing to take chances with unknown directors. He had been totally unfamiliar with *Bandini's* helmer Dominique Deruddere but found him "just wonderful."

Fred Lombardi

Recent and Forthcoming Films

(For various reasons some of last year's titles missed our late summer deadline and are included here when noted while some of this year's films were already listed on our last chart.)

The Adventures of Ford Fairlane. Script: Dan Waters, James Cappe, David Arnott. Dir: Renny Harlin. Phot: Oliver Wood. Players: Andrew Dice Clay, Wayne Newton, Priscilla Presley. Prod: Silver Pic./Fox.

After Dark, My Sweet. Script: Robert Redlin, James Foley from Jim Thompson's novel. Dir: James Foley. Phot: Mark Plummer. Players: Jason Patric, Rachel Ward, Bruce Dern. Prod:

George Gund Films
1821 Union Street
San Francisco, CA 94123
415/921-4929 Fax: 415/921-6019

Avenue Pictures. Int'l Sales: Samuel Goldwyn Co.
Air America. Script: John Eskow, Richard Rush. Dir: Roger Spottiswoode. Phot: Roger Deakins. Players: Mel Gibson, Robert Downey Jr., Nancy Travis, Lane Smith. Prod: Carolco/Tri-Star.
Alice. Script and Dir: Woody Allen. Phot: Carlo DiPalma. Players: Mia Farrow, William Hurt, Alec Baldwin, Judith Ivey, Joe Mantegna, Cybill Shepherd. Prod: Orion.
Almost An Angel. Script: Paul Hogan. Dir: John Cornell. Phot: Russell Boyd. Players: Paul Hogan, Linda Kozlowski. Prod: Paramount.
The Ambulance. Script and Dir: Larry Cohen. Pht: Jacques Haitkin. Players: James Earl Jones, Eric Roberts, Red Buttons, Janine Turner. Prod: Esparza-Katz Prods./Triumph Releasing.
Another 24 Hours. Script: John Fasano, Jeb Stuart, Larry Gross, from Fred Braughton story. Dir: Walter Hill. Phot: Matthew F. Leonetti. Players: Eddie Murphy, Nick Nolte. Prod: Paramount.
Arachnophobia. Script: Don Jakoby, Wesley Strick, Al Williams. Dir: Frank Marshall. Phot: Mikael Salamon. Players: Jeff Daniels, Harley Jane Kozak, John Goodman, Julian Sands. Prod: Amblin Ent./Disney (Buena Vista).
Aunt Julia and The Scriptwriter. Script: William Boyd from Isabelle Allende's novel. Dir: Jon Amiel. Phot: Andrew Dunne. Players: Barbara Hershey, Keanu Reeves, Peter Falk. Prod: Cinecom.
Avalon. Script and Dir: Barry Levinson. Phot: Allen Daviau. Players: Aidan Quinn, Elizabeth Perkins, Armin Mueller-Stahl, Joan Plowright. Prod: Tri-Star.
Awakenings. Script: Steven Zaillian. Dir: Penny Marshall. Phot: Miroslav Ondricek. Players: Robert De Niro, Robin Williams. Prod: Columbia.
Back to the Future Part III. Script: Bob Gale from story by Robert Zemeckis and Gale. Dir: Robert Zemeckis. Phot: Dean Cundey. Players: Michael J. Fox, Christopher Lloyd, Mary Steenburgen. Prod: Amblin Entertainment/Universal.

Jamie Lee Curtis in *Blue Steel*
photo: Joel Warren/MGM/UA

Bad Influence. Script: David Koepp. Dir: Curtis Hanson. Phot: Robert Elswit. Players: Rob Lowe, James Spader. Prod: Triumph Releasing.
Bail Jumper. Script: Christian Faber, Josephine Wallace. Dir: Faber. Phot: Tomasz Magierski. Players: Eszter Balint, B.J. Spalding. Prod: Angelika Films.
Basket Case 2. Script and Dir: Frank Henenlotter. Phot: Robert M. Baldwin. Players: Kevin Van Hentenryck, Annie Ross, Kathryn Meisle, Jason Evers. Prod: Shapiro Glickenhaus Entertainment.
Betsy's Wedding. Script and Dir: Alan Alda. Phot: Kelvin Pike. Players: Alan Alda, Madeline Kahn, Molly Ringwald, Ally Sheedy, Anthony LaPaglia, Joe Pesci. Prod: Disney (Touchstone).
The Big Bang. (documentary feature) Dir: James Toback. Phot: Barry Markowitz. Prod: Triton.
Blue Steel. Script: Kathryn Bigelow, Eric Red. Dir: Kathryn Bigelow. Phot: Amir Mokri. Players: Jamie Lee Curtis, Ron Silver, Clancy Brown. Prod: MGM/UA/Vestron.
Bonfire of the Vanities. Script: Michael Cristofer from Tom Wolfe's novel. Dir: Brian DePalma. Phot: Vilmos Zsigmond. Players: Tom Hanks, Melanie Griffith, Bruce Willis, F. Murray Abraham, Morgan Freeman. Prod: Warner Bros.
Boris and Natasha. Script: Charles Fradin, Linda Favila, Anson Downs. Dir: Charles Martin Smith. Phot: Daryn Okada. Players: Sally Kellerman, Dave Thomas. Prod: MCEG.
Bright Angel. Script: Richard Ford. Dir: Michael Fields. Players: Valerie Perrine, Sam Shepard. Prod: Hemdale.
Bullseye. Script: Leslie Bricusse, Laurence Marks, Maurice Gran, Ed Naha. Dir: Michael Winner. Phot: Alan Jones. Players: Michael Caine, Roger Moore, Sally Kirkland. Prod: 21st Cent./Col.
Career Opportunities. Script: John Hughes. Dir: Bryan Gordon. Phot: Donald McAlpine. Players: Frank Whaley, Jennifer Connelly. Prod: Universal.
Chains of Gold. Script: John Petz, Linda Favila, Anson Downes. Dir: Rod Holcomb. Players: John Travolta, Marilu Henner, Bernie Casey. Prod: MCEG.

Jessica Tandy and Morgan Freeman in the Oscar-laden Warner release, *Driving Miss Daisy*

Child's Play II. Script: Don Mancini. Dir: John Lafia. Phot: Stefan Czapsky. Players: Alex Vincent, Jenny Agutter, Gerrit Graham. Prod: Universal.
Class Action. Script: Samantha Shad, Carolyn Shelby, Christopher Ames. Dir: Michael Apted. Phot: Conrad Hall. Players: Gene Hackman, Mary Elizabeth Mastrantonio. Prod: Interscope/Fox.
Cold Heaven. Script: Allan Scott. Dir: Nicolas Roeg. Phot: Francis Kenny. Players: Theresa Russell, Mark Harmon, Talia Shire. Prod: MCEG.
Come See the Paradise. Script and Dir: Alan Parker. Phot: Michael Seresin. Players: Dennis Quaid, Tamlyn Tomita, Sab Shimono, Stan Egi. Prod: Fox.
Convicts. Script: Horton Foote from his play. Dir: Peter Masterson. Phot: Toyomichi Kurita. Players: Robert Duvall, James Earl Jones, Luke Haas. Prod: MCEG.
Crazy People. Script: Mitch Markowitz. Dir: Tony Bill. Phot: Victor J. Kemper. Players: Dudley Moore, Daryl Hannah, Mercedes Ruehl. Prod: Paramount. (Note: Last year's chart listed John Malkovich later replaced during filming by Moore.)
Crash and Burn. Script: J.S. Cardone. Dir: Charles Band. Phot: Mac Ahlberg. Players: Ralph White, Paul Ganus. Prod: JGM Enterprises.
Crimes and Misdemeanors. Script and Dir: Woody Allen. Phot: Sven Nykvist. Players: Woody Allen, Martin Landau, Mia Farrow, Alan Alda, Anjelica Huston, Jerry Orbach. Prod: Orion. (released 10/89)
Daddy's Dying, Who's Got The Will. Script: Del Shores based on his play. Dir: Jack Fisk. Phot: Paul Elliott. Players: Beau Bridges, Beverly D'Angelo, Tess Harper, Judge Reinhold, Amy Wright. Prod: MGM/UA.
Dance of the Damned. Script: Andy and Katt Shea Ruben. Dir: Katt Shea Ruben. Phot: Phedon Papamichael. Players: Starr Andreef, Cyril O'Reilly. Prod: Concorde/New Classics.
Dances with Wolves. Script: Michael Blake. Dir: Kevin Costner. Phot: Dean Semler. Players: Kevin Costner, Mary McDonnell. Prod: Tig Prods./Orion.
Daredreamer. Script: Pat Royce, Barry Callier, Tim Noah. Dir: Barry Callier. Phot: Christopher G. Tufty. Players: Noah, Alyce LaTourelle. Prod: Lensman Co.
Darkman. Script: Sam Raimi, Ivan Raimi, Chuck Pfarrar. Dir: Sam Raimi. Phot: Bill Pope. Players: Liam Neeson, Frances McDormand, Larry Drake. Prod: Universal.
Days of Thunder. Script: Robert Towne from story by Towne, Tom Cruise. Dir: Tony Scott. Phot: Ward Russell. Players: Tom Cruise, Robert Duvall, Nicole Kidman, Randy Quaid. Prod: Paramount.
Def by Temptation. Script and Dir: James Bond 3d. Phot: Ernest Dickerson. Players: James Bond, Kadeem Hardison, Bill Nunn, Cynthia Bond. Prod: Troma.
Defending Your Life. Script and Dir: Albert Brooks. Phot: Allen Daviau. Players: Albert Brooks, Meryl Streep, Rip Torn, Lee Grant. Prod: Warner Bros.
Delirious. Script: Lawrence J. Cohen, Fred Freeman, Doug Claybourne. Dir: Tom Mankiewicz. Phot: Robert Stevens. Players: John Candy, Muriel Hemingway. Prod: MGM/UA.
The Desperate Hours. Script: Michael Cimino, Lawrence Konner, Mark Rosenthal from Joseph Hayes' novel and 1955 screenplay. Dir: Michael Cimino. Phot: Robert Stevens. Players: Mickey Rourke, Anthony Hopkins, Mimi Rogers, Lindsay Crouse. Prod: MGM/UA.
Die Hard 2. Script: Steven E. Souza, Doug Richardson. Dir: Renny Harlin. Phot: Oliver Wood. Players: Bruce Willis, Bonnie Bedelia, Franco Nero. Prod: Fox.
Dogfight. Script: Bob Comfort. Dir: Nancy Savoca. Phot: Bobby Bukowski. Players: River Phoenix, Lili Taylor. Prod: Warner Bros.
The Doors. Script and Dir: Oliver Stone. Phot: Robert Richardson. Players: Val Kilmer, Meg Ryan, Kevin Dillon, Kyle MacLachlan. Prod: Carolco/Tri-Star.
Don't Tell Her It's Me. Script: Sarah Bird. Dir: Malcolm Mowbray. Phot: Reed Smoot. Players: Shelley Long, Steve Guttenberg, Jami Gertz, Kyle MacLachlan. Prod: Hemdale.
Duck Tales – The Movie: The Treasure of the Lost Lamp. (*animated feature*) Dir: Bob Hatchcock. Prod: Buena Vista (Disney).
Eating. Script and Dir: Henry Jaglom. Phot: Hanania Baer. Players: Mary Crosby, Lisa Blake Richards, Gwen Welles. Prod: International Rainbow Pictures.
Edward Scissorhands. Script: Caroline Thompson. Dir: Tim Burton. Phot: Stefan Czapsky. Players: Johnny Depp, Winona Ryder,

Dianne Wiest, Kathy Baker, Alan Arkin. Prod: Fox.
Eminent Domain. Script: Andrzej Krakowski, Richard Gregson. Dir: John Irvin. Players: Donald Sutherland, Anne Archer. Prod: SVS.
Enid is Sleeping. Script: A.J. Tipping, James Whaley, Maurice Phillips. Dir: Phillips. Phot: Affonso Beato. Players: Elizabeth Perkins, Judge Reinhold, Jeffrey Jones. Prod: Davis Ent./Vestron.
Eve Of Destruction. Script and Dir: Duncan Gibbins. Phot: Alan Hume. Players: Gregory Hines, Renée Soutendijk. Prod: Interscope/Orion.
Exorcist III: Legion. Script and Dir: William Peter Blatty. Phot: Peter Fisher. Players: George C. Scott, Sylvia Sidney, Brad Dourif. Prod: Morgan Creek/Fox.
The Feud. Script: Bill D'Elia, Robert Uricola based on novel by Thomas Berger. Dir: D'Elia. Phot: John Beymer. Players: Rene Auberjonois, Ron McLarty, Joe Grifasi, Scott Allegrucci. Prod: Castle Hill Prods.
The Fifth Monkey. Script and Dir: Eric Rochat. Phot: Gideon Porath. Players: Ben Kingsley, Mika Lins. Prod: 21st Century.
The Five Heartbeats. Script: Robert Townsend, Keenan Ivory Wayans. Phot: Bill Dill. Players: Robert Townsend, Leon Robinson, Michael Wright. Prod: Fox.
Flatliners. Script: Peter Filardi. Dir: Joel Schumacher. Phot: Jan DeBont. Players: Kiefer Sutherland, Julia Roberts, Kevin Bacon. Prod: Columbia.
Flight of the Intruder. Script: John Milius, David Shaber. Dir: John Milius. Phot: Fred J. Koenekamp. Players: Danny Glover, Willem Dafoe, Brad Johnson, Rosanna Arquette. Prod: Paramount.
Fools of Fortune. Script: Michael Hirst. Dir:

Joel (left) and Ethan Coen, the talented brothers responsible for *Miller's Crossing* and *Barton Fink*
photo: Bonnie Schiffman/Circle Films

Pat O'Connor. Phot: Jerzy Sielinski. Players: Mary Elizabeth Mastrantonio, Iain Glen, Julie Christie. Prod: Polygram/New Line.
The Fourth War. Script: Stephen Peters, Kenneth Ross. Dir: John Frankenheimer. Phot: Gerry Fisher. Players: Roy Scheider, Jurgen Prochnow, Harry Dean Stanton. Prod: Cannon/Pathe.
Frankenhooker. Script: Robert Martin, Frank Henenlotter. Dir: Frank Henenlotter. Phot: Robert M. Baldwin. Players: James Lorinz, Patty Mullen. Prod: Shapiro Glickenhaus.
Frankenstein Unbound. Script: Roger Corman, Ed Neumeier. Dir: Roger Corman.

FINANCE PRODUCTION WORLDWIDE DISTRIBUTION

CINETRUST
ENTERTAINMENT

2121 Avenue of the Stars, 6th Floor, Los Angeles Ca, 90067
Phone: (213) 551 6504 Fax: (213) 551 6622 Telex: 698218 HQ CCLSA
Contact: Kelly Ross

"Michelangelo" visiting the Metropolitan to see his namesake's work, in *Teenage Mutant Ninja Turtles*
photo: Timothy White

Phot: Players: John Hurt, Raul Julia, Bridget Fonda. Prod: Fox.
The Freshman. Script and Dir: Andrew Bergman. Phot: William A. Fraker. Players: Marlon Brando, Matthew Broderick, Bruno Kirby, Penelope Ann Miller, Maximilian Schell. Prod: Tri-Star.
Funny About Love. Script: Norman Steinberg, David Frankel. Dir: Leonard Nimoy. Phot: Fred Murphy. Players: Gene Wilder, Christine Lahti, Mary Stuart Masterson, Farrah Fawcett. Prod: Paramount.
F/X 2. Script: Bill Condon. Dir: Richard Franklin. Phot: Victor Kemper. Players: Bryan Brown, Brian Dennehy, Philip Bosco, Joanna Gleason. Prod: Orion.
The Game. Script: Julia Wilson, Curtis Brown. Dir: Brown. Phot: Paul Gibson. Players: Brown, Richard Lee Ross. Prod: Aquarius.
Ghost. Script: Bruce Joel Rubin. Dir: Jerry Zucker. Phot: Adam Greenburg. Players: Patrick Swayze, Demi Moore, Whoopi Goldberg. Prod: Paramount.
The Godfather Part III. Script: Mario Puzo, Francis Coppola. Dir: Francis Coppola. Phot: Gordon Willis. Players: Al Pacino, Diane Keaton, Talia Shire, Andy Garcia, Eli Wallach, Bridget Fonda, Sofia Coppola, Joe Mantegna. Prod: Paramount.
Good Fellas. Script: Nicholas Pileggi, Martin Scorsese from Pileggi's novel 'Wise Guy.' Dir: Martin Scorsese. Phot: Michael Ballhaus. Players: Robert De Niro, Ray Liotta, Lorraine Bracco, Joe Pesci, Paul Sorvino. Prod: Warner Bros.
Graffiti Bridge. Script and Dir: Prince. Phot: Bill Butler. Players: Prince, Morris Day, Ingrid Chavez. Prod: Warner Bros.
Green Card. Script and Dir: Peter Weir. Phot: Geoff Simpson. Players: Gérard Depardieu, Andie MacDowell. Prod: Buena Vista (Disney).
Gremlins 2: The New Batch. Script: Charlie Haas. Dir: Joe Dante. Phot: John Hora. Players: Zach Galligan, Phoebe Cates, John Glover, Robert Prosky, Christopher Lee. Prod: Amblin Ent./Warner Bros.
The Handmaid's Tale. Script: Harold Pinter from a novel by Margaret Atwood. Dir: Volker Schlöndorff. Phot: Igor Luther. Players: Natasha Richardson, Robert Duvall, Faye Dunaway, Elizabeth McGovern. Prod: Cinecom.
Hard To Kill. Script: Steven McKay. Dir: Bruce Malmuth. Phot: Matthew F. Leonetti. Players: Steven Seagal, Kelly Le Brock. Prod: Warner Bros.
Havana. Script: Judith Rascoe. Dir: Sydney Pollack. Phot: Owen Roizman. Players: Robert Redford, Lena Olin, Alan Arkin, Thomas Milian. Prod: Universal.
Heart Condition. Script and Dir: James D. Parriott. Phot: Arthur Albert. Players: Bob Hoskins, Denzel Washington, Chloe Webb. Prod: New Line Cinema.
Henry and June. Script: Philip Kaufman, Rose Kaufman from Anaïs Nin's journals. Dir: Philip Kaufman. Phot: Philippe Rousselot. Players: Maria de Meideros, Fred Ward. Prod: Universal.
The Hider in the House. Script: Lem Dobbs. Dir: Matthew Patrick. Phot: Jeff Jur. Players: Gary Busey, Mimi Rogers. Prod: Vestron.
Highway to Hell. Script: Brian Helgeland. Dir: Ate de Jong. Phot: Robin Vidgeon. Players: Patrick Bergin, Chad Lowe. Prod: Hemdale.
Home Alone. Script: John Hughes. Dir: Chris Columbus. Phot: Julio Macat. Players: Macaulay Culkin, Joe Pesci, Catherine O'Hara, Daniel Stern. Prod: Fox.

Hot Spot. Script: Charles Williams, Nona Tyson. Dir: Dennis Hopper. Phot: Ueli Steiger. Players: Don Johnson, Virginia Madsen, Jennifer Connelly, Charles Martin Smith. Prod: Orion.
The Hunt for Red October. Script: Larry Ferguson, Donald Stewart from Tom Clancy's novel. Dir: John McTiernan. Phot: Jan de Bont. Players: Sean Connery, Alec Baldwin, Scott Glenn, Sam Neill. Prod: Paramount.
If Looks Could Kill. Script: Darren Star. Dir: William Dear. Phot: Doug Milsome. Players: Richard Grieco, Linda Hunt. Prod: Warner Bros.
Impulse. Script: John De Marco, Leigh Chapman. Dir: Sondra Locke. Phot: Dean Semler. Players: Theresa Russell, Jeff Fahey, George Dzunda. Prod: Warner Bros.
In the Spirit. Script: Jeannie Berlin, Laurie Jones. Dir: Sandra Seacat. Phot: Dick Quinlan. Players: Elaine May, Marlo Thomas, Berlin, Peter Falk, Melanie Griffith. Prod: Castle Hill.
Jacob's Ladder. Script: Bruce Joel Rubin. Dir: Adrian Lynne. Players: Tim Robbins, Elizabeth Peñz, Danny Aiello. Prod: Tri-Star.
Joe Versus the Volcano. Script and Dir: John Patrick Shanley. Phot: Stephen Goldblatt. Players: Tom Hanks, Meg Ryan, Lloyd Bridges, Robert Stack, Abe Vigoda, Ossie Davis. Prod: Amblin/Warner Bros.
Kindergarten Cop. Script: Murray Salem, Timothy Harris, Herschel Weingrod. Dir: Ivan Reitman. Phot: Michael Chapman. Players: Arnold Schwarzenegger, Penelope Ann Miller, Pamela Reed, Linda Hunt. Prod: Imagine/Universal.
The King of New York. Script: Nicholas St John. Dir: Abel Ferrara. Phot: Bojan Bazelli. Players: Christopher Walken, David Caruso, Larry Fishburne, Victor Argo. Prod: Carcolco/New Line Cinema.
King Ralph I. Dir: David S. Ward. Player: John Goodman. Prod: Universal.
A Kiss Before Dying. Script and Dir: James Dearden from Lawrence Roman's 1956 screenplay. Phot: Mike Southon. Players: Matt Dillon, Sean Young, Max von Sydow. Prod: Universal. **Late for Dinner**. Script: Mark Andrus. Dir: W.D. Richter. Phot: Peter Sova. Players: Brian Wimmer, Peter Berg, Peter Gallagher. Prod: Columbia.
The Lemon Sisters. Script: Jeremy Pikser. Dir: Joyce Chopra. Phot: Bobby Byrne. Players: Diane Keaton, Carol Kane, Kathryn Grody,

Arnold Schwarzenegger in Carolco's megahit, Total Recall

Elliott Gould. Prod: Miramax.
Letter to the Next Generation. (*Documentary*) Dir: James Klein. Phot: Don Lenzer. Prod: New Day Films.
Listen Up: The Lives of Quincy Jones. (*Documentary*) Dir: Courtney Sale Ross. With: Quincy Jones, Barbra Streisand, Ray Charles, Ella Fitzgerald, Lionel Hampton. Prod: Warner Bros.
The Long Walk Home. Dir: Richard Pearce. Phot: Roger Deakins. Players: Sissy Spacek, Whoopi Goldberg. Prod: New Century Vista.
Love at Large. Script and Dir: Alan J. Rudolph. Phot: Elliot Davis. Players: Tom Berenger, Elizabeth Perkins, Anne Archer. Prod: Orion.
Love Field. Script: Don Roos. Dir: Jonathan Kaplan. Phot: Ralf Bode. Players: Michelle Pfeiffer, Dennis Haysbert. Prod: Orion.
Marked for Death. Script: Victor Grais. Dir: Dwight H. Little. Phot: Ric Waite. Players: Steven Seagal, Elizabeth Gracen, Joanna Pacula. Prod: Fox.
The Marrying Man. Script: Neil Simon. Dir: Jerry Rees. Phot: Donald E. Thorin. Players: Kim Bassinger, Alec Baldwin. Prod: Disney (Buena Vista)

Meet the Applegates. Script: Michael Lehmànn, Redbeard Simmons. Dir: Michael Lehmann. Phot: Mitchell Dubin. Players: Ed Begley Jr., Stockard Channing, Dabney Coleman. Prod: Triton.

Men at Work. Script and Dir: Emilio Estevez. Players: Charlie Sheen, Emilio Estevez, Leslie Hope. Prod: Triumph.

Memphis Belle. Script: Monte Merrick. Dir: Michael Caton-Jones. Phot: David Watkin. Players: Matthew Modine, Eric Stolz, John Lithgow. Prod: Enigma Prods./Warner Bros.

Mermaids. Script: June Roberts. Dir: Richard Benjamin. Phot: Howard Atherton. Players: Cher, Bob Hoskins, Winona Ryder. Prod: Orion.

Misery. Script: William Goldman from Stephen King's novel. Dir: Rob Reiner. Phot: Barry Sonnenfeld. Players: James Caan, Kathy Bates, Frances Steenhagen, Lauren Bacall. Prod: Columbia.

Mr & Mrs Bridge. Script: Ruth Prawer Jhabvala from Evan S. Connell's novels. Dir: James Ivory. Phot: Tony Pierce-Roberts. Players: Paul Newman, Joanne Woodward, Kyra Sedgwick, Blythe Danner. Prod: Miramax.

Mr Destiny. Script: James Orr, Ernest Cruickshank, Susan Landau. Dir: Orr. Phot: Alex Thompson. Players: James Belushi, Michael Caine, Linda Hamilton. Prod: Buena Vista (Disney).

Mr Frost. Script: Philippe Setbon, Brad Lynch. Dir: Philippe Setbon. Phot: Dominique Brenguier. Players: Jeff Goldblum, Alan Bates, Kathy Baker. Prod: SVS

Mr Hoover And I. (*Documentary*) Script and Dir: Emile DeAntonio. Phot: Morgan Wesson, Matthew Mindlin. Prod: Turin Film/Ch.4 (U.K.).

Mister Johnson. Script: William Boyd from Joyce Cary's novel. Dir: Bruce Beresford. Phot: Players: Pierce Brosnan, Edward Woodard, Denis Quilley, Beatie Edney, Maynard Ezaishi. Prod: Avenue Pictures.

Mo' Better Blues. Script and Dir: Spike Lee. Phot: Ernest Dickerson. Players: Denzel Washington, Spike Lee, Wesley Snipes, Giancarlo Esposito, Joie Lee, Cynda Williams, Robin Harris. Prod: Universal.

Moon Over Miami. Script: Mitch Glazer. Dir: Edward Bianchi. Phot: Andrzej Bartkowiak. Players: Cyndi Lauper, David Keith, Richard Belzer. Prod: Orion.

Mortal Passions. Script: Alan Moskowitz. Dir: Andrew Lane. Phot: Christian Sebaldt. Players: Zach Galligan, Michael Bowen, Krista Errickson. Prod: MGM/UA.

Mortal Thoughts. Script: William Reilly, Claude Kerven. Dir: Alan Rudolph. Phot: Elliot Davis. Players: Demi Moore, Glenne Headly, Bruce Willis. Prod: Columbia.

My Blue Heaven. Script: Nora Ephron. Dir: Herbert Ross. Phot: John Bailey. Players: Steve Martin, Rich Moranis, Joan Cusak. Prod: Warner Bros.

Narrow Margin. Script, Dir. and Phot: Peter Hyams. Players: Gene Hackman, Anne Archer, James Sikking, M. Emmet Walsh. Prod: RKO/Tri-Star.

Navy Seals. Script: Chuch Pfarrer, Gary Goldman. Dir: Lewis Teague. Phot: John A. Alonzo. Players: Charlie Sheen, Michael Biehn, Joanne Whalley-Kilmer, Cyril O'Reilly. Prod: Orion.

Night of the Living Dead. Script: George Romero. Dir: Tom Savini. Players: Pat Tallman, Tony Todd. 21st Century/Columbia.

Nobody's Perfect. Script: Annie Korzen, Joel Block, Steven Ader. Dir: Robert Kaylor. Phot: Claus Loof. Players: Chad Lowe, Gail O'Grady. Prod: Moviestore Entertainment/TMS Pictures.

The Nutcracker. (*Animated*) Script: Patricia Watson from E.T.A. Hoffmann story. Dir: Paul Schibli. Voices: Peter O'Toole, Kiefer Sutherland, Phyllis Diller. Prod: Warner Bros.

The Object of Beauty. Script and Dir: Michael Lindsay-Hogg. Phot: David Watkin. Players: John Malkovich, Andie MacDowell, Lolita Davidovich. Prod: Avenue Pictures.

Once. (*Animated feature*) Dir: Richard Williams. Prod: Warner Bros.

Once Around. Script: Malia Scotch Marmo. Dir: Lasse Hallström. Phot: Theo Van De Sande. Players: Richard Dreyfuss, Holly Hunter, Danny Aiello, Gena Rowlands, Laura San Giacomo. Prod: Universal.

Pacific Heights. Script: Daniel Pyne. Dir: John Schlesinger. Phot: Amir Mokri. Players: Melanie Griffith, Matthew Modine, Michael Keaton. Prod: Morgan Creek/Fox.

Postcards from the Edge. Script: Carrie Fisher from her novel. Dir: Mike Nichols. Phot: Michael Ballhaus. Players: Meryl Streep, Shirley MacLaine, Richard Dreyfuss, Dennis Quaid, Gene Hackman. Prod: Columbia.

Predator 2. Script: James Thomas, John

Thomas. Dir: Stephen Hopkins. Players: Danny Glover, Gary Busey, Ruben Blades, Maria Conchita Alonso. Prod: Fox.
Presumed Innocent. Script: Frank Pierson, Alan J. Pakula from Scott Turow's novel. Dir: Pakula. Phot: Gordon Willis. Players: Harrison Ford, Brian Dennehy, Raul Julia, Bonnie Bedelia, Paul Winfield, Greta Scacchi. Prod: Mirage/ Warner Bros.
Pretty Woman. Script: J.F. Lawton. Dir: Garry Marshall. Phot: Charles Minsky. Players: Richard Gere, Julia Roberts, Ralph Bellamy, Laura San Giacomo, Hector Elizondo. Prod: Disney (Touchstone).
Puppet Master. Script: Joseph G. Collodi from story by Charles Band, Kenneth Hall. Dir: David Schmoeller. Phot: Sergio Salvati. Players: Paul Le Mat, Irene Miracle, William Hickey. Prod: JGM Enterprises.
Pump Up the Volume. Script and Dir: Allan Moyle. Phot: Walt Lloyd. Players: Christian Slater, Samantha Mathis, Ellen Greene. Prod: New Line Cinema.
Q&A. Script: Sidney Lumet from novel by Edwin Torres. Dir: Lumet. Phot: Andrzej Bartkowiak. Players: Nick Nolte, Timothy Hutton, Armand Assante, Patrick O'Neal, Lee Richardson, Charles Dutton. Prod: Tri-Star.

Queens Logic. Script: Tony Spiridakis. Dir: Steve Rash. Phot: Amir Mokri. Players: Jamie Lee Curtis, Linda Fiorentino, John Malkovich, Joe Mantegna, Spiridakis. Prod: New Century/ Vista.
Quick Change. Script: Howard Franklin. Dir: Howard Franklin, Bill Murray. Phot: Michael Chapman. Players: Bill Murray, Geena Davis, Randy Quaid, Jason Robards, Philip Bosco. Prod: Warner Bros.
Quigley Down Under. Script: John Hill. Dir: Simon Wincer. Phot: David Eggby. Players: Tom Selleck, Laura San Giacomo. Prod: Pathe/ MGM/UA.
The Rescuers Down Under. (*Animated*) Dir: Hendel Butoy, Michael Garbriel. Voices: Bob Newhart, Eva Gabor. Prod: Disney (Buena Vista).
Revenge. Script: Jim Harrison, Jeffrey Fishkin, from Harrison's novella. Dir: Tony Scott. Phot: Jeffrey Kimball. Players: Kevin Costner, Anthony Quinn, Madeleine Stowe, James Gammon, Slly Kirkland. Prod: Columbia.
Reversal of Fortune. Script: Nicholas Kazan. Dir: Barbet Schroeder. Phot: Luciano Tovoli. Players: Ron Silver, Jeremy Irons, Glenn Close. Prod: Warner Bros.
Roger and Me (*Documentary feature*) Dir:

Jack Nicholson and Harvey Keitel in *The Two Jakes*

photo: Elliott Marks

Michael Moore. Phot: Chris Beaver, John Prusack, Kevin Rafferty, Bruce Schermer. Prod: Dog Eat Dog Films/Warner Bros. Released 12/89.
Robocop II. Script: Frank Miller, Walon Green. Dir: Irvin Kershner. Phot: Mark Irwin. Players: Peter Weller, Nancy Allen, Dan O'Herlihy, Gabriel Damon. Prod: Orion.
Robert Jox. Script: Joe Haldeman, Stuart Gordon. Dir: Gordon. Phot: Mac Ahlberg. Players: Gary Graham, Anne-Marie Johnson, Paul Koslo. Prod: Triumph Releasing.
Rocky V: The Final Bell. Script: Sylvester Stallone. Dir: John G. Avildsen. Phot: Steven Poster. Players: Sylvester Stallone, Talia Shire. Prod: MGM/UA.
The Rookie. Script: Boaz Yakin, Scott Spiegel. Dir: Clint Eastwood. Phot: Jack N. Green. Players: Clint Eastwood, Charlie Sheen, Raul Julia, Sonia Bragia. Prod: Warner Bros.
Rosencrantz and Guildenstern Are Dead. Script and Dir: Tom Stoppard from his play. Phot: Peter Biziou. Players: Richard Dreyfuss, Gary Oldman, Tim Roth, Ian Richardson. Prod: Cinecom Pictures.
Rover Dangerfield (*Animated Feature*) Script: Rodney Dangerfield. Dir: James George, Bob Seeley. Voice: Rodney Dangerfield. Prod: Warner Bros.
Run. Script: Dennis Shyrack, Michael Blodgett. Dir: Geoff Burrowes. Phot: Bruce Surtees. Players: Patrick Dempsey, Kelly Preston. Prod: Buena Vista.
The Russia House. Script: Tom Stoppard from John Le Carré's novel. Dir: Fred Schepisi. Phot: Ian Baker. Players: Sean Connery, Michelle Pfeiffer, Roy Scheider, Klaus Maria Brandauer. Prod: Pathe/MGM/UA.
Scenes from a Mall. Script: Paul Mazursky, Roger L. Simon. Dir: Paul Mazursky. Phot: Fred Murphy. Players: Bette Midler, Woody Allen, Bill Irwin. Prod: Disney (Touchstone).
Shattered. Script: Wolfgang Petersen, Andrew Birkin from Richard Neely's novel 'The Plastic Nightmare.' Dir: Wolfgang Petersen. Phot: Laszlo Kovacs. Players: Tom Berenger, Bob Hoskins, Greta Scacchi. Prod: Pathe/Warner Bros.
The Sheltering Sky. Script: Mark Peploe from Paul Bowles' novel. Dir: Bernardo Bertolucci. Phot: Vittorio Storaro. Players: Debra Winger, John Malkovich, Campbell Scott. Prod: Film Trustees/Warner Bros.

A Shock to the System. Script: Andrew Klavan from Simon Brett's novel. Dir: Jan Egleson. Phot: Paul Goldsmith. Players: Michael Caine, Elizabeth McGovern, Peter Riegert, Swoosie Kurtz. Prod: Corsair.
A Show of Force. Script: Evan Jones, John Strong. Dir: Bruno Barreto. Phot: James Glennon. Players: Amy Irving, Andy Garcia, Lou Diamond Philips, Robert Duvall. Prod: Golden Harvest/Paramount.
Sibling Rivalry. Script: Martha Goldhirsch. Dir: Carl Reiner. Phot: Reynaldo Villalobos. Players: Kirstie Alley, Jami Gertz, Bill Pullman, Carrie Fisher. Prod: Columbia.
Sidewalk Stories. Script and Dir: Charles Lane. Phot: Bill Dill. Players: Charles Lane, Nicole Alysia. Prod: Island Pictures.
The Silence of the Lambs. Script: Ted Tally from Thomas Harris's novel. Dir: Jonathan Demme. Phot. Tak Fujimoto. Players: Jodie Foster, Anthony Hopkins, Scott Glenn, Ted Levine. Prod: Orion.
Sketches. Script: Paul W. Shapiro. Dir: Neal Israel. Phot: James Hayman. Players: Jason Bateman, C. Thomas Howell, Annie Potts. Prod: MCEG.
State Of Grace. Script: Dennis McIntyre, David Rabe. Dir: Phil Joanou. Phot: Jordan Cronenweth. Players: Sean Penn, Ed Harris, Gary Oldman, Robin Wright, John Turturro, Michael Gambon. Prod: Orion.
Stephen King's Graveyard Shift. Script: John Esposito from King story. Dir: Ralph S. Singleton. Phot: Peter Stein. Players: David Andrews, Stephen Macht, Brad Dourif. Prod: Orion.
Streets. Script: Katt Shea Ruben, Andy Ruben. Dir: Katt Shea Ruben. Phot: Phedon Papamichael. Players: Christina Applegate, David Mendenhall, Eb Lottimer, Starr Andreeff. Prod: Concorde.
Strike It Rich. Script: James Scott from novella by Graham Greene, 'Loser Takes All.' Dir: Scott. Phot: Robert Paynter. Players: Robert Lindsay, Molly Ringwald, John Gielgud. Prod: Miramax.
The Taking of Beverly Hills. Script: Rick Natkin, David Fuller. Dir: Sidney J. Furie. Players: Ken Wahl, Harley Jane Kozak. Prod: Columbia.
Taking Care of Business. Script: Jill Mazursky, Jeffrey Abrams. Dir: Arthur Hiller.

Continued on page 411

INTER VIDEO

Your One Stop Source for Video Equipment Rentals, Post Production and Stage Facilities
733 No. Victory Blvd., Burbank, CA 91502 (818) 569-4000 FAX: (818) 843-6884

- CCD Betacam SP
- Online Bays
- Standards Conversion/Duplication

Look for our work in TOTAL RECALL, ROBOCOP 2 and FIRE BIRDS, or call for reel!

Video Round-up: Gathering in Silents

Like other theatrical ventures silent films are now having a rebirth through video. Theatrical exhibitions live on through groups like The Silent Society of the Hollywood Heritage Inc. but in the 1990's vid companies are awakening to a specialised audience at their disposal. Kino Video and MGM Video have been spearheading the current drive with video copies from master prints and sometimes orchestral scores. Smaller companies operating with fewer technical resources vary in quality of visuals and musical background but some are quite dogged in their pursuit of best possible prints.

Cinephiles who've trekked many miles for a rare silent screening now have an opportunity to view even some of the more obscure silents at home. Though many of these titles may not be available at the local video store they can usually be purchased from distributors at reasonable prices.

Viewers have a chance to catch stars and directors who spent all or part of their careers in the speechless medium. Those wishing to view the late Greta Garbo in her formative years can scrutinise video prints of the 1924 Swedish *Story of Gösta Berling* (Video Yesteryear), the German 1925 *The Joyless Street* (Kino) or the 1926 American

TOP GROSSING FILMS IN U.S. & CANADA: 1989

	Rentals
Batman	$150.5 million
Indiana Jones and the Last Crusade	$115.5 million
Lethal Weapon 2	$79.5 million
Honey, I Shrunk the Kids	$71 million
Rain Man	$65 million
Back to the Future, Part II	$63 million
Ghostbusters II	$61.6 million
Look Who's Talking	$55 million
Parenthood	$48.6 million
Dead Poets Society	$47.6 million

"They didn't need voices. They had faces then." Louise Brooks in *Diary of a Lost Girl* and Lon Chaney in *The Hunchback of Notre Dame*, both released on video by Kino International

Flesh and the Devil (MGM). *Wild Orchids* (1929) is also available from MGM and the 1928 *A Woman of Affairs* is among the titles being considered by Metro for its next batch of silent releases.

All of the three foreign silents starring the legendary Louise Brooks are also available on video: *Pandora's Box* (Nelson Ent. & Video Dimensions), *Diary of a Lost Girl* (Kino) and *Prix de Beauté* (Interama Video Classics), the latter a hybrid containing some post-synchronised dialogue. It remains for Brooks' American features to be exploited on video.

Rudolph Valentino can be espied early in his career when he appeared briefly in the 1919 *Eyes of Youth* (VY). Valentino can also be seen in *The Eagle* (Kino) and *Monsieur Beaucaire* (Grapevine Video). The latter type contains not only an orchestral score but is advertised as having Valentino singing on the soundtrack.

It is doubtful that anyone will turn up with a tape featuring Lon Chaney Sr. singing on the track but he has remained more in sync with audience tastes and his *Phantom of the Opera* is one of the most popular of all silent titles on video (Kino & others). Kino is touting a two-strip Technicolor sequence in its print and is also releasing Chaney's *Hunchback of Notre Dame*. Sinister Cinema's Chaney collection includes *Oliver Twist* with Jackie Coogan in the title role opposite Chaney's Fagin, *Shadows* and an early Tod Browning effort, *Outside the Law* (1921). A number of macabre features Browning and Chaney did at MGM remain untapped on tape including the bizarre classic *The Unknown*.

More eerie fare can be found among the German expressionist silents now available on video such as *The Cabinet of Dr. Caligari* (Kino), *The Golem* (VY), Fritz Lang's *Destiny* (VY), *Waxworks* (Sinister Cinema), *Warning Shadows* (VY) and *Metropolis* (Kino & others). Rare foreign films on tape also include Carl Dreyer's *Leaves from Satan's Book* (Grapevine Video) and René Clair's *The Crazy Ray* (Sinister Cinema).

Films of America's first star director D.W. Griffith include selected shorts, *Birth of a Nation*, *Intolerance*, *Broken Blossoms*, *Way Down East*, *True Heart Susie* and *Dream Street* all available from Video Yesteryear. *Isn't Life Wonderful?* is available from Danny Burk while *The White Rose* and *Orphans of the Storm* can be purchased from Grapevine Video. Classic Video Cinema Collectors Club offers a print of *Birth* preceded by a discussion shot in the early 1930's between Griffith and actor Walter Huston on the film's controversy.

As made evident in these listings Video Yesteryear is prolific among distributors of silents. It also labours to have its films unspooled at the closest equivalent to silent projection speed and provides organ scores. Among its many riches is a collection of Alfred Hitchcock silents including *Easy Virtue*, *The Manxman* and *The Lodger*. It has Chaplin and Keaton shorts and some features and even a tape of beer commercials Keaton did in the 1960's. The four comic L's of that period are also represented with a smattering of work from Harold Lloyd, Max Linder, Harry Langdon and Stan Laurel, the latter in a two volume collection called *Stan without Ollie*. A youthful W.C. Fields can be seen flexing his misanthropy in *Pool Shark* (1915).

Since so many of the silents are public domain titles they are often found on several labels but there are some small companies which take extra care to manufacture rare films. CVCCC distributes such rarities as Maurice Tourneur's *The Last of the Mohicans*, Jean Renoir's *Charleston* and Italian silents such as *Cinema*, the only film made by diva Eleonora Duse. Its prints are often provided with orchestral scores and preceded by a background intro. Danny Burk's big find is an ultra-rare Marlene Dietrich silent, *The Woman Men Yearn For* (1928), while Grapevine has *Uncle Tom's Cabin* (1914). Among the majors Paramount released a handful of films on its 75th anniversary and more recently *The Covered Wagon* but is just beginning to assess its silents potential.

Kino International has released *The Cabinet of Dr. Caligari* on video

The obvious need for optimal visual quality in silents is being addressed by their appearance on videodiscs. Lumivision and Image Entertainment have both issued discs of *The Phantom of the Opera* both using the 1929 re-release print of maximum quality. Image is also producing discs of Keaton's *Our Hospitality*, *The Thief of Bagdad* and Victor Sjöström's *The Outlaw and His Wife* among other titles. The Voyager Co. will be releasing silents on laser in 1991 but titles have yet to be firmed.

Finally, those wishing to keep up with new releases by the small vid companies can check two periodicals, *Big Reel* and *Classic Image*. *Big Reel* deals with the whole area of movie collecting with more emphasis on celluloid than on tape. *Classic Image* is a nostalgia publication with the accent on video.

Fred Lombardi

Silents Video Distributors

Danny Burk
2316 Mishawaka Avenue
South Bend
Indiana 46615

Cable Films
PO Box 7171 Country Club Sta.
Kansas City
Missouri 64113
Tel: 913–362–2804

Classics Video Cinema Collector's Club (CVCCC)
6945 Pebble Park Circle
West Bloomfield
Michigan 48033

Facets Video
1517 West Fullerton Avenue
Chicago
Illinois 60614
Tel: 1–800–331–6197

Grapevine Video
PO Box 46161
Phoenix
Arizona 85063
Tel: 602–245–0210

HBO Video
1370 Avenue of the Americas
New York
N.Y. 10019
Tel: 212–977–8990

Image Entertainment Inc.
9333 Oso Avenue
Chatsworth
California 91311–6089
Tel: 818–407–9100

Interama Video Classics
301 West 53rd Street
Suite 19E
New York
N.Y. 10019
Tel: 212–977–4830

Kino Video
333 West 39th Street
New York
N.Y. 10018
Tel: 212–629–6880

Lumivision Corporation
1490 Lafayette Street
Suite 305
Denver
Colorado 80218
Tel: 303–860–0400

MGM/UA Entertainment
10000 Washington Boulevard
Culver City
California 90232–2728
Tel: 213–280–6000
or:
1350 Avenue of the Americas
New York
N.Y. 10019
Tel: 212–408–0500

Nelson Entertainment Inc.
Embassy Home Entertainment
335 N. Maple Drive
Beverly Hills
California 90210–3899
Tel: 213–285–6000

Paramount Home Video
5555 Melrose Avenue
Hollywood
California 90038
Tel: 213–468–5000

Sinister Cinema
PO Box 777
Pacifica
California 94044
Tel: 415–359–3292

Video Dimensions
530 W. 23rd Street
New York
N.Y. 10011
Tel: 212–929–6135

Video Yesteryear
Box C
Sandy Hook
Connecticut 06482
Tel: 1–800–243–0987

The Voyager Co.
1351 Pacific Coast Highway
Santa Monica
California 90401

Big Reel
c/o Empire Publishing
Route #3, Box 83
(Highway 220 South)
Msfidon
North Carolina 27025
Tel: 919–427–5850

Classic Image
PO Box 809
Muscatine
Iowa 52761
Tel: 319–263–2331

Film Producers

Amblin Entertainment
Building 477 First floor
100 Universal City Plaza
Universal City, California 91608
Tel: (818) 777 4600

Carolco Pictures
8800 Sunset Blvd.
Los Angeles
California 90069
Tel: (213) 850 8800
Fax: (213) 657 1629
Telex: 234337

Castle Rock Pictures
335 North Maple Drive
Suite 135
Beverly Hills
California 90210
Tel: (213) 285 2300
Fax: (213) 285 2345

Cinecom
1290 Ave. of the Americas

New York, N.Y. 10104
Tel: (212) 830 9700
Fax: (212) 245 4173

Columbia Pictures
10202 West Washington Blvd.
Culver City
California 90232
Tel: (213) 280 8000
Fax: (213) 204 1300
Telex: 842 9348

Tri-Star Pictures
(A Columbia Pictures
Entertainment Company)
Columbia Plaza
Burbank
California 91505
Tel: (818) 954 6000

Concorde Pictures
11600 San Vicente Blvd.
Los Angeles
California 90049
Tel: (213) 820 6733

Walt Disney Company
(*Walt Disney Pictures, Touchstone Pictures,
Hollywood Pictures all
released through Buena
Vista*)
500 Buena Vista Street
Burbank
California 91521
Tel: (818) 560 1000
Fax: (818) 560 1930

Hemdale
7966 Beverly Blvd.
Los Angeles
California 90048
Tel: (213) 966 3700
Fax: (213) 651 3107

Imagine Films Entertainment
1925 Century Park East
Suite #2300
Los Angeles
California 90067
Tel: (213) 277 1665
Fax: (213) 785 0107

Interscope
10900 Wiltshire Blvd.
Suite 1400
Los Angeles
California 90024
Tel: (213) 208 8525
Fax: (213) 208 1197

Largo Entertainment
10201 West Pico Blvd.
Bldg. 86, Room 206
Los Angeles
California 90035
Tel: (213) 203 3600
Fax: (213) 203 4133

Lucasfilm
P.O. Box 20009
San Rafael
California 94912
Tel: (415) 662 1800

MGM/UA
10000 West Washington Blvd.
Culver City
California 90232
Tel: (213) 280 6000
Fax: (213) 836 1680
Telex: 6831385

Morgan Creek Productions
1875 Century Park East
Los Angeles
California 90067
Tel: (213) 284 8884
Fax: (213) 282 8794

New Line Cinema
116 North Robertson Blvd.
Los Angeles
California 90048
Tel: (213) 854 5811
Fax: (213) 854 1824

Orion Pictures
1325 Avenue of the Americas
New York, N.Y. 10019
Tel: (212) 956 3800
Fax: (212) 956 9449

Paramount Pictures
5555 Melrose Avenue

Los Angeles
California 90038
Tel: (213) 956 5000
Fax: (213) 956 5555
Telex: 3715855

Pathé Communications Corporation
640 San Vicente Blvd.
Los Angeles
California 90048
Tel: (213) 658 2100
Fax: (213) 658 2111

Twentieth Century Fox
10201 West Pico Blvd.
Los Angeles
California 90035
Tel: (213) 277 2211

Universal Pictures
100 Universal City Plaza
Universal City
California 91608
Tel: (818) 777 1000
Fax: (818) 777 6431

Warner Bros.
4000 Warner Blvd.
Burbank
California 91522
Tel: (818) 954 6000
Fax: (818) 954 2464
Telex: 6718514

Distributors

Angelika Films
110 Greene Street
Suite 1102
New York, N.Y. 10012
Tel: (212) 274 1990
Fax: (212) 966 4957

Avenue Pictures
12100 Wiltshire Blvd.
Suite 1650
Los Angeles
California 90025
Tel: (213) 442 2200
Fax: (213) 207 1753

Buena Vista
See production listing for Disney

Castle Hill Productions
1414 Avenue of the Americas
New York, N.Y. 10019
Tel: (212) 888 0080
Fax: (212) 644 0956

Cinecom
See production listing

Columbia Tri-Star Film Distributors
711 Fifth Ave.
New York, N.Y. 10022
Tel: (212) 751 4400
Fax: (212) 688 2738

Triumph Releasing Corp.
(A Columbia Pictures Entertainment Co.)
Same as listing for Columbia Tri-Star

Concorde Pictures
See production listing

Fries Entertainment
6922 Hollywood Blvd.
Hollywood
California 90028
Tel: (213) 466 2266
Fax: (213) 466 9407
Telex: 401954

Samuel Goldwyn Company
10203 Santa Monica Blvd.
Los Angeles
California 90067
Tel: (213) 552 2255
Fax: (213) 284 8463

Hemdale
See production listing

International Film Exchange
201 West 52nd Street
New York, N.Y. 10019
Tel: (212) 582 4318
Fax: (212) 956 2257
Telex: 420748

Island Pictures
8920 Sunset Blvd.
Los Angeles
California 90069
Tel: (213) 276 4500
Fax: (213) 271 7840

MGM/UA
See production listing

Miramax
375 Greenwich Street
New York, N.Y. 10013
Tel: (212) 941 3800
Fax: (212) 941 3949

New Century Vista
5757 Wiltshire Blvd.
Suite 723
Los Angeles
California 90036
Tel: (213) 936 6161
Fax: (213) 936 6127

New Line Cinema
See production listing for California operations
Also:
575 Eighth Avenue
New York, N.Y. 10018
Tel: (212) 239 8880
Fax: (212) 239 9104

Seven Arts
(New Line distributor for Carolco Pictures)
Same listing as New Line

New Yorker Films
16 W. 61st Street
New York, N.Y. 10023
Tel: (212) 247 6110
Fax: (212) 307 7855

Orion Pictures
See production listings

Orion Classics
See Orion Pictures production listings

Paramount
See production listing

Pathé
See production listing

Skouras Pictures
1040 North Las Palmas Avenue
Hollywood
California 90038
Tel: (213) 467 3000
Fax: (213) 467 0740
Telex: 160777

Triton Pictures
9000 Sunset Blvd
Suite 500
Los Angeles
California 90069
Tel: (213) 275 7779
Fax: (213) 275 7334

Universal Pictures
See production listing

Warner Bros.
See production listing

Useful Addresses

Academy of Motion Picture Arts and Sciences
8949 Wiltshire Blvd.
Beverly Hills
California 90211
Tel: (213) 278 8990
Fax: (213) 859 9351
Telex: 698614

Motion Picture Association of America (MPAA)
1133 Avenue of the Americas
New York, N.Y. 10036
Tel: (212) 840 6161
Fax: (212) 391 9239

Motion Picture Export Association of America
Same as MPAA

Directors Guild of America
7920 Sunset Blvd.
Los Angeles
California 90046
Tel: (213) 289 2000

U.S.S.R.

by Verina Glaessner

More liberal times have left the cinema in the Soviet Union with the problem of defining for itself a new role. It is a task made doubly difficult by the need simultaneously to provide wholesale a set of industrial under-pinnings to replace the erstwhile model of monolithic centralisation. This is crucially important as the kind of industrial infra-structure now being devised will determine the kind of films produced in the Soviet Union's constituent republics in the future.

The last year has been a transitional one. Certain things have definitely changed. Film-makers talk with quite palpable relief of the entirely new sensation of shooting a film without having to double-guess the outcome of the hitherto inevitable bureaucratic struggles. "Compared with doing the rounds of the bureaucrats' offices, raising money from a number of different sources is child's play," one remarked. The automatic release of completed films regardless of opinions of their quality may be a fact but it is still not taken for granted and objections continue to be voiced.

Projects are initiated by a diverse range of sources. The studios play an active part here, hiring personnel and selling their own product with the rules being more or less worked out as they go along. Hence the unpleasantness between Mosfilm, who laid claim to a large number of titles hitherto sold by Sovexportfilm and that organisation at the Cannes Film Festival. Slowly the need to professionalise the marketing and promotion of films is being acknowledged, with Mosfilm, again leading the way by hiring its own international PR and its own representation in the United States.

With independence comes financial accountability and although the need to ensure the continued production of films of artistic merit is widely recognised there is general dismay at the small number of films that are able currently to recoup costs. According to *Soviet Film* magazine only three of some 38 titles succeeded in the previous year (*Cold Summer of '53*, *Assa* and *Blackmail*).

In part this has to do with low ticket prices and the incursions made into the audience by the remarkable revival of Soviet television (Leningrad TV has already made moves towards independence and discussions about establishing an alternative TV channel in Moscow too are taking place) and in part with the largely unchecked advance of video. Apart from video cafés there are video libraries where one borrows and views films, and video buses visiting remote areas. Although legislation to curb video piracy has been mooted for some time, there has been as yet no move to implement it. To an extent, a Sovexport spokesman explained, this has been due to the strength of the movement opposing any such legislation backed as it is by the trades unions and the Young Communist League who make a tidy profit leasing premises to video café managers.

But there is also a reluctance to curb illicit distribution before the release of Western films through legitimate means has become more extensive. This desire in turn is subject to an awareness of the harmful effect a flood of imported product could have on the local industry. But an increasing number of Western films are being distributed alongside an increasing number of "showcase" events. Last year a Festival of

Director Sergei Soloviev with Soviet pop star Boris Grebenchikov on *Red Rose Stands for Sadness, Black Rose Stands for Love*

American films was screened at several cinemas in Moscow and there was a Pasolini retrospective.

Meanwhile there has been no shortage of prosecutions – most of which have in the end been dropped – against the video establishments for showing exploitation material that offends against public taste.

Changing Patterns of Exhibition
Decentralisation is also occurring within distribution and a series of separate networks, like the Lenkinvideo company, which buy films at the various national film markets. Some are tied to exhibition outlets, others resell to exhibitors or to other distributors. Patterns of exhibition are also changing. Although ticket sales are down the average Soviet citizen still makes some thirteen and fourteen visits to the cinema a year, and new ones are being built, like the 2,000 seater with attached bowling alley under construction in Leningrad.

Following its meeting in May the Film-Makers' Union was reorganised as a confederation of film unions from the whole of the Societ Union. It was also dramatically slimmed down. There are no figure-heads and a small group of three working secretaries in place of its previous large secretariat.

It is led by Davlat Khudonazarov, formerly President of the Tajikistan Association of Film-Makers'. Khudonazarov, elected for two years, intends to oversee the drafting of a body of law relating to film and the cinema by way of permanently removing it from the realms of personal diktat. "Progress will not be as fast as it has been but I shall leave a solid foundation," he says.

Watching current Soviet films, Western viewers may be forgiven for imagining themselves having been returned to the 1960's, so redolent are they of the permissive spirit of that time. Irony, the great weapon of "stagnation," has been abandoned and almost everything can be said or shown unfettered at the moment by either the stringent constraints of a market economy or the behest of an artistic establishment. (A rudimentary system of film classification copes with the problem of minors.) A rather large slice of the 150 odd titles produced in the course of the year for the cinema (another 150 odd are shot in the studios for showing on TV) fall into the youth culture exposé category with a familiar (to us) mix of sex (nudity is remorselessly obligatory), drugs and rock (for example **The Needle** from Khazakfilm Studios of **Blue Skies**). Others rework Jodorowski or Makavejev territory as does Soloviev's **Red Rose Stands for Sadness, Black Rose Stands for Love**, a heavy excursion into erstwhile surrealism. Elsewhere history's sacred monsters are turned to figures of fun as in Yuri Kara's **Balthassar's Feast** or **My Night with Stalin**, which boasts a performance of smirking sanctimoniousness from its lead but little else. Ogorodnikov's **Prishvin's Paper Eyes**, about a television producer who becomes involved in an inquest into events of the 1940's and 1950's, however, has its supporters. Karate rather than culture is on the agenda for co-operative film production companies.

Others take a more deliberately critical path. **That's All the Love There Is**, directed by Anatoly Vasilyev, casts an eye back at the Brezhnev era in its story of a girl who works in a factory and wins the prize of meeting the man himself, and **Braking in the Sky** reveals a sense of disillusionment with perestroika itself administered, it argues, as a charade by an implacable bureaucracy. It was directed by Victor Buturlin, scripted by Roman Solnstev and made at Lenfilm Studios.

Vasilyev's film was written by Sergei Bodrov whose *Freedom Is Paradise*, documented the lives of social outcasts and was filmed with a reticence that made it all the more shocking. It won deserved prizes at Berlin and Montreal. Bodrov's new and different **The Gambler**, about gambling, gangsterism and romance, occupies territory visually reminiscent of Welles at some points, early Godard at others and conjures a sense of unease as much existential as strictly a function of events. It also reveals a film-maker far more cinematically literate than the workaday likes of Abdrashitov or Shaknazerov.

Film of the Decade?

For certain Russians, and perhaps especially for certain Russian women, the film of the year, and even of the decade, was Kira Muratova's **The Asthenic Syndrome**. The rise of Kira Muratova to recognition following the "unshelving" of *Short Meetings and Long Farewells* and the controversy surrounding her latest films (she has made only eight films in some thirty years) marks her as emblematic of the times, as indeed does her self-indulgence. In *The Asthenic Syndrome*'s central character, a disaffected teacher subject to fits ofn somnolence under stress, she draws on a very familiar Russian male stereotype, and in its unflinching and disillusioned look at unsatisfactory relationships, and its anger and despair it is felt to speak for a generation of Russian women. Its release has not been without problems stemming in part from its strong language if not its frank

Still from Igor Minaiev's *Ground Floor*, released via Primodessa Film

male nudity. It will be awarded a limited release.

It has been cheering indeed to witness the end of the isolation of Soviet cinema, and from the vast amount of puffery concerning co-productions and joint ventures a number of interesting projects has materialised. Serge Silberman is producing Rustam Khamdamov's **Anna Karamozov** (it stars Jeanne Moreau), a project put his way by Elem Klimov. Khamdamov is seen in Soviet film critical circles as expressing a hitherto suppressed potential for Soviet film. His graduating film, *My Heart Is in the Mountains*, was shot in the style of silent Russian cinema. His second, *Slave of Love*, had him barred from film-making and has attained legendary status. Peter Fleischman has shot **It Is Hard To Be God** from a science fiction novel by the Strugatski brothers. It is a Dovzhenko Studios Hallelujah Film co-production. Gleb Panfilov has written the script of a study of the final days of the Romanovs, *Je vous aime*, which sees the family as the first victims "of terror which bathed the country in blood, the moment when the Russian ship of state sank in sight of the harbour," as he has said. It will be produced by two British companies. The co-production team of Lenfilm, American– Soviet Film Initiative and Marin Karmitz's MK2 company have signed Pavel Longuin to make three more features, following his success at Cannes with *Taxi Blues*. Alexei German is scripting a film on the last days of Stalin for the same company.

Other co-productions include Alexei Mitta's *Lost in Siberia* with Anthony Andrews and *Assassin of the Tsar* with Malcolm McDowell.

Meanwhile an ambitious plan is awaiting Culture Minister Gubenko's consideration. It will establish a fund to provide a series of cultural centres in the name of the Soviet Union's most popular actor/director of the 1970's, Vasily Shukshin – a contemporary of Tarkovski's. Shukshin's widow, the actress Lydia Fedosova Shukshina (who plans to produce Shukshin's unrealised final project on the peasant rebel Stenka Razin, *I Came to Bring You Freedom*), sees the centres as providing a grassroots focus for the revival of Russian film and more broadly, Russian culture.

Astenichesky Sindrom (The Asthenic Syndrome)

Script: Sergei Popov, Alexander Chernyk, Kira Muratova. Direction: Kira Muratova. Players: Olga Antonova, Sergei Popov, Galina Zakhurdayeva. Produced by Odessa Studios.

With its first (black-and-white) section dealing with a woman in somewhat Chekhovian mourning for her life, and its second bursting affectingly into colour for the story of incidents in her frequently catatonic protagonist's existence, *The Asthenic Syndrome* is evidence of an extraordinary eye and considerably more artistic discipline beneath the surface than we may at first suspect. The situations might be desperate, the male protagonist slumped apparently lifeless in the metro station, the woman in an excess of self-contempt accepting the sexual advances of a derelict, but they are honed to a sharp edge of black Beckett-like absurdity. The man's prone body becomes the subject of incongruous attentions from passers-by. The woman's sexual encounter has a moment of ridiculousness (the apartment door is left open accidentally.) It is not only irreverence that Muratova shares with Vera Chytilová, but also her feminist concerns, elaborated in celebratory scenes, reminiscent of Agnès Varda, which offer a fine vindication of female sexuality. But, at heart, Muratova is quite sui generis, darker than either of the above and, if this film is anything to go by, in the grip of a rather intoxicating love affair with cinema. One wonders how she will proceed.

Verina Glaessner

New and Forthcoming Films

Diversia (Subversive Action). Script: Eldar Kuliyev, Ramiz Fataliyev. Dir: Eldar Kuliev. Players: Elkhan Jafarov, Arzu Ojaguerdiyev. Prod: Azerbaijan Film Studios.
Lichnoye delo Anny Akhmatovoy (The Story of Anna Akhmatova). Script: Semyon Aranovitch, Elena Ignatova. Dir: Semyon Aranovitch. Prod: Lenfilm.
Semeinye fotografi (Family Album). Script and Dir: Valentin Kuik. Players: Allan Kuljus, Merle Tiaje. Prod: Tallinn Film Studios.
Trudno byt Bogom (It's Hard To Be God). Script: Peter Fleischman, Jean-Claude Carrière, Dal Orlov. Dir: Peter Fleischman. Players: Edvard Zentara, Alexander Filippenko, Pierre Clémenti. Prod: Dovzhenko Studios/Hallelujah Film GmbH.
Vitebskoye Delo (The Vitebsk Case Part One: The Crime). Script and Dir: Viktor Dashuk. Prod: Belarusfilm.
Zakon (The Law). Script: Leonid Zorin, Alexander Alev, Vladimir Naumov. Dir: Vladimir Naumov. Players: Yuri Shlykov, Boris Shcherbakov, Natalia Belikhvostikova. Prod: Mosfilm.

Mat (Mother). Script and Dir: Gleb Panfilov. Players: Inna Churikova, Lubomiras Lautsavichus, Victor Rakov. Prod: Mosfilm.
Katala (The Gambler). Script: Valery Barakin, Sergei Bodrov. Dir: Sergei Bodrov, Alexander Buravski. Players: Valeria Garkavina, Yelena Safonova, Nodar Mgaloblishvili, Victor Pavlov. Prod: Mosfilm.
Piry Valtasara Ili Noch so Stalinim. Script: Fazil Iskander. Dir: Yuri Kara. Players: Alexei Petrenko, Yevgeny Yevstigneev. Prod: Gorki Studios.
Gran (On the Verge). Script and Dir: Nadezhda Repina. Players: Arnis Licitis, Olga Sirina. Prod: Katarsis/Mosfilm.
Drugoi i Stalin (Others and Stalin). Script and Dir: V. Lopatin. Prod: Tsentrnauch Film Studio.
Je vous aime. Script and Dir: Gleb Panfilov. Prod: Westbourne Film/Harris Film.
Zhili-Byli Sem' Simeonov (Once Upon a Time There Lived Seven Simeons). Script and Dir: Hercs Franks, Vladimir Eisner. Prod: Eastern Siberia Newsreel Studios.
Nochi Chorni v Sochi (Nights Are Dark in Sochi). Script: Maria Khmelik. Dir: Vasily Pichul. Players: Natalia Negoda. Prod: Podarok.
Muzh i doch Tamari Alexandrovny (Tamara Alexandrovna's Husband and Daughter). Script: Nadrzhda Kozhushanaya. Dir: Olga Narutskaya. Prod: Mosfilm.
Bumazhniye Glaza Prishvina (Prishvin's Paper Eyes). Script: Valery Ogorodnikov. Dir: Valery Ogorodnikov. Players: Alexander Romantsov, Oleg Kovalov. Prod: Lenfilm. *Surreal exploration of Stalin's hypnotic power.*
Coma. Script: Nijele Adomenaite, Yuri Makusinsky, Mikhail Konovalchuk. Dir: Nijele Adomenaite, Boris Gorlov. Players: Natalia Nikulenko, Alexander Bocharov. Prod: Lenfilm. *A distinctive account of a woman's incarceration in a 1950's labour camp.*

Still from Gleb Panfilov's new version of *Mother*

Useful Addresses

Film-makers' Union of the U.S.S.R.
13 Vassilevskaya Uliza
Moscow 123825

Sovexportfilm
14 Kalashny per.
Moscow 103869
Fax: 200 1256
Telex: 411 143

Mosfilm
1 Mosfilmovskaya ul.
Moscow 119858
Fax: 938 20 83
Telex: 411293 mzflm su
Publicity in the U.S.A.
Dennis Davidson
211 South Beverly Drive
Suite 200
PO Box 5519
Beverly Hills
CA 90210/0519
Fax: (213) 275 6030

Primodessa
Cuvilliesstrasse 8
D-8000 Munich 80
Federal Republic of Germany
Fax: (089) 9828 506
or:
Tshishikova 62
270023 Odessa
U.S.S.R.

Primodessa represents the Interdet co-operative association of which Lenfilm, Leningrad, Gorky TV, Moscow, Grusya Film, Tbilissi, Azerbaijan Film, Baku and Odessa Film, Odessa are members.

Soviet-British Creative Association
46 Charlotte Street
London W.1.
Tel: (071) 637 4602

Association of Film Education Workers of the U.S.S.R.
5-3-41 K. Simonov Street
Moscow 125167
U.S.S.R.

VERINA GLAESSNER is a freelance film critic and arts correspondent with a special interest in Soviet cinema.

VENEZUELA
by Paul Lenti

Venezuela's film community entered the new decade with hopes to recapture the heyday of the mid-1980's, with annual production up to almost 20 features. When petroleum prices fell, the film industry suffered a concurrent recession, with domestic production limited to only a handful of independent ventures by 1988.

Formerly the richest country in Latin America, Venezuela was caught unawares by the 1981 oil glut when petroleum dropped from approximately $40 a barrel to as low as $9. For the first time, Venezuelans were suddenly forced to tighten belts. When state subsidies on staples and transportation were cut sharply in 1989, following Carlos Andrés Pérez's return to the presidency, the situation exploded. Large-scale rioting in the capital left around 300 people dead.

Burdened with a US$29-billion foreign debt, the country has been forced to devalue the bolivar drastically over the past seven years (from 4.3 to about 50 x US$1). This has taken its toll on the national film industry. The preferential exchange rate – where distributors paid foreign remittances

Still from Luis Alberto Lamata's *Land of Grace*

at a lower ratio – was dissolved in 1989, making distributors more selective with films they bring into the country. And while box-office figures are up, an 80% inflation rate in 1989 (estimated at only 25% for 1990) cut into profits as a government-imposed low ceiling on ticket prices (under $1) make recoupment for domestic film-makers nearly impossible. The Gross Domestic Product, the broadest measure of total economic output, fell 8.1% in 1989, the largest such slump in memory.

In contrast to most Latin American countries, Venezuelan film-goers have always supported their cinema. For example, while distributors released only 17 national features in 1985 (representing a mere 4% of all films distributed in the country), these movies managed to capture 17% of the gross revenues. Yet, Venezuela's relatively small population makes it virtually impossible for producers to recuperate investment within the national territory alone. According to Julio Sosa Pietri, head of the state production agency Foncine (Fondo de Fomento Cinematográfico de Venezuela), a national film must attract more than 1,000,000 people at domestic box-offices to break even, something which has been achieved by only two films in the last decade: *Macu, the Policeman's Wife* and *Homicidal Guilt*.

Latino Common Market

Recognising the need for external markets, Venezuela has taken a leading role in promoting the establishment of a so-called Latin American Common Market for Spanish-and Portuguese-language films, that will allow free passage of movies between signatory countries. Inspired by Europe's 1992 economic unification, various Latin American countries are currently working to change national laws governing their film industries to function on a region-wide basis.

To advance this initiative, Foncine hosted the Foro Iberoamericano de Integración Cinematográfica (Ibero-American Cinema Integration Forum) in November 1989. The purpose of the meeting was to develop strategies unifying production and distribution measures throughout Latin America in an effort to amplify natural markets for films in Spanish-and Portuguese-speaking countries. Protectionist measures found in some national legislations currently impede co-productions with other Latin countries.

Documents establishing a *mercomun* (common market) – in which Latino films pass freely between signatory countries – and promoting co-productions between nations were signed by representatives from a dozen countries. These documents are at present being debated by respective countries for their incorporation into national legislation.

Attending the meet were officials from Argentina, Brazil, Chile, Colombia, Cuba, the Dominican Republic, El Salvador, Ecuador, Italy, Mexico, Nicaragua, Panama, Paraguay, Peru, Portugal, Puerto Rico, Spain and Venezuela, along with representatives from the Cuban-based Foundation for New Latin American Cinema, the Miami Film Commission and the Sundance Institute.

(Although film-makers are optimistic, an earlier such meet to establish a common market for Latino films was held in Brasilia in 1977 with no long-term results.)

As for business at home, Sosa Pietri notes Venezuela is attempting to recapture the level of its film production, which had fallen drastically in recent years. Film-makers, faced with diminishing funds, have developed new production strategies and 1989–90 saw many new film starts, mostly in co-production with Latin American or European companies.

With the verbal support of President Pérez, Foncine is currently attempting to consolidate the various film-related companies into an industry through new legislation, of which Sosa Pietri notes four main points:

1. Establish the state's acknowledgement of a responsibility for domestic production as an expression of national culture. This would also give the government the responsibility to protect all sectors of the industry: production, distribution and exhibition.

2. Stabilise the diverse sectors of the industry – laboratories, distributors, publicity, exhibitors, etc. – which is important for the economic growth of the industry as a whole.

3. Create a National Film Institute, one in which Foncine could be incorporated into its production section. The institute would supervise and co-ordinate all film-related activity. It would also promote Venezuelan locations for foreign companies and attract co-productions with Venezuelan companies. (If a foreign company currently wishes to film in Venezuela, it must arrange everything through a multitude of people. A central office could reduce this to one person.)

4. Overhaul the tax structure concerning film. Through the creation of tax shelters, the private sector could be attracted to invest in production. Also, a new 10% tax on ticket sales could go to finance production. (This figure is similar to the existing 6.6% Foncine tax, but it would be shifted from the distributor to the consumer.) Municipal taxes on cinemas could be eliminated and duties leveled on professional film-related imports could be re-classified and lowered. (At present, a recreational super-8 camera for private use has the same import duties as professional 16mm and 35mm equipment.)

Prolific Output

While waiting for legislators to debate this proposed plan, film-makers have not been idle. By mid-1990, around ten new features have been finished and await commercial release with an approximate equal number of new films either under camera or slated to begin production in the near future.

For the most part, Venezuelan filmmakers can be divided into two types: those working specifically for the art market such as Roque Zambrano, whose **The Other Illusion** picked up the best photography prize at the 1989 Havana Film Festival, and commercial directors whose films tend to imitate American and Mexican models. The latter movies are characterised by an abundance of sex and violence.

Currently awaiting domestic release are: *The Other Illusion*, originally shot in 1988; *The Mixed-Blood*, a Cuban–Venezuelan co-production by Uruguyan Mario Handler; *Amongst Blows and Boleros*, by John Dickinson; *Black River*, a French–Spanish–Venezuelan co-production by Atahualpa Lichi; *The Caracas Contact*, by Philippe Toledano; *Land of Grace*, by Luis Alberto Lamata, shot in 1988; and *Joligud*, by Agusto Pradelli, and *Lady Bolero*, by Marilda Vera, both produced in 1989.

Roman Chalbaud, director of the acclaimed *The Smoking Fish*, also completed work on his new film *Flaming Knives*, a Venezuelan–Spanish Television co-production based on the play "Todo Bicho de Uña." The film was premiered at the San Sabastian Film Festival.

Either under camera or in pre-production are: *Tender Is the Night*, a co-production with France by Leonardo Henríquez; *New Land*, a co-production with Italy by Calogero Salvo; *Shoot To Kill*, a co-production with Televisión Española (TVE) by Carlos Ozpurua; *Full Moon*, by Ana Cristina Henríquez; *On Foreign Shores*, a co-production with France by Jacobo Penzo; and *Latino Bar*, a co-production between Venezuela, Mexico, Cuba and Spain by Mexican director Paul Leduc.

Sosa Pietri notes that four further features were slated to begin production in 1990, including one by Joaquín Cortez. Foncine also plans to produce an original made-for-TV miniseries to be shot on videotape.

Foncine has also been trying to attract foreign producers to Venezuela. The year began with Amblin Entertainment and Hollywood Pictures using locations in the Venezuelan jungles for the U.S. production *Arachnophobia*, about a town invaded by spiders.

Foncine also changed addresses in August, moving into the Centro Colgate Building.

Because of financial problems, the film department at the Universidad de los Andes (ULA) in Mérida has fallen back in production and other related activities in recent years. Although it formerly operated a biennial film festival, it has been four years since the last event.

And besides the National Cinémathèque, there is one art house in Caracas, the Sala de Arte y Ensayo "Margot Benacerraf" of the Ateneo de Caracas, directed by María Helena Ascanio. The Ateneo offers various film programmes and retrospectives throughout the year and maintains approximately 30 affiliates around the country. In addition, the Caracas Cine Prensa offers art films and three capital cinemas feature "Martes selectos," with special fare on Tuesdays. All cinemas are half price on Mondays.

Miguel Angel Landa and Marisela Berti in Flaming Knives, *directed by Roman Chalbaud*

Recent and Forthcoming Films

Cuchillos de Fuego (Flaming Knives). Script: Roman Chalbaud, David Suárez. Dir: Roman Chalbaud. Phot: José María Hermo. Music: Rederico Ruiz. Players: Miguel Angel Landa, Marisela Berti, Gabriel Fernández, Javier Zapata. Prod: Miguel Angel Landa. 93 mins.
En Territorio Extranjero (On Foreign Shores). Script: Jacobo Penzo, Frank Baiz. Dir: Jacobo Penzo. Phot: José Gregorio González. Player: Franklin Virguez. 90 mins.
Contacto en Caracas (The Caracas Contact). Script: Philippe Madral. Dir: Philippe Toledano. Phot: Johnny Semeco. Music: Miguel Angel Fuster. Players: Philippe Caroit, Ruddy Rodríguez, Pierre Dux, Herriete Lesser, Miguel Angel Landa. 90 mins.
Joligud: Crónicas de El Saladillo (Joligud: Chronicles from the Saladillo Neighbourhood). Script: Consuelo González, Augusto Pradelli. Dir: Augusto Pradelli. Phot: Ricardo Rubio. Music: Daniel Castro. Players: Marau Robelo, Vidal Figueroa, Fatima Colina. 87 mins.
Tierna es la noche (Tender Is the Night). Script and Dir: Leonardo Henríquez. Phot: Césare Jaworski. Music: José Vinicio Adames. Players: Víctor Cuica, Constanza Giner. 93 mins.
Río Negro (Black River). Script: Antonio Laneta, Atahualpa Lichi, Joaquín González, Eduardo de Gregorio. Dir: Atahualpa Lichi. Phot: Mario García Joya. Music: José María Vitter, Rafael Salazar. Players: Angela Molina, Frank Ramírez, Daniel Alvarado. Prod: Venezuela–French Culture Ministry-French Foreign Relations-Televisión Española- ICAIC. 100 mins.
Señora Bolero (Lady Bolero). Script: Marilda Vera, Milagros Rodríguez, David Suárez. Dir: Marilda Vera. Phot: Hernán Toro. Music: Carlos Moréan. Players: Carlota Soca, Héctor Mayerston, Marcelo Romo. Prod: Cinematográfica Macuto. 93 mins.
Tierra de Gracia (Land of Grace). Script and Dir: Luis Alberto Lamata. Phot: Andrés Augusti, Carlos Tovar. Players: Cosme Cortázar, Francis Rueda, Alexander Milic, Armando Gota. Prod: Thalia Producciones. 90 mins.
Entre Golpes y Boleros (Among Blows and Boleros). Script and Dir: John Dickinson. Phot: Césare Jaworski. Music: Eduardo Valls. Players: María Alejandra Martin, Vladimir Torres, William Mujica, Marcos Moreno. 93 mins.
La Otra Ilusín (The Other Illusion). Script and Dir: Roque Zambrano. Phot: Césare Jaworski. Music: Juan Carlos Nuñez, Grupo Sentimento Muerto. Players: Julie Restrifo, Javier Vidal, Luz Urdaneta. Prod: R.Z. Cine y Video-Departamento de Cine de la Universidad de los Andes (ULA). 112 mins.
La Mujer Ajena (The Other Woman). Script: Edilio Pena. Dir: Livio Quiroz. Phot: Carlos Tovar. Players: Pedro Lander, Carlos Carrero, Bettina Grand. Prod: Livas Films. 90 mins.

Useful Addresses

Foncine *(Fondo de Fomento Cinematográfico de Venezuela)*
Edificio Centro Colgate, piso 2, Ala Sur.
Oficina 2.B. Los Ruices
Caracas 1071
Telex: 29457 FONCI VC
Fax: 239–4786.

Dirrección de Industria Cinematográfica Avd. Libertador, Edificio Nuevo Centro, Chacoa
Caracas.
Tel: 32-4045.

Ateneo de Caracas
Apdo. 662
Caracas 1010
Tel: 573–4622
Telex: 29316 ATENA VC

Cinemateca Nacional de Venezuela
Edificio Anexo al Museo de Ciencias Naturales
Plaza Morelos
Caracas
Tel: 571–7533, 571–176, 571–5220

PAUL LENTI is a freelance journalist specialising in Latin American cinema. In addition to working eight years as a film critic for the Mexico City News and seven years with the trade paper Variety, he more recently co-ordinated the film section of the 1990 New York Festival Latino.

VIETNAM
by Fred Marshall

Importing films into Vietnam remains tricky. The country has its own language and culture; it also has a powerful television network and purchasing of foreign films is frowned upon. If films are donated by Foreign Missions, that is a different matter. But the problem of subtitling remains, and Chinese is the only language apart from their own that the Vietnamese understand. The People's Republic of China is not one of the allies of Vietnam, so this means that Hongkong and Taiwanese films are still in strong demand. Many Hongkong productions (e.g. *Better Tomorrow Part 3*) have been sent here. All films by Chow Yuen Fatt have been brought into Vietnam.

Vietnamese film weeks have formed part of recent festivals in India and Hawaii, and are popping up all around the festival circuit. The subject of such films is usually hardship and suffering in the midst of social reforms. *The Peasant*, directed by Ho Quong Minh, is one of the better and more realistic film to have emerged in recent years. Ho was educated in Switzerland and made an impact with his first film, *Kharma*. Other interesting titles are *Confronting the Sea*, *The Left Turn on the Lane*, and *The River of Aspiration*.

The Flood Season examines the guerrilla warfare that took place in the Mekong Delta during the Vietnam War. The film takes a direct look at the military strategies, organisation, and operations of the PLA. *Co-ordinates of Death*, directed by Nguyen Shang Tyan, is a propaganda movie showing the American actress and singer Kate Francis, moving along the Ho Chi Minh trail and seeing ruined Vietnamese villages and dead old folk. Other Vietnamese films on the subject of the conflict with the Americans are *The Wild Field*, *When the Tenth Month Comes*, and *Brothers and Relations*.

There are two studios in Vietnam, one in Ho Chi Minh City and the other in Hanoi. Their annual output is 17 films, half of these being in colour. Two or three films of the annual crop are selected for subtitling and sending abroad to festivals. Films are shown throughout the country in aging cinemas at low admission prices and with five performances each day, so that workers can have an opportunity to see the films.

Vietnamese director Ho Quong Minh

YUGOSLAVIA

by Maja Vlahović

Another one of Yugoslavia's hopeless directors with a perfect but neglected producer's gift, Goran Paskaljević (president of the Federal Film-Makers' Association) couldn't have chosen a better title for his pretentious feature which marked the first half of the year. Indeed, **The Time of Miracles** is the best tag for another Yugoslav political experiment. For the major part of the year, the Yugoslavs have lived in a country with a twofold system, the Western parts (Slovenia and Croatia) exalting in an attempted capitalism with nationalistic and separatist tendencies, compared to the comic version of "democracy" to which the remaining four communist republics still pathetically cling. The only reasonable trend has been the stubborn efforts of the Government to maintain the unity and reform the economy, their actions sabotaged by literally every regional administration. Still, as promised, the Government has managed to cut down the 1989 inflation rate raging at 2,000% by Christmas time, to its wondrous negative value, as early as April 1990.

Kusturica's *Time of the Gipsies* continues to open around the world after record-breaking business at home

The loose federation and its eight different legislative systems have always resulted in fine diversity and impressive quantity of film production. This year, the quarreling republics don't even try to mimic unity. When the Serbian screenwriter and director Srdan Karanović was granted a share of Croatian funds to shoot his ten-year-old script *Virgina, a Kind of a Woman*, the Croatian professionals launched a campaign to overturn the decision.

Six Systems

Yugoslavia at the moment experiences six different production systems. Serbia, once the most prolific film industry in the country, regularly making half of the federal corpus of features (15–18 out of 35), plans in future to produce only 6 to 8 titles per year, severely discouraging some 25 applicants who recently submitted scripts to the newly established Film Fund. The two dozen demands range from $200,000 to over $1 million per project, but the Fund has enough money for one average feature only. The solution seems to dwell in defrosted bank initiatives to co-invest money with a rightful percentage of the profit in mind, as well as in co-productions with foreign investors or producers. The Croatian production has been severely cut, since the most reliable company, Jadran Film, apparently decided to concentrate on co- productions for the foreign market and has completed only one feature for domestic distribution, compared to ten completed and ten more discussed foreign projects. The Bosnian production, lately resembling a private domain of Emir Kusturica's favourite screenwriter, Abdulah Sidran, is being artificially blown up: half of it is old TV features, transferred on film tape.

More and more Yugoslav projects are being taken over by TV, whether as material for future TV series or as plain TV features, shot on 16mm, a trend easily understandable for two compatible reasons. Television is still financed through a monthly fee, pre-collected from some 4 million households altogether and are at the same time burdened by thousands of employed but unused professionals. Extensive shootings for the time being resemble a solution, while the funds don't appear to shrink. However, it is precisely with the television companies that gross waste of funds has occurred. It seems that the incompetence of their legal representatives could cost the Novi Sad and Belgrade Televisions a tremendous lot of money already invested in two abandoned projects: one an A-production period drama with European cast (Saša Petrović's **Migrations**) and the other a charming comedy starring Agostina Belli and Jamie Lee Rose, (Miloš Radović's **Happy End**). The two wasted films show Yugoslav producers find it hard to adapt to the new business procedures, since they were never accustomed to having their fanciful deals investigated by the public eye.

The natural result of the communist regime's decline is the re-investigation of several official court decisions taken in the past against some forty films that were consequently banned from distribution and confiscated. The bureaucracy, which never much bothered with the rules, now finds it extremely hard to bypass the rigid protocol, leaving these now politically naïve films to float in a legal limbo.

Video Piracy Still Rampant

Yet the worse obscenity still to plague the Yugoslav motion pictures industry is the unsolved video piracy problem. The country is rapidly trying to catch up with the western legal systems, new regulations are being introduced almost each day (often interfering with other, still valid ones) but a single solid law that would regulate video copy rights still hasn't seen the light of day. The united distributors of Hollywood and Yugoslavia tried to undermine the illegal market with a succession of fresh box-office hits from U.S., but forgot to install decent equipment and change the staff, introducing perfect copies of alluring images into unventilated theatres, often with wooden stools instead of seats. Thus, attendances remain low, slowly turning Yugoslav audiences, once an army of astute film lovers, into numb video consumers, unable to chose between popcorn and chips. In extremis, the film-makers in Yugoslavia may find themselves producing films only they will want to watch.

MAJA VLAHOVIĆ is a journalist and radio and TV host of cultural programmes in Yugoslavia, and has co-written a feature film in production, Sixteen and Three-quarters.

Profile: Dušan Prelević Prele

Born in 1948 in Belgrade. After finishing high school, he started a professional musical career, as a jazz singer. In 1969 he starred in a prestigious version of *Hair* in Atelje 212 Theatre, later recognised as the highlight of the Company's rich production. An active hockey and football player in youth, a weary hedonist by his late thirties, Prelević published in 1986 a collection of short stories on the last Belgrade romantics, losers and bohemians, an overnight best-seller. Given even a regular column in a popular newspaper, he concentrated on writing rather than music. *Last Circle in Monza* is his first screenplay, showing definite signs of a rare writer's gift combined with a film-maker's sense for simplicity, visualisation, rhythm and clever dialogue, qualities seriously lacking in most

TOP TEN GROSSING FILMS IN BELGRADE: JANUARY – JUNE 1990

(estimated attendance in Yugoslavia in brackets)

Batman	67,000	(500,000)
Dead Poets Society	52,000	(400,000)
Indiana Jones and the Last Crusade	49,000	(400,000)
Last Circle in Monza	42,000	(300,000)
Dangerous Liaisons	40,000	(350,000)
The Abyss	39,000	(300,000)
When Harry Met Sally	38,000	(250,000)
Working Girl	37,000	(220,000)
The War of the Roses	36,500	(200,000)
Who Framed Roger Rabbit	33,000	(225,000)

of Yugoslav features. An admirer of Coppola's *Godfather* films and the early Peckinpah, Prelević admits having spent much of his youth in Belgrade cinemas, often able to quote in English the dialogue of an entire classic Western, while not speaking a word of the language! Nicknamed "the Belgrade Bukowski," he has just finished his second script, scheduled for production in Fall 1990.

Recent and Forthcoming Films

Adam Ledolomac (Adam The Ice Breaker). Script: Duško Trifunović. Dir: Zlatko Lavanić. Phot: Danijel Sukalo. Prod: Sutjeska Film (Sarajevo).
Belepok (Belle Epoque). Script & Dir: Nikola Stojanović. Prod: Bosna Film (Sarajevo).
Cubok (A Little Something Extra). Script & Dir: Dragan Nikolić. Phot: Miloš Soldatović. Players: Danilo Lazolić, Ljiljana Blagojević, Dara Džokić. Prod: Avala Film (Belgrade)/FDU (Belgrade).
Čaruga (Charuga). Script: Ivan Kušan, Rajko Grlić. Dir: Rajko Grlić. Phot: Slobodan Trninić. Players: Ivo Gregurović, Davor Janjić, Ena Begović. Prod: Viba Film (Ljubljana)/Maestro Film (Zagreb)/TV Zagreb.
Čudesni san Dzige Vertova (The Amazing Dreaming of Dziga Vertov). Script & Dir: Miroslav Petrović. Phot: Zoran Veljković. Players: Zlatko Dukić, Ana Vujović, Dragoslav Ilić. Prod: Avala Film (Belgrade).
Dan za tetoviranje (A Day for Tattooing). Script: Mirko Kovac (Zivojin Pavlović, Stole Popov). Dir: Stole Popov. Phot: Miša Samuilovski. Players: Meto Jovanovsk, Ljiljana Medeši. Prod: Vardar Film (Skopje).
Decembarski dez (The December Rain). Script & Dir: Božo Sprajc. Phot: Radovan Čok, Boris Turković. Players: Saša Pavćek, Boris Ostan, Radko Polič, Roman Končar. Prod: Viba Film (Ljubljana)/TV Ljubljana.
Do konca in naprej (Till the End and Onward). Script: Nebojša Pajkić. Dir: Jure Pervanje. Phot: Tomislav Pinter. Players: Matjaž Tribušon, Janez Hocevar, Lučka Počkaj, Barbara Lapajne. Prod: Viba Film (Ljubljana).
Dr (Doctor). Script: Milan Sećerović, Vul Babić. Dir: Vuk Babić. Phot: Dorde Nikolić, Miša Samuilovski. Players: Dragomir Bojanić, Branislav Lečić, Radmila Živković. Prod: FIT (Belgrade).
Gluvi barut (Wet Powder). Script & Dir: Bata Čengić. Phot: Tomislav Pinter. Players: Mustafa Nadarević, Branislav Lečić, Fabijan Sovagović, Mira Furlan. Prod: Forum Film (Sarajevo)/Sutjeska Film (Sarajevo)/Beograd Film (Belgrade)/Jadran Film (Zagreb)/TV Sarajevo.
Granica (Border). Script: Ferenz Deak. Dir: Zoran Maširević. Phot: Dušan Ninkov. Players: Mirjana Joković, Marko Ratić, Davor Janjić. Prod: Tera (Novi Sad)/TV Novi Sad/Avala Film (Belgrade).

Karneval, andeo i prah (Carnival, Angel and Dust). Script & Dir: Anton Vrdoljak. Phot: Vjeko Vrdoljak. Players: Boris Dvornik, Ivica Vidović, Tonko Lonza. Prod: Jadran Film (Zagreb)/TV Zagreb.
Kontesa Dora (Countess Dora). Script & Dir: Zvonimir Berković. Phot: Goran Trbuljak. Players: Alma Prica, Rade Serbedžija, Zdravka Krstulović. Prod: Croatia Film (Zagreb)/TV Zagreb.
Ljeto za secanje (A Summer To Remember). Script & Dir: Bruno Gamulin. Phot: Enes Midžić. Players: Branislav Lečić, Suzanna Nikolić, Luka Milas, Dora Lipovčan. Prod: Zagreb Film (Zagreb).
Orao (The Eagle). Script: Pavao Pavličić. Dir: Zoran Tadić. Phot: Goran Trbuljak. Players: Vlatko Dulić, Božo Orešković, Ivica Vidović. Prod: Marjan Film (Split)/Color 2000 (München).
Početni udarac (Initial Kick). Script: Gordan Mihić. Dir: Darko Bajić. Phot: Boris Gortinski. Players: Nikola Kojo, Anita Mančić, Danilo Lazović. Prod: Avala Film (Belgrade).
Poslednji krug u Monci (Last Circle in Monza). Script: Dušan Prelević. Dir: Aleksandar Bošković. Phot: Miloš Spasojević. Players: Dragan Nikolić, Olivera Marković. Prod: Beograd Film (Belgrade)/TV Beograd.
Praznik u Sarajevu (A Festive Day in Sarajevo). Script: Abdulah Sidran, Ademir Kenović. Dir: Ademir Kenović. Phot: Mustafa Mustafić, Prod: Forum Film (Sarajevo).

Sex – partijski neprljatelj br 1 (Sex, Party Enemy No 1). Script & Dir: Dušan Sabo. Phot: Šahim Šišić. Players: Branko Vidaković, Olivera Ježina, Velimir Bata. Prod: Avala Film (Belgrade)/Bosna Film (Sarajevo).
Stela (Stella). Script & Dir: Petar Krelja. Prod: Avala Film (Belgrade)/Urania Film (Zagreb).
Umetni raj (Artificial Paradise). Script: Branko Vučićević. Dir: Karpo Godina. Phot: Tomislav Pinter. Players: Jurgen Morche, Vlado Novak, Dragana Mrkić, Željko Ivanek. Prod: Viba Film (Ljubljana).
Vampiri su medu nama (Vampires Among Us). Script & Dir: Zoran Ćalić. Phot: Aleksandar Petković. Players: Velimir Bata Živojinović, Žarko Radić, Boro Stjepanović. Prod: TRZ Viktorija (Belgrade).
Vetar v mrezi (The Wind in the Web). Script & Dir: Filip Robar-Dorin. Phot: Jure Pervanje. Players: Milan Stefe, Rene Medvešek, Robert Prebil. Prod: Viba Film (Ljubljana).
Volio bih da sam golub (I Wish I Was a Dove). Script: Wolfgang Held. Dir: Miomir Miki Stamenković. Phot: Danijel Šukalo. Players: Marina Marković, Vanja Drah. Prod: Sutjeska Film (Sarajevo)/Defa Film (Potsdam).
Vreme Čuda (The Time of Miracles). Script: Borislav Pekić, Goran Paskaljević. Dir: Goran Paskaljević. Phot: Radoslav Vladić. Players: Predrag Miki Manojlović, Dragan Maksimović, Ljuba Tadic, Svetozar Cvetković, Mirjana Joković. Prod: Singidunum (Belgrade)/Centar Film (Belgrade)/Film Four Int'l (London).

Useful Addresses

Institut za film
Čika Ljubina 15/II
11000 Belgrade
Tel: (38 11) 62 51 31
Fax: (38 11) 62 41 31

CFS Avala Film
Kneza Višeslava 88
11000 Belgrade
Tel: (38 11) 55 94 55
Fax: (38 11) 55 94 74
Telex: 12088

Jadran Film
Oporovečka 12
41040 Zagreb
Tel: (38 41) 25 12 22
Fax: (38 41) 25 13 94
Telex: 21460

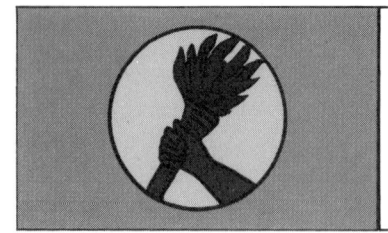

ZAIRE

by Roy Armes

Zaire has a long involvement with cinema, even though its feature film output is virtually non-existent. As early as 1897 the first footage was shot there, but this material and indeed most of the documentary footage shot in what was then the Belgian Congo was not destined for local screenings or even for normal commercial distribution in Europe. From the first such films were used in Belgium to foster the idea of colonisation, as part of a spectrum of media used at manifestations, exhibitions etc. Imported films were first shown in the major towns of Leopoldville (Kinshasa), Elisabethville (Lubumbashi) and Stanleyville (Kisangani) in 1910 and a permanent commercial cinema was installed as early as 1916.

By 1925 the double pattern which has shaped the whole development of film in the state up to and beyond independence became apparent, when the existing outlets were supplemented by the first cinema run by missionaries. Eventually the 35mm theatres in the towns were reinforced by portable 16mm equipment taken from village to village. These shows proved overwhelmingly popular with Congolese audiences, but the missionaries became increasingly frustrated by the values that imported films portrayed, and so turned to production themselves. As in some parts of Africa colonised by the British, the authorities (and here the missionaries too) increasingly tried to "protect" Africans from what were felt to be the excesses of Western commercial cinema. The resultant films – particularly those of the principal proponent of "films for Africans", Father Alexandre Van Den Heuvel – have proved controversial. Catholic publications, such as those issued by the Organisation Catholique Internationale du Cinéma (OCIC) tend to praise this work for its human values. This is the case in the book *Le cinéma au Zaire, au Rwanda et au Burundi* by Rick Otten, from which much of the material for the present article is drawn. On the other hand, the younger African critics have been harsh in their condemnation of the paternalism apparent in films which treat their adult Congolese audiences as no more than children. Whatever the case, OCIC based in Brussels, remains a major force in African cinema, publishing a series of books (twelve in all so far) on all aspects of African film making and awarding prizes at the major black African film festival, FESPACO in Ougadougou.

Since independent, distribution and exhibition have followed the pattern of development customary elsewhere in Africa. In the big towns there are perhaps a couple of dozen first class cinemas, operating in 35mm and showing recent imports from the U.S.A. and Europe at prices which exclude the bulk of the population. Beyond this there are perhaps five or six hundred 16mm outlets, many little more than converted bars or open spaces, operating without the constraints of numbered tickets or regular accounting procedures. Here as elsewhere in Africa the films shown are the cheapest western imports (cowboy films, action dramas etc) supplied to importers by the major international distribution companies which control the flow of films worldwide.

Soon after independence, a Zairean company, Exebo Films, set up an international co-production agreement to make *Konga Yo* (1962), directed by the well-known French film-maker Yves Allégret. The film represented the country at Cannes but was promptly banned in Zaire by the censor and it has remained without successors. There is virtually no state help for production and even the making of documentaries and newsreels is hesitant.

In 1972 an Organisation of Zairean Cinéastes (OZACI) was founded, but has made little headway. In the absence of any national film office, all production is in the hands of private companies, who have generally lacked the resources to complete those projects they have begun. Ndomanuele Mafuta Nlanza's 16mm fictional feature, *Pour une infidelité* (1972) is a rare exception, but remains the director's sole completed film. Significantly the only films of the 1980's to receive any international attention were those whose funding came partly from abroad: the feature-length study of a martyred nun, *Soeur Anuarite, une vie pour Dieu* (1983), directed by Madenda Kiesse Masekela and produced by the Missionary Society of San Paolo in Rome; the short documentary on Kinshasa, *Ken-Kiesse* (1982) made by Ngangura Mwese, who studied film in Brussels and made this film with the help of French television and the French Ministry of Foreign Relations; and, in quite a different vein, *La Vie est belle* (1986). This Franco-Belgian co-production, co-directed by Ngangura Mwese and the Belgian Benoit Lamy, stars the popular Zairean singer Papa Wemba in an unpretentious rags-to-riches comedy with plenty of music and songs. Though the film touches on issues such as prostitution, corruption, poverty, exploitation and impotence, the tone remains light-hearted and the characters stereotyped. Any pretensions to social significance are lost beneath the slick westernised technique, but the film remains a popular entertainment.

Continued from page 388

Phot: David M. Walsh. Players: Charles Grodin, James Belushi. Prod: Buena Vista.
Tales from the Darkside: The Movie. Screenplay: Michael McDowell, George A. Romero. Dir: John Harrison. Phot: Robert Draper. Players: Deborah Harry, Christian Slater, David Johansen, Rae Dawn Chong, James Remar. Prod: Paramount.
Teenage Mutant Ninja Turtles. Script: Todd W. Langen, Bobby Herbeck. Dir: Steve Barron. Phot: John Fenner. Players: Judith Hoag, Elias Koteas, Joch Pais. Prod: Golden Harvest/New Line Cinema.
The Tender. Script: Robert Stitzel. Dir: Robert Harmon. Players: John Travolta, Ellie Rabb. Prod: Triumph Releasing.
Texasville. Script: Peter Bogdanovich, Larry McMurtry. Dir: Peter Bogdanovich. Phot: Players: Jeff Bridges, Cybill Shepherd, Cloris Leachman, Timothy Bottoms, Randy Quaid, Eileen Brennan, Annie Potts. Phot: Nicholas Von Sternberg. Prod: Nelson Films/Cine-Source/Columbia.

Three Men and a Little Lady. Script: Charlie Peters, Josann McGibbon, Sara Pariott. Dir: Emile Ardolino. Phot: Adam Greenberg. Players: Tom Selleck, Steve Guttenberg, Ted Danson, Nancy Travis. Prod: Disney (Buena Vista).
To Sleep With Anger. Script and Dir: Charles Burnett. Phot: Walt Lloyd. Players: Danny Glover, Richard Brooks, Paul Butler, Mary Alice, Vonetta McGee. Prod: SVS.
Too Much Sun. Script: Al Schwartz, Robert Downy, Laura Ernst. Dir: Downy. Phot: Robert Yeoman. Players: Jim Haynie, Howard Duff, Eric Idle, Andrea Martin, Robert Downy Jr. Prod: New Line Cinema.
Total Recall. Script: Ronald Shussett, Dan O'Bannon, Gary Goldman, Jon Povill inspired from short story 'We Can Remember It For You Wholesale' by Philip K. Dick. Dir: Paul Verhoeven. Phot: Jost Vacano. Players: Arnold Schwarzenegger, Rachel Ticotín, Sharon Stone, Ronny Cox. Prod: Caroloco/Tri-Star.
True Colors. Script: Kevin Wade. Dir: Herbert

Ross. Phot: Dante Spinotti. Players: James Spader, John Cusack, Imogen Stubbs, Richard Widmark. Prod: Paramount.
Two Evil Eyes. Script: George Romero, Dario Argento, Franco Ferrini. Dir: Romero/Argento. Phot: Peter Reniers. Players: Adrienne Barbeau, E.G. Marshall, Harvey Keitel, Madeleine Potter. Prod: Taurus.
The Two Jakes. Script: Robert Towne. Dir: Jack Nicholson. Phot: Vilmos Zsigmond. Players: Nicholson, Harvey Keitel, Meg Tilly, Madeleine Stowe, Eli Wallach. Prod: Paramount.
Twister. Script and Dir: Michael Almereyda from novel 'Oh!' by Mary Robison. Phot: Renato Berta. Players: Harry Dean Stanton, Suzy Amis, Crispin Glover. Prod: Vestron.
Underworld. Script and Dir: Joseph Strick. Players: Paul Zimet, Louise Smith. Prod: Angelika Films.
Valkenvania. Script and Dir: Dan Akroyd. Phot: Dean Cundey. Players: Chevvy Chase, Dan Akroyd, John Candy, Demi Moore. Prod: Warner Bros.
Venice, Venice. Script and Dir: Henry Jaglom. Phot: Hanania Baer. Players: Henry Jaglom, Helly Alard. Prod: International Rainbow Picture.
Vietnam, Texas. Script: Tom Badal and C. Courtney Joyner. Dir: Robert Ginty. Phot: Robert M. Baldwin. Players: Robert Ginty, Haing S. Ngor. Prod: Trans World Entertainment.
Vincent and Theo. Script: Julian Mitchell. Dir: Robert Altman. Phot: Jean Lepine. Players: Tim Roth, Paul Rhys, Jip Wijngaarden. Prod: Hemdale.
Wait Until Spring, Bandini. Script: Dominique Deruddere from John Fante's novel. Dir: Dominique Deruddere. Players: Joe Mantegna, Ornella Muti, Faye Dunaway, Michael Bacall. Prod: Orion Classics.
Waiting for the Light. Script and Dir: Chris Monger. Phot: Gabriel Beristain. Players: Shirley MacLaine, Teri Garr. Prod: Triumph.
Welcome Home, Roxy Carmichael. Script: Karen Leigh Hopkins. Dir: Jim Abrahams. Phot: Paul Elliott. Players: Winona Ryder, Jeff Daniels. Prod: Paramount.
White Hunter, Black Heart. Script: Peter Viertel, James Bridges, Burt Kennedy from novel by Viertel. Dir: Clint Eastwood. Phot: Jack N. Green. Players: Clint Eastwood, Jeff Fahey, George Dzunda, Alun Armstrong, Marisa Berenson. Prod: Malpaso/Rastar/Warner Bros.
White Palace. Dir: Luis Mandoki. Players: Susan Sarandon, James Spader. Prod: Universal.
Wild at Heart. Script: David Lynch from novel by Barry Gifford. Dir: David Lynch. Phot: Fred Elmes. Players: Nicolas Cage, Laura Dern, Diane Ladd, Willem Dafoe, Isabella Rossellini. Prod: Samuel Goldwyn Co.
Wild Orchid. Script: Zalman King, Patricia Louisianna Knop. Phot: Gale Tattersall. Players: Mickey Rourke, Jacqueline Bisset. Prod: Vision Int'l./Triumph Releasing.
The Witches. Script: Allan Scott from Roald Dahl's book. Dir: Nicolas Roeg. Phot: Harvey Harrison. Players: Anjelica Huston, Mai Zetterling, Jasen Fisher. Prod: Jim Henson Prods./Lorimar/Warner Bros.
Without You I'm Nothing. Script: Sandra Bernhard, John Boskovich. Dir: John Boskovich. Players: Sandra Bernhard, Steve Antin, John Doe. Prod: Sterling Ent./MCEG.

Guide to International Locations

As film production becomes increasingly cosmopolitan in its topography, the art of selecting (and marketing) locations is taking on considerable significance. We launch herewith a succinct guide to regions that welcome film and TV productions, and (for those responding to our questionnaire) details of climate, access, local union regulations etc. More general information may be obtained from the Association of Film Commissioners International, c/o Wyoming Film Office, I–25 & College Drive, Cheyenne, WY 82002. Tel: (307) 637.3601.

AUSTRALIA
New South Wales

Diverse region encompassing the famous beaches and coastal areas of Australia, farming lands with vast sheep and cattle herds, desert regions (e.g. Broken Hill), vineyards, rain forests, open-cut mines, and green-belt suburban areas. The capital, Sydney, has a population of 5 million.

Climate: average temperatures in Sydney in December through March are around 22 C; these drop to around 12 C in June and July. Snowfalls on the high mountains and plateau, June to August.

Access: Sydney airport (Mascot) is main entry point.

Labour Factors: actors covered by Actors Equity awards, and crews work under ATAEA Union awards (700 skilled freelance crew available in Sydney region).

Information: NSW Film and Television Office, Level 2, 10 Quay Street, Haymarket, Sydney, NSW 2000. Tel: (02) 281.8711. Fax: (02) 281.8710.

Western Australia

Enormous state comprising spectacular national parks, rugged coastlines, forests, farmlands, "ghost towns" from goldrush days, and superb coral reefs.

Climate: Perth, the capital, enjoys 250 days of sunshine each year. Rain in the cooler winter months (May through August) in north and south, but minimal precipitation inland.

Access: Perth is a major airport.

Labour Factors: Actors Equity and ATAEA both have branch offices in Perth. Heads of departments are permitted to enter Australia for a foreign production being shot there. All foreign technicians must be members of an equivalent union in his/her own country.

Recent Shoots: *Dead Calm, Quigley Down Under.*

Information: Western Australian Film Council, Suite 8, 336 Churchill Avenue, Subiaco, Perth, Western Australia 6008. Tel: (09) 382.2500. Fax: (09) 381.2848.

AUSTRIA

Spectacular yet intimate Alpine country, with rolling wooded hills as well as mountain peaks, from the flat land of the Puszta with Europe's only steppe lake, to glacier lakes as well as architecturally attractive towns and quaint villages.

Climate: summer days can be hot, but summer evenings are always cool. Winter snow lasts from late December through March in the valleys, from November through May at about 6000 ft, and becomes permanent above 8500 ft.

Access: Vienna and Salzburg.

Labour Factors: obtain information from ORF (Austrian TV), individual film companies, or Cine Austria.

Recent Shoots: *Red Heat, Amadeus, The Hotel New Hampshire, The Sound of Music.*

Information: Cine Austria, Margaretenstrasse 1, A–1040 Vienna. Tel: (0222) 25 71 13/14. Fax: (0222) 257.1315.

BAHAMAS

Information: Bahamas Film Promotion Bureau, P.O. Box N 3701, Nassau. Tel: (809) 326.0635. Fax: (809) 328.0945.

CANADA
Nova Scotia

Abundant in historical associations, both French and English. The province contains some 50 museums as well as numerous converted sites still in commercial, residential and recreational use. Spectacular shorelines.
Climate: moderate conditions due to proximity of the Atlantic. Summer highs around 25 C, winter lows −6 to −13 C.
Access: Halifax International Airport.
Labour Factors: union and non-union labour available.
Recent Shoots: *Little Kidnappers, The Midday Sun, The Bruce Curtis Story*.
Information: Film Nova Scotia, P.O. Box 2287, Stn M, Halifax, Nova Scotia B3J 3C8. Tel: (902) 422.3402. Fax: (902) 424.0563.

Other Regions

Information: Ontario Film Development Corporation, 81 Wellesley Street East, Toronto, Ontario M4Y 1H6. Toronto Film Liaison, 18th floor, East Tower, City Hall, Toronto, Ontario M5H 2N2. Montreal Film Commission, 425 Place Jacques Cartier, Suite 300, Montreal Quebec H2Y 3B1.

CAYMAN ISLANDS

Information: Cayman Island Film Liaison, Government Tower Building, Grand Cayman, Cayman Islands, BWI. Tel: (809) 949.7999. Fax: (809) 949.8487.

COSTA RICA

Ideal mix of location backdrops: beaches, mountains, jungle, deserts, volcanoes, rapids, waterfalls, and plantations.
Climate: sunshine 6 A.M. to 6 P.M. daily. Rains late May through late October, but only a few hours each day. No snow.
Access: flights originate from Miami, Mexico City, New York, Los Angeles, New Orleans, Houston.
Labour Factors: supporting actors and extras available at very reasonable rates. Cameras and sound equipment not available in Costa Rica.
Information: Costa Rican Film Commission, 9000 West Sunset, Suite 1000, Los Angeles, CA 90069. Tel: (213) 271.5858. Fax: (213) 273.5566.

ISRAEL

Long Mediterranean coastline, religiously charged region of the Galilee, Jerusalem, Bethlehem, Nazareth etc.
Climate: no rain from mid-April to mid-October, and a Californian style diet of sunshine for most areas.
Access: Tel Aviv, Jerusalem, Haifa etc.
Labour Factors: most manpower is non-union and multi lingual.
Recent Shoots: *Iron Eagle, Delta Force 3, Rambo III*.
Information: Ministry of Industry and Trade, P.O. Box 299, 94190 Jerusalem. Tel: (02) 210433, 210297. Fax: (02) 245110.

JAMAICA

Information: Jamaica Film Office, 35 Trafalgar Road, Kingston 10. Tel: (809) 929.9450. Fax: (809) 926.7326.

LUXEMBOURG

Mini-scale European nation with medieval towns, castles, and natural forests.
Climate: up to 200 hours of sunshine between March and September. Some snow in winter.
Access: Luxembourg int'l airport.
Labour Factors: non-union crews, limited selection of other types of film personnel.
Recent Shoots: *The Saint, Dracula* (the series), local feature films.

NEW ZEALAND

Information: New Zealand National Film Unit, P.O. Box 46–002, Lower Hutt. Tel: (4) 672.059. Fax: (4) 673.450.

THAILAND

Information: Thailand Film Promotion Center, 599 Bumrung Muang Road, Bangkok 10100. Tel: (662) 223.4690. Fax: (662) 223.2568.

U.S.A.

Alabama

Information: Alabama Film Office, 340 North Hull Street, Montgomery, AL 36120. Tel: (205) 242.4195. Fax: (205) 265.5078.

Alaska

Information: Alaska Film Office, 3601 C Street, Suite 700, Anchorage, AK 99503. Tel: (907) 562.4183. Fax: (907) 563.3575.

Arizona

Anyone familiar with John Ford's westerns will recognise one of Arizona's finest locations – Monument Valley. In addition, the state boasts the Grand Canyon, Montezuma's Castle, Sunset Crater, Sedona, and several national monuments.
Climate: the warm dry desert climate of the far West and Southwest portions of Arizona result in high temperatures, low humidity and sparse rainfall. An annual average of more than 200 clear days.
Access: Phoenix and Tucson.
Labour Factors: both union and non-union labour available (see Arizona Productions Services Directory).
Recent Shoots: *Midnight Run, Back to the Future III, Young Guns II, Rambo III*.
Information: Arizona Film Commission, 1700 West Washington Avenue, Phoenix, AZ 85007. Tel: (602) 542.5011. Fax: (602) 255.2146.

Arkansas

Information: Arkansas Motion Picture Development Office, 1 State Capitol Mall, Room 2C–200, Little Rock, AR 72201. Tel: (501) 682.7676. Fax: (501) 682.7691.

California

The world's most popular source of film locations. According to recent estimates, 60% of all U.S. films are shot in this state. Year-round sunshine, combined with mountain and desert landscapes as well as lush urban and coastal topography.
Climate: contact CFC with specific inquiries.
Access: dozens of major airports, with Los Angeles, San Francisco, and San Diego the favourite entry points.
Labour Factors: largest pool of union and non-union talent in the U.S.A. Permits for filming state-owned property are issued speedily and without undue formality.
Information: California Film Commission, 6922 Hollywood Boulevard, Suite 600, Hollywood, CA 90028. Tel: (213) 736.2465. Fax: (213) 736.3159.

Colorado

Information: Colorado Motion Picture and Television Commission, 1313 Sherman Street, Suite 500, Denver, CO 80203. Tel: (303) 866.2778. Fax: (303) 866.2251.

Connecticut

Enjoys four distinct seasons: a cool, colourful spring; a warm, green summer; an autumn filled with dazzling foliage; and a snow-covered winter. Connecticut is famed for its colonial villages, river valleys, and English-style rolling hills.
Climate: few extremes, and the relatively mild weather is interrupted on average by only 12 days of temperatures above 90 F. Frosts occur from mid-October to mid-April.
Access: Bradley International Airport, 20 mins north of Hartford.
Labour Factors: all covered in the "Connecticut Production Manual," available on request.

Recent Shoots: *Jacknife*, *Mystic Pizza*, *Stanley & Iris*.
Information: Connecticut Film Commission, 865 Brook Street, Rocky Hill, CT 06067. Tel: (203) 258.4301. Fax: (203) 563.4877.

Delaware

Information: Delaware Development Office, 99 Kings Highway, Dover, DE 19903. Tel: (302) 736.4271.

District of Columbia

Information: Mayor's Office of MP/TV, 1111 E Street Northwest, Suite 700, Washington, DC 20004. Tel: (202) 727.6600.

Florida

Sunshine state featuring marine locations (Gulf of Mexico, Atlantic seaboard), tranquil rivers and lakes, the exotic Everglades, as well as the urban charisma of Miami.
Climate: probably the best in the world for filming purposes, although temperatures soar during the summer months.
Access: Miami, Ft. Lauderdale.
Labour Factors: producers can choose union, non-union or mixed crew at negotiated wages and benefits.
Recent Shoots: over 17,000 TV commercials, almost 50 major features and TV projects.
Information: Motion Picture & Television Bureau, Division of Economic Development, 101 East Gaines Street, Tallahassee, Florida 32399–2000. Tel: (904) 487.1100. Fax: (904) 487.3014.

Georgia

Mountains, beaches, coastal islands, swamps, and undulating hills. Period towns, metropolitan areas and historical cities also located within the state.
Climate: quite mild winters, but quite high precipitation (dry periods occur mainly during the late summer and early autumn).
Access: primary hub is Atlanta, the world's second busiest airport.
Labour Factors: Georgia is a right-to-work state so both union and non-union technical talent are available. It is also a permit-free state.
Recent Shoots: *Driving Miss Daisy*, *Glory*, *Career Opportunities*.
Information: Georgia Film & Videotape Office, 285 Peachtree Center Avenue, Marquis Two Tower, Suite 1000, Atlanta, GA 30303. Tel: (404) 656.3544. Fax: (404) 651.9063.

Hawaii

An exceptionally benevolent climate, and lush, exotic landscapes have made Hawaii one of the world's most popular film locations. Sandy beaches, steep ocean cliffs, volcanic terrain, and rain forests – all scattered over a comparatively small spread of islands.
Climate: the persistent pattern is a combination of cooling trade winds and equable temperatures throughout the year. Enormous range of rainfall, with the windward side of the islands being generally wetter than the leeward.
Access: Honolulu, Oahu.
Labour Factors: information available from local branches of IATSE, Screen Actors Guild, Screen Extras Guild etc.
Recent Shoots: *War and Remembrance*, *Fists of Steel*, *Jake and the Fatman*.
Information: Film Industry Branch, P.O. Box 2359, Honolulu, Hawaii 96804. Tel: (808) 548.4535. Fax: (808) 548.2189.

Idaho

Information: Idaho Film Bureau, 700 West State Street, Boise, ID 83720. Tel: (208) 334.2470. Fax: (208) 334.2631.

Illinois

Information: Illinois Film Office, 100 West Randolph, Suite 3–400, Chicago, IL 60601. Tel: (312) 814.3600. Fax: (312) 814.6732.

Indiana

Information: Indiana Film Commission, Department of Commerce, 1 North Capitol, Indianapolis, IN 46204. Tel: (317) 232.8829. Fax: (317) 232.4146.

LOCATIONS | 417

Pier at Old Orchard Beach, Maine

The spectacular Chimney Rock, Nebraska

Civil War games at Carnifax Ferry, West Virginia

View over Utuado in Puerto Rico

Iowa

Information: Iowa Film Office, Department of Economic Development, 200 East Grand Avenue, Des Moines, IA 503009. Tel: (515) 288.1360. Fax: (515) 281.7276.

Kansas

Information: Kansas Film Commission, 400 West 8th Street, Topeka, KS 66603. Tel: (913) 296.4927. Fax: (913) 296.5055.

Kentucky

Information: Kentucky Film Office, Berry Hill Mansion on Louisville Road, Frankfort, KY 40601. Tel: (502) 564.3456. Fax: (502) 564.7588.

Louisiana

Information: Louisiana Film Commission, P.O. Box 94361, Baton Rouge, LA 70804. Tel: (504) 342.8150.

Maine

Picturesque villages, rugged coastlines, and verdant countryside attest to Maine's New England heritage.
Climate: 83% of Maine days are sunny, although it is very much a four-season state.
Access: Bangor and Portland int'l airports.
Labour Factors: union, non-union, and mixed crews available in ample numbers.
Recent Shoots: *Pet Sematary, A Cry for Life, All My Children.*
Information: Maine Film Office, Office of Tourism/Economic Development, State House Station, Augusta, ME 04333. Tel: (207) 289.5710. Fax: (207) 289.2861.

Maryland

Information: Maryland Film Commission, 217 East Redwood, Baltimore, MD 21202. Tel: (301) 333.6633. Fax: (301) 333.6643.

Massachusetts

The original New England imagery distinguishes Massachusetts, with elegant Boston only 3 hours distance from any location in the state. Wetlands, farmlands, coastlines, of every type and description, and everywhere the Pilgrim memories.
Climate: more than 50% chance of sunshine on every day of the year in Boston. Temperatures can climb to 100 F in the summer and dip as cold as −10 F in December and January.
Access: Boston's Logan Airport the main entry point (fog can be a problem in winter).
Labour Factors: many productions hire as much as 90% of their labour within the state. In 1989 and 1990 local labour crewed up to three full-scale motion picture projects shooting concurrently with local production.
Recent Shoots: Dad, Glory, Once Around, Unsolved Mysteries.
Information: Massachusetts Film Office, The Transportation Building, 10 Park Plaza, Suite 2310, Boston, MA 02116. Tel: (617) 973.8800. Fax: (617) 973.8810.

Michigan

Information: Michigan Film Office, P.O. Box 30107, Lansing, MI 48909. Tel: (517) 373.3456. Fax: (517) 373.3872.

Minnesota

Information: Minnesota Film Board, 401 North 3rd Street, Suite 460, Minneapolis, MN 55401. Tel: (612) 332.6493.

Mississippi

Information: Mississippi Film Office, 1200 Walter Sillers Building, Box 849, Jackson, MS 39205. Tel: (601) 359.3297. Fax: (601) 359.2832.

Missouri

Information: Missouri Film Commission, P.O. Box 118, Jefferson City, MO 65102. Tel: (314) 751.9050. Fax: (314) 634.5472.

Montana

Information: Montana Film Commission, 1424 Ninth Avenue, Helena, MT 59620. Tel: (406) 444.2654. Fax: (406) 444.2808.

Nebraska

Nebraska's geography features rolling hills, flat prairies, lakes and rivers, bluffs and rock formations and the vast Sandhills and Pine Ridge areas. Especially noted for its pioneer and agricultural heritage (Pony Express and Oregon Trail sites, for example).
Climate: well-defined seasons. Everything from spring blossoms, to sultry summers, to colourful autumns and blustery winters.
Access: Lincoln and Omaha have the state's largest airports.
Labour Factors: ample creative, technical, and support personnel available through the Film Office. Nebraska is a right-to-work state.
Recent Shoots: Terms of Endearment, Home Fires Burning.
Information: Nebraska Film Office, P.O. Box 95143, Lincoln, NE 68509–4666. Tel: (402) 471.2593. Fax: (402) 471.3778.

Nevada

Information: Motion Picture & Television Development, McCarran International Airport, 2nd floor, Las Vegas, NV 89158. Tel: (702) 486.7150. Fax: (702) 486.7155.

New Jersey

New Jersey is by no means merely the backdoor to New York. There is the Victorian resort of Cape May, the Great Gorge ski resort area, Atlantic City, and the Meadowlands Sports Complex.
Climate: fairly even temperatures in the 70's F throughout the summer months. New Jersey boasts few extremes of weather.
Access: Newark International Airport is expanding and increasing in importance with each passing year.
Labour Factors: skilled labour is readily available, and full details are included in the state's Production Services Directory.

Recent Shoots: *Presumed Innocent, She-Devil, Mortal Thoughts, A Kiss Before Dying*.
Information: New Jersey Motion Picture & Television Commission, One Gateway Center, Suite 510, Newark, NJ 07102–5311. Tel: (201) 648.6279. Fax: (201) 648.7350.

New Mexico

Topography ranges from the low desert to alpine mountains; there are state and national parks as well as historical sites, national forests, and wilderness areas. Wide diversity of architecture representing the Native American Indian, Spanish, and Anglo.
Climate: semi-arid with light precipitation, abundant sunshine and low relative humidity. 85% of New Mexico is over 4000 ft high.
Access: Albuquerque International Airport, centrally located in the state.
Labour Factors: large talent pool for print, commercial, TV and feature work. Film Commission publishes a business personnel directory.
Recent Shoots: *Twins, Indiana Jones and the Last Crusade, Lonesome Dove, Enid Is Sleeping*.
Information: New Mexico Film Commission, 1050 Old Pecos Trail, Santa Fe, NM 87503. Tel: (505) 827.8580. Fax: (505) 827.8584.

New York

Information: New York State Governor's Office for MP/TV Development, 1515 Broadway, New York, NY 10036. Tel: (212) 575.6570. Fax: (212) 840.7149.

North Carolina

Information: North Carolina Film Office, 430 North Salisbury Street, Raleigh, NC 27611. Tel: (919) 733.9900. Fax: (919) 733.0110.

North Dakota

Widely varied terrain across the state, with the Theodore Roosevelt National Park an outstanding location.
Climate: 2,800 hours of sunshine per year.

Precipitation ranges from 13″ in the west to 20″ in the east. Generally low humidity.
Access: Bismarck, Fargo, Grand Forks and other cities.
Labour Factors: see Film and Video Services Directory, available through the EDC (address below).
Recent Shoots: commercials and documentaries. No features.
Information: EDC/Tourism Promotion Division, Liberty Memorial Building, Bismarck, ND 58505. Tel: (701) 224.2525. Fax: (701) 223.3081.

Ohio

Information: Ohio Film Bureau, 77 South High Street, 28th floor, Columbus, OH 43266–0101. Tel: (614) 466.2284. Fax: (614) 644.1789.

Oklahoma

Information: Oklahoma Film Office, P.O. Box 26980, Oklahoma City, OK 72316–0980. Tel: (405) 841.5135. Fax: (405) 841.5199.

Oregon

Oregon has 400 miles of spectacular coastline on the Pacific, as well as 1,600 lakes, 4 mountain ranges, and Hells Canyon, the deepest gorge in the world.
Climate: widely varied, with areas of minuscule rainfall and regions where wet weather is frequent. Sunshine also varies, with 20–27 days during the summer in most parts of the state.
Access: Portland int'l airport.
Labour Factors: both union and non-union personnel available.
Recent Shoots: *Drugstore Cowboy, Come See the Paradise, Breaking In*.
Information: Oregon Film Office, 595 Cottage Street Northeast, Salem, OR 97310. Tel: (503) 373.1232. Fax: (503) 581.5115.

Pennsylvania

Information: Pennsylvania Film Bureau, Forum Building, Room 455, Harrisburg, PA 17120. Tel: (717) 783.3456. Fax: (717) 234.4560.

Crater Lake in Oregon

Whiskey Creek in Ft. Myers, Florida

The Obernberg region of Austria

Oak Creek Canyon, Arizona

Puerto Rico

272 miles of beaches, 11 forest reserves, and Spanish Colonial relics in plenty.
Climate: Mostly sunny, with an average temperature of 77 F throughout the year.
Access: Luis Munoz Marin International Airport is the main point of entry.
Labour Factors: no unions that affect filming in Puerto Rico. Local talent is sufficient to supply an entire feature film production on location.
Recent Shoots: *Jacob's Ladder, Cat Chaser, Q & A.*
Information: Puerto Rico Film Institute, P.O. Box 2350, San Juan, PR 00936. Tel: (809) 758.4747. Fax: (809) 754.7110.

Rhode Island

Information: Rhode Island Film Commission, 150 Benefit Street, Providence, RI 02903. Tel: (401) 277.3456. Fax: (401) 277.6046.

South Carolina

A state of three natural divisions: rolling mountains, unspoiled forests upstate; midlands region, more heavily populated; and the "Low Country" known for its subtropical beaches, marshes, and swamplands. There are over 400,000 acres of lakes and some 45 State Parks in S.C.
Climate: 61 F annual average temperature. Average of 11.41 daylight hours of sunshine/shooting time.
Access: main air hubs are Columbia, Charleston, and the Greenville/Spartanburg area.
Labour Factors: S.C. is a right-to-work state and welcomes both union and non-union productions. Crews can be located within 24 hours by the Film Office.
Recent Shoots: *The Abyss, Chattahoochie, Shag.*
Information: South Carolina Film Office, P.O. Box 927, Columbia, SC 29202. Tel: (803) 737.0400. Fax: (803) 737.0418.

South Dakota

Information: South Dakota Film Commission, Capitol Lake Plaza, Pierre, SD 57501. Tel: (605) 773.3301. Fax: (605) 773.3256.

Tennessee

Information: Tennessee Film/Entertainment/Music Commission, 320 Sixth Avenue North, 7th floor, Nashville, TN 37219. Tel: (615) 741.3456. Fax: (615) 741.5829.

Texas

Texas contains two National Parks, a national seashore, 10 national wildlife refuges, four national forests, more than 100 State Parks, a biological preserve, and numerous historic sites and memorials.
Climate: sunshine throughout the state all-year round. Most years, winter only bites in January and February. Snow falls only in the High Plains.
Access: 1,276 airports function in Texas, with main hubs being Dallas–Fort Worth, Houston, San Antonio, Austin, and El Paso.
Labour Factors: Texas is a right-to-work state. The *Texas Production Manual* lists 653 individuals and companies providing film and video services.
Recent Shoots: *Dark Angel*, *Indiana Jones and the Last Crusade*, *Neurotic Cabaret*.
Information: Texas Film Commission, P.O. Box 12728, Austin, TX 78711. Tel: (512) 469.9111. Fax: (512) 473.2312.

Utah

No more spectacular state exists in the United States. Famed for its canyons, its exceptionally clear air, and its awesome buttes and outcrops.
Climate: mountain climate, with fine skiing at resorts like Park City, and scorching heat in the sandstone canyons.
Access: Salt Lake City, St. George (from Las Vegas).
Labour Factors: experienced union and non-union crew are available as well as skilled labour.
Recent Shoots: *Wait Until Spring, Bandini*, *Halloween V*, *Indiana Jones and the Last Crusade*.
Information: Utah Film Commission, 324 South State Street, Suite 230, Salt Lake City, UT 84111. Tel: (801) 538.8740. Fax: (801) 538.3396.

Vermont

Information: Vermont Film Bureau, 134 State Street, Montpelier, VT 05602. Tel: (802) 828.3236. Fax: (802) 828.3230.

Virginia

Information: Virginia Film Office, P.O. Box 798, Richmond, VA 23219. Tel: (804) 786.8204. Fax: (804) 786.1211.

Virgin Islands

Information: United States Virgin Islands Film Production Office, P.O. Box 6400, Saint Thomas, USVI 00804. Tel: (809) 775.1444 Fax: (809) 774.4390.

Washington

Famous for the Cascade and Olympic mountain ranges, Seattle and its Space Needle, the ferry boats, the rain forests, and the rugged ocean coast. Plus momentoes of the Old West.
Climate: very little precipitation by comparison with regions at similar latitudes. There is plenty of sunshine during the summer months, and extended "sun breaks" during autumn and winter.

Skyline of Atlantic City, New Jersey

Access: Seattle is the major international airport.
Labour Factors: experienced pool of production personnel from cinematographers to property masters, plus fully-equipped sound stages, labs, and equipment.
Recent Shoots: *The Fabulous Baker Boys, Bird on a Wire, The Hunt for Red October, Twin Peaks*.
Information: Washington State Film & Video Office, 2001 Sixth Avenue, Suite 2700, Seattle, WA 98121. Tel: (206) 464.7148. Fax: (206) 464.7222.

West Virginia

Rich in Civil War and 19th century history. Harper's Ferry National Park, New River Gorge National Park, and evocative Richmond itself are excellent locations.
Climate: four distinct seasonal changes.
Access: Charleston, Clarksburg, and Huntington.
Labour Factors: West Virginia publishes a production services directory on personnel, transportation, caterers, lodging etc.
Recent Shoots: *Matewan, Strangest Dreams*.
Information: West Virginia Film Industry Development Office, 2101 Washington Street E, Charleston, WV 25305. Tel: (304) 348.2286. Fax: (304) 348.0108.

Wisconsin

Known for its profusion of lakes (15,000+) and rivers, Wisconsin contains huge forests, prehistoric burial grounds, and a state capitol that resembles the one in Washington, D.C.
Climate: sunshine averages between 50% and 60% year round. Winter weather can begin in early November and last through to March, with most rivers and lakes in the north of the state frozen during this spell.
Access: Madison, Milwaukee, Green Bay.
Labour Factors: no special restrictions.
Information: Wisconsin Film Office, P.O. Box 7970, Madison WI 53707. Tel: (608) 267.3456. Fax: (608) 266.3403.

Wyoming

Contains some of the cinema's most memorable landmarks – Devil's Tower National Monument, Yellowstone and Grand Teton National Parks, Wind River Indian Reservation, South Pass City, Old Trail Town.
Climate: arid with four distinct seasons. Over 200 days of sunshine yearly. Snowfall heaviest in February and March.
Access: main hub cities are Cheyenne, Casper and Jackson.
Labour Factors: both union and non-union. Wyoming is a right-to-work state. Computer listing of talent and technicians throughout the state/region is available.
Recent Shoots: *Dances with Wolves*, Japanese documentary *The World Is Calling*, and not forgetting *Shane* and *Close Encounters of the Third Kind*.
Information: Wyoming Film Office, I–25 at College Drive, Cheyenne, WY 82002–0660. Tel: (307) 777.7777. Fax: (307) 777.6904.

WEST GERMANY

Bavaria/Munich

Largest German federal state in the south, known for its monasteries, castles, lakes, mountains and the historic city of Munich.
Climate: winter with snowfall, hot summers, beautiful autumns.
Access: Munich int'l airport.
Labour Factors: about 20,000 skilled personnel in the region. Mostly union members.
Recent Shoots: *Last Exit to Brooklyn, Seven Minutes, Abraham's Gold*.
Information: Film Information Office, Türkenstrasse 93, D-8000 Munich 40, F.R.G. Tel: (89) 38 19 04 30–31. Fax: (89) 38 19 04 26.

TRIBUTE:
The Toronto Festival of Festivals

In just fifteen years, the Toronto Festival of Festivals has become one of the most successful events of its kind in North America boasting a public avid for the best films contemporary cinema produces, and international attention from distributors, producers and buyers. Toronto is the third most important film market in North America, behind New York and Los Angeles, and this fact has fuelled its success. Perceived as an ideal platform to launch films into the English-language North American market, the Hollywood majors and, increasingly, European companies now look to Toronto to premiere their films. With a public numbering in the hundreds of thousands jamming upwards of ten cinemas every day, the industry gets an accurate perception of what films are popular and destined for further success. Neither a purely commercial showcase nor an exclusively highbrow one, Toronto represents an uncommonly successful fusion of two impulses. A smoothly-running business boasting strong corporate ties and support, it is also an event for cinephiles seeking out new, challenging trends.

In the early days, things were much different. Toronto had never had a film festival in the city, unlike Vancouver and Montreal which both began events in the 1960's, only to see them expire before being revived. Prior to the establishment of the Toronto Festival of Festivals, there had been scattered attempts at starting an international film festival in the province of Ontario. But, if Stratford and the Ottawa festivals proved successful, neither of them had Toronto's advantages: a large and enthusiastic population base, and industry support from which to draw both organisational and financial support.

At the time that entertainment entrepreneurs William Marshall, Dusty Cohl and Henk van der Kolk established the first Festival of Festivals in 1976 (the title implying a kind of 'best of' event), the Toronto film industry was enjoying an unprecedented boom. The centre of gravity of Canadian production had shifted from Montreal to Toronto. Producers and directors wanted to place themselves on the international map and emerge from a cloistered regional parochialism. What better way than to start a film festival and attract the players to Toronto?

Mix of Big Budget and Serious Art Films

The first event was a mix of big budget films, designed to attract media attention, and serious art cinema. The Festival opened with Jean-Charles Tacchella's *Cousin, Cousine* while critic Jan Dawson programmed an eye-opening selection of new German films centred around a retrospective of Wim Wenders' films. This formula would be extended and

John Cassavetes and Gena Rowlands at the 1982 Festival of Festivals

photo: Tim Fletcher

strengthened in subsequent years. A Gala section was created for the high profile films, while the European art cinema was programmed in a variety of sections. It was decided from the beginning to keep the festival a non- competitive event even though, at that time, there was no competitive festival in North America apart from Chicago. Film-makers would not be pitted against each other but brought together in mutual celebration, and quality would always be the final criterion for selection.

The festival, child as it is of the Canadian film industry, has always been careful to reciprocate in a substantial and practical manner. Even in the very first festival (which cost $211,000 to produce, compared to $3 million in 1989), events such as conferences and workshops were designed to support and assist the domestic film industry. This remains a crucial and significant component within the festival to this day. Each year the festival addresses the major issues and developments facing the Canadian industry in the form of an annual, three-day Trade Forum. More recently, the Festival formalised its status as a marketplace (it is considered a crucial place to test the commercial potential of studio as well as alternative and independent cinema) by establishing a bureau specifically for dealmaking: the Sales Office. This functions as a facilitator, bringing buyers from around the world together with producers and film-makers seeking to sell their films.

Yet, crucial as the festival's commercial and industrial connections have been to its development and increasing success, they should not be emphasised in isolation. The festival, for all its marketing experience and savvy, is hardly a triumph of commerce over content. In fact, if there is one thing which must stand as its most remarkable achievement, it is the sustained balance it has maintained between these two impulses.

This too is evident from the event's earliest steps. Alongside the industrial workshops and seminars mentioned above, the first festival featured films from the Soviet Union, Germany, France and Japan; and programmes ranging from *Kid's Stuff* and *Silent Classics* to *New German Cinema* and a programme of feminist works called *Womenscene*. By any standards a liberal and eclectic mix, evincing not only a healthy interest in world cinema and movie history, but with matters of social and political concern as well.

The same kind of scrupulous range, not to mention the seriousness about film's cultural status, is even more boldly evident in the most recent festivals. In 1989, for example, patrons of the Festival could choose between three programmes with a national bent (*Perspective Canada, Contemporary World Cinema* and *Polish Cinema*) one with an auteurist inclination (a retrospective of Krzysztof Kieślowski's work) or two programmes of convention-shirkers (*The Edge* and *Midnight Madness*). There were even programmes bound to induce, particularly if you'd be around the festival since year one, a sense of déjà vu: *Kid's Flicks* and *Surfacing: Canadian Women's Cinema*.

Idiosyncratic Roster

As proud as the festival is of its commercial and financial viability, it is fastidious in its concern with offering patrons an annual selection of the best and most unusual movies its team of programmers can track down. This has been demonstrated not only by the manner in which the festival has attracted establish programmers, but in the way it has nurtured an idiosyncratic roster of its own.

While an interest in daring programming and non-mainstream fare was evident even from the first festival it wasn't until 1978

Warren Beatty at the 1984 tribute to him at the Festival of Festivals

that the festival's commitment to institutionalising itself as an ongoing cultural event was agreed. That year Marshall stepped down as Festival Director, and S. Wayne Clarkson stepped in. A programmer, teacher and student of film history and theory, Clarkson brought the background and the connections necessary to establish the festival as an ongoing entity. It was under his guidance that the current festival, with its constant emphasis on a carefully programmed selection of culturally significant material, began to develop.

Much of his legacy is in evidence today: it was Clarkson who first initiated the practice of comprehensive retrospectives, which evolved from an initially auteurist bent (featuring the works of people like Jean-Luc Godard, Yilmaz Güney and John Cassavetes), to genre programmes of horror and comedy. Publications began to make an appearance to support these series. Dawson had produced a valuable monograph on Wenders for the first festival. This was followed by an anthology on the horror film edited by Robin Wood: *The American Nightmare*, a collection of essays on David Cronenberg to accompany a retrospective of his films in 1983: *The Shape of Rage*, and two ambitious books to support the massive Canadian retrospective in 1984: a reader entitled *Take Two*, and the first dictionary of Canadian cinema, Peter Morris's *The Film Companion*.

It was also during Clarkson's tenure that the annual Tributes began. Designed as an in-person showcase for the work of a noteworthy individual, the Tributes were celebrity-laden affairs, which featured people like Martin Scorsese, Robert Duvall and Warren Beatty attending This-Is-Your-Life-like ceremonies in their own honour. Hosted by Roger Ebert and Gene Siskel, these popular evenings attracted considerable attention.

Arguably, howeve, the most significant programming development of Clarkson's directorship was the instigation of the Perspective Canada programme. The time was propitious. The festival had always demonstrated a commitment to the programming of Canadian cinema but 1984 marked a special break. That year, the festival not only mounted the largest retrospective of Canadian Cinema ever attempted, to great public and critical success, but it also introduced a separate programme of films selected from the Canadian industry's annual production. Dedicated to the principle that the best new Canadian cinema must be sought out in all forms (and that all forms of Canadian film

Sonia Braga and Raul Julia arrive for *Kiss of the Spider Woman* at the 1984 Festival of Festivals

Kate Reid and Dustin Hoffman at a press conference for the 1985 closing night presentation of *Death of a Salesman*

need the promotional break), Perspective Canada is possibly the most varied programme within the festival including, as it regularly does, short films, animated works, experimental cinema, television drama and documentary, as well as feature films.

While regarded somewhat sceptically when it started, Perspective Canada has quickly become the premiere showcase of new Canadian cinema of the world. As a programme that places Canadian movies on a par equal to films from Hollywood or anywhere else, Perspective Canada not only infuses Canadian cinema with a hard-sought sense of legitimacy, it does so in front of an audience of international critics and film industry representatives. It is hardly a coincidence that, since the programme began, Canadian cinema has been more frequently visible at national and international festivals – such as Berlin, Cannes and Venice – than ever before.

Most film-makers now hold their premieres for Toronto and then release the films directly into the marketplace.

Moreover, many of the directors who have been lauded internationally in recent years, such as Atom Egoyan (*Next of Kin, Family Viewing, Speaking Parts*), Patricia Rozema (*I've Heard the Mermaids Singing, White Room*), Guy Maddin (*Archangel*), Ron Mann (*Poetry in Motion, Comic Book Confidential*), Anne Wheeler (*Loyalties, Bye Bye Blues*), Sandy Wilson (*My American Cousin, American Boyfriends*), Bill MacGillivray (*Stations, Life Classes*) all premiered their first works here. A cash prize of $25,000, juried by international and Canadian film-makers and critics, is annually awarded for excellence in Canadian cinema to the best feature film in this programme. In 1989 a prize for the best Canadian short film, supported by the National Film Board, was inaugurated at the festival.

Spike Lee at a press conference for *She's Gotta Have It* in 1986

Canadian Opening Night

Further support was given to the local industry by starting a tradition of offering opening night to a Canadian film with all the accruing publicity and attention. Films like Denys Arcand's *The Decline of the American Empire*, David Cronenberg's *Dead Ringers*, Patricia Rozema's *I've Heard the Mermaids Singing* and Yves Simoneau's *Perfectly Normal* have occupied this prime position in the past five years. Government film agencies like Telefilm Canada and the recently created Ontario Film Development Corporation (OFDC) began to recognise the marketing value of this commitment and responded in kind.

The festival also experienced significant growth in other areas. The Gala programme regularly premieres major films. *Chariots of Fire* and *The Chant of Jimmy Blacksmith* were two of the early successes. Many others followed: *Bad Timing*, *Montenegro*, *Veronika Voss*, *The Big Chill*, *Carmen*, *Paris, Texas*, *The Official Story*. Among them were films which went on to win Academy Awards. A public's award was started in 1978. Distributors sat up and paid notice. In 1989 it was won by a documentary with no distributor and no advance word-of-mouth: *Roger and Me*. By 1982 a Critic's Award had been instituted. But, the temptation to join the ranks of other international competitive film festivals was still resisted.

By the mid-1980's, Wayne Clarkson had joined the newly created OFDC, but the team of Helga Stephenson and Piers Handling continued his legacy. National cinema programmes of increasing scope were presented: Canada (1984), the world's largest retrospective of Latin American cinema (1986), Eastern Asia (1987), the Soviet Union (1988), Poland (1989), Portugal (1990). Priding itself as being on the cutting edge and anticipating trends, a highly successful 'Spotlight' series on a director was begun. Pedro Almodóvar, Aki and Mika Kaurismäki, Krzysztof Kieślowski and Mitsuo Yanagimachi electrified audiences with their impassioned work, and created further demand to see their films at subsequent festivals.

The increasing scope of the festival's programming resulted in the creation of two international programmes: 'Contemporary World Cinema' and 'The Edge,' the latter designed to premiere first, audacious works. Every year approximately 100 new films from around the world are screened, many of which are world premieres. Special emphasis has always been given to Asian and Latin American cinema, but the core of this section remains films from Europe and the United States. Numerous films went onto considerable success after Toronto screenings, some plucked from anonymity: Jean-Jacques Beineix's *Diva*, Paul Verhoeven's *The Fourth Man*, the Coen brothers' *Blood Simple*, Hal Hartley's *The Unbelievable Truth*. A midnight series was reintroduced. The public still crammed the

Faye Dunaway and Barbet Schroeder at their press conference for *Barfly*

David Cronenberg and Geneviève Bujold at the world premiere of *Dead Ringers* at the Toronto Festival of Festivals in 1988

Shirley MacLaine and John Schlesinger arrive for the closing night screening of *Madame Sousatzka* in 1988

Dušan Makavejev, Helga Stephenson (Executive Director of Festival of Festivals), and Eric Stoltz at the 1988 screening of *Manifesto*

Denys Arcand and Atom Egoyan at the 1989 Toronto Festival of Festivals

ten or eleven public cinemas, ranging in size from theatres seating 200 to 1250. Separate cinemas for the press and the industry now run all day. Guests have included such luminaries as Clint Eastwood, Diane Keaton, Faye Dunaway, Julie Christie, and directors like Stephen Frears, Alan Pakula, Jim Jarmusch, Wim Wenders, Norman Jewison, John Schlesinger, Paul Newman, Ruy Guerra, Bertrand Tavernier, Hou Hsiao-hsien, Fernando Solanas, Dušan Makavejev, Luis Puenzo, Paul Schrader, and Fred Schepisi.

Fifteen years on, it remains remarkable how adroitly the Toronto festival has managed to juggle both corporate credibility and cultural vitality. Now a larger, more expensive and better attended event than ever before, the festival is nonetheless still seeking ways to keep the flame of film-as-culture alive. Last year, it took over the operations of the decades-old Ontario Film Institute. Renamed Cinémathèque Ontario, its mandate extends to year-round programming, a documentation centre specialising in the history of the cinema and Canadian film, a regional outreach programme, and eventually publications and archiving.

The future for the Toronto Festival of Festivals seems both promising and secure. Looked to with increasing frequency as one of the world's major film festivals, it has not lost touch with its local public. Indeed, this receptive and enthusiastic audience is remarked upon without fail by virtually every visiting film-maker. As Kieślowski exited a sold-out screening of *A Short Film About Killing* to a rousing standing ovation he was overheard saying, 'You have a wonderful public.' This is Toronto's calling card and the secret of its success.

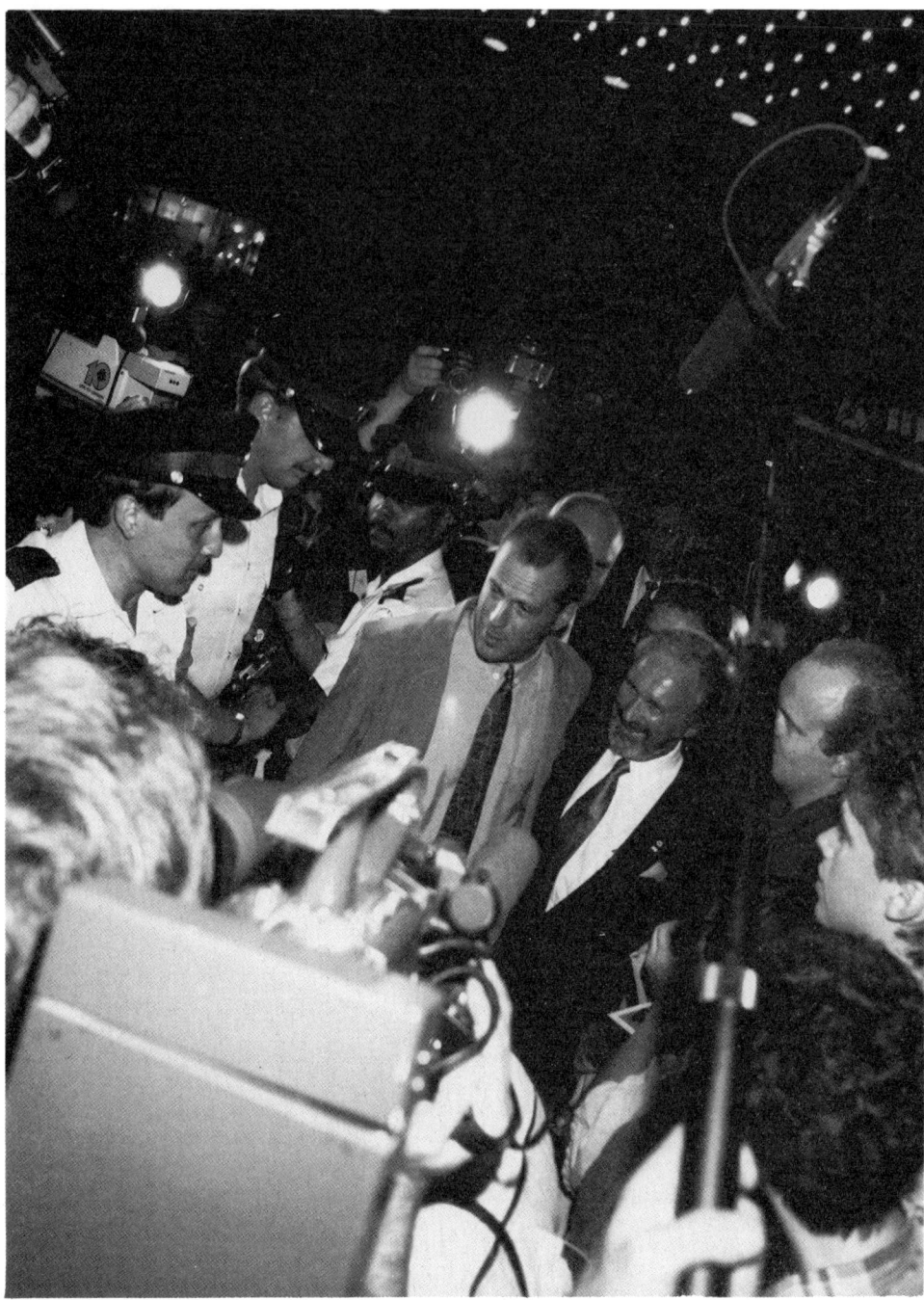

Bruce Willis and Norman Jewison arrive for the world premiere of *In Country* at the 1989 Toronto Festival of Festivals

Guide to Leading Festivals

Annecy
June 1–6, 1991

Long hailed as the first love of animators around the world, Annecy's idyllic setting makes for the perfect festival rendezvous, where animators can mingle and screen their latest works in congenial mood. There is a competitive section, as well as a Market for Animation which is on the upswing. *Inquiries to*: Journées Internationales du Cinèma d'Animation, B.P. 399, 74013 Annecy Cedex, France. Telex: 309267.

Berlin
February 15–26, 1991

Berlin is generally recognised to be the most efficiently-organised of the world's major festivals, under the leadership of Moritz de Hadeln and Ulrich Gregor. The dramatic changes in Eastern Europe have added immense significance to the Berlinale, and the Film Market is prospering under Beki Probst. In addition to the competitive programme and information section, there is a Retrospective, screenings of all new German films, and of course the Forum of Young Cinema, directed by Ulrich Gregor, where many of the most imaginative films are screened. *Inquiries to*: Berlin International Film Festival, Budapester Strasse 50, 1000 Berlin 30. Tel: (30) 254890. Telex: 185255. Fax: (30) 25489249.

AWARDS 1990
Golden Bear (features): **Music Box** (U.S.A.), Costa-Gavras/**Larks on a String** (Czechoslovakia), Menzel.
Silver Bear (Special Prize): **Coming Out** (G.D.R.), Carow.
Special Jury Prize: **The Weakness Syndrome** (U.S.S.R.), Muratova.
Best Director: Michael Verhoeven for **The Nasty Girl** (F.R.G.).
Best Single Performance: Iain Glen for **Silent Scream** (U.K.).
Best Joint Performance: Jessica Tandy and Morgan Freeman for **Driving Miss Daisy** (U.S.A.).
Special Achievement Award: Xie Fei (director) for **Black Snow** (China).
Alfred Bauer Prize: **The Guard** (U.S.S.R.), Rogoshkin.
International Film Critics Prize: **The Guard** (U.S.S.R.), Rogoshkin.
Golden Berlin Camera Award: Oliver Stone.

Cambridge
July 11–28, 1991

A film festival in this historic university town can call on considerable local and student interest, and now deserves ranking alongside London and Edinburgh as the best festival in the U.K. Now in its 15th year the event is non-competitive and screens both shorts and feature films. *Inquiries to*: Tony Jones, Cambridge Film Festival, PO Box 17, Cambridge CB2 3PF, U.K. Tel: (223) 462666. Telex: 81574. Fax: (0223) 46255.

Cannes
May 9–20, 1991

Cannes remains the world's top festival, attracting the American studios and personalities as well as entries from the more obscure countries. Its only problem is assimilating the mass of delegates and buyers. Cannes includes three major sections: the competition, the Directors' Fortnight, and the "Certain Regard" screenings. There is also the Critics' Week, and innumerable other useful screenings (e.g. the Australian, New Zealand and Scandinavian films). The great advantage of Cannes is that everyone of importance attends the event. *Inquiries to*: 71 rue du Faubourg Saint-Honoré, 75008 Paris, France. Tel: (1) 42 66 92 20. Telex: 650765. Fax: (1) 42 66 68 85. Marché International du Film: Fax: (1) 45 62 60 25.

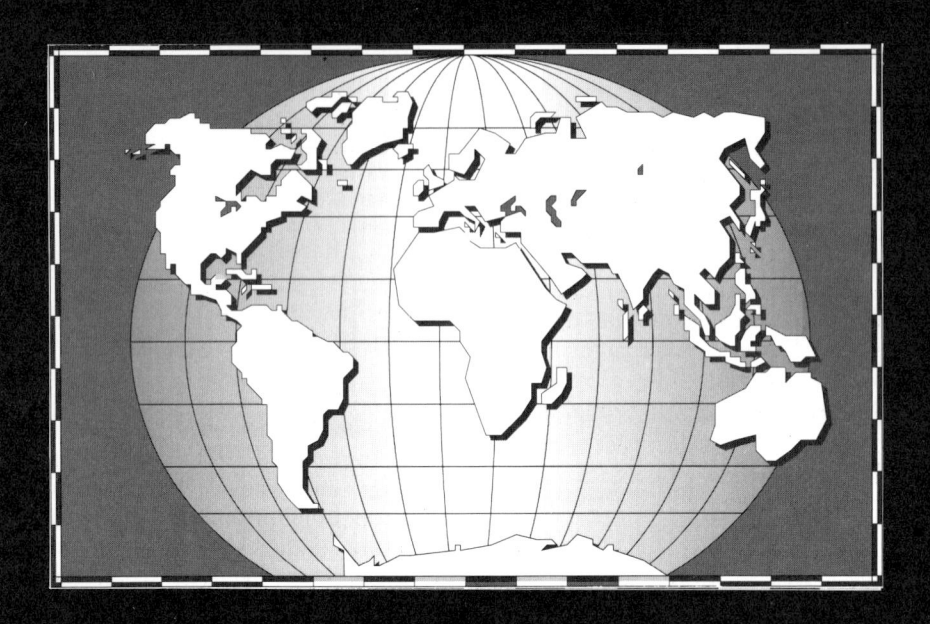

No matter where you're headed, we can get you there for less.

Whether you're scouting your next production location or scheduling production troop movement, call us first. Our expertise is in last minute bookings that don't require an advance purchase and that won't cost you an arm and a leg.

When you call ask for David Rezaieh.
He's an expert at dealing with production travel.

Air Services
(213) 854-8570 • (800) 527-5657
(213) 854-3915 fax • 188-617 telex

AWARDS 1990

Palme d'Or: **Wild at Heart** (U.S.A.), Lynch.
Special Grand Prix du Jury: (shared) **The Sting of Death** (Japan), Oguri and **Tilai** (Burkina Faso), Ouedraogo.
Best Director: Pavel Lounguine for **Taxi Blues** (U.S.S.R./France).
Best Actor: Gérard Depardieu for **Cyrano de Bergerac** (France).
Best Actress: Krystyna Janda for **The Interrogation** (Poland).
Best Artistic Contribution: **Mother** (U.S.S.R./Italy), Panfilov.
Prix du Jury: **Hidden Agenda** (U.K.), Loach.
Caméra d'Or: **Don't Move, Die and Recover** (U.S.S.R.), Kanevski.
FIPRESCI Awards: **The Sting of Death** (Japan) (official section), and **Swan Lake** (U.S.S.R.) (non-official section).
FIPRESCI Special Prize: Manoel de Oliveira.

CINETEX International Comedy Film Festival

September, 1991

America's only comedy film festival is held annually in Las Vegas as part of the CINETEX event, which also includes a film market, trade show, a seminar series and location exposition. The funniest films from around the world are invited to compete for awards handed out by an international jury. The Grand Prize in 1989 went to Great Britain's **The Tall Guy**. *Inquiries to*: AFI Festivals, 2021 N. Western Avenue, Los Angeles, CA 90027, U.S.A. Tel: (213) 856 7707. Fax: (213) 462 4049. Telex: 372 9910 FILM LSA.

Clermont-Ferrand

February 1–9, 1991

The ideal destination for anyone who wants to explore around 200 of the best short films of the year, the volcanoes of the Auvergne, and the exquisite cuisine of the region. This competitive event has enhanced its reputation recently (39 countries in 1990) and has really displaced such former festivals as Tours and Lille. *Inquiries to*:

15th CAMBRIDGE FILM FESTIVAL
8 MARKET PASSAGE, CAMBRIDGE CB2 3PF

11-28 JULY 1991

As in recent years, Cambridge will present première screenings of new British films and major titles from the Cannes and Berlin Festivals. With a programme of over 70 features, the **CAMBRIDGE FILM FESTIVAL** is based at the Arts Cinema in the centre of the historic town. The programme is complemented by retrospectives and archive revivals and has additional screenings in the refurbished Cambridge Corn Exchange.

Since its inception in 1977, the **CAMBRIDGE FILM FESTIVAL** has grown from modest beginnings to its present position as a leading event in Britain's regional film calendar. Attendances by major filmmakers in recent years have featured *Philip Kaufmann, Francesco Rosi, Peter Greenaway, Derek Jarman, Wim Wenders, Jean-Claude Carrière, Neil Jordan, Percy Adlon, Mike Hodges, Thaddeus O'Sullivan, David Hare, John McGrath, Jim Sheridan* and *Rangel Vulchanov*.

Highlights from the 1990 Festival included British premières of David Lynch's *WILD AT HEART*, Woody Allen's *CRIMES AND MISDEMEANORS*, Thaddeus O'Sullivan's *DECEMBER BRIDE*, Whit Stillman's *METROPOLITAN*, Andrzej Wajda's *KORCZAK* and Ryszard Bugajski's *INTERROGATION*. A retrospective of Italian Cinema from the 30s to the 80s and a season of Almodóvar completed a very successful programme.

Entries and applications for the 1991 Festival should be sent to **1991 CAMBRIDGE FILM FESTIVAL, 8 Market Passage, Cambridge CB2 3PF.**
Telephone **(0223) 462666/350871**
Fax **(0223) 462555**
by March 31 1991.

In Cannes: contact
TONY JONES,
Le Floriana Apartments,
Avenue du Grand Pin or
via British Pavilion.

R.I.S.C., 26 rue des Jacobins, 63000 Clermont-Ferrand, France. Tel: 73 91 65 73.

Denver

October 1991

More than 100 film programmes from around the world make up the 14th Denver International Film Festival for eight days in October. New international features, documentaries, new American cinema and critic's programmes are screened and more than 40 directors are due to attend the event in Colorado's delightfully spacious and uncrowded capital. Denver is non-competitive, but presents two achievement awards. *Inquiries to*: DIFF, PO Box 17508, Denver, CO 80217, U.S.A.. Tel: (303) 298 8223. Telex: 710 1111 406. Fax: (303) 292 6486.

DUTCH FILM DAYS

DUTCH FILMDAYS

ANNUAL SCREENING OF ALL NEW DUTCH FEATURES, SHORTS, ANIMATIONS AND DOCUMENTARIES

RETROSPECTIVES, SEMINARS, TALKSHOWS AND THE 'CINEMA MILITANS-LECTURE'

GRAND PRIX OF THE DUTCH FILM

INCLUDING THE HOLLAND FILM MEETING

SEPTEMBER 1991

PLEASE CONTACT:
THE DUTCH FILMDAYS
HOOGT 4 3512GW UTRECHT
THE NETHERLANDS
TELEPHONE: (31) 30-322684
TELEX: 43776 INCO EXT 19019

Dutch Film Days
September 19–25, 1991

Now established as an important occasion during which the entire output of Dutch film-making may be assessed, in the attractive old town of Utrecht. All new Dutch features and shorts are screened and judged, and there is a Golden Calf award for the Best Film. Useful for festival directors, film buffs, distributors and critics. *Inquiries to*: Stiching Nederlandse Filmdagen, Hoogt 4, 3512 GW Utrecht, Holland. Tel: (31) 30 322684.

AWARDS 1989
Golden Calf (Best Film): **Secret Wedding** (Netherlands), Agresti.
Best Director: Frans Weisz for **Polonaise**.
Best Actor: Pierre Bokma for **Polonaise**.
Best Actress: Annet Nieuwenhuijzen for **Polonaise**.
Special Jury Prize: Anneke Blok for **Your Opinion Please** (Netherlands).

Edinburgh
August 10–25, 1991

One of the world's oldest film festivals now going through a period of adjustment and rejuvenation after director of eight years Jim Hickey stepped down following the 1988 event. British critic David Robinson took over the reigns for 1989 and 1990 with virtually new staff, and his version has met with a good response. Emphasis on U.K. films and young directors, with retrospectives and seminars. *Inquiries to*: The Film House, 88 Lothian Road, Edinburgh EH3 9BZ, Scotland. Tel: (31) 228 4051. Telex: 72166. Fax: (31) 229 5501.

Fajr International Film Festival
February 1991

The Fajr festival has flourished as a competitive event and is now the leading Iranian film festival. Catering mainly for Iranian films, although screenings of

---

annecy 91
haute-savoie/france

1er juin - 6 juin 1991
festival international
du cinéma d'animation
international animated
film festival

1er juin - 4 juin 1991
marché international
du film d'animation
international animated
film market

information
boîte postale 399
74013 annecy cedex
téléphone 50 57 41 72
télex 309267 f
fax 50 67 81 95

15th Denver International Film Festival
October 10–17, 1991

INQUIRIES TO:
Ron Henderson
Denver International Film Festival
P.O. Box 17508 • Denver, CO 80217 USA

Tele: (303) 298–8223   Telex: 710 1111 406   Fax: (303) 298 0209

international films are on the increase. The festival also plays host to foreign guests and industry figures. *Inquiries to*: Farhang Cinema, Dr. Shariati Ave., Gholhak, Tehran 19139. Tel: 265 086. Fax: 678 155.

Festival des 3 Continents
November 1991

This is the only annual competitive festival for films emerging solely from Africa, Asia, and black and Latin America. Over the past eight years, the event has acquired prestige as well as public following in the French town of Nantes. The retrospectives, devoted to such artists as Glauber Rocha, Xie Jin, and Nelson Pereira dos Santos, are also significant. Essentially for those interested in both the culture and the society of the developing countries. *Inquiries to*: Alain Jalladeau, Director, Festival des 3 Continents, BP 3306, 44033 Nantes Cedex, France. Telex: 700610.

Festival de Genève
October 1991

Previously known as Stars de Demain, this festival dedicates itself to seeking out future talents in the film industry. A programme of seminars and debates led by professionals provide valuable contacts for younger, more inexperienced participants. *Inquiries to*: Promoguide SA, 2 rue Bovy-lysberg, Case postale 418, 1211 Geneva 11. Tel: (022) 21 54 66. Fax: (022) 21 98 62.

Festival International Nouveau Cinéma et de la Vidéo
October 1991

This long-established festival in Montréal seeks to discover and promote films of outstanding quality produced as an alternative to the conventions and commercialism of the established film

CLERMONT FERRAND
SHORT FILM FESTIVAL

3rd International Festival · 13th National Festival · 6th Short Film Market · Additional programmes · British short films · Short films about dance

VICE VERSA ▼ CLERMONT-FD

1-9 FEBRUARY 1991

For information: 26 rue des Jacobins - 63000 Clermont-Ferrand
France   Tel. 33.73.91.65.73 - Fax : 33.73.92.11.93

Denver Festival director Ron Henderson (left) and actor Seymour Cassel present Steven Soderbergh with the first John Cassavetes Award

photo: Larry Laszlo

industries. There is emphasis on the formal structure and experimental nature of film-making. Note the Québec Film and Video Market, held during the festival. *Inquiries to*: 3724 Boulevard Saint-Laurent, Montréal, Québec, Canada H2X 2V8. Telex: 5560074.

!IMAGFIC
FESTIVAL INTERNACIONAL
DE CINE DE MADRID
APRIL 19–27, 1991

IMAGFIC
Gran via 62
Madrid 28013, Spain

Tel: 5413721
5415545
Fax: 5425495

FESTIVAL DES 3 CONTINENTS

NANTES 20-27 NOVEMBER 1990

ASIAN, AFRICAN, LATIN & BLACK AMERICAN CINEMATOGRAPHIES IN COMPETITIVE & NON COMPETITIVE SECTIONS

Festival Internazionale Cinema Giovani

November 9–17, 1991

This well-organised event takes place in Turin each autumn and focuses exclusively on films made by young directors. There is a competitive section and retrospectives, and the festival aims to act as a forum where people discuss aspects of the film world reflecting youthful behaviour. *Inquiries to*: Festival Internazionale Cinema Giovani, Piazza San Carlo 161, 10123 Torino, Italy. Tel: (11) 547171. Telex: 216803. Fax: (11) 519796.

Festival of Festivals

September 1991

Claiming to be the world's largest public film festival. Toronto's event offers films and film-makers from all over the world to an eager Canadian audience. Few can match the range of this festival's international programmes – Galas, Tributes, Contemporary World Cinema, and the Documentary series. There is also a Trade Forum and an annual industry trade conference. (See special tribute earlier in this section.) *Inquiries to*: Festival of Festivals, 70 Carlton Street, Toronto, Ontario, Canada M5B 1L7. Tel: (416) 967–7371. Fax: (416) 967–9477.

Filmfest München

June 22–30, 1991

Over the past eight years the Filmfest München has found its place among non-competitive festivals, with attendances of over 100,000. Munich is after all regarded as the capital of the new German cinema. The event is funded by the City of Munich and the Free State of Bavaria. The Bayerische Rundfunk (Bavarian Broadcasting and TV) and the SPIO are

Presented by
the Urban Council, Hong Kong

15th HONG KONG INTERNATIONAL FILM FESTIVAL

March 28 – April 12, 1991

Information:
Hong Kong International Film Festival,
Level 7, Administration Building,
Hong Kong Cultural Centre,
10 Salisbury Road, Tsim Sha Tsui,
Kowloon,
Hong Kong.
Tel.: (852) 7342900-6
Fax: (852) 3665206
Telex: 38484 USDHK HX
Cable: FESTUSD HK

Festival
OF FESTIVALS
TORONTO INTERNATIONAL FILM FESTIVAL

★ SEPTEMBER 5-14, 1991 ★

70 Carlton Street
Toronto, Ontario
Canada, M5B 1L7
Tel: (416) 967-7371 Fax: (416) 967-9477 Telex: 06-219724

Expanded Entertainment invites animators everywhere to submit films for North American and Worldwide DISTRIBUTION

New Features for 1990-91
The new "Allegro Non Troppo"
"The Third Animation Celebration"
"The British Animation Invasion"
"Zagreb's Animation Fascination"
"The 23rd International Tournee of Animation"
"Too Outrageous Animation"

Television Sales
Representing more than 350 films for domestic and worldwide television distribution

Home Video Distribution
22 programs in release including *"The International Tournees of Animation"* Volumes 1, 2 & 3

Film Festival Management
The Fourth Los Angeles International Animation Celebration
May 1990

Non-Theatrical Distribution
Representing more than 400 films for libraries and schools in the U.S. and Canada

Call or write Terry Thoren, President
Expanded Entertainment
2222 S. Barrington Ave., Los Angeles, CA 90064
Phone (213) 473-6701 • Fax (213) 444-9850
Telex 247770 ANIM UR

co-associates. There is also a "Film Exchange" programme. *Inquiries to*: Eberhard Hauff, Director, Internationale Münchner Filmwochen GmbH, Türkenstrasse 93, D–8000 Munich 40, Federal Republic of Germany. Tel: (89) 3819040. Telex: 5214674. Fax: (89) 38190426.

Flanders-Ghent

October 1991

The International Filmgebeuren has been held in the Belgian city of Ghent for 16 years now, and takes as one of its main themes the use of Music in Film (with cash awards). Scores of new films receive their Belgian premiere in Ghent, and the event has proved both popular and efficiently organised. *Inquiries to*: The House of Communication, Kortrijksesteenweg 1104, B–9820 Ghent, Belgium. Tel: (91) 21 89 46. Telex: 12750. Fax: (91) 21 90 74.

French Film Festival in Sarasota

November, 1990

Supported by the French film trade, this event has a quality programme selected by Molly Haskell, and serves as an admirable showcase for French cinema not just in Florida but also in the United States as a whole, for films screened here are often picked up for distribution. *Inquiries to*: French Film Festival, 5555 North Tamiami Trl, Sarasota, Florida 34243, U.S.A. Tel: (813) 351 9010).

Göteborg

January 25–February 3, 1991

A genuine success story. In a mere decade Göteborg has established itself as not only the best film festival in Norden but as one of the key events in Europe, with more than

9° FESTIVAL INTERNAZIONALE CINEMA GIOVANI TORINO-ITALIA

9th TURIN INTERNATIONAL FILM FESTIVAL

NOVEMBER 8-16, 1991

OFFICIAL COMPETITION:
Feature and short films

HORS CONCOURS SECTION

ITALIAN INDIPENDENTS

RETROSPECTIVE

SPECIAL EVENTS

Recognized by the International Federation of Film Producers Associations

FESTIVAL INTERNAZIONALE
CINEMA GIOVANI

Festival Intenazionale Cinema Giovani
Piazza San Carlo,161
10123 Torino, Italia
Phone (11) 547171-513703-513287
Fax: (11) 519796
Telex: 216803 FICG I

de Silva Associati

14th GÖTEBORG film festival

JANUARY 25 - FEBRUARY 3 1991

1991

THE LEADING INTERNATIONAL FILM FESTIVAL IN SCANDINAVIA

SUPPORTED BY THE SWEDISH FILM INSTITUTE

MAIL: BOX 7079, 402 32 GÖTEBORG, SWEDEN
PHONE: 46 - 31 - 41 05 46   FAX: 46 - 31 - 41 00 63   TLX: 28674 FIFEST S

XIV

INTERNATIONAL FLANDERS FILM FESTIVAL GHENT - BELGIUM

Belgium's most prominent yearly film event presents films from all over the world to some 45,000 spectators, in association with TV stations. More than 60,000 $ prizes.

FOR ALL INFORMATION CONTACT

INTERNATIONAL FLANDERS FILM FESTIVAL - GHENT
1104, Kortrijksesteenweg,
B-9051 ST. DENIJS-WESTREM

In 1991, the INTERNATIONAL FLANDERS FILM FOUNDATION will support and co-ordinate the GHENT and ANTWERP film festivals.

60,000 eager and discriminating spectators who warm the cockles of a nervous director's heart with their spontaneous applause. Hotels and cinemas are close to one another. Swedish TV selects one film daily for simultaneous telecasting, a symbol of the prestige which the event carries in Sweden. *Inquiries to*: Göteborg Film Festival, PO Box 7079, S–402 32 Göteborg, Sweden. Tel: (31) 41 0546/47. Telex: 28674. Fax: (31) 410063.

Hongkong

March 28–April 12, 1991

The usual selection of Asian product is included among about 150 films on show at various venues in Kowloon and on Hongkong mainland. The festival has become even more valuable in recent years as the West has discovered the riches of Chinese cinema. *Inquiries to*: Festival

› FESTIVALS | 445

MUNICH GIVES THE MOVIES A FUTURE

FILMFEST MÜNCHEN & FILM EXCHANGE
JUNE 22 – JUNE 30, 1991
ACCREDITED BY THE INTERNATIONAL
FEDERATION OF FILM PRODUCERS ASSOCIATIONS

**INTERNATIONALES FESTIVAL
DER FILMHOCHSCHULEN MÜNCHEN**
11TH COMPETITION
OF INTERNATIONAL FILM SCHOOLS

INTERNATIONALER MEDIENMARKT MÜNCHEN
INTERNATIONAL MEDIA MARKET
FOR CULTURAL AND EDUCATIONAL AV
AND COMPUTER PROGRAMMING

INFORMATIONSBÜRO FILM
MUNICH FILM INFORMATION OFFICE
YOUR PARTNER IN THE
BAVARIAN FILM INDUSTRY

INTERNATIONALE MÜNCHNER FILMWOCHEN GMBH
TÜRKENSTRASSE 93 · D-8000 MÜNCHEN 40
PHONE: 89/38 19 04-0
TELEX 5 214 674 imf d · FAX 89/38 19 04 26
DIRECTOR: EBERHARD HAUFF

Coordinator, Cultural Services Dept., USD, HK Coliseum Annex Bldg., Parking Deck Floor, KCR Kowloon Station, 8 Cheong Wan Road, Kowloon, Hongkong. Tel: (3) 642217. Telex: 38484. Fax: (3) 639849.

Houston

J. Hunter Todd is a professional survivor, having started his "Festival of the Americas" more than twenty years ago back in Atlanta. It then moved to the Virgin Islands, and finally to Houston. The festival is competitive and in 1989 (the 11th Houston International Film Festival) featured 110 features, along with shorts, documentaries, TV productions and experimental films. *Inquiries to*: PO Box 56566, Houston, Texas 77256. Tel: (713) 965 9955. Telex: 317 876. Fax: (713) 965 9950.

Isabella Rossellini and J. Hunter Todd, Chairman of the Houston International Film Festival, meet to discuss a special retrospective of the actress's mother, Ingrid Bergman

photo: Larry Jouett

Imagfic

April 19–27, 1991

This Madrid international film festival screens around 140 new and classic films and more than a hundred guests from around the world attend the event. Its theme is the imaginative nature of the cinema. *Inquiries to*: Rita Sonlleva, Director, IMAGFIC, Gran Via 62–8, 28013 Madrid, Spain. Tel: 541 3721/241 5545. Telex: 42710. Fax: 341 5425495.

India

January, 1991

The Indian film festival is held each year (Madras in 1991) and is non-competitive (recognised by FIAPF). There are retrospectives, information sections, and a Film Market, as well as a most valuable panorama of recent trends in Indian cinema. *Inquiries to*: Mrs. Deepak Sandhu, Directorate of film festivals, Lok Nayak Bhawan, Khan Market, New Delhi 110003, India.

International Hofer Filmtage

October, 1991

Dubbed 'Home of Films' by Wim Wenders, Hof is famous for its thoughtful selection of some 40 features. Founded by the directors of the New German Cinema, Hof enjoys a high reputation among German film-makers and American cult figures like Roger Corman, Monte Hellman, John Sayles and Henry Jaglom, all of whom have attended retrospectives in their honour. The real applause should go to the peripatetic Heinz Badewitz, who had the idea for the festival over 20 years ago. A screening in Hof can often result in a distribution deal. Director Henry Jaglom was guest of honour at the 1989 event.

Istanbul
March 16–31, 1991

The Istanbul International Film Festival is now recognised as a specialised competitive event acting as a valuable showcase for distributors – not just Turkish. Attendances reach 150,000. The festival focuses on features dealing with arts (literature, music, dance etc) with sections dealing with tributes, selection of world festivals and a panorama of national cinema. *Inquiries to*: Vecdi Sayar/Hülya Ucansu, Yildiz Kultur ve Sanat Merkezi, Besiktas 80700, Istanbul, Turkey. Telex: 26687. Fax: (1) 1618823.

AWARDS 1990
Golden Tulip: **The Flame of Pomegranate in the Cane** (Iran), Ebrahimifar.
Special Jury Prize: **All the Doors Were Closed** (Turkey), Ün.
Special Prize: **Berlin Jerusalem** (Israel), Gitai.
Best Turkish Film of the Year: **Blackout Nights** (Turkey), Kurçenli.

Henry Jaglom visiting the Hof Film Days for a retrospective in 1989

Inquiries to: Postfach 1146, D–8670 Hof, F.R.G. or Heinz Badewitz, Lothstr. 28, D–8000 Munich 2, F.R.G. Tel: (89) 1297422. Telex: 5215637

ISTANBUL FOUNDATION FOR CULTURE AND ARTS

10th INTERNATIONAL ISTANBUL FILM FESTIVAL
16-31 MARCH 1991

Features of the 10th Anniversary Edition:
- INTERNATIONAL COMPETITION
- COLORS, SOUNDS & IMAGES
- SILENCE IS GOLDEN
- ALTMAN ON THEATRE
- FROM MASTERS OF OUR 10 YEARS
- IN MEMORIAM: HUSTON/IVENS/GABOR/GERASIMOV/PARADJANOV
- FILMS WE COULDN'T SHOW
- CINEMA OF A POET: PIERRE PAOLO PASSOLINI
- HOMAGE TO AKIRA KUROSAWA
- THREE WOMEN: VARDA/MURATOVA/VON TROTTA
- FREEDOM FOR CINEMA
- GOLDEN PALMS OF ITALY
- FROM WORLD FESTIVALS
- YOUNG STARS OF THE WORLD CINEMA
- COMEDIES FROM THE MEDITERRANEAN
- HOMAGE TO WALT DISNEY
- POWER OF THE DOCUMENTARY
- A COUNTRY, A CINEMA: POLAND
- TURKISH CINEMA '90 - '91

Accredited by the INTERNATIONAL FEDERATION OF FILM PRODUCERS ASSOCIATIONS as a "Specialized Competitive Festival" (Films on Art). In 1990, 184 films from 42 countries participated and attendance raised to 150,000.

Contact: Mrs. HÜLYA UÇANSU (Director)

Yıldız Kültür ve Sanat Merkezi, Beşiktaş 80700 Istanbul TURKEY
Tel: (1) 160 45 33 - 160 90 72 Fax: (1) 161 88 23
Tlx: 26687 iksv tr

International Tournée of Animation

Now in its 23rd annual programme, this feature-length touring showcase of international short animated films is exhibited in over 400 specialised theatres and art centres in the United States and Canada. Since 1985 the Tournée has been on the Top Ten list of the highest grossing speciality pictures. Typically the Tournée includes 15 to 20 film selections including each year's Academy Award-winner, the prizewinners from the major festivals, and the best new work of independent animators. *Inquiries to*: 2222 S. Barrington Avenue, Los Angeles, California 90064, U.S.A. Tel: (213) 473 6701. Telex: 247770. Fax: (213) 444 9850.

12ᵉ FESTIVAL INTERNATIONAL DU CINEMA MEDITERRANEEN
Montpellier-France · 26 octobre - 4 novembre 1990

CINEMA MEDITERRANEEN MONTPELLIER

Hôtel des Festivals • 7, bd Henri IV, 34000 Montpellier, France
Téléphone (33) 67 04 29 39 • Fax (33) 67 04 29 41

SiFF SEATTLE INTERNATIONAL FILM FESTIVAL

May 16 - June 10, 1991

Cinema Seattle, The Egyptian Theatre
801 East Pine Street, Seattle, Washington 98122
Phone (206) 324-9996 Facsimile (206) 324-9998
TELEX 329 473 BURGESS SEA

XIXᵉ FESTIVAL INTERNATIONAL DU FILM DE LA ROCHELLE

directed by jean-loup passek   **JULY 2nd - JULY 12th**

100 LONG FEATURES FILMS - 300 SCREENINGS - NON COMPETITIVE

3 MAIN SECTIONS

- Retrospectives devoted to the work of past filmmakers
- Tributes to contemporary directors, in their presence
- Le Monde tel qu'il est (The World as it Is), a selection of unreleased films from all over the world

for any information, please contact:

**Festival International du Film de La Rochelle
28, bd du Temple 75011 Paris
Phone: (1) 43 57 61 24 Fax: (1) 48 06 40 22**

Dušan Hanak, Eva Zaoraleva and festival director Jean-Loup Passek during the 1990 La Rochelle event
photo: Regis d'Audeville

La Rochelle

July 2–12, 1991

Jean-Loup Passek builds a bright and enthusiastic bridge between past and future cinema with his popular and distinguished festival in this French resort, where only the superlative seafood may distract one from a wealth of restrospectives (always some discoveries among the silents), new features and thematic programmes. Passek coaxes many a director to his event, and 1990 guests included Jancsó, Menzel, Passer, and several figures from the Asian Republics. *Inquiries to*: Festival International du Film de La Rochelle, 28 Boulevard du Temple, 75011 Paris, France. Tel: (1) 43 57 61 24.

Locarno

August 8–18, 1991

Under the direction of David Streiff, Locarno has triumphantly achieved its aim to be a meeting point for film-makers from around the world, in a location where new features may be viewed in a peaceful atmosphere. Locarno awards are much prized, and can often go to films unjustly ignored at the more glamorous festivals. Locarno now also offers visitors a useful chance to catch up on recent Swiss films. *Inquiries to*: Festival Internazionale del Film, Casella Postale, CH–6600 Locarno, Switzerland. Tel: (93) 31 02 32. Telex: 846565. Fax: (93) 31 74 65.

London

November, 1991

The London Film Festival has now ranged out well beyond the National Film Theatre with screenings in various venues (including major West End screens) and around 150 films or so shown during the event. Directors are encouraged to discuss films with the audience. All programmes are open to the public. *Inquiries to*: National Film Theatre, South Bank, London SE1. Tel: (1) 928 3535. Telex: 929220. Fax: (1) 633 9323.

Los Angeles International Animation Celebration

February 8-17, 1991

This "festival of festivals" is a new concept for animation, and more than 400 films are showcased at the event. A panel of experts presents cash prizes and awards of more than $100,000 to the best in 15 categories. The festival is open to films in 16mm, 35mm, video (almost all standards), completed since January 1988. There are also restrospectives and artist tributes. *Inquiries to*: Terry Thoren, Director, Expanded Entertainment, 2222 S. Barrington Avenue, Los Angeles, California 90064, U.S.A. Tel: (213) 473 6701. Telex: 247770. Fax: (213) 444-9850.

Los Angeles European Community Film Festival

June, 1991

AFI EuroFest takes place every June in Los Angeles, Washington, D.C., New York and Minneapolis. The best new films from each of the member countries of the European Community are shown with stars and film-makers in attendance. Recent festivals have spotlighted films by Ermanno Olmi, Jacques Rivette, Margarethe von Trotta, Derek Jarman, Luigi Comencini, Mario Camus, and Reinhard Hauff. *Inquiries to*: American Film Institute, PO Box 27999, 2021 North Western Avenue, Los Angeles, California 90027, U.S.A. Tel: (213) 856 7707. Fax: (213) 462 4049.

Los Angeles International Film Festival

April, 1991

Continuing the tradition started by Filmex, this event is the largest of its kind in the United States, though only in its fifth year. Collaborating with over 30 film and arts organisations, the L.A. FilmFest is each year dedicated to different aspects of film-making (the producer, writer and cinematographer were honoured in the first three years). Over 200 feature films, shorts and documentaries from 45 countries are screened, with gala premieres, seminars, workshops and on-stage tributes. *Inquiries to*: AFI Festivals, 2021 N. Western Avenue, Los Angeles, CA 90027. Tel: (213) 856 7707. Fax: (213) 426 4049. Telex: 372 9910 FILM LSA.

Mannheim

October 8-13, 1991

One of the world's liveliest festivals, specialising for almost forty years in first features, long and short documentaries, featurettes and animation films. Known as

THE 14TH ANNUAL

MILL VALLEY FILM FESTIVAL

OCTOBER 3-10, 1991

Eight Days of Movie Magic!

FOR INFORMATION
38 MILLER AVENUE #6 • MILL VALLEY
CALIFORNIA • 94941 USA
TEL: (415) 383-5256 FAX: (415) 383-8606
TLX: 282 696

> # MANNHEIM FILM FESTIVAL
> – 40th International Filmweek Mannheim –
> ## Germany October 1991
> West-Germany's oldest film festival changes · Ask for information!
>
> Collini-Center-Galerie · D-6800 Mannheim 1 · Phone: 06 21 - 10 29 43 · Telex: 463 423 · Fax: 06 21 - 2 93 28 68

"fixed star for all Third World filmmakers." A Grand Prize of DM 10,000 is awarded for the best feature; another award to the best film from a Third World country (DM 10,000); the Josef von Sternberg prize of DM 3,500 to the most original film; and there are also awards of five Mannheim Film Ducats, each accompanied by DM 2,000. *Inquiries to*: Filmwochenbüro, Collini-Center-Galerie, D–6800 Mannheim, F.R.G. Tel: (621) 102943. Telex: 463423. Fax: (621) 101452.

AWARDS 1989
Grand Prize: **China Lake** (U.S.A.), Weihl.
Jury Prize: **Growing up in America** (Canada), Markson.
Josef von Sternberg Prize: **The Dead Fish** (Austria), Synek.

Melbourne

June 6–22, 1991

Now flourishing again under the direction of Tait Brady, Melbourne is respected for the attention it gives to quality short films as well as to the major features of the year, culled from various countries and festivals around the world. *Inquiries to*: Melbourne Film Festival, GPO Box 2760EE, Melbourne 3001, Australia. Tel: (3) 663 1395. Telex: 152613.

AWARDS 1990
Grand Prix: **Swimming** (Australia), Chayko.
Best Fiction Film: **He Was Once** (U.S.A.), Hestand.
Best Documentary: *(shared)* **Senso Daughters** (Australia), Sekiguchi, **Elefanti** (Canada), Hayes.
Best Animation Film: **Deadsy** (U.K.), Anderson.
Best Experimental Film: **Jolicoeur Touriste** (Canada), Bourque.
Best Australian Film: **Night Cries** by Tracey Moffat.
Best Children's Film: **The Water Trolley** (Australia), Price.
Best Student Film: **A Rat in the Building** (Australia), Horne.

MIFED (Milan)

October 20–27, 1991

Long established film market held in the expansive Milan Trade Fair, particularly well attended by the European buyers and sellers. Third of the year's big three film markets – preceded by the American Film Market and Cannes Film Festival – the atmosphere is all business, but Milan is still attractive, even in gloomy October. *Inquiries to*: E.A. Fiera Internazionale di Milano, Largo Domodossola 1, 20145 Milano, Italy. Tel: (02) 4997267–270. Telex: 331360. Fax: (02) 49977020.

Mill Valley

October 3–10, 1991

The Mill Valley Film Festival has a managable programme with range and variety that is shaped by a commitment to cultural and artistic excellence. An intimate event of unusually high calibre and

FESTIVAL DE GENEVE
(Stars de Demain)

Automne 1991

LES ESPOIRS DU CINEMA EUROPEEN

> **40th MELBOURNE INTERNATIONAL FILM FESTIVAL**
> **JUNE 6–22, 1991**
> - Entree to Australasian theatrical, video and non-theatrical buyers
> - 29th International Short Film Competition (Open to films up to 60 minutes in length)
>
> Entry deadline for features and shorts – March 23rd
> **Melbourne International Film Festival**
> BOX 12367 A'Beckett Street P.O. Melbourne 3000 Australia
> Fax (03) 662 1218 Telex 152613 Phone (03) 663 1395

dedication set in the beautiful small town just north of San Francisco. A non-competitive event including a large selection of seminars as well as a video sidebar. *Inquiries to*: Mill Valley Film Festival, 38 Miller Avenue, Suite 6, Mill Valley, California 94941, U.S.A. Tel: (415) 383 5256. Fax: (415) 383 8606.

Montpellier

October 26–November 4, 1990

Unusual event focusing on "Mediterranean" cinema, and awarding financial prizes for both features and shorts. Now in its 12th year, Montpellier also mounts a useful Information section. The 1990 programme ranged from Albania to Portugal, from Yugoslavia to the countries of the Maghreb. There is also a major symposium. *Inquiries to*: International Festival of Mediterranean Film, Hôtel des Festivals, 7 Bd Henri IV, Montpellier, France. Tel: (33) 67 04 29 39. Fax: (33) 67 04 29 41.

Montreal World Film Festival

August 1991

Serge Losique has established a major competitive festival in Montréal in late summer, and it is the only such event recognised by FIAPF in America. There are several categories, public attendance is extremely high, and the number of foreign personalities swells each year. Montréal is the ideal location for such an event, with its bilingual facilities and its proximity to all major North American outlets. *Inquiries to*: Serge Losique, World Film Festival, 1455 Boulevard de Maisonneuve Ouest, Montréal, Québec, Canada H3G 1M8. Tel: (514) 848 3883. Telex: 05–25472. Fax: (514) 848 3886.

AWARDS 1989

Best Film: **Freedom Is Paradise** (U.S.S.R.), Bodrov.
Special Jury Award: (shared) **Forever Mary** (Italy), Risi, **Indian Nocturne** (France), Corneau.
Best Actor: Daniel Day Lewis for **My Left Foot** (Ireland).
Best Actress: Danielle Proulx for **Portion d'Eternité** (Canada).
Best Short Film: **Juke-Bar** (Canada), Barry.
Best Director: Jiří Menzel for **The End of Old Times** (Czechoslovakia).
Best Screenplay: Elisio Subelia for **Last Images of the Shipwreck** (Argentina/Spain).
Best Artistic Contribution: **Rikyu** (Japan), Hiroshi Teshigahara.
FIPRESCI Prize: *(shared)* **Save and Prosper** (U.S.S.R.), Sokurov, **The Philosopher** (F.R.G.), Thome.

Moscow

July, 1991

Biannual event that in terms of statistics usually defeats all the other film festivals (the main hotel alone accommodates literally thousands of delegates). While some of the official programmes may be rather ponderous, there is always the opportunity to catch up on recent Soviet productions of note, and to meet with visitors from a wider range of countries than ever in this era of glasnost. *Inquiries to*: Sovinterfest, State Committee for Cinematography, 10 Khokhlovsky pereulok, Moscow 109028, U.S.S.R.

New York

September–October, 1991

Back in the heady days of the 1960's, when

Richard Roud and (especially) Amos Vogel pioneered the event, the NY Fest was a lodestone for film-makers like Truffaut and Godard. Now the sheen has dulled, and although attendances at Lincoln Center remain high, one feels that New York as a festival is uncertain of its own identity and forte. But a screening here can certainly help the cause of a foreign film as well as that of an American independent. *Inquiries to*: Film Society of Lincoln Center, 140 West 65th Street, New York, NY 10023, U.S.A.

Nordic Filmfestival

March–April, 1991

The 9th Nordic Filmfestival will be held in Kristiansand, on the south tip of Norway. The festival presents new Nordic titles, attracting creative film-makers of all categories and is regarded as a meeting place for film producers from Nordic countries. Also popular for foreign

33. NORDISCHE FILMTAGE LÜBECK

vom 31.10–3.11, 1991

Scandinavian and Baltic feature films, shorts and documentaries

Information screenings of Scandinavian children's and young people's films

Retrospective

Discussion

Seminar

Information:
**Nordische Filmtage Lübeck
Postfach 2132
D-2400 Lübeck 1
Tel. (0451) 1224105
Fax. (0451) 1221331**

There is a life outside Haugesund ... but who cares

"I would encourage any of my colleagues who haven't been here before to come, and I certainly will come again and again and again, because it seems to me this festival is a festival entirely to do with craft".
Ben Kingsley

"If someone asks you to go to Haugesund, say yes – yes, please!"
Roger Moore

"Bravo! Pour le Festival et pour l'amitié"
Fernando Solanas

"I am looking forward to my next visit. Long live Norway!"
Gabriel Axel

THE NORWEGIAN FILM FESTIVAL   AUGUST 18–25 1991
P O BOX 145, 5501 HAUGESUND, NORWAY

9th International Odense Film Festival
2nd - 8th August 1991

The International Odense Film Festival held in the spirit of Hans Christian Andersen invites imaginative, experimental and creative films to participate i 1991.

Films in competition must have been produced since July 3Oth 1987, maximum length 60 minutes.

The International Odense Film Festival is organized by the City Council of Odense and the Association of Danish Film Directors.

Further information:

International
Odense Film Festival
Vindegade 18
5000 Odense C
Denmark

Phone: +45 66 13 13 72 ext. 4294
Telefax: +45 65 91 4318

producers looking for co-productions and location scouting in Scandinavia. Offers one public award. *Inquiries to*: Nordic Filmfestival, PO Box 356, N–4601 Kristiansand, Norway. Tel: (47) 42 21629. Fax: (47) 42 20390.

Nordische Filmtage
November, 1991

This annual event held in the charming medieval town of Lübeck (north of Hamburg), throws a spotlight on the Scandinavian cinema exclusively, and enables members of the Nordic trade, critics, and other visitors to see the best of the new productions. *Inquiries to*: Nordische Filmtage, Postfach 1889, D–2400 Lübeck 1, Federal Republic of Germany. Tel: (451) 1224105. Fax: (451) 1221331.

Norwegian Film Festival
August, 1991

Held in the west coast port of Haugesund every summer, the Norwegian film festival has now become the country's major film event attended by many international visitors along with about 800 representatives from the Norwegian film world. The festival is run by festival director Gunnar Johan Løvvik and programme director is Nils Klevjer Aas. Honourable President is Liv Ullmann. The Norwegian 'Amanda Statuettes' are presented there. *Inquiries to*: PO Box 145, N–5501 Haugesund, Norway. Tel: (47) 28 422.

Nyon
October 1991

For over 20 years, Nyon has been a focus for the world's documentaries to aim at. There are awards for the best entries and an indispensable retrospective section as well as informative screenings, all under the diligent stewardship of Erika de Hadeln. *Inquiries to*: Festival International de Cinéma – Nyon, Case postale 98, CH–1260 Nyon, Switzerland. Telex: 28163.

Oberhausen
April 24–30, 1991

Oberhausen still has a just claim to be the world's premier short film festival. Not only is there a wider selection of shorts from all over the world (with special emphasis on productions from the Third World and Latin America in particular), but also an opportunity to attend the "Information Days" devoted to West German short films. *Inquiries to*: Westdeutsche Kurzfilmtage, Christian-Steger-Strasse 10, D–4200 Oberhausen 1, F.R.G. Tel: (208) 8252652. Telex: 856414. Fax: (208) 28159.

AWARDS 1990
Grand Prize: **Soviet Elegy** (U.S.S.R.), Sokurow. *Main Prizes*: **Ad Rem** (Hungary), Cako; **Alois Camenzind, Klauenschneider** (Switzerland), Weber; **Crofton Road SE5** (F.R.G.), Gockell; **Foutaises** (France), Jeunet; **Count and Countess** (U.S.S.R.), Jachina; **You Can Drive The Big Rigs** (U.S.A.), Pierce.

Odense
August 2–8, 1991

Originally launched as a "fairy-tale" film festival in the spirit of the town's greatest son, Hans Christian Andersen, Odense has broadened its appeal to cover "imaginative, experimental and creative film," of all kinds. There is a competition, restricted to films no longer than 60 mins. *Inquiries to*: Odense International Film Festival, Vindegade 18, DK–5000 Odense C, Denmark. Tel: (9) 131372. Telex: 59853. Fax: (9) 914316.

Pesaro
June, 1991

The "Mostra" Internazionale del Nuovo

German and Italian guests at the traditional Round Table during the 21st International Cinema Week in Verona

> Grand retrospective:
> **The DeMilles**
>
> **10th PORDENONE SILENT FILM FESTIVAL October 1991**
>
> LE GIORNATE DEL CINEMA MUTO
>
> For information, send international reply coupon c/o
> La Cineteca del Friuli, via Osoppo 26,
> I-33014 Gemona (UD) Italia. Tel: 0432-980458 Fax: 0432-970542

Cinema" is particularly concerned with the work of new directors and emergent cinemas – in other words, with innovation at every level of the film world. For the past 23 years this Mediterranean resort has been the centre for some lively screenings and debates, and in recent seasons the festival has been devoted to a specific theme. Pesaro also tries hard to arrange commercial distribution for films during the festival. *Inquiries to*: Mostra Internazionale del Nuovo Cinema, Via Yser 8, 00198 Roma, Italy. Telex: 624596.

Pordenone
October, 1991

Impeccably organised and meticulously researched tribute to the silent cinema, held each year in this small Italian town with love and devotion. In 1988 the festival screened 60 features and 30 shorts from the American 1910's and 1989 saw a rare programme of Russian and Soviet silents. Pordenone devoted its most recent edition to the treasures of German silent film, and met with even greater success than ever. *Inquiries to*: La Cineteca del Friuli, Via Osoppo 26, 33014 Gemona (UD), Italy. Tel: (0432) 950458. Fax: (0432) 970542.

Rotterdam
January 24–February 3, 1991

This is the 20th annual festival. Its aim is to create a focal point for directors, festival programme heads (Rotterdam being one of the earliest events of the season), and the Dutch public. There are no awards, but a distribution guarantee is given to the film regarded as best in a poll among critics and public. More than half the programme is chosen from outside the United States and Europe. Rotterdam is an immediately friendly and informal festival where guests can talk to visiting directors and personalities in pleasant conditions. There is a "Cinemart" for the buying and selling of film and video rights. *Inquiries to*: Rotterdam Film Festival, PO Box 21696, 3001 AR Rotterdam, Netherlands. Tel: (10) 4118080. Telex: 21378. Fax: (10) 4135132.

San Francisco
April, 1991

North America's oldest international film festival celebrated its 30th anniversary in 1987, but seems to grow younger and more

---

"The Way to the Neighbour"

April 24-30, 1991

37th Westdeutsche Kurzfilmtage Oberhausen

"The World's Premier Short Film Festival" – IFG

Director: Karola Gramann   Address: D-4200 Oberhausen, Christian-Steger-Str. 10
Telephone: (0208) 8252652   Telex: 0856414

audacious with each passing year. The Golden Gates Awards competition has expanded to include features made for TV, as well as documentaries and shorts. Peter Scarlet is the much respected and widely-travelled Artistic Director, and his team triumphed over the after-effects of the 1989 earthquake to achieve their most popular festival to date. *Inquiries to*: San Francisco International Film Festival, 1560 Fillmore Street, San Francisco, California 94115, U.S.A. Tel: (415) 567 4641. Telex: 6502816427. Fax: (415) 567 0432.

Sanremo

March, 1991

This distinguished event exists to promote original cinema in all its forms, and also organises admirable retrospectives. The Gran Premio carries a substantial cash award. *Inquiries to*: Nino Zucchelli, Director, Mostra Internazionale del Film d'Autore, Rotonda dei Mille 1, 24100 Bergamo, Italy.

San Sebastian

September, 1991

Held in an elegant Basque seaside city, only 20 kilometers from the French border, San Sebastian is still by far the most important film festival in Spain in terms of budget, glitter, sections, facilities, attendance, competition, partying and number of films. Key movers at the festival are longtime Secretary, Pilar Olascoaga, and festival co-ordinator Antonio Ezeiza. The city is known for its superb gastronomy, beautiful beaches and quaint streets. The festival usually attracts a number of international celebrities, as well as a wide selection of national and international press, talent, and buffs. *Inquiries to*: International Film Festival, PO Box 397, 20.080 San Sebastian, Spain. Tel: (43) 481–212. Telex: 38145. Fax: (43) 285979.

FILM FESTIVAL ROTTERDAM 20th

JANUARY 24 - FEBRUARY 3, 1991

P.O. Box 21696
3001 AR Rotterdam
The Netherlands
Telephone (0)10-4118080
Telefax (0)10-4135132
Telex 21378 filmf nl

INTERVAL TIDINGS,
newsletter of the Film Festival Rotterdam.

Interval Tidings is a quarterly publication.
You can receive it simply by sending in
your address

SAN SEBASTIAN

THE SEPTEMBER FESTIVAL

SAN SEBASTIAN INTERNATIONAL FILM FESTIVAL

Apartado de Correos, 397
Tel.: 43-42 96 25. Fax: 43-28 59 79
Tx.: 38145 FCSS E
20080 **SAN SEBASTIAN
SPAIN**

AWARDS 1989
Golden Shell (Best Feature): *(shared)* **Homer and Eddie** (U.S.A.) Konchalovsky, **The Secret Nation** (Bolivia), Sanjinés.
Silver Shell (Best Director): Miroslaw Bork for **Konsul** (Poland).
Special Jury Prize: **The Sea and Time** (Spain), Gómez.
Best Actress: Mirjana Jokovic in **Eversmile, New Jersey** (Argentina/U.K.).
Best Actor: Ari Berry in **Hostages' Story** (Hungary).
San Sebastian Prizes: **Days of Smoke** (Spain), Ezeiza, **True Love** (U.S.A.), Savoca.

Sydney
June, 1991

Australia has become an ever-more important market for both English and foreign language films, and Sydney has been proving for decades that an efficient and lively festival can introduce even the most recondite of works to an enthusiastic public. New director, critic Paul Byrnes, looks like carrying on the good work from former globe-trotting director Rod Webb. *Inquiries to*: Paul Byrnes, PO Box 25, Glebe, NSW 2037, Australia. Tel: (2) 660 390. Telex: 75111.

Taipei
December, 1991

International Film Exhibition Taipei is run every year alongside Taiwan's Golden Horse Awards for offshore Chinese cinema, and is organised by the city's Film Library. *Inquiries to*: International Film Exhibition Taipei, Film Library, 4/F., 7 Ch'ingtao East Road, Taipei, Taiwan.

Tampere
March 6–10, 1991

The most important short film festival in the Nordic area (celebrating its 21st anniversary), and an event that attracts entries from all over the world, especially Eastern Europe. The international competition consists of categories for documentaries, animation, and fiction and experimental films. In addition there is a full retrospective programme. *Inquiries to*: Tampere Film Festival, PO Box 305, SF–33101 Tampere, Finland. Tel: (31) 35681. Telex: 22448. Fax: (31) 196756.

AWARDS 1990
Main Prizes: **Kitchen Sink** (New Zealand), Maclean: **Thin Ice** (Denmark), Graaböl; **The Bun Boy** (Finland), Prepula; **Rage** (Finland), Lindholm; **Cuisine** (France), Harel.

Telluride
August–September, 1991

Over the past 17 years, this friendly gathering in a spectacular location in the mountains of Colorado has become one of the world's most influential festivals, with the town of Telluride virtually doubling in size as famous directors, players, and critics descend on the Sheridan Opera House. It is a formula that others have tried to emulate –

Scene
91
Take
38
Location
Sydney

38th Sydney Film Festival

7-21 June 1991

Fax: 02-692 8793
Phone: 02-660 3844
Address: PO Box 25 Glebe
NSW 2037 Australia

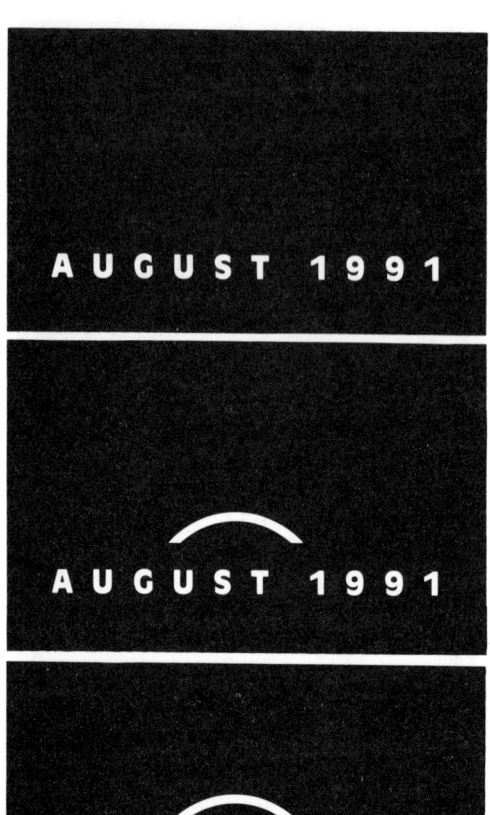

and always fail, because the team of Bill and Stella Pence and Tom Luddy blend wit and wisdom and bathe the festival in a mood of discovery. *Inquiries to*: The National Film Preserve, PO Box B1156, Hanover, New Hampshire 03755, U.S.A. Tel: (603) 643 1255.

Tyneside

October, 1991

A lively festival now in its thirteenth year, it established a reputation as a major British forum for new international independent cinema. Changing direction in the mid 1980's it now focuses on European cinema and for six years has showcased new and retrospective Spanish cinema with visiting directors. Discussion and television events are also featured. *Inquiries to*: Tyneside Film Festival, 10–12 Pilgrim Street, Newcastle upon Tyne, NE1 6QK, U.K. Tel: (91) 232 8289.

Uppsala

October, 1991

With a local audience of around 11,000 plus journalists, Uppsala is yet another Swedish event that covers both features and shorts. Awards to three titles annually. The festival composes its programmes so as to show how certain types of film-making are achieved, or how certain topics are handled. Note also the Children's section. *Inquiries to*: Uppsala Film Festival, PO Box 1746, S–751 47 Uppsala, Sweden. Tel: (18) 16 22 70. Telex: 76020.

Valladolid

October 18–26, 1991

Now firmly established as one of Spain's leading festivals, Valladolid offers an Official section with features and shorts in competition, special tributes, restrospectives

```
┌─────────────────────────────────────────────────────┐
│                                    18/26 Oct'91    │
│  ┌──────────────────────────┐                       │
│  │ 36th VALLADOLID          │  P.O. Box 646         │
│  │                          │  Tel.: (34-83) 305700/77/88 │
│  │   Intl. FILM FESTIVAL    │  Fax: (34-83) 309835  │
│  └──────────────────────────┘  Telex: 26304 FONCAB E │
│                                 47003 VALLADOLID    │
│                                                     │
│              S     P     A     I     N              │
└─────────────────────────────────────────────────────┘
```

and documentaries. In 1990, events included a tribute to the Ealing Comedies, one on Spanish playwright Miguel Mihura and films made from his plays, another on UCLA (silent classics), one on Romanian cinema and a tribute to the Berlin Film School. *Inquiries to*: Semana Internacional de Cine de Valladolid, Spain. Tel: (3483) 305700/77/88. Telex: 26304. Fax: (3483) 309835.

Vancouver

October, 1991

Now in its tenth year, this festival has grown into an event of some stature. About 75,000 people attend more than 200 screenings, and the Canadian city's natural beauty adds to the hospitality offered guests. Areas of special focus are Canada, the Pacific Rim, U.K. and the Soviet Union. Overlapping events include the Fifth Annual Trade Forum, international section and special showcase events. *Inquiries to*: Alan Franey, 303–788 Beatty Street, Vancouver, B.C., V6B 2M1, Canada. Tel: (604) 685 0260/6. Telex: 045 08354. Fax: (604) 688 8221.

Venice

August–September, 1991

During his four-year regime, Guglielmo Biraghi promises to renovate the inadequate building of the Palazzo del Cinema – why not transfer the Mostra itself to downtown Venice? – and to give new life to the bureaucracy of the Biennale. Its cultural power should be expanded soon by year-long activities that could penetrate into the dull commercial market. Most pictures screened in Venice achieve distribution in Italy. *Inquiries to*: La Biennale Cinema, Cà Giustinian, 30100 Venezia, Italy. Tel: (41) 5200311. Telex: 410685.

AWARDS 1989

Golden Lion: **A City of Sadness** (Taiwan), Hsiao-hsien.

Special Grand Prize: **And There Was Light** (France), Ioselliani.

Silver Lion: *(shared)* **Recollections of the**

```
┌─────────────────────────────┐
│            THE              │
│           14th              │
│         TYNESIDE            │
│      INTERNATIONAL          │
│       FILM FESTIVAL         │
│        AUTUMN 1991          │
│      TYNESIDE CINEMA        │
│       10 Pilgrim Street     │
│    Newcastle upon Tyne      │
│          England            │
│          NE1 6QG            │
│     Tel: (091) 232 8289     │
│     Fax: (091) 221 0535     │
└─────────────────────────────┘
```

TAMPERE • XXI • INTERNATIONAL • SHORT • FILM • FESTIVAL •

6-10 March 1991

• Box 305, 33101 Tampere, Finland •
• tel +358-31-196149, -235681 • fax -230121 • tlx 22448 •
Now contact also for:

MIDNIGHTSUN FILM FESTIVAL June 1991

5th WINE COUNTRY FILM FESTIVAL
July 12 – 21 1991
Northern California
"one of the top film celebrations in the US" Screen International
Entry Deadline: April 10, 1991
Features, docs, animation, shorts welcome
WCFF, Box 303, Glen Ellen, Ca 95442 707-935
FILM for ticket, program & entry info

Yellow House (Portugal), Monteiro, **Death of as Tea Master** (Japan), Kuami.
Best Actor: Marcello Mastroianni and Massimo Troisi for **What Time Is It?** (Italy).
Best Actress: Peggy Ashcroft and Geraldine James for **She's Been Away** (U.K.).
Best Screenplay: Jules Feiffer for **I Want To Go Home** (France), Resnais.
Best Photography: Yorgos Arvanitis for **Australia** (Belgium/France/Switzerland).
Best Music: The cast of **Street Kids** (Italy).
FIPRESCI *Awards*: **Dekalog 1-10** (Poland), Kieślowski, **A World Without Pity** (France), Rochant.

independent films. Past winners include Hemdale, Orion Classics and Miramax. Not surprisingly, the festival also presents special events featuring the culinary arts and the finest of wines, as well as the related arts of dance, painting, photography and music to tie in with special screenings. *Inquiries to*: PO Box 303, Glen Ellen, CA 95442, U.S.A.

Wellington

July, 1991

Attractive festival that twins with Auckland in offering New Zealand's best festival showcase. *Inquiries to*: Wellington Film Festival, Box 9544, Te Aro, Wellington, New Zealand. Tel: (64) (4) 850162. Fax: (64) (4) 8017304

Wine Country Film Festival

July, 1991

Set in the heart of Northern California's premium wine country, this event showcases new films, with special series' of independent features and international films. Non-competitive, but an award is given each year to the film company of the year, acknowledging their commitment to

10th International Uppsala Film Festival 18 – 27 Oct. 1991
Address: P. O. Box 1746, S-751 47 Uppsala, SWEDEN
Tel: (46)18-50 30 10 Fax: (46)18-50 15 10 Telex: 76020

Other Festivals and Markets of Note

American Film and Video Festival, 920 Barnsdale Road, LaGrange Park, Illinois 60625, U.S.A. (*Formerly in New York, this is the definite round-up of documentaries and animated films in the States – June.*)

American Film Market, 10000 Washington Boulevard, Culver City, California 90232. (*Efficiently-run market primarily for English-language theatrical films. Buyers must be accredited – February.*)

American Independent Feature Film Market, 21 West 86th Street, New York, NY 10024. (*Showcase for independently produced American films – October.*)

Amiens, Marché International du Film, 36 rue de Noyon, 80000 Amiens, France. Telex: 140754. (*Film Market, with workshops and co-production finance deals being negotiated, plus competitive section – November.*)

Belgrade, Sava Center, M. Popovica 9, 11070 Belgrade, Yugoslavia, (*Cream of world cinema, exceptionally well attended – January–February.*)

Bergamo Film Meeting, Via Pascoli 3, 24110 Bergamo, Italy. (*Useful gathering aimed at the specialist distributors interested in buying quality films for Italy – competitive cash prizes – July.*)

Biarritz Festival du Film Ibérique et Latino-American. Comité du tourisme et des fêtes, Cité administrative, 64200 Biarritz, France. (*Film in Spanish and Portuguese language from Europe and the Americas – September.*)

Birmingham Film and Television Festival, c/o Birmingham City Council, Dept. of Recreation and Community Services, Auchinleck House, Five Ways, Edgbaston, Birmingham B15 1DS, U.K. Tel: (21) 4402543/4221. Fax: (21) 440 4372. (*Growing provincial festival – October–November.*)

British Industrial and Sponsored Film Festival, BISFA, 26 D'Arblay Street, London W1V 3FH. (*Annual presentation of awards to best sponsored documentaries produced in Britain – June.*)

Bristol Animation Festival, 41B Hornsey Lane Gardens, London N6 5NY, U.K. (*Retrospectives, new animated films, exhibitions seminars – October.*)

Brussels International Festival of Fantasy and Science Fiction Films, 144 avenue de la Reine, B–1210 Brussels, Belgium. (*Dedicated to the gruesome and outlandish – March.*)

Cairo International Film Festival, 17 Kasr El Nil Street, Cairo, Egypt. Tel: 3923562/3923962. Telex: 21781. Fax: 3938979. (*Non-competitive, aimed at showing major international films not usually available at local cinemas. There is also a Children's film festival in Cairo – December.*)

Canadian Film Celebration, PO Box 2100, Station "M" (No. 300), Calgary, Alberta T2P 2M5, Canada. Tel: (403) 268 1370. Fax: (403) 233 8327. Telex: 038 27873. (*Exclusively for Canadian films, giving the public the chance to see and participate behind the scenes – March.*)

Cherbourg, Festival de Cinéma Franco-Britannique, Association Travelling, 1 rue

---

Twentieth Wellington Film Festival
Twenty-Third Auckland International Film Festival

July 1991

Box 9544, Te Aro Wellington, Fax 64 4 801 7304, Phone 64 4 850 162
Courier address, 1st floor, 30 Courtenay Place, Wellington, New Zealand

Raymond Rajaonarivelo, from Madagascar, presenting his film *Tabataba* at the Uppsala Festival

du Fourdray, 50100 Cherbourg, France. (*Charming and enthusiastic small festival focusing on British film – October.*)
Chicago International Film Festival, 415 North Dearborn, Chicago, Illinois 60610, U.S.A. Telex: 936086. (*Oldest competitive event in the States – October.*)
Cine Espoo, PO Box 96, SF–02101 Espoo, Finland. Tel: (0) 446 599. Fax: (0) 446 458. (*New, partly competitive festival focusing on the Baltic and related countries – August.*)
Cleveland International Film Festival, 6200 SOM Center Road C20, Cleveland, Ohio 44139, U.S.A. Telex: 980131. (*Round-up of new and classic films from all major countries – April.*)
Cork Film Festival, 38 MacCurtain Street, Cork, Ireland. (*Annual competitive, for documentaries, animation, art films, fiction and sponsored shorts – October.*)
Cracow, Festival Bureau, Pl. Zwyciestwa 9, PO Box 127, 00–950 Warsaw, Poland. (*Poland's only international film festival and respected short film showcase – June.*)
Dance on Camera, Dance Films Association Inc., 241 East 34th Street, New York, NY 10016, U.S.A. (*16mm and video films on various aspects of dancing. Competitive – January.*)
Dublin Film Festival, 1 Suffolk Street, Dublin 2, Eire. Tel: (001) 792937/792939. (*Amicable Irish festival focusing on world cinema with special emphasis on Irish film – October–November.*)
Europa Cinema, Via Giulia 66, 00186 Roma, Italy. (*Successor to the Rimini festival, concentrating on European product, now down near the heel of Italy at Bari – September.*)
Fantasporto, Porto Film Festival, Rua Diogo Brandão, 87, Porto 4000, Portugal. Tel: (3512) 320 759. Fax: (3512) 383 679. (*Competitive festival for science fiction and fantasy films – February 8–17.*)
Festival du Film Strasbourg, L'Institut International des Droits de l'Homme, 1 quai Lezay-Marnesia, 67000 Strasbourg, France. (*Concentrates on European films with a humane slant. Competitive – March.*)
European Environmental Film Festival, 55 rue de Varenne, 75341 Paris Cedex 7. Telex: 201220. (*Films and discussions about environmental issues – April.*)
Festival dei Popoli, Friedensallee 7, D–2000 Hamburg 50, F.R.G. (*Documentaries on social issues, films on history etc., in part competitive – November–December.*)
Festival International de Créteil et du Val de Marne, Maison des Arts, Place Salvador Allende, 94000 Créteil, France. Tel: (1) 4980 9050. Fax: (1) 4399 0410. (*Features, shorts, animated films all made by women, annual spotlight on an actress – April.*)
Festival International du Film de Comédie, Place de la Gare 5, Ch–1800 Vevey, Switzerland. Tel: (021) 921 8282. Fax: (021) 921 1065. (*Screenings of new and old films, as long as they are amusing – August.*)
Festival of Films and Photographs, No.

20, 19th Alley, Gandhi Ave., Tehran, Iran. Tel: 762 280. (*November.*)
Festival International du Film Nature, WWF-Genève, CP28, CH–1212 Grand-Lancy, Switzerland. (*Films on 16mm and Super 8, devoted to nature and the environment – November.*)
Festival International du Film sur l'Ecologie et l'Environment, AFIFEE, Domaine de Grammont, route de Mauguio, 3400 Montpellier, France. (*Films on ecology and natural resources – April.*)
Festival du Cinéma International en Abitibi-Témscamingue, 215 Avenue Mercier, Rouyn-Noranda, Québec J9X 5WB, Canada. Tel: (819) 762 6212. Fax: (819) 762 6762. (*Competitive for features and shorts held in northwestern Québec – October–November.*)
Festival Internacional de Cinema de Animacão ('Cinanima'), rue 62, No. 251–1/ Apart. 43, P–4500 Espinho. (*Animation.*)
Festival of Three Continents, c/o Oxfam Wereldwinkel, Gelmuntstraat 8, 8000 Bruges, Belgium. (*Small but dedicated Third World specialist event – March.*)
FestRio, 362 rua Paissandu, 22210 Laranjeiras, Rio de Janeiro, Brazil. (*Huge Latin American event covering film, TV, and video – November.*)
Figueira da Foz, rua Luis de Cameos 106, 2600 Vila Franca de Zira, Portugal. (*Competitive festival on the Portuguese coast – September.*)
Filmfest DC, PO Box 21396, Washington DC 20009, U.S.A. Tel: (202) 727 2396. Telex: 440 732. Fax: (202) 347 7342. (*Improving non-competitive American event, which focuses on innovative films and individual countries – April.*)
Florence Film Festival, c/o Assessorarto alla Cultura, Comune di Firenze, Diapartimento Arti Visive, Via Sant'Egidio 21, 50122 Florence, Italy. (*Review of independent cinema – features only – May–June.*)
Gay and Lesbian Film Festival, National Film Theatre, South Bank, London SE1 8XT. Tel: (71) 928 3535. Fax: (71) 633 9323. (*Films made by, or about, gays and lesbians – March.*)
Giffoni Film Festival, Piazza Umberto 1, 84095 Giffoni Valle Piana (Salerno), Italy. Tel: (89) 868544. Telex: 721585. (*Annual survey of films for youths and children – July–August.*)
Gijón, Cerinterfilm, Paseo de Begoña, 24 entlo, Gijón, Asturias, Spain. Tel: (85) 343 739. Fax: (85) 354152. Telex: 87443 FICG E. (*Concentrates on films for young people, with competitive and non-competitive sections – July.*)
Greek Film Festival (Thessaloniki), Valaonitou 9, Athens 106 71, Greece. Tel: 364 2129. Fax: 364 6544. (*30th anniversary of event. Complete panorama of new Greek films – October.*)
Havana International Film Festival, ICAIC, Calle 23 No. 1155, Plaza de la Revolucion, Habana 4, Cuba. Tel: 3 4400/ 4711. Telex: 511 419 ICAIC. (*Excellent, immense Latin American festival with many celebrities on hand – December.*)
Hawaii International Film Festival, 1777 East-West Road, Honolulu, Hawaii 96848, U.S.A. Telex: 989171. Fax: (808) 944 7970. (*Aims to bring East and West together through film; all screenings free – November–December.*)
Hiroshima Animation Festival, 1–1 Nakajima-cho, Naka-hu, Hiroshima 730, Japan. (*Competitive event for animation – August 8–13, 1990.*)
Holland Animation Film Festival, Hoogt 4, 3512 GW Utrecht, Holland. (*Unique biannual competitive survey of applied animation, with 1989 focus on Japan as well as computer animation.*)
Humboldt Film Festival, Humboldt State University (Theatre Arts), Arcata, California 95521. (*For student and independent films under 60 minutes, and on 16mm – May.*)
Iberoamerican Film Festival, Hotel Tartessos, Huelva, Spain. Tel: (55) 245

611. Fax: (55) 250 617. (*Survey of films from Latin America and the Spanish peninsula – December.*)
Indonesian Film Festival, National Film Council, Jalan Merdeka Barat no. 9, Jakarta, Indonesia. (*Colourful annual survey of Indonesian cinema – November.*)
International Children's Film Festival, Communal Cinema Oulu, Rantakatu 30, SF–90120 Oulu, Finland. (*Non-competitive annual event covering children's films, with retrospectives – November.*)
International Festival of Films for Children and Young Adults, Farhang Cinema, Dr. Shariati Ave., Gholhak, Tehran 19139, Iran. Tel: 265 086. Fax: 678 155. (*November.*)
International Filmwochenende Würzburg, Filminitiative Würzberg, Gosbersteige 2, D–8700 Würzburg, F.R.G. Telex: 680070. (*Non-competitive event screening some 20–25 features, emphasis on dialogue between film-makers and audience – January.*)
Internationales Kinderfilmfestival im Frankfurt am Main, Kinder- und Jugendfilmzentrum in der Bundesrepublik Deutschland, Kuppelstein 34, D–5630 Remscheid 1, F.R.G. Tel: (2191) 794 233. Fax: (2191) 71810. (*New films for, or featuring, children, judged by children and professionals. Plenty for parents too – September.*)
International Roshd (Educational) Film Festival, No. 8, Semnan Alley, Bahar Ave., Tehran, Iran. Tel: 762 280. (*November.*)
International Film and TV Festival of New York, 5 West 37th Street, New York, NY 10018, U.S.A. (*Annual competitive survey of films and videotape productions, TV programmes, industrial and educational productions, TV and cinema commercials – November.*)
International Film School Festival, Münchner Filmwochen GmbH, Türkenstrasse 93, D–8000 Munich 40, Federal Republic of Germany. (*Highly regarded event that's a kind of 'Junior Championships' for film school students and graduates – November.*)
Jerusalem Film Festival, PO Box 8561, Jerusalem 91083, Israel. (*Broad spread of new films from throughout the world, retrospectives – June.*)
Junior London Film Festival, National Film Theatre, South Bank, London, SE1 8XT. Tel: (71) 928 3535. Fax: (71) 633 9323. (*Prior to the London Film Festival, a half-term treat for children of all ages – October.*)
Kaleidoscope, PO Box 2260, S–103 16 Stockholm, Sweden. (*International Immigrant Film Festival, competitive – April.*)
Karlovy Vary, Ceskoslovensky Film, Jindriska 34, 110 00 Praha 1, Czechoslovakia. Tel: 236 5385–9. Telex: 122 259. (*Biannual, major competitive festival in Eastern Europe, emphasis on Czechoslovakian features – July.*)
Leipzig Festival, Chodowieckistr, 32, 1055 Berlin, G.D.R. Telex: 512455. (*Documentaries and animation. Competitive – November.*)
Lille International Festival of Short and Documentary Films, 26–34 rue Washington, 75008 Paris, France. (*Competitive for shorts, with additional panorama of recent French production in the field – March.*)
Miami Festival, Film Society of Miami, 7600 Red Road, Suite 307, Miami, Florida 33143, U.S.A. Tel: (305) 377 3456. Telex: 264047. (*Non-competitive, with emphasis on Hispanic cinema – February.*)
Midnight Sun Film Festival, Vainämöisenkatu 19A, SF–00100 Helsinki, Finland. Fax: (0) 413541. (*Long weekend for film lovers in the Midsummer beauty of Finland, and above the Arctic Circle! – June.*)
Mostra Internacionnais de Cinema & Video, NCV, Rua Eng. Ewbank Camera, 78 Bela Vista, CEP 90.420, Porto Alegre/ RS, Brazil. (*Films and videos from abroad as well as South American programmes – September.*)
Mostra Internacional de Cinema, Al.

Lorena 937 cj., 302–1424, São Paulo, Brazil. Telex: (11) 25043. (*Non-competitive panorama of best films of year, plus critics and audience awards – October.*)

New Orleans Film and Video Festival, PO Box 70556, New Orleans, LA 70172, U.S.A. Tel: (504) 581 3420. (*October/November.*)

New York International Home Video Market, Knowledge Industry Publications Inc., 701 Westchester Ave., White Plains, NY 10604, U.S.A. (*Showplace for video retailers, distributors, publishers, media buyers etc. – April.*)

Norwegian Short Film Festival, Storengveien 8b, N–1342 Jar, Norway. (*Local shorts in competition, plus selection of titles from other international festivals – held in Grimstad every June.*)

Österreichische Filmtage, Columbusgasse 2, A–110 Vienna, Austria. Tel: 604 0126. Fax: 602 0795. (*Annual survey of new Austrian features, documentaries, TV, avant-garde, and video productions – October.*)

Palm Springs International Film Festival, 401 South Pavilion Way, PO Box 1786, Palm Springs, CA 92263, U.S.A. Tel: (619) 322 8389. Fax: (619) 320 9834. (*Glamorous new festival spearheaded by Palm Springs' mayor Sonny Bono – January.*)

Piccadilly Film and Video Festival, 177 Piccadilly, London W1V 9LF, U.K. (*Growing festival focusing on off-beat, with stress on retrospectives – June.*)

Polish Film Festival, Piwna 22, PO Box Nr. 192, 80–831 Gdańsk, Poland. Telex: 0512153. (*15th edition of the festival focusing on Polish film – September.*)

Pula Festival, Festival jugoslavenskog igranog filma, Marka Laginje 5, 52000 Pula, Yugoslavia. (*Annual screening of all new Yugoslavian features – July.*)

Rencontres Internationales du Jeune Cinéma, 70 rue Faider, 1050 Brussels, Belgium. (*Accent on films for and by young people.*)

Restoration Festival, National Film Theatre, South Bank, London SE1 8XT. Tel: (71) 928 3535. Fax: (71) 633 9323. (*First of an annual, reciprocal event between the UCLA and National Film Theatre, a tribute to preservation and restoration of archive material – August.*)

Rivertown (Minneapolis/St. Paul) International Film Festival, University Film Society, Minnesota Film Center, 425 Ontario Street SE, Minneapolis, MN 55414. Tel: (612) 627 4431. (*Event built up over 26 years by the reliable Al Milgrom. Scores of unusual foreign films on display – April–May.*)

Rouen, Festival du Cinéma Nordique, 91 rue Crevier, 76000 Rouen, France. Tel: 35 98 28 46. Telex: 771444. (*Competitive festival of Nordic cinema, including retrospective and information sections – March.*)

San Juan Film Festival, Apartado 4543, San Juan, Puerto Rico 00905. Tel: (809) 721 5676. Telex: 383 9686. (*New festival*

WORLD FESTIVAL OF ANIMATED FILMS

ZAGREB '92
& ANIMARKET

41000 Zagreb, Nova ves 18, Yugoslavia
Phone: (041) 412–651 · Telex: 21790
Cable: FESTANIMA Zagreb · Fax: (041) 275–994

focusing on the film and video harvest of the Caribbean countries – October.)
Santa Barbara International Film Festival, 1216 State Street, Suite 201, Santa Barbara, CA 93101, U.S.A. Tel: (805) 963 4408. (*Non-competitive, usually focusing on a single country – March.*)
Seattle International Film Festival, 801 East Pine Street, Seattle, Washington 98122, U.S.A. (*Unusual Northwest Pacific coast event that has done a great deal to establish Dutch cinema in the States – May–June.*)
Settimana Cinematografica Internazionales di Verona, Via S. Giacomo Alla Pigna 6, 37121 Verona, Italy. Telex: 434339. (*Features, new and retrospective – June.*)
Short and Documentary Film Festival, Farhang Cinema, Dr. Shariati Ave., Gholhak, Tehran 19139, Iran. Tel: 265 086. Fax: 678 155. (*New Iranian event – July.*)
Singapore International Film Festival, 11 Keppel Hill, Singapore 0409. Telex: 38283. Fax: 2722069. (*Biannual non-competitive event showcasing international films – January.*)
Sitges Festival, Diputación 279, Barcelona 08007, Spain. Tel: (3) 317 3585/418 4858. (*Decades-old science fiction and fantasy film festival, competitive, usually attended by celebrities and directors, set in charming seaside town – October.*)
Solothurn Filmtage, Postfach 92, CH–4500 Solothurn, Switzerland. (*Screenings of all new Swiss films – January.*)
Taormina International Film Festival, Comitato 'Taormina Arts,' Palazzo Corvaja, Taormina, Sicily. Telex: (in Rome) 625673. (*Competitive and non-competitive event in Sicily with stress on films by new directors, plus retrospectives and discussions – July.*)
Tokyo International Film Festival, No. 3 Asano Building, 2–4–19 Ginza, Chuo-ku, Tokyo 104, Japan. Telex: 34548. Fax: 81–35636310. (*New mammoth event with competition and other sidebar events – September 27–October 6.*)

Torremolinos Film Festival, Avendia Carlota Alessandri 27, Aloha Torre 6, Torremolinos, Spain. Tel: (52) 374 292. Fax: (52) 376 826. (*New non-competitive festival dedicated to comedies, run by former head of the Benalmádena festival – December 28–January 5.*)
Troia Film Festival, 2901 Setúbal Codex, Portugal. Tel: (35165) 44121. Fax: (35165) 44123. (*Wide variety of categories in this competitive festival. Held in a Summer recreational area on the tip of a peninsula – June.*)
Umeå Film Festival, Box 43, S–901 02 Umeå, Sweden. Tel: (46) 90 140150. Telex: 540 84. Fax: (46) 90 132791. (*Busy festival featuring international panorama, films for children, and obscure films section – September.*)
USA Film Festival, PO Box 3105, Dallas, Texas 75275, U.S.A. (*Collection of new and old American movies – March.*)
Valencia: Mostra of Mediterranean Cinema, Plaza Arzobispo, 2 acc. B., Valencia 46003, Spain. Tel: (96) 332 1506. Fax: (96) 3315156. Telex: 63427. (*Major tributes for films made in and around the Mediterranean – October.*)
Viennale, Würzburggasse 30, A–1136, Vienna, Austria. Tel: (222) 8291 4515. Fax: (222) 8291 2200. (*Non-competitive festival for features – March.*)
Women in Cinema, International Festival of Films made by Women, Lavalle 1578 9 "B", Buenos Aires, Argentina. Tel: 467 318. Fax: (54 11) 12559. (*April.*)
Women in Film Festival, 6464 Sunset Blvd., Suite 600, Los Angeles, California 90028, U.S.A. (*Dedicated to the improvement of women's image in film and TV. Various categories – October.*)
Zagreb Animation, Zagreb Film, Nova ves 18, 41000 Zagreb, Yugoslavia. Telex: 21790. (*Competitive festival in hospitable surroundings, concurrent market for animated films – June.*)

THE HOUSTON INTERNATIONAL FILM FESTIVAL

THE 24TH ANNUAL FESTIVAL OF THE AMERICAS

WORLDFEST 91! AMERICA'S MOST IMPORTANT FESTIVAL!
APRIL 19-28, 1991

Houston Worldfest 91 offers you the largest film and video competition in the world in terms of entries. We present a complete film market with program book, plus competition and awards in six major categories: features, shorts, documentary, TV commercials, experimental/independent and TV production. No other festival or film market provides you so much!

FOR THE COMPLETE ENTRY & INFORMATION KIT, PLUS POSTER, CONTACT:
J. HUNTER TODD, CHAIRMAN & FOUNDER — THE HOUSTON INTERNATIONAL FILM FESTIVAL, P.O. BOX 56566 HOUSTON, TEXAS 77256 USA TELEPHONE (713) 965-9955 FAX: (713) 965-9960 TELEX: 317-876 (WORLDFEST-HOU)

THE LONDON
•INTERNATIONAL•
FILM SCHOOL

• Training film makers for over 30 years •
• Graduates now working worldwide •
• Located in Covent Garden in the heart of London •
• Recognised by A.C.T.T. •
• 16mm documentary & 35mm studio filming •
• Two year Diploma course in film making
commences three times a year: January, April, September •

London International Film School, Department IG10, 24 Shelton Street, London WC2H 9HP
071-836 0826

FILM SCHOOLS

AUSTRALIA
Australian Film, Television and Radio School, PO Box 126, North Ryde, NSW 2113. The Australian national centre for professional training in film, television and radio production. The School conducts one and three year full-time courses training in both film and video, a six-month full-time commercial radio course, and a nation-wide program of specialist short and part-time courses through its Industry Program. The three-year Bachelor of Arts course and one-year extension courses offer specialisations in scriptwriting, producing, directing, sound, editing, cinematography and production design. There are no specific educational requirements for entry. Places are limited and applicants are judged on previous experience, commitment and attitude. Applications close at end June for the following year's full-time courses. For course details, contact the Student Centre on 02 805 6444.

AUSTRIA
Hochschule für Musik und angewandte Kunst, Abteilung für Film und Fernsehen, Metternichgasse 12, A-1030 Vienna. Director: Prof. Mag. Robert Schöfer.

BELGIUM
Koninklijke Academie voor Schone Kunsten – Gent, Academiestraat 2, B-9000 Gent. Director: Pierre Vlerick. Animation department: Director: Raoul Servais assisted by Jean Marie Demever, Dirk de Paepe, Rembrand Hoste as workshop teachers. The department focuses on the animated cartoon technique, although other animation techniques, such as puppet, pixillation and cut-out animation, are also taught.

Institut National des Arts du Spectacle et Techniques de diffusion (I.N.S.A.S.), Rue Thérésienne, 8 à 1000 Bruxelles-Belgium. Director: Raymond Ravar. 215 students and 120 staff. Tel: 02/511.92.86. Fax: 02/511.02.79. Four year course leading to a degree, concerned with all aspects of film/radio/television production, or three-year course giving more specialised instruction in photography, sound, writing or acting.

Institut des Arts de Diffusion, (I.A.D.), Rue des Wallons No. 77, B 1348 Louvain-la Neuve, Belgium. Chairman: Jean-Marie Delmée. 250 students and 100 staff. Four-year course in direction, production in film, television, radio and the theatre. Three-year course in photography, sound, editing and writing. Films made by students include features, documentaries and animated shorts.

Hoger Rijksinstituut voor Tonell en Cultuurspreiding (RITCS), 8, Theresiënstraat, 1000 Brussels. Dutch four-year course in film/radio/television/theatre.

BRAZIL
Escola Superior de Cinema, Faculdade São Paulo.

Escola Superior de Cinema, Pontificia Universidade Catolica, Av. Brasil 2033, Belo Horizonte, Minas Gerais.

Instituto de Arte e Communicação Social, Universidade Federal Fluminense, Rua Professor Lara Villela 126, 24.210 – Niterói, Rio de Janeiro.

CANADA
Sheridan College of Applied Arts & Technology, School of Visual Arts, Trafalgar Road, Oakville, Ontario L6H 2L1. Dean: Scott Turner. This 14-week Summer diploma programme which runs from May until August is equivalent to one college academic year, and is primarily a foundation devoted to an understanding and application of basic production techniques. Studies examine both contemporary and traditional approaches to animation. Applicants should have two years' post-secondary art school study or equivalent. Competence in English is also required.

York University, Faculty of Fine Arts, Film & Video Department, 4700 Keele Street, North York, Ontario M3J 1P3. Offers studies in Film, Video, Screenwriting, and Theory over a 4-year Honours BA of BFA course. 2-year MFA.

Simon Fraser University, School for the Contemporary Arts, Burnaby, B.C., Canada V5A 1S6. Tel: (604) 291 3363. Fax: (604) 291 3039. The film programme consists of a blend of

16mm film and video productions, theory and analysis courses within an interdisciplinary context allowing contact with students in theatre, music and the visual arts. The programme focuses on the development of skills valuable to independent film-makers and appropriate to cinematic expression as an art form. Potential students can pursue either an interdisciplinary Fine and Performing Arts major programme with a concentration in film or a Film major programme with lead to a Batchelor of Arts degree. In addition, students may pursue a M.F.A. interdisciplinary degree specialising in an aspect of Film or Video production.
Emily Carr College of Art & Design, 1399 Johnstone St., Vancouver, BC V6H 3R9. Animation, Video.
Univ of British Columbia, Film & T.V. Studies Programme, Dept., of Theatre, Vancouver, BC V6T 1W5. Film & TV Advanced and Comprehensive.
University of Alberta, Television & Film Institute, Box 90, Sub 11, U of A Edmonton, Alberta T6G 2EO. Tel: (403) 437–5171. During 1990 the Institute will conduct a series of seminars concentrating on writing for film and TV. Past instructors have included: Gerry Davis, Syd Field and Linda Seger. Courses are designed for professionals or those aspiring to careers in the film industry. Top students are selected for a programme using computers to link them with top screenwriters, worldwide. As a companion programme, the TFI operates a computer bulletin board dedicated to both amateur and professional screen and TV writers.
Univ of Regina, Regina, Sask S4S 0A2. Film and Video.
Univ of Manitoba, 447 University College, Winnipeg, Man R3T 2N2. Basic film-making.
Humber College, 205 Humber College Blvd, Rexdale, Ont M9W 5L7. Film, TV & A/V.
Queen's University, 160 Stuart St, Kingston, Ont K7L 3N6. Film Production.
Ryerson Polytechnical Institute, 50 Gould St, Toronto, Ont M5B 1E8. Film and TV advanced and comprehensive.
Seneca College, 1750 Finch, E Toronto, Ont M2J 2X5. TV & Video.
Wilfrid Laurier University, Waterloo, Ont N2L 3C5. Production courses.
University of Windsor, Windsor, Ont N9B 3P4. Film, Radio, TV.
Concordia University, Production & Animation 1395 Dorchester Blvd W, Montréal, Qué H3G 2M5. Dept. of Cinema and Photography.
Niagara College, Welland Campus, PO Box 1005, Welland, Ont L3B 5S2. Film, TV & Radio.

CZECHOSLOVAKIA
Faculty of Film and Television (FAMU), Academy of Arts, Smentanovo nábřeži 2, Prague 1. Regular day-study courses in film and TV directing, film and TV photography, artistic photography, film and TV documentaries, film and TV film editing. Foreign nationals may apply through Ministerstvo školstvi, zahraniční odbor, Kármelitská 7, Prague 1. Before starting they must take a year's course in the Czech language.

DENMARK
Danish Film School, Danish Film Institute, Store Søndervoldstr., DK-1419 Copenhagen K.

EGYPT
Egyptian Film Institute, City of Arts, Pyramids, Giza. Established 1959. Higher Studies. Sections devoted to Direction, Production, Editing and Photography. Dean: Dr. Shawki Ali Mohamed.

FINLAND
Taideteollinen korkeakoulu, elokuvataiteen laitos, University of Industrial Arts, Department of Cinema and TV, Pursimiehenkatu 29–31, SF-00150 Helsinki. Chief Instructors: Juha Rosma, Raimo Paananen, Tove Idström. Approximately 60 students (14 per year), 6 full-time and 25 part-time staff. Qualifications for admission: matriculation exam and the admission course of one week. Foreign students admitted with knowledge of Finnish. Average duration of studies: five years. Main subjects: directing, camerawork, screenwriting, sound, editing, documentary, producing. Production on 16 and 35mm films plus videotape. Production facilities: professional film equipment and TV studio and photographic equipment.

FRANCE
Fondation Européenne des Métiers de L'Image et du Son (FEMIS), Palais de Tokyo, 2 rue de la Manutention, 75116 Paris. Chairman: Jean-Claude Carrière. Director: Jack Gajos.
Conservatoire Libre du Cinéma Français (C.L.C.F.), 16 rue de Delta, 75009 Paris.

Institut Supérieur de Cinéma, Radio et Télévision (I.S.C.R.T.), 65 Bd. Brune, 75014 Paris.

GERMANY
Deutsche Film- und Fernsehakademie Berlin GmbH, DFFB, Pommernallee 1, 1000 Berlin 19. Director: Prof. Dr. Thomas Koebner. Four year course dealing with theories of film-making, film-history, and all aspects of practical film and television production; script-writing, direction, camerawork, editing and special effects. Students make films and videos and are encouraged to gain experience in as wide a variety of techniques as possible.

Hochschule für Fernsehen und Film, Frankenthaler Strasse 23, D-8000 München 90. President: Prof. Dr. Helmut Oeller. Approx. 160 students, 50 staff. Four-year course providing instruction in the theory and practice of film and television. Facilities provide for work in 16 and 35mm as well as video equipment. Studies are free. Two-step admission process; ask for details in January each year. Studies begin each Autumn.

Hochschule für Film und Fernsehen der Deutschen Demokratischen Republik, "Konrad Wolf," Karl-Marx-Strasse 27, 1590 Potsdam-Babelsberg. Rector: Prof. Dr. sc. Lothar Bisky.

HUNGARY
Szinház-es Filmmüvészeti Föisskola, Vas u. 2/c, 1088 Budapest. Rector: Dr. Jenö Simó. General Secretary: László Vadász.

INDIA
Film and Television Institute of India, Law College Road, Poona 411 004. Director: K.G. Varma. 87 students in Film wing. Experienced teaching staff. The Institute conducts three-year courses in (1) Film Direction, (2) Motion Picture Photography, (3) Sound Recording and Sound Engineering, (4) Film Editing (two year duration). All four courses include one year integrated training.

Film and Television Institute of Tamil Nadu, Department of Information and Public Relations, Government of Tamil Nadu, Madras, Adyar, Madras-600 020.

ISRAEL
Department of Film and Television, Tel Aviv University, Tel Aviv. Offers a two track curriculum, one with emphasis on film and TV production, the other with film theory.

ITALY
Centro Sperimentale di Cinematografia (C.S.C.), Via Tuscolana 1524, Rome. Director: Ernesto G. Laura.

Instituto di Storia del Cinema e dello Spettacolo, Universitá di Torino Facoltá di Magistero, Via Sant'Ottavio 20, 10124 Torino. Comprises courses in the history and appreciation of cinema.

JAPAN
Nihon University College of Art, Asahigaoka 2-42, Nerimaku, Tokyo, 176. Head of Film Department: Professor Toru Otake.

NETHERLANDS
Nederlandse Film- en Televisie Academie, De Lairessestraat 142, 1075 HL Amsterdam. Managing Director: Henk Petiet. 150 students, 30 staff. Four years.

POLAND
Pańswowa Wysza Szkola Filmowa, Telwizyjna e Teatralna, im Leona Schillera, ul. Targowa 61/63, 90 323 Lódz.

ROMANIA
Institutul de Artă Teatrală şi Cinematografică "I.L. Caragiale", str. Matei Voievod nr. 75–77 sect. 2 cod 73226, Bucharest. Dean: Professor Dr. Ileana Berlogea.

SPAIN
University of Valladolid, Cátedra de Historia y Estética de la Cinematografica, Palacio de Sta. Cruz, Valladolid. Director: Sr. Dr. Francisco Javier de la Plaza. Diploma Course on Film Theory, History, and Criticism.

SWEDEN
Dramatiska Institutet (College of Theatre, Film, Radio and Television), Borgvägen, Box 27090, S-102 51 Stockholm. Head of School: Janos Hersko. Formed in 1970, the Institute is intended to provide instruction in production techniques for theatre, film, radio and television. A three year course (Theatre, Film and T.V.); a two year course (Radio); and a one year course providing insight into the various media and their production methods; and continuing and advanced education in the form of extension courses. The Institute is equipped with film and TV studios, 14 editing rooms for 8, 16 and 35mm, sound mixing studios and portable video equipment.

Department of Theatre and Cinema Arts, University of Stockholm, Filmhuset, Borgvägen 1-5, Box 27062, S-102 51 Stockholm. Stockholm University is the only university in Sweden offering both Theatre and Cinema. Tuition in Cinema Arts is provided for between 300-350 students, and the curriculum offers courses in the history of the cinema, film analysis and mass media studies.

TURKEY

Sinema-TV Enstitüsü Kişlaönü, Beşiktas, Istanbul. Director: Sam Sekeroğlu. Film and TV school offering applied and theoretical training.

U.K.

National Film and Television School, Station Road, Beaconsfield, Bucks. HP90 1LG. Tel: (0494) 671234. Fax: (0494) 674042. Director: Colin Young. Approximately 100 students. 15 full-time teaching staff complemented by a large number and variety of part-time tutors, all experienced professionals. Three year full-time course with the emphasis on creative production for the cinema and television, through practice and instruction, designed to equip graduates for employment in the industry. Admission is through open competition. The studios are fully equipped for 16mm films with some 35mm, and professional video facilities. The School operates a positive equal opportunities policy.

London International Film School, 24 Shelton Street, London WC2H 9HP. Principal: Martin M. Amstell. Two year Diploma Course to professional level recognised by the British Film Technicians' Union – A.C.T.T. On average, half each term is devoted to film production and half to practical and theoretical tuition. The School has two cinemas, two shooting stages with professional lighting equipment, two rehearsal stages and fifteen cutting rooms. Comprehensively equipped departments use Bolex, Arriflex and Panavision cameras, Nagra, Westrex and Perfectone recorders, Steenbeck and Moviola editing tables and U-matic Portapacks and editing suites. Productions are on 16mm and 35mm film and video tape. Tuition is by permanent and visiting professionals. Entrance requirements: a degree or an art or technical diploma. Less qualifications accepted in cases of special ability or experience. All applicants must submit examples of their work and be proficient in English. New courses start three times a year.

Middlesex Polytechnic, Faculty of Art and Design, Cat Hill, Barnet, Herts EN4 8HT. Tel: (081) 368 1299. Course Leader: David Furnham. MA in Video. This one year course (48 weeks, full-time) offers graduate students who already have considerable experience in low-band video production the opportunity to think creatively and critically about video production, to acquire detailed knowledge of professional practice in the television and video industries, to work as part of a team to produce a video tape of fully professional standard for a stated context. It also allows each student to produce, as an individual project, a fully developed script. This course replaces the previous Post-graduate Diploma.

Polytechnic of Central London, School of Communication, 18/22 Riding House Street, London W1P 7PD. MA in Film and Television Studies: advanced level part-time course (evenings and study weekends) concerned with theoretical aspects of film and TV. Modular credit and accumulation scheme, with exemption for work previously done. Postgraduate Diploma normally awarded after two years (70 credits), MA after three years (120 credits). Modules offered: Authorship, Structuralism, Realism and Anti-Realism, the Film and TV Audience, Problems of Method, Hollywood, British Cinema History, Psychoanalysis, Third World Cinema, Issues in British Film Culture, Public Service Broadcasting, TV Genres and Gender, the Documentary Tradition, British TV Drama, Soviet Cinema, Production Studies. No practical component. Course leader: Dr. Robert E. Peck.

Royal College of Art, Department of Film, Queen's Gate, London SW7. 40 students. Two-year post-graduate course.

Bournemouth and Poole College of Art, Department of Photography, Film and Television, Wallisdown Road, Poole, Dorset BH12 5HH. B/Tec Higher National Diploma in Photography, Film & Television. Qualifications for admission are minimum age 18, with five G.C.S.E. passes, two of which must be at 'A' level, or appropriate B/Tec Diploma or satisfactory completion of a foundation course or approved commercial/industrial experience.

Bristol University, Department of Drama, Radio, Film and Television Studies, 29 Park Row, Bristol BS1 5LT. Director of Film Studies: John Adams. Undergraduate courses leading to BA in practical criticism, history, theory and practice of film and TV. Postgraduate: higher degree by dissertation leading to M.Litt and Ph.D.; Certification in Radio, Film and Television, predominantly practical, provides an introduction to a wide range of technical skills, followed by production of films and TV programmes in the Department's studio and on location. Normally one year. Film production entirely on 16mm; video production on VHS and U-matic; 4 colour-camera Studio; rostrum facilities.

Derbyshire College of Higher Education, Kedleston Road, Derby DE3 1GB. Course Leader: John Fullerton. Linked Postgraduate Diploma and MA in Film Studies. The PgDip is a two year course and the MA a one year dissertation. Screening facilities on city-centre site at the Metro Cinema, Derby's regional film theatre. Supported by the work of the Centre for the Study of Early Film plus range of materials in Faculty Library.

University of East Anglia, School of English and American Studies, Norwich NR4 7TJ. Offers Film as a BA Hons Major in combination with English Studies, and as a BA Hons Minor in combination with other Arts subjects: also offers a taught MA in Film Studies, with or without a new option in Film Archive work based on collaboration with the East Anglian Film Archive. The MA is awarded 50% on individual dissertation. Students are also accepted for the research degrees of M.Phil and Ph.D. Staff: Charles Barr, Thomas Elsaesser, Andrew Higson (Archive work: David Cleveland).

Newport Film School, Faculty of Art and Design, Gwent College of Higher Education, Clarence Place, Newport, Gwent NP9 0UW. Film and Television Practice – A two-year H.N.D. practical course in film and video production with an opportunity to specialise in either live action, 2D or 3D animation techniques. Course director: Henry Lutman. Senior lecturers: Peter Turner and Cyril Moorhead.

Harrow College of Higher Education, Northwick Park, Harrow HA1 3TP. Three year full- time BA Hons in Photography, Film and Video. The course offers an integrated approach, combining theory and practice and encouraging students to explore a range of media. Years one and two teach basic skills in photography film (16mm and S8), video (Umatic and VHS), a-v and computer animation in the context of a wide-ranging core of theoretical studies. Year three students work on a self-initiated project which may be in any – or a combination of – media and includes a long contextual study.

University of Stirling, Film and Media Studies, Stirling FK9 4LA. Head of Department: Professor P.R. Schlesinger. Undergraduate Film and Media Studies is designed at Stirling to give a grounding in the theory and criticism of film, television, radio and the press together with some practical experience. Also offers Postgraduate studies in the same areas.

West Surrey College of Art and Design, Falkner Road, Farnham, Surrey GU9 7DS. CNAA BA (Hons) in Photography. 3 years full time. Intake is 35. Course leader Peter Hall. CNAA BA (Hons) in Animation. 3 years full time. Course accredited by ACTT. Intake is 25. Course leader Roger Noake. CNAA BA (Hons) in Film & Video. 3 years full time. Course accredited by ACTT. Intake is 25. Course leader Claire Mussell. Entry requirements for each course in accordance with CNAA regulations.

URUGUAY

Escuela de Cinematografia, 18 de Julio 1265 p. 2, Montevideo. Director: Juan José Ravaioli.

U.S.A.

The International Film Workshops, Rockport, ME 04856. Summer film workshops on camera-work, lighting, editing, directing etc. with some of the industry's leading artists and craftsmen.

Brooks Institute of Photography, 801 Alston Road, Santa Barbara, California 93108. Founded in October, 1945 by Ernest H. Brooks, Brooks Institute in Santa Barbara has become one of the leading schools of its kind in the world, training aspiring professional photographers and cinematographers to fill roles in a growing, diversifying industry.

U.S.S.R.

Vsesoyuzni Gosudarstvenni Institut Kinematografi (VGIK) (All-Union State Institute of Cinematography), ulitsa Vilgelma Pika 3, Moscow 129226. Director: Vitali Nikolayevich Zzhdan. No. of students: 1,500. No. of instructors: 250. Length of courses: actors, economists – 4 years; cameraman – 4 years; writers, directors – 5 years; designers – 6 years. Specialisation is always taken into account during training. The various disciplines taught can be divided into three groups; socio-economic (e.g. philosophy – 140 hours), general knowledge (e.g. history of Fine Arts – 160 hours – history of theatre. Soviet and foreign literature), and specialist instruction (e.g. for cameramen; 320 hours on operating, 110 on lighting). Practical work undertaken on all courses. The Institute has a training studio (with four stages totalling 1,000 sq. metres and 100 cameras of various types), an information department, its own textbooks, and teaching manuals, and also auxiliary instruction quarters for Soviet cinema, foreign cinema operating, direction, etc.

YUGOSLAVIA
Fakultet dramškíh umetnosti (pozorišta, filma, radija i televizije), Ho Si Minova 20, 11070 Beograd. Vladan Slijepčević. Four-year course equivalent to undergraduate level; specialisation in direction, production, photography, dramaturgy, acting or editing (as well as a fine *animation* and *special effects* division). Students make films on 8 and 16mm, and a final diploma film on 35mm.

FILM ARCHIVES

ALBANIA
Arkivi Shtetöror i Filmit i Republikes Populor Socialiste të Shquipërisë, Rruga Alexandre Moisiu Nr-76, Tirana. Tel: 77–94/51-6. Director: Abaz Hoxha. Stock: 5,000 film titles, 10,000 film stills, 1,025 posters.

ALGERIA
Cinémathèque Algerienne, rue Larbi-Ben-M'Hidi, Algiers. Tel: 638301. Telex: 67437. Director: Boudjemaa Kareche. Stock: 15,000 film titles, 30,000 film stills, 3,000 posters.

ARGENTINA
Cinemateca Argentina, Corrientes 2092, 2nd floor, 1045 Buenos Aires. Tel: (54–1) 953 3755/953 7163. Fax: (54–1)3110562. Telex: 24569 Sicvil Ar. Established in 1949. Stock: 11,000 film titles, 5,500 books, collection of film periodicals, 330,000 film stills, 6,000 film posters. The collection of micro-filmed clippings hold 30,000 files on individual films, 15,000 on foreign film personalities, 5,000 on Argentine personalities. The library is open to researchers and students. The Cinemateca operates two film theatres with daily screenings.

AUSTRALIA
National Film and Sound Archive, McCoy Circuit, Acton, Canberra A.C.T. 2601. Tel: (61–6) 2671711. Telex: AA 61930. Director: Graham Gilmour. Deputy Director: Ray Edmondson. Stock: 52,000 film and video titles, 315,000 stills, 8,500 scripts, 56,000 posters, 400,000 publicity items, 2,500 memorabilia items. Research and viewing facilities available by appointment.
State Film Archives, Library and Information Service of Western Australia. Alexander Library Building, Perth Cultural Centre, Perth, WA 6,000. Tel: 427 3303. Film Archivist: Robin Faulkner. Stock: 1,800 film titles.

AUSTRIA
Österreichisches Filmarchiv, A–1010 Vienna, Rauhensteingasse 5, Film stores and theatre: Laxenburg, Altes Schloss. Tel: 5129936. Fax: 513 5330. President: Prof. Dr. Alfred Lehr. Director: Dr. Walter Fritz. Stock: 37,224 titles, 8,790 books, 1,006 periodicals, 221,000 film stills, 5,586 posters. Regular Summer exhibitions and retrospectives at Laxenburg, Altes Schloss.
***Österreichisches Filmmuseum**, A–1010 Vienna, Augustinerstr. 1, Tel: 533 70 54–0. Fax: 533 70 56 25. Telex: 111768 fma. Directors: Peter Konlechner and Prof. Peter Kubelka. Stock: app. 10,000 film titles, and an extensive library. A non-profit institution, the Museum now has 15,000 members and holds daily

Theo Angelopoulos visiting the new vaults at the Swiss Cinémathèque in April 1990, and seen here with curator Freddy Buache

screenings in its invisible cinema at the Albertina Gallery. The shows have created a hungry audience for cinema in spite of the unimaginative programming of Vienna's commercial cinemas. "One of the most active cinémathèques in Europe" (Der Spiegel).

BELGIUM
*Cinémathèque Royale, 23 rue Ravenstein, 1000 Brussels. Tel: 5134155. Telex: 23022. Stock: more than 45,000 film titles, 25,000 books, 200,000 film stills and a large collection of posters. Publishes useful catalogues and screens three sound and two silent films daily. A preserving archive, where films can only be consulted for research purposes.

BOLIVIA
Cinemateca Boliviana, Pichincha esq. Indaburo, s/n-Casilla 20271-La Paz. Tel: 325346. Director: Pedro Susz K. Stock: 5,850 film titles, 850 books, 8,200 film stills, 1,900 posters, 8,000 clippings. The Cinemateca operates one film theatre with daily screenings at 16.00 and 19.30 hours.

BRAZIL
Cinemateca Brasileira, Caixa Postal 12900, 04092 São Paulo. Tel: 5774448. Telex: 1153714. Director: Maria Rita Galvão. Stock: 30,000 film titles, 33,220 photos, 3,610 posters. Mainly concerned with Brazilian films, this archive has laboratory facilities to preserve and restore films, and all the nitrate in the country is deposited here.
Cinemateca do Museu de Arte Moderna, Caixa Postal 44, CEP 20021, Rio de Janeiro, RJ. Tel: (021) 2102188. Telex: 21-22084 FTVR BR. Director: João Luiz Vieira. Stock: 10,000 film titles, 4,500 books, 2,570 periodicals, 75,000 film stills, 4,800 posters. Daily screenings are held in the archive's 185 seat theatre. The archive publishes a monthly bulletin, restores and preserves its collections and provides facilities for researchers.
Bulgarska Nacionalna Filmoteka, ul. Gourko

36, 1000 Sofia. Tel: 802749. Director: Vladimir Ignatovski. Stock: 12,400 film titles, 6,360 books, 2,110 bound volumes of periodicals, 111,300 stills, 25,155 posters, 21,100 unpublished film scripts. The Filmoteka holds four regular screenings a day in its own cinema and organises film seasons and seminars in Sofia and the provinces as well as Bulgarian film weeks abroad.

CANADA
National Archives of Canada, Moving Image and Sound Archives, 395 Wellington Street, Ottawa, Ontario K1A 0N3. Tel: (613) 996 6009. Telex: 0533367. Director: Jana Vosikovska. Stock: 300,000 film, video and sound recording titles, 9,000 books, 1,060 periodicals, 600,000 stills, 7,000 posters. Title index of 500,000 films. Reference dossiers on 95,000 personalities, films and subjects. The collection concentrates on Canadian film and television production and oral history, but the Archives are building up an international collection and expanding facilities are available for researchers and students.
La Cinémathèque Québécoise., 335 boul. de Maisonneuve est, Montréal, Québec H2X 1K1. Tel: (514) 842 9763. Curator: Robert Daudelin. Stock: 23,000 film titles, 250,000 stills, 12,000 posters. The Cinémathèque specialises in preserving the work of animators and of Canadian film-makers and this collection is on show at thirteen screenings a week, together with other aspects of world cinema.
Conservatoire d'Art Cinématographique de Montréal, 1455 de Maisonneuve West, Montréal, Québec. Director: Serge Losique. Stock: 3,000 film titles, 1,000 books, 100 periodicals, 2,000 film stills.

CHILE
Cinemateca Chilena en al Exilio, Padre Xifré 3, oficin 111, Madrid 2, Spain. Director: Pedro Chaskel. Curator: Gaston Angelovici. The Cinemateca is continuing in exile the work of Chile's principal archive, the Cinemateca Universitaria. Member of the Union de Cinematecas de América Latina.

CHINA
Cinémathèque Chinoise, 25B rue Xin Wai, Beijing. Tel: 2014316. Telex: 22195. Director: Xu Zhuang. Stock: 21,000 films, 11,000 stills.

COLOMBIA
Fundacion Patrimonio Filmico Colombiana, Carrera 13, n° 13–24, piso 9°, Bogota. Tel: 281–5241. Exec. Director: Claudia Triana de Vargas. Curator: Jorge Nieto. Stock: 27,500 films and newsreels, 3,300 stills, 400 posters, 400 books, 280 periodicals. Also scripts, documents, apparatus. Library and viewing services.

CUBA
Cinemateca de Cuba, Calle 23 no. 1155, Vedado, Havana. Tel: 34719. Telex: 511419. Interim Director: Pastor Vega. Stock: 6,300 film titles, 110,500 film stills. Members of the Co-ordinated Latin American de Archivos de Imagenes en Movimiento (CLAIM).

CYPRUS
Kypriaki Tainiothiki, PO Box 5314, Nicosia. Curator: Panikkos Chrysanthou. Stock: 230 films.

CZECHOSLOVAKIA
Ceskoslovenský filmový ústav-filmový archiv, Národni 40, 11000 Praha 1. Tel: 260087. Telex: 122259. Fax: 261618. Curator: Vladimír Opěla. Stock: about 15,000 features, plus the same number of shorts and documentaries, incl. newsreels, 82,000 books, 12,000 periodicals, 430,000 stills, 50000 posters.

DENMARK
Det Danske Filmmuseum, Store Søndervoldstraede, DK-1419 Copenhagen K. Tel: 31576500. Telex: 31465. Fax: 31541312. Director: Ib Monty. Stock: 13,000 film titles, 42,000 books, 350 periodicals subscribed to, 1,800,000 film stills, 15,000 posters. 158-seat cinema used for three daily screenings for researchers and students. Small changing exhibitions. The Museum also publishes a magazine "Kosmorama" and occasional leaflets and books on film.

EQUADOR
Cinemateca Nacional del Ecuador, Avenida 6 de Diciembre y Tarqui, Quito. Tel: 543748. Director: Ulises Estrella. Stock: 298 film titles, 3,600 film stills, 250 posters.

Cinematheque ONTARIO / Festival OF FESTIVALS

As anyone who has ever attended the Festival of Festivals, Toronto's International Film Festival, can attest, the city boasts one of the most informed, dedicated and adventurous film-going audiences in the world. Which is why the transformation of the festival into a year-round operation has been greeted with such enthusiasm by Toronto's discerning cinephiles. Cinematheque Ontario, as this new organisation is known, was founded by Gerald Pratley in 1969 as the Ontario Film Instute. Now operating under the aegis of the Festival, the Cinematheque recently relocated along with its parent organisation to the heart of the film exhibition and distribution scene in downtown Toronto. Previously the home of Warner Bros. Pictures Canada, the renovated building is ideally situated for public accessibility, an important factor for the many researchers who use the Cinematheque's burgeoning collection.

Within six weeks of its transformation and relocation, the Cinematheque initiated all three of its major functions.

SCREENING PROGRAMMES: The programming division of the Cinematheque confirmed its commitment to ensuring the continuity and exploring the complexity of world cinema with its two inaugural programmes. The first, a complete retrospective of the films of Italian director Pier Paolo Pasolini arranged by Laura Betti and the Fondo Pasolini, sold out virtually all of its screenings and prompted passionate debate amongst the city's film community. The second, a tribute to the great Japanese actress Kinuyo Tanaka, who was also her country's first woman film director, treated Toronto audiences to a number of familiar classics and overlooked masterworks by Ozu, Mizoguchi and Naruse. Also on the Cinematheque's slate for 1990 are retrospectives of the films of Akira Kurosawa, the early works of Andy Warhol, eight films starring Ingrid Bergman before she went to Hollywood, 21 of Gerald Pratley's favourite films by way of tribute to 21 years of programming at the Ontario Film Institute, and an intensive survey of recent films from Ontario, run concurrently with the Cinematheque Francaise.

DOCUMENTATION CENTRE: The non-circulating collection including 20,000 books, 6,000 posters, 25,000 stills, 350 videocassettes, over 4,000 sound recordings, more than 75,000 vertical files and 100 periodical subscriptions was recently christened the Pratley Collection. With the recent undertaking to recatalogue and automate much of the collection, the Documentation Centre will be an even more invaluable resource for film scholars, students, media and the general public. As with the programming division, emphasis is placed on the documentation of Canadian cinema.

MEMBERSHIP: A major membership drive has been designed to develop a broad base of support for the Cinematheque.

Cinematheque Ontario, drawing on the diverse audience which both the Festival of Festivals and the Ontario Film Institute have created for classic and contemporary international cinema, will play a key role in the development of film culture in Canada as both a focal point and a catalyst for the study, appreciation and enjoyment of cinema.

EGYPT

National Film Archive, c/o Egyptian Film Centre, City of Arts, Pyramids Road, Guiza Tel: 854681. Telex: 93661. Curator: Abdel Gawad el Dani. Stock: 1,500 film titles, 700 film stills, 600 posters.

FINLAND

Suomen elokuva-arkisto, Pursimiehenkatu 29–31 A, P.O. Box 177, SF–00150 Helsinki. Tel: + 358.0.171417. Telex: 125960. Fax: + 358.0.171544. Director: Kaarle Stewen. Programmer: Antti Alanen. Stock: 8,000 feature film titles, 20,000 shorts and advertising film (spots), 6,000 videocassettes, 14,000 books, 132 magazines (currently subscribed), 7,000 dialogue lists and scripts, 320,000 different stills, 110,000 posters and 30,000 documentation files. The archive arranges regular screenings in Helsinki and seven other cities.

FRANCE

Cinémathèque Française, 29 rue de Colisée, 75008 Paris. President: Jean Rouch.
Cinémathèque de Toulouse, 3 rue Roquelaine, 31000 Toulouse. Tel: 489075. Curator: Raymond Borde. Stock: 13,000 film titles, 400,000 photos, 38,000 posters.
Service des Archives de Film du Centre National de la Cinématographie, 7 bis rue Alexandre Turpault, 78390 Bois d'Arcy. Tel: 34602050. Curator: F. Schmitt. Stock: 97,000 film titles, 150,000 stills, 15,000 posters, 24,700 screenplays, 1,200 apparati. Founded in 1969. Film vaults capable of holding 1,200,000 reels of film, and laboratory for restoration of old films. Documentation department.
Cinémathèque Universitaire, UER d'Art de d'Archéologie, 3 rue Michelet, 75006 Paris.
Institut Lumière, 25 rue du Premier-Film, 69008 Lyon. Tel: 78.00.86.68. Director: Bernard Chardère. Admirable institution that screens precious old films, organises exhibitions, preserves films, and publishes monographs.
Musée du Cinéma de Lyon, 69 rue Jean Jaurès, 69100 Villeurbanne. Tel: 8532769. Curator: Paul Génard. Stock: 1,600 film titles, 1,000 film stills, 50 posters.

GERMANY

Münchner Filmmuseum, St.-Jakob-Platz 1, 8000 München 2. Tel: 2332348. Curator: Enno Patalas. A municipal archive devoted to the restoration of German classics and to the preservation of the New German Cinema.
Stiftung Deutsche Kinemathek, Pommernallee 1, 1000 Berlin 19. Tel: 30307234. Fax: 3029294. Director: Dr. Hans Helmut Prinzler. Stock: 8,000 film titles, 1,000,000 film stills, 15,000 posters, 60,000 film programmes, 10,000 scripts etc. The Kinemathek's library of books and periodicals is now amalgamated with that of the Film-und Fernsehakademie, in the same building.
Bundesarchiv-Filmarchiv, Potsdamerstrasse 1, POB 320, D 5400 Koblenz. Tel: 261–5050. President: Prof. H. Booms. Stock: 51,900 film titles, including 45,200 documentary films and newsreels and 3,820 long film features, exclusively of German production. Co-operation with Stiftung Deutsche Kinemathek and Deutsches Institut für Filmkunde.
Deutsches Filmmuseum, Schaumainkai 41, 6000 Frankfurt am Main 70. Director: Prof. Walter Schobert. Curator: Jürgen Berger. Film Archive: Rainer Schang. Stock: 2,500 film titles, 14,000 books, 110 current periodicals subscribed to, 300,000 stills, 15,000 posters, thousands of items of cinema equipment, cameras, projectors, ephemera plus musical scores of silent films. The museum incorporates the Kommunales Kino Frankfurt. It has a permanent exhibition on two floors and exhibitions on various themes (up to five per year). It screens 3 different films a day and publishes books and a magazine.
Deutsches Institut für Filmkunde, Schaumainkai 41, 6000 Frankfurt am Main 70. Tel: 617045. Telex: 4–189969. Telefax: 069/62 0060. Director: Dr. Gerd Albrecht. Deputy Director: Eberhard Spiess. Administrative Director: Peter Franz. Stock: 4,200 film titles, 54,000 books, 260 periodicals, 1,000,000 film stills, 30,000 posters, 16,000 dialogue lists, 5,000 scripts. Also programmes, newspaper clippings, advertising material.
Arsenal Kino der Freunde der Deutschen Kinemathek. V, Welserstrasse 25, D-1000 Berlin 30. Tel: 213–6039. The nearest equivalent of Britain's NFT. Became a model for all "Communal Cinemas" in the Federal Republic of Germany. Programming: Ulrich and Erika Gregor, Alf Bold. The Freunde (chairmen: Ulrich Gregor, Gerhard Schoenberner, Sylvia Andresen) also run a non-commercial distribution of about 800 films, most of them from the International Forum of

Young Cinema, the independent second main programme of the Berlin Film Festival, organised by the Freunde.
Staatliches Filmarchiv der Deutschen Demokratischen Republik, Hausvogteiplatz 3–4, 1080 Berlin. Tel: 2124324. Telex: 112712. Curator: Wolfgang Klaue. Stock: 57,000 film titles, plus documentation material on about 25,000 titles, 1,500,000 stills and 14,000 posters. With its own theatre, the Filmarchiv holds exhibitions and a yearly retrospective on documentaries at the Leipzig festival.

GREECE
Tainiothiki tis Ellados, 1 Canari Street, Athens 106 74. Tel: 3612046. President of D.C.: Aglaya Mitropoulos. Curator: Mona Mitropoulos. Director: Theodore Adamploulos. Stock: 3,800 film titles, 6,000 photos of Greek and international cinema, 500 posters of Greek and 2,500 posters of international cinema, 1,500 film stills. Expanding collection of magic lanterns, praxinoscopes, etc.

HUNGARY
Maygar Filmintézet, Budakeszi ut 51/b, 1021 Budapest. Tel: 17.67.106. Director: József Marx. Stock: 1,931 feature titles, 8,611 documentaries, 3,693 newsreels, 13,224 books, 3,710 periodicals, 2,708 scripts, 5,381 manuscripts, 143,159 stills, 15,365 posters. The institute, besides housing the archive (Budakeszi ut 51/b, 10 21 Budapest. Head of archive: Mrs Vera Gyürey) also does research into the history of the cinema, particularly the Hungarian cinema, and encourages the development of film culture in Hungary.

ICELAND
Kvikmyndasafn Islands (Icelandic Film Archive), Laugavegur 24, 101 Reykjavík. (Postal: P.O. Box 320, 121 Reykjavík.) Tel: 10940. Fax: 627171. Nearly 400 titles in the collection, documentaries being the larger part of it. Numerous sources of information regarding Icelandic films and the national film history.

INDIA
National Film Archive of India, Ministry of Information and Broadcasting, Government of India, Law College Road, Poona 411004. Tel: 51559. Director: P.K. Nair. Stock: 10,798 films, 17,991 books, 214 periodicals, 1,678 disc-records, 108 audio tapes, 1,951 microfilms, 48,685 stills, 4,864 posters, 4,638 song booklets, 19,999 shooting scripts, 5,244 pamphlets and folders and 56,644 press clippings. Daily screenings for Film & TV Institute students at Poona; weekly public screenings at Poona and Bombay, regular special screenings.

INDONESIA
Sinematek Indonesia, Pusat Perfilman "H. Usmar Ismail," Jalan H.R. Rasuana Said, Jakarta Selatan. Tel: 516891. Director: H. Misbach Yusa Biran. Stock: about 257 features plus 114 shorts. Indonesian film titles (50% negatives). Earliest film dates from 1938.

IRAN
National Iranian Film Archive, Baharestan Square, Tehran. Tel: 324 1601. Director: Mohammad Hassan Khoshnevis.

ISRAEL
The Doran Cinema Center (Tel Aviv Cinémathèque), 2 Sprintzak Street, Tel Aviv. Tel: 43854/438220.
Israel Film Archive (Jerusalem Cinematheque), Hebron Road, P.O. Box 8561, Jerusalem 91083. Tel: 724131. Telex: 26358 CANJR IL. Fax: 733076. Director: Lia van Leer. Stock: 13,000 prints in international, Israeli and Jewish collection. Books, periodicals, stills, posters and scripts. Jewish Film Centre, extensive Israeli and Jewish theme collection. Permanent exhibition of early cinema apparatus. 1,000 screenings yearly, extensive morning educational programme for schools. Facilities for film research. Organisers of the Jerusalem International Film Festival (July).

ITALY
Cineteca Italiana, Via Palestro 16, 20121 Milano. Tel: 799224. Sec. General: Gianni Comencini. Stock: 30,000 film titles, 600,000 stills, 8,000 posters.
Museo Nazionale del Cinema, Palazzo Chiablese, Piazza. S. Giovanni 2, 10122 Torino. Tel: 4361148/4361387. President: Roberto Morano. Stock: 2,000 film titles, 300,000 stills, 20,000 posters. The Museum is temporarily closed. Films screened every day 4 to 12 pm in three rooms at Cinema Massimo, Via Montebello 8.
Cineteca Nazionale, Via Tuscolana N. 1524, 00173 Rome. Tel: 746941. Curator: Dr. Guido Cincotti. Stock: 20,000 film titles, 28,000 books

and periodicals, 190,000 stills, 2,000 posters. The Cineteca is a department of the Centro Sperimentale di Cinematografia.
Cineteca del Friuli, 26 via Osoppo, 33014 Gemona del Friuli (Udine). Excellent Italian archive that conceived the idea for the Pordenone Silent Film Festival, and organises regular screenings. Stock: 1,500 film titles, 3,000 newsreels, 5,000 books.

JAPAN
Japan Film Library Council/Kawakita Memorial Film Institute, Ginza-Hata Building, 4–5, 4-chrome, Ginza, Chuo-ku, Tokyo. Director: Mrs. Kashiko Kawakita. Secretary: Akira Shimizu. Stock: 500 film titles, 3,000 books, 6,000 periodicals, 50,000 film stills, 100 posters. The Council co-operates with archives throughout the world in supplying Japanese films for screening, makes available stills for publication and publishes documentation of its collection.
National Filmcenter, 7–6, 3 chome, Kyobashi, Chuoku, Tokyo. Curator: Masatoshi Ohba. Stock: 2,100 film titles, 6,000 shorts, animation and newsreels, 4,000 books, 25,000 magazines, 100,000 stills, 1,800 posters, 20,000 scripts. Screenings held twice on Saturday and Sunday.

KOREA (NORTH)
*The National Film Archive of the Democratic People's Republic of Korea, 15 Sochangdong, Central District, Pyongyang. Tel: 34551. Telex: 5345. Director: Pak Sun Tae. Stock: 17,200 film titles, 6,300 stills, 1,100 posters.

KOREA (SOUTH)
Korean Film Archive, 34–5, 3-ka, Namsan-Dong, Chung-ku, Seoul 100. Tel: 755.92915. Telex: 28385. Director: Chung Yun-Koo. Stock: 2,236 film titles, 6,550 stills. Initiated in the mid-1970's and a full board member of FIAF since 1984. Though an independent body, it is funded by the Motion Picture Promotion Corporation.

LUXEMBOURG
Cinémathèque Municipale de Ville de Luxembourg, 19 rue de la Chapelle, L-1325 Luxembourg. Tel: (352) 4796–2644. Fax: (352) 45 93 75. Curator: Fred Junck. Founded in 1977, the Cinémathèque Municipale is entirely subsidised by the City of Luxembourg. It specialises in unearthing rare French and American films – *Variety* calls Fred Junck the "Flatfoot" of film archives – and is well appreciated by historians in adjacent countries. Stock: some 8,000 titles (9.5, 16, 35 and 70 mm prints), numerous stills, posters and books. Two screenings per day in a comfortable, Dolby-equipped 180-seat auditorium. Organises "Live Cinema" presentations of silent classics with full orchestra accompaniment, in association with composer–conductor Carl Davis.

MEXICO
Filmoteca de la Universitad Nacional Autonoma de Mexico, San Ildefonso 43, 06020 Mexico D.F. Tel: 522 4665. Telex: 1777429. Director: Carlos Gonzalles Morantes. Stock: 7,500 film titles, 120,000 stills.
Cinemateca Mexicana, Museo Nacional de Antropologia, Calzada M. Gandhi, México 6, D.F. Director: Galdino Gomez Gomez. Stock: 1,000 film titles. 500 books, 500 film stills, 300 posters. The Cinemateca Mexicana also has a collection of early apparati dating from 1900.
Cinemateca Luis Buñuel, Calle 5, Oriente 5, Apdo. Postal 255, Puebla, Pue. Curator: Fermando Osorio Alarcon. Established in 1975, this archive has a stock of 100 films, some of them made entirely in Puebla, belonging to the silent period; 300 posters, 500 stills, 200 film books.
Cineteca Nacional, Av. Mexico-Coyoacán 389, 03330 Mexico. Tel: 688 8814. Telex: 1760050 RTCME. Director: Mercedes Certucha. Mexico's main film archive, supported by the Federal government. Stock: 3,700 film titles, 22,000 reels. Documentation department: 21,000 books, 3,000 stills folders, 3,000 posters. Library, bookshop, gallery and four film theatres open Tuesday to Sunday to the public, 14 screenings daily.

NETHERLANDS
Stichting Nederlands Filmmuseum, Vondelpark 3, 1071 AA Amsterdam. Tel: (020) 5891.400. Fax: (020) (6)8334.01. (The number 6 to be used from March 1, 1991) Director: Hoos Blotkamp. Deputy Director: Eric de Kuyper. Stock: about 25,000 films, 25,000 film stills, 30,000 posters. The museum has a theatre of 95 seats.
Audiovisual Archive of the Netherlands Information Service, Baden Powellweg 5,2583 KT The Hague; Postbus 20006, 2500 EA The

Hague. Head: Mr. R.H.J. Egeter van Kuyk. Permanent collections of films and photographs of the central Government. Mostly documentary material since 1898.

NEW ZEALAND
The New Zealand Film Archive, P.O. Box 9544, 82 Tory Street, Wellington. Tel: 847647. Fax: 829595. Telex: 30386. Director: Kate Fortune. Stock: 4,500 film titles, 35,000 stills, 25,000 posters. The collection includes New Zealand silent and sound films and some features from 1901 to the present day, as well as a proportion of foreign material. Also held are periodicals, books, apparati and special collections.

NORWAY
Norsk Filminstitutt, Militærhospitalet, Grev Wedels plass, Postboks 482, Sentrum, 0105 Oslo 1. Tel: 472 428740. Fax: 472 332277. Director: Jan Erik Holst. Curator: Arne Pedersen. Head of Cinémathèque: Kjell Billing. Stock: 11,000 film titles, 13,000 books, 130 periodicals and a large collection of stills and posters. Also over five hundred pieces of early cinema apparatus and a fine theatre for screening films. The cinémathèque of the film institute is run by the organisation "The Friends of the NFI."
Henie-Onstad Art Centre, 1311 Hovikodden, Oslo. Director: Per Hovdenakk. Stock: 200 film titles, 100 video works, 500 books and periodicals, 4,000 film stills, 600 posters. A large collection of documentary material on experimental film, and regular screenings.

PANAMA
Cinemateca del GECU, Apartado 6–1775, Estafeta El Dorado, Panama. Telex: 2643 Decla PG. Director: Edgar Soberón Torchia. Stock includes films, books, periodicals, film stills and posters. It has a small theatre in the University of Panama, with three daily screenings.

POLAND
Filmoteka Polska, ul. Pulawska 61, 00–975 Warszawa, skr, poczt. 65. Tel: 455074. Telex: 813640. Director: Waldemar Piatek. Stock: 13,000 film titles, 15,500 books plus programmes, leaflets and press cuttings, 970 periodical titles, 150 of which are currently subscribed to, stills from 25,000 films, 45,000 posters, 23,000 scripts, 1,000 film scores, 300 archive materials, reference indexes and a collection of early equipment. Publishes a quarterly film magazine, *Iluzjon*.

PORTUGAL
Cinemateca Portuguesa, Rua Barata Salgueiro 39, 1200 Lisboa. Tel: 546279/547732. Telex: 15308. Director: Luís De Pina. Stock: 5,300 film titles, 18,300 books, 170 current periodicals, 40,000 stills. Daily screening sessions, retrospective cycles, publication of film books. New nitrate vaults under construction.

ROMANIA
Archiva Nationala de Filme, Bd. G.H. Gheorghiu dej 68/65 Bucharest. Director: Marin Paraianu. Stock: 7,500 feature titles, 22,500 shorts, 5,350 books, 3,500 stills, 20,000 posters and reference index. Archive also has a collection of clippings, scripts and periodicals.

SOUTH AFRICA
South African National Film, Video and Sound Archives, Private Bag X236, Pretoria 0001. Director: J.H. de Lange. Enormous variety of 35mm and 16mm footage, video and sound material as well as stills, scripts, books, posters and other material. The Archive is a State controlled organisation, dedicated to the classification and preservation of all items relating to the film, video and sound industries.

SPAIN
Filmoteca Española, Carretera Dehesa de la Villa, s/n. 28040 Madrid. Tel: 549 00 11. Fax: 549 73 48. Director: José María Prado. Stock: 11,819 film titles, 4,000 newsreels, 13,500 books, 3,000 posters, 130,000 still files. Thirty screenings a week in Cine Doré. Publishes monographs and useful brochures. Library open to the public.
Filmoteca de la Generalitat de Catalunya, Diputació 281, 08007 Barcelona. Tel: 317 35 85. Excellent Catalan archive that arranges screenings of foreign films also.

SWEDEN
Cinemateket, Svenska Filminstitutet, Filmhuset, Box 27 126, S-102 52 Stockholm. Tel: (46–8) 665 1100. Telex: 13326 FILMINS S. Fax: 08–6611820. Curator: Rolf Lindfors. Head of Documentation: Margareta Nordström.

Stock: 12,500 film titles, 35,000 books, 280 periodicals, 1,500,000 film stills, 30,000 posters, and unpublished script material on 6,000 foreign films and 1,700 Swedish films. The collection of microfilmed clippings holds 49,000 jackets on individual films, 15,000 jackets on film personalities and 6,500 jackets on general subjects classified under 700 headings. Cinemateket has two theatres and four daily screenings in Stockholm. A selection of the yearly programme is also shown in Gothenburg and Malmö. There is also a film club for teenagers, *Filmögat*, with weekly screenings of film classics in four cities.

Asta Nielsen Filmmuseum, Vapenkroken 29, 222 47 Lund. Established in 1946 by G.D. Postén, Head of the Film History section at the Dept. of History, University of Lund. This is one of the biggest, private, non-commercial international collections of published, written materials on motion pictures and the film industry. Included in the collection are stills, programmes, books, magazines, posters, historical materials, etc. with the emphasis on the silent screen. Also the most complete collection of material on Asta Nielsen.

SWITZERLAND
Cinémathèque Suisse, 3 Allée Ernest Ansermet, 1003 Lausanne. Tel: 237406. Telex: 24430. Curator: Freddy Buache. Stock: 25,000 titles (300,000 reels), 260 apparati, 35,000 posters, 300,000 film references, 12,000 books, and 708,000 stills. Three projections each day (except Sunday).

THAILAND
The National Film Archive of Thailand, 4 Chao Fa Road, Bangkok 10200. Director: Penpan Jarernport. Stock: 1,680 film titles, 5,000 stills.

TAIWAN
Tien-ying t'u-shu-kuan (Film Library of The Motion Picture Development Foundations R.O.C.), 4th floor, 7 Ch'ingtao East Road, Taipei. Director: Ray Jiing. Opened in January 1979, this archive already has a book collection of some 5,759 titles (in 6,836 copies) and a print deposit of 2,134 films and a video section with five viewing machines and 2,671 tapes, 5,103 stills and 2,708 posters. The library holds regular screenings and special programmes (at 4th floor, 7 Ch'ingtao East Road, Taipei) and organises the annual International Film Exhibition, held in mid December.

TURKEY
Sinema-TV Enstitüsü, 80700 Kislaönü-Besiktas, Istanbul. Tel: 166 983031. Telex: 26439. Director: Sami Şekeroğlu. Stock: over 3,000 film titles, 300,000 stills, original negatives of early Turkish films, 500 books, collections of major world periodicals, 10,000 posters, 12 years' collection of press cuttings, 100 scripts, film music tapes.

U.K.
National Film Archive, 21 Stephen Street, London W1P 1PL. Tel: (71) 255 1444. Telex: 27624. Curator: David Francis OBE. Deputy Curator: Michelle Snapes. Stock: 100,000 film and television titles, 2,500,000 black-and-white stills, 350,000 colour transparencies, 10,000 posters, 2,000 set designs. Viewing service for students and researchers, production library for film-makers.

Imperial War Museum, Lambeth Road, London SE1 6HZ. Tel: (71) 735 8922. Keeper of the Film Department: Anne Fleming. The museum's collection now includes over 40,000,000 feet of film, the main emphasis being on non-fiction film.

The Scottish Film Archive, Scottish Film Council, 74 Victoria Crescent Road, Dowanhill, Glasgow G12 9JN. Tel: (041) 334 4445. Curator: Janet McBain. Established in 1976, the Archive is mainly concerned with the filmed history of Scotland. Stock: 8,000 reels of film, varied collection of non-film material. Viewing facilities for students and researchers *by appointment only*.

URUGUAY
Cinemateca Uruguaya, Lorenzo Carnelli 1311, Casilla de Correo 1170, Montevideo. Tel: 482 460, 494 572, or 495 795. Telex: 22043. Curator: M. Martinez Carril. Stock: 6,500 film titles, 4,115 books, 11,000 periodicals, 13,500 posters.

Archivo Nacional de la Imagen-Sodre, Sarandi 430, Montevideo. Tel: 955758. Telex: 41134. Director: Eugenio Hintz. Stock: 550 film titles, 2,000 stills.

U.S.A.

American Film Institute/National Center for Film and Video Preservation, John F. Kennedy Center for the Performing Arts, Washington, DC 20566. Archivist: Susan Dalton. Stock: 24,000 film titles; no research facilities. All titles in the AFI Collection are housed at the Library of Congress or other American archives where the films are available for study. Screenings are held twice nightly in the AFI Theater at the Kennedy Center.

Harvard Film Archive, Carpenter Center for the Visual Arts, Harvard Univ, 24 Quincy Street, Cambridge, MA 02138. Tel: (617) 495 4700. Curator: Vlada Petrić. Films (16mm and 35mm): 1,000 titles including the Film Study Center collection (Robert Gardner, Producer/Director). Library: 1,100 books, 6,000 clippings files, 700 video tapes. Researchers and scholars may have access by appointment. Public film screenings which are designed in conjunction with Visual Studies courses take place six nights weekly.

The Library of Congress, Motion Picture, Broadcasting and Recorded Sound Division, Washington, DC 20540. Tel: (202) 707 5840. Telex: 64198. Director: Robert Saudek. Stock: 150,000 film and television titles, 4,000 books, 150,000 stills, descriptive material for more than 200,000 films and television programmes registered for U.S. copyright since 1912. Much more extensive book and periodical collection in the Library's general collection. Individual screening facilities are available to serious researchers and scholars by appointment.

Museum of Modern Art, Department of Film, 11 West 53rd Street, New York, NY 10019. Tel: (212) 708 9602. Telex: 62370. Director: Mary Lea Bandy. Curators: Eileen Bowser, Adrienne Mancia, Larry Kardish. Stock: 10,000 film titles, 2,500 books, 250 periodicals, 4,000,000 film stills. The excellent research and screening facilities of the department are available to serious students only by appointment with the supervisor, Charles Silver. 1,000 of its films are available for rental, sale, and lease. Stills Archive open by appointment with Mary Corliss.

George Eastman House/International Museum of Photography, 900 East Avenue, Rochester, N.Y. 14607. Tel: (716) 271 3361. Film Dept. Dr. Jan-Christopher Horak, Curator of Film: George Pratt, Curator Emeritus. Film collections, including nitrate, rich in American and foreign silents, German, French and American classical studio work, poverty-row and independent documentary. Over 2.5 million stills, posters, scripts and documents related to history of film.

Academy of Motion Picture Arts and Sciences, 8949 Wilshire Boulevard, Beverly Hills, California 90211. Academy Film Archive. Curator of Film and Artifacts: Daniel Woodruff.

National Museum of Natural History/Human Studies Film Archives, Rm E307 Smithsonian Institution, Washington DC 20560. Tel: (202) 357–3349. Asst. Dir: Wendy Ann Shay. More than 2,000,000 feet of original film.

The Wisconsin Center for Film and Theatre Research, 816 State Street, Madison, Wisconsin 53706. Tel: (608) 262–585. Head of Archive: Maxine Ducey. Stock: 5,500 feature films, 8,500 short films and television programmes, 2,000,000 stills, 12,000 posters.

Pacific Film Archive, University Art Museum 2625 Durant Avenue, Berkeley, California, 94720. Stock: 6,000 films, 75 periodicals, 3,000 books, 10,000 stills, and 40,000 files of clippings organised by title, person, subject and festival. The PFA's daily international film exhibition programme presents over 750 films per year and covers the history of the cinema, highlighting rediscoveries and rare points, works by independent film-makers, frequent personal appearances by film-makers and scholars, and films for children. The film collection emphasises Japanese features, Soviet silents, international animation, and avant-garde films. Library and research screening facilities are open to the public weekday afternoons by appointment.

American Cinematheque, 1717 N. Highland Ave. (at Hollywood Blvd.), Hollywood 90028. Artistic Director: Gary Essert. A viewer-supported arts complex of state-of-the-art theatres, galleries and gathering places (including a cafe and bookstore) dedicated *exclusively* to the public exhibition of film and video. Scheduled to open in 1992. Meanwhile, regular film and video programming for the public is underway now at the new Directors Guild theatre complex in Hollywood.

UCLA Film and Television Archive, 1438 Melnitz Hal, University of California, 405 Hilgard Avenue, Los Angeles CA 90024. Tel: (213) 206–8013. Telex: 910 3427597. Director: Robert Rosen. Stock: 55,000 film and television programmes, 5,000,000 stills.

SOUTH AFRICAN NATIONAL FILM, VIDEO AND SOUND ARCHIVE

The aims of this Archive are the acquisition, preservation, storage, adaptation and supply of available films, video and sound material of archival value, with specific reference to South Africa. Further, to provide an information service with regard to film, video, sound material and photographs.

It is a division of the State Archives of the Department of National Education.

Private Bag X236
PRETORIA
0001

South Africa

U.S.S.R.

Gosfilmofond, Stantsia Byelye Stolby, Moskovskaya Oblast. Tel: 546 05 16. Telex: 411417. Director: Mark Strotchkov. Stock: 48,000 film titles, 7,082 books, 15,728 periodicals, 332,000 film stills, 52,000 posters. Shows film publicly and has viewing facilities for the serious student.

Moscow Film Centre, Museum Dept. of the Film Centre of the Filmmakers' Union of the U.S.S.R., Druzjinnikovskaya 15, Moscow 123376. Curator: Naum Kleiman. Admirable work in restoring Russian and Soviet classics and lost films.

The Central State Archive of Cinema and Photo Documents of the USSR, Krasnogorsk, near Moscow. Director: O.N. Tyagunov.

VENEZUELA

Cinemateca Nacional, Musco de Ciencias Naturales, Edf. Anexo, Plaza Morelos, Los Caobos, Aptdo. Postal 17045, Caracas. Tel: 571 5220. Director: Rodolfo Izaguirre. Stock: 1,012 film titles, 5,000 books, pamphlets and documentation, 12,000 stills, 500–card index.

YUGOSLAVIA

Jugoslovenska kinoteka, Knez Mihailova 19, 11000 Belgrade. Tel: 622 555. Director: Sloboden Šijan. Foreign Relations Consultant: Žika Bogdanović. Stock: 64,610 films, 17,700 books and periodicals, 9,334 scripts, reference index of 200,000 cards, 100,000 newspaper clippings, 185,716 stills, 64,342 negative photos, 10,830 posters, 2,395 programmes.

Stock Footage Libraries

The following is a listing of the major U.S. independent stock footage libraries:

John E. Allen, Inc., North Avenue, Park Ridge, N.J. 07656. Tel: (201) 391–3463.

Archive Films Inc., 530 West 25th Street, New York, NYT 10001. Tel: (212) 620– 3955. Invaluable source of film extracts, newsreels, cartoons etc. Patrick Montgomery's archive contains a vast assortment of material from 1894 through the 1960's.

Producing everything from commercials to full-length documentaries, **Archive Films Inc.** specialises in the use of historical footage. Experts in the utilisation of existing films and tapes, the firm houses a vast collection of archival footage as well as maintaining exclusive arrangements throughout the world with other distributors, archives and libraries. All footage has been transferred to video cassettes for reference purposes and is available on all film and video formats for use.

By definition, historical or "archival" footage is any type of footage, film or videotape, colour or b&w, 16mm or 35mm shot as early as 1898 or as recently as yesterday. Archive Films locates its footage from a number of different origins – acquiring clips from newsreels, silent film comedies and dramas. Hollywood feature films (primarily those shot outside of the studio systems) and cartoons.

Cameo Film Library, 10620 Burbank Boulevard, North Hollywood, Ca. 91601. Tel: (818) 980–9700. Represents stock footage from NBC Productions, Tri-Star, Viacom and others.

Larry Dorn Associates/World Backgrounds, 5550 Wilshire Boulevard, Los Angeles, Ca. 90036. Tel: (213) 935–6266.

Film Bank, 3306 West Burbank Blvd., Burbank, CA 91505. Tel: (818) 841 9176. Fax: (818) 567 4235. President: Paula Lumbard. Stock footage, research, camera service.

Film Search Inc., 232 Madison Avenue, New York, N.Y. 10016. Tel: (212) 532–600.

Sherman Grinberg Film Libraries, Inc., 630 Ninth Avenue, New York, NY 10036. Tel: (212) 765 5170. Fax: (212) 262 1532. Also, 1040 North McCadden Place, Hollywood, CA 90038. Tel: (213) 464 7491. Fax: (213) 462 5352.

Killiam Shows, Inc., 6 East 39 Street, New York, N.Y. 10016. Tel: (212) 679–8230.

Producers Library Service, 1051 North Cole Avenue, Hollywood, CA 90038. Tel: (213) 465 0572. Houses more than 5 million feet of 35mm colour film from the 1950's to the present, 1 million feet of 16mm colour film from the 1940's and 1950's, and more than 1 million feet of 35mm black-and-white film from the 'teens through the 1940's; it represents stock footage from the productions of ABC Circle, Orion and the Spelling-Goldberg TV series, specialises in Hollywood history and has direct access to stock footage from all Hollywood studios.

The Stock House, 6922 Hollywood Boulevard, Suite 621, Hollywood, Ca. 90028. Tel: (213) 461–61.

PHENOMENAL FOOTAGE.™

It's just a phone call away. Stock footage from silent films, feature films, newsreels, documentaries, industrial films and more. Fully cleared for use in your productions.

Our computerized system insures fast access. Call or write for a free brochure and sample reel.

ARCHIVE FILMS™
STOCK FOOTAGE LIBRARY

212-620-3955

Archive Films, Inc., Dept. IFG,
530 W. 25th St. NY, NY 10001 USA Fax 212/645-2137

Toronto	London	Paris
416-591-1541	071-383-0033	01-40-30-11-47
Rome	Stockholm	Amsterdam	Tokyo
06-359-5056	46-8-660-2700	20-234-219	03-561-2391

Sherman Grinberg Film Libraries, Inc.
1040 North McCadden Place, Hollywood, CA 90038
(213) 464-7491   LA FAX (213) 462-5352
630 Ninth Avenue, New York, New York 10036
(212) 765-5170   NY FAX (212) 245-2339

BOOK REVIEWS

Many general publishers, having dipped their toe gingerly into the currents of film literature, are leaving the scene. Faber and Faber in Britain, and the Centre Georges Pompidou in France, have emerged as the most reliable specialist imprints. American houses have the flair and the wallets to commission an increasing number of books on Hollywood – with the emphasis as much on malfeasance as on myths and mythmakers.

BOOKS OF THE YEAR

The most enthralling as literature must be **Francois Truffaut: Letters** (Faber, London, 1989), which we reviewed in our 1989 edition after the original had appeared in France. The competent translation by Gilbert Adair contrives neither to abridge nor to bowdlerize, and for anyone who ever fell under the spell of the French New Wave in the 1960's, this is a golden treasury of memories and references.

In terms of pioneering research and criticism, **Silent Witnesses: Russian films 1908–1919** (British Film Institute, London, 1989) is outstanding. Published in connection with the Pordenone Silent Film Days, this bilingual volume (English and Italian) covers the hitherto unknown quantity of pre-revolutionary Russian cinema. The archivist Yuri Tsivian presents and analyses a host of sparkling revelations. Frame blow-ups and a wealth of reference material make the book indispensable.

THE INDUSTRY

Peter Bart's **Fade Out: The Calamitous Final Days of MGM** (William Morrow & Co., New York, 1990) paints a scabrous portrait of financier Kirk Kerkorian and his acolytes as they seek first to save and then to sell the most celebrated of all Hollywood studios. Bart, a senior studio executive who worked at MGM during these horrendous years, writes with an astringent objectivity and brings his many villains to life with a sardonic turn of phrase.

On the European side of the water, Jake Eberts and Terry Ilott's **My Indecision Is Final** (Faber, London, 1990) chronicles a similar debacle. The ill-fated Goldcrest was never a studio, but its enthusiastic board championed such British triumphs as *Chariots of Fire*, *Gandhi*, and the Cannes winner *The Mission*. Eberts, a Canadian who loves England, writes in a tone of anguish and regret. The book suffers from excess (678 pages), but its meticulous recreation of each and every error serves as an invaluable primer for anyone entering the production side of the business.

Iain Johnstone's **Cannes, The Novel** (Chatto and Windus, London, 1990) gives fictional flesh to similar goings-on, but is stronger on details of a film festival's organisation than on human behaviour when faced with terrorist blackmail. In the best passages there lurks something of the spirit of Douglas Sirk and Vincente Minnelli, the shabby compromises and the whiff of disgrace under pressure.

Bengt Forslund, an accomplished Swedish producer in his own right, has written the first authentic study of the role of the producer, how he functions, and what traits are required to achieve the greatness of Thalberg, Braunberger, Korda, or even Joseph E. Levine. Unfortunately this book, **Drömfabrikens Verklighet** (Natur och Kultur, Stockholm, 1990) is available at present only in Swedish.

On the practical side, a word of congratulation for **How To Sell Your Short Films** (published by the International Short Film Conference), in which the Dutch-born, Canadian sales agent Jan Röfekamp tells the innocent exactly which pitfalls to avoid and which clients are most likely to buy a short or featurette.

BIOGRAPHIES AND MONOGRAPHS

The Hustons (Scribner's, New York, 1989) attests to enormous diligence on the part of its author, Lawrence Grobel, and despite his patent enthusiasm for the life of John Huston and his father Walter in particular, Grobel does not shirk from maligning their excesses and their selfishness. Not so hot, however, on criticism of John's movies.

The director is not always his own best critic, and **Scorsese on Scorsese** (Faber, London 1989) presents rather a pedestrian stream of interviews with a man whose demons surface on screen rather than in conversation. Some of the minor details of how films came to fruition, however, are intriguing.

An accolade for the most sumptuous packaging of the year should go to Harry N. Abrams of New York (André Deutsch in Britain), for **David Lean**. Stephen Silverman's pedestrian prose is skilfully concealed in some spectacular pages, in full-colour and monochrome, that chart the epic progress of Britain's most austere and retiring director. The book is useful also in that Lean has talked to the author at length. Katharine Hepburn contributes an introduction.

Andrew Robinson's **Satyajit Ray** (André Deutsch, London, 1989) functions on an altogether more profound level. As biography it searches diligently among the gifted ancestors of India's best director, and portrays Ray in a sympathetic light (who wouldn't?). Ray remains one of the world's most articulate film-makers, able to dissect in words his own aims and errors, as well as being a marvellous draughtsman (many of his sketches grace the pages of Robinson's book).

Even more scholarly is Edvin Kau's **Dreyers Filmkunst** (Akademisk Forlag, Copenhagen, 1989), although the Danish language will mask this brilliant assessment from all but the most ardent specialist. Few books have used frame blow-ups in quite so intense and rewarding a fashion.

For those with a mastery of Italian, **Il Cinema di Augusto Genina** (Edizioni Biblioteca dell'Immagine, Friuli, 1990) provides a lavish assessment of the distinguished director for whom Louise Brooks made *Prix de beauté* in 1930.

Three commendable books have emerged from the Centre Georges Pompidou in Paris this past year. **Révoltes, Révolutions, Cinéma**, edited by Marc Ferro, assesses the cinema's attitude to political upheaval in various countries. **Le Cinéma Cubain**, edited by Paulo Antonio Paranagua, provides the best possible survey of that country's film-making, and the chronology of political events at the front of the book casts much light on the themes and incidents that colour Cuban cinema. **Le Cinéma des Pays Nordiques**, edited by Peter Cowie, tracks the development of film-making in Denmark, Finland, Iceland, Norway, and Sweden. All these volumes contain extensive reference sections and a wealth of filmographies.

Finally, Jacek Fuksiewicz's **Le Cinéma Polonais** (Les Editions du Cerf, Paris, 1989) seems all the more timely for its appearance in a western language, and takes the story right up to Kieślowski. Intelligently written, concisely expressed, this book is among the best of its kind.

SCREENPLAYS

Faber have taken up where Lorrimer left off (and where France's L'Avant-Scène continues to publish). They are releasing around a dozen scripts each year. Most of them do not describe the *finished film* (no indication of music, camera angles etc), but they are useful in showing how screenplays are constructed and how dialogue is written on the printed page. Titles since our last edition include Malle's **Milou in May**, Lang's **Metropolis**, and collections of films by comedians like Woody Allen and W.C. Fields. Most fascinating are those scripts accompanied by detailed reminiscences, such as Steven Soderbergh's "diary" that runs alongside the screenplay for **sex, lies, and videotape**.

Sometimes you do not need the script at all. Michael Powell's genial account of the making of **Edge of the World** (Faber, London, 1990) brings effortlessly to life a sublime summer in the Shetlands, and all the muddled romance of shooting a movie on location.

Abel Gance's **Napoléon** (Faber, London, 1989) lists every single shot in that sprawling masterpiece, while the reprint of Sidney Howard's screenplay for **Gone with the Wind** contains an illuminating introduction by Richard Harwell.

GENERAL

Budding critics would do well to read **The Golden Screen, Fifty Years of Films** (Pavilion/Michael Joseph, 1989), which collects the best reviews by Dilys Powell, who contributed a column to the London *Sunday Times* for half a century. Enthusiastic, matter-of-fact, occasionally sardonic, these columns set a benchmark by which other regular reviews must be judged.

A welcome for the updated and expanded edition of **The Cinema as Art** (Penguin, London, 1989), by Ralph Stephenson and Guy Phelps. Few textbooks read so smoothly, and for anyone approaching the cinema with serious intent, this is the primer to buy.

Vision and Persistence (University of Waterloo Press, Waterloo, Ontario, 1990) is by Jan Uhde and charts the twenty-year history of the Ontario Film Institute and its indefatigable founder, Gerald Pratley. The story represents the victory of hope over experience, for Pratley convinced officialdom to support his dream, and thousands of filmgoers in Canada have benefited since.

Also worth collecting is Wolfgang Jacobsen's sumptous history of the Berlin Film Festival: **Berlinale** (Argon Verlag, Berlin, 1990). Beautifully composed in flawless English, and with a plethora of evocative photos.

James Spader in *sex, lies and videotape*. Faber publish the screenplay

Film Bookshops, Posters and Records

Australia

Electric Shadows Bookshop, *Upper Level, Boulevard Shopping Centre, Akuna Street, Civic Act 2608. Tel: (062) 488342. Fax: (062) 491640.*
Gaumont Book Company, *123 Little Collins Street, Melbourne 3000. Tel: (03) 63–2623.*
Readings Records and Books, *P.O. Box 434, South Yarra 3141. Tel: (03) 267–1885.*
Soft Focus, *P.O. Box 508, Hawthorn, Victoria 3122.*

Catalogue available listing movie books, magazines, posters, and memorabilia.

Canada

Broadway and Hollywood Books, *17 Yorkville Avenue, Toronto, M4W 1L1. Tel: (416) 926–8992.*

Bookstore specialising in stage and screen, and with a comprehensive stock of *biographies*, and out-of-print items. Excellent catalogue available.

Theatrebooks, *25 Bloor Street W, Toronto, M4W 1A3. Tel: (416) 922-7175.*

Founded first as a source of theatre, opera, and dance books, Theatrebooks has since 1982 also developed a first-class film book collection. Worldwide mail order is handled.

Lux, *5220 boul. St-Laurent, Montréal.*

Large stock of European movie posters. Open daily 10 a.m. to 4 p.m.

France

Atmosphère, Librairie du Cinéma, *7–9 rue F. de Pressensé, 75014 Paris. Tel: 45.42.29.26.*

Situated in a leisure complex that includes an art cinema and a café, Atmosphère offers a wide range of film publications, with a special emphasis on science-fiction, fantasy, comics, and pop music as related to the cinema. Also back issues of magazines. Open every day except Tuesday, from 2 p.m. to 8 p.m.

Cinédoc, *45–53 Passage Jouffroy, 75009 Paris.*

Posters, pressbooks, magazines etc.

Ciné-Folie, *14 rue des Frères-Pradignac, 06400 Cannes. Tel: 93.39.22.99.*

Stills, books, posters, postcards.

Cinémagence, *12 rue Saulnier, 75009 Paris. Tel: 42.46.21.21.*

Stills, posters, magazines, books. Mail Order service.

Librairie Contacts, *24 rue de Colisée, 75008 Paris. Tel: 43.59.17.71.*

Bookshop established since 1966 in the film production companies' neighbourhood off the Champs-Elysées. Amply stocked with French and foreign-language books on technique, theory, history, and director monographs. Also magazines. Mail order service. Free "new acquisitions" list. Open year round.

Librairie de la Fontaine, *13 rue Médicis, 75006 Paris.*

ATMOSPHERE / LIBRAIRIE DE CINEMA

7 / 9 RUE FRANCIS DE PRESSENSÉ, 75014 PARIS.
MÉTRO: PERNETY. TÉL: 45 42 29 26.
OPEN DAILY: 2 PM / 8 PM.
CREDIT CARDS WELCOME.

OLD AND RARE POSTERS

Le Réverbère, *4 rue Neuve, 69002 Lyon.*
Zreik, *68 rue du Cardinal Lemoine, 75008 Paris.*
Tel: (1) 46.33.65.73.
Outstanding collection of rare European posters, both films and stars, with more than 300 postcards created from same. Also celebrity pins and other memorabilia items.

Germany

Buchhandlung Dialog, *Gutleutstr. 15, D–6000 Frankfurt 1. Tel: (0611) 23 52 80.*
Filmland Presse, *Aventinstr. 4–6, D–8000 Munich 40.*
Founded in 1977 by H.K. Denicke, this establishment is among the largest film bookshops in Europe, and circulates lists.
Buchhandlung Walther König, *Ehrenstr. 4, D–5 Köln 1.* Also at: *Deutschen Filmmuseum, Schaumainkai 41, D–6000 Frankfurt/Main 70.*
Useful source for anyone in Europe looking for that out-of-print book or magazine. Write for superb catalogue.
Buchhandlung Langenkamp, *Beckergrube 19, D–2400 Lübeck. Tel: (0451) 76479.*
H. Lindemanns Buchhandlung, *Nadlerstr. 4, D–7000 Stuttgart 1.*
Sautter & Lackmann, *Klosterstern 8, D–2000 Hamburg 13.*
Marga Schoeller Bücherstube, *Knesebeckstr. 33, D–1000 Berlin 12.*
One of the fabled literary haunts of western Europe, Marga Schoeller's shop is justly proud of its film book selection.
Verlag für Filmschriften Christian Unucka, *Am Kramerberg 71, D–8061 Hebertshausen. Tel: (08131) 13922.*

Italy

Libreria dello Spettacolo, *via Terraggio 11, 20123 Milano. Tel: (02) 800752.*
"Il Leuto," *via Di Monte Brianzo 86, 00186 Rome. Tel: (06) 656.9269.*

Netherlands

Cine Qua Non, *Staalstraat 14, Amsterdam. Tel: (40) 255588.*
Posters, stills, new and second-hand film books, scripts, and magazine back issues. Specialises in French and Italian cinema.

Spain

Biblioteca del Cinema Delmiro de Caralt, *Escuelas Pias 103, 08017 Barcelona.*
El Espectador, *Consejo de Ciento 475 bis, 08013 Barcelona. Tel: (93) 231 65.16.*
Specialising in cinema and video books, magazines etc.
Filmoteca Nacional, Cine Doré, *Santa Isabel 3, Madrid.*
Well-stocked bookstore dealing with movie topics.
Libreria del Espectaculo, *Almagro 13, 28010 Madrid.*
Specialises in film and theatre books. Wide selection of books from all major countries. Compact and modern.
R. Seriña, *Calle Ariban 114, Barcelona 11.*
A specialist collection of books, photos, magazines, press books, posters and programmes on sale to the public in Spain and abroad.

Switzerland

Filmbuchhandlung Hans Rohr, *Oberdorfstr. 3, CH–8024 Zürich.*
Hans Rohr is one of those rare birds – an advertiser in all 28 years of our book! Over all that time, the shop has remained a paragon of Swiss efficiency and courtesy when it comes to dealing with mail order inquiries for literally any film book or magazine. Libraries and institutions rely on Rohr – even beyond Switzerland.
Librairie du Cinéma, *9 rue de la Terrassière, CH–1207 Genève. Tel: (022) 736.8888.*
Immaculate display of posters, books, stills, film postcards, soundtrack CD's, and videos. A veritable treasure trove for the movie buff. Closed Monday mornings.

U.K.

The Cinema Bookshop, *13–14 Great Russell Street, London WC1. Tel: (071) 637.0206.*
Fred Zentner's film bookshop close to the British Museum has succeeded by virtue of prompt and friendly service, and an eye for rare items. People come from all over the world to browse and buy at the Cinema Bookshop.
Cox, A.E., *21 Cecil Rd., Itchen, Southampton SO2 7HX. Tel: 0703.447989.*
This long-established dealer specialises in books, magazines, and ephemera on both theatre and cinema.

Film Magic, *18 Garsmouth Way, Watford, Herts.*
Mail order service for colour and black-and-white stills of film and TV stars, plus books, magazines and posters.

MOMI Shop, *Museum of the Moving Image, South Bank, London SE1. Tel: (071) 928 3535.*
Recently expanded, this shop offers posters, postcards, toys, videos and film books.

Anne FitzSimmons, *The Retreat, The Green, Wetherall, Carlisle, Cumbria CA4 8ET. Tel: 0228.60675.*
A useful source for second-hand and out-of-print books on the cinema, as well as the theatre, puppeteering, etc.

58 Dean Street Records, *58 Dean Street, London W1V 5HH. Tel: (071) 437 4500, 734 8777.*
Specialising in soundtracks, original cast shows (incl. imports), personalities, and nostalgia. Over 7,000 titles both current and deleted items; LP's, cassettes, and CD's. (Mail Order service.)

David Henry, *36 Meon Road, London W3 8AN. Tel: (081) 993.2859.*
Mail-order business.

Ed Mason, *Shop 5, Chelsea Antique Market, 253 King's Road, London SW3. Tel: (071) 352.9695.*
Large and carefully-assembled stock of memorabilia from the silents to the 1980's. Plus stills, pressbooks, posters. Customers served by post.

Movie Finds, *4 Ravenslea Road, Balham, London SW12 8SB. Tel: (081) 673.6534.*
Teddy Green has built this small firm into a treasure trove of film stills and memorabilia. The range is huge, and the catalogue contains innumerable posters and movie scenes.

Dress Circle, *57–59 Monmouth Street, Upper St.*

Zwemmer
for books on the cinema.

We specialise in providing an efficient and informed service for books on the cinema. If you wish to receive our catalogue of English and foreign titles please inform us and we will add your name to the mailing list.

A. ZWEMMER LTD
80 CHARING CROSS ROAD
LONDON WC2H 0BB
Tel 071–379 7886
Fax 071–836 7049

'58 Dean St. Records'
58 DEAN STREET
LONDON
W1V 5HH

Phone:
01-437 4500
01-734 8777

"THB" Specialists for Soundtracks
Original Cast Shows (including imports)
Personalities and Nostalgia

A RELIABLE WORLD RECORD MAIL ORDER SERVICE

Warsaw 1939: women harvesting moments before a Nazi attack. From Archive Films' library of stock footage

photo: Julien Bryan

SOUNDTRACKS...
6000 PLUS ITEMS ON CD, LP AND SINGLE.
EUROPE'S LARGEST STOCKISTS OF IMPORTS, NEW RELEASES AND DELETIONS.

VIDEOS...
6000 PLUS TITLES (NEW) AVAILABLE ON VHS ONLY. LATEST RELEASES AND ALL CURRENTLY AVAILABLE TITLES.

FILM MEMORABILIA...
THOUSANDS OF FILM POSTERS, STILLS (SETS) AND BOOKS ETC.

CATALOGUES...
FOR EACH CATALOGUE PLEASE SEND EITHER A CHEQUE OR P.O. FOR £1.00 OR 4 IRC'S (OVERSEAS).

MOVIE BOULEVARD LTD.
Dept (VAR).
Baker House,
9 New York Road,
Leeds LS2 9PF, England.
Telephone:- (0532) 422888
(10am - 6pm)

---

businesses that have survived to advertise in all 28 editions of IFG – a tribute to their solid, professional approach to stocking, and dealing efficiently with mail order inquiries. Location near Leicester Square is also handy.

Movie Boulevard, *Baker House, 9 New York Road, Leeds LS2 9PF. Tel: (0532) 422888.*

Welcome north of England addition to the ranks of shops specialising in soundtracks, videos, and movie memorabilia. Headed by the enthusiastic Robert Wood.

U.S.A.

Martin's Lane, London WC2H 9DG. Tel: (071) 240.2227, (071) 836.8279.

Flashbacks, *6 Silver Place, (Beak St.), London W1R 3LJ. Tel: (071) 437.8562.*

Most impressively stocked establishment, which, in London's West End, caters for those interested in movie ephemera – posters, stills, pressbooks – from many countries and every period of cinema history. Also extensive Mail Order service: 4 catalogues per annum.

Zwemmer, A., *80 Charing Cross Rd., London WC2. Tel: (071) 379.7886.*

Zwemmers are of one of the handful of

Books of Latin America, *P.O. Box 1103, Redlands, California 92373. Tel: (714) 793–8423.*

Specialist in works on Latin American cinema, and Spanish and Portuguese cinema in general.

Cinema Books, *4753 Roosevelt Way NE, Seattle, Washington 98105. Tel: (206) 547-7667.*

Fine selection of film books and magazines, with space also devoted to TV and theatre. Mail Orders welcome.

Cinema Collectors, *1507 Wilcox Avenue, Hollywood, California 90028. Tel: (213) 461–6516.*

Establishment in Hollywood featuring over

SAMUEL FRENCH
THEATRE & FILM BOOKSHOPS
PLAYS, and BOOKS on FILM, THEATRE and the MOTION PICTURE INDUSTRY

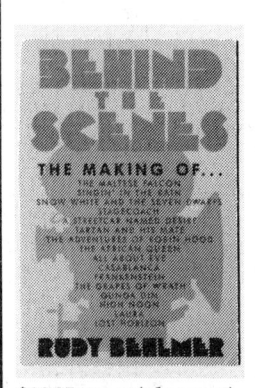

**7623 Sunset Blvd.
Hollywood, CA 90046
(213) 876-0570**

EVERYTHING FOR THE FILMMAKER,
PRODUCER, ACTOR & FILM BUFF

Business of Film, Screenplays, Acting, Screenwriting, Industry Directories, Video, Reference, Directing, Editing, Animation, Special Effects, Cinematography, Music, Television, History, Biographies...and more

WORLDWIDE MAIL ORDER VISA, MC, Am EX
FILM BOOK CATALOGUE on request

$14.95 paper (plus post) $18.95 paper (plus post)

Samuel French, Inc. *Play Publishers and Authors Representatives*   Founded 1830 • Incorporated 1899

1,700,000 stills (many in colour), 350,000 posters and banners, and marvellous runs of *Photoplay*.

Cinemonde, *1932 Polk Street, San Francisco, California 94109. Tel: (415) 776–9988.*

Installed in a capacious loft-like HQ on Polk Street, Cinemonde may well be the world's leading poster store for cinema buffs. Items are immaculately displayed and stored, and the colourful catalogue is a collectors' item ($8 incl. airmail costs).

Collectors Book Store, *1708 N. Vine Street, California 90028. Tel: (213) 467–3296.*

As well as a commendable range of posters, stills, lobby cards, and magazines, Collectors Book Store stocks movie costumes, set drawings etc.

Samuel French's Theatre & Film Bookshop, *7623 Sunset Boulevard, Hollywood, California 90046. Tel: (213) 876–0570.*

The world's oldest and largest play publisher (est. 1830) operates a separate film bookshop. Complete range of new movie books available: directories, reference, writing, acting, biography, screenplays etc.: 3,000 titles and growing! Worldwide mail order service. Note that French's also have a store at 11963 Ventura Blvd, Studio City, California 91604. Tel: (818) 762–535. Gwen Feldman prepares some meticulous catalogues that include more data than most similar efforts.

Gotham Book Mart, *41 West 47th St., New York, NY 10036.*

As its regular "GBM Film Bulletins" will testify, Gotham has achieved a remarkable prominence in the film bookshop field, and has been flourishing since 1920. Philip Lyman, the General Manager, has worked hard to expand the film section.

Larry Edmunds Bookshop, *6658 Hollywood Blvd., Hollywood, California 90028. Tel: (213) 463.3273. Also at 11969 Ventura Blvd, Studio City, California 91604.*

Larry Edmunds is the world's nearest equivalent to a film-book supermart. The stills collection alone is a goldmine for any film buff. Back numbers of movie annuals always available.

Limelight Film and Theatre Bookstore, *1803 Market Street, San Francisco, California 94103. Tel: (415) 864–2265.*

Roy A. Johnson runs this lively store for film and theatre books. Collection includes plays, screenplays, biographies, history and criticism of film etc.

Movie Madness, *1222 Wisconsin Avenue NW, Washington, DC 20007.*

Posters etc. available at this tiny store adjacent to the Key (one of Washington's best repertory cinemas).

Jerry Ohlinger's Movie Material Store Inc., *242 West 14th Street, New York, NY 10011. Tel: (212) 989–869.*

Jerry Ohlinger's emporium stocks a wealth of stills from the 1960's through the 1980's, specialising in colour material. Posters are also plentiful and there are some magazines as well.

Sound Track Album Retailers, *P.O. Box 7, Quarryville, Pennsylvania 17566. Tel: (717) 284–2573.*

Specialists in new and out of print soundtrack albums. Lists issued.

FILMBUCHHANDLUNG ROHR

- International film bookshop stocking a large range of books and magazines
- International film-bibliographic quarterly listing new publications (second-hand offerings listed occasionally)
- Mail-order service (ask for our catalogues)

Oberdorfstr. 3, CH-8024 Zürich/SWITZERLAND Tel. (01) 251 36 36

continued from p. 246

Place about a Buddhist nun won for 24-year-old actress Kang Soo Yeon the best actress citation at the Moscow Festival in 1989. Her performance in Im's 1987 **Surrogate Mother** won the ubiquitous actress – she even turned up on the jury of last year's Tokyo International Film Festival – a best acting award at the Venice Festival. Im is a proven star-maker, and a commercial force at home. His **Son of the General** was one of Korea's most popular films in the first half of 1990, pulling in more than 300,000 paying customers in Seoul in two months.

Im's international renown broadens. A retrospective of nine of hi films beginning with 1978's *Genealogy* through to *Come, Come...* was mounted recently at the Munich International Film Festival.

For her part, Kang managed to remain Korea's most active leading performer. At home, she copped best actress prize at the 1989 Grand Ball Film Festival, an event that is Korea's equivalent of the Academy Awards, for her role in director Chang Gil-Su's **All That Falls Has Wings**. The budget for this melodrama, based on a Lee Moon-yol novel about a young man who kills his beautiful lover in order to fully possess her, was much larger than usual for a Korean feature. There was location shooting in Europe and in the U.S.

The extra investment paid off since *All That Falls* swept the Grand Bell ceremonies, winning seven awards including a best director nod for Chang. The film also proved commercially successful in the first half of 1990. It played the "Cinema of Today and Tomorrow" section of this Montreal Festival.

Also at that same event in competition was director Shin Seung Soo's **The Rooster**, with another attractive actress, newcomer Choe Yoo Ra, topcast. It's a comedy with a feeling about the plight of men in a largely matriarchal society.

To provide a glimpse of the range of Korean popular cinema, the last year saw the emergence of a film about an American soldier stranded in during the Korean War in an orphanage run by nuns (**Soldiers of Innocence** was directed by an American expatriate living in Korea) and star-producer Shin Sung-il's examination of the drug traffic involving police and politicians among the bad guys. No problems here from the government's censor board, the Public Performance Ethics Committee, a marked shift from the bad old days. Korean cinema is alive with new possibilities. As Im himself suggests, "We are about to leave a long, dark tunnel of limits...."

Useful Addresses

Korean Motion Pictures Promotion Corp.
34–5, 3KA, Namsan-Dong
Chung-Ku
Seoul
Tel: 755 9291(5)
Telex: K28385
Fax: (822) 774 0531

Korea Public Performance Ethics Committee
51–1, Dowha-Dong, Mepo-ku
Seoul
Tel: (0) 715 0187

Dae Jong Film Co. Ltd.
58–2, 3-Ka, Chungmu-Ro
Chung-Mu
Seoul
Tel: 273 2201(2)
Fax: (822) 273 6012
Telex: K32995

MAGAZINES

The following list amounts to a selection only of the world's hundreds of film publications. Editors wishing to receive a free listing must send sample copies (preferably opening a sample subscription for us). Address: IFG, Variety, 34–35 Newman Street, London W1P 3PD, U.K.

AFTERIMAGE, 1 Birnam Road, London N4 3LJ, U.K. Attractively-produced and intelligent occasional British journal.
AMERICAN CLASSIC SCREEN, P.O. Box 7150, Overland Park, Kansas 662070, U.S.A. Bi-monthly devoted to the preservation of old films; filled with useful addresses.
AMERICAN FILM, 6671 Sunset Blvd., Suite 1514, Hollywood, CA 90028, U.S.A. Glossy monthly featuring articles on video and television, as well as film.
AMERICAN PREMIERE, 8421 Wilshire Blvd., Penthouse, Beverly Hills, CA 90211, U.S.A. Bi-monthly industry magazine, free to members of the Academy of Motion Picture Arts and Sciences.
ANIMATOR, Filmcraft Publications, 13 Ringway Road, Park Street, St. Albans, Herts AL2 2RE, U.K. Entertaining and informative magazine for animators and animation buffs.
L'AVANT SCENE CINEMA, 16 rue des Quatre-Vents, 75006 Paris, France. Meticulously researched full screenplays of classic films, ancient or modern. Twenty issues a year.
BIANCO E NERO, 1524 via Tuscolana, 00173 Rome, Italy. Italian quarterly that boasts a reputation for scholarship second to none in its country.
CAHIERS DU CINEMA, Editions de l'Etoile, 9 passage de la Boule Blanche, 75012 Paris, France. Celebrated French journal now enjoying a second lease of life after a long spell in the wilderness.
CAMERA OBSCURA, The Editors, Rush Rhees Library, University of Rochester, Rochester, NY 14627, U.S.A. A journey of feminism and film theory, encourages written responses to issues raised in articles.
CHAPLIN, Box 27 126, S–102 52 Stockholm, Sweden. The most regular of the Swedish film journals, sponsored by the Swedish Film Institute and also covering world cinema.
CIAK SI GIRA, C. so I. Europa 5/7, 20122 Milan, Italy. Glossy Italian monthly, well established, full of lively articles. Similar to France's *Première*.

CINE AL DIA, Apartado 50, 446 Sabana Grande, Caracas, Venezuela. Venezuelan monthly.
CINE ACCIÓN NEWS, 3181 A Mission St., San Francisco, CA 94110, U.S.A.
CINEASTE, P.O. Box 2242, New York, NY 10009, U.S.A. Perhaps the finest anti-establishment movie magazine, never afraid to tackle controversial issues and never prone to Hollywood worship. Interviews are especially good in *Cineaste*.
CINE-BULLES, 4545 avenue Pierre-de-Coubertin, CP 1000, Succursale M, Montréal, Canada H1V 3R2. Remarkable and informative Québécois quarterly that may just be the best in Canada.
CINE-BULLETIN, Clarastrasse 48, Postfach 4005, Basel, Switzerland. Serious Swiss monthly in French and German.
CINE CUBANO, Calle 23 no. 1155, Havana, Cuba. Vital information on all Latin American cinema, unfortunately only in Spanish.
CINEFANTASTIQUE, P.O. Box 270, Oak Park, Ill. 60303, U.S.A. An enthusiastic, well-written, beautifully produced bi-monthly with a special emphasis on fantasy films.
CINEINFORME, Grand Via 64, 28013 Madrid, Spain. Bi-monthly that covers Spanish and international film development.
CINEMA 2002, Ardemans 64, Madrid 28, Spain. First-class Spanish monthly packed with pictures, serious articles and interviews, and a great many news items.
CINEMA & CINEMA, 1 via Battibecco, 40123 Bologna, Italy. Respected quarterly.
CINEMA CANADA, Box 398, Station Outremont, Montréal H2V 4NF, Canada. Large-format monthly.
CINEMA IN INDIA, 1 Dalamal Towers, Ground Floor, 211 Nariman Point, Bombay, India. Quarterly published by India's National Film Development Corporation.
CINEMA INDIA INTERNATIONAL, A–15 Anand Nagar, Juhu Tara Road, Bombay 400 400 049, India. Indian quarterly (in English) packed with articles, reviews and interviews.
CINEMA JOURNAL, Film Division, Northwestern University, Evanston, Illinois 60201, U.S.A. A scholarly and respected American magazine, now published twice a year.
CINEMA NOVO, Apartado 78, 4002 Porto Codex, Portugal. Bi-monthly Portuguese magazine dealing with international and Portuguese topics.
CINEMA NUOVO, 110 via Giacinta Pezzana, 00197 Rome, Italy. Polemical, academic Italian bi-monthly with excellent reviews.

CINEMA PAPERS, 43 Charles Street, Abbotsford 3067, Australia. Excellent large-format Australian bi-monthly is back, packed with information and pictures, useful for anyone monitoring the industry in Oz.

CINEMATECA REVISTA, Lorenzo Carnelli 1311, Casilla de Correo 1170, Montevideo, Uruguay. Bright magazine with international slant published by Cinemateca Uruguaya. Ten times a year.

CINEMATHEQUE, P.O. Box 20370, Tel Aviv 61203, Israel. Fine monthly Israeli magazine (with summary in English) dwelling on seasons at the Tel-Aviv Cinémathèque but also reporting on world festivals etc.

CINEMAYA, B 90 Defence Colony, New Delhi 110 024, India. Informative, elegant new magazine on all aspects of the Asian film industry.

CLASSIC IMAGES, P.O. Box 4079, Davenport, Illowa 52808, U.S.A. Formerly "Classic Film Collector," a good source for film buffs eager to enlarge their library of movies. Bi-monthly.

CULTURE AND CINEMA, No. 20, 19th Alley, Gandhi Ave., Tehran, Iran. Monthly magazine featuring Iranian cinema.

DIRIGIDO POR..., Rbla. de Catalunya, 108 3. 1. Barcelona 8, Spain. This handsomely-produced Spanish monthly throws the spotlight each issue on a particular director of international renown.

DOCUMENTO CINEMATOGRÁFICO LATINOMERICANO, Cra. 19 No. 31–47 of. 205 A.A. 89133–Bogotá, Colombia.

EMPIRE, 42 Great Portland Street, London W1N 5AH, U.K. Glossy new magazine with international slant, heavy on reviews and behind-the-scenes. Monthly.

ENTERTAINMENT HERALD, Corrienres 2817 3-A 1015, Buenos Aires, Argentina.

FARABI, 55 Sie-Tir Ave., Tehran 11358, Iran. Quarterly periodical issued by the Farabi Cinema Foundation.

FATAL VISIONS, P.O. Box 133, Northcote 3070, Victoria, Australia. Lively "junk media" magazine on trash cinema, video and television.

FILM, Friedrichstrasse 2–6, D-6000 Frankfurt 17, F.R.G. Evangelical monthly that covers contemporary cinema well, especially the festival scene.

FILM, 21 Stephen Street, London W1 1PL, U.K. Much improved, nicely-printed monthly, issued on behalf of the British Federation of Film Societies.

FILM, ul. Pulawska 61, 02–595 Warsaw, Poland. Popular Polish weekly with international slant.

FILM (Yeonghwa), Motion Picture Promotion Corporation of Korea, 34–5, 3-ga, Namsan-dong, Junggu, Seoul. South Korea's only serious film magazine, packed with information. Bi-monthly.

FILMHAFTET, Storgatan 15, 753 31 Uppsala, Sweden. Egghead monthly with features on international directors, retrospectives, and Scandinavian television.

FILMS IN REVIEW, P.O. Box 589, New York, NY 10021, U.S.A. Compact bi-monthly journal, reviewing notable new releases with interviews, retrospective articles and television/video reports.

FILM A DOBA, Václavské nám. 43, Praha 1, Czechoslovakia. The principal Czech film monthly.

FILM APPRECIATION (Tien-ying hsin-shang), Film Library, 4th floor, 7 Ch'ingtao Road, Taipei, Taiwan. Taiwan's premier serious film journal, published as a bi-monthly. Wide range of material, with the emphasis on the theoretical.

FILM EN TELEVISIE + VIDEO, Haachtsesteenweg 35, 1030 Brussels, Belgium. Extensive reviews of major new film and video releases, profiles and interviews.

FILM BULLETIN, Postfach 137, Hard 4, CH–8408 Winterthur, Switzerland. Informative, straightforward look at international cinema, with useful Swiss material also.

FILM CRITICISM, Allegheny College, Meadville, PA 16335, U.S.A. In-depth articles on international cinema in this quarterly journal.

FILM-DIENST, Am Hof 28, 5000 Cologne, F.R.G. Fortnightly. Lists all films in West German cinemas and television screenings, with news, credits, reviews, articles.

FILM DOPE, 45 Lupton Street, London NW5 2HS. Not so much a magazine, more a part-work film dictionary, this irregular British quarterly is to be welcomed for its exhaustive research.

FILMIHULLU, c/o Suomen elokuvakerhojen-liitto, Annankatu 13 B 11, SF–00120 Helsinki 12. Finnish film and TV magazine with critical approach, appearing eight times a year.

FILM LITERATURE QUARTERLY, Salisbury State University, Salisbury, MD 21801, U.S.A. Manuscripts invited for submission, reviews, interviews or analysis.

FILM MONTHLY, No. 12, Sam Alley, Hafez Ave., Tehran, Iran. Reviews and features on the latest releases.

FILM QUARTERLY, University of California Press, Berkeley, California 94720. Now much improved visually, this magazine neatly straddles the barrier between the glossy journals and academic tomes.

FILM REPORT, No. 242, Vali-e Asr Ave., Tehran, Iran. Reports and interviews on international cinema.

FILM THREAT, 6646 Hollywood Boulevard, Suite 205, Los Angeles, CA 90028, U.S.A. The world's most outrageous and anarchic movie magazine, lashing out zestfully at all and sundry. Some of it sticks, by the way. The cartoon work is great.

FILM UND FERNSEHEN, Oranienburgerstr. 67–68, 104 Berlin, G.D.R. Monthly edited by Association of Film- and TV-Makers in the G.D.R. Broad surveys, extensive interviews, etc.

FORMATO DIECISEIS, Apartado 6–1775, Estafeta El Dorado, Panama.

FILM MAGAZINES | 501

FOTOGRAMAS & VIDEO, Consell de Cent 83, 6ª planta, 08015 Barcelona, Spain. Glossy monthly, packed with colourful articles and photographs, also video reviews and television film listings.
FRAMEWORK, 40A Topsfield Parade, London N8 8QA, U.K. Substantial, occasional British magazine, with wide-ranging international essays.
GRAND ANGLE, rue d'Arschot 29, B–6370 Mariembourg, Belgium. Belgian bi-monthly.
GRIFFITHIANA, Cineteca del Friuli, 26 via Osoppo, 33014 Gemona del Friuli (Udine), Italy. Quarterly – living up to its name.
GUIA DE FILMES, Rua Mayrink 28–5 andar, Rio de Janeiro, Guanabara, Brazil. Bi-monthly Brazilian magazine, an equivalent to Britain's *MFB*.
HOLLAND ANIMATION BULLETIN, Stevinstraat 261, 2587 EJ The Hague, Netherlands. Authoritative Dutch bulletin edited by Nico Crama.
HOLLYWOOD, P.O. Box 38010, Los Angeles, CA 90038, U.S.A. A mixture of features, not all cinema-based, for Californians who live in *Hollywood*, not L.A.
IMAGEN, Casilla 1733, La Paz, Bolivia. Magazine of the Bolivian New Cinema Movement.
IMAGENES DE ACTUALIDAD, Rambla de Cataluna 108, 08008 Barcelona, Spain. Glossy, well presented magazine with strong Hollywood bias. Monthly.
IMMAGINE, 1522 via Tuscolana, 00173 Rome, Italy. Much-admired Italian magazine, full of articles and notes on the history of the cinema.
THE INDEPENDENT FILM/VIDEO GUIDE, EFLA, 45 John Street, New York, NY 10038, U.S.A. Quarterly index to the works exhibited by non-commercial film-video show-cases in New York City and New York State.
ISKUSSTVO KINO, 9 ulitsa Usievich, 125319 Moscow, U.S.S.R. Chunky, theoretical, officially blessed Soviet monthly.
JUMP CUT, P.O. Box 865, Berkeley, California 94701, U.S.A. Published only once or twice a year, this tabloid contains an extraordinary amount of closely-woven text.
KINO, c/o Holloway, Helgoländer Ufer 6, 1000 Berlin 21, F.R.G. Excellent quarterly devoted to both German and other cinema, with interviews, credits and comment.
KINO, ul. Kredytowa 5/7, 00–56 Warsaw, Poland. Culturally-inclined Polish magazine edited by much-travelled Dr. Jerzy Plazewski.
KOSMORAMA, The Danish Film Museum, Store Søndervoldstræde, DK–1419 Copenhagen K, Denmark. One of the most beautifully-designed and lovingly-edited of Nordic film magazines. Bi-monthly.
KUVA & ÄÄNI, Ruoholahdenkatu 23, SF–00180 Helsinki 18, Finland. Excellent monthly on technical matters.
MACGUFFIN, Paradisgade 7–9, D–8000 Århus C, Denmark. Solid, slim Danish quarterly.
MAKING BETTER MOVIES, 28 Great James Street, London WC1N 3HL, U.K. Film and video monthly that concentrates on the craft of making your own films.
MEDIUM, Friedrich Strasse 2–6, 6000 Frankfurt am Main 17, F.R.G. Monthly including articles about mass media politics, TV interviews and portraits of directors, festival reports etc.
MONTHLY FILM BULLETIN, British Film Institute, 21 Stephen Street, London W1 1PL, U.K. Full credits (plus reviews and background) of all new films released in Britain. Monthly.
MOVIE, 6/F D, Formost Building, 19–21 Jordan Road, Kowloon, Hongkong. Bright new arrival (since summer 1988) on Hongkong's serious movie magazine scene, combining best of the defunct Film Bi-weekly and China & Overseas Movie News.
MOVIES U.S.A., 8010 Roswell Road, Atlanta, GA 30350, U.S.A. Lightweight American monthly, two or three main features and lots of paparazzi.
MOZGO KEPEK, P.O. Box 223, H–1906 Budapest, Hungary. Monthly covering film, TV, and video in tabloid form.
NUOVO CINEMA EUROPEO, Via Castelfidardo, 50137 Firenze, Italy. Chunky bi-monthly report on Italian film industry, in English with Italian summary. Includes industry news, such as box-office, markets and foreign sales.
NZ FILM, P.O. Box 11–546, Wellington, New Zealand. News from the New Zealand Film Commission, a monthly round-up of the country's film industry.
ONFILM, P.O. Box 6374, Wellington, New Zealand. A film, television and video magazine for New Zealand, with location reports and a production survey.
PHOTOGRAPH, No. 20, 19th Alley, Gandhi Ave., Tehran, Iran. A monthly magazine by the Young Iranian Cinema Society.
PICTURE HOUSE, 44 Warlingham Road, Thornton Heath, Surrey CR4 7DE, U.K. Admirable quarterly devoted to the cinema buildings of the past.
POLISH FILM, Film Polski Ltd., Mazowiecka 6/8, 00–048 Warsaw, Poland. News and reviews of Polish films in this colourful monthly. In English.
POPULAR CINEMA (Dazhong dianying), 22 Beisanhai Donglu, Peking, China. Leading mainland Chinese monthly, also carrying pieces on Hongkong, Taiwan and foreign cinema.
POSITIF, Nouvelles Editions Opta, 1 quai Conti, 75006 Paris. In-depth interviews, articles, all immaculately researched and highly intelligent. The best film magazine in France.
PREMIERE, 23–25 rue de Berri, 75388 Paris Cedex 08, France. France's glossiest and most wide-ranging monthly, packed with information, reviews, interviews and filmographies.
PREMIERE, 2 Park Avenue, New York, NY 10016, U.S.A. The major American monthly that with its

large-format, zesty approach to mainstream movies bids fair to make it the *Rolling Stone* of the movie world.
PRESENCE DU CINEMA FRANÇAIS, Les Editions de l'Expression, 22 rue Plumet, 75015 Paris, France. On-the-ball, colourfully illustrated bi-monthly that verges on being an industry journal.
PRODUCER, 162–170 Wardour Street, London, W1V 4LA, U.K. Welcome voice for the independent British producer.
PROJEKTIO, Annankatu 13 B 11, SF–00120 Helsinki 12, Finland. The magazine of the Finnish Federation of Film Societies, appearing quarterly.
QUADERNI DI CINEMA, Via Benedetto Varchi 57, 50132 Florence, Italy. Wide-ranging Italian bi-monthly striving to match cultural politics with an enthusiastic appreciation of film.
RECTANGLE, Case postale 66, CH–1211 Geneva 7, Switzerland. Only film magazine in the Suisse romande, and admirably poised between the theoretical and researchist approach to the cinema.
RIVISTA DEL CINEMATOGRAFO, Via Giuseppe Palombini, 6–00165 Rome, Italy. Important Italian monthly.
SEGNOCINEMA, Via G. Prati 34, Vicenza. Italian bi-monthly, with particularly useful September issue that lists complete guide to all films released the previous season.
SIGHT AND SOUND, British Film Institute, 21 Stephen Street, London W1 1PL, U.K. The most august of British periodicals, mixing theory, TV and the historical byways of cinema.
SIGHTLINES, Educational Film Library Association, 45 John Street, Suite 301, New York, NY 10038, U.S.A. Excellent quarterly magazine dealing with film education in the United States.
SKOOP, Postbus 11377, Amsterdam, Netherlands. The well-known Dutch movie magazine, with a spectrum of news, reviews, interviews, and a lavish selection of pictures.
SKRIEN, p/a Filmmuseum, Vondelpark 3, 1071 AA Amsterdam, The Netherlands. Excellent Dutch magazine that appears with regularity and enthusiasm.
SORUSH, Motahari Ave., Jam-e Jam Building, Tehran, Iran. Weekly magazine issued by Islamic Republic of Iran Broadcasting.
SOUNDTRACK! Astridlaan 171, 2800 Mechelen, Belgium. Excellent quarterly (in English) for film music collectors.
SOVYETSKI EKRAN, ul, Chasovaya 5–6, Moscow A–319, U.S.S.R. Popular Soviet fortnightly.
SPEKTRI, Box 142, SF–00101 Helsinki, Finland. An independent quarterly aiming at Finnish film buffs. Fresh opinions, no prejudices.
STILL, P.O. Box 432, SF–33101 Tampere, Finland. Lively, very well-informed Finnish quarterly.
STUDIO MAGAZINE, 116 bis, avenue des Champs-Elysées, 75008 Paris, France. Glossy, beautifully designed monthly with reviews, articles and interviews.

TRAVELIN, Valázquez 10, Madrid, Spain. New Spanish fortnightly that sparkles with colour stills and lively articles.
TUSIND ØJNE, Frederiksberg Alle 18, 4 sal., DK–1820 Frederiksberg C, Denmark. Invaluable for anyone passing through Copenhagen – a tabloid guide to the major films and the issues emerging from them.
24 IMAGES, 3781, rue Laval, Montréal, QC H2W 2H8, Canada. Exceptionally attractive French-Canadian quarterly.
VE CINEMA, Hil Yayinlari, Cagaloglu, Istanbul, Turkey. Quarterly published in Turkish.
THE VELVET LIGHT TRAP, University of Texas Press, P.O. Box 7819, Austin, Texas 78713 U.S.A. Bi-annual journal featuring critical essays analysing the history and criticism of the American Cinema.
VIDEO PROFESIANAL, Consell de Cent 83, 6°, 08015 Barcelona, Spain. A monthly look at the Spanish video industry, with comprehensive listings of new releases.
VISIONS, 9 rue Traversière, 1030 Brussels, Belgium. Richly-illustrated Belgian monthly.
WIDE ANGLE, The Johns Hopkins University Press, Baltimore, Maryland 212180, U.S.A. Scholarly thematically arranged journal. Wide range.
Z FILMTIDSSKRIFT, Teatergt. 3, 0180 Oslo 1, Norway. Reliable, polemic, and enthusiastic Norwegian quarterly issued by Norsk Filmklubb-forbund.

National Organs

AFC INFORMATION UPDATE, 8 West Street, North Sydney, NSW 2060, Australia. Monthly.
BULGARIAN FILMS, Film Bulgaria, 96 Rakovski Street, Sofia, Bulgaria. Eight times a year.
CHINA SCREEN, China Film Export and Import Corporation 25 Xin Wai Street, Peking, China. Quarterly.
CINEMA, CINEMA, Ministère de la Culture Française avenue de Cortenbur 158, 1040 Brussels, Belgium.
CZECHOSLOVAK FILM, 28 Václavské náměsti, Prague 1, Czechoslovakia.
HUNGAROFILM BULLETIN, Báthori utca 10, Budapest V, Hungary. Five times a year.
ISRAEL FILM CENTRE INFORMATION BULLETIN, Ministry of Commerce and Industry, 30 Agron Street, Jerusalem, Israel.
KINO, Türkenstrasse 93, 8000 München 40, F.R.G. Monthly.
NFDC NEWS, Dalamal Towers, 211 Nariman Point, Bombay 400 021, India. Monthly.
POLISH FILM, Film Polski, ul. Mazowiecka 6/8, 00–054 Warsaw, Poland.
THE ROMANIAN FILM, 25 Julius Fucik Street, Bucharest, Romania.
SOVIET FILM, Sovexportfilm, 14 Kalashny pereulok, Moscow 103009, U.S.S.R. Monthly.

Trade and Technical

AMERICAN CINEMATOGRAPHER, ASC Agency Inc., 1782 North Orange Drive, Hollywood, California 90028, U.S.A. Monthly.
BKSTS JOURNAL, 110–112 Victoria House, Vernon Place, London WC1B 4DJ, U.K. Monthly.
BLICKPUNKT-FILM, Oberhachingerstrasse 44, 8022 Grünwald, F.R.G. Strong on box-office returns and marketing, West German weekly also covers Austria.
BRITISH NATIONAL FILM & VIDEO CATALOGUE, 21 Stephen Street, London W1 1PL, U.K. Quarterly that provides essential particulars of all nonfiction films (British and foreign) becoming available in Britain.
CINEMA D'OGGI, viale Regina Margherita 286, 00198 Rome, Italy. Fortnightly. Interviews with producers.
LE FILM FRANÇAIS, 12 avenue George V, 75008 Paris, France. Weekly.
FILM-ECHO/FILMWOCHE, Wilhelmstrasse 42, 62 Wiesbaden, F.D.R. Doyen of West German trade.
FILM OG KINO, Stortingsgaten 16, 0161 Oslo 1, Norway. Wide-ranging and well illustrated, covering trade matters but often controversial issues too.
GIORNALE DELLO SPETTACOLO, via di Villa Patrizi 10, 00161 Rome, Italy. Box-office data, legal requirements, technical information etc.
HOLLYWOOD REPORTER, 6715 Sunset Blvd., Hollywood, California 90028, U.S.A. Daily.
MONITEUR DU FILM, 36 rue des Framboisiers, 1180 Brussels, Belgium. Monthly.
MOVIE TV MARKETING, Box 30, Central Post Office, Tokyo, 100–91 Japan. Monthly from Japan – in English.
SCREEN INTERNATIONAL, 6–7 Great Chapel Street, London W1V 4BR, U.K. Weekly. Daily edition at Cannes.
THEMATA, Athinon 64, Aharnai Attikis, Greece. Fortnightly.
VARIETY, 475 Park Avenue South, New York, NY 10016, U.S.A. The world's foremost newspaper of the entertainment business.

Still from Satyajit Ray's latest film, *Family Reunion*, screened at the Venice and London festivals
photo: Nemai Ghosh

Index to Advertisers

Air Services 434
American Cinematheque 366
American European Entertainment 165
American Film Institute 364
Archive Film 489
Atmosphere 493
Australian Film Commission 66
Australian Film Finance Corporation 73
Avalon TV Center 282
Bamboo 3
Berlin International Film Festival *Outside back cover*
Cambridge Film Festival 435
Camera Film/Grand Cinema 139
Capricorn Pictures 70
Catalan Films 320
Centre National de l'Audiovisuel 250
Ceskoslovensky Filmexport 132
Cinevideo 342
Cinetrust 383
Clermont-Ferrand Short Film Festival 438
Danish Film Institute 136
Danish Filmstudio *Inside back cover*
Denver International Film Festival 438
El Deseo 318
Dutch Film Days 436
Entertainment Data 4
European Film Development Office 17
Expanded Entertainment 442
Farabi Cinema Foundation 212, 436, 450
Festival des 3 Continents 439
Festival du Film D'Animation d'Annecy 437
Festival Internazionale Cinema Giovani 443
Festival of Festivals 441
Festival de Genève 453
Festival International de Cinéma Méditerranéen de Montpellier 448
Festival International du Film de La Rochelle 449
Film Australia 75
Film Fonds, Hamburg 175
Finnkino 150
Finnish Film Foundation 148
French Film Festival 2
58 Dean Street Records 495
French's, Samuel, Theatre & Film Bookshop 496
Ghent Film Festival 444
Göteborg Film Festival 444
Greek Film Centre 180
Gund, George 380
Holland Film Promotion 266
Hong Kong International Film Festival 440
Houston International Film Festival 471
Hungarofilm 191
Iberoamericana Films 316
Icelandic Film Fund 200
Imagfic 439
Inter Video/Tri Tronics 389
International Film Exchange *Spine*, 1
Internationale Hofer Filmtage 448
Internationale Münchner Filmwochen 445

Israel Film Centre 226
Istanbul International Film Festival 447
J & M Entertainment *Spine*
Locarno Film Festival 15
London International Film School 472
Manfred Durniok Filmproduktion 8
Mannheim Filmwoche 452
Melbourne Film Festival 454
Mill Valley Film Festival 451
Ministerio de Cultura (Spain) 314
Movie Boulevard 496
National Film Board of Canada 94
New Zealand Film Commission 280
Nordische Filmtage Lübeck 455
Norwegian Film Festival 455
Norwegian Film Institute 286
Oberhausen Kurzfilmtage 458
Odense International Film Festival 456
Palace Entertainment Corporation 64
Pordenone Silent Film Festival 458
Pro Helvetia, Zurich 337
Productions La Fête *Spine*
Rohr, Hans 497
Rotterdam Film Festival 459
Rotterdam Films 267
San Sebastian International Film Festival 460

Seattle Film Festival 448
Shell Film & Video Unit 352
Sherman-Grinberg Film Libraries 489
Shibata Organization 244
Shochiku Co *Inside front cover*
South African National Film Archive 488
Statens Filmcentral 142
Stockholm Film Festival 462
Swedish Film Institute 326
Swedish Institute 329
Swiss Film Centre 333
Sydney Film Festival 461
Tampere International Short Film Festival 464
Tyneside Film Festival 463
Uppsala Film Festival 464
United International Pictures 12
Valladolid Film Festival 463
Wellington Film Festival 465
Western Australia Film Council 67
Wine Country Film Festival 464
York University 504
Zagreb Festival 469
Zwemmer's Bookshop 495

YORK FINE ARTS

York University • Toronto, Canada

Film & Video
Fall/Winter '91

- Four-year degree programs: BFA and BA
- Film and video production and film studies
- Graduate studies: MFA in film and video production, writing, and film studies
- SUMMER program: day and evening courses in film studies, film production, and screenwriting (May to August)

Programs also offered in Dance, Fine Arts Studies, Music, Theatre, and Visual Arts.

For further information, contact:
Room 216F, Fine Arts Centre Phase II,
Faculty of Fine Arts,
York University, North York,
Ontario, Canada M3J 1P3
Telephone: (416) 736-5135